INTRODUCTION TO
CHINESE LAW

Recommended Stockists

Australia
LBC Information Services Ltd
Brisbane, Sydney, Melbourne, Perth

Canada and USA
Carswell
Ottawa, Toronto, Calgary, Montreal,
Vancouver

Hong Kong
Bloomsbury Books Ltd

India
N.M. Tripathi (Private) Ltd
Bombay

Eastern Law House (Private) Ltd
Calcutta

M.P.P. House
Bangalore

Universal Book Traders
Delhi

Aditya Books
Delhi

Japan
Kinokuniya Co. Ltd
Tokyo

Kokusai Shobo Ltd
Tokyo

Maruzen Co. Ltd
Tokyo

Yushodo Co. Ltd
Tokyo

New Zealand
Brooker's
Auckland

Pakistan
Pakistan Law House
Karachi, Lahore

Singapore & Malaysia
Thomson Information (S.E. Asia)

South Korea
Information & Culture Korea
Seoul

Thailand
DK Book House Co. Ltd
Bangkok

Nibondh & Company Ltd
Bangkok

Pasit Limited Partnership
Bangkok

UK/Europe
Sweet & Maxwell Ltd
London

THE CHINA LAW SERIES

INTRODUCTION TO CHINESE LAW

Edited by

Wang Chenguang, M.A., M.L., LL.M.

Associate Professor, Department of Law
City University of Hong Kong

and

Zhang Xianchu, J.D., M.C.L., LL.B.

University Lecturer, Department of Law
City University of Hong Kong

HONG KONG • SINGAPORE
SWEET & MAXWELL ASIA
1997

Published in 1997 by
Sweet & Maxwell Asia
a division of
The Thomson Corporation (Hong Kong) Ltd
17/F Lyndhurst Tower, 1 Lyndhurst Terrace
Central, Hong Kong

Affilated Companies

AUSTRALIA
LBC Information Services Ltd
44–50 Waterloo Road, North Ryde
NSW 2113

CANADA
Carswell
Corporate Plaza,
2075 Kennedy Road
Scarborough, Ontario M1T 3V4

NEW ZEALAND
Brooker's
PO Box 6343, Auckland

SINGAPORE / MALAYSIA
Thomson Information (S.E. Asia)
30 Prinsep Street, #05-02
LKN Prinsep House, Singapore 188647

UNITED KINGDOM EUROPE
Sweet & Maxwell Ltd
100 Avenue Road, London NW3 3PF

Typeset by Best-set Typesetter Ltd.,
Hong Kong

Printed in China

Index prepared by
Francoise Parkin

A CIP catalogue record for this book is available from the British Library

ISBN 0 421 56080 0

PREFACE

Looking at the recent dramatic changes in Chinese law, the speed and extent of the resurrection of the Chinese legal system is really quite impressive. Even up to 30 years ago, during the Cultural Revolution, a countless number of people were charged or persecuted without formal legal charges or the due process of law, with many of them even dying as a result. Since the official termination and denouncement of the "Cultural Revolution" in 1976 however, China has embarked on massive legal reconstruction.

The original impetus for this change stemmed directly from Deng Xiaoping who said that:

> "To ensure people's democracy, we must strengthen our legal system. Democracy has to be institutionalized and legalized, so as to make sure that institutions and laws do not change whenever the leadership changes, or whenever the leaders change their views or shift the focus of their attention. The trouble now is that our legal system is incomplete, with many laws yet to be enacted." (Deng Xiaoping: *Select Works of Deng Xiaoping*, Vol. 2, Beijing, People's Press, p. 146)

Nevertheless, the dilemma generated by the theoretical and practical conflicts between the idea of an impersonal, highly institutionalized legal system expressed above and the insistence on maintaining the Communist Party's leading position, have slowed down the pace of political reform. However, the momentum of the fast economic development and the reform of the national economic structure on a market basis have fuelled the modernization of the legal system in China. This is probably the reason why the current legal reforms have focused mainly on the economic field. The authors nevertheless believe that along with further economic development, further political reforms will sooner or later be invoked. The current problems of local protectionism, the difficulty of reforming state-owned enterprises, the reform of judicial adjudication by the courts, and the extended powers of the people's congress, shall surely bring about and further promote changes in the current political structure. In short, the framework of the Chinese legal system has now been established.

Needless to say, in this nascent legal system, there are numerous problems that both puzzle and frustrate legal scholars and practitioners. The malpractice of government officials, judges and lawyers, irregularities in implementing the law, widespread corruption, the function of *guanxi*, and inconsistencies in various laws and regulations are but a few of these problems. To a great extent, the future direction of Chinese law depends on the interplay as well as variations of all of these forces.

Those who are faced with such a complex and volatile legal system, have been demanding more information on Chinese law. It is hoped that this book on Chinese law will help those who are conducting research or practise Chinese law. At the same time, we are fully aware that there are many scholars and practitioners working in this field who can provide a broader outlook on this topic. This book is meant as an introduction only. Taking into consideration the speed of development of the subsisting Chinese legal system, and the volatility of the legal system determined by the transitional nature of the society towards a "socialist market economy" and a "socialist legal system", it is unfortunately the case that it is not always possible to keep abreast at all of these changes. *The Criminal Procedural Law* was substantially revised last spring; a new comprehensive contract law is close to its final outline; more laws and regulations are in the course of being drafted or revised such as the *Criminal Law, Agency Law, Law on Property, Bankruptcy Law, Legislative Process Law*, etc. Therefore, it is inevitable that some of the chapters do not allow for a broad coverage of all the new legislations, especially new administrative regulations and rules on both central and local levels, and judicial interpretations. In this regard, we would appreciate any comments or suggestions as to how the text can be improved.

We would also like to state that this book is truly a group effort. Most of the contributors are law teachers at the Law Department, City University of Hong Kong, teaching or researching Chinese law. We, as editors of this book, are grateful for their generous contribution and co-operation. In the process of writing, they have encountered many difficulties, *inter alia*, the tight teaching schedule and the difficulty in collecting materials, particularly relevant legal rules. The editors provided preliminary comments to each of the chapters, but the authorship of each chapter goes to their respective contributors, and they are responsible for their own work.

We would like to take this opportunity to express our sincere appreciation to the Research Centre of Chinese Law and Comparative Law, City University of Hong Kong for its encouragement for this book. The faculty of law as well as the Law Department of the University provided the same encouragement and facilities for research. Our thanks also go to the secretaries who work quietly but efficiently in the General Office of the Law Department and for their logistical assistance. Last but not the least, our sincere and special thanks go to Ms. Paula Harris and Ms. Kate Wyllie and their hard-working colleagues at Sweet & Maxwell. Without them and their generous assistance and strong encouragement for this project, this book would not have become a reality. Their roles have been indispensable for the completion of this project.

Wang Chenguang
Zhang Xianchu
City University of Hong Kong
August, 1996

CONTENTS

Chapter 4
Criminal Law
(Ian Dobinson)

Chapter 5
Criminal Procedure Law
(Fu Hualing)

Chapter 6
Civil Law
(Ling Bing)

Chapter 7
Contract Law
(Zhao Yuhong)

Chapter 8
Foreign Investment Law
(John S. Mo)

Chapter 9
Family Law
(Zhang Xianchu)

Chapter 10
Law of Business Organizations
(Yu Guang Hua and Zhang Xianchu)

Chapter 11
Alternative Dispute Resolution
(John S. Mo)

Chapter 12
Law of Civil Procedure
(Zhang Xianchu)

Chapter 13
Intellectual Property Law
(Bryan Bachner)

Chapter 14
Labour Law
(Lin Feng)

Chapter 15
Laws on the Financial System
(Stephen Foo)

TABLE OF CASES

TABLE OF LEGISLATION

CHAPTER 1

INTRODUCTION: AN EMERGING LEGAL SYSTEM

Wang Chenguang

City University of Hong Kong

Wang Chenguang, M.A., LL.M. (Beijing University), LL.M. (Harvard University School of Law), Associate Professor of Law at the City University of Hong Kong, Member of the PRC Bar, Arbitrator of China International Economic and Trade Arbitration Committee; Formerly Associate Professor and Vice-Dean, Law Department, Peking University.

Introduction

China is a country with one of the longest histories in the world. **1.01** Nevertheless, throughout its history, the concept of law and the notion of the rule of law have never taken centre stage in society until the late 1970s, when the People's Republic of China (hereafter the PRC) decided to rebuild and modernize its socialist legal system after the turmoil of lawlessness generated by the ultra-leftist thoughts and especially by "the Cultural Revolution". In this sense, the existing Chinese legal system is a nascent system emerging from the decease of long-sustained Chinese traditional law. Institutionally and ideologically, there are no direct links between traditional law and contemporary law in China.

Nevertheless, the impact and influence of traditional law, especially the traditional legal culture, on contemporary law cannot be disregarded or underestimated. The law is a set of rules formally adopted by a state authority, and backed up by coercive sanctions, with the functions of institutionalising and standardising the social behaviours of individuals, organisations and governments. The behaviours in a particular society are bound to be shaped, modified and transformed by the people in the course of historical development. In this sense, the law governing these behaviours inevitably has intrinsic links with historical tradition, cultural heritage and social customs, as well as with ideological doctrines, the economic and political structure and the social milieu. In short, law cannot be understood outside the context of the entire social scenario of a particular community, of which law is only a part. In the case of Chinese law, the approach of sociology of law is even more important. The unique history, culture and social structure of China should be taken into consideration in order to have insightful understandings of the relationship between law and other social factors, of the actual operation of the legal system in the society, and of its future directions. Therefore, it is necessary, before diving into the substantive rules and concrete fields of law, to have a bird's eye view of Chinese legal history and the legal legacy, the characteristics and structure of the Chinese legal system.

Following such an understanding, this chapter attempts to examine the history of Chinese law, and the salient features and the structure of the sustaining legal system of the PRC.

Historical Survey of Traditional Chinese Law

Division of Traditional Chinese Law and Modern Chinese Law

1.02 Historical records show that the earliest law in China appeared more than 4,000 years ago during the Xia Dynasty, the first dynasty in Chinese history. The ancient historical book *Zuo Zuan* says: "Due to political disorders in Xia, Law of Yu was formulated".[1] As commonly accepted, its long history of law is divided into two parts, namely the part of the traditional Chinese law ranging from Law of Yu to the Codes of the Qing Dynasty, and the part establishing a modern legal system, starting from the legal reforms in the late Qing Dynasty to the present time.

The Primitive Stage of Traditional Law

Traditional Chinese law, lasting from the 21st century B.C. to the end of the last century, constitutes the major part of Chinese legal history. It may be further divided into two major stages. The first stage was the primitive stage of traditional law covering the Xia Dynasty (the 21st century B.C. to the 16th century B.C.), the Shang Dynasty (the 16th century B.C. to the 11th century B.C.) and the Western Zhou Dynasty (the 11th century B.C. to 711 B.C.). These three dynasties were slavery societies built on patriarchal and aristocratic systems. Under such systems, the King of the country granted royal titles, lands and powers to his family members and his favourite generals and ministers, who in return pledged allegiance to the King. This division of powers and privileges was preserved by the primogeniture regime. In such a social context, the rules institutionalising the above systems and social arrangements put substantial emphasis on maintaining the distinct ranks and orders among the nobles, in addition to controlling the populace. As a result, "li" (ritual rules, etiquette) meant mainly the norms governing the conduct of the royal family members and nobles; while "xing" (law), a set of secret and draconian rules, meant the rules governing the slaves.

Thus, a dual system of governance was created, namely the dual system of "li" and "xing". As well as the cruelty and the arbitrariness of the law of this period, the principle that "li never descends to the plebeian class and xing shall by no means ascend to touch nobles"[2] constitutes a far-reaching legal legacy in Chinese legal history. Although this principle was gradually phased out during later periods, the privileges of nobles and officials, especially the exemption for the distinguished from harsh punishment under the law was sustained throughout the entire span of traditional Chinese law.

Stage of Formation and Fortification of Traditional Law

The second stage was the formation and fortification stage of traditional law, which started with the Eastern Zhou Dynasty (770 B.C. to 221 B.C.) and continued through the first unified feudal country, the Qin Dynasty (221 B.C. to 207 B.C.), all the way up to the last dynasty, the Qing Dynasty (1644 to 1911). This period was the most important one for the formation and entrenchment of traditional Chinese law.

The Eastern Zhou Dynasty, divided into the Spring-Autumn Period (770 B.C. to 476 B.C.) and the War Period (475 B.C. to 221 B.C.), witnessed the decline of the slavery system and the vicissitudes of small kingdoms, which caused enormous social unrest and upheavals. In such a social context, changing the archaic law became one of the popular social demands by the newly-arising feudal lords and the populace, who had no political powers and privileges in the patriarchal and aristocratic system. Under the demand for social reforms, the former secret law was replaced by publicly-displayed legal documents. The representatives of this change were the Bronze Tripod bearing rules of Xing (Xingding) designed by Zi Chan of the Zheng Kingdom in 536 B.C., the Bamboo Book of Xing (Zhuxing) by Deng Xi of the Zheng Kingdom around 504 B.C., and the Bronze Tripods bearing rules of Xing in the Jin and other kingdoms in the following years.[3] During the War Period, more profound changes in the law took place. Among the changes, the most significant ones were:

(1) the development of comprehensive codes (a typical example is the legislation by Li Kui of the Wei Kingdom);

3

    (2) the legal reforms launched by Shang Yang of the Qin Kingdom in 361 B.C.; and

    (3) the debates over issues of the functions, purposes and effects of law, and the issue of the importance of law in society among different schools, particularly Confucianism (its founder was Confucius (551 B.C. to 479 B.C.)) and the Legalistic School (Shang Yang was one representative).

These changes facilitated legal reform and the development of the legal system, and elevated the status and functions of the law in society. The Qin Kingdom implemented the most profound reforms promoted by the apologists of the Legalistic School, and the kingdom became the most powerful one during the late War Period. It finally conquered all the other kingdoms establishing the first unified State in Chinese history. The First Emperor of Qin upheld the Legalistic School and vehemently prohibited the ideas and books of Confucianism and other schools by burning all other scholarly books and slaying the disciples of Confucius. This extreme approach of the Legalistic School which emphasised the cruel and excessive punishment of those who dared to show even the slightest resentment, in conjunction with the depletive expenditure resulting from the building of the Great Wall and of the royal palaces, caused nationwide peasant uprisings, and led to the subsequent collapse of the short-lived Qin Dynasty.

    Drawing lessons from the collapse of Qin, the rulers of the Han Dynasty that replaced Qin adopted lenient laws in the hope of winning support from the populace. It later banned the Legalistic School and other schools by elevating Confucianism to the position of the official orthodoxy of the country at the suggestion of Dong Zhongshu (179 B.C. to 104 B.C.), an ardent disciple of Confucianism. From then on, Confucian concepts and ideas were promoted to be the dominant orthodoxy and permeated through all the legal rules and codes as the underpinning spirit of traditional Chinese law throughout the entire feudal society. The Han Code formed a solid foundation for the codes of later dynasties. The subsequent Tong Code (during the Tong Dynasty, one of the most prosperous periods in Chinese history) and the Qing Code (the last dynasty) are considered the most representative pieces of traditional Chinese law.

The Characteristics of Traditional Chinese Law

1.04 Since the Qin Dynasty, China has basically remained a unified country, and the traditional law, started more than 4,000 years ago and fortified by Confucianism in the Han Dynasty, persisted until the beginning of this century. Its stability and sinew of subsistence certainly contributed to the stable and obstinate feudal regime in China and pose an enigma to legal historians. This long-lasting legal system has been labeled as the 'Chinese Legal Tradition" (*zhonghua faxi*)[4], distinct from common law and civil law traditions in the West. This tradition has the following features, which are different from common law and civil law traditions and, to a great extent, are contrary to the concepts of modern law.

Traditional Chinese law overtly recognizes and protects the unequal status of persons. It is constructed on the feudal system based on a patriarchal system and the *ancien regime*. Under such social settings, social status which is pre-determined by pedigrees or by official ranks is the crucial determinant of individuals' rights and obligations. Equality before law was never officially accepted as a legal principle and as a legal practice. Social status has apparently been more important than legal rules. The system of exemption of eight categories of persons from criminal prosecution (*ba yi*) and the system of exemption from criminal punishment by giving up official positions (*guandang*) are formally-recognized legal devices that provide different legal treatment on the basis of different social status and grant privileges above law to the privileged classes in society. Some practices of inequality before the law in contemporary China, such as the necessity to seek approval from a higher authority before investigating and prosecuting high-ranking officials (the most recent example of this practice being the bribery case of Chen Xitong, the former Party Secretary in Beijing), may be attributable to this legacy.

This traditional legal system is not founded on the democratic system but on a totalitarian system. The emperors are enthroned as sons of heaven by the orthodox theory of the feudalism and by military powers. Any utterance of the emperor is taken as law. The feudal rulers have absolute control over the entire country. This totalitarian system generates the concept of the rule of man and its irrational practices which have persisted throughout history and still exert influence over the present legal system. The centralized power structure constitutes a closed pyramid style system of dominance by man which excludes any possibility of joint rule or rules from any other sources. Unlike Western civilisation, where the secular and religious powers and legal systems co-existed and fostered a tradition of plurality and the supremacy of law, the traditional Chinese legal system, which is a subordinate sub-branch of the power structure, has never encountered strong counterparts, and therefore never tolerated the existence of any alien powers and legal rules other than those of the emperor. In such a political milieu, the supremacy of law in society can hardly be generated and embraced.

Traditional law is constructed on the basis of a monolithic and comprehensive code that contains all types of rules, with criminal law as the backbone of the entire system. It is no exaggeration to say that traditional law is of the same nature as criminal law as it depends on criminal punishments to structure the system. As a result, all types of litigation are subject to criminal procedures which are represented by torture and corporal punishment and deter the populace from using the legal apparatus. Therefore, the law is viewed by both the ruling class and the ruled as a cruel instrument of suppression. The agricultural-autarchic economy can by no means promote concepts of freedom and equality, but ideas of hierarchy and obedience. Therefore, the concept of private law which reflects the patterns and spirits of market exchanges among equal persons has never appeared in the traditional legal system. In a broader sense, the emphasis on criminal law and disregard for civil law is the only natural product of the agricultural-autarchic economy and the totalitarian regime. This phenomenon poses a striking contrast with Western legal tradition, which is based to a great extent on private law such as the *jus civile* in ancient Roman law, and the "law merchant" in European countries. The lack of private law in Chinese legal history, and the dominance of the monolithic code backed by criminal law, may explain the generally hostile attitude towards litigation in Chinese society, which still exists to a certain extent.

1.05   In the traditional legal system, there is no separate judicial branch. The administrative officials exercise both the power of administration and the power of adjudication. In the process of adjudication, they take the role and the responsibility of both prosecutor and judge at the same time. The typical format of a trial is an inquisitional process backed by physical torture to obtain a confession. This irrational practice of law is not able to establish impartiality but rather prejudice against parties to litigation (especially defendants). Since this irrational process defeats people's expectations and hopes for the law, they are compelled to place their expectations and hopes in the illusory rationality of individual officials. Therefore, throughout history, the popular concept is that justice cannot be found in the law, but from the intelligence and honesty of individual officials. This may be a partial explanation for the deeply-rooted distrust of the legal system and the formal justice in Chinese culture, and for the practice of finding personal connections and substantive justice outside of the formal procedure.

A distinct legal profession never emerged in the traditional legal system. To start litigation or to be sued by the government or other persons means to be left at the discretion of officials, without any legal assistance from any other people. There are a few self-trained shysters (*song shi*), but their role is no more than drafting complaints or other legal documents for the litigants. They are not permitted to defend or argue for the litigants as independent legal experts during trials. Most of the shysters are ex-clerks working in governmental offices. Economic profits are their primary concern in providing the limited legal assistance to litigants, therefore, they enjoy no respectable reputation. The lack of a systematic legal education system also contributes to the absence of a distinct legal profession and the lack of qualified legal officials. Although there was a tradition of learning from officials (*yi li wei shi*) in the Qin Dynasty, legal education by private institutes has never occurred in traditional law.

The law is interwoven with confucianism and feudal ethical rules. "Taking moral means as the primary, and legal means as the secondary"[5] has long been the ideal way of governance by the ancient rulers. In this system, moral standards are sanctioned by the legal rules. The persistent rules concerning the ten gross evils (including *inter alia* conspiracy for rebellion, treason, assault and killing of elderly family members and relatives, failure to perform filial piety, disturbing patriarchal orders, etc.) represent the moral values imbued in the legal system. The law intends to regulate not only ostensible behaviours but also internal patterns of thinking.

The emphasis of law is on the protection of government powers and social interests rather than on the protection of individual rights and private interests. The patriarchal system and the totalitarian regime does not allow or even tolerate the existence of individual rights or interests that may foster rebellion against the regime. The feudal rulers, in the name of the ultimate head of the entire patriarchal system and the paramount leader of the totalitarian regime, assume their interests to be the legitimate public interests and substitute them for individual interests. "To preserve heavenly theorem and to eradicate human lusts" is the dominant spirit of law. As a result of this assertion, State, community and family, which constitute the different levels of the fabric of feudal society, are the primary concerns of the law. The notion of the ten gross evils mentioned above demonstrates this emphasis of traditional law. To a great extent, private interests and rights have never been the concern of the law. This historical feature has been ingrained in Chinese legal culture and continues to influence the current development of the legal system.

Nevertheless, traditional law also has its contributions and values, **1.06** including the mixed system of codification and precedents,[6] an emphasis on the educational function of the law, the rich experience in legal practice, and the stable function of the law in maintaining social harmony. The mixed system refers to the role of precedents in the traditional legal system. Although Chinese law is based primarily on codified documents, in many periods of history, precedents do play an important role in analysing legal rules and providing detailed standards to officials who are responsible for adjudication. To a certain extent, the cases published by the Supreme People's Court and those by the provincial high courts have the same effect in the current legal system. Likewise, the educational function and the stable function of law also have their impacts on the contemporary legal system.

Generally speaking, the strengths and values of the traditional law have been overshadowed by its backwardness and demerits.

Traditional Chinese law and legal culture constituted an insurmountable obstacle in the historical course of transition towards modernisation. So much so that the modern legal system must now demolish the entire traditional legal system. This irreconcilable contradiction between the two systems demands the termination of the traditional legal system and the inception of a new era of Chinese legal development.

Chinese Law in Modern Times

1.07 The second part of Chinese legal history has been the transition towards a modern legal system compatible with an industrialized and modernized society. To date, this transition is far from being completed.

Legal modernization was triggered by foreign powers during the Opiate War (1840) and the signing of the unequal treaties by the Qing Imperial Court. It was at this time that ancient China found it had been surpassed by the superior material instruments and superior systems of modern Western countries, amongst which the legal system occupied an important position. With humiliation, China started to learn from the Western legal system. Shen Jiaben (1840 to 1913), the Minister in Charge of Legal Reform in the late Qing Dynasty, invited Japanese legal scholars to assist the legal reform process. Despite the failure of the reform process, these scholars translated some foreign laws and legal works and prepared many drafts of important new laws of the Qing Dynasty. These legal reforms exerted a significant impact on later reforms. The reasons for the failure were multiple — one was the incompatibility of the newly-designed legal system with the old and obstinate social structure. Without changing the entire social system through a revolution or a reform, the mere changing of black-letter laws could hardly achieve any significant and sustainable results.

Later on, the Nationalist Government continued the course of legal reform and drafted new laws by copying Western patterns on a broader basis. But these laws again were never effectively implemented throughout the country, due to the failure of the Nationalist Government to unify the country and to make thorough social changes.

The legal reform scheme, regardless of its form and results, has attempted to replace the Chinese legal tradition by introducing modern Western types of law. The tremendous pressure and demands triggered by the need to modernize the country and to transform the archaic social infrastructure are so alien to the traditional law, that it can hardly co-exist with the new legal regime. The new legal regime based, on totally different social and economic structures, is on the whole antagonistic to the traditional law and culture. In this sense, it may be asserted that there is no inherent connection between the traditional Chinese law and the modern legal regime in China. Institutionally, the long-lasting Chinese legal tradition has died.[7] Nevertheless, the traditional legal culture continues to exert its influence on contemporary society. The above-mentioned features pose constant obstacles to the legal system in China. Any explanation of the "grotesque" practices and "peculiar" problems of the existing legal system cannot ignore the results of the traditional and cultural values existing underneath the formal legal system. In this sense, the traditional legal system is extinct, but the traditional legal culture, in the sense of ingrained consciousness and customary behavior, has persisted obstinately despite the institutional changes and the legal reform endeavors.

Historical Development of the PRC

The Nature of the Legal System in the PRC

The PRC legal system was established in 1949 upon the founding of   **1.08**
the PRC, which had its embryonic form in the "liberated areas" occupied by the communists. This new legal system was based on entirely different political, economic and ideological structures. In February 1949, the Central Committee of the Communist Party of China (hereafter the CPC) issued the Instruction on Abolition of the Nationalist Six Codes and on Affirmation of the Legal Principles of the Liberated Areas, which officially abolished the Nationalist legal system in the mainland and attempted to establish a brand new legal system of a socialist nature.

Stage of Legal Construction

The period from 1949 to 1956 was the stage of legal construction. In   **1.09**
this period, China faced many problems and tasks, inter alia, recovery from the war-demolished economy, strengthening of its new regime, reform of capitalist ownership, construction of a socialist system and the Korean War. The nature of this period was the transition from "New Democracy Revolution" to "Socialist Revolution", as described by official statements. The purpose of this transition was to establish a socialist system, which required, in the economic field, public ownership and a centralized-planned economy; in the political field, people's democratic dictatorship and the supremacy of the Party;

and in the cultural and ideological field, the dominance of Marxist theory.

One striking feature of this period was the constant social reforms and movements launched throughout the country, such as the Land Reform from 1950 to 1952, the Movement of Suppression of Counter-revolutionaries from 1950 to 1953, the Movement Against the Three Evils (corruption, waste and bureaucracy in the Party and the government) in 1952, the Movement Against Five Evils (bribery, tax evasion, theft of State property, cheating on government contracts, and stealing State economic information, mainly by private business-men and entrepreneurs) in 1952, and the Movement of Judicial Reform starting from 1952. In the process of these movements, relevant laws and regulations were drafted and promulgated to meet the needs of these movements, among which the most important step was the promulgation of the first PRC Constitution in 1954. In order to establish the socialist regime, socialist reform was launched in both urban and rural areas. In the cities, after the confiscation of bureau-cratic capitalist property, national capitalist ownership and small private business became the major forms of ownership which were alien to socialist ownership. The socialist reform in urban areas, following the policy of redemption, intended to transform capitalist ownership and private ownership into socialist ownership by persuading or forcing private proprietors to establish public and private joint ventures with the State. In rural areas, after the confiscation of land from landlords and distributing it among the peasants, the Movement of Agricultural Co-operation was initiated. It went through several stages and finally led to the establishment of People's Communes in 1958.

On the whole, this period was the major period for legal construc-tion, in the sense that many laws and regulations, especially the Constitution, were promulgated. Many basic legal institutions were also established, such as the judicial structure, the procuratorial struc-ture, the governmental structure and the legal profession. Though the movements may have been necessary and were probably the most efficient means to inaugurate and promote such a rapid and fundamen-tal social change, they nevertheless had certain negative impacts on the development of the new legal system. These included the idea that the policies of the Party and the State should be more important than legal rules, and the tendency of neglect or even violation of rules and procedures for the sake of social reform. As a result, law was perceived as something flexible and manipulable. To a certain extent, this is still the dominant attitude, which may be demonstrated by different inter-pretations of the law on the basis of policy. Therefore, in analysing and applying legal rules in China, it is necessary to understand the current policies of the Party and the State that serve as the parameters for legal interpretation and operation.

Decline and Suspension of the Legal System

The second period started from 1956 and ended in 1966, during which **1.10**
legal development was virtually suspended. The turnabout was triggered by the Hungarian Incident and the severe criticism and castigation of the Party and the government expressed during the Movement
of Rectification in 1957. This was taken as an alarm signal by the Party
and entrenched the "leftist" thoughts embraced by Mao Zedong and
other communist leaders. Therefore, they turned the Rectification
Movement, intended to rectify the working style of the Party, into an
Anti-rightist Movement, intended to repulse criticism. During the
Movement, many intellectuals and cadres were punished and purged
for their alleged attacks against the Party. The concepts of legality,
equality before the law and the independence of the judiciary were
labelled as bourgeois ideas and discarded completely. As a result of the
surging leftist thoughts, the Party's policy to concentrate on economic
construction formulated by the Party's Eighth National Congress was
replaced by the concept of class struggle, which was prioritised by Mao
as the major task in China. During this period, the National People's
Congress virtually suspended its legislative function, and only a few
regulations were passed. The already feeble legal profession suffered a
fatal blow and was disbanded, except in the limited field of foreign
trade. What became accepted and dominant ideas were the contempt
for the old legal regime and the tendency to neglect law and to subject
law to Party policy and mass movements. Law was not regarded as a
necessary instrument in social life. Although important laws such as
the Civil Code, the Criminal Code and the Procedural Code were
deliberated by the legislative body during this period, they were never
formally enacted due to the "Anti-Rightist Movement" and the subsequent "Cultural Revolution". The policies of the Party and the State
were the most authoritative guidance for behavior, especially for
political activities. This tendency paved the way for the "Cultural
Revolution".

The Destruction of the Legal System

The third stage was the period of the "Cultural Revolution", which is
considered as a period of disaster in the PRC history. During this stage,
the extreme left-wing approaches called for "Continuous Revolution
under the Proletarian Dictatorship". Endless fights among different
groups of people and brutal castigation and corporal torture of numerous individuals ranging from ordinary citizens to senior intellectuals
and cadres were instigated by the leftists under the name of the "Cultural Revolution". The spirit of rebellion and lawlessness was praised.
It is no exaggeration to say that the country was in a complete chaos

and social development was suspended during the ten years of the "Cultural Revolution". Against such a background, law commensurate with order and justice was labelled a capitalist device restricting the hands of the revolution. The law was literally abolished and the legal apparatus, which was already inert, was completely smashed. The Party's policies and Mao's works were the only sources of rules in the country.

Legal Reconstruction and Reform

1.11 The disastrous economic consequences and the protracted political fighting made the people expect an end to the leftist dominance — this was brought about by the arrest of the "Gang of Four", the ultra-leftist group in power. After the nightmare of the Cultural Revolution, China began to engage in unprecedented legal reconstruction. Law was regarded as the most efficient and institutionalised means to safeguard people's democracy, to prevent sudden social changes brought about by the whims of leaders and to maintain the sustained economic development of the country.[8] This ideological change paved the way to the fourth stage of the development of the country's legal system.

The current fourth stage of legal reconstruction has been unveiled in the context of the profound social changes throughout the country. In the political field, economic construction has replaced the class struggle as the basic task of the country; democracy and the protection of citizens' rights have been emphasised by the Party and the government; decentralization has been introduced into the power structure; and the governmental organs have been streamlined around the people's congress system. In the economic field, the policy of structural reform and opening up to the outside world has been introduced and implemented; the rigid planned economy has been abandoned and replaced by a "Socialist Market Economy". Private ownership has been allowed and protected; foreign investment and foreign trade have been encouraged and promoted. The nature and fundamental purposes of socialism have been defined by Deng Xiaoping as being: to promote productivity, to eliminate exploitation and to reach the final goal of prosperity for all.[9] Despite the enormous changes, there has been a lot of criticism of the inertia in political change, poor protection of human rights and the inadequacy of economic reforms.

Corresponding to such a social scenario, the legal system has been redesigned for the purpose of implementing, institutionalising and strengthening the reform enterprise. The achievements of the legal reconstruction include the following:

    a) The awareness of the importance of law by the populace and the government represents a watershed in China's legal development. The ideological change has to a great extent changed the popular view towards law. The subsisting legal debates have invigorated the legal discourse and paved the way for reforming the legal system. The debates have been conducted over the issues of the nature of the law, right-centred theory, the dichotomy between Party policy and the law, the antagonism of the rule of law and the rule of man, the division between private law and public law, the presumption of innocence, etc. Many ideas discussed by legal scholars have been incorporated into the laws and regulations, such as the Constitution, civil law, administrative law, procedural law. The recent revision of the PRC Criminal Procedure Law is one of the positive consequences of such debates.

b) Since 1979, China has embarked on a large-scale legislative endeavour which has brought about 200 laws and 80 decisions of the National People's Congress; more than 700 administrative regulations of the State Council and its ministries, commissions and other branches; about 3,000 local regulations, and more than 10,000 local administrative rules of the local governments and their agencies.[10] This ever-expanding constellation of laws and regulations in a nascent but growing legal regime embraces almost every aspect of society and constitutes a complex hierarchy of law in China.

c) A legal structure has been established throughout the country. It includes the system of the people's courts, the system of the people's procuratorates — these two are the judicial branches established by the people's congresses — and various governmental law enforcement organs such as public security organs, tax bureaux, administrative reconsideration offices, arbitration committees, etc. Taking the judicial branch as an example, by 1994, there were, under the Supreme People's Court, 30 high courts, 391 intermediate courts and 3,074 basic courts.[11]

d) The legal profession has been restored. By June of 1995, there were 89,000 lawyers and 7,200 law firms which are in the forms of partnership, co-operation and State sponsorship.[12] Legal education has also flourished. The number of law schools has risen from two by the end of 1977 to more than 80.

Problems in the PRC Legal System

Despite the achievements mentioned above, it is important not to overlook the negative side of the system. There are problems due to profound contradictions and issues wrought by rapid social reform and   **1.12** structural problems. The problems and deeply rooted contradictions create a big gap between the law on paper and the law in practice.

The concepts of supremacy of law and the rule of law are still not fully accepted by governmental officials. Although the issues of rule of man and the rule of law constituted the first nationwide legal debate in the early stage of legal reconstruction, official documents have not formally adopted the concept of "the rule of law". The term used in official documents is "legal system". (Although the two terms have the same pronunciation of "fa zhi" in Chinese, the literal meanings of them are different.) The General Secretary of the Party, Jiang Zemin recently called for "governing the country according to law"[13] which rekindled the desire of legal scholars to push for formal recognition of the concept of the rule of law. The crucial issue involved in this discussion is whether the Party and the government are subject to law or whether law is merely an instrument of the government in governing the country.

There is no doubt that law has to a great extent been elevated to the centre stage of society, but this elevation does not guarantee the supremacy of law in society. Party policies, governmental powers, the network of all kinds of social relations and the rampant local protectionism often render law a secondary authority. Therefore it is naive to rely purely and solely on legal rules to solve all issues encountered in the country. Since China has a long history of feudal and patriarchal systems, a tradition of dependency on wise and charismatic leaders and a long practice of the planned economy and the old socialist system which concentrates on the supremacy of the Party and rule of man have a tenacious influence on both officials and populace. In such a social context, the real supremacy of law shall continue to remain in legal rhetoric for a long period of time.

The proliferation of laws and regulations is a parameter of the rapid development of the legal system. But ambiguity about the division of legislative powers among people's congresses at different levels, and among the governmental branches with different functions and at different levels, makes legal rules inconsistent and even contradictory among themselves. Legislative power has become a lever for governmental organs to get more control of funds or more power. Differences among legal rules of different organs and levels create confusion in complying with law. Furthermore, the constant changes promoted by reform and social transition make some of the existing legal rules out of touch with social reality; new amendments and supplementary provisions, especially the judicial opinions, render the legal rules too complicated. Despite the legislative explosion, there are in some fields no adequate legal rules. Lack of legal expertise is common. Since many administrative rules and local regulations are not published systematically, there is no comprehensive and authoritative way for rule-finding and there is no sufficient and effective way to challenge legal rules on the basis of the constitution.

Notwithstanding the large number of laws and regulations enacted in the PRC, implementation of law remains a major challenge to the nascent legal system. The gap between laws on the statute books and those enforced in practice tarnishes the credibility of the system. The tenacious plague of "triangle debts", the difficulty in enforcing verdicts and arbitral awards and the impotence of the Bankruptcy Law and the Copyright Law are well known examples of this problem. The difficulty in implementing laws is the result of many factors which reflect far deeper social problems and contradictions. These factors include the influence of Party policy, the rapid social and structural changes, abuses of official powers, widely spread favouritism and local protectionism, corruption, symbolic legal rules, selective implementation, the coexistence of both the old and new mechanisms, implementation of law in the form of mass movements, etc. Many legal scholars and officials in China have realized that the implementation of law shall be the major task for the next stage of the legal development in China.

These problems are pernicious and pose an imminent threat to the future of Chinese law. From a practical perspective, realizing the existence of them can help us to understand how to use legal rules and other means of solving legal issues encountered in China.

Hierarchy of Chinese Law

Chinese law follows the continental legal tradition, therefore, the sources of law are mainly statutes and written legal documents. As discussed above, the increasing number and complexity of legal rules make legal research more difficult. Therefore, to understand the hierarchy of Chinese law is a prerequisite for studying and applying it.   **1.13**

Structure of the State Organs

The hierarchy of laws relates closely to the structure of the Chinese government. As a socialist country, China's formal political structure is centred on the system of people's congresses which are responsible for creating and supervising all administrative, judicial and procuratorial organs at all levels. Since China adopts the unitary system as the organic form of the state and the principle of democratic centralism, all local government organs function under the unified leadership of the central authorities and within the scope of power delegated by the central authorities. (See Chart 1.)

There are five levels of the PRC governmental structure:

a) the central level,
b) provincial level,
c) prefectural level (in most places, there are no governmental organs at this level except autonomous prefectures and large cities.),
d) country and city level,
e) township and village (*xiang*) level. At the grass root level, natural village (*cun*), there are no governmental organs, but an assembly of villagers which is an autonomous mass organization.

At the above mentioned five levels, legally speaking, the people's congresses are the most authoritative state organs enjoying exclusive state power at a corresponding level. For example, at the central level, the National People's Congress (hereafter the NPC) is the highest state organ in the country enjoying exclusive state power such as legislation, establishing and organizing other state organs at the central level, appointing important leaders of the country, supervising the work of other state organs, etc. Since the NPC convenes only one meeting annually, its Standing Committee carries many of its powers and functions.

Below the Congress, there are three branches. They are the State Council, Supreme People's Court and Supreme People's Procuratorate. The State Council (the central government) is the highest state administrative organ. Within the State Council, there are ministries, commissions and bureaux responsible for the administration of particular fields or state affairs. According to the Constitution, the State Council has the legislative power to make administrative regulations; its ministries, commissions and bureaux have the power to issue administrative rules. All the laws and administrative regulations are mandatory for the people's courts to follow, but the administrative rules may be subject to examination by the courts in the administrative litigation process. The Supreme People's Court is responsible for exercising the state power of adjudication and the Supreme People's Procuratorate for exercising the legal supervision power. They also have the power to issue judicial interpretations relating to legal rules in the course of their adjudication or legal supervision work. Since their interpretations intend to answer specific and detailed questions raised in the process of application of law, they constitute a very important part of the legal hierarchy, especially the interpretations by the Court. It is a controversial issue as to whether the Court and the Procuratorate should have such a quasi law-making power.

At each lower level, the same pattern of structure can be observed.

Chart 1

LEGAL SYSTEM OF THE PRC
GOVERNMENTAL STRUCTURE OF THE PRC

(1) Central Level;   (2) Provincial Level;
(3) Prefectural Level (not existing);   (4) County Level;   (5) Township

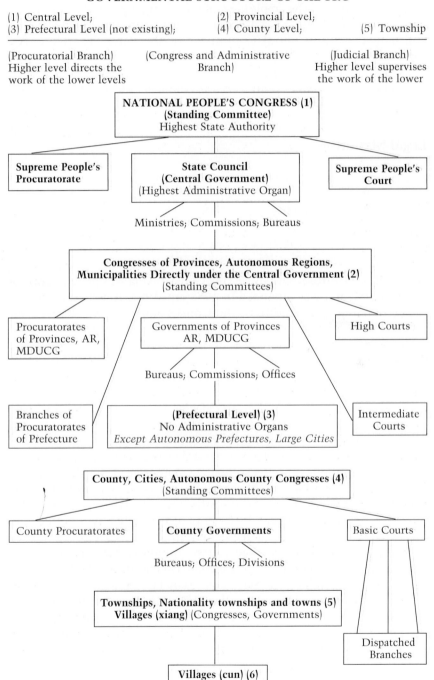

(Procuratorial Branch)   (Congress and Administrative   (Judicial Branch)
Higher level directs the   Branch)   Higher level supervises
work of the lower levels   the work of the lower

NATIONAL PEOPLE'S CONGRESS (1)
(Standing Committee)
Highest State Authority

Supreme People's Procuratorate

State Council (Central Government) (Highest Administrative Organ)

Supreme People's Court

Ministries; Commissions; Bureaus

Congresses of Provinces, Autonomous Regions, Municipalities Directly under the Central Government (2) (Standing Committees)

Procuratorates of Provinces, AR, MDUCG

Governments of Provinces AR, MDUCG

High Courts

Bureaus; Commissions; Offices

Branches of Procuratorates of Prefecture

(Prefectural Level) (3) No Administrative Organs *Except Autonomous Prefectures, Large Cities*

Intermediate Courts

County, Cities, Autonomous County Congresses (4) (Standing Committees)

County Procuratorates

County Governments

Basic Courts

Bureaus; Offices; Divisions

Townships, Nationality townships and towns (5) **Villages (xiang)** (Congresses, Governments)

Dispatched Branches

Villages (cun) (6)

17

Nevertheless, beside the formal structure of the state organs described by law, it cannot be overlooked that the Communist Party, as
the leading and only political party possessing state power, has the
decisive role in making, applying and reforming legal rules. No important statute has been passed without discussion or scrutiny by the
Politbureau of the Central Committee of the Party. Therefore, the
comprehension and interpretation of legal rules should be done in line
with the Party's policy and instructions. Party organizations which
parallel the state organs at all levels are the institutional guarantee for
the Party's guidance.

Legal Structure

1.14   The legislative structure in such a regime is described by scholars as "a
monistic system with several levels", which means that the NPC as
the highest state organ has the unitary legislative power over the entire
nation and it delegates certain legislative powers to local people's
congresses and the central and local governments. (See Chart 2.)
   The sources of legal rules are as follows:

   a) **Constitution.** The subsisting Constitution was promulgated in
      1982 and was amended in 1988 and 1993. In a broad sense, it
      includes the statute of the Constitution, law of election, or-
      ganic laws of the people's congresses, of the State Council, of
      the local governments, of the people's courts and of the
      people's procuratorates.
         Although the Constitution is regarded as the paramount
      law in the country, it nevertheless cannot be quoted in judicial
      verdicts and administrative decisions as a direct legal ground
      for solving concrete disputes and problems. It is therefore out
      of direct touch with daily legal practice and operation and is
      regarded as being of a general and vague nature. Since it has no
      direct applicable effects, review of other legal rules and govern-
      mental practice on the basis of constitutionality have been
      both politically and technically problematic.

   b) **Law (*falu*).** All legal documents promulgated by the NPC and
      its Standing Committee belong to the category of law which
      includes laws, decisions (often containing state policies) and
      ratified international treaties. Law could be further divided
      into two sub-categories, one is basic laws which are enacted by
      the general meetings of the NPC and have a general impact
      throughout the nation; the rest are non-basic laws which are
      enacted by the Standing Committee of the NPC and have a
      wide impact in certain areas only.

   c) **Administrative Regulations (*xingzheng fagui*).** This refers to
      the legal documents made by the State Council (sometimes

Chart 2

STRUCTURE OF THE CHINESE LAW

PARTY POLICY

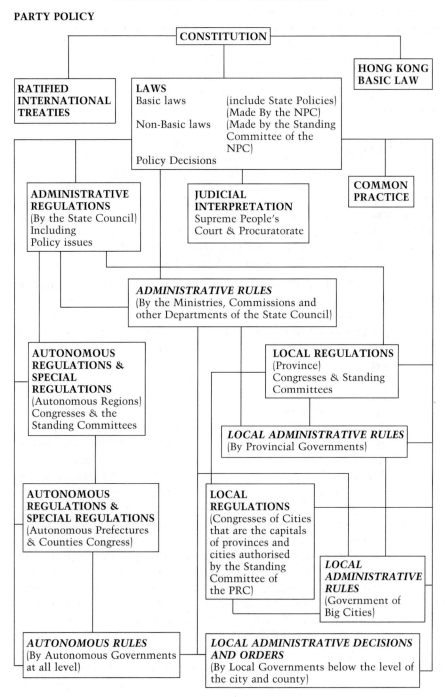

19

together with the Party). As the central administration of the country, the State Council has the power to enact rules concerning important issues of the country provided they shall not contravene the Constitution and the law. On most occasions, they are detailed rules for implementing laws; on other occasions, they are experimental rules where there are no governing laws.

d) **Administrative Rules (*xingzheng guizhang*).** This category includes regulatory rules issued by the ministries, commissions and departments of the State Council. These governmental organs are administrative branches which have the power to issue rules regulating affairs and matters under their respective administration. From a practical perspective, this set of rules is very important for it provides detailed procedures, standards and requirements for practitioners. For example, rules issued by the Ministry of Foreign Trade and Economic Cooperation are most useful for practical issues regarding foreign investment and foreign trades.

e) **Local Regulations (*difang fagui*).** Local regulations are enacted by local people's congresses and their respective standing committees. Their effects shall be confined within their respective geographical territories. The local people's congresses and their standing committees include the levels of provinces, counties, large cities and cities which are the capitals of provinces and are authorized by the Standing Committee of the NPC.

f) **Local Administrative Rules (*difang xingzheng guizhang*).** This category includes regulatory rules issued by provincial, city and county governments and their administrative branches. They are detailed rules for implementing national laws and regulations and local regulations in their respective areas.

g) **Autonomous Regulations and Special Regulations (*difang zizhi tiaoli he danxing tiaoli*).** According to the Constitution, the people's congresses and their respective standing committees of autonomous areas of all levels (autonomous regions, prefectures and counties), have the power to enact autonomous regulations and special regulations which shall not contravene the Constitution but may adopt flexible and different rules accordaning to their special local conditions and customs.

h) **Autonomous Rules (*difang zizhi guizhang*).** Although there are no specific provisions defining the legislative powers of the autonomous governments, they in practice, have similar power to the local governments to make rules regulating affairs and matters under their daily administration.

1.15 i) **Regulations by Special Economic Zones (*jingji tequ fagui*).** Special economic zones are the places circumscribed by the

Standing Committee of the NPC for the purpose of promoting foreign investment and attracting foreign technology. In such places, the economic structure may be different from other places in terms of preferential treatment for foreign business, powers of import and export, more radical measures of reform and experiments. By the authorization of the NPC, Hainan provinces and Shenzhen, Xiamen, Zhuhai and Shantou as well as Pudong Developing Zone have acquired the power of enacting special economic zones' regulations which institutionalize the economic practices in these areas.

j) **Judicial Interpretation (*sifa jieshi*).** Judicial interpretation consists of detailed rules for implementing laws and regulations, judicial guidance to resolve issues encountered in the process of application of law, answers to specific questions raised by lower courts and procuratorates, etc. by the Supreme People's Court and the Supreme People's Procuratorate. According to law, the Supreme People's Court and the Supreme People's Procuratorate have the power to issue judicial interpretations on questions concerning specific application of laws and regulations in judicial proceedings. Despite the criticisms on the broad power of judicial interpretation, two supreme judicial organs have played important roles in shaping the legal regime and have provided the lower judicial organs with urgently needed gap-fillers. In theory these interpretations are only binding over the judicial branches, but in practice they have a wider range of application in all kinds of dispute resolutions throughout the country, such as administrative proceedings and arbitration.

Judicial decisions are not legally binding over later cases, but the decisions published or approved by the two supreme judicial organs have *de facto* influence over the thinking of all judges and prosecutors and their effects as reference can not be ignored. In times when there are no explicit legal rules, judicial verdicts inevitably provide some guidance.

k) **Hong Kong Basic Law (*xianggang jiben fa*).** Hong Kong Basic   **1.16**
Law (hereafter HKBL) is a new category which has occurred with the invention of the policy of "one country two systems". After the return of the sovereignty of Hong Kong, the judicial system previously practised in Hong Kong shall be maintained, which is distinct from the system in the mainland, but it shall function under the PRC Constitution and within the framework of one country. Since it provides the foundation for safeguarding the Common Law System of Hong Kong and serves as a bridge between two entirely different legal systems, its position in the PRC legal system is unique. Judging from its nature (semi-constitution), its contents (provisions concerning

political, economic, social structure and basic rights of residence), its effects (applicable nationwide), its relations with
other national laws and regulations (without particular procedure at the NPC, other laws shall not be effective in Hong
Kong), it is proper to posit it below the Constitution and above
other national laws. The direct application of the HKBL in
concrete cases and the particular procedure of interpretating
the HKBL by the Standing Committee of the National People's
Congress after consultation with its Committee for the HKBL,
may influence the future development of the Chinese Constitutional Law.

l) **Common Practice.** In every jurisdiction, there are informal
parts or elements within the formal legal system. In the Chinese legal system, these informal elements also exist as hidden
rules or procedures. For example, the law does not explicitly
stipulate whether lawyers can meet the judges before open
trials. In practice, many lawyers try to meet judges to discuss
their cases in order to influence the judges' opinions. In the
process of adjudication, division chiefs and presidents of courts
often ask the judges responsible for certain cases to report to
them on issues of these cases. Their opinions often influence
the outcome of the cases. Without knowing these common
practices, parties and their legal counsels find it difficult to
apply the legal rules efficiently and effectively.

m) **International treaties.** Once China becomes a signatory party
to an international treaty, the treaty shall become an integral
part of the system except for the articles over which China
makes reservations.

Among the constellation of legal rules, the principles of
determining their effects are as follows:

(i) higher rules prevail over lower rules;
(ii) later rules prevail over the previous rules;
(iii) special rules prevail over general rules.

In the process of adjudication, laws and regulations
have greater effects than rules. According to Administrative
Litigation Law, people's courts must follow laws, administrative regulations and local regulations, but may take administrative rules and local rules as references. In this sense, courts
may decide whether a rule is enforceable or not in the process
of a litigation on the grounds of contradicting higher legal
rules.

From a practical perspective, administrative rules and local regulations are more useful in the sense that they provide for more detailed
guidelines and procedures on concrete legal issues. The problem is that
these rules and regulations are not published in a systematic way,

therefore it is difficult to find proper and applicable rules in legal practice.

Again one point that should not be overlooked is the Party policy as mentioned above, which has significant impacts on law but not formally a part of the legal system.

Judicial Structure and Practice

Judicial structure in the Chinese sense does not only refer to courts,   **1.17** but also to procuratorates and public security organs. The security organ is one branch in the administrative system; the other two branches are created by the people's congresses and, in the legal sense, are on an equal footing with the administrative branch. The presidents of courts and the procurator-generals of procuratorates are selected and appointed by the people's congresses on the same levels. The judges and procurators are selected and appointed by the standing committees of the respective people's congresses, and assistant judges and assistant procurators are appointed by the respective courts and procuratorates.

The people's courts are state organs exercising exclusive state adjudicatory power. The people's procuratorates are the organs for legal supervision (initiating criminal indictments, supervising the practise of other judicial organs) on behalf of the state. According to the Constitution, within the judicial branch, the higher level courts supervise the work of the lower courts and the courts at various levels are responsible to the respective people's congresses that created them. But within the structure of the procuratorate, the higher level procuratorates direct the work of those at lower levels. The procuratorial organs at lower levels are responsible to both the corresponding people's congresses which created them and the people's procuratorates at higher levels. We will examine the structure of the courts which are the most important in terms of settling legal disputes.

The people's courts have four levels, namely the Supreme People's Court at the national level, high courts at provincial level, intermediate courts at prefectural level (that is a level between the levels of province and county and there are no administrative branches at this level except in autonomous areas and in big cities.), basic courts at county and city level. In many places, the basic courts establish branches for the sake of convenience of the people. Within each court, there are usually several divisions, such as civil, economic, criminal, administrative and enforcement divisions. A court has one president and several vice-presidents, a division has one chief and several associate chiefs. Each court also has a judicial committee which is composed of the presidents, division chiefs and experienced judges. The members of the committee are appointed by the standing committees of the courts at the corresponding level. The judicial committee is the most authoritative body in a court, which is responsible for discussing important or difficult cases, making decisions concerning other judicial matters and reviewing and summing up judicial experiences. Its decision shall be followed by judges and collegial panels. In case of differing opinions, the majority's opinions shall be adopted.

Collegial panels are the basic units in each court. They are not permanent bodies but organised to adjudicate individual cases. A collegial panel is composed of three to seven judges, the number of which must be odd. Simple civil cases, economic cases, minor criminal cases and cases that are otherwise provided for in law can be tried by a single judge. Cases of second trial are heard by a collegial panel of three to five judges. The presiding judge of the panel is appointed by the president of the court or the division chief. When a president or a division chief participates in a trial, he/she shall be the presiding judge of the panel.

The standing committees of local people's congresses may appoint people's assessors and provide a list of them to the courts at the corresponding level. Courts may select people's assessors to participate in cases of first trial. The function and position of the people's assessors in collegial panels are the same as judges. Since nowadays economic interests are a major concern of the populace, it is increasingly difficult to find those who are willing to serve as people's assessors. As a result, collegial panels for the first trial may be composed of judges and people's assessors or of judges exclusively. The people's assessors system is different from the jury system in common law jurisdiction, in that the people's assessors are not selected on the basis of citizenship, they function as judges, and have the authority to decide both issues of facts and law.

The trial process is the crucial part of adjudication and is greatly influenced by the civil law jurisdiction in which the judge is the dominant party in conducting a trial. Recently, "the reform of adjudication format" has tried to bring an adversarial pattern into the Chinese adjudication process. The recently revised Criminal Procedure Law will also further the reform.

1.18 According to law, each case shall have at the most two trials, which means that litigants to a case and their legal representatives who challenge the judgements or orders made by a local court in the trial of first instance have the right to appeal the case to the next higher level court only once. Once an appeal is filed the next higher court must try the case again. The judgement of the second trial shall be final and cannot be appealed. However, the parties to a litigation may challenge the final decision or the effective decision through the trial supervision procedure. They may appeal to the appellate court or a higher court. After reviewing the complaint, the president may ask the judicial committee to make a decision to accept or reject the appeal. Under no circumstances does the re-trial initiated by trial supervision procedure suspend the enforcement of the effective judgement that is challenged.

The Constitution and the Organic Law of Courts allow the people's courts to exercise state adjudicatory power independently, free from interference from any organizations or individuals. The word "court" is of pivotal importance and, according to the authoritative explanation, means that the individual judges do not have the adjudicatory power but the courts where the judges perform their duties do. The collegial panels are the trial units not the individual judges and the judgements by the collegial panels are made in the name of the courts. Therefore, the independent power of adjudication is vested in courts and not in judges. Based on this explanation, presidents and division chiefs may have a legitimate right to review and suggest changes in draft judgments prepared by collegial panels. This practice constitutes an internal interference with the independent adjudication of collegial panels and, strictly speaking, has no direct legal grounds except for the above. Another internal interference with collegial panels comes from the judicial committees. If a case is considered complicated or important, the final decision may be concluded by the judicial committee of a court rather than the designated collegial panel. This mechanism is said to be designed to safeguard the correct and impartial exercise of judicial powers, but in practice it may also be used as a device by some committee members to interfere improperly with the collegial panel's function and to provide favours to one side of a litigation.

As well as internal interference with collegial functions, there is **1.19** often interference from outside sources.

    a) **Interference from the Party and governmental organs and officials.** Although courts are created by and responsible for people's congresses, their financial resources as well as other social benefits are provided and supplied by central or local governments, and the Party's personnel offices have the power to nominate candidates for judges, upon which people's congresses have the power to appoint and remove judges. Thus, the independence of courts and judges is in fact limited. Take rampant local protectionism as an example which has aroused national attention. Very often judgments are entered under pressure from local governments to bend justice for local interests or economy.

    b) **The interference exerted by corruption.** The procedural laws clearly state that judicial personnel shall not receive gifts from any parties to a litigation and their representatives. But in some places, taking gifts from participants is not an uncommon practice. As criticisms say "litigation (*da guansi*) has been turned into finding connections (*da guanxi*)". On these occasions, lawyers sometimes exert negative influences by abusing the privilege of meeting judges before trials. Recently, the Law of Judge has imposed certain restrictions on judges. For example, a judge is not allowed to accept gifts from or have meals with any party and his legal counsel involved in the case he is handling. But the actual results have yet to be seen.

c) **Interference from other organizations.** These include security organs, army units and other powerful organizations. Among them, the Party's Working Committees of Politics and Law at all levels have a direct influence over the judicial practice, which are responsible for legal work within the Party organization. They mainly exercise controls over policies and important issues of judicial works by way of convening meetings of four heads (president of court, chief procurator, police chief and head of justice bureau). Except in the most influential and sensational cases, the committees do not get directly involved in the adjudication of cases. Their political and ideological control over the courts and judicial personnel represents the Party's leading role in the legal field.

The interference with the independence of judicial practice poses a great obstacle for realizing the rule of law in China. But it must be pointed out that this interference represents only a fraction of the whole legal system and can perhaps be seen as inevitable in the transitional period towards the rule of law.

Theoretical Issues in Contemporary Chinese Law

1.20   Since the beginning of the legal reconstruction, there have been many theoretical debates in the legal field. The following are some important ones:[14]

a) **Rule of law and rule of man.** Rule of man is the heritage of the traditional legal culture and the legacy of the Cultural Revolution. Along with the legal development, the concept of the rule of man has been castigated and abandoned. But as discussed above, the debate is still going on since the official version sticks to the "legal system" rather than the rule of law and the lingering idea of the rule of man still influences the thinking and practice of officials in a latent way.

b) **Party's leadership and the supremacy of law.** The legal reform has enhanced the status of law and brought the relationship between the Party and law into a theoretical debate. Indeed, the Constitution and the Party's Constitution respectively stipulate that "all political parties . . . must abide by the Constitution and law" and that "the Party must operate within the framework of the Constitution and law". The popular comprehension of these articles is that the Party is a leading political authority but is not a governmental organ, therefore it should not play any governmental power, and the people's congress should become a true authoritative body. This theoretical and legal approach is still far from the real practice and will not be completely or quickly implemented. Needless to say this contradiction constitutes a challenge to the legal reform.

c) **Market economy and law.** Market economy as the ultimate purpose of reform is widely believed as the social and economic foundation of the new legal system in China. The notion that, "market economy must be an economy based on law" has proposed to denounce not only the planned economy based on the whims of government, but also the corresponding legal regime and ideology. Therefore, Chinese legal scholars are trying to advocate the rules of predictability, calculability and accountability of market operation, principals of freedom and autonomy, considerations of equal value and efficiency, and ideas of democracy and human rights, etc. and try to incorporate them into the emerging legal system.

d) **Nature of law.** Law was defined as a tool in the class struggle for a long time. In the current course of reform and economic development, this idea has been rejected by the majority of people. But the debate over the nature of law as the will of the ruling class or the will of the whole society, as a subjective violition of the people or objective norms of the society, are still ongoing.

e) **Division of private law and public law.** Before the reform, private interests and ownership were prohibited in China. Along with the flourishing of private ownership and increasing individual autonomy (especially in the economic field), those legal rules emphasising private rights and autonomy become important. The proposal to divide private law and public law has been widely accepted. Some scholars even boldly advocate the idea of "supremacy of private law". This division, if sustained, shall exert a great impact on the future legislation and legal operation.

f) **Democracy and law.** It has been accepted by most scholars that the modern rule of law cannot be achieved without establishment of democracy. Democracy shall be the foundation of legislation and legal operation. Any discrimination on the basis of class, gender and ethical group should be eliminated completely. This debate also involves the issue of the relationship between political reform and economic reform. Some scholars believe that slow political reform shall delay or even hinder further economic development; and others think they may be separated for a period in order to make the economy develop first.

g) **Spirits of modern law.** Many scholars advocate that there are spirits of modern law, which are based on modern market economy. These spirits are more important and decisive than the wills of the ruling classes who are averted by the old orthodox theory. The spirits of modern law include emphasis on individual rights, freedom of contract, efficacy, humanity and macro intervention of government.

h) **Legal transplant.** Since China is building a market economy, the legal rules of other countries with an established market economy could be introduced to, and transplanted in China. The legislative practice has accepted the idea of legal transplant and borrowed extensively from many foreign jurisdictions. Nevertheless, many scholars have realised that legal transplant needs to consider the relevant social factors of the recipient rather than to copy blindly the black letters of law. Simple copying of rules may not necessarily change the behaviour pattern of people as changes of the social structure and legal culture can.

There are many other issues under the theoretical debate, such as human rights, constitutionalism, equality in legislation process, presumption of innocence, civil society, etc. All these theoretical considerations represent the fundamental changes in the minds and the ideology of the people. They may look abstract or distant from reality, but they constitute an enlightenment in Chinese legal thinking and herald the bigger changes in the legal reform ahead.

The Chinese legal system has been developing rapidly since the start of reform. As discussed in this chapter it cannot be denied that it is still full of contradictions, problems and setbacks. However, it is equally true to say that it has achieved a lot in many respects over a relatively short period of seventeen years. The legal system works, though not smoothly; it moves forward, though unevenly. The most important factor is that this emerging legal system has embarked on the correct path to the rule of law ideal.

Notes

[1] Editing Group, *Chinese Legal History*, Mass Press, Beijing, 1982, p. 17.
[2] Shen Zongling, *General Theory of Comparative Law*, Peking University Press, Beijing, 1987, p. 329.

[3] See above n. 1, p. 58.
[4] See above n. 1, p. 1.
[5] Zhang Guohua, *History of Chinese Legal Thoughts*, Legal Press, Beijing, 1982, p. 56.
[6] Wu Shuchen, *Chinese Traditional Legal Culture*, Peking University Press, Beijing, 1994, p. 746.
[7] See above n. 6, p. 6, p. 15; see above n. 1, p. 1. Whether the Chinese Legal Tradition is an extinct legal tradition is very much under debate.
[8] Deng Xiaoping, *Selected Works of Deng Xiaoping (1975–1982)*, People's Press, Beijing, 1983, p. 136.
[9] Deng Xiaoping, *Selected Works of Deng Xiaoping*, Vol. 3, People's Press, Beijing, 1993, p. 373.
[10] Yue Xiang, Presentation at City University of Hong Kong, 1994.
[11] Supreme People's Court, *The People's Courts of the People's Republic of China*, 1995, p. 4.
[12] Data provided by the Legislative Affairs Commission of the NPC, 1996.
[13] Xin Pao, "Jian Zemin Emphasises Governing the Country According to Law". [February 9, 1996.]
[14] Zhang Wenxian, "Market Economy and Law", *China Law Journal*, 1994, Vol. 2; Guo Daohui, "Market Economy and Reform of Legal Theory and Ideas", *Legal Science*, 1994, Vol. 2; Wang Chenguang, "Market Economy and the Division of Private Law and Public Law", *China Law Journal*, 1993, Vol. 6.

CHAPTER 2
CONSTITUTIONAL LAW

Zhu Guobin

City University of Hong Kong

ZHU Guobin, Research Assistant Professor, City University of Hong Kong; B.A. (the People's University of China, Beijing), M.A. in History (the People's University of China), Certificate of Administrative Engineering Class (Ecole Nationale d'Administration, Paris), LL.D. (University of Aix-Marseilles, France). Guest Associate Professor, the People's University of China; Managing Editor, *Journal of Chinese and Comparative Law*; Member, the Chinese Society of Public Administration and the French Society of Comparative Legislation. Formerly, Lecturer at the People's University of China; Associate Research Fellow in Comparative Law at the National Centre of Scientific Research, Paris; and Associate Professor (part-time) at the Faculty of Law and Political Science of University of Aix-Marseilles, France.

Introduction

The Concept of Constitution

The word "Constitution" is derived from a Latin word *Constitutio*, **2.01** which in the civil law means, "an imperial ordinance, decree, or constitution, distinguished from *lex, senatus-consultum*, and other kinds of law and having its effect from the sole will of the emperor", or "an establishment or settlement".[1]

Constitution, *xianfa* in Chinese, has two meanings, depending on its everyday usage. In its broader sense, it is equivalent to "constitutional law", a branch of public law of the State which treats the organization, power, form of government, the distribution of political and governmental authorities and functions, the fundamental principles which regulate the relation between government and citizen and the administration of public affairs. In modern China, the *Imperial Constitutional Outline* (1908), the *Provisional Constitution of the Republic of China* (1902) advocated by Dr. Sun Yat-sen, the *Provisional Constitution of the Titulary Period of the Republic of China* (1931) and the *Common Program of the Chinese People's Political*

Consultative Conference (1949) after the foundation of the People's Republic of China (PRC) are examples of constitutional law.

In an narrower sense, *xianfa* is only directed at the constitution, the organic and fundamental law of a nation which may be written or unwritten, for example *The Constitution of the United States of America*, *The Constitution of the People's Republic of China* and *The Constitution of French Republic*, etc.

Since the constitution is one of the laws promulgated by a state, it possesses a legal nature as any other laws. However, as the fundamental law of the state and the supreme legal authority, a constitution has distinctive features.

First of all, provisions of a constitution differ from that of ordinary laws. A constitution defines the fundamental political regime, the form of government, the structural relationship among state institutions and the basic principles of social and economic systems of a state. They cover the most fundamental issues.

Secondly, a constitution has the supreme authority over other laws. Any laws which are in violation with the constitution are null and void. In China, "no laws or administrative or local rules and regulations may contravene the Constitution".[2]

Thirdly, the procedure of enactment and amendment of a constitution is much more vigorous, cautious and stringent than any other laws. This is to guarantee the stability of the constitution. The PRC has adopted successively four constitutions since its foundation in 1949; this phenomena reflects the political instability in the state. According to the present Constitution, any amendment has become more difficult than before as it provides: "Amendments to the Constitution are to be proposed by the Standing Committee of the National People's Congress ("the Standing Committee") or by more than one-fifth of the deputies to the National People's Congress (the NPC) and adopted by a vote of more than two-thirds of all the deputies to the Congress."[3] While enacting and amending the basic laws governing criminal offences, civil affairs, the state organ and other major matters, the NPC only has to obtain a majority vote of all deputies for such amendment or enactment. Moreover, the Standing Committee has achieved from the 1982 Constitution a great deal of power, through legislation by delegation, in enacting and amending laws.

Finally, special provisions are provided for interpretation and supervision of implementation of constitution. According to the Constitution, the NPC has power to "supervise the enforcement of the Constitution"[4] and its Standing Committee not only has power to "interpret the Constitution", but also to "supervise its enforcement".[5]

Traditionally, Chinese scholars hold that, as the fundamental law of a state, the Constitution is "the concentrated expression of balance of all political forces",[6] and mainly reflects "will and interests of the dominant class".[7] Therefore, the nature of a constitution is basically moderated by the changing relationship amongst the forces of different classes. The scholars quoted Lenin's standpoint on the nature of constitution to justify their argument, as Lenin said: "the crux of constitution lies in: all basic laws of the state and laws relating to the power of election of the representative institutions and to the competence of the latter express a contrast of all forces in class struggle".[8]

Meanwhile, more and more scholars in China today believe that "a constitution is the legalisation of democratic system"[9] and confirm that constitutions in both capitalist and socialist society embody some democratic principles, although the concrete forms are quite different from one another. A well-established constitutional law scholar points out that the following principles must be observed in constitution: the ultimate people's sovereignty, fundamental human rights, rule of law, and separation of powers, or unification of legislative and executive powers (which is illustrated by the Chinese constitutional regime).[10]

To distinguish the Chinese socialist constitution from the Western constitutions, a constitutional law professor highlighted in his textbook the following principles on which a socialist constitution should rely: socialist public property; unity of the proletarian dictatorship and socialist democracy; all power of the State belonging to the people; democratic centralism and socialist legality.[11] Since the open door policy and the economic reforms were implemented in 1979, some of the more traditional constitutional principles have been challenged, in particular those concerning the State-owned property system, while a powerful private and collective economy continues to grow rapidly.

The Historical Development of the Constitution of the People's Republic of China

Ever since the foundation of the PRC, China has adopted four Consti-   **2.02**
tutions respectively in 1954, 1975, 1978 and 1982, without including the *Common Program of the Chinese People's Political Consultative Conference* promulgated in 1949, which was the first document of constitutional law in nature in contemporary China.

Of these documents, the 1954 Constitution which totalled 106 articles was more comprehensive than that of 1975 and that of 1978. The 1982 Constitution carries on its basic internal structure with 138 articles. The practical basis of the 1954 text was very fragile since the enactment was based on only five years' experience of state construction after the foundation of China. China at that time was constrained by Western countries for ideological reasons, so it naturally paid its attention to the experiences of other socialist countries in the world, particularly the Soviet Union. This is why some scholars thought this document was closely modelled on the 1936 Constitution of the Soviet Union and emphasised the principles of "socialist legality". The 1954

Constitution had laid the foundation for the Chinese legal system and consolidated the Chinese political structure that is still in place today. However, this document hardly played an active role later on, due to several political campaigns and movements, including the catastrophic Cultural Revolution (1966–1976). These movements had obviously and inevitably shaken the authority of modern constitutionalism in China. This situation lasted for more than 20 years until a new Constitution was adopted in 1982.

The 1975 Constitution, comprising of only 30 articles, was a sharp reflection of the state of a "no law, no heaven" and the dominant ideology at that time, that is, "the continuing revolution under the proletarian dictatorship". This document as an abnormal document recorded China's political turbulence at an abnormal time.

Three years later in 1978, a new constitution was enacted to replace that of 1975. The number of articles was doubled, but it still was not worthy of esteem for the following reasons: the contents were highly politicised and abstract, certain leftist slogans were still kept in the text such as "the continuing revolution under the proletarian dictatorship" and the party organs of the Communist Party of China (the CPC) were completely integrated into the system of the State.

The fourth Constitution, currently in force, was adopted at the Fifth National People's Congress and promulgated on 4 December 1982. It basically retains the structure of the 1954 Constitution but embodies a new spirit.

First, it adheres to the "Four Fundamental Principles" as its general guiding ideology. Those principles are to maintain the socialist road, to maintain the people's democratic dictatorship, to maintain the leadership of the Communist Party of China, and to maintain the guidance of Marxism-Leninism and Mao Zedong thought. These principles, usually abbreviated as "Four Maintenances", are explicitly prescribed in the Preamble of the Constitution.

Secondly, Chinese people must make more effort to construct a socialist spiritual civilisation while building up a high degree of socialist material civilisation. This is a new "creation" when compared to the three previous constitutions. The articles in Chapter II entitled "Fundamental Rights and Duties of Citizens" have frequently stressed this principle.

Thirdly, development of socialist democracy and improvement of socialist legality in China represent one of the most important constitutional developments. According to the Constitution, all power of the PRC belongs to the people. "The NPC and the local people's congresses at various levels are the organs through which the people exercise State power"; "The people administer state affairs and manage economic, cultural and social affairs through various channels and in various ways in accordance with the law."[12] Through the electoral system, Chinese citizens have the right to participate in the political life of the State and in the administration of State affairs. In the light of the experience of the PRC and the lessons given by the Cultural Revolution, this document not only reaffirms systematically the right of citizens established by the 1954 Constitution, but also enlarges the scope of the rights and the means of enforcement.

Another area that should be stressed, is that "The people of all   **2.03** nationalities, all State organs, the armed forces, all political parties and public organizations and all enterprises and institutions in the country must take the Constitution as the basic standard of conduct, and they have the duty to uphold the dignity of the Constitution and ensure its implementation."[13] "All political parties" here obviously include the CPC. Furthermore, Article 5 of the Constitution further provides that: "All state organs, the armed forces, all political parties and public organizations and all enterprises and institutions must abide by the Constitution and the law. All acts in violation of the Constitution or the law must be investigated"; and "No organizations or individual is privileged to be beyond the Constitution or the law." To embody this spirit into the organization of the CPC, the final paragraph of the General Programme of the Constitution of the CPC, adopted at its 12th Congress in 1982, states: "The Party must conduct its activities within the limits permitted by the Constitution and the laws of the State." Such direct and clear provisions on constitutionalism "must be understood as a giant step towards the gradual establishment of the rule of law in China and, therefore, deserves our support."[14] This fundamental change demonstrates, for the first time, the determination of China to construct a country under the rule of law.

Finally, the 1982 Constitution puts forward the unification of the country, the unity of all nationalities, and the maintenance of independence of the country. With regard to the unification of the country, Hong Kong and Macau will be integrated into mainland China respectively in 1997 and 1999 under the principle of "One Country, Two Systems". The reversion of the sovereignty of Hong Kong and Macau and the administration of these two regions are governed by two Basic Laws enacted for this purpose: *The Basic Law of the Hong Kong Special Administrative Region of the PRC*, adopted by the NPC in April 1990, *and The Basic Law of the Macau Special Administrative Region of the PRC*, adopted by the NPC in December 1993. Although the issue of Taiwan is much more complicated than those of Hong Kong and Macau, the Constitution clearly states, "Taiwan is part of the sacred territory of the PRC. It is the inviolable duty of all Chinese people, including our compatriots in Taiwan, to accomplish the great task of reunifying the motherland."[15]

Almost all Chinese constitutional law scholars agree that the 1982 Constitution is the "best" among the four constitutions in PRC history in terms of its content and forms. Considering that China is a socialist country led by the CPC, any further radical changes to its policy may not be possible within the current framework. However, the rapid economic reform has touched many fields in the political, social and economic life of the nation, especially the current economic and political structure. As a result, the 1982 Constitution has been amended, without making entire changes to its structure and basis, first in 1988 and then in 1993.

The first amendment related to private economy and the property of land; the second concerned a larger scope of reform which involved the following aspects: redefining the "State economy" as the "State-owned economy"; the organization and management of collective economy; applying "socialist market economy"; the operation and management of State enterprises; and the modification of the terms of office of the local people's congresses, etc. The most important change is that Chinese authorities have decided to establish a market economy in China.

The significance of these two amendments is quite evident. Without any brave breakthrough in law-making and strong legislative support, other reforms simply may not be effectively carried out.

The Basic Political and Economic Systems

The System of the People's Democratic Dictatorship

2.04 China is a socialist country where the CPC is the permanent ruling party. The first sentence of the General Programme of the Constitution of the CPC states that: "The Communist Party of China is the vanguard of the Chinese working class, the faithful representative of the interests of the people of all nationalities in China, and the force of the core leading China's cause of socialism."[16] This definition helps us to understand the nature of the State: China is "a socialist state under the people's democratic dictatorship led by the working class and based on the alliance of workers and peasants".[17] The State system of China is thereby determined. Compared to the past constitutions, the replacement of "the proletarian dictatorship" by "the people's democratic dictatorship" "has more explicitly defined the nature of the Chinese State."[18]

Most Chinese scholars of Constitutional Law argue that "the people's democratic dictatorship is by nature an exchangeable term with the proletarian dictatorship" as "the essence of Marxism". In this regard, they point out that "the theory of the people's democratic dictatorship is the creative development of the Marxist theory in proletarian dictatorship under the Chinese concrete circumstances".[19] Briefly, this dictatorship comprises two indivisible aspects: to practise democracy to the people, to exercise dictatorship to the enemy. In conducting the dictatorship, the working class exercises, through the Communist Party, its leadership on the basis of the alliance of workers and peasants.

In the current framework, the patriotic united front plays an important role in ensuring a large participation of people from all sectors, all classes and all parts of the country in the management of State affairs. At the current stage, this patriotic united front is an alliance under the direction of the CPC, including the people from all democratic parties and all popular organizations. A larger united front only aiming at the unification of the country includes the patriotic people among the compatriots of Taiwan, Hong Kong, Macau and the overseas Chinese. In China, there exist eight small democratic parties. They are the participants of the Patriotic United Front. As the CPC is the permanent governing party, these parties can only partake in the political life of the State by sending their members to assume leading functions in the state organs at all levels.

The organization underlying this large united front is the Chinese People's Political Consultative Conference (CPPCC). Since its first Congress in September 1949, the CPPCC has engaged directly in the political life of the State by providing consultation to the government, by supervising public administration, and by engaging in the management of State affairs.

The System of the People's Congress

The form of government in China is the system of the People's Congress which also reflects the nature of the State. The Constitution states that the system of the People's Congress is the fundamental form of organization of political power under the people's democratic dictatorship.

Article 2 defines this system explicitly: "All powers in the PRC belong to the people. The NPC and the local people's congresses at various levels are the organs through which the people exercise state power." Article 4 stipulates: "The NPC and the local people's congresses at various levels are constituted through democratic elections. They are responsible to the people and subject to their supervision." In addition, the People's Congress system concerns not only the "people's congresses" themselves, but also the organization of the overall state organs such as the central and local governments, the people's courts and the people's procuratorates. The People's Congresses are by nature the organs of state power, all other state organs find their legal foundation of establishment and operation from the People's Congresses.

For example, "the State Council, that is, the Central People's Government, of the PRC is the executive body of the highest organ of state power; it is the highest organ of state administration."[20] "The State

Council is responsible and reports on its work to the NPC or, when the NPC is not in session, to its Standing Committee."[21] "Local people's governments at various levels are the executive bodies of local organs of state power as well as the local organs of state administration at the corresponding levels."[22] They are responsible and report on their work to people's congresses at the corresponding levels. Based on the same principle, the Supreme People's Court and the Supreme People's Procuratorate are responsible to the NPC and its Standing Committee. Local people's courts and local people's procuratorates at various levels are responsible to the local people's congresses which create them.

As an integral part of the people's congress system, the electoral system has been greatly improved since the adoption of the first Electoral Law in 1953 entitled *Electoral law of the NPC and Local People's Congresses.* This law has been revised three times since 1979. The last amendment was made on 28 March 1995. The right to vote and to stand for election is the inviolable and inalienable political right of the citizens of the PRC.

There coexist two forms of election, that is, direct election and indirect election. The people's deputies are directly elected at levels of municipality without internal division, districts directly under the authority of municipality, township, nationality township, county and autonomous county. Deputies at levels of the NPC, of provinces, autonomous regions, municipalities directly under the Central Government, and of autonomous prefectures and municipalities within which districts are created are indirectly elected by the deputies at the lower level.

During the process of election, a secret ballot system is practised in order to ensure objectivity and legality. People can choose the person they prefer from the proposed candidates. As China is still under the direction of an omnipotent party, it is not clear to what extent people may be able to choose candidates of their own free will against the monopoly of nomination by the party. The question which is worthy of in-depth analysis is how to maintain a representative participation from all classes with different political and economic backgrounds in the administration of State affairs, and how to choose candidates fairly. Along with further political and economic reforms, the Chinese electoral system should be further improved in order to suit the changing situation.

The System of Administrative Division

2.05   The preamble of the Constitution defines China as "a unitary multinational state created jointly by the people of all its nationalities". A unitary system means that a state is composed of different administrative units or autonomous units which have no independent position, and all these units are inseparable parts of the state. Under this regime, the state has only one Constitution and one organ of state power which exercises legislative power and policy-making power in a unified manner. All administrative units accept the unified leadership of the Central Government; they are prohibited to declare independence from the country.

The reason China has chosen to be a unitary state is rooted in its history. China has been a highly centralised country since the first unified dynasty of Qin from the year 221 BC to the present. During that period divided situations happened but were of relatively short duration. China also has 56 nationalities scattered in different regions all over the country, who display a large disparity in their ways and standards of living. Due to their uneven political and economic development, it is not seen as suitable to adopt a federal or confederate regime within the state. Instead, a system of regional autonomy of the minority nationalities is being practised in China, which is aimed at an overall solution of current national problems. As national problems are quite complicated in China, the government promulgated the *Law on the Regional Autonomy of Minority Nationalities* on 31 May 1984 as a legal solution. This allows the establishment of self-government organs with larger powers of autonomy in accordance with the Constitution and laws. It is now unlikely that under the current constitutional framework other systems of government will be adopted.

Article 30 provides that:

a) The country is divided into provinces, autonomous regions and municipalities directly under the Central Government;
b) Provinces and autonomous regions are divided into autonomous prefectures, counties, autonomous counties and cities;
c) Counties and autonomous counties are divided into townships, nationality townships, and towns.

Further it adds that:

d) Municipalities directly under the Central Government and other large cities are divided into districts and counties.
e) Autonomous prefectures are divided into counties, autonomous counties, and cities. All autonomous regions, autonomous prefectures and autonomous counties are national autonomous areas.

In addition, Article 31 stipulates:

f) The State may establish Special Administrative Regions when necessary.

Based on the provisions above, horizontally, there are three types of administrative divisions: normal administrative units, national autonomous areas and special administrative regions. Vertically, there are three levels: the provincial level including autonomous regions and municipalities directly under the Central Government, county level including autonomous counties and municipalities corresponding to this level, and the township level including nationality townships and towns. An intermediate level exists in some cases between province and county. This is an autonomous prefecture level, which includes some important municipalities that have counties under their direction. (See the diagram that follows.)

Article 31 is designed for the reversion of sovereignty of Hong Kong and Macau to China. "Special Administrative Region" (SAR) can be understood as another expression of the idea of "One Country, Two Systems" to ensure a smooth hand-over of the sovereignty of the two colonies to China. The Article continues that "the systems to be instituted in special administrative regions shall be prescribed by the law enacted by the NPC in the light of their special conditions". It also provides the legal basis for the two Basic Laws governing the future Hong Kong and Macau SARs which were adopted by the NPC respectively in 1990 and 1993.

Hong Kong and Macau SARs enjoy a special legal position. The socialist political and economic systems shall not be practised there, and the previous capitalist system and way of life shall remain unchanged for at least 50 years. Moreover, the NPC authorizes the Hong Kong and Macau SARs to exercise a high degree of autonomy and enjoy executive, legislative and independent judicial power. However, the governments of the SARs are by nature the local governments directly under the Central Government. The Central Government shall be responsible for foreign affairs relating to, and the defence of, these two SARs.

The Chinese government is willing to apply the idea of "One Country, Two Systems" to resolve the problem of Taiwan, although the situation between mainland China and Taiwan is more complicated. According to Chinese authorities, a peaceful way to resolve the problem of Hong Kong and Macau should serve as a model for the unification of Taiwan into China.

The Social and Economic Systems

2.06   Article 6 of the Constitution states that "The basis of the socialist economic system of the PRC is socialist public ownership of the means of production, namely, ownership by the whole people and collective ownership by the working people".

Ownership by the whole people, an essential form of public ownership, also known as "state ownership", has been considered as an advanced form of socialist ownership for a long time. However, Article 7 was amended in 1993 to provide that: "The State-owned economy,

DIAGRAM OF CHINA'S LEGISLATIVE SYSTEM
AND LEGAL HIERACHY

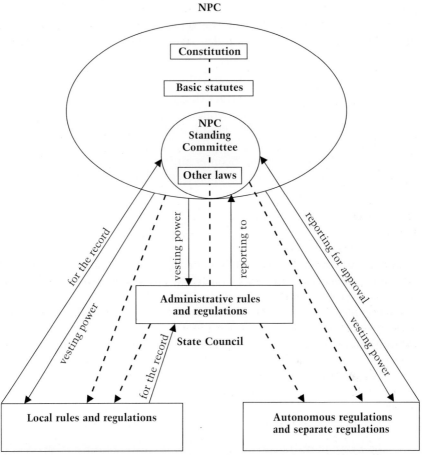

Legend:
——— Relationship line
− − Legal authority and supervision line

namely, the socialist economy under ownership by the whole people, is the leading force in the national economy." This amendment has in fact recognised the existence of other forms of economy in addition to the State-owned economy, such as collective economy and private economy. But the Article again affirms that "the State ensures the consolidation and growth of the State-owned economy", aiming at maintaining the dominant position of this economy within the whole national economy and maintaining the socialist nature of the Chinese state.

The collective ownership of the working people, also known as the "collective economy" includes two integral parts according to Article 8:

> a) in the rural areas the responsibility system, the main form of which is household contract that links remuneration to output, and other forms of co-operative economy, such as producers', supply and marketing, credit and consumers' co-operatives, belong to the sector of socialist economy under collective ownership by the working people; and
>
> b) the various forms of co-operative economy in the cities and towns, such as those in the handicraft, industrial, building, transport, commercial and service trades, all belong to the sector of socialist economy under collective ownership by the working people.

The State protects the lawful rights and interests of the urban and rural economic collectives and encourages, guides and helps the growth of the collective economy.

At the time of the 1982 Constitution, the individual economy of both urban and rural areas was already permitted by law. Under Article 11, individual economy is considered as "a complement to the socialist public economy". "The State guides, assists and supervises the individual economy by administrative control." Seven years later, the picture of national economy changed a great deal and private economy began to exist and to develop rapidly. As a result, Article 11 was amended in 1988 to the effect that:

> "the State permits the private sector of the economy to exist and develop within the limits prescribed by law. The private sector of the economy is a complement to the socialist public economy. The State protects the lawful rights and interests of the private sector of the economy, and exercises guidance, supervision and control over the private sector of the economy."

Thus, the private sector of economy has officially occupied a place in the Constitution. The amendment represents not only a clear recognition of the existence of such an economic sector, but also shows a great theoretical breakthrough in China.

In addition to individual economy and private economy, direct and indirect foreign investment in various forms in China is playing an increasing role in the national economy. Article 18 states that China "permits foreign enterprises, other foreign economic organizations and individual foreigners to invest in China and to enter into various forms of economic cooperation with Chinese enterprises and other Chinese economic organisations". The Chinese legislature and government have already enacted a series of laws and regulations aiming at protecting foreign investment. Of course, foreign enterprises in China should conduct their activities within the limits prescribed by the law.

It is worth noting that the 1993 Amendment of Article 15 revolutionised the previous planned economic system. It provided for the first time in the history of the PRC that: "The State practises socialist market economy. The State strengthens economic legislation, improves macro-regulation and control." The significance of this change is obviously tremendous simply because the new direction of the country has been confirmed by the supreme legal authority of the nation.

The People's Congress and Legislative System

China has attempted to establish the authority of law by using the concept of "socialist legality" which is considered to be one of the fundamental principles in the course of drafting the 1982 Constitution. Unlike most Western countries, China does not practise a state system in which legislative, executive and judicial functions are separated from each other. This system is often regarded as "a capitalist element" by some orthodox politicians and scholars and hence cannot be transplanted in China. Instead, a state system is built on the basis of the NPC by combining together the functions of parliament and government. The national and local people's congresses are the organs of state power, and exercise the legislative power of the State.

2.07

Legislative Order and Legal Hierarchy

China's legal system consists of three major parts: constitution, laws, and administrative regulations and rules. They are different from each other in nature and in their scope of application. Constitution is the general chart of the State, defining the basic structure and systems of the State. Law means the basic statutes enacted by the NPC Standing Committee. Administrative regulations and rules include those established or approved by the State Council, its ministries as well as local and autonomous regulations formulated by local people's congresses and their standing committees.

The NPC and its Standing Committee are vested by the Constitution with the legislative power of enacting the Constitution, basic statutes and other laws. Meanwhile, Article 85 provides, "The State Council, that is, the Central People's Government of the People's

Republic of China, is executive body of the highest level of State power; it is the highest institution of State administration." Therefore the Constitution empowers the State Council to formulate administrative rules and regulations aiming at enforcing laws and running State administrative affairs. This authority is restricted by law. For example, the NPC has the right to abolish any administrative rules and regulations of the State Council that contradict the Constitution and laws. If the local rules and regulations are in conflict with the State Council's administrative rules and regulations, they will be abolished or modified by the NPC Standing Committee and not by the State Council.

Provincial people's congresses and their Standing Committees, as the local organs of State power, establish and promulgate local rules and regulations. This power, however, is restricted not only by the Constitution, basic statutes and other laws, but also by administrative rules and regulations formulated by the State Council. In this regard, the provincial people's congresses have the duty to ensure the observance and implementation of the Constitution, the statutes and the administrative rules and regulations in their respective administrative areas.

China's unified legislative system can be illustrated by the following diagram.[24]

This diagram shows that the NPC and its Standing Committee are the controlling centre and are at the core of the legislative system. They are the source of power for all other state institutions. All the essential elements of this legislative system connect with and act on each other to form a unified entity, involving the central and local authorities, institutions of power and legislative and executive bodies.

NPC: its Structure and Functions

2.08 China's NPC system is an unified legislative system which concentrates legislative power within the central authority and has the absolute power of enacting laws. According to Article 58, the NPC and its Standing Committee exercise legislative power of the State. They may amend the constitution and enact basic statutes and other laws.

The NPC is made of deputies elected from the provinces, national autonomous regions, municipalities directly under the Central Government, and those elected from the armed forces. All the minority nationalities are entitled to appropriate representation. In addition, there are deputies representing the people of Hong Kong, Macau and Taiwan.

The NPC is elected for a term of five years. Should extraordinary circumstances prevent such an election, it may be postponed and the term of office of the current NPC extended by the decision made of a vote of more than two-thirds of all those on the Standing Committee

ADMINISTRATIVE DIVISION OF THE PRC[23]

```
                        The People's Republic of China

    Province   Autonomous Region   Municipality directly    Special Administrative
                                    under the Central        Region
                                    Government

            Autonomous      City (large)
            Prefecture

  Autonomous   City   County   Urban Districts      County      Urban District
  County

  Town   Township   Nationality Township        Town    Township
```

of the current NPC. The election of deputies to the succeeding NPC must be completed within one year after the termination of such extraordinary circumstances.

The NPC meets in session once a year and is convened by its Standing Committee. A session of the NPC may be convened at any time the Standing Committee deems necessary or when more than one-fifth of the deputies to the NPC so propose. When the NPC meets, it elects a Presidium to conduct its session.

According to Article 62, the NPC, as the supreme source of the State power in China, has power in the following four aspects:

a) *Legislative Power*

(i) **Amending the Constitution**

Only the NPC has the power to amend the Constitution. Any amendment to the Constitution is to be proposed by the Standing Committee or by more than one-fifth of the deputies of the NPC and is adopted by a majority vote of more than two-thirds of all the NPC deputies. Practically, after working out the draft of the Constitution or of the revised Constitution, the NPC must solicit opinions

45

from all social circles for revision before it is finally discussed and adopted by the NPC.

(ii) Enacting and amending criminal and civil laws

Criminal and civil laws and their procedures form the most important part of the basic statutes. By enactment and amendment of these laws, the NPC protects the people's democratic rights, their personal and property rights, the property rights of the State and the collectives, and preserves the order of the State and the safety of citizens. The amendment of the Criminal Procedure Law on 17 March 1996 by the Eighth NPC at its Fourth Session is the latest example.

(iii) Enacting and amending the basic statutes of state institution

These basic statutes are organic laws defining legal status, organizational structure, state administrative institutions, judicial and procuratorial institutions.

(iv) Enacting and amending other basic statutes

These laws promulgated under this category harmonise some essential relationships of political and social life, and play an important part in ensuring normal order in the society. Such examples include the *Marriage Law, Electoral Law,* etc.

b) *Managing Power of High Rank State Personnel*

To elect the president and vice-president of the PRC; decide on the choice of the premier of the State Council upon nomination by the president; decide on the choice of the vice-premiers, state councillors, ministers, and other important staff of the State Council upon nomination by the premier; elect the chairman of the Central Military Commission and, upon nomination of the chairman, decide on the choice of all the others on the Central Military Commission; elect the president of the Supreme People's Court and the procurator-general of the Supreme People's Procuratorate.

The NPC also has the right to recall or remove these personnel from office according to law.

c) *Power of Legal Supervision*

To supervise the enforcement of the Constitution and the work of the NPC Standing Committee. The NPC has the right to alter or annul inappropriate decisions of its Standing Committee.

d) Decision-making Power

To examine and approve the plan for national economic and social development and the report on its implementation, the state budget and the report on its implementation and other important affairs of the State.

The Constitution stipulates that the NPC may establish a number of special committees in order to assist the NPC in exercising its State power. The major work of these special committees is to examine, discuss and draw up relevant bills and to draft resolutions under the direction of the NPC and its Standing Committee. The 1982 Constitution enumerates the following committees under the NPC: Nationalities Committee, Law Committee, Finance and Economic Committee, Education, Science, Culture and Public Health Committee, Foreign Affairs Committee, the Overseas Chinese Committee. These committees are led by the NPC and, when the NPC is not in session, by the NPC Standing Committee. Meanwhile, the NPC and its Standing Committee may, when they deem it necessary, appoint committees of inquiry into specific questions and adopt relevant resolutions in the light of their reports.

On the proposal of the Drafting Committee for the Basic Law of Hong Kong SAR, the Seventh NPC decided at its Third Session on 4 April 1990 to establish the Committee for the Basic Law of the Hong Kong SAR under the NPC Standing Committee, when the Basic Law of the Hong Kong SAR of PRC will come into effect as scheduled on 1 July 1997. According to the original proposal, this Committee will function as a working committee of the NPC Standing Committee. The same principle is applicable to the future Macau SAR when the change of sovereignty takes place in 1999.

The NPC Standing Committee

When the NPC is not in session, it leaves many affairs to the NPC   **2.09**
Standing Committee as its permanent organ. According to the Constitution and the *Organic Law of the National People's Congress* (10 December 1982), the Standing Committee is composed of a chairman, vice-chairmen, a secretary-general and a number of members. They are elected from the deputies of the NPC. No one on the Standing Committee shall hold a post in any of the administrative, judicial or procuratorial institutions of the state. This is to ensure that they can concentrate fully on their duties and work independently.

In line with the Constitution and the NPC Organic Law, the Standing Committee primarily exercises the following functions and powers:

a) Legislative Power

This involves the enactment and amendment of laws other than those enacted by the NPC. Actually, the Standing Committee has the right, when the NPC is not in session, to make non-fundamental partial amendment to laws enacted by the NPC, and to interpret the Constitution and laws.

b) Power of Legal Supervision

The Standing Committee has the right to annul those administrative rules and regulations, decisions or orders of the State Council that contravene the Constitution and basic statutes. It can also annul those regulations or decisions adopted by the local people's congresses and governments that contravene the Constitution, statutes, or administrative rules and regulations. Articles 73, 89, 94, 128 and 133 also respectively provide that the Standing Committee supervises the work of the State Council, the Central Military Commission, the Supreme People's Court and the Supreme People's Procuratorate.

c) Decision-making Power

The Standing Committee decides, upon nomination by the premier of the State Council, on the choice of the ministers, the auditor-general and the secretary-general of the State Council; upon nomination of the chairman of the Central Military Commission, on the choice of the members of the commission. It passes on the ratification and abrogation of treaties and agreements concluded with foreign countries; on conferring state medals and titles of honour; on instituting systems of titles and ranks for military and diplomatic personnel and of other specific titles and ranks; on granting of special pardons; on the proclamation of war; on general or partial mobilisation; on the enforcement of martial law throughout the country or in particular regions.

When the NPC is not in session, the Standing Committee is entitled to examine and approve partial adjustments to the plan for national economic and social development and to the state budget when it deems it necessary in the course of their implementation.

d) Managing Power of High Ranking State Personnel

The Standing Committee has the power to appoint or remove, on the recommendation of the president of the Supreme People's Court, the vice-presidents and judges of the Court, members of its Judicial Committee and the president of the Military Court; to appoint and remove, at the recommendation of the procurator-general of the Supreme People's Procuratorate, the deputy-procurator-general and procurators of the Procuratorate, members of its Procuratorial Committee and the chief procurator of the Military Procuratorate. It also has the right to approve the appointment or removal of the chief procurators of the people's procuratorates of provinces, autonomous regions, and municipalities directly under the Central Government; and to decide on the appointment or recall of plenipotentiary representatives abroad.

The Standing Committee meets once every two months, whereas the NPC meets once a year. Thus, the Standing Committee handles a large amount of legislative work, especially in recent years after the transformation of the State's planned economy into a market economy. The leadership of the Standing Committee has made many initiatives in drafting and enacting new laws in order to adapt to unprecedented new circumstances.

Local People's Congresses

Following the constitutional provisions, people's congresses are estab-   **2.10**
lished in provinces, municipalities directly under the Central Government, counties, cities, municipal districts, townships, nationality townships, and towns.

The term of office of the provincial people's congresses is five years. The term of office of the people's congresses in counties and townships is three years.

Before 1979, there were no standing committees of the local people's congresses. Their functions and powers were executed by the respective people's governments. The Fifth NPC amended the *Organic Law of the Local People's Congresses and the Local People's Governments* in 1979[25], and decided that people's congresses at and above the county level should establish their standing committees.

The functions and powers of the local people's congresses and their standing committees are as follows:

a) Decision-making Power

They discuss and decide on major issues in all fields in their respective administrative areas, examine and approve the plans for local economic and social development and the budgets of their respective administrative areas, and as well as the reports on their implementation.

b) *Power of Supervision*

They have the power to ensure the observance and enforcement of the Constitution, laws, decrees and policies, to alter or annul inappropriate decisions of their standing committees and the people's governments at the corresponding levels, and inappropriate resolutions of the people's congresses at the next lower level. They have the power to supervise the work of the people's governments, people's courts and people's procuratorates at the corresponding levels.

c) *Managing Power of Local Government Personnel*

They elect and recall the leaders of the people's governments, people's courts and people's procuratorates at the same levels as defined by the Constitution and concerned laws.

d) *Legislative Power*

People's congresses and their standing committees at the provincial level, people's congresses of the capitals of provinces or autonomous regions and of major cities approved by the State Council, as well as people's congresses of autonomous regions, autonomous counties and autonomous prefectures, enjoy the corresponding power of enacting administrative rules and regulations under the condition that the legislation must not contravene the Constitution, the laws and the administrative rules and regulations.

In addition, the NPC and its Standing Committee have delegated legislative power to Shenzhen, Xiamen and Shantou Municipal People's Congresses and their Standing Committees, and the Municipal People's Governments of these three cities to make their own laws and regulations to be implemented respectively in 1992, 1994 and 1996. All laws and regulations passed by the designated organs of these three cities as Special Economic Zones must be reported to the NPC Standing Committee, the State Council and the Standing Committees of Provincial People's Congresses.

The Fifth NPC Standing Committee, by a decision on 26 November 1981, also allowed the People's Congresses of Guangdong and Fujian provinces and their Standing Committees the power of enacting various economic rules and regulations for their special economic zones. This was a landmark decision in delegating legislative power to the local organs of state power and made an active contribution to the construction of local legislation. However, in practice after Shenzhen, Shantou, Zhuhai and Xiamen have obtained their special legislative power, the legislative power vested on Guangdong and Fujian provinces seems obsolete.

With the rapid development of local legislation, the Constitution must be supervised, in order to combat the trends of localism and regionalism which are widespread in China these days. Although the Constitution has already defined some mechanisms to control local rules and regulations, for example, the system of records and reports; the NPC and its Standing Committee apparently are still looking for an effective way to exercise their supervisory power over local legislation.

Head of State — The President of the People's Republic of China

A Brief Retrospect

The President of the PRC is one of the central State organs and an 2.11 independent State organ. The system of Head of State in China went through a difficult evolution before the 1982 Constitution. In addition to the first constitutional document *Common Programme of the Chinese People's Political Consultative Conference* (1949), each of the four Constitutions in history of the PRC has brought some changes to the system. According to the *Common Programme* and the *Organic Law of the Central People's Government* (1949), the Commission of the Central People's Government acted on behalf of the PRC in directing State affairs with extensive powers and functions. Hence some scholars think that "the Commission collectively exercised the functions of the Head of State, it was the collective Head of State."[26]

Under the 1954 Constitution, two State organs had been established: the NPC Standing Committee and the President of the PRC, replacing the Commission of the Central People's Government. The President was not a component of the NPC, nor a part of the State Council. It was a relatively independent organ with the function of Head of State in conducting external and internal affairs.

The third Constitution, adopted in 1975 before the official termination of the Cultural Revolution, simply removed the post of the President of the Republic. All powers and functions once belonging to the President were respectively attributed to the Standing Committee, the Central Committee (CC) of the CPC and its Chairman. The 1978 Constitution did not restore the position of the President, but granted important functions to the President of the

NPC Standing Committee. The restoration of the President of the Republic was completed with the 1982 Constitution, according to which the President enjoys extensive powers and functions as the real Head of State.

Election and Legal Status

2.12 The President and Vice-President[27] of the PRC are not elected through general election, but elected by the NPC. According to Article 79, candidates for the President and Vice-President should fulfil the following conditions:

a) be Chinese citizens;
b) have the right to vote and to stand for election; and
c) have reached the age of 45.

The term of office of the President and Vice-President is five years, the same as that of the NPC. For the first time, the 1982 Constitution stated that the President and Vice-President should serve no more than two consecutive terms. The restriction of terms corresponds to the practice imposed on the other State leaders and important members of the government.

Article 82 stipulates that the Vice-President assists the President in his work. The Vice-President may exercise such functions and powers of the President as the President may entrust to him. In case of office vacancy, the NPC shall elect a new President and a new Vice-President. Prior to such election, the President of the NPC Standing Committee shall temporarily act as the President.

An interesting situation exists in China. After Jiang Zemin was elected Secretary General of the CC of the CPC in 1989, he was then elected President of the State in 1993. This practice reveals that after the Tiananmen Square incident in June 1989, Chinese authorities hoped to reinforce political control and the leading role of the Party in administrating State affairs.

Functions and Powers of the President

As the Head of State, all functions and powers granted to the President by the Constitution can be divided into two parts: internal affairs and foreign relations.

a) Internal Affairs
In pursuance of the decisions of the NPC and its Standing Committee, the President has the following functions and powers:

(i) to promulgate statutes. Promulgation of laws is the final step in legislative procedure. But promulgating a law does not mean "approving" a law, so this action is not considered as a legislative power;

(ii) to appoint and remove the Premier, Vice-Premiers, State Councillors, Ministers, the Auditor-General and the Secretary-General of the State Council;

(iii) to confer State medals and titles of honour;

(iv) to issue orders of special pardon;

(v) to proclaim martial law throughout the country or in particular provinces and regions of the country. (According to the Constitution, the State Council has the power to decide on the imposition of martial law in certain provinces or regions);[28]

(vi) to proclaim a state of war; and

(vii) to issue mobilisation orders.

b) Foreign Relations

As a major part of his functions, the President, on behalf of the PRC, conducts the following activities:

(i) to receive foreign diplomatic representatives;

(ii) to go on official visits to foreign countries as the Head of the State;

(iii) in pursuance of the decisions of the NPC Standing Committee, to appoint or recall plenipotentiary representatives abroad; and

(iv) to ratify or abrogate treaties and important agreements concluded with foreign states.

The People's Government and the Executive Power

The executive and judicial branches in China are responsible to the   **2.13** NPC and its Standing Committee under a system of "unity of legislative and executive power" (*yixing heyi*). This can be traced back to the short experience of the Commune of Paris after the 1789 French Revolution. It also characterises the current Chinese political system.

At the central level, the State Council is the executive body of the highest organ of State power; it is qualified as the highest organ of State administration. Relying on the same principle, local people's governments at various levels are executive bodies of local organs of State power as well as the local organs of State administration at the corresponding levels.

The State Council — the Central People's Government

As stipulated by the Constitution and the *State Council Organic Law* of 1982, the State Council is responsible for organizing and managing national political, economic, cultural and defence affairs, and giving unified guidance to national administration. Local organs of state administration are directly under the leadership of the State Council. The term of office of the State Council is the same as that of the NPC.

The State Council is composed of the premier, vice-premiers, state councillors, ministers, the auditor-general and secretary-general. The premier, vice-premiers and state councillors shall serve not more than two consecutive terms. The premier, assisted in his work by the vice-premiers and state councillors, is responsible for directing the work of the State Council. In accordance with *the Decision of the NPC on the State Council Organic Reform Programme*, adopted by the Seventh NPC at its First Session on 9 April 1988, the State Council is composed of 41 ministries and commissions, plus the Xinhua News Agency.

State administrative functions and working environments have been changing since the introduction of a market economy in China. To meet the demand for the establishment of this new economic structure, an internal structural reorganization took place in 1993. On 22 March 1993, the Eighth NPC decided at its First Session to rationalize the division of work among the then existing ministries and commissions. Numerically the State Council still has 41 ministries and commissions today. In line with the general organizational adjustment, the obvious changes took place in reforming other institutions and agencies. For example, the State Council decided on 19 April of the same year to cut 19 institutions directly subordinate to it to 13, and also reduce the number of working bodies from nine to five and create eight public institutions directly under it.

Article 89 states in detail the State Council's functions and powers as follows:

a) Power of Making Administrative Regulations and Rules
The State Council has powers: to adopt administrative measures, enact administrative regulations and rules and issue decisions and orders in accordance with the Constitution and the law; to submit proposals to the NPC or its Standing Committee; to alter or annul inappropriate orders, directives and regulations issued by the ministries or commissions; to alter or annul inappropriate decisions and orders issued by local organs of state administration at various levels.

b) Power of Decision-making on Major State Administrative Affairs

These rights include:
- (i) to formulate the tasks and responsibilities of the ministries and commissions of the State Council, to exercise unified leadership over the work of the ministries and commissions and to direct all other administrative work of a national character that does not fall within the jurisdiction of the ministries and commissions.
- (ii) to exercise unified leadership over the work of local institutions of state administration at different levels throughout the country, and to establish the detailed division of functions and powers between the Central Government and the local governments.
- (iii) to draw up and implement the plan for national economic and social development and the State budget; to conduct foreign affairs and conclude treaties and agreements with foreign states; to approve the geographic division of provinces, autonomous regions and municipalities directly under the Central Government, and to approve the establishment and geographic division of autonomous prefectures, counties, autonomous counties, and cities.
- (iv) to examine and decide on the size of administrative organs and, in accordance with the law, to appoint or remove administrative officials, to train them, to appraise their performance and to reward or to punish them.
- (v) to decide on the imposition of martial law in those parts of the provinces, autonomous regions and municipalities directly under the Central Government.

c) Administrative Power of State Affairs

The State Council has the right:
- (i) to direct and administer economic affairs and urban and rural developments;
- (ii) to direct and administer the affairs of education, science, culture, public health, physical culture and family planning;
- (iii) to direct and administer civil affairs, public security, judicial administration, supervision and other related matters;
- (iv) to direct and administer the building of national defence;
- (v) to direct and administer affairs concerning the nationalities and to safeguard the equal rights of minority nationalities and the right to autonomy of the national autonomous areas;
- (vi) to protect the legitimate rights and interests of Chinese nationals residing abroad and protect the lawful rights and interests of returned overseas Chinese and of the family members of Chinese nationals residing abroad.

In accordance with the 1982 Constitution, the State Council enjoys more powers than before in making administrative regulations and rules on national economic matters. In recent years, the State Council has made full use of these powers to meet a variety of practical needs and to suit the changing economic and political environment of the country. This will certainly help to promote the development of a practical and sound legal framework and working environment which is required for the construction of a market economy in China.

The Local People's Governments

2.14 According to the Constitution, the local people's congress at various levels are local organs of state power; local people's governments at various levels are executive bodies of the former as well as the local organs of state administration at the corresponding levels. Local people's governments have the right to issue decisions and orders, to appoint or remove local civil servants, to appraise their performance and reward or punish them.

Local people's governments at various levels are responsible, and report their work to people's congresses at the corresponding levels. Those at and above the county level are responsible, and report their work to the standing committees of the people's congresses at the corresponding levels when the congresses are not in session. Moreover, local people's governments at various levels are responsible, and report their work to the people's governments at the next higher level. In this sense, all local people's governments throughout the country are the state administrative organs under the unified leadership of the State Council.

China is a state with 56 nationalities. China applies a self-governing system in all national areas. The organs of a self-government of an autonomous area enjoy a high degree of autonomy in directing and managing internal affairs within their administrative areas. For example, the organs of a self-government have the power of autonomy in administrating the financial affairs of their areas. All revenues accruing to the national autonomous areas under the financial system of the State shall be managed and used by the organs of a self-government of those areas. This power is not granted to any other provincial governments.

Following the principle of self-government, these organs can independently administer educational, scientific, cultural and public health affairs in their respective areas, protect the cultural heritage of the nationalities and work towards the development of their cultures.

The first law concerning the national regional autonomy in China entitled *Law Relating to the Autonomy of Minority Nationality Re-*

gions was promulgated on 31 May 1984, and became effective on 1 October of the same year. This law ensured the principle of self-government fixed by the Constitution and the State.

The Central Military Commission

Unlike other countries, the President of the PRC, Head of State, is not the Commander-in-Chief of all the armed forces of the country. The 1982 Constitution thus created another State organ to direct the armed forces including the People's Liberation Army (PLA), the People's Armed Police and the People's Militia; this organ is the Central Military Commission, which is the highest military commanding organ.[29]   **2.15**

The 1954 Constitution stipulated that the President of the PRC also commanded the national armed forces and assumed the office of the Chairman of the National Defence Commission. The President held the power of direction of the armed forces, but the Commission was only a consultative organ.[30] In the same year, the CC of the CPC decided to establish the Military Commission under the CC with the mission of directing the PLA and other armed forces. This practice was in response to the Party's idea of "the Party directs the gun", as Mao Zedong often repeated: "Political power grows out of the barrel of a gun". Mao Zedong, Hua Guofeng, Deng Xiaoping and Jiang Zemin have successively held the post of the Chairman of the CC Military Commission.

The 1975 and 1978 Constitutions removed the Central Military Commission from the State structure and defined in their "General Principles" that: "the Chairman of the CC Military Commission of the CPC commands the armed forces of the country."[31] This resulted in the functions of the Party and the State becoming interwoven, with the Party often substituting for the government. This led to serious malpractice in the Chinese political structure before 1982.

Article 93 of the 1982 Constitution allows for the Central Military Commission of the PRC to direct the armed forces of the country. Article 62 further provides that the NPC elects the Chairman of the Commission and, upon nomination by the Chairman, decides on the choice of the Vice-Chairmen and members of the Commission. In addition, Article 67 States that, when the NPC is not in session, the Standing Committee has the power to decide, upon nomination by the Chairman of the Commission, on the choice of other members.

The Chairman of the Central Military Commission assumes overall responsibilities for the work of the Commission. In return, the Chairman is responsible to the NPC and its Standing Committee.

Furthermore, the NPC has the power to remove from office the Chairman and other members of the Commission. The term of office of the Commission is the same as that of the NPC. Through the above mechanisms, it is hoped to establish a new command structure for the armed forces in China.

It is worth noting, however, within the CPC, a structure that directs the armed forces is also existing and runs parallel to that existing within the State structure. In fact, the 1982 Constitution of the CPC decided to establish a Military Commission under the CC. The members of the Military Commission of the CC are decided on by the CC. The Chairman, who is elected by the CC, must be a member of the Standing Committee of the Political Bureau of the CC.[32]

In practice, the Central Military Commission of the PRC and the CC Military Commission of the CPC are identical in their formation, functions and powers. This system is often popularly known as "a group of the same personnel with two signboards" (*yitao renma liangkuai paizi*) which means that there are two institutions who share the same staff. The Chinese authorities have adopted this system in order to confirm the direction of the armed forces by the Party on one hand, and to normalize the structure of the State organs.

For example, Deng Xiaoping was elected Chairman of the Military Commission of the CC in September 1982, and then Chairman of the Central Military Commission of the PRC in June 1983. He continued his second term of office in March 1988. The current Chairman of both Commissions is now Jiang Zemin, who is also the President of the PRC and the Secretary General of the CC of the CPC.

The Judicial System and Institutions

2.16   In theory and in practice, China's judicial system is quite different from that of most Western democratic countries. Generally China's judiciary is made of the people's courts, people's procuratorates, public security, State security and administration of justice. The people's courts and people's procuratorates are studied below.

Public security branches lead and direct the people's police, as functional departments of the people's governments. They are responsible for maintaining social and public order and State security, and also for conducting investigations, arrests and preliminary hearings in criminal cases. The administrative institutions of justice are also functional departments under the people's governments which supervise the administration of justice, including the administration of prisons and implementation of the system of transformation through labour.[33] According to the Constitution, leaders of public security, State security and administration of justice are appointed by the people's congresses, or by their standing committees when the congresses are not in session, at the corresponding levels.

People's Courts

The people's courts are judicial organs exercising judicial power on behalf of the State. According to the Constitution and the *Organic Law of the People's Courts* of 1979 as amended in 1983, China practices a system of courts characterised by "four levels and two instances of trials". The judicial authority of the PRC is exercised by the following people's courts: local people's courts at various levels; military courts and other special people's courts and the Supreme People's Court. The local people's courts are divided into: basic people's courts, intermediate people's courts and higher people's courts.

In the administration of adjudication, the people's courts adopt the system whereby a case should be finally decided after two trials. This means, first, a judgment or orders of a first instance must come from a local people's court, and a party may bring an appeal only once to the people's court at the next higher level. The people's procuratorate may present a protest to the people's court at the next higher level. Secondly, judgments or orders of the first instance of the local people's courts at various levels become legally effective if, within the prescribed period for appeal, no party makes an appeal. Thirdly, judgments and orders of the court of the second instance shall be seen as final decisions of the case. However, any judgments and orders rendered by the Supreme People's Courts as the court of the first instance shall become immediately legally effective.

In conducting judicial work, all people's courts and special courts must rely on the following constitutional principles:

a) All citizens are equal before the law;
b) The people's courts shall exercise judicial power independently and are not subject to any interference by the administrative institutions, public organizations or individuals;
c) Open trials should be conducted;
d) No one is guilty until proven before the people's court;
e) The accused has the right of defence;
f) Citizens of all nationalities have the right to use their own spoken and written languages in the court proceedings.

In accordance with Article 11 of the *Organic Law*, "people's courts at all levels set up judicial committees" with the task of summing up judicial experience and discussing important or difficult cases and other issues relating to judicial work. Members of judicial committees of local people's courts at various levels are appointed and removed by

the standing committees of the people's congresses at the corresponding levels, upon the recommendation of the presidents of these courts.
The presidents of the people's courts preside over the meetings of
judicial committees at all levels; the chief procurators of the people's
procuratorates at the corresponding levels may attend such meetings
without voting rights.

The Supreme People's Court

The Supreme People's Court is the highest judicial organ of the State.
The president of the Supreme People's Court is elected by the NPC. He
is responsible and reports on his work to the NPC and its Standing
Committee. His term of office is five years and he may serve for not
more than two consecutive terms. The NPC Standing Committee
appoints or dismisses vice-presidents, head and associate heads of
divisions, and judges.

The Supreme People's Court has a criminal division, a civil division,
an economic division. It may have such other divisions as it deems
necessary. Generally, it has jurisdiction over the following cases:

(i) cases of first instance assigned by laws and other cases which
it considers it should try itself;
(ii) appealed and protested cases against judgments and orders of
higher people's courts and special people's courts;
(iii) protested cases filed by the Supreme People's Procuratorate.

The Supreme People's Court supervises the work of the local people's courts at various levels as well as the special courts. "The Supreme People's Court gives interpretation on questions concerning
specific application of laws and decrees in judicial proceedings."[34] In
reality, the practice of interpreting laws and decrees by the Supreme
People's Court has developed in recent years to an extent that is called
"judicial legislation". This was not previously defined in the Constitutional Law. However, the legislation does require guidance in order to
fill gaps and to solve conflicts and some vagueness among the laws so
that effective enforcement can be carried out by the judicial branch.

The High People's Courts

The high people's courts are courts of provinces, autonomous regions
and municipalities directly under the Central Government. The internal structure is almost the same as that of the Supreme People's Court
according to the definition of the *Organic Law*.

A high people's court deals with: cases of the first instance assigned
by laws and decrees, cases of the first instance transferred from peo-

ple's courts at the next lower level, cases of appeals and of protests lodged against judgments and orders of people's courts at the next lower level, and cases of protests lodged by people's procuratorates.

The Intermediate People's Courts

They are the courts established in capitals or prefectures in a province level. The scope of jurisdiction by an intermediate people's court covers cases of first instance assigned by laws and decrees, cases of first instance transferred from the basic people's courts, and appealed and protested cases from the lower court.

The Basic People's Courts

The basic courts, as the lowest level, are normally located at the county, municipal districts and autonomous counties. A basic people's court may set up a number of people's tribunals according to the conditions of the locality, population and cases involved. A people's tribunal is a component of the basic people's court, and its judgments and orders are considered as judgments and orders of the basic people's court with the same legal effects. In practice, a tribunal of this nature is often set up in big towns or townships where there is a concentrated population.

As defined in the *Organic Law*, the basic people's court adjudicates all criminal and civil cases of the first instance except where the law provides otherwise. Besides trying cases, a basic people's court is also responsible for settling civil disputes, handling minor criminal cases that do not require formal handling, and directing the work of the people's mediation committees.

The Special Courts

The special courts include military courts, railway courts and maritime courts. The military court which is established within the PLA is in charge of hearing criminal cases involving servicemen. This is a relatively closed system.

The railway and transport court deals with criminal cases and economic disputes relating to railways and transportation.

Five maritime courts have been established by the Supreme People's Court at the port cities of Guangzhou, Shanghai, Qingdao, Tianjin and Dalian. These courts have jurisdiction over maritime cases and maritime trade cases of the first instance, including any other disputes of this category taking place between Chinese and foreign citizens, organizations, and enterprises. Nevertheless, they have no jurisdiction over criminal cases and other civil cases belonging to the ordinary courts. The high people's court in the locality where a maritime court is located shall have jurisdiction over appeals against the judgments and orders of the maritime court.

The People's Procuratorates

2.17   Under Article 129, China's people's procuratorates are "state organs for legal supervision". To define the tasks, functions and organizations of the people's procuratorates, the Standing Committee of the Sixth NPC adopted at its Second Session on 2 September 1983 the *Organic Law of the People's Procuratorates.*

Article 5 of the *Organic Law* states the functions and powers of the people's procuratorates at all levels as the following:

a) to exercise procuratorial authority over cases of treason, cases involving acts to dismember the state and other major criminal cases severely impeding the unified enforcement of state policies, laws, decrees and administrative orders;

b) to conduct investigations of criminal cases handled directly by themselves;

c) to review cases investigated by public security organs and determine whether to approve arrest, and to prosecute or to exempt from prosecution;

d) to exercise supervision over the investigatory activities of public security organs to determine whether their activities conform to the law;

e) to initiate public prosecutions of criminal cases and support such prosecutions;

f) to exercise supervision over the judicial activities of people's courts to ensure they conform to the law;

g) to exercise supervision over the execution of judgments and orders in criminal cases and over the activities of prisons, detention houses and organs in charge of transformation through labour to ensure such executions and activities conform to the law.

The Supreme People's Procuratorate is set up at central level. The local people's procuratorates are divided into three levels and include: people's procuratorates of provinces, autonomous regions and municipalities directly under the Central Government; branches of the people's procuratorates in prefectures and cities directly under the provincial governments; and people's procuratorates of counties, cities, autonomous counties and municipal districts.

Procuratorial committees are created inside the people's procuratorates at different levels. According to Article 3 of the *Organic
Law*, "The procuratorial committee shall apply the system of democratic centralism and, under the direction of the chief procurator, hold
discussions and make decisions on important cases and other major
issues."

People's procuratorates at all levels shall have a chief procurator, a
number of deputy chief procurators and procurators. The chief procurators exercise unified leadership over the work of the procuratorates.
The term of office of the chief procurators shall be the same as that of
the people's congresses at corresponding levels.

The Supreme People's Procuratorate

The Constitution defines it as "the highest procuratorial body". Unlike the Supreme People's Court, it leads the people's procuratorates at
lower levels in order to safeguard the independence of the system.

The procurator-general of the Supreme People's Procuratorate shall
be elected and removed by the NPC. The deputy procurator-general,
members of the procuratorial committee and procurators of the Supreme People's Procuratorate shall be appointed and removed by the
Standing Committee of the NPC upon the recommendation of the
procurator-general. The Supreme People's Procuratorate is responsible
to the NPC and its Standing Committee. The Supreme People's
Procuratorate may establish a number of procuratorial departments
and other professional departments as needed.

According to the *Organic Law*, if the Supreme People's Procuratorate discovers some errors in a legally effective judgment or
order of a people's court at any level, it shall file a protest in accordance
with the procedure of judicial supervision.

Today, the judicial interpretations of the Supreme People's Procuratorate, as well as that of the Supreme People's Court, have, *de
facto*, the legal effect and are binding upon the judicial activities of
people's procuratorates of lower levels throughout China even though
China is not a common law country.[35]

The Local People's Procuratorates

The local people's procuratorates apply the system of dual leadership
and the principle of democratic centralism.

The chief procurators of people's procuratorates of provinces, autonomous regions and municipalities directly under the Central Government and their branches shall be elected and removed by the

correspondent people's congresses; the deputy chief procurators, members of procuratorial committees and procurators shall be appointed and removed by the standing committees of the people's congresses upon the recommendation of the chief procurators.

Nevertheless, the appointment and removal of the chief procurators of the local people's procuratorates must be reported to the procurator-general of the people's procuratorate at the next higher level, who should then submit the matter to the correspondent standing committee of the people's congresses for approval.

The chief procurators, deputy chief procurators, members of procuratorial committees and procurators of people's procuratorates set up, in industrial and mining areas, agricultural reclamation areas and forest zones, by people's procuratorates at the provincial or counties level shall be appointed and removed by the standing committee of the people's congress at the corresponding level, upon the recommendation of the chief procurators of the dispatching people's procuratorates.

The Fundamental Rights and Duties of Citizens

2.18 According to Article 33, "all persons holding the nationality of the PRC are citizens of the PRC." "Every citizen is entitled to the rights and at the same time must perform the duties prescribed by the Constitution and the law."

Two other terms are often used in China, they are "national" and "people". The word "national" was generally used before the promulgation of the Electoral Law in 1953 to refer to the person who had Chinese nationality. As "national" is not a common word in China, "citizen" was thus introduced in the 1953 Electoral Law and in the 1954 Constitution to replace the former. Contrary to the term "citizen" which is principally a legal word, the term "people" is rather a political concept which has specific meaning in China. It has been agreed that the concept of "citizen" includes both law abiding people and also criminals. "Even those who have been legally deprived of political rights and who do not belong to the category of 'people' as the majority of citizens, are still citizens of the State".[36]

The Fundamental Rights of Citizens

All Citizens Being Equal before the Law

Article 33 explicitly provides that "all citizens of the PRC are equal before the law". Equality is not only a fundamental right of Chinese citizens, but also a basic principle of the socialist legal system. Right of equality means all citizens are entitled to the political, economic and social rights prescribed by law. Article 34 further stipulates that citizens should not be discriminated against because of differences in ethnic status, race, sex, occupation, family background, religious beliefs, education, property status, or length of residence.

Political Rights and Freedom

Under the Constitution, "the political rights and freedom" of citizens means that all citizens have the right to take an active part in the political affairs of the State and have the liberty to freely express their personal opinions and views. For example, Chinese citizens who have reached the age of 18, except those who are deprived of their political rights by law, have the right to vote and stand for election.

The freedom of expression has been particularly emphasized since 1979. Constitutionally, citizens of China "enjoy freedom of speech, of the press, of assembly, of association, of procession and of demonstration".[37] However, a gap does exist between the legal provisions and reality. Today, people would like to have a better quality and degree of freedom of expression. The textual definition can no longer satisfy people's needs. In reality, the Chinese government has much to do to improve its record in this field. This topic is now quite sensitive for the Chinese government which is concerned about any criticism from the outside world. Along with the worldwide trend towards democracy and economic liberalization, the Chinese people are demanding more real freedom of expression, and freedom of political rights.

Based on the current Constitution, citizens do not have the freedom to strike, a right they once had under previous constitutions and a right that is generally upheld by people outside China.

The Freedom of Religious Belief

It is quite clearly stated in Article 36 that Chines citizens "enjoy freedom of religious belief". Further, the state policy on religion is defined in the Constitution as follows:

(i) No state organ, public organization or individual may compel citizens to believe in, or not to believe in, any religion; or they may not discriminate against citizens who believe in, or do not believe in, any religion;

(ii) The state protects normal religious activities. No one may make use of religion to engage in activities that disrupt public order, impair the health of citizens or interfere with the educational system of the state;

(iii) Religious bodies and religious affairs are not subject to any foreign domination.[38]

As China is a huge country with 56 nationalities, almost each of them has its own religion or popular religious beliefs. There are basically four religions: Buddhism, Taoism, Christianity and Islam; the believers are widespread, but do not represent the majority of the population. During the last decade, together with the opening of China to the outside world, the Chinese government is facing new situations and must reconsider its policy on religion. At the forefront extreme nationalism and separatism which both have a strong religious background are difficult issues which are perplexing the Central Government of China today.

The Freedom of Person

The freedom of person is an essential prerequisite for citizens participating in all kinds of social activities. In recent years, Chinese legislature has promulgated a number of laws for the purpose of protecting freedom of the citizens. But still, the situation is not satisfactory, because the notion of "Rule of Law" has not been well established in the political and judicial practice in China. For example, abuse of police power is fairly common; public administration often oversteps judicial power by making arbitrary decisions and by abusing the discretional power granted by laws.

Article 37 clearly guarantees that the freedom of a person can not be violated by providing:

> "No citizen may be arrested except with the approval or by decision of a people's procuratorate or by decision of a people's court, and arrests must be made by a public security organ." "Unlawful detention or deprivation or restriction of citizen's freedom of the person by other means is prohibited, and unlawful search of the person of citizen is prohibited."

Moreover, the personal dignity of citizens is inviolable. Article 38 confirms: "Insult, libel, false accusation or false incrimination directed against citizens by any means is prohibited". Further, the residence of citizens is protected as Article 39 stipulates that: "Unlawful search of, or intrusion into, a citizen's residence is prohibited". And finally, freedom and privacy of correspondence of citizens are protected by law. Article 41 stresses that:

> "No organization or individual may, on any ground, infringe upon citizens' freedom and privacy of correspondence, except in cases where, to meet the needs of the State security or of criminal investigation, public security or procuratorial organs are permitted

to censor correspondence in accordance with procedures prescribed by law."

The Right of Supervision and Compensation

The right of supervision is one of the essential ways for citizens to take   **2.19**
an active part in the management of the State's political and social
affairs. All citizens are therefore encouraged to keep an eye on public
administration and its civil servants. Under Article 41,

> "Citizens of the PRC have the right to criticise and make s
> uggestions regarding any State organ or functionary. Citizens have
> rights to make to relevant State organs complaints or charges
> against, or exposures of, any State organ or functionary for viola-
> tion of the law or dereliction of duty; but fabrication or distortion
> of facts for purposes of libel or false incrimination is prohibited";
> "The State organ concerned must deal with complaints, charges or
> exposures made by citizens in a responsible manner after ascer-
> taining the facts. No one may suppress such complaints, charges
> and exposures or retaliate against the citizens making them."

To implement this article, relevant laws and regulations have been
adopted and put into force. Examples are *Administrative Procedure
Law*, promulgated by the NPC on 4 April 1989 which came into effect
on 1 October 1990; *Administrative Supervision Regulation*, issued by
the State Council on 9 December 1990; *Administrative Reconsideration Regulation*, issued by the State Council on 24 December 1990;
and the *Law on Administrative Sanctions*, adopted on 17 March 1996
by the NPC which became effective on 1 October 1996. A series of
rules and measures implementing the above laws and regulations have
been published, aimed at establishing a legal system which puts the
administration under the watchful eye of the people.

The right to compensation is also guaranteed by Article 41: "Citizens who have suffered losses as a result of infringement of their civil
rights by any state organ or functionary have the right to compensation
in accordance with the law." In addition to the above cited *Administrative Procedure Law*, the NPC passed another law on 12 May 1994
which was of great importance, the *State Compensation Law*. This law
has filled a gap in legislation in protecting the legal rights of citizens by
establishing a system to compensate them for the government's
wrongdoing.

Economic and Social Rights

Citizens' economic and social rights provided by the Constitution
include:

    (i) the right of property. "The state protects the right of citizens to own lawfully earned income, savings, houses and other lawful property."[39]

   (ii) the right to inherit. "The state protects according to law the right of citizens to inherit private property."[40]

  (iii) the right to work, which means that those who are physically and mentally capable of working have the right to get a job and thus to be remunerated according to their work.

   (iv) the right to rest. Citizens make use of this right in order to keep a good health and improve working efficiency. China started a five-working-day system in 1995.

    (v) the right of retired people to social help and insurance. The government is trying to reform the social welfare system in order to improve the livelihood of the aged.

   (vi) the right to get material help from the State. This is mostly directed to those who are old, ill and disabled. The State has promised to "develop social insurance, social relief and medical and health services that are required for citizens to enjoy this right."[41]

These constitutional rights are not fully realized today. In fact, some of the new rights, including unemployment insurance and social relief, have yet to be established and are still at a stage of experimentation. The State is being challenged in the course of these economic and social reforms.

The Right and Freedom to Education and in the Fields of Sciences and Culture

Chinese citizens have the right, as well as duty, to receive education. To achieve this goal, the state promotes the all-round development of children and young people, morally, intellectually and physically. In practice, Chinese legislature adopted on 12 April 1986 the *Compulsory Education Law* which aimed at setting up a nine-year compulsory educational system. The State will develop all the necessary facilities for implementing this law. Apart from this significant step, citizens are also entitled to join other educational programmes at various educational institutions.

    Moreover, two other important laws were successively promulgated in order to improve national educational system, i.e., the *Teachers Law* (adopted on 31 October 1993 by the Standing Committee of the NPC) and the *Education Law* (adopted on 18 march 1995 by the NPC). The former defines the rights and duties of teachers, and all related working systems concerning the management of teachers. The latter is a document guiding the organization of the national educational system. It describes the respective roles and responsibilities of educational institutions, State and society in conducting educational activities, and stipulates the rights of those receiving education.

Chinese citizens have the freedom to engage in scientific research, literary and artistic creations and other cultural pursuits. The State encourages and assists citizens' creative endeavours conducive to the interests of the people in education, science, technology, literature, art and other cultural work.

Other Rights Enjoyed by Citizens

Women in China enjoy equal rights with men in all spheres of life including political, economic, cultural, social and family life. The State protects the rights and interests of women, implements the principle of equal pay for equal work, and selects cadres among women.

To this end, the NPC promulgated on 3 April 1992 *the Law on the Protection of the Rights and Interests of Women* with its main objective to safeguard women's political rights, rights and interests in culture and education, labour, property, marriage and family. Legal responsibilities are imposed against violation of these rights and interests.

Marriage, family, mothers and children are specially protected by the State. There are laws stipulating that violation of the freedom of marriage is strictly prohibited. Maltreatment of old people, women and children is also strictly prohibited. Such provisions are derived from the *Marriage Law* of 1980, the *Law on the Protection of Minors* of 1991, and the, above-cited, *Law on the Protection of Rights and Interests of Women.*

The legitimate rights and interests of overseas Chinese are also protected by the Constitution and laws. Since the economic reform in the late 1970s, many overseas Chinese have been returning to the motherland for business or to live. The Chinese government considered it necessary to make laws to protect the rights and interests of these people. The Standing Committee of the NPC enacted the *Law on the Protection of the Rights and Interests of the Returned Overseas Chinese and the Relatives of Overseas Chinese* on 7 September 1990. The State also published a number of regulations implementing this law.

The Fundamental Duties of Citizens

In theory as well as in practice, rights coexist with duties. No one **2.20** enjoys rights and freedom without assuming corresponding duties.

Thus, Article 51 expressly states that "Citizens of the PRC, in exercising their freedoms and rights, may not infringe upon the interests of the State, of society or of the collective, or upon the lawful freedoms and rights of other citizens".

According to the Constitution, Chinese citizens should perform the following duties:

Concerning the Unification of the Country

As the Preamble of the Constitution states, the PRC is a "unitary multinational State" created jointly by the people of all its nationalities. Any action destroying or weakening the unification or unity of the country will be subject to the suppression of the State apparatus. Any activities of national separatists are prohibited by law.

As the handover of sovereignty of Hong Kong and Macau to China is imminent, the question of Taiwan is already on the agenda for the Chinese government. It is described in the Preamble of the Constitution that "it is the inviolable duty of all Chinese people, including our compatriots in Taiwan, to accomplish the great task of reunifying the motherland". Under the guiding principle of "one China", it is hoped that the two sides of the Strait can come together and discuss the question of how "one China" can be realized and built.

Concerning State Secrets and State Security

To enforce this constitutional duty, the State has made certain laws and regulations, for example the *Law on Guarding State Secrets* of 1988 and the *Law on State Security* of 1993. The detailed rules for implementing these two laws have already been put into practice.

Concerning Labour Discipline

Under the guidance of the Constitution, the *Labour Law* was adopted in 1994 by the Standing Committee of the NPC. The State Council and the Ministry of Labour have passed a series of regulations and rules for implementation to establish a legal system governing labour discipline and to regulate the growing market of employment.

Concerning the Social Ethics

To strengthen the conscience of social ethics is part of the construction of a "socialist spiritual civilisation" promoted by the Chinese government and society. Article 24 of the Constitution says that "the State advocates the civil virtues of love of the motherland, of the people, of labour, of science and of socialism". As a general policy, the Chinese government insists on the construction of a spiritual civilisation whilst stressing the progress of material civilisation. Article 24 also emphasises the "education among the people in patriotism and collectivism, in internationalism and communism and in dialectical and historical materialism", and demands to "combat capitalism, feudal and other decadent ideas".

Safeguarding the Security, Honour and Interests of the Country

Any acts detrimental to the above are not allowed. Moreover, according to the Constitution, it is the sacred duty of every citizen to defend the motherland and resist aggression. And it is an honourable duty for citizens to perform military service and join the militia. In line with this, the State has published a number of laws and regulations relating to military service and the organization of the militia at a national level. In the early 1950s, the legislature passed the *Law on the Military Service* (1955). This law was revised by the NPC in July 1984. Then, *Regulations Governing the Work of the People's Militia* were jointly issued by the State council and the Central Military Commission on December 24, 1990.

Concerning Tax Payment

The 1954 Constitution established the provision of tax payment. But that provision was removed from the 1975 and 1978 Constitutions. In 1980, the NPC adopted the first law on personal income tax. The 1982 Constitution thus restored the provision of tax payment. In 1995, the NPC Standing Committee amended the *Law on Taxation Administration* originally adopted in 1992 to reinforce the management of tax payment. As income tax is becoming the main source of State financial revenue, the question of how to implement the laws and organize tax administration and supervision still remains a legal, as well as a practical issue in today's China.

Conclusion

Constitutional law is a branch of law enacted by the State legislative **2.21** organ, but its form, content and legal effect differ from those of other

71

kinds of laws. China is a nation with a civil law tradition and thus all constitutional laws are written laws, which date from the first Constitution of the late Qing Dynasty to the latest 1982 Constitution.

The 1982 Constitution directly records the experiences in State construction achieved after the foundation of the PRC and generally corresponds to the current political, economic and social conditions of the country. The nature of the Sate, its structure, form of government, and fundamental rights and duties of citizens are explicitly provided in this document, which is the basic charter of the country.

China has experienced tremendous historical changes since the late 1970s when the open door policy and economic reform were implemented. Two amendments of the Constitution in 1988 and 1993 witnessed this significant development. A number of political, economic and social systems currently in place need to be reformed or restructured in order to suit the new trends of development.

In terms of the fundamental rights and duties of Chinese citizens, the 1982 Constitution redefined and widened the areas of rights and freedoms enjoyed by Chinese citizens. In addition, the Constitution was drafted on a realistic basis to ensure the enforceability of these rights and freedoms.

As economic reforms are still continuing in China, a clash between the old structure and the new market economy system is inevitable. Thus, the 1982 Constitution is being challenged in many respects. New constitutional changes or constitutional reforms should be thought about and put on the agenda of the Chinese government, so as to respond to the development of the market economy and the gradual process of democratisation which is now taking place in China.

Notes

[1] *Black's Law Dictionary*, fifth edition, West Publishing Co., 1979, p. 282.
[2] Art. 5 of the *Constitution of the PRC (1982)*. All citations of Chinese Constitution hereafter are derived from the Constitution of 1982.
[3] Art. 64.
[4] Art. 62.
[5] Art. 67.
[6] XU Chongde, *Chinese Constitutional Law*, the People's University of China Press, 1989, p. 24.
[7] WU Jialin, *Constitutional Law*, the Press of Masses, 1985, p. 37.
[8] Cited from WU Jialin, *op. cit.*, p. 36.
[9] *Ibid.*, p. 28.
[10] *cf.* Xu Chongde, *op. cit.*, p. 41, 44, 46 and 49.
[11] *cf.* Wu Jialin, *op. cit.*, p. 35.
  As to the concept of "democratic centralism", it was developed by Mao Zedong as a guiding principle in handling the relations "between democracy and centralism" and "between freedom and discipline" among the people. The idea was expressed in a

speech entitled *Correct Handling of Contradictions among the People* given on February 27, 1957. This principle is also regarded as a guiding principle for the "intra-party democratic life", it is thus confirmed in the General Programme of the 1982 Constitution of the Communist Party of China.

The democratic centralism exercised at the "state organs" is interpreted differently. Here the principle is primarily for handling the relations "between the people and government", "between a high ranking office and its subordinates", and "between the central and local governments". The General Principle of the 1982 Constitution of China embodies this orientation. *cf. A Glossary of Political Terms of the People's Republic of China*, compiled in Chinese by Kwok-sing Li and translated into English by Mary Lok, The Chinese University Press, Hong Kong, 1995, pp. 279–280.

[12] Art. 12.

[13] Preamble.

[14] Byron S. J. Weng and Chang Hsin, *Introduction to Chinese Law* (Bilingual), Ming Pao Publishing Co., Hong Kong, 1989, p. 28.

[15] Preamble.

[16] *The Twelfth National Congress of the CPC* (September 1982), Foreign Languages Press, Beijing, p. 96.

[17] Art. 1.

[18] *A Course for the Qualification Examination of Lawyers of China*, edited by the Centre of the Qualification Examination of Lawyers of China and the Faculty of Law of the People's University of China, the Press of the Public Security University of China, Beijing, 1994, p. 256.

[19] *Ibid.*, p. 256.

[20] Art. 85.

[21] Art. 92.

[22] Art. 105.

[23] This diagram is designed in accordance with Articles 30 and 31 of the 1982 constitution.

According to the *Basic Law of the Hong Kong Special Administrative Region of the PRC* (adopted by the NPC on April 4, 1990) and the *Basic Law of the Macau Special Administrative Region of the PRC* (adopted by the NPC on March 31, 1993), Hong Kong and Macau Special Administrative Regions will be established respectively on July 1, 1997 and on December 20, 1999.

[24] This diagram is adapted from Du Xichuan and Zhang Lingyuan, *China's Legal System: a General Survey*, New World Press, Beijing, 1990, p. 33.

[25] This Law was amended on December 2, 1986

[26] Pu Xinzu, *Political System of the People's Republic of China*, Joint Publishing (H. K.) Co., Ltd, Hong Kong, 1995, p. 154.

[27] The official English version of the 1982 Constitution prepared by the Legislative Affairs Commission of the NPC Standing Committee refers to the "Vice-President" in the singular. We follow hereafter this translation.

[28] *cf.* Arts. 80, 67(20) and 89(16).

[29] Art. 93.

[30] Art. 42 of the 1954 Constitution.

[31] Art. 15 of the 1975 Constitution and Art. 19 of the 1978 Constitution.

[32] Art. 21 of the 1982 Constitution of the CPC.

[33] Concerning the functions and structures of public security, state security and administration of justice, please refer to The General Office of the State Commission of Organisation and Establishment, ed., *Outline of the Organisational Structure of the State Council of the PRC (1988)*, the Press of Northeast Industrial Institute, Shenyang, 1989, pp. 41–42, 52–54; and the Secretariat of the General Office of the State Council, ed., *The Organisational Structure of the Central Government*, the Press of China Development, Beijing, 1995, pp. 114–116, 125–129. No description of state security institutions was provided in these two books perhaps for reasons of "state security".

[34] Art. 33 of the *Organic Law*.

[35] This phenomena has attracted much attention from both legal scholars and practitioners; for example, an article titled *Chinese Judicial Interpretation and Precedent of Common Law Countries* gives us certain explanations on this matter. *cf.* Guo Keqiang

and Tao Kaiyuan, in *Journal of Chinese and Comparative Law* (Bilingual), Vol. I (1995), No. 2, pp. 128–141 (in English) and 142–151 (in Chinese).

[36] Xu Chongde, *op. cit.*, p. 392.

[37] Art. 35.

[38] Art. 36.

[39] Art. 13.

[40] Art. 13.

[41] Art. 45.

CHAPTER 3
ADMINISTRATIVE LAW

Lin Feng

City University of Hong Kong

Lin Feng, Assistant Professor of Law, Faculty of Law, City University of Hong Kong; formerly Assistant Professor of Law, Faculty of Law, Fudan University, Shanghai, China; LL.M., Victoria University of Wellington, New Zealand, 1992; LL.B., Fudan University, 1987; B.Sc. in Physics (equivalent), Fudan University, 1985.

Introduction

Administrative law has been widely accepted in the last two decades as a fully-fledged law subject. Unlike the approach generally accepted in common law jurisdiction where, administrative law is almost equivalent to judicial review, the concept of administrative law in China is much wider. Various definitions have been provided.[1] Each of them approaches the subject from a different angle. An examination of those definitions shall reveal that they all include three ingredients, namely administrative law theory, substantive and procedural administrative law. Most textbooks and monographs on administrative law deal with the historical development and general principles of administrative law, administrative legal relationships, administrative organs and their personnel, administrative activities, administrative supervision and so on. Some textbooks may also cover part of substantive administrative law, such as laws on military administration, external administration, civil affairs administration, public security administration, education and culture administration, land administration, national economic administration, judicial administration and so on. More frequently, substantive administrative legislation is dealt with in other law subjects such as economic law, land law, customs law and so on.

Apart from substantive administrative legislation, procedural administrative law has developed well over the last two decades. Different legal procedures have been established to address grievances

75

3.01

against the administration or its personnel for any decisions under-taken in the process of administration, upon which this chapter will focus. This chapter first examines an important concept in procedural administrative law, *i.e.* administrative acts. It then analyses the proce-dure available within the administration for the handling of griev-ances, *i.e.* administrative reconsideration. Afterwards, the chapter moves to examine external procedures, for the handling of grievances against the administration by judiciary, *i.e.* judicial review. The next part of the chapter looks at the handling of compensation claims against the administration by the judiciary. The chapter concludes with a few comments on the development of the system for the control of the exercise of executive power.

Administrative Acts

3.02   Administrative acts refer to any administrative activities undertaken by the administrative organs. They should be distinguished from legis-lative and judicial acts which are undertaken by the legislature and judiciary respectively. Administrative acts can be classified in different ways. These classifications are essential to the understanding of the scope of administrative reconsideration and judicial review.

Concrete Administrative Act versus Abstract Administrative Act

The concept of the concrete administrative act is the most important one in Chinese procedural administrative law because only concrete administrative acts are subject to administrative reconsideration and judicial review. However, neither the *Regulation on Administrative Reconsideration* (RAR) nor the *Administrative Litigation Law* (ALL) provide any definition as to what will constitute a concrete adminis-trative act. But section 1 of the Opinions of the Supreme People's Court on the Interpretation of the ALL states that:

> "A concrete administrative act is a unilateral act undertaken by an administrative organ or its personnel, legally authorized organiza-tion, or organization or individual entrusted by an administrative organ, in exercising administrative authority in the process of administration, targeting at a specific citizen, legal person or other organization with regard to his rights and obligations."

Concrete and abstract administrative acts are a set of concepts. An abstract administrative act refers to the activity of administrative organs to make administrative regulations, regulations, decisions and orders which have a general binding effect in a certain area. Compared with a concrete administrative act, the target and the scope to which an abstract administrative act is applicable are quite different, as an abstract administrative act aims at all kinds of citizens, legal persons or organizations instead of a specific one. To include abstract administrative acts under administrative reconsideration will make it difficult to converge with the existing legal system of supervision.[2] However, that does not mean that an abstract administrative act will not be subject to proper legal supervision. Instead, alternative means have been provided by laws to deal with the issues of their illegality and inappropriateness. The Constitution and *Organic Law of Local People's Congresses and Local People's Governments* provide that abstract administrative acts shall be subject to the supervision of legislature (at both national and local levels) and the administrative organ at the next higher level. Furthermore, the ALL has also provided certain means to deal with certain kinds of problems concerning abstract administrative acts.

Internal Administrative Act versus External Administrative Act

Internal administrative acts refer to various measures taken by administrative organs against their own personnel, including warning, recording a demerit, removal from position, probation, dismissal and any other disciplinary actions. Disputes with regard to these internal acts are expected to be resolved within the original administrative organ, the organ at the next higher level or supervisory organ. External administrative acts refer to actions taken by administrative organs towards citizens, legal persons or other organizations not within the same administrative organ. The scope of external administrative acts is quite wide and not all external administrative acts are subject to administrative reconsideration and judicial review.

Act of State

Acts of State are a unique kind of administrative act. They are those undertaken in the name of the State and are sovereign actions. In order to protect national interests, every state grants special status to the Acts of State. China is not an exception. There are mainly two common categories. One relates to national defence, such as war and military practice. The other relates to diplomatic relationships, such as relationships with other countries or international organizations, establishment, severance of diplomatic relationships with foreign countries, and conclusions of treaties. Besides, Acts of State also include other important acts relating to state interests, such as the imposition of curfew by the State Council in certain areas or regions. Complaints against Acts of State can be brought neither for administrative reconsideration nor for judicial review. Instead they can only be duly addressed through other means.

Administrative Reconsideration

3.03 Administrative reconsideration is a procedure through which grievances against the decision of an administrative organ can be reconsidered by another administrative organ either at the same level or at the next higher level. Upon the application of the aggrieved party, the original concrete administrative act, with which a citizen, legal person or any other organization is not satisfied and appeals against, will be reconsidered by another administrative organ.

With the adoption of the ALL, the importance of administrative reconsideration has become even more obvious and the requirement of administrative reconsideration has been enhanced. One source has revealed that about 70% of administrative litigation cases have been through the stage of administrative reconsideration before their submission to the people's court.[3]

Administrative reconsideration was available well before the adoption of the RAR in 1990. However, many important issues regarding administrative reconsideration, such as the conditions for application, jurisdiction, scope of reconsideration, and procedures etc. were not stipulated in any other legislation. They are provided for in the RAR for the first time.

The Legal Sources of the RAR

The 1990 RAR is a secondary legislation enacted by the State Council. Its legal status is lower than primary legislation adopted by the National People's Congress or its Standing Committee. Section 1 of the RAR states that the Constitution and other pertinent laws are its legal source. Other pertinent laws include the 1989 ALL, the *Organic Law of the State Council of the People's Republic of China 1982*, the *Organic Law of the Local People's Congresses and Local People's Governments of the People's Republic of China 1986* and other laws which have incorporated provisions on administrative reconsideration. The *Land Administration Law of the People's Republic of China 1986* is one of them. After the promulgation of the 1982 Constitution and before the adoption of the 1990 RAR, the system of administrative reconsideration had already been provided in more than 100 laws and regulations. These legal provisions had contributed to the effective resolution of administrative disputes and the strengthening of supervision by administrative organs themselves.

The RAR has clarified those provisions in primary legislation. It has provided for the scope of administrative reconsideration and makes it unnecessary to stipulate the availability of administrative reconsideration in every primary or subsidiary legislation, apart from those not falling within the listed categories in the RAR.

The Administrative Reconsideration Law is at present under draft and is very likely to be enacted soon.

Its Nature and Function

The purpose of administrative reconsideration is to safeguard and supervise administrative organs in exercising their functions and powers, to prevent and rectify any malfeasant or improper concrete administrative acts, and to protect the lawful rights and interests of citizens, legal persons and other organizations.

In modern society, public administration is becoming more and more complicated and diversified. Administrative organs are involved in all sorts of activities. Whenever a decision is made by an administrative organ, it is bound to affect the interests of citizens, legal persons and other institutions in one way or another. In every country, especially a developing country like China, it is quite natural that certain administrative tortious activities may be committed. Furthermore, it will not be surprising that some administrative organs or their functionaries may, while exercising their authorities, misuse or even abuse their powers.

Therefore, the State should provide remedial measures for the aggrieved parties to redress their grievances and get compensation wherever it is appropriate. Administrative reconsideration is one such remedial measure. It is of an administrative nature as it is an administrative organ at the same level or the next higher level that will, through reconsidering the original decision, maintain, rescind or change an illegal or inappropriate concrete administrative act so as to effectively protect the legitimate interests of the aggrieved parties.

Another function of administrative reconsideration is to supervise the administrative organs in exercising their functions and powers. Through administrative reconsideration, administrative organs at the next higher level may examine the concrete administrative act undertaken by the organ at the lower level in order to see whether it is illegal or inappropriate. In so doing, the illegal or inappropriate concrete administrative act can be rectified within the system of administration. There are obvious advantages, such as the reduction of the

workload on the people's courts, the increase of the grievance addressing speed and the increase of the efficiency of administration.

Administrative reconsideration has another equally important role
to play, *i.e.* to protect and maintain administrative acts undertaken
according to law. Administrative reconsideration is provided by legislation and it has to be conducted according to the conditions and
procedures laid down by the RAR. The aggrieved party has to strictly
follow those conditions and procedure. For example, section 5 of the
RAR provides that administrative reconsideration shall usually apply a
single-level system of reconsideration. It can prevent the aggrieved
party from endlessly bothering an administrative organ and the legality
of a concrete administrative act can be recognized in time and the
efficiency of administration can be guaranteed.

Conditions for Administrative Reconsideration

In order to bring a case for administrative reconsideration,the aggrieved party must prove that the following conditions are satisfied.
Firstly, the party at which the complaint is directed against must be an
administrative organ, legal person or other organization which is authorized by laws or regulations to exercise administrative authority.
This covers two situations. One is that the administrative organ is
directly involved in disputes with the aggrieved party through exercising its administrative authority. The other is that the party at which
the complaint is directed against is a non-governmental organ or other
organization which is nevertheless authorized by laws or regulations
to exercise administrative authority. For example, professional banks
are authorized to exercise certain management authority. If an aggrieved party is not satisfied with their decisions, it can appeal to the
people's bank at the same level for reconsideration.

Secondly, an aggrieved party can only apply for administrative reconsideration when it believes its own lawful rights or interests have
been infringed upon by the concrete administrative act of an administrative organ or its functionary. This is a subjective test and there does
not have to be a real infringement. It does not imply that the administrative organ involved has committed tortious action and the applicant
is therefore entitled to compensation.

Thirdly, only concrete administrative acts can be reconsidered. For
example, the refusal by a land administration bureau to grant land-use
rights illegally or unreasonably. Excluded are abstract administrative
acts and other acts. The latter includes actions of administrative organs in handling civil disputes as a third party or any civil activities
conducted by the administrative organs themselves.

Sometimes relevant laws and regulations may also provide that the
aggrieved party must fulfil the obligations imposed by the concrete

administrative act before bringing a case against that decision. Taxation law provides a typical example.

Administrative Reconsideration Organs

The administrative reconsideration organs refer to those which accept   **3.04**
applications for reconsideration, and shall, according to law, conduct
reviews of the concrete administrative acts, and make decisions accordingly. Not all administrative organs will undertake the task of
administrative reconsideration. For example, State Council, as the
highest administrative organ, will not undertake administrative reconsideration. The purpose is to relieve it from becoming too involved in
specific matters. Therefore, any complaints against provincial, autonomous regional, and autonomous municipal people's governments will
be handled by themselves. Similarly any complaints against any Ministries will be dealt with by themselves. Any departments under
county people's government, which do not have any further established institutions under their control, will not bear the responsibility
of administrative reconsideration. For those departments which have
further established institutions under their control, they will still not
have the responsibility if the further established institutions do not
perform the concrete administrative acts in their own names. The
responsibility remains in the hands of county people's government.
Township people's governments do not have the responsibility because they are at grassroots level and do not have any working departments under their control.

It is not those administrative organs that actually reconsider the
original concrete administrative acts. Instead, there are reconsideration offices which are set up within the administrative reconsideration
organs who are responsible for this. Such offices are internal components of administrative organs and do not have the status of independent legal persons. They cannot therefore make any decisions in their
own names. All decisions have to be made in the name of the administrative organs to which they belong.

Grounds for Administrative Reconsideration

There are two main grounds for administrative reconsideration. One is
illegality and the other is inappropriateness. The administrative reconsideration organ can review whether or not a concrete administrative
act is legal or appropriate. Legality covers three different aspects. The
first one is whether or not the administrative organ undertaking
the concrete administrative act has exceeded its legal authority; the
second is whether the administrative act complies with the provisions

of the relevant laws and regulations; the third is whether the administrative organ undertaking the concrete administrative act has followed the proper legal procedure. Moreover, a concrete administrative act undertaken without sufficient evidence, with abuse of power or *ultra vires* elements are also regarded as illegal acts. It is therefore not difficult to see that the concept of illegality in China's administrative reconsideration is much wider than its counterpart in common law.

The other ground is inappropriateness of a concrete administrative act. It is impossible for laws and regulations to make detailed provisions in every aspect. There are bound to be discretions left in the hands of administrative organs. If an administrative organ exercises its discretionary power within its limits, the concrete administrative act undertaken will be lawful. But it may not be appropriate or reasonable. That is how the issue of inappropriateness arises. The RAR grants the authority to the administrative reconsideration organ to review the appropriateness of a concrete administrative act. If a concrete administrative act is inappropriate or unreasonable, then the administrative reconsideration organ may alter or change that act partially or completely, depending on the necessity. As an inappropriate act is lawful, review of inappropriateness will only take place after the review of the legality of the act. It is at the secondary level.

Scope of Administrative Reconsideration

The scope of administrative reconsideration deals with the kinds of concrete administrative acts which are reviewable by the administrative reconsideration organ. It determines the breadth and depth of administrative supervision and remedy. Chapter two of the RAR has listed the categories of concrete administrative acts subject to and not subject to reconsideration.

The first category is administrative sanction, including detention, fine, rescission of a permit or a licence, or order to suspend production or business operations or confiscation of property, which a citizen, legal person or other organization refuses to accept. Administrative sanction is imposed by administrative organs or other organizations authorized by laws or regulations to punish any citizens, legal persons or other organizations for violation of laws, regulations or rules. These are just a few main forms of administrative sanction. They are by no means the only ones subject to administrative reconsideration. In fact, there are many other kinds of administrative sanctions, such as the circulation of a notice of criticism, warning, order of destruction of food products which are prohibited to be produced, confiscation of illegal income and fake medicines and so on. They are all subject to administrative reconsideration.

The second category is compulsory administrative measures, including restriction of personal freedom or the sealing up, distraint, or freezing of property, which one refuses to accept. This category has two components. One is compulsory measures taken against personal freedom, which include the following main measures. Education through labour is a compulsory educational reform measure. The duration is between one to three years and can be extended for another year if necessary. Education has duel functions, *i.e.* both in terms of education and punishment. It is not an administrative sanction and should be distinguished from reform through labour which is targeted at criminals and executed by prison or labour reform teams. Detention is a compulsory administrative measure to restrict personal freedom. For example, under *Customs Law*, suspected smugglers can, after the approval of the head of the Customs office, be detained for 24 hours which can be extended to 48 hours under special circumstances, if the Customs office intends to transfer the case to the judicial organs. There are also other kinds of compulsory administrative measures such as segregation, which can also be brought to administrative organ for reconsideration.

The second component is restriction on property, including the sealing up, distraint and freezing of property in order to prevent its owner from disposition. The property concerned is sealed at its location and will not be transferred to the administrative organ. The seal cannot be removed by the property owner without the permission of the administrative organ. Restraint is a measure to take movable property under the control of the administrative organ either for the purpose of collecting evidence or preventing the party concerned removing the property. Freezing is a measure to freeze the bank account of the party concerned by the bank in order to prevent the party from disposing of the money in its account.

The third category is infringement upon a managerial decision-making authority, which is held to have been perpetrated by an administrative organ. This provision aims to protect the managerial decision-making authorities of all kinds of enterprises. Managerial autonomy, including the right to possess, to use, and to dispose of property, is essential to the success of any enterprise. Various legislation has now been passed to separate ownership from managerial authority. Any unlawful or inappropriate infringements of such autonomy may be challenged through administrative reconsideration.

The fourth category is refusal by an administrative organ to issue a permit or licence, which one holds oneself legally qualified to obtain, or a failure to respond to an application. Whether or not a certain kind of activity needs a licence or permit is governed by legislation. Currently, licence or permit systems are widely used in many areas, such as in the protection and maintenance of important resources and the ecological environment, the protection of public safety and health, the maintenance of normal economic order, the management of cultural activities and so on. There are several conditions which have to be satisfied by an applicant in order to obtain a licence, *e.g.* the relevant administrative organ must have the authority to grant the licence, the applicant must apply within the law and so on.

The fifth category is refusal by an administrative organ to perform its statutory duties with regard to protecting one's personal or proprietory rights, as one has applied for, or its failure to respond to the application. Only those organs which have the legal responsibility to protect personal and proprietory rights can be complained against under this provision.

3.05   What has been discussed above is one aspect of the authority enjoyed by administrative organs, *i.e.* the authority to grant or deprive the party concerned of its rights. The next category is about the other aspect, namely the authority to impose upon or relieve someone from an obligation. It is where an administrative organ is held to have illegally demanded the performance of duties. All duties to be imposed should have clear legal basis. However, this is not the case in practice. Reports are often heard about unlawful collection of fees and imposition of other duties. The parties concerned can not only refuse to pay but also apply for administrative reconsideration. However, it is claimed that no application for administrative reconsideration is allowed if the administrative organ concerned requests the citizens, legal persons or other organizations to pay in terms of a donation provided that no administrative authority is used. This is not logical. When an administrative organ is involved, it is quite natural that the people will believe that administrative authority will be invoked if they do not pay the so-called donation. It is better to prohibit administrative organs from requesting donations. Moreover, section 9(8) provides that all kinds of concrete administrative acts are subject to administrative reconsideration if they have infringed upon either other personal rights or other proprietary rights which are not covered in the above categories.

Section 9(9) further broadens the scope of administrative reconsideration by providing that application for administrative reconsideration can be lodged against any other concrete administrative acts against which, according to the laws and regulations, an administrative lawsuit or an application for reconsideration may be instituted. One kind of application which could be lodged under section 9(9) is complaints against infringement upon rights other than personal or proprietary rights, such as civil and political rights. Election right is one example. As the RAR was enacted after the promulgation of the ALL, it is obvious that the intention of the State Council is to bring the RAR in line with the ALL. Certain concrete administrative acts which are not judicially reviewable may also be subject to administrative reconsideration as long as a specific law or regulation so provides. It is reasonable that remedial measures should be provided as long as the rights or interests of the party concerned are infringed upon. The *1989 Law of the People's Republic of China on Assemblies, Processions and Demonstrations is* one such example where judicial review is not allowed but administrative reconsideration is nevertheless allowed. *Regulations on Registration and Management of Social Organizations* is another one. In this sense administrative reconsideration can be said to be complementary to judicial review.

There are four kinds of administrative acts which are not subject to administrative reconsideration. They are abstract administrative acts, internal administrative acts, Acts of State and arbitration, conciliation or other dispositions of civil disputes. However, any decisions made by administrative organs concerning the ownership of or the right to use land, mineral resources, forests and so on are subject to administrative reconsideration.

Applicable Legislation

The concept of legislation in its broad sense covers the laws enacted by the NPC, the administrative regulations adopted by the State Council, local regulations promulgated by local legislatures, regulations, decisions and orders with a general binding force formulated and promulgated by administrative organs at higher levels according to law, and the regulations passed by autonomous regions. The legal effects of these normative documents are different. The issue is whether they can all be applied by the administrative reconsideration organ in handling cases. There is no argument with regard to the applicability of laws, administrative regulations, and local regulations. Controversy focuses mainly on the applicability of regulations, decisions and orders with a general binding force formulated and promulgated by administrative organs at higher levels according to law.

As far as regulations are concerned, the Constitution and *Organic Law on Local People's Congresses and Local People's Governments* provide that certain administrative organs have the authority to make universally binding regulations. They include various Ministries and Commission of the State Council, Provinces, Autonomous Regions and Municipalities under direct control of the Central Government. These regulations will normally work out the details of the laws and administrative regulations and they therefore play an essential role in the implementation of the laws and administrative regulations in social life and in the enhancement of administrative efficiency. Practice also reveals that a large quantity of concrete administrative acts are undertaken by relying on various regulations. In certain areas more than 70% of applicable normative documents are these regulations and given this fact, administrative reconsideration must apply those

regulations. Otherwise, people will doubt the legal effect of regulations, especially when concrete administrative acts are undertaken
according to these regulations. Therefore the RAR provides that
regulations should also be applied by the administrative reconsideration organ. One pre-condition is of course that the regulations
must be made according to laws and are therefore lawful and effective
regulations.

The next issue to look at are decisions and orders. These play an
important role in filling the vacuum left by laws, administrative regulations and regulations, especially in cities which do not have the
authority to make local regulations. However, existing decisions and
orders from different departments or governmental organs sometimes
contradict each other and no sound system has been developed to
improve on the making of decisions and orders. The RAR has provided
that decisions and orders should be relied upon in administrative
reconsideration cases. In theory this means that the lower administrative organs should obey the decisions and orders from higher administrative organs, as opposed to concrete legal decisions.

Concern has been expressed about the different provisions in this
aspect between administrative reconsideration and judicial review.
The ALL provides that laws and administrative regulations are to be
relied on whereas regulations can only be referred to. The issue then
arises of applications of different standards in dealing with the same
case. If the decisions or orders relied upon by the administrative reconsideration organ are themselves lawful or effective, then those decisions or orders are consistent with the laws and administrative
regulations, and so reliance upon the decisions and orders will make it
easier to resolve the case in dispute.

What is left is a more complicated issue. That is what the administrative reconsideration organ is supposed to do if it finds that the
regulations, or decisions or orders with a general binding force, which
serve as the basis for a concrete administrative act, are in conflict with
the laws, administrative regulations or other regulations?

It is clear that no application for reconsideration can be lodged
against any decisions or orders with a general binding force because
they are abstract administrative acts. Even worse, they need to be
relied upon by the administrative reconsideration organ. Neither is it
possible to bring a case for judicial review against these decisions or
orders. However, procedures do exist to redress such problems. The
first is an administrative procedure, based on the supervisory role
played by a higher administrative organ or people's government over a
lower administrative organ or people's government. If the decisions or
orders fall within the scope of functions and powers of the competent
administrative reconsideration organ, it can then decide to nullify or
change the decisions or orders.

The administrative reconsideration organ, will not have the power to handle the matter and has to report to the administrative organ at the next higher level if the regulations, decisions, or orders with a general binding force, which serve as the basis for a concrete administrative act, are made by an administrative organ or people's government enjoying a higher status than itself. If the administrative organ at the next higher level does not have the power to handle the case either, the case shall be submitted to an organ which does have the power. Once the inconsistency between the normative documents is resolved by the administrative organ with authority, the administrative reconsideration organ may resume the hearing of the case.

Remedies

As far as a concrete administrative act is concerned, if the application of laws, administrative regulations, regulations as well as the decisions and orders with a general binding force are correct, the facts are clearly ascertained, and the statutory limits of authority and procedures are duly complied with, then the applicant shall not have a case for administrative reconsideration. The concrete administrative act, which has been challenged, will be sustained. On the other hand, if the applicant has got a case, there are various kinds of remedies available through administrative reconsideration. The defending party may be required to rectify procedural inadequacies, or a fixed time may be set for the defending party to perform the duty, or the concrete administrative act may be annulled or changed. Even a specific performance can be required of the defending party.

Judicial Review

Administrative litigation (judicial review) refers to the litigation activity under which a citizen, legal person or other organization, believing that his legitimate rights or interests have been infringed by a concrete administrative act of an administrative organ or its personnel, applies to the people's court for judicial protection. The court will then exercise its power of review of the administrative act concerned and adjudicate upon it. This is a kind of judicial control over the exercise of administrative power by the executive branch of the government. Different countries have different constitutional structures due to their different historical, political and cultural backgrounds. The relationship between the three main branches of the government, *i.e.* legislature, executive and judiciary, differs from one country to another. Judicial control of executive power is concerned with the relationship between the judiciary and the executive. It is quite natural **3.06** that the organs responsible for judicial review, the scope, grounds and remedies for judicial review may differ from one country to another. The main legislation in China governing judicial review is the 1990 ALL.

The Objective of the ALL

The ALL intends to achieve two kinds of objectives namely the procedural and substantive objectives. The direct (procedural) objective of the ALL is to ensure the correct and prompt handling of administrative cases by the people's courts. The ALL lays down the procedural requirements as to how a litigation against the administration should be conducted. It has not only defined the authority of the courts in adjudicating administrative cases, but also laid down certain restrictions on the judicial control of administration. These procedural requirements are enacted to achieve correctness and accuracy of adjudication in administrative cases.

However, procedural legislation is to ensure the proper application and implementation of substantive legislation. The ALL has two substantive objectives to achieve. One is to protect the lawful rights and interests of citizens, legal persons and other organizations. The other is to safeguard and supervise the exercise of administrative powers by administrative organs. Through the adjudication of specific administrative cases, the people's courts will examine the legality of administrative acts undertaken by the administrative organs. If the acts undertaken are illegal, the courts have the responsibility to rectify them and exercise their authority accordingly and issue an order of rectification or nullification.

The two substantive objectives of the ALL are in theory not contradictory, but they have a different emphasis and in practice it is very difficult to achieve the balance between the two. Judicial practice has shown that the proper exercise of authority by the administration has often been over-emphasized.

Sources of Judicial Review

As China adopts a continental legal system, the jurisdiction of the courts over lawsuits against administration has to be prescribed by legislation.

The constitutional source of judicial review in China is section 41, which has to be brought into operation by other legislation. The direct source of judicial review has therefore to be provided for by specific laws or administrative regulations. Section 2 of the ALL provides that:

"If a citizen, a legal person or any other organization considers that his or its lawful rights and interests have been infringed upon by a specific administrative act of an administrative organ or its personnel, he or it shall have the right to bring a suit before a people's court in accordance with this Law."

This provision has provided for the three essential conditions for a case to qualify as an administrative case. Firstly, the plaintiff must be one who believes that his lawful rights or interests have been infringed upon by administrative activities. Secondly, the defendant must be an administrative organ or its functionary which or who is authorized to exercise administrative authority. None of the people's courts, legislative organs, Party's branches and military organs can be sued as defendants. Thirdly, the administrative activities to be sued against must be concrete administrative acts.

Scope of Jurisdiction

Section 2 of the ALL only provides for the general condition under which a person may bring a case to the people's court for judicial review. However, not all concrete administrative acts are judicially reviewable by the people's courts. The concept of scope of jurisdiction is concerned with the categories of administrative acts which are, and are not, subject to judicial review.

Chapter two of the ALL lays down the categories of administrative acts which are reviewable and non-reviewable. The Opinions of the Supreme People's Court on the Implementation of the ALL provide more detailed provisions with regard to the scope of jurisdiction. The general principle is that the people's courts can only accept lawsuits against those concrete administrative acts which are reviewable according to legislation. If a concrete administrative act is not specifically mentioned by any legislation as reviewable, then it is not subject to judicial review. Section 11 of the ALL lists eight categories of concrete administrative acts which are reviewable. They are exactly the same as those categories for administrative reconsideration.

Section 12 of the ALL lists four kinds of matters which are not subject to judicial review. The first three that are excluded, are also excluded from administrative reconsideration. If a person is not satisfied with arbitration awards or any other disposition of civil disputes, he cannot bring a case for judicial review either. Instead, he can bring the matter to the relevant people's court as a civil case. If any concrete administrative acts shall, as provided by law, be finally decided by an administrative organ, they shall not be subject to judicial review.

Grounds for Judicial Review

3.07   Grounds for judicial review refer to the legal basis upon which a concrete administrative act may be lawfully challenged. They are the legal grounds upon which the judiciary may review a concrete administrative act. There are altogether seven specific grounds for judicial review.

Illegality

Section 5 of the ALL lays down the principle of legality, *i.e.* the people's courts shall examine the legality of a concrete administrative act. That means the people's courts shall normally only review whether or not an administrative organ has breached any legislation in undertaking a concrete administrative act. But the scope of illegality seems to be very wide. It covers insufficiency of evidence, inaccuracy in the application of legislation, failure to comply with legal procedure, and *ultra vires*. In principle, the people's courts will not review a concrete administrative act falling within administrative discretion. Any complaints against the appropriateness of the exercise of discretionary powers should usually be handled through administrative reconsideration. But this does not mean that the courts can never review inappropriate administrative decisions. In fact, the people's courts have been granted certain jurisdiction to scrutinize the improper exercise of discretionary power, based on the grounds of abuse of power, and delay or failure in the performance of statutory duty, obvious unfairness, which will be discussed in the section on judicial control of discretionary power.

Lack of Evidence

It must first be established whether the evidence is accurate and sufficient, which is the pre-condition and basis for the legality of a concrete administrative act. Deviation from this basis and pre-condition will make it impossible for the application of legislation to be correct.

Evidence can be classified as ordinary and essential evidence. The former refers to all kinds of materials and methods as provided under the ALL to be used to prove the facts of the case. The latter must satisfy three requirements. Firstly, it must be objective. Secondly, it must be relevant. The people's courts will examine the submitted evidence to see whether or not it is directly related to the case and therefore essential to the adjudication of the case. Thirdly, the evidence must be lawfully obtained. If the methods adopted to obtain the evidence are unlawful, then the evidence, even though essential to the case, cannot be used as evidence for the adjudication.[4]

In order to ensure that the concrete administrative act is lawful, the facts relied on by the administrative decision-maker must be accurate, reliable, sufficient and conclusive. Failure in this respect may make the decision unlawful.

Sufficiency and conclusiveness are closely related. Sufficiency of evidence means that there must be enough evidence to prove all the material facts of the case. If any of the material facts do not have any evidence, this will be regarded as insufficient evidence. All the evidence used must be coherent and must point to one conclusion. We are only concerned with key evidence which is essential for the undertaking of the concrete administrative act. Conclusiveness of evidence refers to the importance of evidence, upon which the people's court can review whether or not the decision undertaken by the administrative organ is lawful.

Section 32 of the ALL provides that the defendant shall bear the burden of proof for the concrete administrative act he has undertaken and shall provide the evidence and regulatory documents in accordance with which the act has been undertaken. If the defendant cannot provide the court with the key evidence or the normative documents before the completion of the trial at the first instance, then the people's court may annul the concrete administrative act. If the defendant fails to provide evidence or the evidence provided does not include key evidence, then the people's court can rule against the defendant. If the defendant only submits evidence which is to his own advantage, then the plaintiff can rebut by providing his own evidence. There is one issue worthy of discussion, *i.e.* when the defendant is supposed to discharge his burden of proof and whether late submission of evidence should be accepted. Section 43 of the ALL states that the defendant shall provide the people's court with the documents on the basis of which a concrete administrative act has been undertaken and file defence pleadings within ten days of receiving the copy of the plaintiff's pleadings. It is made very clear that the defendant is required to submit his defence before the actual hearing. However, section 30 of the Opinions allows the defendant to submit evidence at any time before the completion of the trial at the first instance. That provides a contradiction between two different sources of law. According to the hierarchy of legislation, the provision in the ALL should prevail over the Opinions issued by the Supreme People's Court.

Errors in the Application of Legislation

The exact meaning of inaccuracy in the application of legislation is not explained either in the Opinions or the ALL. One scholar suggests that application of legislation should refer to the application of both substantive and procedural legislation.[5] The people's courts should review not only the errors in the application of substantive legislation but also errors in the application of procedural legislation. It is correct to say that legislation includes both substantive and procedural ones. It seems better to restrict the erroneous application of legislation to substantive legislation. In other words, the inclusion of both substantive and procedural legislation under 52(2)(b) would make the provision of 52(2)(c) redundant.

Errors in the application of legislation may be caused by various factors. Firstly, China adopts a unilateral legal system and there are different levels of legislation. Central legislature (the NPC), local legislature, central government, local government, and various governmental organs have respective authorities to promulgate legislation (law, administrative regulations, regulations, and other normative documents). It happens sometimes that two pieces of legislation are contradictory. If that is the case, the administrative organ concerned has to choose one, which is often a difficult task especially if the two pieces are at the same level of the legal hierarchy.

Secondly, Chinese legislation is, compared with legislation in the United Kingdom or Hong Kong, very general and the provisions in the legislation only lay down the principles in the areas concerned and normally lack detailed provisions. This has something to do with the tradition of the continental legal system which normally emphasizes the importance of legal principles. Furthermore, China has, since 1978, started to develop from a planned economy to a market economy and therefore many former legislations are no longer suitable for the growing needs of economic development. During a transitional period, it is not surprising to find gaps in legislation. It is therefore almost unavoidable that errors will occur in the process of application of legislation.

Thirdly, the quality of law enforcement officers is also essential to the accurate application of legislation because any legislation must be implemented by people.

3.08 Errors in the application of legislation can be classified into different categories.

a) Application of a Wrong Piece of Legislation

Application of a wrong piece of legislation may be caused by several different factors. The first could be that the administrative act undertaken is according to legislation A while the applicable legislation should be legislation B. This may occur when several pieces of legislation govern the same kind of administrative activities, or one legislation grants different authorities to more than one administrative organ or several authorities to the same administrative organ. Therefore it often happens that one kind of activity is governed by several pieces of legislation, or several administrative organs. The second factor could be that the administrative organ has applied a legislation which has not come into force yet. The third possibility is that the administrative organ has, in undertaking the concrete administrative act, applied a legislation which has already lost its legal effect. The fourth possibility is that the administrative organ has applied a legislation which it does not have the authority to apply. Normally, every piece of legislation stipulates its law enforcement organ to exercise administrative authority. That organ is empowered to apply the relevant legislation within the scope defined by the legislation. If an administrative organ has applied a legislation which it is not authorized to apply, then it will be deemed to have committed an error in the application of legislation. For example, if a municipal planning Administrative division handles the violation of municipal planning by a resident according to Land Administration Law, not City Planning Law, that decision may be set aside by the court. The fifth possibility is that the administrative organ intentionally avoids the application of an appropriate piece of applicable legislation. This may occur when there are several pieces of legislation. The administrative organ will choose the legislation that is to its advantage. Another possibility is that the administrative organ is supposed to apply special legislation, but it applies ordinary legislation.

b) Application of Wrong Provisions of Correct Legislation
   There are two possibilities. One is that the administrative organ should apply one section or sub-section, but it actually applies another section or sub-section. The second possibility is that the administrative organ should apply several sections in the legislation, but it only applies one of them.

c) Application of Correct Legislation to Wrong Subject
   This refers to situations under which the administrative organ either grants rights to, or imposes administrative penalties upon, those who are not entitled to receive such rights or penalties. Typical examples include the issue of licences to unqualified person(s), failure to issue licences to qualified person(s), and improper imposition of taxes.

Compliance with Legal Procedure

Administrative procedure refers to the specific methods and steps for an administrative organ to undertake a concrete administrative act. An administrative decision needs to be made through one or other kind of procedure. Administrative procedure may be classified in different ways. According to the nature and function of administrative acts, it may be classified into administrative legislative procedure, administrative enforcement procedure and administrative judicial pocedure. It may also be classified into legal procedure, *i.e.* the procedure is laid down in legislation, and non-legal procedure, *i.e.* customs or traditions formulated from time to time by the administrative organ for making a particular kind of administrative decisions.

The necessity of judicial review of procedural legality can be illustrated as follows. Firstly, the rule of law principle requires administration according to legal requirements which include both substantive as well as procedural legal requirements. The rule of law principle demands that the administration complies with procedural legal requirements. Though China does not have a uniform administrative procedural law, some general principles on proper administration have been laid down in China's Constitution. Section 5 of the Constitution requires all state organs (including administrative organs) to abide by the law. Section 27 of the Constitution requires all state organs to carry out the principle of simple and efficient administration. However, these are only general principles. Their implementation in practice requires their incorporation into other legislation. The enactment of the *Administrative Penalty Law 1996* has set down the legal procedures for the establishment and imposition of administrative penalties.

Secondly, the breach of procedural requirement is itself an infringement of the rights of the aggrieved party. However, not enough attention has been paid to legislation on administrative procedural requirements. It is true that most substantive administrative legislation such as that on administration of commerce and industry, taxation, customs, public security and so on, has incorporated certain procedural requirements on the exercise of administrative authority. They are however, mainly very general and lack detailed provisions. There are often more procedural requirements for those under administration than those on administrative organs. Consequently, some important administrative procedures have not been incorporated into any legislation. These procedures are the customs formulated over the years in practice and are by no means arbitrary. They are normally followed in practice by the administrative organs in undertaking concrete administrative acts. In principle, the compliance with non-legal procedural requirements is purely voluntary. Whether or not the administrative organ follows the non-legal procedures will not affect the validity and effect of the decisions. Any concrete administrative acts undertaken accordingly will be non-reviewable.

Excess of Legal Authority (*Ultra Vires*)

Various attempts have been made by Chinese scholars to define the concept of *ultra vires* in China. Some define the concept according to the contents of *ultra vires* while others define it according to the categories of different kinds of *ultra vires* activities. There are mainly two different views. One approach holds that the concept of *ultra vires* refers to the concrete administrative acts undertaken by the administrative organs, or its personnel, or other organizations either legally authorized, or entrusted by those administrative organs which exceed the scope of authority, either legally prescribed or authorized or entrusted. The other approach maintains that *ultra vires* refers to the circumstances under which the administrative organs either exercise the administrative power which is not legally granted to them or exceed the scope of legally authorized administrative power.

The main difference between the two approaches is whether or not the concept of *ultra vires* should include 'no authority' which refers to if the administrative organs have exercised administrative authority which is neither within their jurisdiction nor entrusted to them by other administrative organs. But both approaches agree that *ultra vires* is only about substantive *ultra vires*, which means that the administrative organs have actually undertaken activities which are in excess of their legal authority.

According to the above discussion of the concept of *ultra vires*, *ultra vires* administrative activities may be classified firstly into two categories. One is the exercise of authority which is not related to the functions of the administrative organs concerned (no authority). The other is the exercise of authority which is within the types of authority which the administrative organs may exercise but exceeds the scope of the jurisdiction of the specific administrative organ. The second may be further divided into

    i) vertical ultra vires, *i.e.* lower administrative organs usurp the authority of the higher administrative organ or vice versa;

    ii) horizontal *ultra vires*, *i.e.* one administrative organ usurps the authority of another administrative organ at the same level either because they are in different geographical locations or they are in charge of different administrative functions;

    iii) *ultra vires* in content, *i.e.* the exercise of administrative power exceeds the legal scope.

Judicial Control of Discretionary Power

Discretionary power is authorized by legislation and should be **3.09** exercised within its defined legal scope and its exercise should be consistent with the objective and fundamental aim of the relevant legislation. Apart from this requirement, the administrative organ may choose to make decision A, which it believes to be accurate, instead of decision B.

As administrative discretionary power is a kind of administrative power, any decision made through the exercise of discretionary power is a unilateral act. The administrative organ has the authority to order the person (natural or legal) concerned to do or not to do something.

The person concerned has the obligation to follow such an order. The relationship between the administrative organ and the person under administration is therefore unequal. The improper exercise of discretionary power may infringe upon the legitimate interests of the person concerned.

Administrative discretionary power is very flexible as the administrative organ is granted the authority to choose among different alternatives and the relevant legislation normally does not provide clear guidance with regard to which alternative should be chosen and how to choose. This feature has been claimed to be the essence of discretionary power. Because of this flexibility, an administrative organ may arbitrarily exercise its discretionary power which may lead to obviously unfair results or abuse of its authority. Both of which are the grounds recognized under the ALL upon which a concrete administrative act may be challenged through judicial review.

The traditional approach is that the exercise of discretionary power can only be appropriate or inappropriate. There does not exist the issue of illegality. Therefore discretionary power is not subject to judicial control. The current approach is that there are certain legal requirements upon the exercise of discretionary power, including its legal scope, the legislative objective and fundamental principles. If the exercise of discretionary power exceeds the legal scope or is against the legislative objective or fundamental principles, then that exercise of discretionary power should be regarded as illegal.

Apart from illegal exercise of discretionary power, there also exists inappropriate exercise of discretionary power which is not subject to judicial control. That does not mean no remedies are available to redress inappropriate exercise of discretionary power. If any person has any complaints in this aspect, he may bring the case to the relevant administrative organ at the next higher level for administrative reconsideration. If the inappropriateness attains a certain degree, they may also be subject to judicial review. According to section 54 of the ALL, there are three grounds under which discretionary power can be challenged.

Abuse of Powers

Abuse of powers in administrative law mainly refers to abuse of administrative discretionary powers. Usually, an administrative organ is granted the discretion to undertake a concrete act when certain legal conditions are satisfied. The discretion concerns the activities, not the identification of facts. It may be granted in all kinds of activities. It could be about whether or not to undertake a concrete administrative act, what kind of acts should be chosen, the measures to be chosen, the scope of choice, the time limit or the methods of activities and so on. Two tests need to be satisfied. The first is a subjective one, *i.e.* it must be intentional. In other words, negligent acts can never be classified as abuse of power. The second is an objective test. The concrete administrative act undertaken by an administrative organ is, though within its discretion, against the purpose and principle of the relevant legislation and unreasonable. More specifically, three essential elements must be satisfied for a concrete administrative act to constitute abuse of power. They are: the concrete administrative act exceeds legal authority; the concrete administrative act is against or deviates from the objective and principle of the relevant legislation; the act undertaken is unreasonable. Unreasonableness is caused by improper exercise of discretionary power by an administrative organ.

Abuse of power may be caused by different factors. An unreasonable decision can be classified as abuse of power if it is made due to bad judgment on behalf of the decision-maker. For example, the decision-maker knows that the specific decision is against the objective of the relevant legislation but still makes the decision. It is also abuse of power if the decision-maker, in undertaking a concrete administrative act, does not take into account the relevant considerations which should usually be considered, and arbitrarily takes an unreasonable concrete administrative act. Likewise, if the decision-maker takes into account irrelevant factors which are usually not taken into account, it also constitutes abuse of power.

Obvious Unfairness

Obvious unfairness is another ground upon which action can be taken to challenge the exercise of discretionary power. According to section 54(4), this ground is rather limited. In order to invoke this ground, two conditions need to be satisfied. One is the concrete administrative act can only refer to administrative penalties as mentioned in section 11(1), not any other kinds of concrete administrative acts. The other is that the concrete administrative act must be obviously unfair. There is no legislative interpretation on the meaning of "obvious unfairness". One academic interpretation is that obviously unfair administrative penalties refer to those imposed on the wrongdoers which are, though with the scope of penalties provided by law and regulation, extremely unfair and incompatible with the wrongs committed.[6] Firstly, the penalty imposed upon the wrongdoer is incompatible with the wrong committed. It could either be too heavy or too light. Secondly, quite different penalties are imposed upon persons with the same responsibility in the same case. Thirdly, in the same case the person committing serious wrong receives a light penalty while the person committing a minor offence receives a heavy penalty. Another scholar has suggested three principles in determining whether or not a concrete administrative act is obviously unfair. They are the principles of proportionality, equal application and compatibility.[7]

Discretionary power may appear or exist anywhere and at any time. Due to the impossibility of legislation to provide for details in every aspect and also the difficulty to foresee what may happen in the future, administrative organs are often granted discretion. On the one hand, they enjoy discretionary power in making decisions as to whether or not to undertake concrete administrative acts either through imposition of penalties or any other punishment. On the other, they also enjoy discretionary power in undertaking abstract administrative acts. For example, Chinese national legislation often stipulates that detailed rules for implementation shall be made by the relevant authority in charge in accordance with the laws, and be submitted to the State Council for approval. There is no requirement as to whether or not and when the detailed rules for implementation should be made. In this sense, the administrative organs enjoy discretionary power in making subsidiary legislation, *i.e.* regulations or rules. Such discretion may also be abused.

However, the ALL clearly provides that only concrete administrative acts are judicially reviewable and abstract administrative acts are not reviewable. That does not mean discretion in undertaking abstract administrative acts are not subject to any control. Instead, different procedures of supervision exist. The control is by the administrative authority in charge or at the next higher level, and the legislature, both local and national.

Failure or Delay in the Performance of Statutory Duty

The third ground for legal control of discretionary power is the failure or delay in the performance of statutory power, which is stated in section 54(3) of the ALL. This is concerned with inaction of the relevant administrative organs. There is not much academic writing on this ground. Even in Professor Luo's book on judicial review, judicial review of administrative inaction was only mentioned in passing, while each of the other six grounds of judicial review was discussed in a separate chapter. This ground is rather straightforward and simple in the sense that it is only related to the time when the concrete administrative act should be undertaken and nothing else. But it is at least equally important as any other grounds since failure or delay in the performance of statutory duty may also infringe upon the legitimate rights of those under administration. Much legislation does not stipulate the exact time limit for the performance of statutory duties by administrative organs. They are granted the discretion to determine when they shall undertake the concrete administrative acts. If an administrative organ intentionally delays or fails to commence performance, it will amount to the unlawful exercise of discretionary power. Such an exercise of discretion will not only affect the efficiency of administration but also cause damage to those under the administration.

There are several conditions which need to be satisfied in order to rely on this ground to challenge the administrative organ concerned. The first is that the administrative organ must owe a statutory duty towards the applicant, either to issue a licence or to provide protection. Without the existence of statutory duty, the administrative organ cannot be sued under this ground. Secondly, the statutory time limit must have been passed or a reasonable time period must have passed if there is no statutory time limit. Thirdly, the administrative organ must have refused or failed to respond during the time limit. Fourthly, there are no defences.

Judicial Remedies

If an applicant has successfully challenged the concrete administrative acts undertaken by the relevant administrative organ, one of the following remedies may be granted.   **3.10**

Order of Rectification

The defending party is supposed to undertake the concrete administrative act in accordance with legal procedures. The pre- condition is that there should be a legal procedure available. However, there are no systematic or comprehensive systems on administrative procedures. As a result, there are no existing procedures to be followed for many administrative activities. That is one of the main reasons why administrative organs neglect procedural requirements. But if there are procedural requirements in the relevant legislation, they should be followed. Failure to do so is deemed to be procedural inadequacy. This normally refers to such situations as failure of the defending party to reveal its own identity, or failure to inform the applicant of its rights, or a mistake in the date of the written decision etc. But the ascertaining of facts and application of laws are correct, and the breach of procedural requirements have not directly affected the substantive rights of the applicants. The defending party will only be required by the courts to make up or improve the procedural inadequacy in the concrete administrative act, which remains effective.

This is quite different from the western legal system where procedural justice is so cherished that breach of procedural legal requirements will lead to the act concerned being deemed void. This is because procedural fairness is the only thing which can definitely be achieved and everybody is regarded as equal before the same procedural requirements. Whereas different people will have different perceptions of substantive justice which is influenced by a number of factors such as ideologies, social and economic backgrounds, religious beliefs and so on.

Specific Performance

If the defending party fails to perform the obligations imposed by laws, administrative regulations or regulations, it is a derelict activity. Two situations could arise. One is the defending party's refusal to perform the obligation; the other is the undue delay on the side of the defending party to perform the duties falling within its scope of obligations. The courts may set a fixed time for the defending party to perform the duty.

Nullification or Change of the Concrete Administrative Act

If the defending party commits substantive mistakes in the process of undertaking a concrete administrative act, the act shall be annulled, or changed or the defending party may be required by decision to undertake a new concrete administrative act. Substantive mistakes include ambiguity of the main facts, erroneous application of the laws, regulations, rules, or of decisions and orders with a general binding force, violation of legal procedures which affects unfavourably the lawful rights and interests of the applicant, the excess of authority or abuse of powers and obvious inappropriateness of the concrete administrative act.

Relationship between Administrative Reconsideration and Judicial Review

Administrative reconsideration and judicial review are different means to redress wrongs committed by administrative organs and to restore justice to the applicant while at the same time protecting the lawful exercise of executive authority by administrative organs. Sometimes the provisions of some laws and administrative regulations stipulate that the person concerned shall first apply for reconsideration and only bring a suit before a people's court if the person concerned does not accept the reconsideration decision. If that is the case, administrative reconsideration is compulsory and a pre-requisite for judicial review. That means all administrative remedies should be exhausted before resorting to judicial remedies. The relatively simple procedure of administrative reconsideration is convenient to both parties and may reduce the burden of the people's courts by solving most administrative disputes at the level of administrative reconsideration. If the applicant does not accept the decision made by the administrative reconsideration organ to reject his application, the applicant may, within fifteen days from the date of receiving the written decision of rejection, bring a lawsuit before the people's court. If the laws or administrative regulations provide otherwise, then those provisions have to be followed. For example, if the laws provide that the administrative reconsideration decision is final, no application for judicial review will be accepted.

Some laws or administrative regulations do not stipulate administrative reconsideration as the prerequisite for judicial review. The applicant shall then have the choice, either to lodge an application for administrative reconsideration or to bring a case directly to the people's court for judicial review. If an application for judicial review has already been accepted, then no application for reconsideration will be accepted. On the other hand, if the applicant has lodged an application for administrative reconsideration which has been accepted, then no application for the same case can be filed before the people's court within the statutory time limit for administrative reconsideration.

State Compensation

The *State Compensation Law* (SCL) was adopted by the Standing **3.11** Committee of the NPC on May 12, 1994 and came into effect on January 1, 1995. The law has for the first time clearly defined the legal basis for claiming compensation from state organs, including the scope and procedure of state compensation. The adoption of the SCL has not only contributed to the establishment of a comprehensive system of state responsibility in China but also filled a gap in the existing legislation of procedural administrative law.

Legislative Development

The principle that the state has the responsibility to pay compensation is stated in China's first Constitution (1954) and reappears in the 1982 Constitution with only minor changes. The relevant provision now reads, "Citizens who have suffered losses as a result of infringement of their civic rights by any state organ or functionary have the right to compensation in accordance with the law". This is regarded as the constitutional basis for the establishment of a state compensation system. As specific laws and regulations are needed to implement the constitutional principle. The *Economic Contract Law of the PRC* (1981) and *Regulations of the PRC on Administrative Penalties for Public Security* (1986) are two examples incorporating provisions on the state's responsibility to pay compensation. *The General Principle of Civil Law (GPCL)* (1986) reaffirms the same constitutional principle. Section 121 of the GPCL imposes civil liability on state organs or their functionaries that, while executing their duties, encroach upon the lawful rights and interests of citizens or legal persons and cause damages.

In order to apply section 121 of the GPCL, many issues still have to be sorted out and tested, such as the relation between state organs and their functionaries concerning compensation, the liability of government organs for damages caused by public utilities, the necessity and procedure of compensation for illegal imprisonment and so on. These issues of common concern have perplexed the judiciary. It has become obvious that the broad constitutional principles and section 121 of the GPCL cannot meet the needs of China's changing society. More detailed legal provisions are needed.

The 1989 ALL provided some guidance on the handling of suits brought by citizens, legal persons or other organizations against government organs on "concrete administrative acts". It contains several clauses on the liabilities of state administrative organs to pay compensation. However, the ALL is in nature a procedural law and therefore focuses on procedural issues (such as the criterion for determining, and method of calculating state compensation) rather than substantive provisions. Moreover, the ALL is restricted to concrete administrative acts only, and does not cover either abstract administrative acts or acts carried out by non-administrative organs which nevertheless participate in administration. Therefore, in order to secure the implementation of the ALL, the SCL was finally adopted in May 1994.

Scope of Application

The SCL does not include legislative compensation. Several concerns have contributed to the exclusion of legislative compensation from the SCL. Firstly, it is common practice with legislation in China that matters shall not be included if the legislators are uncertain as to whether or not and how they should be covered. Secondly, legislative acts have been claimed by some scholars as State Acts and therefore should be immune from responsibility for compensation. Thirdly, compatibility with the ALL and other legislation demands the exclusion of legislative compensation.

Different opinions have been expressed with regard to whether military compensation should be covered by the SCL. Damages caused by military acts may be classified into three categories. One is those caused by military exercises or training, which are, according to one source, the main ones. They are within the scope of civil disputes and can be recovered through civil claims according of section 121 of the GPCL and the procedure laid down by the *Civil Procedure Law (CPL)*. The second concerns actual military action consisting of lawful acts, and therefore should not be within the scope of the SCL. The compensation for those acts should be provided through administrative indemnity. The third category is concerned with the damages caused by illegal exercise of military power. It has been suggested that these may in the future be governed by a separate military law or other regulations. The main reason for the exclusion of provisions on military compensation, according to a distinguished scholar, Professor Pi Chunxie, is the exclusion of acts of national defence from the ALL. However, as Professor Pi argues, military acts are not equal to acts of national defence, and furthermore military organs were put under state organs under the 1982 Constitution. It is therefore reasonable to subject them to the regulations of the SCL. It has also been claimed that doing so is beneficial to the unification and consistency of the state compensation system nationwide.

As China moves towards a market economy, many public utilities are still owned by the State. How to deal with the damages caused by mismanagement of public utilities, such as roads and bridges, is essential to the protection of the lawful interests of the public. One argument is that there are some provisions in the GPCL on the compensation for damages caused by public utilities. Under those provisions, victims can claim compensation from the enterprises in charge of the administration of the public utilities according to the CPL. They are therefore classified as civil disputes. However, many public utilities are managed by state organs and the damages caused are sometimes enormous. The other argument is that damages caused by public utilities should be covered by the SCL so long as they are still under the management of the state government. But bearing in mind the SCL requirement of the existence of special relationship between the claimant and the state organ concerned, it does not seem easy to prove the existence of a special relationship between a road-user, for example, and the state organ administering the road. It is therefore much easier for the road-user to bring a claim by relying on Article 121 of the GPCL.

The scope of application of the SCL has finally been restricted to administrative and criminal fields. Administrative compensation covers infringement upon both personal and property rights. The infringement upon personal rights includes illegal detention, adoption of compulsory administrative measures, illegal custody of citizens or deprivation of personal freedom by other means, infliction of physical injury or causing death by violent acts or illegal use of weapons and so on. The infringement upon property rights includes illegal use of administrative penalties, illegal institution of compulsory administrative measures, illegal collection of property charges or financial contributions, and "any other illegal acts."

Procedure for State Compensation

The SCL combines substantive and procedural provisions. Claimants, **3.12** including any aggrieved citizens, legal persons and other organizations, must demand compensation according to the procedures provided in the SCL. Before the enactment of the SCL, as far as administrative compensation was concerned, lawsuits could be brought relying on Chapter 9 of the ALL. That chapter, however, contains only three sections setting out general principles. The SCL procedure of compensation (Section 3 of Chapter 2) is therefore a noticeable development on the basis of the ALL general principles. Under the SCL a two-step procedure is provided. Claimants must first file their claims in the form of an application with the state agencies responsible for compensation, which could be any one of the state agencies jointly responsible. The agency which assumes obligation of compensation shall accept the claim and calculate the amount of compensation according to the methods laid down in Chapter 4 of the SCL. If claimants are not satisfied with the amount of compensation, they may then file suit with the people's court within a limited period of time.

Section 14 of the SCL provides that state agencies may seek full or partial indemnity against its functionaries under only two situations, *i.e.* the functionaries either intentionally committed errors or negligently committed grave errors. In other words, if no intention to commit errors can be proved, the functionaries will only be held responsible in negligence if they committed grave or serious errors, not for committing ordinary errors. That is to say that negligence has been divided into two categories, serious negligence and ordinary negligence. The former refers to the condition that the functionaries failed to notice the tortious behaviour which the ordinary persons noticed and were able to prevent happening and their failure leads to the tortious consequence. The main reason to hold the functionaries liable for serious negligence, is to make sure that they do their work properly and exercise their authorities according to law. However, if the functionaries are held liable to pay either full or partial indemnity for all negligent behaviour, then the efficiency of administration will be hampered as they will be over-cautious. It is therefore a balancing exercise between judicial supervision of administration and administrative efficiency. Furthermore, section 14 also provides that the functionaries will face administrative penalties for committing intentional errors or negligently committing grave errors. They may even face criminal penalties if their intentional or negligent conduct constitutes a crime.

The procedure concerning criminal compensation was also very controversial during the legislative process as it involved a series of issues, such as the criminal law system, legal supervision system and reform of judicial and supervision systems. The focus was on whether it was necessary to have pre- trial procedures and if so, which organ should be in charge. The procedure finally adopted by the SCL is a three-step one. The first step is the same as the procedure for claims of administrative compensation. In the second step the claimants may apply to the next higher agency for a review if they object to the amount of compensation. Thirdly, the claimant may apply to the compensation committee of the people's court at the corresponding level for a decision on compensation. This procedure for criminal compensation is a special one which combines administrative reconsideration with administrative litigation. Whether this procedure will work remains to be seen. It is questionable in theory whether this procedure is appropriate, since the fundamental principle of fairness is breached, because the causes of criminal compensation are illegal acts. Both review and litigation will therefore be of little value to the claimant.

Partial or even full indemnity can also be claimed, under section 24 of the SCL, after criminal compensation by the body responsible for paying compensation from the functionaries under certain circumstances. The same is true under section 14 for administrative compensation. As the conduct mentioned under section 24 of the SCL is expressly prohibited by law, it is logical to hold the law enforcers who committed the illegal conduct, responsible for paying indemnity. Moreover, in order to prevent this illegal conduct from happening, those reoponsible will also face administrative penalties, or even criminal penalties if their conduct constitute crimes.

Observation

Though the SCL has a narrow scope of application. The adoption of the **3.13** SCL is a great achievement towards the improvement of the legal system, especially the public law system in the PRC. The SCL has recognized the uniqueness of the torts committed by state organs for the illegal exercise of power and subjected them to legal regulation. In so doing, not only the lawful interests of the citizens, legal persons and other organizations are better protected, but also the accountability of those state organs regulated by the SCL is enhanced.

The enactment of the SCL has also contributed to the completion of the administrative law structure in China. The ALL was enacted in 1989 with the aim to subject the administrative organs to judicial control in civil affairs. The 1990 RAR promulgated by the State Council is a supplement to the ALL. In the same year, the *Regulation on Administrative Supervision in the PRC* was promulgated by the State Council, under which the Ministry of Supervision shall supervise the work of other administrative organs. However, the Ministry of Supervision is within the executive branch of the Government. Its function is similar to that of Ombudsman in some western countries. The focus of this legislation has been on state organs, *i.e.* to control the exercise of power by state organs. The protection of lawful interests of the claimants and victims and the exact remedies available to them have never been laid down in any detailed legislation. The SCL has filled that gap. In this sense, the adoption of the SCL is a great achievement in the protection of the lawful rights and interests of the citizens, legal persons and other organizations against illegal infringement of their rights or interests by state organs or their personnel.

Conclusion

3.14   From 1989 to 1996, China promulgated legislation aimed at the supervision and control of the exercise of administrative authority by administrative organs or their functionaries. There are both internal supervision (administrative reconsideration) and external supervision (judicial review). The aggrieved parties can go through the relevant legal procedures to seek appropriate compensation, including financial compensation. Moreover, the importance of procedural legality has gradually been realized in China. The enactment of the 1996 *Administrative Penalty Law* is sufficient evidence of this. The proper operation of the established system shall contribute to the implementation of the rule of law principle in public administration.

Notes

[1] See Xu Chongde and Pi Chunrie, *An Overview of Administrative Law in the People's Republic of China*, Legal Science Press, 1991, Beijing, pp. 32–36.
[2] The ALL was enacted one year before the RAR.
[3] See Legislative Affairs Bureau, *The Interpretation of the Regulation on Administrative Reconsideration*, China Legal System Press, Beijing, 1990, p. 2.
[4] See Luo Haocai, *Judicial Review System in the People's Republic of China*, Peking University Press, Beijing, 1993, pp. 324–349.
[5] See Luo Haocai, pp. 350–352.
[6] See Huang Jie, *Interpretation of the Administrative Litigation Law of the PRC*, the People's Court Press, Beijing, 1994, pp. 184–185.
[7] See Hua Yang, *Judicial Control of Discretionary Power*, in *Collection of Legal Essays (Administrative Law)*, 1992, Vol. 2, pp. 191–193.

CHAPTER 4

CRIMINAL LAW

Ian Dobinson

City University of Hong Kong

Ian Dobinson, B.A., LL.B., Associate Professor, City University of Hong Kong, Solicitor (Supreme Court of New South Wales), formerly Barrister (Supreme Court of New South Wales), Visiting Lecturer, Charles Sturt University and Research Officer, New South Wales Bureau of Crime Statistics and Research.

Introduction

Criminal law has traditionally dominated the Chinese legal system. In **4.01** ancient times, it often formed the legal framework around which much of the system was structured. In the history of China, this central position was based on the theory that law was the instrument of the ruling class. Although the criminal law has changed significantly from these earlier times, the impact of the old system is still substantial. It is not intended to discuss such issues here, however, and the purpose of this chapter is to introduce the reader to Chinese criminal law and provide some analysis of the general principles and concepts that form the basis of its interpretation and application. In this sense, the analysis is descriptive rather than critical, and many of the criticisms that have been leveled at Chinese criminal law and procedure are not discussed.

From a comparative perspective, especially that of common law, Chinese criminal law would appear to be very different. This may be true when observing specific provisions and offences, but a closer analysis shows that many of the general principles of criminal liability and the way in which they are applied are very similar to common law traditions. Chinese criminal law is mostly contained in one large code (the *Criminal Law of the People's Republic of China*) which forms the focus of most of the discussion — it stipulates the basic principles, concepts and most of the offences. The code is supplemented, however, by much ancillary legislation from the Standing Committee of the National People's Congress. The code and Standing Committee enactments are further interpreted and detailed by the directions, interpretations and decisions of the People's Supreme Court. Any comprehensive analysis of Chinese criminal law, therefore, would need to consider all these sources.

Except for several discrete regulations, there had not been any criminal code before the start of the legal reconstruction. *The Criminal Law of the PRC* was one of the first laws enacted at the beginning of the period that followed the death of Mao and the trial of the "Gang of Four". It was adopted formally by the Fifth National People's Congress on July 1, 1979 and became effective on January 1, 1980. Along with six other laws, including the fourth Constitution, *The Criminal Law* had an important role in the reconstruction of the Chinese legal system as it exists today.

The constitutional foundation of *The Criminal Law* lies in Article 28 of the Constitution, which states that: "The State maintains public order and suppresses treasonable and other counter-revolutionary activities; it penalizes criminal activities that endanger public security and disrupt the socialist economy as well as other criminal activities; and it punishes and reforms criminals." In accordance with this article and Article 2 of *The Criminal Law*, the code emphasizes the protection of the socialist revolution and socialist development, as well as public order and citizens' rights.

Therefore, *The Criminal Law* not only contains all the classic offence categories, such as murder, theft, rape and assault, but also stipulates the offences deemed counter-revolutionary. It is these offences that distinguish *The Criminal Law* most from other codes and offence categories in Western jurisdictions.

This dichotomy of underlying legal functions also pervades the administration of justice. Article 3 of the *Organic Law of the People's Courts* entrusts the courts, when trying criminal cases, with safeguarding the system of the dictatorship of the proletariat, maintaining the socialist legal system and public order and protecting the legal rights of citizens. Article 4 of the *Organic Law of the People's Procuratorates* contains a similar provision.

To properly understand both the determination of criminal liability in China and criminal procedure, one must acknowledge the overriding importance of this philosophical underpinning and its effect on the objectives of *The Criminal Law* and its administration by both the courts and the procuratorates.

In recent years, however, discussions and criticisms of "counter-revolutionary offences" have been widely aired and published. The basis for this criticism is that such offences are political in nature rather than legal and therefore should not be included as part of *The Criminal Law*. This view has become popular and it is believed that in the new criminal code, which is currently being drafted, these offences will be changed, along with many other reforms.

Structure of Criminal Law

As mentioned earlier, *The Criminal Law*, which was first promulgated   **4.02** in 1980, remains unchanged. It has been supplemented, however, by numerous decisions and regulations enacted by the Standing Committee of the NPC. As will be seen from the overview set out below, many of the provisions of *The Criminal Law* are expressed in very general terms. This is true for both general principles as well as the specific offences. The Decisions and Regulations passed by the Standing Committee tend to serve two purposes. The first is to provide additional detail for specific offence categories. The second purpose is to direct the courts on the enforcement of certain offences and the imposition of severe punishment on those who commit these crimes. In some cases this may involve an increase in the maximum penalty which often includes the death sentence. The Supreme People's Court of the PRC also plays an important role in the interpretation and implementation of *The Criminal Law*. The legislative function of the Standing Committee and the role of the Supreme People's Court are discussed later.

First, however, we can look at the various parts of *The Criminal Law*. In this respect, it is not unlike the codes of many other countries. It is divided into two Parts and 13 Chapters. Part I (Chapters I–V) deals with general principles and punishment, while Part II (Chapters I–VIII) sets out the specific offence provisions.

Conceptual Analysis

Crime and Non-crime

An interesting dichotomy exists in PRC law, which distinguishes   **4.03** between serious offences and those offences covered by administrative regulations and practice. The most prominent of the administrative or "non-crime" regulations is the *Regulations of the PRC on Security Administration and Punishment* (SAPR) adopted by the Standing Committee of the NPC on September 5, 1986. This does not mean that individuals are arbitrarily punished, rather that a distinction has been drawn between less and more serious crimes. This is not unlike the felony/misdemeanor or indictable/summary dichotomies in common law, although in China offences covered by the SAPR are not labeled as criminal. In many cases, a decision as to whether an offence will be tried as a crime or dealt with under the SAPR will be decided by the likely penalty or punishment to be imposed. Article 2 of the SAPR states that:

> "Whoever disturbs social order, endangers public safety, infringes upon citizens' rights of the person or encroaches upon public or private property, if such an act constitutes a crime according to the *Criminal Law of the People's Republic of China*, shall be investigated for criminal responsibility; if such an act is not serious enough for criminal punishment but should be given administrative penalties for public security, penalties shall be given according to these regulations."

The standards for distinguishing crimes from non-crimes are outlined in Article 10 of *The Criminal Law*, which states that "an act that is clearly of minor importance and little harm shall not be considered a crime." Article 10 further defines a crime as any act that:

> "endangers the sovereignty and territorial integrity of the state; endangers the system of the dictatorship of the proletariat; undermines the socialist revolution and socialist construction; disrupts public order; violates property owned by the whole people or collectively owned by the working people; violates the citizens' privately owned lawful property or infringes upon the citizens' rights of the person and their democratic and other rights; and any other act that endangers society and is punishable according to the law."

The distinction between crime and non-crime, however, is vague, and whether, for example, theft is charged as a crime or under the SAPR is often determined simply by the amount of money involved. Other offences covered by the SAPR include minor assaults, public order infringements, vandalism, traffic violations, failure to register residence and prostitution. Penalties under the SAPR include a warning, a maximum fine of 200 yuan and 15 days' imprisonment. Offenders may also have their property confiscated and be deprived of their political rights. Certain other sanctions may also be applied. These include "re-education through labour" (*laodong jiaoyang*) and "sheltering for investigation"(*shourong shencha*). The responsibility for the investigation, determination and punishment of "minor" offences lies with the Public Security Bureau. At the lowest levels of administration the system could be operated by the local police station, or, where there is no station, the town or village governing body.

Constitution of a Crime

4.04   There are many terms used in *The Criminal Law* that would be very familiar to common law lawyers. These include intention, recklessness, negligence, foreseeability and causation. Much of the code, both in terms of general principles and specific offences, contains much which is similar to common law jurisdictions. In fact, Chinese academics tend to use many of these terms in the same way as their common law counterparts. According to Chinese criminal law theory, four basic elements are required to establish criminal liability. These are: the Subject — the person who performed the criminal act, the Subjective Aspect — the person's intention or negligence, the Object — the type of crime, and the Objective Aspect — the harm caused. If any one of these elements is missing or deficient then this will affect criminal liability.

The Subject

First, the age of criminal responsibility is 14. Someone under this age will lack the capacity to take criminal liability (Article 14). Those between 14 and 16 are only responsible for serious crimes, and those between 14 and 18 are to be given lighter or mitigated punishment. Insanity is covered by Article 15, whereby a person ("mental patient") who commits a crime "when he is unable to recognize or control his conduct" bears no criminal responsibility. Intoxication, however, is no defence (Article 15).[1] Deaf-mutes or blind persons who commit crimes may receive lighter or mitigated sentences (Article 16). For certain crimes, only those with special status shall be eligible to be subjects, such as crimes of embezzlement (Chapter V) and deriliction of duty (Chapter VIII) which require the subjects to be persons in official positions.

The Subjective Aspect

Articles 11 and 12 tell us that crimes can be intentionally or, where specified, negligently committed. A person intentionally commits an act where he clearly knows it will produce socially dangerous consequences and (1) he desires such consequences (direct intention); or (2) he allows them to occur (indirect intention). An offender will be negligent when he commits an act (1) which he should have foreseen would possibly produce dangerous consequences, but failed to foresee (negligence by recklessness); or (2) having foreseen such consequences, he decided to proceed believing that the consequences could be avoided but in fact they did occur (negligence by self-confidence). Under Article 13, a harmful act which is not intentional or negligent by virtue of it being unavoidable or unforseeable will not be deemed a crime.

If the mental element cannot be established then no crime has been committed. In *He Liannu*,[2] the accused was convicted of fraud contrary to Article 152 of *The Criminal Law*. The facts showed that the defendant had acted as middleman for two swindlers involved in a fake "gold grit" business. On appeal, it was argued that although the accused had introduced the swindlers to the victim, she was unaware of the others' intention and only became suspicious at the very end. In upholding her appeal, the Intermediate Court ruled that although the accused had played a role, there was no way to decide whether she knew that the gold grit was false and that she was therefore part of conspiracy to defraud. As the two principals had fled, there was no evidence to prove the allegation.

For some crimes, the courts draw a connection between what was intended and what in fact occurred. If certain harm occurs but this was not the offender's purpose then they may not be liable for the result, even though it was foreseeable. Thus for murder, an intention to kill must be proved, and an intention to injure may therefore be insufficient to substantiate this crime. In *Yang Xiaohong*,[3] the accused killed her father during the course of an argument and subsequent fight. The court ruled that while she intended injury (she stabbed her father), she did not intend to kill, and accordingly her crime was one of intentional injury causing death (Article 134) rather than intentional homicide (Article 132). In this sense, some crimes require that the harm caused be the purpose of the offender's conduct (for example murder). Another example is Article 100, which makes it an offence to, amongst others, cause explosions and set fires for the purposes of counter-revolution. This offence carries a maximum penalty of life imprisonment, but if such activity was not for the purpose of counter-revolution (or this cannot be proved), then liability may be covered by Article 105, which carries a maximum of 10 and a minimum of three years' imprisonment.

For some crimes, however, the harmful consequence need not be the accused's specific purpose. If a person intentionally or negligently commits an offence and this causes a harmful consequence then this will usually be sufficient to establish criminal liability. Thus the offender who intentionally or negligently fails to carry out his duty, causing injury to others, will be criminally liable, even though the injury was never his purpose. This does not mean individuals are liable regardless of the circumstances. As mentioned above, Article 13 states that there is no crime where the consequences of the accused's conduct were unavoidable or unforeseeable.

Negligence, as referred to in Article 12, appears to cover situations of reckless behaviour as well as a breach of a duty of care. In *Zhang Zhongmin*,[4] the accused was a policeman who during the course of chasing a suspected offender shot and killed this person. In finding the accused guilty of negligent killing under Article 133, the People's Court of Wucheng District held: "As a policeman, the defendant should have knowledge and experience in the use of a pistol. He should have foreseen that being armed with a pistol on duty could result in a person's death, but he failed to do so because of his nervousness and carelessness, consequently causing the victim's death."[5]

Apart from a general notion of duty of care, negligence is also concerned with specific or legal duties. In the cases of *Zhang Bingfu*[6] and *Yang Kaiwang*,[7] the courts considered a duty owed by an exploder to other workers and a quarry contractor to his employees. In the first case, the court found negligence due to a failure to adhere to certain operating regulations, while in the second, the defendant had failed in his general duty to ensure that the site was safe.

The Object

This refers to the rights or social values violated by the offences. In the   **4.05** case of murder, for example, the object is not the victim, but the right to life of the victim. Therefore, it reveals the social consequence or social harm of the offence. Where crimes have the same or similar object, then they can be grouped together as the same kind of crime. This is reflected by the various chapters which cover the specific offence categories. The object of each group of offences is called the common object. Chapter IV, for example, is entitled "Crimes of Infringing upon the Rights of the Person and the Democratic Rights of the Citizen." This category deals mainly with offences against the person such as homicide, assault and rape, but also includes the offences of unlawful surveillance and searching and criminal defamation. The common object at first may be difficult to identify. All the offences, however, can be seen as having the common thread of either being an infringement of personal or democratic rights. Personal rights, for example, are infringed when an individual is subject to violent and unwarranted attack. This is also true when their right to privacy is infringed or they are defamed. As such rights are protected by the State then this is also an infringement of one's democratic rights.

Specific offences also have their objects. The offence of theft, for example, violates public and private property rights. The offence of robbery violates both property rights and the rights to life and health of the victim(s). Therefore, the punishment for robbery is much more severe than that for theft. Identifying the different objects of offences helps to select the appropriate offence to be charged. If there is no identifiable object then there is no crime.

The Objective Aspect

The objective aspect in Chinese criminal law is very similar to the concept of *actus reus* in a common law jurisdiction. It includes an act of offence, a harmful consequence and causation between them. Criminal acts consist of positive *acts* and *non-acts* (omissions). The distinction between an act and non-act can be demonstrated by the cases of *Zhang Zhongmin*[8], *Zhang Bingfu*[9] and *Yang Kaiwang*[10] mentioned above. In the first case the accused had negligently shot a suspect during the course of a chase while in the last two cases, the accused people had failed (omitted) to carry out their duties to ensure the safety of a site where explosives were being used.

A harmful consequence refers to the consequences specified by the criminal law. As stated earlier, Article 10 stipulates that those acts with apparently less harmful consequences shall be deemed not to be criminal (but dealt with by administrative regulations such as the SAPR). Some offences, however, do not require that the harmful consequence actually materialize, such as defamation and most counter-revolutionary offences.

The third crucial requirement is that there must be a causal link between the act or omission and the harmful consequence. In one case (unreported), for example, a female student was unjustifiably scolded by her teacher. While walking home in a distressed state, she was struck and injured by a car. She was taken to hospital but later died as a result of negligent medical treatment. Her initial injuries were not serious. In holding the doctor liable for the schoolgirl's death, the court ruled that the direct and intrinsic cause of death was the negligent medical treatment. The driver of the car, however, was only responsible for the injuries caused by the car accident. Even though the injuries he caused led to the victim being hospitalised, there was no causal link between the victim's death and the injuries sustained when she was struck by the car. As far as the teacher's liability was concerned, the act of scolding was wrong but not criminal. It had not caused the harmful consequence as there was no direct or intinsic relationship between the scolding and the death.

Preparation, Attempt and Discontinuation

4.06 The next general principles relate to preparation for, attempt and discontinuation of a crime (Articles 19–21). The first point to note is the distinction which is drawn between acts which are preparatory, *e.g.* the obtaining of instruments and the creation of the conditions for a crime, and acts which amount to an attempt.

Preparation for a crime can include activities which could give rise to charges of conspiracy, but Article 19 seems to imply that an individual, acting alone, can be liable. The important factor appears to be the creation of conditions by the accused which, if allowed to continue, would have resulted in the commission of a substantive offence, for example robbery. The prevention of the continuation of the preparation must also be independent of the accused's will. If the offender discontinues preparation for a crime voluntarily then this appears to be covered by the provisions of Article 21, and may result in an exemption from punishment or a mitigated sentence.

A similar approach is taken for attempt. Article 20 refers to a situation where the crime has already begun but, for reasons unconnected to the accused's will, it is prevented from occurring. In *Wang Haizhi*,[11] the defendant was unhappily married. The facts showed that she had purchased poison and then put this in her husband's eggs. The husband, noticing that the eggs smelt bad, gave them to his mother's dog, which died immediately. While the court did not take this approach, it may be assumed that the purchase of the poison was a preparatory act, while the giving of the poisoned eggs to the husband was attempted murder.

An attempt is also to be distinguished from an act which is voluntarily discontinued by the accused (Article 21). In *Chen Longjian*,[12] the accused was charged with attempted rape (Article 139). The facts were that the accused attacked the victim, forcing her into a field and grabbing her around the neck. The victim struggled and, fearing that he might kill the victim, the accused released her and assisted her back to the road. In ruling that this was a valid discontinuation, the court distinguished this from a situation where a crime was prevented from taking place due to outside intervention or the victim being able to escape. In such circumstances, it must be shown that it was the accused who took preventative steps by discontinuing his actions.

Joint Crimes

Conspiracy is a regularly-used term in many cases involving multiple **4.07** offenders, but it is not specifically referred to in *The Criminal Law*. Instead, Article 22 states that a joint crime relates to an intentional offence committed by two or more persons, jointly. A negligent crime cannot be committed jointly and must be dealt with individually. It is also not a joint crime where one party has acted intentionally and the other negligently.

While the notion of conspiracy is not clear under the criminal law, one interpretation could be that it relates to preparatory or attempted crimes, where such crimes are committed by two or more persons as part of a joint enterprise. The approach taken by the courts in charging all participants with the substantive offence appears to show that no distinction is made between those involved in an actual agreement to commit a crime and those who play various participatory roles in bringing about the commission of a crime. The principal purpose of the provisions in Articles 22–26 is to differentiate between those who are principal offenders, organizers or leaders, and those who play a secondary or ancillary role. The cases also indicate the identification of certain types of criminal group, notably the criminal gang. Such groups are viewed as having an organic structure, with a hierarchy of leadership. Gangs are also involved in regular criminal activities which involve a degree of planning in their commission.

While the extent of the role played by each joint offender is determined by the facts, there is a general requirement of knowledge of the circumstances of the offence. Therefore, if knowledge cannot be proved then the offender is not liable (see for example *He Liannu*[13] above), in other words there is no intention.

The determination of whether joint parties are principals or accomplices also has an important effect on the sentence imposed. Principal offenders, such as ringleaders or organisers, should receive heavier sentences compared to an accomplice (Articles 23 and 24), while someone who is compelled or induced to participate is to have their punishment mitigated or may be exempt from punishment (Article 25). The following case demonstrates the general approach. In *Dai Jun and Others*,[14] three defendants planned to rob tourists at a popular scenic spot. The third defendant was required to keep watch, while the other two committed the robbery. During the course of the robbery, the second defendant hit the victim with a rock resulting in fairly minor injuries, while the first stabbed him several times causing severe injuries. In convicting all three defendants, the courts (trial and appeal) held the first and second defendants to be principals while the third defendant was an accomplice. The differing degrees of involvement were reflected in the sentences for each defendant: the first defendant was sentenced to death, the second to 15 years' fixed-term imprisonment and the third to three years' fixed-term imprisonment, suspended for four years. It should be noted that the third defendant had not reached 18 years of age at time of the offence.

Legitimate Defence and Aversion of Imminent Danger

4.08   A number of defences are specified by *The Criminal Law*. Under Article 17 it is a legitimate defence to act in one's own defence or to prevent the commission of a crime. The use of excessive force may give rise to a mitigated sentence or may be evidence that the force used by the accused was not for the purposes of self defence. In *Yan Wenzhi*[15] for example, the accused and the victim had quarreled and fought over allegations that the victim had been involved in stealing. The accused stated that the victim had attacked him first with a chisel and that in response he hit the victim on the head with a steel bar. Thereafter, the accused had repeatedly chopped the victim around the face and neck, killing him. He had also tried to conceal the corpse. Apart from there being no corroborative evidence of an attack by the victim, the Higher People's Court held that; "even if the defendant had been attacked by the victim, such danger ceased when the victim fell to the ground. The defendant could easily have taken other measures to avoid being attacked. Repeatedly chopping the victim could not be viewed as an attempt to avoid attack."[16]

Article 18 provides for a defence where an offence is committed in an emergency and in order to avert an immediate public danger. A defence under Article 18 is only available where legitimate interests are in danger, the danger is imminent or ongoing and there are no other reasonable means to prevent it. Determination of these defences, as with other questions of criminal liability, however, often appear to be pre-trial considerations. From the cases available, there is little judicial guidance on their interpretation and definition. An example of where self defence was successfully pleaded was in *Wang Haifeng*.[17] The accused in this case was tricked by others to go to a specified location, where the plan was to beat him up. Having reached the designated location he was attacked by others, including the victim. During the course of the attack, the accused pulled out a dagger he had brought with him and stabbed the victim, resulting in his death.

Other concepts such as provocation are often raised in mitigation, and the cases provide an insight into how such principles are applied. Provocation can result from the act of the victim, such as an initial assault[18] or the mistreatment of a wife by her husband[19], or threats by the victim against the accused.[20] In other cases, however, the provocation is not so clear. In *Dai Chengua and Another*,[21] two brothers intentionally killed their mentally disabled brother, who for many years had been a significant psychological burden. The facts were that the victim was prone to periods of wandering off, stealing and property damage. Having planned to kill their brother, the two defendants took some rope and after a struggle, strangled the victim by hanging him from a beam in their house. The court convicted both defendants, sentencing the first to 10 years' fixed-term imprisonment and the second to three years with a four-year suspension.

Punishments

Chapter III divides the types of punishment into two groups: principal **4.09** and supplementary. The principal types are public surveillance, criminal detention, fixed-term imprisonment, life imprisonment and death. The supplementary punishments are fines, deprivation of political rights and confiscation of property. Offenders may also be required to compensate the victim (or in some cases, such as homicide, the victim's relatives) in cases where economic loss is caused by the offences (Article 31). Both principal and supplementary punishments can be applied independently or jointly (Article 29).

The penalty of public surveillance is uniquely Chinese. It is punishment without putting the offender in prison, but keeping them under the control of state organs and mass supervision. The purpose of this punishment is to reform less harmful persons in society. The term of public surveillance is from three months to two years. Other restrictions on the offender include freedom of movement (change of residence or leaving the area) and the requirement of reporting regularly to enforcement agencies.

Criminal detention is between 16 days and six months. This can either be served in prison or "reform through labour centres". Such punishment is administered by the local public security organ. Fixed term imprisonment and life imprisonment can also be served in prison or "reform through labour centres". Fixed terms are between six months and 15 years.

Where the death penalty is imposed, it must first be confirmed by the Supreme People's Court. It is not to be imposed on those under 18 (when they committed the offence) or pregnant women. If the crime is particularly serious, the death penalty with two years suspension may be imposed on those between 16 and 18. In other circumstances, it can either be carried out immediately (by shooting) or again suspended for two years. If during the period of suspension an offender shows true repentance then the sentence may be commuted to life. If in addition the offender performs meritorious service, then the sentence can be commuted to between 15 and 20 years.

Fines are a supplemental punishment. There is no set scale of fines and they are to be imposed according to the circumstances of the offence. The offender can be required to pay in a lump sum or be given the opportunity to pay by instalments.

Part of most sentences is the deprivation of political rights. These include the right to vote and stand for election, rights under Article 45 of the Constitution (social welfare), the right to hold public office and the right to hold a leading position in any enterprise, institution or people's organization.

Finally, an offender's property may be confiscated and liquidated, particularly for the purposes of compensation.

Sentencing

4.10   Chapter IV sets out certain general sentencing principles. The degree of punishment is to be determined by "the facts, nature and circumstances of the crime, the degree of harm done to society and the relevant provisions of this law." (Article 58). Where it is prescribed by law, an offender can receive a heavier or lighter sentence (Article 58) or due to the circumstances have his punishment mitigated, even to a point lower than the specified minimum (Article 59). All property which is illegally obtained by an offender shall be recovered and all things used for the purposes of the crime confiscated.

Any person who commits another crime punishable by imprisonment within three years of their release from prison is deemed to be a recidivist and subject to a heavier penalty (Article 61). The serious nature of counter-revolutionary offences is emphasized by the provision that a person is a recidivist where they commit another counter-revolutionary crime at any time after a previous conviction (Article 62).

Voluntary surrender is rewarded by an exemption from or mitigation of punishment (Article 63). Articles 64–66 set out the rules regarding combined sentences, the limitations on consecutive sentences and the use of concurrent terms of imprisonment. A sentence of fixed-term imprisonment may also be suspended (Articles 67–70). Public surveillance, fixed-term imprisonment and life terms may also be commuted where an offender demonstrates "true repentance". An offender must, however, have served half of his original sentence or 10 years of a life term before commutation can be considered (Articles 71–72). After similar "minimums", criminals may be granted parole. Supervision is provided by the public security organs and will be revoked if another crime is committed (Articles 73–75).

Finally, the limitation periods for prosecution and other related provisions are set out in Articles 76–78. Where no person is arrested, the prosecution of crimes will not proceed after certain periods have elapsed. This varies depending on the maximum penalty imposed for the crime as specified by Article 76. For a crime carrying a maximum penalty of five years there shall be no prosecution after five years, for a crime carrying a maximum penalty of five to 10 years, the period is 10 years, for a crime carrying a maximum penalty of not less than 10 years it is 15 years, and for a crime carrying a penalty of life imprisonment or death, the period is 20 years. There is no limitation period where an offender has escaped from investigation or trial once measures have been commenced by the courts, procuratorates or public security organs (Article 77).

Specific Offences

The specific offences are set out in Part Two, but before briefly describing these, special note should be made of the mechanism of analogy specified by Article 79. This states that where an act is not clearly defined within the criminal code, it "may be determined and punished according to whichever article in the Specific Provisions of this Law that covers the most closely analogous crime. . . ." Approval for   **4.11**

119

the judgment, however, must be obtained from the Supreme People's Court. To date, the use of this provision has been largely restricted to cases involving the disruption of marriage and the family (Chapter VII)[22] but there have been calls for its repeal based on the potential for abuse and its incompatibility with current policy on criminal law.

There are altogether about 150 offences. In order to put them into a systematic arrangement, *The Criminal Law* uses the objects of the crimes as factors to put them into different categories. If several offences infringe the same object (social relations or legal rights) such as property rights, then they are put in the same category such as crimes violating property rights. In some cases, however, the distinction is not clear and there appears to be an overlap between some categories and some offences. There are eight categories of offences stipulated by *The Criminal Law*, outlined below, plus one category concerning crimes committed by military personnel, covered by separate regulations.

Offences of Counter-Revolution

The importance of protecting the State and the socialist revolution is emphasized by the first group of specific offences. These are set out in Chapter 1 of Part Two under the general heading of crimes of counter-revolution. Such crimes are defined in Article 90 as "any act that is committed with the aim of overthrowing the political power of the dictatorship of the proletariat and socialist system and endangers the People's Republic of China."

The offences in Chapter 1 are expressed in somewhat convoluted terminology, but appear to relate to crimes such as treason, espionage, terrorist acts (such as causing explosions) and sabotage. It is also an offence to organize, lead or participate in a counter-revolutionary group (Article 98). What is unclear is what characterizes such a group, especially as this could be very broadly defined, given the provisions of Article 90. Similar broad provisions are also found in Article 102, which makes it an offence to:

a) incite the masses to resist or sabotage the implementation of the State's laws or decrees; or

b) propagandize for and incite the overthrow of the political power of the dictatorship of the proletariat and the socialist system, through counter-revolutionary slogans, leaflets or by other means.

As such, the publication of any anti-government material might be deemed to be an offence under this Article.

Offences of Endangering Public Security

Chapter II is entitled "Crimes of Endangering Public Security" and at first sight appears not to be significantly different to counter-revolutionary crimes (*e.g.* sabotage, arson, causing explosions). The term "endangering public security" is not defined but Meijer[23] suggests that the difference between offences under Chapter I (counter-revolution) and those of Chapter II is that the underlying premise for crimes under Chapter I is the purpose of overthrowing the State, whereas it is not for those in Chapter II.

Chapter II also makes it an offence to illegally manufacture, trade or transport guns or ammunition (Article 112).

Those employed in safety-sensitive areas, such as communications or transportation, factories, mines or construction, or who are responsible for the use or handling of dangerous (explosive, poisonous, radioactive) materials, will also be liable if they violate the rules or regulations, thereby causing an accident that results in serious injury or death (Articles 113–115).

Offences of Undermining the Socialist Economic Order

Chapter III includes the familiar offences of smuggling, counterfeiting (money and other items of value, *e.g.* train tickets) and tax evasion (Articles 116, 118–119, 120 and 122–124). Other less familiar or unique offences include speculation in violation of laws and regulations on the control of monetary affairs (Article 117), destroying or injuring property or livestock in order to sabotage collective production for reasons of retaliation or spite (Article 125), misappropriating funds or materials for disaster relief (Article 126), trademark violations (Article 127), illegal cutting of trees (Article 128), illegal fishing (Article 129) and illegal hunting (particularly rare species) (Article 130).

Offences of Infringing upon the Rights of the Person and the Democratic Rights of Citizens

This category suggests offences which infringe upon or contravene a person's political or non-political rights (civil liberties). While Chapter IV includes some offences such as, for example, sabotage of elections or obstruction of voting, unlawful arrest, detention and search, defamation (insult by "big or small character posters"), false charges and false accusations, and tampering with the mail (Articles 138 and 142–149), it also deals with offences against the person, including homicide, assault, torture and rape (Articles 132–136 and 138). Such crimes are also seen as an infringement upon a person's rights, in that the person has a right to be protected against such things and an offender is therefore preventing the State from providing such protection.

For homicide and assault a differentiation is also made between intentional and negligent crimes. For homicide, this appears to create the murder/manslaughter division (although these common law offences are not specifically mentioned). Other offences include those relating to riots, "beating, smashing and looting" (Article 137), forcing a woman into prostitution (Article 140) and abducting and trafficking in human beings (Article 141).

Offences of Property Violation

This category contains all the classic property crimes including theft, robbery, fraud and embezzlement. It also refers to the old crime of swindling, and differentiates between the first-time offender who steals or swindles a large amount of money or property (Article 151) and the habitual thief or swindler who steals, swindles or forcibly seizes a "huge" amount of money or property.

What might be called simple criminal damage, as compared to offences under Chapters I or II, is covered by Article 156.

Offences of Obstructing the Administration of Public Order

Chapter VI covers a number of loosely-connected crimes whose linkage may be simply described as offences which in some way adversely affect both public and social order. In this regard, the Chapter includes offences relating to public disturbances such as affray and demonstrations which disrupt traffic or work. It also includes the offence of damaging boundary tablets or markers or permanent survey indicators. A number of offences also relate to the violation of border regulations including illegal crossing, illegal transportation of others and the violation of health and quarantine regulations. Offences relating to social order include the selling of bogus medicines, swindling by sorcery or witchcraft, gambling, luring women into prostitution, manufacturing, selling or trafficking in narcotic drugs, and illegally exporting and damaging or destroying cultural relics.

Offences of Disrupting Marriage and Family

The importance of marriage and the family, as these relate to the maintenance of social order, is emphasized by the offences in Chapter

VII, "Crimes of Disrupting Marriage and the Family". While not defined, it is a crime to forcibly interfere with another person's freedom of marriage (Article 179). Bigamy is covered by Article 180 and Article 181 makes it an offence to cohabit with or marry the spouse of a member of the armed forces knowing that the other is away on duty. Maltreatment of family members (*i.e.* one member of another) is also prohibited (Article 182) as is refusal to properly support someone who is old, young or sick (Article 183). It is also an offence to abduct a child (different to kidnapping under Article 141), thus "cutting the child off" from his family or guardian (Article 184).

Offences of Dereliction of Duty

Crimes by public servants associated with their duties are set out in Chapter VIII. These include bribery, divulging State secrets, neglect of duty causing public loss, judicial malpractice and violation of prison rules, unauthorized release of prisoners (by judicial functionaries) and the tampering with or destruction of mail by a postal or telecommunications worker.

Supplementary Sources

Supplementary Decisions by the Standing Committee of the NPC

As mentioned earlier, many of the above offence provisions have been   **4.12** supplemented by Standing Committee Decisions. In this sense the central provisions of *The Criminal Law* are not amended but added to by these enactments. Some examples include the Decision of the NPC Standing Committee on the Prohibition Against Narcotic Drugs (1990), Decision of the NPC Standing Committee on the Severe Punishment of Criminal Elements Who Abduct for Sale or Kidnap Women and Children (1991), Decision of the NPC Standing Committee on the Strict Prohibition of Prostitution (1991), Decision of the NPC Standing Committee on Punishing Crimes Violating Company Law 1995) and Decision of the NPC Standing Committee on Punishing Crimes of Issuing, Making and Illegally Selling Fake Invoices of Value-added Tax (1995).

Looking at the first example, the Decision on the Prohibition of Narcotic Drugs, we can see how this operates. Article 171 of *The Criminal Law* makes it an offence to manufacture, sell or transport narcotics, with a maximum penalty of five years and a fine. If the quantities are large then a minimum of five years is to be imposed. The provisions of the Standing Committee Decision on Narcotic Drugs set out the various minimum quantities of opium and heroin and the different sentence ranges to be imposed. Under Article 2, for example, the person who smuggles, transports or manufactures opium of not less than 1,000 gm or heroin of not less than 50 gm is subject to a minimum of 15 years' imprisonment with a maximum of life or the death penalty.

An offender involved in amounts of between 200–1,000 gm of opium and 10–50 gm of heroin is subject to a fixed term of seven years' imprisonment. There are numerous other detailed provisions which expand upon the elements of various drug offences and the punishments to be imposed.

Judicial Interpretations

Guidance in the interpretation of *The Criminal Law* and its application is also provided by the Supreme People's Court and the Supreme People's Procuratorate (separately or jointly) through various directions on interpretation.[24] This can take a variety of forms. The first type of directions or interpretations result from a single question (*pifu* or *fuhan*) posed by a lower court. On other occasions, the Court may give a combined direction through a reply to a much larger number of questions posed by a number of courts but relating to the same area of law. This often gives rise to a more formal document and direction to the lower courts in general. Similar directions may result not from questions about a particular case but rather questions for future reference and guidance. Other statements by the Court appear to be in the form of policy, while others are bordering on legislative enactments which are sometimes necessary to fill in the gaps in existing or new legislation. This is often in the form of circulars.

Examples of the above include the Circular Regarding Severe Crackdown on Illegal Hunting, Purchase, Speculative Selling and Smuggling of Wild Life (December 15, 1990), Explanations on the Concrete Application of Law in Handling the Criminal Offences of Tax Dodging and Refusal to Pay Tax (March 16, 1992), Opinions on the Application of Law in Handling Joint Theft Cases (April 12, 1991) and Answers to Several Questions on Unauthorized Lumbering and Denudation Cases (October 17, 1991).

Conclusion

4.13 The purpose of this chapter is to provide an overview of Chinese criminal law and the application of the general principles of criminal liability. To date, little has been written attempting to analyse the conceptual framework of Chinese criminal law. This is particularly true for Western literature. Much has been written on the Chinese criminal justice system, but this has mostly focused on procedure.[25] A number of articles[26] were published on or around the date of the promulgation of *The Criminal Law*, but these were by and large simple descriptions of the various Parts and Articles.

Since these publications, little, if anything, has been written on the actual principles and practices that underpin the Chinese criminal law. In many ways, however, this is not surprising. As Lubman[27] notes, this aspect of the study of Chinese law is what is often lacking from much of the literature. From a common law perspective, any analysis of the practical application of legal principles would be largely framed around an analysis of cases and the operation of precedent. In China, however, case law and case reporting, in a form familiar to those from common law jurisdictions, is simply non-existent. Cases are reported but tend to be mainly in the form of "commentaries" on what occurred. As observed by Lubman,[28] "Chinese judicial decisions are terse summaries with little analysis of the reasoning that underlies the result, so their value for observers, foreign or otherwise, is necessarily limited".

Unlike common law case reports, there is no written judgment which sets out the judge's written interpretations of legal concepts and principles. China has no history past or present of a legal system based on the judicial determination of principle and the doctrine of precedent that is so basic to the study and practice of the common law in the West.

Recent developments, however, have greatly improved the possibilities of researching Chinese law. This includes the recent production in English of the first volumes of the *Chinese Law Reports*,[29] which contain "commentaries" on approximately 140 criminal cases. In 1994, the first volume (1992) of principal cases, *Zhongguo Shenpan Anli Yaolan*, by the People's University, Beijing was also published. This volume will also be translated into English in the very near future,[30] with other volumes and translations to follow annually. Other sources include "casebooks" and other texts published by academics primarily for teaching purposes.[31] These publications are also now easily obtained.

While, therefore, case reporting as a common law lawyer would recognize it does not exist, the situation continues to improve. The *China Law Reports*, for example, provide a previously unavailable (in English) source and insight into the practice of Chinese criminal law, with close analysis demonstrating some of the aspects of the general principles of criminal liability.

Many of these principles will be familiar to the common law lawyer both in name and application. One should not be surprised by this, however, as crime is generally universal in nature and the liability of an offender who steals will be determined in much the same way regardless of whether the theft takes place in Beijing or London. A closer analysis, even one as limited as above, however, does demonstrate some differences in interpretation and application. One Chinese approach to liability, for example, appears to be one of establishing responsibility for the crime and thereafter to vary the punishment depending on the proximity of the offender's responsibility to the final offence. Responsibility in such terms may be established simply by the offender's status as being the official in charge. In *Yang Kaiwang*,[32] for example, the facts were that the defendant had entered into a contract for the quarrying of limestone, one of the conditions stipulating that he was responsible for safety management and administration. He thereafter employed relatives and others from his hometown and placed two of these persons in charge. These persons had no experience in quarrying, and even though the defendant was an experienced exploder, he had also handed over this responsibility to others who had no experience. Three workers were killed after being crushed by falling rocks when they were sent into the site to clear away rocks after the use of explosives. Even though the accused was not at the site at the time and it was another who ordered the men to clear the rocks, the Intermediate Court (on appeal) ruled that the accused had ultimate responsibility and that he had breached regulations by employing inexperienced workers and allowing them to carry out explosives work. In holding him liable under Article 114, the courts accepted that while he was not the one directly responsible, in that he personally had not ordered the men to clear the rocks, he had breached regulations and had failed to take proper steps to ensure the safety of the site.

What most distinguishes the Chinese criminal law from other codes, even socialist, however, are the counter-revolutionary offences. They are the first of the specific crimes (Chapter I, Part Two), which reflects their importance in the overall code. They are, however, the major source of concern for many both in and outside China. For those outside China, they represent the basis for much of China's abuse of human rights, particularly when combined with reform and re-education through labour sentences. Even within China, there are calls by those involved in reforming *The Criminal Law*[33] for the repeal of many of these laws due to their incompatibility with China's economic development and "open-door" policy. As mentioned earlier, the belief is that such offences are political rather than legal, and accordingly should not be covered by *The Criminal Law*.

There have also been calls for the repeal of the "analogy" provisions in Article 79. The counter-revolutionary offences, Article 79 and the frequent use of the death penalty are those aspects of *The Criminal Law* which appear most "foreign" in comparison to other jurisdictions and are, accordingly, seen as an impediment to China's development and its full integration into the international community. Indeed the repeal of the counter-revolutionary offences, Article 79 and a reduction in the use of the death penalty are major changes currently being considered by those responsible for the drafting of a new criminal law.[34]

Other aspects of the code are also in need of reform. In many cases there is an overlap between offences, which, on paper at least, appears to create difficulties in offence selection.[35] Some case reports reflect this by describing the role of the appeal courts in remedying what appears to have been incorrect offence selection by the prosecution. Procedurally, it is of interest to note that appeal courts are empowered in this regard simply to replace one offence with another and thereafter to confirm the guilty decision of the lower court.

This raises a number of important comparative issues regarding Chinese criminal procedure, and it is here that the most significant differences exist between China and Western jurisdictions. Many of these procedural differences are of a practical nature, while others are fundamental to a consideration of the determination of criminal liability. Such legal precepts include the burden of proof and the presumption of innocence, and the Chinese approach[36] to such principles has also led to criticism. The recent enactment of the new *Criminal Procedure Law* (see Chapter 5), however, has introduced many major reforms to the Chinese criminal justice system. Any detailed and comprehensive conceptual analysis of Chinese criminal law must therefore include a detailed consideration of these and other legal principles.

Notes

[1] See *Wang Genyang* [1991] China L.R. 221.
[2] [1991] 1 China L.R. 348.
[3] [1991] 1 China L.R. 207.
[4] [1991] 1 China L.R. 190.
[5] *Ibid.*, p. 193.
[6] [1991] 1 China L.R. 35.
[7] [1991] 1 China L.R. 41.
[8] See above n. 2.
[9] See above n. 3.
[10] See above n. 4.
[11] [1991] 1 China L.R. 130.
[12] [1991] 1 China L.R. 236.
[13] See above n. 2.
[14] [1991] 1 China L.R.
[15] [1991] 1 China L.R.
[16] *Ibid.*, p. 137.
[17] *Wang Haifeng* Criminal Case No. 243 of 1992.
[18] *Chen Yunming* [1991] 1 China L.R. 144.
[19] *Li Guihua* [1991] 1 China L.R. 148.
[20] *Wen Lixian* [1991] 1 China L.R. 176.

[21] [1991] 1 China L.R. 158.

[22] [1991] 1 China L.R. 500.

[23] Meijer, M.J. "The New Criminal Code of the People's Republic of China" 1980, 6(2) *Review of Socialist Law* 125–139.

[24] See discussion in Chen, Albert *An Introduction to the Legal System of the People's Republic of China* 1992 Butterworths, Hong Kong, pp. 98–102.

[25] See for example Gelatt, T.A. "The People's Republic of China and the Presumption of Innocence" 1982, 73(1) *Journal of Criminal Law and Criminology*, pp. 259–316.

[26] See for example Meijer n. 23 above and Zhu Qiwu "General Aspects of the Chinese Criminal Code and Code of Criminal Procedure" 1985, 2 *Pacific Basin Law Journal*, pp. 65–75.

[27] Lubman, S. "Studying Contemporary Chinese Law: Limits, Possibilities and Strategy" 1991, 39 *American Journal of Comparative Law* pp. 293–340.

[28] *Ibid.*, p. 327.

[29] Published by Butterworths, Asia.

[30] Project of the Law Faculty, City University of Hong Kong.

[31] See for example *Xin si yi an yan jin* by Chen Xin Niang, People's University, Beijing.

[32] See above n. 7.

[33] Zhao Binzhi and Bao Suixian "The Present and Future of Criminal Law Reform in China" 1995, 1(1) *Journal of Chinese and Comparative Law*, pp. 133–144.

[34] The latest estimation for the completion of the new *Criminal Law* is the middle of 1998.

[35] Note for example the number of offences that relate to criminal damage to property. These include Articles 100, 105–111 and 156.

[36] See above n. 25.

CHAPTER 5
CRIMINAL PROCEDURE LAW

Fu Hualing

City University of Hong Kong

Fu Hualing, LL.B. (Southwestern University of Political Science and Law, PRC); M.A. (Criminology, University of Toronto); D.Jur. (York University, Toronto); Assistant Professor (City University of Hong Kong).

Introduction

Criminal procedure in the People's Republic of China (PRC) is gov-   **5.01**
erned by the 1979 *Criminal Procedure Law* (CPL 1979).[1] CPL 1979
divides the Chinese criminal process into three distinctive stages:
criminal investigation; public prosecution; and trial. Three independent
systems govern their own respective parts in the criminal procedural law. First, the public security system (the police), headed by the
Ministry of Public Security (MPS), together with other investigative bodies are responsible for criminal investigations. Second, the
procuratorial system led by the Supreme People's Procuratorate (SPP)
is responsible for instituting public prosecutions. Third, the court
system, led by the Supreme People's Court (SPC), is responsible for the
adjudication of cases prosecuted.

CPL 1979 has been recently amended by the new CPL 1996.[2] The
new statute will take effect on January 1, 1997. The Amendment
introduces inportant changes to the existing procedures and significant
redistributes the existing division of powers within the system. The
most striking feature of the Amendment is the recognition of the
presumption of innocence on the part of the accused. CPL 1996 no
longer refers to a suspect as an offender. It expressly states that: "no
one is guilty of a crime without a people's court rendering a judgment
according to law" (Article 12, CPL 1996).

The purpose of this chapter is to explore in some detail the salient
provisions of criminal procedures in the PRC as they are set out in the
1996 Amendment. In doing so, it discusses the provisions of the new

statute in light of similar provisions in CPL 1979 and parses on the significance and on the limitations of the amending statute.

Investigative Powers

Jurisdiction

5.02 The provisions in CPL 1979 on jurisdictions of the authorities related to investigations are very loosely stated. They created overlapping jurisdictions among the investigative bodies, thus causing conflicts of institutional interests among them. The 1996 Amendment attempts to clearly circumscribe the jurisdictional boundaries.

The Jurisdiction of Public Security Organs

Under article 18 of CPL 1979, a public security organ (the police) has jurisdiction in the investigation of all criminal offences, save and except where the jurisdiction is assigned to other bodies under law. The other authorities having jurisdiction in this matter include the procuratorate, national security organs, and the Military Protection Department (MPD).

Jurisdiction of the Procuratorate

According to article 13 of CPL 1979, cases involving crimes of corruption, violation of citizens' democratic rights and dereliction of duty as well as other cases that the people's procuratorate considers necessary to handle directly themselves shall be placed on files by the people's procuratorate. It shall conduct investigations and decide whether or not to initiate public prosecutions (Article 13, CPL 1979).

What has been disputed between the procuratorate and the police is the inclusive clause that allows the procuratorate to investigate any case that it deems necessary to handle itself. This clause has significantly expanded the jurisdiction of the procuratorate.

The 1996 Amendment restricts the ambit of the inclusive clause and narrows the investigative power of the procuratorate. Article 18 of CPL 1996 specifies the procuratorate shall have to investigate allegations of:

(a) corruption;
(b) dereliction of duty by state functionaries;
(c) unlawful detention, administration of torture, taking venge-

ance and making false accusations, and unlawful searches
committed by state functionaries in abuse of their powers; and

(d) other important criminal cases which are committed by state
functionaries through abuse of their powers. But the exercise of
such powers must be authorized by the procuratorate at or
above the provincial level.

Military Jurisdiction

CPL 1979 is silent on the MPD's investigative powers. It is a settled
principle of law in China that military justice is a distinct system that
is parallel to the civilian system and that the MPD has exclusive
jurisdiction over the investigation of all crimes committed by service
personnel on military premises.[3] In cases where crimes are committed
by both service personnel and civilians within those premises, the
MPD has primary responsibility in conducting investigations and the
civilian police only assists in the investigations. After the investigations are completed, the soldiers and the civilians may be prosecuted
and tried under the military and civilian system respectively.

The MPD also has jurisdiction over investigation of crimes committed by military personnel off military premises. The police has no
jurisdiction in investigating crimes committed by service personnel.
Where there is suspicion at the outset that a crime may have been
committed by service personnel outside military premises, a local
police station has preliminary responsibilities in conducting investigations, with the assistance of the MPD. But once there is *prima facie*
evidence that a crime was committed by a member of service personnel, the case transfers to the MPD for further investigations. The
detainee is also transferred to the custody of the MPD.

Jurisdiction of the National Security Organs

The Ministry of State Security (MSS) was set up in 1983 by a Decision
of the Standing Committee of the National People's Congress (NPC).
The MSS took over the responsibility for investigating activities which
are regarded as external threats to China's state security. In 1993, the
Standing Committee of the NPC enacted the State Security Law (SSL).[4]
This statute defines the contours of state security in China and speci-
fies the functions and the powers of the MSS. In 1994, the State
Council passed the *Rules for the Implementation of the State Security
Law* (the Rules).[5] The Rules define some of the terms in the SSL and
provide guidelines for station security work.

Under Chinese law, state security is limited to external interferences as provided for in the SSL. Under Article 4 of the SSL, an act is

prejudicial to China's state security when organizations or individuals outside China commit, or request to commit or support others to commit, or collude with organizations and individuals within China to commit acts which are prejudicial to China's state security. This Article makes abundantly clear that for the purposes of contravening national security, foreign elements must be involved. Purely domestic subversion is left to be dealt with by other agencies of the state. Only organizations or individuals with foreign connections who pose state security threats are dealt with under the SSL.

The subject matter of state security is broadly defined. Article 4 of the SSL lists five categories of state security concerns which include subversion, espionage, stealing state secrets, mutiny and a catch-all provision, namely, any other activities prejudicial to state security.[6]

Filing a Case

5.03 Criminal litigation in China starts when an investigatory agency files a case, *i.e.* to start a formal investigation of a complaint or of a confession. The CPL gives the filing of a case an independent status and treats it as a requisite stage in criminal prosecutions. Each investigative body has detailed provisions on the standards for filing a case and for the requisite procedures.

Filing a case has significant legal and social implications in China. Legally, a case cannot be prosecuted without first being filed by an investigatory agency. The filing of a case evidences legal recognition that a crime in law has taken place. Socially, a complaint or a confession does not enter the official statistics for crime in China unless it is filed. China's official criminal statistics relies totally upon cases filed by its investigatory agencies.

The filing procedures remain the same under the Amendment. Upon discovering a crime or a criminal suspect, government and non-government organizations and citizens may bring a complaint to an investigative organ. That organ accepts all complaints and the voluntary surrender of suspects for possible investigations. If the case is outside a receiving body's jurisdiction, it refers the matter to a competent body and so notifies the complainant (Article 84, CPL 1996).

Article 86 of the CPL 1996 sets out two criteria for filing. After reviewing the materials involving a complaint or a voluntary surrender, an investigative body files a case if it believes there are facts of a crime necessitating the investigation for criminal liability. If it believes there are no facts of crime or that the facts of crime are obviously minor and do not warrant an investigation, it does not file a case. The police has the discretion in making a determination on the facts and on whether to file a case (Article 86, CPL 1996).

The discretion of an investigative body in filing a case is of course not unfettered. The perspective investigative bodies may issue guidelines to specify conclusively the criteria for filing a case for the perspective offences, that is the "filing standard" which an investigative body has to refer to when making a determination on filing.

CPL 1996 renders the police accountable to the procuratorate in making decisions on filing. Where a procuratorate considers the police has failed to file a case for investigation, it has the right to demand a police explanation. The procuratorate may order the police to file a case if the explanation is not satisfactory to itself (Article 87).

Administrative Sanction Powers

Security Administration Punishment Act (SAPA)

The SAPA was enacted by the NPC in 1957 to deal with minor **5.04** unlawful acts that, although they may not have breached the criminal law, nonetheless require the imposition of definite administrative punishment. In 1986, the 1957 Act was replaced by a new *Security Administration Punishment Act*. The law was amended in 1994.

The SAPA falls somewhere between criminal sanction, social mority and organizational discipline. In Chinese Communist jargon, it is the "second defence line" in the battle of preserving social order, with social morality forming the front line and criminal sanction the reserve army. The SAPA represents the intermediate sanctions. But the activities under SAPA jurisdiction are criminal in nature and constitutive elements of the criminal law. They are not subject to criminal law sanctions because the circumstances or consequences are not serious.

The penalty authorized by the SAPA are administrative sanctions exclusively administered by the police. The Act empowers the police to impose sanctions which include a warning, a fine of not more than 5,000 yuan, and/or administrative detention of not more than 15 days. A great number of offenders are penalized by the police under the SAPA. In 1989 for instance, the police processed some two million SAPA offences and penalized more than three million offenders.

Re-education Through Labour (RTL)

Another level of police powers lies between SAPA sanctions and criminal punishment. This level is the administrative penalty called "Re-education through Labour." In 1957, a Decision was promulgated by the state council, with the approval of the NPC, to formalize the system by establishing the RTL institutions. These institutions were "to reform into self-supporting new persons those persons with the capacity to labor who loaf, who violate law and discipline, or who do not engage in proper employment, and in order to further preserve public order and to benefit socialist construction". The application for RTL sanction could be made by "civil affairs and public security departments or the offices, organizations, enterprises, schools or other units to which (the targets) belong; or their parents or guardians". The applications for sanctions were to be approved by the government or the entrusted organizations. According to this Decision, an agency in charge was to be set up. It would be jointly administered by the department of civil affairs and the police.[7]

The term of detention was indefinite in the 1957 Decision. In a 1979 Supplementary Decision of the State Council, the term of incarceration was set at one to three years, with one year extension when "it is necessary". According to the Supplementary Decision, a RTL Committee is to be established in large and medium sized cities and will be composed of persons in charge of the civil administration, public security and department of labour. The target population of RTL is restricted to residents of large and medium sized cities. The rural populace is excluded.[8]

The police force has turned RTL into a crime control mechanism. In a 1982 Regulation passed by the Ministry of Public Security and approved by the State Council, the police can impose RTL on any person who has committed a criminal offence while the circumstances surrounding the offence are not serious. As a result, a great variety of offenders have received RTL sanctions, including parents who hide their fugitive children, lawyers who are suspected of conducting illegal activities in defending their clients, pickpockets, and more recently, political dissidents. RTL is used to incarcerate those whose offences are either not severe enough for criminal punishment, or where the police deem the offence as serious but lacking sufficient evidence to support a charge.[9]

The scope of RTL is expanding. Recently the police power to detain was expanded by the creation of a statutory power to "shelter for education" prostitutes or people who visit prostitutes, for between six months and two years and drug addicts in treatment centres for an unspecified period of time.[10]

Detention and Arrest

Detention under CPL 1979

5.05 Article 41 of CPL 1979 grants the police the power of detention. Article 41 provides:

In any of the following circumstances, the public security organs may detain a suspect:

    a) if he is in the process of preparing to commit a crime, is committing a crime or is discovered immediately after committing a crime;

    b) if he is identified as having committed a crime by the victim or by an eyewitness on the scene;

    c) if he is discovered to have criminal evidence on his person or at his residence;

    d) if, after committing the crime, he attempts to commit suicide or to escape or is a fugitive;

    e) if he may possibly destroy or falsify evidence or collude with others to devise a consistent story;

    f) if his identity is unclear and there is strong suspicion that he is a person who goes from place to place committing crimes; or

    g) if he is engaged in "beating, smashing and looting" and gravely undermining work, production or social order.

Article 48 of CPL 1979 limits the period of such detention to ten days. Criminal suspects who are not formally arrested within ten days of their detention must be released. According to the said article:

> "In cases where a public security organ considers it necessary to arrest a detained person, it shall, within three days after detention, submit a request to the people's procuratorate for review and approval. Under special circumstances, the time for requesting review and approval may be extended by from one to four days. The people's procuratorate shall make its decision to approve arrest or not to approve arrest within three days after receiving the application for approval of arrest from the public security organ."

Arrest by the Police under CPL 1979

Article 40 of CLL sets out three requisites for arrest:

    a) "the principal facts" of the crime must have already been clarified; and there must be a *prima facie* case against a suspect before an arrest may be executed;

    b) the crime committed must be serious and the suspect may be sentenced to a penalty of not less than imprisonment; and

    c) arrest must be necessary, and it should only be effected under the circumstances where adopting such measures allowing the suspect to obtain a guarantor and await trial out of custody, or to reside at home under surveillance, would be insufficient to prevent the occurrence of a danger to society.

Apart from these substantive requirements, an arrest must be executed by the procuratorate at the same level. When the police intend to make an arrest, they should submit a written request for approval of arrest together with the case files and evidence to the procuratorate at the same level for examination and approval (Article 45, CPL 1979). The chief procurator makes a decision after examining the case. The decisions in major cases are made by the procuratorial committee, the leading body in a procuratorate (Article 46, CPL 1979).

The Problems Created by CPL 1979

It is commonly acknowledged that Article 40 of CPL 1979 imposes an unreasonably high standard for arrest. The requirement of procuratorial approval for an arrest is complicated and unsuitable for effective police work. The essence of the problem is that the formal criminal process cannot be initiated without an arrest, and no arrest can be made without the prior written authorization from the procuratorate. Police may not make any arrests in China without a warrant.

Moreover, the police detention powers are not sufficient. A ten day police investigation cannot provide enough evidence to prove the "main facts" of a case which forms the threshold of an arrest. As a consequence the police have been circumventing the CPL 1979 provisions by imposing measures and sanctions outside the court sanctioned criminal procedures.

The Use and Abuse of Shelter for Examination

5.06 The mechanism used by the police to bypass the formal criminal procedure is a procedure called Shelter for Examination (SE). The legislative basis for SE has never been clear. It began as a police initiative for the control of urban transients. By the mid-1970s, the police declared that SE would become a crime control mechanism which involved subjecting roving criminal suspects to compulsory examination. The government intended to control the use of SE after the promulgation of the CPL 1979 but such attempts were abandoned in 1983 when the government formally launched its war on crime.[11]

There have been several regulations and notices issued by both the State Council and by the Ministry of Public Security to regulate the application of SE. Unfortunately, many of the rules are inconsistent and contradictory. In 1985, the Ministry of Public Security issued a Notice which was intended to standardize the use of SE. The Notice confines the target populace into two groups: suspects who commit crime from place to place; and suspects who refuse to reveal their identities, addresses or backgrounds to the police. The Notice stresses

136

that SE is not applicable to local offenders whose identity is known to the police.[12]

The Notice also sets certain procedural requirements in the application of this measure. The regular detention period for SE is one month, which, with the permission of the police department at the next higher level, could be extended to two months if the case is "complicated." An additional one month extension is allowed in an "extremely complicated case." But consent from the provincial police authority is required.[13]

Despite the Notice from the Ministry of Public Security and the consistent plea of restraint by the government, there is a staggering abuse of power that is prevalent within SE. The most serious concern is the flouting of the time limit for detention and the expansion of target groups to be apprehended under SE.[14]

The 1996 Amendment

The most significant change in the 1996 Amendment is the abolishment of SE. There is a national consensus, despite initial resistance from the MPS, that SE is an abusive process and is to be abolished.[15]

The police's concerns relative to its insufficient detention powers and the rigid test of arrests are also addressed in the Amendment. There are two changes in the CPL 1996 Amendment designed to compensate the abolishment of SE:

a) the new test specifies that "there should be evidence to prove that a suspect has committed certain criminal acts". While the precise meaning of this new test is not yet ascertained, it should be equivalent to the common law test of reasonable suspicion.[16]

b) the power to detain a suspect is enhanced. The police is authorized, with the permission of the procuratorate, to detain certain suspects for a period of 30 days if there is "serious suspicion" that a person has committed crimes from place to place, repeatedly, or jointly with others. By the end of the 30 day period, the suspect must be formally arrested, released or subject to other administrative sanctions.

The Amendment is thus a compromise between the SE and CPL 1979. It partially abolishes SE in that:

(i) it has shortened the period of SE detention from three months to one month;

(ii) it subjects the one month police detention to procuratorial review; and

(iii) it limits the target populace.

But given the large proportion of the populace that may be apprehended for 30 days detention, there are sufficient grounds to advance
the claim that at least part of the SE practice has been submerged into
the formal criminal process, and that the police shall be able to do
legally what they can only do now in secret. In this light, the 1996
Amendment legalizes, at least partially, what it intends to abolish.

Procuratorial Approval of Arrest

The procuratorate retains the power to approve arrests made by the
police. Before the police make an arrest, they have to submit a written
application to the procuratorate at the same level for examination and
approval, together with the case file and evidence gathered (Article 66,
CPL 1996). The chief procurator is the only party who is authorized to
examine and to approve the arrest of a suspect. Major cases are submitted to the procuratorial committee for discussion and decision (Article
67, CPL 1996).

After examining the application, the procuratorate shall, within
seven days after receiving the application for arrest, decide, according
to the circumstances, either to approve or to disapprove the arrest. If
the procuratorate disapproves an arrest, it should provide reasons for
the disapproval and advise the police whether the particular case requires supplementary investigation (Article 68, CPL 1996). If the suspect is in police custody, the police, upon receiving notification of the
decision, shall immediately release the detainee. If the case requires
further investigation and the conditions for bail are satisfied, the detainee shall be released on bail.

If the police disagree with the decision to disapprove an arrest, they
may request a reconsideration but must nevertheless immediately
release the detainee. If the application for reconsideration is not accepted, the police may request a review by the procuratorate at the
next higher level. The higher procuratorate shall immediately review
the matter, decide whether or not to vary the decision and to notify the
lower procuratorate and the police (Article 70, CPL 1996).

The procuratorate has broad authority in supervising the investigatory activities of the police. If in examining and approving arrests, the
procuratorate discovers illegalities during the investigation, it shall
advise the police to amend these. The police have the duty to report on
the action taken to the procuratorate (Article 76, CPL 1996).

Search

5.07   An officer may search a person, a person's belongings, residence and
       other relevant places where it is suspected that criminals or criminal

evidence is being concealed. The search must be executed for the purposes of gathering criminal evidence and apprehending criminals (Article 109, CPL 1996).

A search warrant must be shown to the person being searched (Article 111, CPL 1996). A search warrant may be issued by a person in charge of a police station at or above the county level.[17] Searches may also be conducted incidental to a detention or an arrest. In an emergency situation, a search may be conducted without a warrant (Article 111, CPL 1996). The Ministry of Public Security specifies three situations under which a search may be conducted without warrant, if a person:

a) possesses weapons or other instruments which could be used to injure themselves or others;
b) has concealed explosives, poisons or other dangerous materials;
c) is liable to destroy or conceal evidence related to any offence.[18]

There are other rules of conduct in executing a search. A search must be conducted by not less than two officers,[19] searches of women shall be conducted by female personnel (Article 112, CPL 1996); family members, neighbours or other witnesses shall be present during the search (Article 112, CPL 1996); the other witnesses can include the person in charge of the unit where the suspect is working.[20]

Proper documentation on the search shall be made. A transcript shall be made of the circumstances of a search, and the investigative personnel and the person searched or his family members, neighbours or other eyewitnesses shall sign it or place their seals upon it. If the person searched or his relatives refuse to sign, the circumstances and should be noted in the transcript (Article 113, CPL 1996).

Articles and documents discovered during the search that may be used as evidence to prove the guilt or innocence of a defendant shall be seized. The seized articles and documents should be secured and they should not be used or damaged (Article 114, CPL 1996).

Searching Mail

The *Postal Law of the People's Republic of China* has a relevant provision. Article 4 states:

> "Freedom and privacy of correspondence shall be protected by law. No organization or individual shall infringe upon the freedom and privacy of correspondence of other persons for any reason, except when the inspection of correspondence in accordance with legal procedures by the public security organ, the state security organ or the procuratorial organ is necessary for state security or for the investigation of criminal offence."[21]

Article 116 of the CPL authorizes the procuratorate and the police to notify the post office to detain the mail and telegrams of a suspect:

> "When investigative personnel consider it necessary to seize the mail or telegrams of a suspect and upon approval of a public security organ or a people's procuratorate, they may notify the post and telecommunications organs to check for relevant mail and telegrams and turn them over to the investigative personnel for seizure."

There are three requirements for the seizure of mail:[22]

a) police may only seize the mail or telegrams of a person who has been detained, arrested or charged;
b) the seizure must be necessary for the investigation, and
c) whether such seizure is necessary is to be determined by the police or the procuratorate.

The seized articles must be returned to the sending party or to the post and telecommunications organ if it is ascertained they are not apposite to the case under investigation (Article 116, CPL 1996).

The 1996 Amendment introduces a new article which authorizes the procuratorate and the police to examine and freeze the monetary deposits and monetary transactions of a suspect during the course of a criminal investigation. But once funds and the transactions are released, they may not be frozen again (Article 117, CPL 1996).

Power to Question

Questioning of Witnesses

5.08 Upon producing a proper certificate, investigative officers may question any witness at his work place or residence. When necessary, the officers may notify the witness to come to the procuratorate or to the police station to render testimony (Article 97, CPL 1996).

Summons

The issue of summons is provided by both the SAPA and the CPL. Where a person commits an offence under SAPA, the police may summon him to a police station to be interrogated (Article 34(1), SAPA). The test for using such a procedure is that first a person must have committed an offence under SAPA, and secondly, it has been deemed necessary to summon that person to answer questions. A summoning warrant shall be issued by the police to the accused, but if the person was apprehended during the process of committing an offence, he may be summoned verbally. The police may use force to remove the suspect to a station if he refuses to be summoned or avoids summons without reasonable cause.

The CPL authorizes the police to summon a suspect to a specified place within the city or county. The police may hold suspects in a police station for 12 hours, and may not turn summonses into indirect detentions by repeatedly summoning the same suspect (Article 92, CPL 1996).

Interrogating Suspects

Interrogation without Detention or Arrest

The police may question a suspect without detaining or arresting him. Under SAPA, the accused should respond honestly to a police interrogation. The police should make a record of the interrogation which should be checked and signed by both the police and the suspect (Article 34(2), SAPA). Under CPL, a suspect who is not not to be arrested or detained may be summoned to a designated place for interrogation (Article 92, CPL).

Under the SAPA, a suspect may be interrogated for 24 hours without being formally detained or arrested. After being summoned to the public station, the suspect should be interrogated and investigated promptly. The time of interrogation and investigation shall not exceed 20 hours in complicated cases (Article 35, SAPA).

The *Police Law* 1995 gives the police broader powers in questioning a suspect without formal detention or arrest. According to Article 9 of the *Police Law*:

> "For the purposes of maintaining social order, people's police in public security organs may, after producing proper documents, interrogate and examine a crime suspect on the spot; after the interrogation and examination, the police officers may take the suspect to a public security organ, and with the permission of the public security organ, continue to interrogate the suspect, if the suspect:
>
> (1) is accused of having committed an offence;
> (2) is suspected of committing an offence on the spot;
> (3) is suspected of committing a crime and the person's identity is not clear; or
> (4) is found in possession of stolen goods."

The police may question the suspect in the police station for a period not exceeding 24 hours, or in special circumstances, not exceeding 48 hours. The police must release the suspect if no other measures are to be taken against him.

Interrogation after Detention or Arrest

The police shall interrogate the detainee or the arrested person within 24 hours after detention (Article 65, CPL 1996) or arrest (Article 72, CPL 1996). The interrogation must be carried out by police officers and there must be no fewer than two officers present during an interrogation (Article 91, CPL 1996). The interrogation should be recorded and the record should be shown to the defendant for checking. Both the defendant and the interrogating officers should sign the record (Article 95, CPL 1996).

The accused has no right to silence under Chinese criminal procedures. All those involved in Chinese criminal procedures, including investigators, procurators, trial judges, and victims have the right to question the defendant. Furthermore, Article 93 imposes the duty on a suspect to answer questions truthfully which are posed by the investigators, but the suspect shall have the right to refuse to answer questions that are irrelevant to the case (Article 93, CPL 1996).

Reasons for the suspect to refuse to answer questions are not clearly stated in the law. Under the CPL, no penalty may be imposed if the accused refuses to answer questions.

Article 46 of CPL 1996, duplicating Article 35 of CPL 1979, provides that a defendant cannot be found guilty on the basis of his confession only. There must be evidence to support the confession. On the other hand, a defendant may be found guilty if evidence is sufficient and reliable, even without his confession. Theoretically, refusal to answer a question is not by itself punishable in law, neither may the court draw any inference to the detriment of a defendant. Confession is an element that will be considered at the time of sentencing, but not for fixing criminal liability.

There has been much discussion in China's academic circles on implementing exclusionary rules into the criminal process, which allow or even compel the courts to exclude evidence which has been unlawfully obtained. These proposals have not been considered by the legislature, however. CPL 1996 simply states that: "It shall be strictly forbidden to extort confessions by torture and to collect evidence by threat, enticement, deceit or other unlawful means." (Article 43, CPL 1996) The law does not provide any solutions for when unlawful means are used in extracting evidence, unless the circumstances of the case are serious enough to be penalised under Article 136 of *the Criminal Law* 1979.[23]

The Time Limit for Completing an Investigation

5.09 Under CPL 1979, there are three different time limits for completing an investigation. These limits vary between case types:

Nature of the case	Time limit	Approving Authority
ordinary	two months	investigative body
complex	one month	procuratorate at the next higher level
extremely grave and complex	further postponement	Standing committee, NPC

The time limit for investigation was extended by Supplementary Provisions of the Standing Committee passed in 1984.[24] With the consent of a procuratorate at a provincial level, the time limit may be further extended by another two months (after the one month extension) in cases of crimes committed by a group or in major and complex cases involving crimes committed by persons going from place to place, or in the event that major and complex crimes were committed in remote areas with extremely poor communications with the rest of China.

The 1996 Amendment incorporates both CPL 1979 and the 1984 Supplementary Provisions. At the same time, these amendments have created a number of exceptions. The three different time limits provided in the CPL 1979 remain. The circumstances in which another two-month extension is allowed are specified as follows (Article 126, CPL 1996):

a) major and complex cases in remote areas with extremely poor communication;
b) serious cases committed by criminal organizations;
c) serious and complex cases involving persons going from place to place; or
d) serious and complex cases which involve a wide range of places or persons, and it is difficult to obtain evidence.

The Amendment provides for special circumstances which may require further extension (Article 127, CPL 1996):

a) another two month extension may be granted upon the consent of a procuratorate at a provincial level if the extension provided in Article 126 was insufficient and if a suspect may be sentenced to more than ten years of imprisonment.
b) the time limit begins again if, while in custody, a suspect was found to have committed another crime.
c) in a case where the name, address, or identity of a suspect is in doubt, the limitation time begins from the date when such information was ascertained.

Article 127 substantially increases the police power to detain a suspect at the pre-trial stage.

Bail

5.10 Although a person has been charged with an offence, he may be allowed to await trial out of custody. Under Article 51 of the CPL 1996, the court, the procuratorate, and the police may grant bail to any suspect under the following conditions:

a) if a suspect may be sentenced to a penalty of less than imprisonment; or

b) if his conditional release will not endanger society, although he may be sentenced to a penalty of imprisonment.

A suspect has no right to appeal if the application for bail is rejected. There are two types of bail: supervision of residence; and obtaining a guarantor or cash bail. Both types are executed by the police (Article 51, CPL 1996).

Obtaining a Guarantor

Bail is a conditional release of a suspect from custody. Under CPL 1979, a suspect may be released under the condition that he obtains a guarantor, who bears the responsibility of ensuring the suspect observes the conditions attached to the bail. CPL 1979 does not specify the qualifications and responsibilities of a guarantor, nor the conditions under which a suspect is released.

The 1996 amendment completes the gaps in the 1979 law. It provides that a guarantor must have the following four requisites (Article 54, CPL 1996):

a) not related to the case;

b) has the capacity to fulfil the responsibilities assumed;

c) enjoys political rights and personal freedoms; and

d) has a fixed address and income.

There are four conditions that a suspect must observe while on bail. A person on bail (Article 56, CPL 1996):

a) may not leave the city or county where the suspect resides without the consent of the police;

b) must appear immediately before a designated authority when summoned;

c) must not interfere with witnesses in any way; and

d), must not destroy, falsify or otherwise tamper with evidence.

The responsibilities of a guarantor are to ensure the suspect observes the conditions of bail. The guarantor has the responsibility to report to the bail granting authority when the suspect is likely to breach or has breached the conditions of bail. A guarantor is not a surety. He bears no monetary responsibility for a suspect on bail. But a guarantor can be subject to the penalty of a fine and even criminal prosecution if he fails to report in time the breach of conditions by the party on bail. (Article 55, CPL 1996).

Release Under Monetary Conditions

CPL 1979 does not allow release under bail on deposit, and the government has been suspicious of the practise of granting bail to those who are able to pay. The Amendment varies this tradition.

Cash bail is allowed in the Amendment (Article 53, CPL 1996). But a suspect may not be released under recognition of a debt to the granting authority, nor may he be released by arranging for another person to undertake to guarantee the payment if the suspect breaches the conditions of bail. In any event, the provisions governing cash bail are rather skeletal and rules need to be drafted by the respective granting authorities to implement cash bail.

The cash deposited is returned to the suspect if he has not violated the bail conditions during the bail period. If the conditions are breached, the cash will be forfeited. In addition, the following measures may be taken by an appropriate authority (Article 56, CPL 1996):

a) order the suspect to find another guarantor or pay additional cash bail;
b) put the suspect under residential surveillance; or
c) arrest the suspect.

Residential Surveillance

Where release under cash bail may be applied for by a suspect or by his representative, supervision of residence is a penalty that may be imposed only upon the initiative of the authority.

The following five conditions must be observed by a suspect under the supervision of residence (Article 57, CPL 1996):

a) the suspect may not leave the place of domicile or a specific address if the suspect has no fixed residence, save and except upon the consent of the granting authority;
b) the suspect may not conduct any interview with others without the permission of the police;

    c) the suspect must appear immediately before a specified author-
       ity when summoned;

    d) the suspect may not interfere with witnesses in any way; and

    e) the suspect may not destroy, falsify or otherwise tamper with
       evidence.

Where a suspect breaches any of these conditions, and the circumstances of the breach are serious, he should be arrested.

Subsection b) above is a condition that is not attached to cash bail.
What constitutes an interview is not defined. But in imposing this
condition, the law makers apparently have in mind those political
dissidents who were interviewed by foreign journalists.

Procuratorial Powers

Instituting Public Prosecution

5.11 After the police conclude their investigations and transfer the files to
the procuratorate for public prosecution, the procuratorate will review
the case. Where the procuratorate considers the facts are clear, the
evidence is reliable and complete, and the offence is serious enough to
warrant criminal sanction, it shall make a decision to prosecute and
initiate a public prosecution in court with competent jurisdiction.

The procuratorate shall decide whether to prosecute the case within
one month of receiving the file from the police. An extension of half a
month may be allowed for major or complex cases (Article 138, CPL
1996).

The procuratorate should determine the following five issues in
examining a file (Article 137, CPL 1996):

    (a) whether the facts and circumstances of the crime are clear;
       whether the evidence is reliable and sufficient; and whether
       the charge and the nature of the crime have been correctly
       determined;

    (b) whether there were any crimes that may have been omitted or
       if there were persons whose criminal responsibility should be
       investigated;

    (c) whether it was a case in which criminal liability should not be
       investigated;

    (d) whether the case relates to collateral civil action; and

    (e) whether the investigation of the case was being lawfully con-
       ducted.

When examining a case, the procuratorate shall interrogate the
suspect, and consider the allegations advanced by the victim and by
the representative of the suspect and the victim (Article 139, CPL

1996). It may also require the police to produce further evidence which may be tendered at trial (Article 140, CPL 1996).

When it is necessary, the procuratorate may remand the case to the police for supplementary investigations or it may conduct its own investigations. Where the case has been remanded to the police, the supplementary investigation must be concluded within one month of the remand. Two supplementary investigations may be remanded to the police for each case. When a case is sent back to the procuratorate after a supplementary investigation, the limitation of time for the procuratorate begins again. The procuratorate may decide not to institute proceedings if the evidence gathered after the supplementary investigation is deemed insufficient (Article 140, CPL 1996). The Amendment is significant in that it prevents the procuratorate from repeatedly remanding a case to the police for supplementary investigation. It authorizes as well as compels the procuratorate not to institute a public prosecution if two supplementary investigations reveal insufficient evidence.

Exemption from Prosecution Under CPL 1979

Under CPL 1979, the procuratorate, after examining a case, may institute a public prosecution; may decide not to prosecute and free the suspect with a clear record; and may exempt the suspect from criminal prosecution but may find him guilty of a crime. The exemption system has caused much controversy.

A procuratorate may grant exemption from prosecution where it deems it not necessary to impose a criminal punishment (Article 101, CPL 1979). If the prosecution makes the determination before trial that a suspect is guilty of an offence, but due to the circumstances of the offence, the suspect should be exempted from criminal prosecution.

The offences which can be granted exemptions are provided by CPL 1979.[25] There are several provisions in the statute that attempt to control procuratorial discretion in granting the exemption (Article 102, CPL 1979):

    (a) a decision to exempt from prosecution shall be publicly announced;

    (b) where the case was investigated by the police, the decision to exempt shall be delivered to the police. Where the police considers the decision mistaken, they may demand reconsideration. If the procuratorate refuses to vary the decision, the police may request review by the procuratorate at the next higher level, whose decision would be binding;

    (c) where the case involves a victim, the procuratorate shall deliver the decision to the victim. If the victim does not agree, he may demand re-examination;

(d) where the defendant does not agree with the decision, he may demand re-examination.

Given the power the procuratorate possesses as the investigator, as well as the accused and the judge, the control of this discretion cannot be effective. The main criticism is that the procuratorate is not accountable to any public body in granting the exemption and the judicial power to determine guilt or innocence is superseded.

The Amendment

The Amendment abolishes the exemption system. Under the CPL 1996, the procuratorate may decide not to institute a prosecution against a suspect. But it cannot make a determination of guilt without prosecuting the case in court. Article 58 states that the people's procuratorate may decide not to institute a case if, firstly, the suspect is apprehended under one of the circumstances specified in Article 15 of CPL 1996;[26] or, secondly, if the circumstances of the offence are minor and the accused need not be penalised; or he may be exempted by the court from any criminal penalty.

Alternatives to Prosecution

Once the procuratorate decides not to institute a public prosecution, it shall release the materials it has detained or frozen during the investigation.[27] The decision shall be announced in public and the decision shall be sent to the accused and to his work unit. If the suspect is in custody, he should be released immediately (Article 143, CPL 1996).

The Amendment also creates a diversion from prosecution. Where the accused is not prosecuted, but there is some need for administrative sanctions or administrative disciplines, the procuratorate may refer him to a related government department with a procuratorial opinion. The related government department should notify the procuratorate of its decision (Article 142, CPL 1996).

Review

5.12 The decision not to prosecute may be appealed by the police, by the victim or by the suspect himself:

a) where the procuratorate decides not to prosecute a case that was investigated by the police, it shall notify the police of its decision. The police may apply to the procuratorate to reconsider the decision. The police may also request the people's procuratorate at the next higher level to review the decision if the application is rejected (Article 144, CPL 1996).

b) where the procuratorate decides not to prosecute a case which involves a specific victim, it shall send the decision to the victim. If the victim is not satisfied with the decision, it may, within seven days after receiving the decision, appeal to the people's procuratorate and request it to institute a public prosecution. If the people's procuratorate sustains the original decision, the victim may himself institute a prosecution in court. The victim may also institute a prosecution directly in court without appealing to the procuratorate. Once the people's court accepts the case which the procuratorate declines to prosecute, the procuratorate shall transfer the files of the case to the court (Article 145, CPL 1996).

c) a defendant who is referred to another government department for administrative sanction may also, within seven days after receiving the decision, appeal to the procuratorate against the procuratorial recommendation (Article 146, CPL 1996).

The important development in the Amendment is to allow a victim to challenge procuratorial discretion in court. As the court is authorized to review the procuratorial discretion in refusing to institute a public prosecution, the power of the procuratorate will be seriously limited.

Incidental Civil Action

Provisions on incidental civil action remain the same in the   **5.13**
Amendment.

Article 77 of the CPL 1996 provides that: "Where a victim has suffered material losses as a result of the defendant's criminal act, he shall have a right to file an incidental civil action during the course of the criminal proceeding." An apparent limitation is that only material losses are actionable as an incidental civil action. Psychological pain and suffering are not. That limitation is not consistent with the recent development in China's tort laws where psychological damages are recoverable in tort. If a crime has caused the victim mental damage, he may have to initiate two seperate civil proceedings against the same defendant.

The same Article also provides that the procuratorate may bring an incidental civil action if state or collective property is damaged. In addition, the court may place under seal or detain the property of the defendant during trial.

Article 78 requires that an incidental civil action be heard together with the criminal case. The civil action may be heard subsequent to the criminal case to prevent excessive delays of a criminal trial. But the civil case must be tried by the same collegial panel. Furthermore, the civil party in a criminal trial has the right to appeal against the judgment as it relates to the civil action, and the appellant court should review the case as a whole.

Private Prosecution

5.14 A private person or his representative may initiate a private prosecution against a defendant directly in court, in the following circumstances (Article 170, CPL 1996):

    a) cases which may be handled only upon complaint;
    b) minor criminal cases which can be proved by a victim; or
    c) criminal cases in which a victim has evidence to prove that a defendant has infringed his personal or property rights, and the public security organs or the procuratorate have refused to investigate the criminal responsibilities of the defendant.

This Article gives courts the power to review decisions made by the police and by the procuratorate in relation to criminal investigations and prosecutions, and allows the court to accept private prosecutions against all offences.

Upon receiving an application for private prosecution, the court may proceed as follows:

    a) the court may open a session for trial if the facts are clear and the evidence sufficient;
    b) the court may mediate a case in relation to Article 170 (a) and (b);
    c) the court may persuade the private prosecutor to withdraw the prosecution if the evidence is insufficient; or
    d) the court may dismiss the application.

A defendant in a case of private prosecution may raise a counterclaim (Article 173, CPL 1996).

Trial at First Instance

Jurisdictions

5.15 The Basic People's Court (BPC) has jurisdiction as courts of the first instance over ordinary criminal cases, unless the CPL otherwise provides. The Intermediate People's Court (IPC) has jurisdiction as courts of first instance over the following criminal offences:

a) counter-revolutionary offences and offences prejudicial to state security;
b) ordinary criminal cases punishable by life imprisonment or the death penalty; and
c) criminal offences committed by foreign nationals.

The High People's Court (HPC) has jurisdiction as courts of first instance over major criminal cases that pertain to an entire province (or municipality directly under the Central Government, or an autonomous region). The Supreme People's Court (SPC) has jurisdiction as the court of first instance over major criminal cases that pertain to the entire nation.

When necessary a superior court may try cases where an inferior court has jurisdiction as courts of first instance. An inferior court may also apply to traverse a case over which it has jurisdiction as courts of first instance to a superior court for trial if the inferior court considers the case to be a major or a complex case. But under the Amendment, a superior court may no longer remand a case over which it has jurisdiction as courts of first instance to an inferior court for trial.

Criminal Trial under the CPL 1979

Pre-trial Court Investigation

Once the procuratorate initiates proceedings against a suspect, and transfers the case to the court, the court forms a Collegial Panel, composed of judges and people's assessors, to try the case. Before the trial, the panel holds meetings to discuss the case, and to make a decision on the nature of the offence as well as on the sentence. In serious cases, decisions are made by the Judicial Committee, which is the leading body of any court. In Chinese judicial practice, if a case is complicated or important, the opinion of the superior court may also be sought. It is a normal practice in China that a case is decided before trial, and those who try a case may not have the power to render a verdict other than that decided before trial.

The court must try the case unless there is not "clear and sufficient evidence" to support the prosecution, in which case, the court remands the case to the procuratorate for supplementary investigation (Article 108, CPL 1979). The same article also states that the court may ask the prosecution to withdraw its prosecution if no criminal sanctions are necessary. More importantly, when it is necessary to clarify a case, a people's court may initiate its own inquest, examination, search, seizure and expert evaluation although in practice, the judicial investigation is mainly limited to reviewing the evidence provided by the police and procuratorate. The fundamental characteristic of Chinese criminal trials is that through the pre-trial investigation, the judges decide on the facts and on the law involved. With regard to criminal procedures, no court opens a court session if the collegial panel is not certain of the facts, the offence and the sentence (Article 109, CPL 1979).

Dominant Role of the Judge

Throughout the trial, the judge is the dominant figure. The presiding judge opens the session by announcing the subject matter of the case and introducing the participants in the trial (Article 113, CPL 1979). The public procurator then reads the bill of prosecution, which includes the facts of the case, the laws violated and the penalty sought. After the bill of prosecution is read, the judge starts to question the defendant. At this stage, the public procurator may question the defendant with the permission of the court (Article 114, CPL 1979).

Upon completion of questioning the defendant, the judges and the procurator then question the witnesses, present records of testimony of witnesses who are not present in court, and recite the conclusions of expert witness if any, and lead documentary evidence (Article 116, CPL 1979). At this stage, the defence may raise questions. According to Article 115, "The parties and the defenders may request the presiding judge to question the witnesses or expert witnesses, or ask the presiding judge's permission to put their own questions directly." But the court may stop the questioning of the defence if it considers such questioning irrelevant.

During the trial, the defenders may seek leave to call new witnesses and to enter new evidence. But the court has the discretion to refuse such requests (Article 117, CPL 1979).

When the judicial inquisition is over, the procurator is permitted to make a speech to conclude his case; the victim is also permitted to make a statement. Afterwards, the defence is given an opportunity to submit a defence. Then, a "debate" among the participants follows. When the judge regards the issues of fact and law is fully debated, he may declare the conclusion of the debate, and allow the defence to present a final statement (Article 118, CPL 1979).

The Amendment

5.16 The Amendment makes Chinese criminal trials more adversarial in three respects: the changing relationship between the collegial panel and the judicial committee; the burden of proof at trial; and the role of judges in court.

The Role of a Collegial Panel

There is a slight change in the status of the collegial panel. Under CPL 1979, all major or difficult cases that the president of the court believes should be referred to the judicial committee shall be submitted by him to the judicial committee for consideration and decision. The collegial panel is bound to execute a decision reached by the judicial committee before trial.

The Amendment enhances the position of a collegial panel. Article 149 states that a collegial panel has the right and duty to render its decision after trial. If the collegial panel is unable to make a decision on a complex and important case after a trial, it should submit the case to the judicial committee for consideration and decision. The decision of the judicial committee is binding on the collegial panel.

The Burden of Proof

Under the Amendment, the court no longer conducts or participates in any pre-trial investigation. Two important articles of CPL 1979 have been deleted: Article 108 which authorizes a court to remand a case to the procuratorate for supplementary investigation and Article 109 which authorizes the court to conduct its own pre-trial judicial fact-finding. These two articles have been fundamental to China's criminal procedure.

Article 150 of the CPL 1996 specifies the new trial procedure:

> After the people's court examines a case which public prosecution is initiated, it shall decide if it should open the court session and try the case if the Bill of Prosecution has included the alleged criminal activities, together with the lists of evidence, names of witnesses and photocopies or photographs of primary evidence.

This article shifts the burden of leading evidence from the court to the procuratorate. Accordingly, the procuratorate alone will be responsible for the validity of the evidence. The court will no longer examine the evidence prepared by the procuratorate before trial. If this procedural reform provision is faithfully executed, courts in China will be removed from the fact-finding process. The judges may become neutral arbitrators, who decide a case according to whatever evidence is given in court. In the new trial provisions, there will be a more active procuratorate and defence lawyers may undertake more vigorous defences.

153

A Less Active Trial Judge

The trial judge becomes less active when the burden of proof is shifted to the procuratorate. Under the Amendment, after the public prosecutor has read the Bill of Prosecution in court, the defendant and victim may make statements in relation to the crimes alleged in the bill of prosecution. The public procurator may question the defendant.

But trial judges may still dominate at trial. A judge may make rulings on whether a new witness should be summoned, new material evidence be gathered, and a new expert evaluation be made. The judge may also directly question the defendant and witnesses. A judge may also adjourn trial to verify evidence if he is in doubt. A judge under the Amendment may be as powerful as one under CPL 1979. It is the judge's discretion as to whether to take on the role of inquisitor or arbitrator. There is no rule to guide him in making this choice. This ambiguity makes the implementation of certain trial types extremely difficult.

Adjourning a Trial

Under CPL 1979 there are four instances in which a trial may be adjourned (Article 123, CPL 1979):

(a) if it is necessary to summon new witnesses; to collect new materials or evidence, to render a new expert evaluation or to hold another inquest;

(b) if members of the procuratorial personnel find that a case for which public prosecution has been initiated requires supplementary investigations, and they make an application to that effect;

(c) if the collegial panel considers the evidence of a case insufficient or upon discovery of new facts, requiring it to either remand the case to the people's procuratorate for supplementary investigations or conduct its own inquiry; or

(d) if the trial cannot proceed because a party applies for the withdrawal of a judicial functionary.

Subsection (c) has now been deleted in the Amendment. The court will not adjourn a trial simply because it regards the evidence produced by the procuratorate to be insufficient. The case is dismissed if the evidence is insufficient. But the court may still adjourn a trial on its own initiative. If a collegial panel has doubts about the evidence, it may adjourn the trial and conduct its own investigation to verify the evidence (Article 158, CPL 1996).

Verdicts

Article 162 represents the most important change in the 1996 Amendment because it may stop the practice of deciding a case before a trial, a practice that has plagued the Chinese criminal courts for quite some time. Given the vigorous fact finding process at the pre-trial stage and the lack of proper defence, the verdicts that courts of law have arrived at have usually been "guilty". It is often said that a defendant in the Chinese criminal process is presumed guilty until proven innocent. It may be added that because the accusers have been allowed to overwhelm the court with evidence and arguments, few defendants have been able to prove their innocence.

Article 162(1) provides a court may find a defendant guilty if:

(a) the facts of the case are clear;
(b) the evidence is reliable and sufficient, and
(c) the defendant is guilty according to law.

Otherwise, the court should find the defendant not guilty. There are two instances in which the not guilty verdict may be rendered.

(a) if the act committed by the defendant does not amount to criminal offence, the court shall find him not guilty;
(b) if there is insufficient evidence to prove the guilt of the defendant, the court shall render the verdict that the defendant was not guilty because of insufficient evidence to support a conviction.

Time Limit for a Trial

Article 168 of the CPL 1996 specifies that a trial at first instance should be concluded within one month from the date the trial court receives the case, with a possible extension of another half month. While one of the instances specified in Article 126 appears, a one month extension may be allowed with the permission of a HPC.

Summary Proceedings

The 1996 Amendment creates a new procedure, namely, summary proceedings, for the court to try minor cases in a speedy fashion (Article 174–177, CPL 1996).   **5.17**

Cases Eligible for Summary Proceedings

a) cases of public prosecution in which the defendant may be sentenced to a penalty of less than three years' imprisonment; and the procuratorate recommends or agrees to have the case tried through summary proceedings;
b) crimes which are to be handled only upon complaint; or
c) minor criminal offences that are prosecuted by the victim.

Procedure for Summary Proceedings

a) a single judge will try a case in a summary proceeding.
b) where a prosecution is instituted by the procuratorate, the procuratorate has the discretion to decide whether or not to appear in court to pursue the prosecution.
c) where a prosecution is instituted by a private prosecutor, the private prosecutor has to appear in court to pursue the prosecution.
d) a summary proceeding need not follow normal trial procedures. But a defendant has the right to make a final statement before a judgment is rendered.

Time Limit for a Summary Proceedings

The court shall conclude a trial within 20 days after accepting the case (Article 178). If the court, during a summary proceeding, finds out that a case is not suitable for summary proceedings, it shall order a retrial under the regular proceeding (Article 179).

Procedure of Second Instance

The Right to Appeal

5.18 The judgement or order of a trial court (the first instance) may be appealed to the court at the next higher level (the second instance). The decision of a court at the second instance is final, subject to adjudicative review.

A court judgment or order may be challenged in following ways:

(a) a defendant or private prosecutor or their legal representatives may appeal if they are not satisfied with the judgment or order. The defender or his close relatives, with the consent of the defendant, may also appeal (Article 180);

An appellant court may not render a heavier sentence on an appellant if he, his legal representative , defender or near relative appeals against a judgment (Article 190);

(b) the procuratorate may lodge a protest if it considers there is some definite error in the judgment or order (Article 181, CPL 1996); but the procuratorate at the next higher level has the authority to withdraw a protest filed by the subordinate procuratorate, if it considers the protest inappropriate;[28]

(c) the victim or his legal representative, if not satisfied with a judgment of a court at the first instance, may request the procuratorate to protest against judgment. The procuratorate should make a decision whether or not to protest within five days of receiving the request (Article 182),

(d) a party in an incidental civil action or his legal representative may file an appeal against the portion of a judgment or order that deals with the incidental civil action (Article 180).

Power of the Appellant Court

The court at the second instance has the power to conduct a comprehensive examination of the case. Article 186 of the CPL 1996 requires the court to review the facts determined as well as the application of law. It is stressed that the appellate court should not limit itself to considering the issues raised by the appellant and by the respondent. In addition, if an appeal is filed by only some of the defendants in a case of a joint crime, the appellant court must review the case in light of all of the defendants.

The appellant court has the jurisdiction to examine a case from both substantive and procedural perspectives. The court may conduct a substantive review in the following fashions:

(a) it should sustain the original decision and dismiss the appeal or protest if it finds the facts accepted and the law applied are correct and the sentence is appropriate;

(b) it should vary the decision if it finds the facts accepted are correct but the law applied is wrong or the sentence imposed is inappropriate;

(c) where the facts are not certain or the evidence is insufficient, the court may vary the decision after it has clarified the facts. It may also remand the case to the court of first instance for retrial.

The significant improvement in the Amendment is that the law compels the appellant court to conduct procedural review of a case. An appellant court should set aside a conviction and remand the case to the court of first instance for retrial if procedural justice as specified below is violated (Article 191, CPL 1996):

    (a) the requirement for public trial is violated;[29]
    (b) the requirement for withdrawal is violated;
    (c) the parties' lawful rights in litigation are deprived of or unlawfully limited, and such deprivation and limitation may have prejudiced a fair trial;
    (d) the trial organs are not lawfully set up; or
    (e) there are violations of other rules regarding litigation procedures, and the violation may have affected a fair trial.

The implementation of procedural justice in China's criminal procedure under CPL 1996 is a significant step forward in protecting the rights of the defendant. However, it must be remembered that an appellant court has no power to quash a conviction and acquit the defendant for violation of procedural justice. It can only remand the case to the court of first instance for a retrial, even though there is a miscarriage of justice.

Format of the Hearing at Second Instance

There has been strong criticism that an appellant court in China lacks the earnestness and sincerity in hearing an appeal or a protest. The SPP, for instance argues that the practice in China's appellant courts has rendered criminal appeal less than a formality. It is not even a show trial (which is alleged to characterize the trial at first instance). In almost all cases, decisions are made by an appellant court behind closed doors and without the assistance of defence counsel and procurators. The appellant court only reviews the case according to the files provided.

Rarely does an appellant court allow an appeal or protest, just as a trial court almost never finds a defendant innocent. Given the close relation within China's judicial hierarchy and the close consultation between lower and higher courts, there is often a consensus between the trial and appellant courts before a case goes to trial. As a result, an appeal serves no purpose.

Whether or not an appellant court is required to open a session to hear a case under the Amendment depends on whether the case is one of appeal or one of protest. If the case is under appeal, the court is bound to open a session to hear the case only if the facts are not clear. If a case is protested by the procuratorate, the appellant court will have to organize a collegial panel to hear the protest.

If an appellant court decides to open a session to hear a case (whether the case was one of appeal or protest), the procuratorate at the same level as the appellant court should send its representative to attend the hearing. The court at second instance has the duty to notify the procuratorate to peruse the court files ten days before the hearing is held (Article 188, CPL 1996).

Time Limit

Another measure to improve the quality of appeal or protest at the second instance is to impose a time limit within which the appellant court is obliged to render its decision. There are three time limits for trials at the second instance, depending on the nature of the case and on the level of the appellant court (Article 196, CPL 1996):

(a) as a general principle, an appellant court, after hearing an appeal or protest, should render its decision within one month, a half month extension may be granted;

(b) where one of the instances specified in Article 126 materalises, a further extension of one month is allowed. But the approval or decision by an HPC is required;

(c) where the SPC accepts a case of appeal or protest, the time limit will be decided by the SPC.

Right to Counsel

Criminal Defence under the CPL 1979

Legal representation was fundamentally flawed before the 1996 **5.19** Amendment. Article 110 of CPL 1979 states:

After a people's court has decided to convene a court session, it shall proceed with the following tasks:

(2) to deliver to the defendant a copy of the bill of prosecution drafted by the people's procuratorate no later than seven days before the opening of the court session and to inform the defendant that he may appoint a defender or, when necessary, to designate a defender for him.

This seven day rule effectively excludes the possibility of any involvement by defence attorneys at the investigation and at the prosecution stage of a criminal case. No legal representation is allowed until a week before trial.

In the vast majority of cases, there are only one or two days available for a lawyer to prepare a defence. In a complicated case, there may be hundreds of pages of documents. It is impossible for a lawyer to review all the main facts of the case. In 30% of these trials, the cases are already at trial when the lawyer receives the notice. Without legal representation during the investigation and prosecution stages, the police and procurators may, as it happens frequently, force confessions, falsify confessions, or record only those statements favourable to the prosecution's case.[30]

In addition to the time limit, the defence offered at trial is also seriously prejudiced. This is not to say that there is nothing a lawyer can say in court. There are occasionally tense debates in court, and sometimes names are called and insults are exchanged between procurators and lawyers. The most serious problem is that no one seems to take a defence counsel's argument seriously. Given the fact that a case is decided before trial, the trial is really no more than a morality play wherein the parties merely participate in a ritual, knowing that all of their input is too little and too late.[31]

Criminal Defence under CPL 1996

The Amendment introduces substantial changes to China's criminal defence by advancing the time when a suspect may have access to a lawyer and by improving the quality of the lawyer's representation.

The Amendment divides legal representation in the criminal procedure into two stages. At the investigative stage, an accused may retain a lawyer to provide legal consultancy. At the prosecution and trial stages, the accused may hire a lawyer to provide criminal defence. A lawyer's right differs at the two stages.

Article 96 of CPL 1996 recognizes the right to counsel at the investigative stage. A lawyer's right during this stage includes the right:

a) to provide legal consultation, to represent the suspect and to lodge a complaint or accusation either from the first time a suspect is interrogated or from the day when he is put under any restrictive measures imposed by an investigative body.

b) to apply for bail on behalf of a suspect upon arrest.

While the Amendment represents a significant advance in improving China's criminal procedures, it also imposes some severe restrictions on lawyers:

(a) although suspects are offered more time for legal advice prior to trial, the time is not enough. Legal representation is allowed only after the first interrogation or any of the restrictive measures have been executed. Specifically, the term "first interrogation" needs further clarification.

(b) while a lawyer may meet with a suspect in custody to obtain information, he has no right to seek any information from an investigative body, except for inquiring about the name of the alleged offence. The Amendment is designed to ensure that lawyers do not "interfere" with the normal investigative work. As far as CPL 1996 is concerned, an investigative body owes no duty to assist a defence lawyer at the investigative stage.

(c) an investigative body has the power to be present during the lawyer's interview with a suspect according to the necessity and the circumstances of the case. There is no protection for the privacy of the conversation between a lawyer and his client. Furthermore, where a case involves state secrets, a suspect may not retain a lawyer without the permission of the investigative body. When a lawyer is allowed to be retained, he may not meet the suspect without further permission (Article 96).

(d) fatal to the defence may be the absence of substantial improvements in legal aid. While the CPL 1996 recognizes the issue of legal aid, it offers no solution. Without a strong commitment from the government to finance legal aid, most of the suspects would not benefit from the newly implemented legal rights.

A laywer who provides legal consultancy to his client becomes a criminal defender at the procuratorial and trial stages. A criminal defender enjoys more rights. According to Article 36:

A defence lawyer may, from the first day when the people's procuratorate starts to examine a case for the purpose of instituting a public prosecution, read, extract and copy the litigation documents and technical identification materials in relation to the case; and interview and communicate with the criminal suspect.

A defence lawyer has the same right when the procuratorate transfers the case to the court.

A defence lawyer may also interview witnesses and other related persons and organizations, request the procuratorate and court to gather evidence on its own behalf, and request the court to summon witnesses to testify in court. They may also, with the permission of the people's procuratorate or court, collect related information and materials from victims of the case (Article 37, CPL 1996).

It is likely that a defence lawyer can make a difference in a criminal trial under the Amendment. The introduction of some adversary elements into the criminal proceedings means, if anything, the procurators have the burden of proving the guilt. Once this burden is shifted to the procuratorate as the Amendment provides, the procuratorate has to lead evidence under a relatively neutral panel of judges. The defence shall then have a real opportunity to challenge the prosecution's allegations.

The crucial question remains as to what sort of input a defence lawyer is allowed to offer. The Amendment is silent on this point.

While a lawyer has access to files prepared by the procuratorate and by the court, it is still not clear, what is included in the files to which the lawyer may have access, and whether the court continues to exclude the crucial minutes of the Judicial Committee in the files available to the defence. Secondly, do judges take the lawyer's file and submissions seriously?

Adjudicative Review

5.20 The court's judgment after appeal becomes "legally effective," but it is not final. A legally effective judgment may be challenged through the procedure of adjudicative review. During the course of review, execution of the judgment will not be suspended.

Review Applied by the Defendant or Victim

A defendant and a victim of a case, his representatives or relatives may petition the court or the procuratorate for relief (Article 203, CPL 1996). The equivalent article in CPL 1979 also allows "other citizens" to lodge such a petition. Under the Amendment, only persons directly related to a case will be granted standing.

A new trial will be ordered after a review in the following circumstances (Article 204, CPL 1996):

- a) where new evidence proves that the facts found in the original judgment or order are incorrect;
- b) where the evidence used to determine criminal liability and sentencing are uncertain and insufficient, or the evidence which proved the crucial facts in the case contradict each other;
- c) where the original judgment or order has wrongly applied the law; or
- d) where the trial actors during the course of trial have embezzled money; accepted bribes, have indulged in favouritism or have otherwise rendered decisions in breach of the law.

Subsection (d) of the Amendment is an important development in that it allows review on the grounds of violation of procedural justice. A new trial should be ordered if a trial judge is found to have accepted bribes from one of the parties, regardless of the substance of the decision itself. The fact that the judge is involved in corrupt activities in relation to the case renders his decision void in law. But there must be concrete evidence to prove that the judge has actually engaged in acts of corruption.

Review Applied by Courts

If the president of a court finds some errors related to the determination of facts or to the application of law in a legally effective judgment or order, he should refer the matter to the judicial committee for review. If the Supreme People's Court finds some definite errors in a legally effective judgment or order of a court at any level, or if a court at a higher level finds some definite errors in a legally effective judgment or order of a court at a lower level, it may try the case itself or order the lower court to retry the case (Article 205, CPL 1996).

Review Applied by the Procuratorate

If the Supreme People's Procuratorate finds some definite errors in a legally effective judgment in an order of a court at any level, or a procuratorate at a higher level finds some definite errors in a legally effective judgment or order of a court at a lower level, it may lodge a protest in a court at the same level. The court, after receiving the protest, should form a collegial panel to try the case; it may also order the lower court to retry the case where the facts are unclear or where the evidence is insufficient in the original judgment to support the verdict (Article 205, CPL 1996).

Review Procedures

The Amendment imposes a time limit for adjudicative review, which is not included in CPL 1979. A court should complete the review within three months after deciding to try the case itself or to order a lower court to retry the case. An extension of three months is allowed when it is necessary.

Article 206 of CPL 1996 provides review procedures as follows:

- (a) a new collegial panel shall be formed for the retrial of a case by a people's court in accordance with the procedures for adjudicative review.
- (b) if the case was tried in a court of first instance, it should be tried in accordance with trial procedures of the first instance and the new judgment or order may be appealed from or protested against.
- (c) if the case was tried in a court of second instance or was brought up for trial by a people's court at a higher level, it shall be tried in accordance with the procedures of second instance and the judgment or order rendered shall be final.

Death Penalty

5.21 The approval procedures in the Amendment remain the same. Article 199 states that: "Death sentences shall be approved by the Supreme People's Court." But the court has the power to delegate the approval authority to the HPC as it sees fit.

Unless there is a special authorization from the SPC, the following procedures must be observed:

(a) in a case of first instance where an IPC has imposed a death penalty and the defendant does not appeal, the case shall be reviewed by a HPC and reported to the SPC for approval. If the HPC does not agree with the death sentence, it must try the case itself or order the case remanded for retrial (Article 200, CPL 1996);

(b) in a case of first instance where a HPC has imposed the death penalty and the defendant does not appeal, or in a case of second instance where the death sentence has been upheld, it shall be submitted to the SPC for approval (Article 200, CPL 1996);

(c) a HPC in a province has the power to approve a death penalty with a two-year suspension of execution (Article 201, CPL 1996); and

(d) the SPC and the HPC of a province should form a collegial panel to be composed of three judges to review a death penalty or a death penalty with a suspension of execution respectively (Article 202, CPL 1996).

Conclusion

Several concluding comments may be offered on China's criminal procedures under CPL 1979. Firstly, it is a police dominated process. The criminal procedure has been structured in such a way that the police could materially affect criminal prosecution. The police have extremely broad administrative powers even without invoking their powers under the statute. SAPA and RTL together with other forms of administrative detention, offer the police sufficient means to dispose of most of the minor offences without even resorting to its powers under the statute and thus avoiding accountability. The formal criminal procedures could then simply be bypassed.

In addition, the police's ability to affect the formal criminal proceedings is also substantial. The sole purpose of China's criminal procedure is to control crimes. There are few procedural requirements within the investigative process, and there are few protective measures to defend the rights of a suspect. CPL 1979 encourages the police to ascertain what it holds to be the true facts of an offence without any regard to procedural rectitude. Once this "truth" is found, the participants in the later stages are compelled to accept it.

Facts, perceived truth, and substantive justice are thus fundamental to China's criminal procedure. Once the police have found their truth, however perceived, all the subsequent processes become a mere verification of that determination. The files prepared by the police become central to the entire prosecuting process. From the procuratorial reexamination of police files to judicial scrutiny at the pretrial stage and judicial inquisition at trial, the only issue at stake is whether the files can withstand scrutiny and inquisition. The rights of defendants are routinely ignored in the criminal procedure in the rigorous search for "truth" and for the purpose of crime control. A defendant and his defenders are marginalised within the criminal justice system.

The Amendment introduces an element of procedural justice into China's criminal justice system. There are high expectations that the Amendment will better protect the rights of a suspect in China's criminal justice system. The substantial improvements in the law and the symbolic values embodied in it should provide an opportunity for such an improvement. The 1996 Amendment is a statute which provides a start for building a fair criminal justice system in China.

Notes

[1] *Criminal Procedure Law of the People's Republic of China 1979.* Translated into English by the Legislative Affairs Commission, National People's Congress.
[2] *Criminal Procedure Law of People's Republic of China* (Amendment) 1996.
[3] There are two Rules governing military jurisdictions. SPC, SPP, MPS, and the General Political Department of the People's Liberation Army, *Rules on Several Problems Related to Cases Involving the Military and Civilians* (1982); and *Supplementary Rules on the Investigative Works of Cases Involving Both the Military and Civilians* (1987).
[4] Standing Committee, National People's Congress, *State Security Law* (1993).
[5] State Council, *Rules for the Implementation of the State Security Law* (1994).
[6] See H L Fu and Richard Cullen, "China's State Security Law', (1996) 34 *Columbia Journal of Transnational Law* 449.
[7] State Council, *The Decision on the Problem of Re-education through Labour* (1957).
[8] State Council, *Supplementary Decision on Re-education through Labour* (1979).
[9] MPS, *Methods for the Implementation of Re-education through Labour* (1982).
[10] State Council, *The Methods of Sheltering for Education Offenders Who Committed the Offences of Prostitution* (1993); and *Methods of Compulsory Drug Rehabilitation.*
[11] H L Fu, "A Case for Abolishing Shelter for Examination: Juridical Review and Police Powers in China," (1994) 17 *Police Studies: The International Review of Police Development* 41.

[12] *Ibid.*

[13] *Ibid.*

[14] *Ibid.*

[15] The abolishment of SE cannot be seen from the text of the CPL, because the use of SE was never authorized by the CPL. It was a political agreement.

[16] There were serious discussions during the drafting process that police in China should have the power to make an arrest without a warrant, *i.e.* the prior authorization from the procuratorate. But this power was not given to the police. This reflects concerns on the part of senior party and government officials on the abuse of police powers in the absence of checks and balances of another governmental body.

[17] Ministry of Public Security, *Regulations on the Procedures of Investigating Criminal Cases by the Public Security Organs* (MPS Regulations) (1986), Article 74.

[18] MPS Regulations, Article 74, para. 2.

[19] MPS Regulations, Article 75, para. 1.

[20] MPS Regulations, Article 75, para. 2.

[21] Standing Committee, National People's Congress, *Postal Law of People's Republic of China* (1986).

[22] The specific procedures for seizing mail and telegrams are governed by the *Provisional Rules for Seizing Mails and Telegrams of Persons being Detained or Arrested*. The rules were made by the Supreme People's Procuratorate, the Ministry of Public Security and the Ministry of Post and Telecommunication in 1979.

[23] Article 136 states: "It shall be strictly forbidden to extort a confession by torture. Any state functionary who extorts a confession by torture shall be sentenced to a fixed-term imprisonment of not more than three years or to criminal detention. Whoever causes injury or disability to a person through corporal punishment shall be charged with the crime of assault and given a heavier penalty." The meaning of torture is not defined. In addition, Article 136 does not speak to circumstances in which confessions were obtained through threats or deceit.

[24] National People's Congress, *Supplementary Provisions of the Standing Committee of the National People's Congress Concerning the Time Limits for Handling Criminal Cases* (1984).

[25] Article 10 (offences with minor circumstances), Article 16 (deaf, mute and blind suspects), Article 17 (using excessive force in self-defence), Article 18 (committing crimes in an emergency), Article 19 (preparation for a crime), Article 21 (discontinuation of a crime), Article 24 (an accomplliance), Article 25 (a person who is compelled or induced to commit a crime).

[26] Article 15 specifies the following special circumstances:

    1) an act is obviously of minor importance, causing no serious harm, and is therefore not deemed a crime;

    2) the limitation period for criminal prosecution has expired;

    3) an exemption of criminal punishment has been granted in a special amnesty decree;

    4) the crime is to be handled only upon complaint according to *The Criminal Law*, but there has been no complaint or the complaint has been withdrawn;

    5) the defendant is deceased; or

    6) other laws or decrees provide an exemption from investigation of criminal liability.

[27] The procuratorate does not have the duty to do so previously because when a suspect is exempted, he is found guilty.

[28] Article 185. According to Article 183, an appeal or protest against a judgment should be filed within ten days from the second day of receiving it, an appeal or protest against an order should be filed within five days from the second day of receiving it.

[29] Article 28 of the CPL 1996 provides that a member of the judicial, procuratorial or investigative body shall withdraw from the case if:

    (a) he is a party or a near relative of a party to a case;

    (b) he or a near relative of his has an interest in the case;

    (c) he has served as a witness, expert witness or the defender in the current case or represented a party in an incidental civil action; or

166

(d) he has any other relations with a party to the case that could affect the impartial handling of the case.

[30] For a study of criminal defence under the 1979 CPL, see H L Fu, "The Present and Future of Criminal Defence in China," in Wang Guiguo and Wei Zhenying (eds.) *Legal Developments in China: Market Economy and Law* (Hong Kong, Sweet & Maxwell, 1996).

[31] *Ibid.*

CHAPTER 6

CIVIL LAW

Ling Bing

City University of Hong Kong

Ling Bing, Assistant Professor of Law, City University of Hong Kong. SJD candidate, LL.M. (University of Michigan); Diploma (Hague Academy of International Law); LL.B. (Peking University). Member of the PRC Bar. Formerly assistant lecturer, International Law Institute, Peking University.

Introduction

Civil law governs property relations and personal relations between **6.01** subjects of equal status. It is the basic law on social and economic activities by private parties. China, whose legal system largely follows the continental civilian model, has yet to enact a comprehensive civil code. The principles and rules of the civil law of China are primarily contained in the *General Principles of Civil Law* (GPCL) of 1986, specific statutes, administrative regulations, the Supreme People's Court opinions and other authoritative documents issued by various governmental organs.

Chinese civil law is heavily influenced by German law, The influence of German law has come either directly or through other legal systems that are influenced by German law. The Civil Code of the Republic of China closely followed German, Swiss and Japanese codes. The civil law of the People's Republic of China (PRC) has been significantly influenced by Soviet civil law which, in turn, has its roots in German law. Although the influence of the common law system has become noticeable in Chinese law in recent years, the fundamental concepts and principles of Chinese civil law originate essentially from the German paradigm.

This chapter will examine the major concepts and rules of Chinese civil law as embodied in the GPCL, its judicial interpretation, other major laws and scholarly opinion. The chapter will start with a survey of some of the fundamental concepts as well as the history of Chinese civil law. It will then cover the areas of persons, civil legal acts and

169

agency, rights over things, obligations,[1] and civil liability. Several important areas of civil law, such as family, succession, contracts, intellectual property and personal rights, are not discussed here, either because they are dealt with in other chapters of this book, or because the limitation of space does not permit their discussion here.

The Concept of Civil Law

6.02   Civil law refers to a body of various legal principles and rules governing property and personal relations between subjects of equal legal status. Every individual and organization may participate in a social relationship or transaction that is subject to civil law, if he stands on an equal legal status with the other party in that relationship. Penal, administrative and revenue relationships in which one party (the State) essentially controls and directs the conduct of the other party are thus beyond the governance of civil law. The equality in legal status of subjects distinguishes civil law from most other areas of law and it dictates the fundamental postulates of civil law.

Civil law in China is generally understood through the economic perspective. Economic activities and relationships are seen as the main "objects" regulated by civil law. The norms of civil law are largely based on the changing needs of social and economic life in a state. Wang Hanbin, chairman of the NPC Legislative Affairs Commission, stated in his Explanations on the Draft General Principles of Civil Law before the National People's Congress, "Civil law reflects socioeconomic relations, and civil law norms are the expression in a legal form of social and economic living conditions."[2] The economic functions of civil law are markedly reflected in its governance of property relations. Property relations, or economic relations, are defined as social relationships with economic contents or interests that arise from the process of production, distribution, exchange and consumption of material resources. Economic activities governed by civil law are usually carried out by subjects of equal status on a voluntary basis in the form of exchange of equivalent values. The economic relations governed by civil law are thus "horizontal", while "vertical" economic relations in which the State exercises control and discipline of economic activities in the society are governed by economic law. Civil law governance of property relations is, therefore, a major part of the functions performed by the legal system in promoting the development of a socialist market economy.

Another branch of civil law governs personal relations. Personal relations are social relationships comprising specific mental and intellectual interests that are inseparable from individual persons, such as interests in one's life, health, name, reputation, invention and creative works. The personal relations governed by civil law do not necessarily involve economic interests. Unlike property rights and interests, rights and interests in personal relations are usually not transferable to other subjects (except where the law provides otherwise). Civil law imposes civil liability on acts in breach of personal rights and thereby vindicates those basic personal rights that are enshrined in the constitution.

Historical Developments

Civil law was generally underdeveloped in ancient China. Although there were rules dealing with civil matters (land ownership, debt, lease and marriage), the major ancient codes were predominantly penal, and civil law rules were usually enforced through penal punishment. Modern codification of civil law started in 1907 when the Qing government was swamped in crises of foreign invasion and domestic changes in social and economic structure. The Draft Civil Code of the Qing Dynasty was completed in 1911 with the assistance of Japanese jurists. The draft code was never promulgated as the Qing Dynasty was overthrown in the same year. The Nationalist Government promulgated a Civil Code during 1929–1930. The Code included five books on General Principles, Obligations, Rights over Things, Family and Succession. It was based on previous drafts (including the draft Qing code) and incorporated numerous rules from the German, Swiss and Japanese codes. It introduced, for the first time in Chinese history, modern civil law concepts and rules to Chinese law. The code was abolished in 1949 together with all other Nationalist legislation by an order of the Communist Party Central Committee.

The history of the People's Republic of China has witnessed three attempts by the government to draft a comprehensive civil code. Before the catastrophic Cultural Revolution (1966–1969), the National People's Congress (NPC) made two attempts on the drafting work of a civil code, one in the 1950s and the other in the early 1960s. The pre-Cultural Revolution period saw civil law legislation primarily in sparse promulgation of specific laws and regulations such as the 1950 *Land Reform Law*, 1950 *Marriage Law* and various regulations and decrees on enterprise organizations, economic contracts, and trademark registration. The massive growth of civil law legislation in China started only in the late 1970s when the far-reaching reform of the socio-economic system began in earnest. The market-oriented economic restructuring and the development of Sino-foreign economic co-operation called for sophisticated civil law governance. The 1982 Constitution envisaged the development of civil law by empowering the NPC "to enact and amend basic laws governing criminal offences, civil affairs, the state organs and other matters" (Article 62). By 1986, a number of important laws on civil matters had been enacted that included 1979 *Sino-Foreign Joint Venture Law*, 1980 *Marriage Law*, 1981 *Economic Contract Law*, 1982 *Trademark Law*, 1984 *Patent Law*, 1985 *Law of Succession* and 1985 *Foreign Economic Contract Law*.

In late 1979, the Legislative Affairs Commission of the Standing Committee of the NPC created a working group of civil law experts to restart the process of drafting a civil code. The group drew up a fourth draft of the Civil Code in 1982 when the Legislative Affairs Commission concluded that a comprehensive civil code could not be completed in the short term and, in light of the pressing demand for legislation on civil and economic matters, it would be more advisable to work on specific laws governing civil matters. Meanwhile, it was felt necessary to pass into law a set of general principles applicable to all or most civil activities that would aid the courts and administrators in dealing with civil and economic disputes. In 1983, the Legislative Affairs Commission started preparation for the General Principles of Civil Law. The draft was initially prepared by legal scholars and government officials and underwent substantial amendment in light of the comments from the public before it was submitted to the NPC. The *General Principles of Civil Law* (GPCL)[3] was adopted on the fourth session of the Sixth National People's Congress. It was a landmark in the development of Chinese civil law and has been the most important civil law legislation in Chinese history. The GPCL, consisting of nine chapters and 156 articles, is not a Book on General Principles in a German-style civil code. While it contains provisions (such as those on persons, legal acts and agency) that would typically be included in the Book on General Principles, the GPCL contains more specific provisions that would more properly be included in the Books on Rights over Things, Obligations and Family. Although the latter type of provisions lack the kind of generality in application that is enjoyed by the former type of provisions, it is fair to say that, compared with other more specific civil law enactments, the provisions of the GPCL are "general" enough to serve as guidelines for dealing with civil disputes and to establish the foundation upon which future codification may be built up.

In January 1988, the Supreme People's Court adopted an *Opinion (for Trial Use) of the Supreme People's Court on Questions Concerning the Implementation of the General Principles of Civil Law of the People's Republic of China* (hereinafter, "the 1988 Opinion").[4] It is the most important judicial interpretation of the GPCL. For all practical purposes, the 200-section Opinion has become a supplement to the GPCL and assumed binding authority in practice.

Since the adoption of the GPCL, the legal development in China has seen the adoption of a vast number of laws and regulations in the area of civil and commercial law. The Legislative Affairs Commission is currently working on the drafting of *Contract Law* and *Property Law* which forms a crucial part of the codification process. It is foreseeable that a comprehensive civil code will eventually emerge in China on the basis of accumulating theoretical and practical experimentation of civil law in China.

Basic Principles of Chinese Civil Law

Articles 3 to 7 of the GPCL lay down several basic principles of civil law. While couched in the most abstract and generic terms, those principles are the fundamental precepts governing civil activities and serve as the basis for legislation, administration, interpretation and study of Chinese civil law. Many of those principles may seem commonplace to foreign lawyers. But with the backdrop of traditional, statist values and the command economy principles then prevailing in the PRC, these principles introduce fresh legal ideas to a nation that had been without a civil law tradition for over 4,000 years.   6.03

The Principle of Equality

In civil activities, the parties are in an equal position. (GPCL, Article 3) This provision is held to be the cardinal principle of GPCL, manifesting the essence of civil law relationships. Therefore, in civil law relationships, all civil subjects, whether citizens or legal persons, whether government agencies or individuals, whether state-owned enterprises or private firms, are all on a level playing field. Their legal rights have equal protection.

The Principle of Voluntariness

GPCL, Article 4, lays down several principles that civil activities must comply with. The principle of voluntariness holds that civil subjects shall undertake civil activities and create, modify or terminate civil law relationships in accordance with their true will. This principle is the corollary of the principle of equality, for the equality in position of the parties determines that the incidence of civil rights[5] and duties must be based on the free will of the parties. In a civil transaction, no one may impose his will on another and compel the other to act in a certain way. Civil acts that are an untrue expression of intent such as those done in the circumstance of deceit or duress are without legal effects (GPCL, Article 58).

In another sense, the principle of voluntariness is akin to the principle of party autonomy. It confers on a party the freedom to decide whether to enter into a civil transaction and what its form and contents shall be.⁶ This freedom, however, is restricted by several other principles discussed below.

The Principle of Exchange of Equivalent Values

This principle applies mainly to property transactions and is the embodiment in law of the market rule that "one gets what he pays for". It requires a civil subject to give an equivalent value to the other when the latter offers valuable property or service to him. In a civil transaction, a person normally enjoys rights and bears duties at the same time, and no one may deprive another of his lawful rights and interests without compensation. Many scholars consider that the principle does not require the exchange of *equal* values and that the principle may be derogated from by specific provisions of law and by the agreement of the parties.⁷

The Principle of Fairness

Civil activities and the resolution of civil disputes should be in conformity with the community standard of fairness and justice. Given the lack of detailed, specific civil law rules in China, the principle of fairness is particularly important for dispute resolution, as it helps remedy the want of relevant legal rules in many cases. The Chinese notion of fairness is also vague enough to be construed as being synonymous with reasonableness and equity. Thus, in a case where the true intent of a party in performing an act cannot be ascertained, the principle of fairness, it is argued, may lead to the application of the intent that a reasonable person may have in like circumstances.⁸ The principle also has direct bearing on certain specific rules in the GPCL. Therefore, civil acts should not be "obviously unfair" (GPCL, Article 59) and civil liability should be commensurate with fault.

The Principle of Good Faith

The Chinese principle of good faith is literally a principle of honesty and credibility. Civil subjects should have good intentions in carrying out civil activities. The principle of good faith requires the parties to give true expression of intent and faithfully fulfill their promises. They should avoid misrepresentation in negotiating contracts. In exercising their rights and performing their duties, they should pay due regard to the interests of others.

The Principle That the Lawful Civil Rights and Interests of Citizens and Legal Persons Are Protected by Law

The lawful civil rights and interests of citizens and legal persons are protected by law; no organization or individual may violate those rights and interests (GPCL, Article 5). The principle highlights the rights-based approach of the GPCL. The elaborate provisions in the GPCL on civil rights will lose much of their significance if the protection of those rights and interests is not elevated to the status of a basic principle of civil law. This principle is also the basis of a distinctive body of rules on civil liability in the GPCL (GPCL, ch. 6) that establishes legal remedies for the infringement of civil rights.

The Principle That Civil Activities Shall Conform with the Law and State Policy

Civil activities shall conform with the law and, in the absence of provision of law, with State policy. Law and State policy manifest paramount public interest of the State. Civil activities in violation of the law and State policy are void (GPCL, Article 58) and incur legal liability. The term "law" referred to in this principle is not limited to laws passed by the state legislature, but denotes all kinds of normative instruments adopted or approved by various State organs. Presumably, the principle refers only to mandatory rules of law, and parties may freely derogate from permissive rules of law.

The reference to "State policy" betrays the fact that the ongoing economic and social reform in China often outpaces the legislative work, and there are many areas in civil and economic activities that are, for the time, only governed by State policy. For example, the State policy on private enterprises provided the principal guidelines for private businesses before the adoption of GPCL which makes provisions for individual businesses and partnerships. The temporary legal vacuum does not mean that civil subjects may act without any constraint. They must comply with State policy which, in this sense, has quasi-legal effect.

The Principle That Civil Activities Shall Conform with Social Morality and Not Harm the Public Interest

Civil activities shall conform with social morality and shall not harm the public interest, undermine the state economic plan or disrupt the socio-economic order (GPCL, Article 7). This is a principle distinct from the preceding one. It applies to civil activities that do not violate

175

the law or state policy. Therefore, it is essentially a principle against the abuse of rights. The principle, by introducing extra-legal standards to the governance of civil activities, serves to preserve good social morality and safeguard public interest. It is corroborated by several specific rules of the GPCL. For example, civil acts that violate public interest are void (Article 58). If an enterprise engages in activities prohibited by law, causing harm to state or public interest, the legal person and its representative may be subject to civil, administrative or criminal liability (Article 49).

Persons

6.04 Civil activities are carried out by various kinds of civil subjects (persons) which are governed by different legal rules. Citizens (natural persons) and legal persons are the two basic types of civil subjects. Unincorporated organizations that are not legal persons are also important actors in civil activities. The state as a civil subject plays a special role in civil law relationships. The rules laid down in the GPCL and the 1988 Opinion are primarily concerned with citizens, legal persons and partnerships.

Citizens (Natural Persons)

Traditional civil law uses the term "natural person" to indicate individual human beings. Chapter 2 of the GPCL is entitled "Citizens (Natural Persons)", which suggests that the two concepts of citizens and natural persons are synonymous. Technically, the concept of "citizen" denotes individuals with Chinese nationality (1982 Constitution, Article 33) and is thus narrower in scope than "natural persons". However, GPCL, Article 8, para. 2, contains a national treatment clause to the effect that the provisions of the GPCL concerning citizens apply to foreigners and stateless persons within the territory of the PRC, unless the law provides otherwise. So the difference between the two concepts in practice are minimal.

Capacity to Have Civil Rights

Capacity to have civil rights (*Rechtsfähigkeit*) is the personality or standing a citizen possesses in order to assume civil rights and duties. It represents a possibility that the law confers on a citizen to enter into civil law relationships. As a juridical potentiality, the capacity of citizens to have civil rights is completely equal (GPCL, Article 10).

The content and scope of the capacity is determined by law and is free from the will of the citizen. In contrast, the acquired rights that citizens actually possess result from the exercise of their will and are not equal among citizens.

Since the capacity to have civil rights is the prerequisite for a citizen to enjoy civil rights, it is essential for the survival and dignity of every citizen. The capacity to have civil rights subsists for citizens from the time of their birth until their death (GPCL, Article 9). "Birth" indicates the total separation of a living infant from the maternal body, and the commencement of the capacity to have civil rights should be at that time. According to the Supreme People's Court, the time of birth is presumed to be that recorded in the household registration certificate and, in the absence of such certificate, that recorded in the hospital birth certificate. In the absence of both certificates, recourse may be made to other relevant evidence (1988 Opinion, s. 1).

Foetuses do not have the capacity to have civil rights, but their legitimate interests are recognized and protected by the law, especially in the case of succession (1985 Succession Law, Article 28).

The capacity to have civil rights terminates at the time of a citizen's natural or declared death.[9]

Competence to Perform Civil Acts

Competence to perform civil acts (*Handlungsfähigkeit*) is the legal capacity of a citizen to perform civil acts in order to enter into civil law relationships, exercise civil rights and fulfill civil duties. The competence to perform civil acts is linked with one's age and mental condition, and citizens do not have equal competence. While the capacity to have civil rights is a citizen's personality at law amenable to civil rights generally, the competence to perform civil acts is one's ability to engage independently in civil activities that will have effect on one's civil rights and duties specifically. That ability is not recognized by the law unless one has developed normal intelligence and is able to reasonably understand the consequences of his acts. The GPCL provides for three levels of competence that apply to different classes of citizens.

Full Competence

A citizen aged 18 or over has full competence to perform civil acts and may engage independently in civil activities (GPCL, Article 11, para. 1) A citizen with full competence has the legal capacity to perform any civil act independently. A citizen who has reached the age of 16 but not the age of 18 is deemed to have full competence, provided his principal source of support is income from his labour (GPCL, Article 11, para. 2).

The fact that a citizen aged between 16 and 18 participates in social-ized labour and supports himself with his income presumably shows that he is able to manage his affairs independently and is able to bear civil liability with his own property. The standard here is that such a citizen receives income from his own labour and maintains a living standard comparable to that prevailing in the local community (1988 Opinion, s. 2).

It should be noted that a citizen falling within GPCL, Article 11 para. 2, is only *deemed* to have full competence. His having full competence is conditional on the fact that his principal source of support is income from his labour. If that fact ceases to exist, the citizen will lose his full competence.

Limited Competence

Limited competence applies to minors above the age of 10 and citizens with mental illness. The GPCL provides that a minor aged 10 or over may only engage in civil activities which are appropriate for his age and intelligence. In other civil activities he shall be represented by his guardian or he shall participate with the consent of his guardian (GPCL, Article 12, para. 1). A person of mental illness who is unable to understand fully the nature and propriety of his own acts may only engage in civil activities which are appropriate for his state of mental health. In other civil activities he shall be represented by his guardian or he shall participate with the consent of his guardian (GPCL, Article 13, para. 2). The rules on limited competence are designed to protect the interests of those two groups of persons who, due to their youth or mental illness, are unable to properly understand and make proper judgment on sophisticated civil activities. The scope of the activities those persons are permitted to carry out independently, are based on standards laid down by the Supreme People's Court. Generally speak-ing, for a person with limited competence, whether a certain activity is "appropriate for his age and intelligence" or is "appropriate for his state of mental health" is to be determined by considering such factors as the extent to which the act relates to his own daily life, whether his mental capacity or mental condition is sufficient for him to under-stand and foresee the consequences of his activity and the amount of money the activity involves (1988 Opinion, ss. 3–4). A person with limited competence may also engage in activities that are beneficial to him without incurring onerous duties, such as the acceptance of gifts, awards and intellectual property rights.

Incompetence

Minors under the age of 10 and persons of mental illness who are unable to understand the nature and propriety of their own acts are incompetent, and shall be represented by their guardians in all civil activities (GPCL, Article 12, para. 2 and Article 13, para. 1). However, an incompetent person may still engage in activities that are purely beneficial to him, such as the acceptance of an award, donation and rewards. The validity of such acceptance is not to be challenged on the ground of the recipient's incompetence (1988 Opinion, s. 6).

For persons of mental illness, the determination of incompetence or limited competence is made through a special procedure. The GPCL provides that a person having an interest with respect to a person of mental illness may apply to the court for a declaration that the person of mental illness is incompetent or has only limited competence (GPCL, Article 19 para. 1). In hearing such an application, the court shall generally base its decision on the result of judicial psychiatric evaluation or refer to hospital medical diagnosis (1988 Opinion, s. 7). If a person is declared to be incompetent or as a person with limited competence, and he subsequently recovers from his mental illness, the court may, upon the application of such a person himself or of an interested person, declare him to be a person with limited competence or a person with full competence based on the state of his recovery (GPCL, Article 19 para. 2). The procedural aspects of this declaration process are governed by the 1991 *Civil Procedure Law*, Articles 170–173.

Guardianship

Guardianship is a civil law institution designed to supervise and pro- **6.05**
tect the lawful rights and interests of persons with incompetence or limited competence. Guardianship, on the one hand, redresses the problem of the lack of full competence of the ward and affords protection for his rights and interests. On the other hand, guardianship requires the guardian to supervise and control the conduct of the ward so as to maintain the security and stability of the society.

The GPCL provides for two types of guardians. The law contains a list of *statutory guardians* who shall serve as guardians if they are competent to do so. In case of a dispute over who shall serve as the guardian, the law authorizes certain organizations to appoint *designated guardians* for the ward.

In the Case of Minors

The parents of a minor are his guardians (GPCL, Article 16 para. 1). Where the parents of a minor are deceased or are not competent to be guardians, one of the following persons shall serve as the guardian if he is competent to do so:

(a) grandparents;
(b) elder brothers or sisters;

(c) relatives and friends with a close relationship to the minor who are willing to serve as guardians, provided the units of the minor's parents or the neighbourhood or village committee at the minor's domicile shall approve (GPCL, Article 16, para. 2).

If none of the above persons exists, the units of the minor's parents, the neighbourhood or village committee or the civil affairs department at the minor's domicile shall serve as guardian (GPCL, Article 16, para. 4).

In case of a dispute over who shall serve as the guardian, the units of the minor's parents or the neighbourhood or village committee at the minor's domicile shall make a designation among the close relatives.[10] If the designation is not accepted and an action is brought to the court, the court shall decide (GPCL, Article 16, para. 3).

In the Case of Persons of Mental Illness

For a person of mental illness who is incompetent or has limited competence, one of the following persons shall serve as the guardian:

(a) spouse;
(b) parents;
(c) adult children;
(d) other close relatives;
(e) other relatives or friends with a close relationship to the ward who are willing to serve as guardian, provided the unit of the ward or the neighbourhood or village committee at his domicile shall approve (GPCL, Article 17, para. 1).

If none of the above persons exists, the units of the ward, the neighbourhood or village committee or the civil affairs department at the ward's domicile shall serve as guardian (GPCL, Article 17, para. 3).

In case of a dispute over who shall serve as the guardian, the units of the ward or the neighbourhood or village committee at the ward's domicile shall make a designation among the close relatives. If the designation is not accepted and an action is brought to the court, the court shall decide (GPCL, Article 17, para. 2).

The Duties of a Guardian

A guardian is the statutory agent of his ward (GPCL, Article 14). He is charged with the responsibility of protecting the person and property as well as other lawful rights and interests of his ward. In particular, a guardian may not dispose of the property of the ward save in the interest of the ward (GPCL, Article 18, para. 1). The Supreme People's Court specifies the duties of a guardian as follows:

(a) protecting the health of the ward;

   (b) caring for the ward in his daily life;

   (c) managing and protecting the property of the ward;

   (d) representing the ward in civil activities;

   (e) supervising and educating the ward; and

   (f) representing the ward in litigation when the lawful rights of the ward are infringed or where the ward has a dispute with another person (1988 Opinion, s. 10).

A guardian who has failed to perform his duties or has infringed the ward's lawful rights or interests shall bear civil liability. He shall pay compensation if he causes damage to the ward's property (GPCL, Article 18, para. 3). The persons and units enumerated in GPCL, Articles 16–17 who have qualification for guardianship may petition to the court, demanding that the guardian bear civil liability or the guardianship be revoked (1988 Opinion, s. 20).

Legal Persons

People engage in civil activities not only as individuals, but also in the form of organizations. The need for the law to endow separate personality to organizations was felt as early as in the Roman period. The German Civil Code lays down detailed rules on *juristiche Person* in Articles 21–89, which had significant influence over the law of other countries. The Chinese GPCL defines a legal person as an organization that has the capacity to have civil rights and the competence to perform civil acts and that independently enjoys civil rights and assume civil duties according to law (GPCL, Article 36). With an independent personality at law, a legal person enjoys its own rights, assumes its own duties, and bears its own liability for its acts that are in breach of civil duties. The founders and members of a legal person are not liable for the debts of the legal person.   **6.06**

   The GPCL divides legal persons into

   (a) enterprise legal persons and

   (b) governmental organs, institutions[11] and social organizations[12] as legal persons.

Enterprise legal persons engage in profit-making business activities. They are subject to more stringent regulations of law. Governmental organs, institutions and social organizations are engaged in non-profit activities. They are mostly funded out of the state budget.

Establishment of a Legal Person

An organization must satisfy four conditions in order to qualify as a legal person (GPCL, Article 37):

(a) It is established in accordance with law. The status of legal person is not inherent in an organization that satisfies all the other conditions for legal personality. That personality is endowed on an organization only through a legally-prescribed formal procedure. Although for some special types of organizations (such as governmental organs), the law may expressly waive the formal requirement of registration, the exception does not apply to most other organizations.

(b) It possesses the necessary property or funds. The "necessary property or funds" are the material basis for the independent conduct of civil activities by the legal person. The law may require enterprise legal persons to have minimum amount of assets for their establishment,[13] while no parallel requirements apply to governmental organs, institutions and social organizations as legal persons. The liability of a legal person is limited to the property it owns or operates. GPCL, Article 48, provides that a state-owned enterprise legal person shall bear liability with the assets that the state has authorized it to operate while an enterprise under collective ownership, and an enterprise with foreign investment shall bear liability with the assets that they own.

(c) It possesses its own name, organizational structure and premises. A legal person shall have a name to distinguish itself from other organizations and an enterprise legal person has the exclusive right to use and transfer its name (GPCL, Article 99). The "organizational structure" of a legal person includes not only its official organ (discussed below) that represents the legal person externally, but also its internal functionary departments as well as its branch offices. The "premises" of a legal person refer to the place where the legal person conducts its operations. Premises are different from the "domicile" of a legal person which is the place where its main administrative office is located (GPCL, Article 39). A legal person may have more than one premises, but may only have one domicile.

(d) It is able to assume civil duties independently. The civil law duties and liabilities of a legal person are those of its own, and the founders and members of a legal person are not bound to pay off the debts owed by the legal person. The independent assumption of civil duties requires the legal person to possess the necessary property and funds to carry out its activities. It does not mean that a legal person shall discharge all the civil duties it undertakes, but that it shall perform its civil duties with all of its own assets.

The establishment of an enterprise legal person is governed by various laws and regulations, depending on the specific type of the legal person.[14] Generally, in order to acquire the status of a legal person, an enterprise shall meet the capital requirements prescribed by the State, prepare a charter and satisfy the above-mentioned conditions for a legal person. Upon the approval and registration by the relevant government authorities, the enterprise will receive a business licence and become a legal person (GPCL, Article 41). In contrast, a governmental organ with independent funds acquires the status of legal person from the time when it is established and there is no requirement for registration (GPCL, Article 50, para. 1). The acquisition of the status of legal person by an institution or social organization is subject to specific regulations which may dispense with the registration requirement, in which case the institution or social organization becomes a legal person from the time when it is established. Otherwise, it becomes a legal person upon approval and registration (GPCL, Article 50, para. 2).[15]

Capacity and Competence of a Legal Person

A legal person has the capacity to have civil rights and the competence to perform civil acts. Both its capacity and competence commence when it is established and cease when it is terminated (GPCL, Article 36). The capacity of a legal person to have civil rights is limited by its objects. As different legal persons have different natures and scope of business, the capacity to have civil rights of legal persons are necessarily unequal. The GPCL expressly provides that an enterprise legal person shall conduct business within its registered scope of business (GPCL, Article 42). The same principle is echoed in other laws and regulations.[16] Acts by a legal person outside its scope of business are in breach of the relevant legal rules and thus void by virtue of GPCL, (Article 5, para. 1, subpara. 5).

The scope of a legal person's competence to perform civil acts is co-extensive with its capacity to have civil rights. They are both limited by the relevant laws and regulations as well as the legal person's registered scope of business. The competence of a legal person is exercised by its *official organ* (*jiguan* in Chinese). An official organ is a component part of a legal person, and its external acts in the name of the legal person are the acts of the legal person itself. The official organ represents the institutional will of the legal person and a legal person acquires rights and performs duties through its official organ.

The official organ is different from an agent of the legal person. Although an agent also performs civil legal acts with third parties in the name of the legal person, it is a separate entity from the principal and has its own independent will. The official organ of a legal person, requires no specific authorization for its acts to bind the legal person. Whether the agent's acts are binding on the legal person depends on the authorization by the principal and the relevant rules of agency law.

The GPCL does not directly provide for the official organ of a legal person. GPCL, Article 43, provides that an enterprise legal person bears civil liability in regard to business activities of its statutory representative and other personnel. The statutory representative of a legal person is the person with management responsibility who, according to law or its charter, exercises authority on behalf of a legal person (GPCL, Article 38). "Other personnel" probably refer to other officers of a legal person who are generally authorized to act for the legal person by law or by its charter. Ordinary staff members may only act for the legal person as its agents. The statutory representative and "other personnel" constitute the official organ of a legal person.

Although a legal person shall be liable for the acts of its statutory representative, the corporate veil of the legal person may be lifted where the legal person engages in certain illegal activities. GPCL, Article 49, provides that the statutory representative of an enterprise legal person shall be subject to administrative and criminal liability in the following events:

(a) the legal person has conducted illegal business operations beyond its registered scope of business;

(b) the legal person has wilfully failed to disclose true information or has committed deception in dealing with the tax or registration authorities;

(c) the legal person has withdrawn funds or concealed property to evade performance of an obligation;

(d) the legal person has disposed of property without authorization after being wound up, dissolved or declared bankrupt;

(e) the legal person has failed to apply for registration and make public announcements in a timely manner at the time of its changes or termination, resulting in significant loss to interested parties;

(f) the legal person has engaged in any other activities prohibited by law, resulting in harm to state interests or public interest.

Termination of a Legal Person

An enterprise legal person terminates in the following events (GPCL, Article 45):

(a) If it is dissolved according to the law. The government may decide to close down an enterprise if the enterprise has engaged in illegal activities or if a State-owned enterprise has been poorly operated with significant losses. Certain national corporations, banks and insurance companies are established under

184

statutory provisions, and their dissolution should also be in accordance with the legal provisions.

(b) If it is wound up. The situations falling within this paragraph are where the members of the enterprise resolve to wind up the enterprise, where the purpose of the enterprise has been achieved, or where the enterprise is wound up in accordance with the provisions of its charter.

(c) If it is declared bankrupt in accordance with the law. When an enterprise is unable to repay its debts that are due, upon the application by its creditors or itself, the court may declare the enterprise bankrupt in accordance with the 1991 *Civil Procedure Law* or the 1986 *Enterprise Bankruptcy Law*.

(d) Other causes. An enterprise will terminate if, for example, it is merged or divided.

Upon the termination of an enterprise legal person, a liquidation organization shall be set up to carry out the liquidation (GPCL, Article 47). In the cases of winding-up and dissolution, the liquidation organization shall be set up by the enterprise itself or the competent government agency. If the enterprise is declared bankrupt, the liquidation organization shall be established by the court (1988 Opinion, s. 59). The liquidation organization will wind up the business operations of the enterprise, assess its assets and liabilities and settle its credits and debts (see 1988 Opinion, s. 60). The liquidation organization shall also cancel the registration of the enterprise and give public notice thereof (GPCL, Article 46).

Partnerships

The GPCL distinguishes between partnerships of individuals and part-   **6.07**
nerships of legal persons. The latter type of partnership is governed by the rules on "joint operation" (GPCL, Article 52). However, the more specific rules on partnerships of individuals apply, *mutatis mutandis*, to partnerships of legal persons as well.

A partnership of individuals is an organization of two or more citizens who, in accordance with an agreement, contribute funds, property, skills and the like, and operate in partnership and work jointly in a business (GPCL, Article 30). Although a partnership may have its own institutional structure and manage its own assets and liabilities, it is not a legal person, and the partners assume unlimited liability for the partnership's debts. A partnership is based on the consensus of the expressions of intent by the partners that is embodied in the partnership agreement. This consensus arises from the personal trust that the partners place on each other and forms the foundation of the partnership agreement and the legal rules on partnerships.

Partnership Agreement

The GPCL, Article 31, requires that the partners shall draw up a
written agreement providing for such matters as the shares of capital
contribution, the distribution of profits, the responsibility for debts,
and the joining in, withdrawal from and termination of the partnership. The requirement of a written agreement was relaxed by the
Supreme People's Court in its 1988 Opinion which states that, where
the parties do not have a written partnership agreement and have not
obtained the certification and registration from the administrative
department for industry and commerce but have satisfied all the other
conditions for a partnership, the court may consider the relationship
among the parties as a partnership if it is proved by the testimony of at
least two persons not directly interested in the partnership that the
oral agreement exists (1988 Opinion, s. 50).

The partnership agreement shall provide for the capital contribution
by the partners which may be in the form of money, tangible property,
technology, labour, and the like. The distribution of profits and responsibility for debts are usually in accordance with the proportion of
capital contributions by the partners, although the parties may agree
otherwise.

The provisions on the joining in, withdrawal from and termination
of the partnership are an important part of the partnership agreement.
The Supreme People's Court set forth certain rules on those matters
that may, however, be modified by the parties' agreement. Under these
permissive rules, the addition of partners to an existing partnership
shall be consented to by all the partners (1988 Opinion, s. 51); the
withdrawal of a partner is permitted in principle, but where such
withdrawal results in loss to the other partners, the withdrawing
partner shall be liable for compensation, the amount of which shall be
determined in light of such factors as the cause and justification for
withdrawal and the degree of fault on both sides (1988 Opinion, s. 52);
upon the termination of a partnership, if the paid-in shares of capital
contribution of all partners are equal, the disposal of the partnership's
assets shall be decided on by the majority of the partners, or, if the
paid-in capital contributions of the partners are not equal, by the
partners whose capital contributions together exceed 50 per cent of the
total paid-in capital of the partnership, but the rights and interests of
the other partners shall be protected (1988 Opinion, s. 55).

Operation of a Partnership

Business activities of a partnership shall be decided on jointly by all the
partners, and the partners have the right to conduct and supervise

these activities (GPCL, Article 34, para. 1). A partnership is a business organization in which every member contributes to its capital and is entitled to participate in its decision-making. But not all decisions have to be made by consensus, and the partnership agreement may adopt the majority rule for the decision-making in the partnership. Also, some partners may make capital contribution to a partnership and agree to share in the partnership's profits, without participating in its management or work (1988 Opinion, s. 46).

The business activities may be jointly carried out by all the partners, but are more typically carried out by one or more partners that are appointed to take charge of the business management. The GPCL, Article 34, para. 2, provides that a partnership may elect a managing partner, and liabilities from business activities of the managing partner and of all other personnel are borne by all the partners. The powers of a managing partner are defined by the partnership agreement or a decision of the partners.

The GPCL divides property of a partnership into two types. "Property contributed by the partners" shall be managed and used in common by the partners, while "property resulting from the operation of the partnership" shall be co-owned by the partners (GPCL, Article 32). This suggests that "property contributed by the partners" may not be co-owned by the partners. When making capital contribution, a partner may decide to assign his rights over things that are short of ownership (e.g., the right to possess or the right to use) to the partnership while retaining the ownership of the property.[17] The legal significance of dividing the two types of property seems relevant to the division of property upon withdrawal from the partnership by a partner. The property to be divided at that time shall include property that the partners contributed when the partnership was formed, assets acquired during the operation of the partnership, and other rights and liabilities arising during the term of the partnership. In principle, the original property that a withdrawing partner contributed at the time he joined the partnership shall be returned to him. If it is difficult to return the original property, it may be returned in money (1988 Opinion, s. 54).

Liabilities of a Partnership

Debts of a partnership shall be satisfied from the individual property of each partner in accordance with his share of capital contribution or the provisions of the partnership agreement (GPCL, Article 35, para. 1). The partners have unlimited liability for the debts of the partnership, and their liabilities are not limited to their capital contribution. The individual property of a partner refers usually to his own property, but may also include family property where the partner used the property co-owned by his family members for his capital contribution to the partnership (1988 Opinion, s. 57),

All partners are jointly liable for the debts of the partnership unless the law provides otherwise. A partner who has satisfied the debt of the partnership in excess of his share is entitled to reimbursement from the other partners (GPCL, Article 35 para. 2). Although internally each partner is only liable for such part of the partnership's debts as is stipulated in the partnership agreement, every partner is externally liable for the whole debts of the partnership *vis-à-vis* the creditors. The sharing of the debts of a partnership is usually in accordance with the provisions in the partnership agreement or with each partner's share of capital contribution. If the partnership agreement fails to make such provisions or specify the capital shares, the debts of the partnership shall be shared in accordance with the ratio by which the partners actually share the profits of the partnership. A partner whose fault results in a loss for the partnership, however, shall bear a greater share of the liability, according to the degree of his fault (1988 Opinion, s. 47).

If a partnership sustains losses in its business operations, a partner who withdrew from the partnership and did not share, or reasonably share, in the partnership's debts as agreed to at the time of his withdrawal, shall be liable for the debts of that partnership. Even if a withdrawing partner has paid his share of the partnership's debts, he shall remain jointly liable for debts of the partnership which arose during the time when he was a partner (1988 Opinion, s. 53).

Civil Legal Acts and Agency

6.08 Civil legal acts and agency are two of the most abstract concepts in the GPCL that originate from the German Civil Code. The theory and rules on civil legal act provide for the basic governance of contracts and unilateral acts, while the law of agency plays a critical role in regulating civil and commercial activities.

Civil Legal Acts

The concept of the civil legal act is based upon the German concept of *Rechtsgeschaeft* which is usually translated as juristic act or legal transaction. The GPCL adds a modifier "civil" in order to distinguish it from acts in other legal contexts (such as administrative acts and procedural acts). But the modifier brings no substantial change to its original meaning.

Concept

A civil legal act is defined as a lawful act by which citizens or legal persons establish, modify, or terminate civil rights and duties (GPCL, Article 54). A civil legal act is, in the first place, a legal event that gives rise to the creation, alteration, or dissolution of civil law relationships. It is the exercise of human will that has civil law consequences. This distinguishes a civil legal act from an incident[18] as a legal event. The person performing a civil legal act has as his purpose to bring about certain legal consequences, and that purpose shapes his intent which is expressed in a certain way in his act. The essence of a civil legal act is the *expression (or declaration) of intent* by the actor that produces the legal effects *intended by the actor*. This distinguishes a civil legal act from other civil acts.

The expression of intent is at the heart of a civil legal act.[19] The formation of expression of intent may starts from the emergence of a *motive* that arises out of certain perceived needs, and moves to the creation of an *intent* that compels the actor to effect the act. It is consummated in the *expression of intent* that commands an act with legal consequences. Generally speaking, the motive of an act is of no legal significance (although in some cases an act may become void because of its illegal motive). The two essential elements of expression of intent are the intent itself and the way of expressing that intent.

Civil legal acts may be classified in several ways. Firstly, civil legal acts may be divided into unilateral acts, bilateral acts and multilateral acts. Unilateral acts require the expression of intent by only one party, such as the making of will and the appointment of an agent. Bilateral acts, such as contracts, require two parties to express their intent that is consensual. Multilateral acts, such as the establishment of a partnership and the incorporation of a company, require consensual expression of intent by more than two parties. Civil legal acts may also be classified into gratuitous acts (such as donation) and non-gratuitous acts (such as sale), or formal acts that require special forms (such as an economic contract or the making of a will) and informal acts that may take any form.

Constitutive Elements

A civil legal act shall satisfy the following conditions (GPCL, Article 55):

The Person Performing the Act has the Appropriate Competence

As discussed earlier, incompetent persons may not perform any civil legal acts. Persons with limited competence may only perform acts that are appropriate for their age, intelligence or state of mental health. Acts performed by a person beyond his competence are void.

The Real Intent is Expressed

A civil legal act will bring about the intended legal consequences only if the real intent of the actor is expressed in the act. If the expression of intent fails to reflect the real intent of the person who makes the expression of intent (the declarant), the act will not qualify as a civil legal act, and the legal consequences caused thereby will usually not be the same as the actor has intended. Expression of intent is real if:

(a) the intent arises from the free exercise of will by the declarant, without extrinsic interference from another; and

(b) the intent thus expressed accords with the intent held by the declarant in good faith.

One may not avoid the legal consequences of his expression of intent simply by alleging that he did not have the intent at the time it was expressed, or that the intent expressed was not the best course of action he should have taken. Only in certain unusual situations that are specifically defined by the law may a party plead expression of false intent to void a civil act.

Chinese civil law divides expression of false intent into that which is caused by one or both parties intentionally and that which is caused unintentionally. Intentional expression of false intent includes expression of false intent due to deceit or duress by another, or due to another's taking advantage of the declarant's distress. It also includes cases where the parties maliciously conspire to injure the interests of another, and where an act is performed in a lawful form to conceal an unlawful purpose. Intentional expression of false intent results in void acts.[20] Unintentional expression of false intent includes expression of false intent due to a significant misconception of the declarant or an incorrect transmission by another.[21] Unintentional expression of false intent results in a voidable act.

There is no Violation of the Law or the Public Interest

A civil legal act is, by its nature, a lawful act. The compliance with mandatory legal norms is a precondition for the intended effects of the act to be recognized by law. Civil acts that violate the mandatory norms of law or the public interest are void; so are acts that violate the mandatory economic plan of the State. This requirement is closely linked with the basic principles of civil law set forth in GPCL, Articles 3–7 (see discussions above). It is often argued, therefore, that a civil legal act shall not only conform with the law and the public interest, but also with state policy and social morality. In fact, the application of those basic principles, particularly the principle of fairness, to civil legal acts leads to another express requirement that a civil legal act shall not be "obviously unfair". Those constraints serve to restrict the autonomy of private parties and are seen as necessary control by the state of the socio-economic activities in China.

The GPCL requires no special form for a civil legal act. Civil legal acts may be in oral or written form, or in any other form, provided that where the law requires a specific form, the provisions of the law shall be followed (GPCL, Article 56). Chinese contract laws normally require economic contracts to be in written form.[22] The law may also require specific acts to be not only in writing, but also notarized by a notary public, or certified by the state administration for industry and commerce, or registered with or approved by specific state authorities. Certain civil legal acts may take the form of tacit conduct or pure silence. For example, on the expiration of a lease, if the lessee continues to pay, and the lessor continues to accept, the rent, the parties, by their conduct, perform a civil legal act of extending the lease. In its 1988 Opinion, the Supreme People's Court states the rule that where one party claims a civil right against another and the latter fails to express his intent orally or in writing but his conduct indicates acceptance, the claim shall be deemed accepted; forbearance may be deemed as expression of intent only if the law so provides or the parties so agree (1988 Opinion, s. 66).

Void Civil Acts

Acts that fail to satisfy the conditions for civil legal acts are ordinary **6.09** "civil acts". The following civil acts are void, and they have no effects *ab initio* (GPCL, Article 58):

(i) An Act Performed by an Incompetent Person, or an Act Performed by a Person with Limited Competence Who According to Law May Not Independently Perform Such an Act

An incompetent person may not perform any civil legal acts and shall be represented by his guardian in all civil activities. Exceptionally, an incompetent person may perform "petty acts" that he is customarily allowed to perform and that are closely connected with his daily life, such as the payment of bus fares or the purchase of a small quantity of sweets. An incompetent person may also perform acts that are purely beneficial to him, such as the acceptance of awards, donations and rewards.

A person with limited competence may perform acts that are appropriate for his age, intelligence or his state of mental health. As for other acts, he shall either be represented by his guardian, or he may perform those acts with the consent of his guardian. The consent of the guardian may be general, but if the person with limited competence causes loss to another, the guardian shall be liable (GPCL, Article 133).

Incompetence and limited competence are attributed to persons of young age or of mental illness (including mental retardation), but an adult person of normal mental health may also at times fall into a state where he is not conscious of the nature and propriety of his acts. Civil acts performed by a person in a state of unconsciousness shall be deemed void (1988 Opinion, s. 67, para. 2). Such acts are void not because the person lacks the necessary competence to perform the acts, but because the intent expressed thereby is not real.

(ii) An Act Performed under Circumstances Where One Party, by Means of Deceit, Induces the Other Party to Act Contrary to his Real Intent

Deceit is an act whereby one party wilfully misrepresents facts or deliberately conceals facts from another party and thereby induces the latter to make a mistaken expression of intent (1988 Opinion, s. 68). A civil act performed due to deceit is void because there is no expression of real intent. The expression of intent is false in that another party improperly induces the declarant to express an intent which he would not express but for the deceit, and that the declarant, in expressing his intent, is prevented from exercising his will freely and voluntarily.

Deceit involves either a wilful misrepresentation of facts, or a deliberate non-disclosure of facts which one is under a legal, contractual or customary duty to disclose. Deceit in this sense must be intentional, *i.e.*, the deceiving party purposefully induces the declarant to give a false expression of intent. As a result, the declarant makes a mistaken expression of intent because of the deceit.

(iii) An Act Performed under Circumstances Where One Party, by Means of Duress, Induces the Other Party to Act Contrary to his Real Intent

Duress is an act whereby a person forces another to make an expression of intent contrary to his true will by threatening harm to such things as the life, health, honour, reputation or property of a citizen or his relatives, or threatening harm to such things as the honour, reputation or property of a legal person (1988 Opinion, s. 69). Expression of intent under duress is one made under improper pressure that often has a terrifying effect on the declarant, the declarant being prevented from freely exercising his will. The lack of expression of real intent causes such an act to be void.

To establish an operative duress, the kinds of threat involved must be unlawful. If both the means and the purpose of the threat are lawful, the threat is not a duress even though it has a terrifying effect on the declarant, and an act performed in such circumstances is not void by virtue of the threat.[23]

(iv) An Act Performed under Circumstances Where One Party, by Taking Advantage of the Other Party's Distress, Causes the Other Party to Act Contrary to his Real Intent

Taking advantage of one's distress is an act whereby a party, in order to secure an unjust benefit, takes advantage of another party's distress to force the other party to make an expression of intent that is contrary to his true will, thereby severely damaging his interests (1988 Opinion, s. 70). Traditional civil law associates taking advantage of one's distress with an act being obviously unfair and requires the establishment of both elements in order to void an act.[24] The GPCL delinks the two concepts and makes them separate grounds for voiding a civil act. An act performed due to another party's taking advantage of the actor's distress is void because the expression of intent is not real. In contrast, an act that is obviously unfair is voidable because the content (not the expression of intent) of the act violates the legal principle of fairness.

Taking advantage of one's distress differs from duress in that distress in which a declarant finds himself is not caused by the other party's threat or other conduct, but is caused by a natural incident or the act of a third party.

(v) An Act That Uses a Lawful Form to Conceal an Illegal Purpose

An act falling within category (ii), (iii) or (iv) above is void because the actor makes false expression of intent that is caused by an intentional act of another party. In contrast, an act that uses a lawful form to conceal an illegal purpose involves false expression of intent that is intentionally made by both parties. It may happen that both parties to an act conceal their real purpose and intentionally express false intent in their act. Their real purpose may be lawful, such as, for example, A intends to give a sum of money to B as a gift, but A and B allege that the transfer of money is in payment for a fictional debt. The real purpose may also be unlawful. For example, A gives gold to B purportedly as a gift and B gives money to A purportedly as another gift. The two acts of donation conceal the real purpose of private sale of gold which violates state regulations. In theory, an act involving intentional expression of false intent by both parties is void, regardless of the lawfulness of the parties' real purpose. The GPCL explicitly provides that an act in lawful form but for an illegal purpose is void.

(vi) An Act That Involves Maliciously Conspiring to Injure the Interests of the State, of a Collective, or of a Third Party

Acts involving malicious conspiracy to injure the interests of the State, a collective or a third party are void not by reason of its possibly illegal content, but by reason of its defective expression of intent. Like an act in lawful form but for an illegal purpose, an act involving malicious conspiracy is also one that involves intentional expression of false intent by both parties. But in the case of an act involving malicious conspiracy, the false expression of intent is made by one party (A) and the agent of the other party (B). It is between party A and the agent of party B that a malicious conspiracy occurs which injures the interest of party B, the principal (who may be the State, a collective or a private person). For example, the agent of a buyer may agree to buy low-quality goods in return for a kick-back. The expression of intent made by the conspiring parties does not accord with the real intent of the party on whose behalf the agent acts, and such an act is therefore void.

(vii) An Act That Violates the Law or the Public Interest and an Economic Contract that Violates the State Mandatory Plan

If the content of an act violates the mandatory rules of law or the public interest, the act is void and will not bring about its intended legal consequences. The significance of State mandatory plan has decreased with the ongoing market-oriented reform, but in certain areas (for example, the production of strategic goods) the State mandatory plan remains an important part of government regulation of the economy. The rule that economic contracts violating the State mandatory plan are void is merely a specific extension of the broader principle that a civil legal act shall not violate the law or the public interest.

Voidable Civil Acts

6.10   The concept of voidable acts are literally called "modifiable or revocable civil acts". in GPCL. A party may request the court or an arbitral tribunal to modify or rescind the following civil acts (GPCL, Article 59):

(i) An Act Where the Person Performing the Act was under a Significant Misconception as to the Contents of the Act

A significant misconception exists where a person performing the act misapprehends the nature of the act, the identity of the other party, or the kind, quality, specification, and quantity of the subject matter, so that the consequences of the act are contrary to his true intent, thereby resulting in significant loss (1988 Opinion, s. 71). In an act involving a significant misconception, a party unintentionally makes a false expression of intent, and the act is thus voidable. A significant misconception is a mistaken understanding of the content of the act, not a mistake in the formation of the motive of the act (such as a miscalculation of the potential profits of the transaction). The Supreme People's Court interpretation enumerates (not exhaustively) several aspects of the act as to which a significant misconception may typically take place, and requires that a significant misconception must result in actual or potential "significant loss" to the party performing the act.

(ii) An Act That is Obviously Unfair

An act is obviously unfair if one party exploits his advantageous position or another party's inexperience in such a way as to violate flagrantly the principles of fairness and of exchange of equivalent values (1988 Opinion, s. 72). Under traditional civil law, an obviously unfair act is voidable only if the act is caused by one party's taking advantage of another party's distress. The GPCL treats the two concepts separately, and declares an obviously unfair act voidable, regardless of the cause of the act. Therefore, an obviously unfair act is voidable not because of any defective expression of intent, but because of its improper content.

The reference by the Supreme People's Court to the principles of fairness and of exchange of equivalent values in GPCL, Article 4, does not lend much help to the comprehension of the seemingly general and ambiguous concept of "obviously unfair". This rule, no doubt, leaves much latitude to the court in applying subjective moral standards to civil cases. Several points may be discussed on this provision. Firstly, in considering whether an act is obviously unfair, the court should examine whether the act confers excessively favourable rights on one party while imposing excessively onerous duties on the other in violation of the principle of exchange of equivalent values. The relevant laws, state policies and customs should be examined to determine whether the benefits and loss of the parties are proper.[25] Secondly, the provision is particularly applicable to cases where the parties have unequal bargaining powers, as the Supreme People's Court stresses the exploitation by one party of his advantageous position or of another party's inexperience. This probably makes the provision not applicable to arm's length transactions. It seems particularly applicable to consumer and employment transactions. Thirdly, the fairness of the act should be weighed under the general circumstances existing at the time the act comes into effect. If a contract is not "obviously unfair" at the time it is concluded, but only becomes so subsequently in the course of its performance, it is not voidable under the "obviously unfair act" rule.[26]

Legal Consequences of Void and Voidable Acts

Void civil acts have no legal effects from the time they occur (GPCL, Article 58, para. 2). Those acts are void automatically, and neither a declaration by a party nor a decision by the court is necessary. But in practice a party or any other person (including the government) may request the court to confirm that an act is void.

Voidable acts may be either rescinded or modified. A rescinded act has no legal effects from the time when it occurred (GPCL, Article 59, para. 2). For some acts (particularly those involving significant misconceptions), modification may be more desirable to the parties as they may wish to carry through the transactions. If a party requests modification of a voidable act, the court shall grant modification; if the party requests rescission, the court may grant either modification or rescission, depending on the circumstances (1988 Opinion, s. 73, para. 1).

The right of rescission is vested only in a party to the voidable act, not in a third party. Although the GPCL provides that rescission (and modification) shall be effected through a request to the court or an arbitral tribunal, some scholars contend that the rescission may also be effected by one party giving notice to the other party.[27] Others argue that whether a significant misconception exists and whether an act is obviously unfair are questions that can only be definitively answered by the court, and no party should be allowed to unilaterally rescind a civil act.[28] A voidable act is valid before it is rescinded or modified, and a request for rescission or modification shall be made to the court within one year after the act is performed (1988 Opinion, s. 73, para. 2). Modification of a voidable act requires the agreement between the parties; failing such agreement, the modification can only be ordered by the court or an arbitral tribunal.

After a civil act is confirmed to be void or is rescinded, no further performance of the act is necessary, and certain steps shall be taken to restore the *status quo ante*. Under GPCL, Article 61, three types of legal consequences may ensue. Firstly, a party shall return property acquired as a result of the act to the party who suffered the loss. Secondly, if one party was at fault in causing the act to become void, he shall compensate the other party for the loss caused thereby; if both parties were at fault, each shall bear appropriate liability. Thirdly, in the case of the parties maliciously conspiring and performing acts harmful to the interests of the state, a collective or a third party, property acquired by them shall be recovered and turned over to the state or the collective or be returned to the third party.

Agency

6.11   Agency is one of the most sophisticated concepts developed by the German Civil Code and adopted by many civil law countries. The law of agency was almost non-existent in China until the GPCL laid down elaborate rules on agency which are discussed below.

Concept

Agency is a set of legal relationships whereby a person (agent) performs civil legal acts in the name of another person (principal) within the scope of his authority and the legal effects of the acts operate directly on the principal. Citizens and legal persons may perform civil legal acts through agents. An agent performs civil legal acts in the name of the principal within the limits of the agent's authority, and the principal shall bear responsibility for acts performed by the agent on his behalf (GPCL, Article 63, paras. 1–2). An agency relationship involves the internal relationship between the agent and the principal and the external relationships between the agent and the third party and between the principal and the third party. As between the agent and the third party, the agent must perform a civil legal act in the name of his principal; otherwise, the legal effects of the act will not directly operate on the principal. In other words, the so-called "undisclosed agency" in which the agent performs an act in his own name, without notifying the third party that he is in fact acting on behalf of another person, is not recognized as an agency relationship. In such a transaction, there has to be a transfer of the obligation from the agent to the principal before the principal may directly demand performance from the third party.

In practice, the acts that an agent may perform on behalf of his principal are not limited to civil legal acts. He may simply make expression of intent that is short of a civil legal act. For example, he may make an advertisement or make an offer to a third party on behalf of his principal. He may also perform acts (such as administrative acts) that have civil law consequences but are not civil legal acts. For example, he may apply for a business licence or file a civil lawsuit on behalf of his principal. Although the GPCL only provides that a person may perform civil legal acts through agents, there is no denying among Chinese scholars that the rules of agency in the GPCL may apply, *mutatis mutandis*, to other agency relationships not involving civil legal acts.

Civil legal acts which by law or by agreement between the parties concerned must be performed by a person himself shall not be performed by an agent (GPCL, Article 63, para. 3). For example, marriage registration shall be effected by the couple personally (1980 *Marriage Law*, Article 7), and an employment contract may require the employee to render his services by himself. If the person entrusts such an act to an agent and fails to perform the act personally, the agent's act is void (1988 Opinion, s. 78).

The GPCL divides agency into appointed agency, statutory agency and designated agency (GPCL, Article 64, para. 1). Statutory agency is established by the operation of law, and mainly refers to the guardian acting as an agent for persons of incompetence or persons of limited competence. Designated agency is a special type of statutory agency, and refers to the relationship between a person of incompetence or limited incompetence and his guardian who is designated by the court or other organizations according to the relevant provisions of the law.[29]

Appointed agency is established by a specific act of appointment by the principal that entrusts certain civil legal acts to an agent. It is the most common type of agency, and the rules of agency in GPCL primarily govern this type of agency.

Authority of an Agent

When a principal appoints an agent, he confers on the agent specific authority to perform civil legal acts on his behalf. The act of appointment itself must satisfy all the conditions for a civil legal act. Appointment is a unilateral act. As such, an appointment does not require the acceptance by the agent or a third party to be effective. When the appointment is validly made, the agent acquires the authority. In practice, however, an appointment is typically made and accepted in a contract of mandate.

An appointment may be in written as well as oral form, save that the law may specifically require the use of a written form. The document of appointment (power of attorney) shall set forth the name of the agent, the subject matter of the agency, the scope and duration of the agency and be signed or sealed by the principal (GPCL, Article 65, paras. 1 and 2).

If the scope of authority in a power of attorney is unclear, the principal and the agent shall bear joint liability toward a third party (GPCL, Article 65, para. 3). This provision seemingly does not apply to appointment in oral form, and difficulties may arise in practice where the delegation of authority is clear in oral form, but is unclearly written in the power of attorney.

In exercising his authority, an agent shall act in the interests of the principal. In the case of appointed agency, this rule requires the agent to follow the principal's intention, whereas in the case of statutory agency and designated agency, it means that the agent's acts should in fact be beneficial to the principal. An agent shall not enter into a transaction in the name of the principal with himself or with another person of whom he is also the agent (1993 *Economic Contract Law*, Article 7, para. 1, s. 3). If an agent conspires with a third party to the detriment of the principal's interests, the agent and the third party shall bear joint liability (GPCL, Article 66, para. 3).

Agency without Authority

Agency without authority refers to a person performing a civil legal act in the name of another without the relevant authority as an agent. The actor may not have any authority from the beginning, or may be exceeding his authority, or may be acting as an agent after the agency has been terminated. In those circumstances, the principal may ratify the act, and the act, upon ratification, operates directly on the principal. As for an unratified act, the person performing the act shall bear the consequences (GPCL, Article 66, para. 1). Ratification may be express or implied. The third party participating in the act may also request the principal to indicate whether he intends to ratify the act. He may also rescind the act before the principal ratifies the act.

If the acts of the principal lead a *bona fide* third party into believing that an agent has the authority to perform a certain act, the act thus performed by the agent will be binding on the principal even though the agent has no actual authority. This rule of so-called "agency by estoppel" is not expressly provided for in the GPCL, but is widely supported by scholars.[30] GPCL, Article 66, para. 1, provides for one of the situations of agency by estoppel, stating that if a person knows that another person is performing a civil act in his name and does not object, he is deemed to have consented.

Agency by estoppel only applies to a *bona fide* third party. If a third party, knowing that an agent performing a civil act is acting without authority, continues to perform the act with the agent, thereby causing loss to the principal, the third party and the agent shall bear joint liability (GPCL, Article 66, para. 4).

Rights over Things

The rules concerning rights over things, or property law, are an impor-   **6.12** tant part of civil law that govern the various relationships involved in the control of things by persons. The GPCL does not have a separate part on rights over things as civil codes in most other countries do, nor does it even mention the concept of rights over things. It does contain rules on "ownership and property rights related to ownership" in the first section of Chapter 5 on civil rights. The GPCL rules on rights over things are not complete, and there has been extensive discussions among Chinese scholars on the subject. New legislative developments have also seen the adoption of the *Security Law* in 1995 and the ongoing drafting of the *Property Law*. This section will examine the GPCL provisions on property rights, while taking into account relevant laws and scholarly opinion that have emerged since the adoption of the GPCL.

Rights over Things in General

Concept

Rights over things (or rights *in rem*) is one of the major categories of civil rights protected by civil law. It is the rights enjoyed by persons to the direct control and management of things to the exclusion of interference by others. No civil or economic activities may be carried out without the operation of rights over things. The right of ownership, in particular, lies at the foundation of economic transactions of all kinds.

Rights over things differ from rights arising from obligations. Rights over things are enjoyed by specific persons and are claimed against the whole world. In other words, rights over things create legal duties for indeterminate persons; every person other than the one holding the rights is bound to refrain from acts that may interfere with the dominion over the things enjoyed by the possessor of the rights. Rights over things are absolute rights, whereas rights arising from obligations are relative rights with specific obligors and obligees. Rights over things have specific things as their object, while the object of obligations is acts.

Rights over things are expressed in the direct control, management and utilization of things. Their realization does not require active performance by others, whereas the fulfilment of obligations requires the performance of the obligors. Rights over things are exclusive in that two persons may not maintain two identical rights *in rem* over the same thing. A right *in rem* also goes with the thing, and the holder of the right may claim his right against anyone who is in possession of the thing.

Things

Things in the civil law sense are material beings that have economic values. Intangible things, such as heat or electricity, exist physically and are things in this sense. Intellectual efforts, emotional manifestations (such as honour and reputation) and legal right as such are not things until they are materialized in physical medium.

Things may be classified in several ways, and different kinds of things may be governed by different legal rules. Firstly, things may be divided into immovables and movables. Immovables include, among others, land, buildings and trees that either cannot be moved or can only be moved with substantial decrease of their economic value. Movables are things that may be moved without substantial change in their economic value. The division between immovables and movables has important legal significance. Special formality and procedures apply to transactions in immovables. The 1986 *Land Administration Law* and the 1994 *Urban Housing Administration Law* are among the most important laws that govern such transactions. Whether a thing is a movable or an immovable will also significantly affect the jurisdiction and applicable law in a dispute.[31]

Secondly, things may be divided into specific things that cannot be replaced by other things in a particular transaction and generic things that are replaceable. Whether a thing is specific or generic affects the passing of risk and the passing of title in a sales contract.

Thirdly, things may be divided into divisible things and indivisible things. This distinction is relevant in the division of property under co-ownership.

Fourthly, things may be divided into original things and fruits. Fruits are benefits that are produced from original things. Fruits include natural fruits that are produced from the original thing in the natural course (for example, offspring of animals and fruits grown from trees) and legal fruits that are produced by operation of law (interest from a loan and rent from a house). Except where the law or the agreement of the parties provides otherwise, the owner of an original thing owns its fruits, and the transfer of an original thing transfers its fruits.

Fifthly, things may be divided into principal things and accessories. Principal things may exist and have their utility independently while accessories must be component parts of the principal thing to facilitate its utilization. For example, doors and windows of a house are accessories while the house is the principal thing. The ownership over the principal thing extends to the accessories, except where the law or the agreement of the parties provides otherwise.

Types of Rights over Things

The GPCL and civil law theory divides rights over things into rights in one's own property (*jus in re propria*) and rights in another's property (*jus in re aliena*). Rights in one's own property is ownership. Rights in another's property may be further divided into usufructuary rights and security rights. Usufructuary rights entitle one to use and benefit from another's property, while security rights are created to secure the performance of an obligation.

Under current Chinese law, usufructuary rights include the right of State-owned enterprises to operate State property, the right to use, the right of a contractor to operate (*chengbao jingyingquan* in Chinese), the right of *dien* and the right to exploit minerals. Security rights include mortgage, pledge and lien.

Ownership

6.13 Ownership is the fundamental right over things from which other types of rights *in rem* stem. It entitles one to the most complete control over a thing. It is also an exclusive right in the sense that the existence of ownership over a thing excludes other claims to ownership over the same thing.

Concept

Ownership is the right in accordance with law to possess, use, benefit from, and dispose of a thing (GPCL, Article 71). An owner, therefore, has four powers in regard to his property. To possess is to take physical control of the thing. Possession may be lawfully transferred to a person not owning the property (such as a lessor), or may be illegally converted by another, in which case different remedies may lie, depending on whether or not the illegal possession is in good faith.[32] To use is to take advantage of the utility of the thing. An owner can also transfer the right to sue to another. For example, the State may allow State-owned units and collective units to use State-owned natural resources (GPCL, Article 81, para. 1). To benefit from a thing is to gain economic interest through the possession, use and transfer of the thing. The owner of an original thing owns the fruits. To dispose of a thing is to factually or legally change the condition or existence of the thing, such as consumption, transfer, placing of security rights and abandonment. The four powers inherent in ownership may be separated and transferred to others, while the owner maintains the right to ownership.

The acquisition of ownership may not violate the law (GPCL, Article 72, para. 1). There are two basic means of acquiring ownership — original acquisition and derivative acquisition. Original acquisition is not based on another's existing ownership, but is established by the creation of new things or by the operation of law. It includes production, gaining of fruits, confiscation by the State, accretion and the acquisition of unclaimed property.

Accretion is the combination of things owned by different persons or the contribution of work by a person to a thing owned by another that results in a new thing. Scholarly opinion and judicial practice hold that the new thing resulting from accretion will usually be under co-ownership. But if one component part of the new thing may be considered as the principal thing, the owner of the principal thing may acquire the ownership of the new thing, but shall compensate the owners of other parts. The interpretation by the Supreme People's Court states that if a non-owner uses the property of another person and makes an addition to the property, the problem of ownership over the new thing shall be solved according to the agreement of the parties.

Failing such an agreement, the addition may be ordered dismantled if it is possible; where dismantling is impossible, the addition may be given to the owner of the property upon his payment of the value of the addition. If the addition or its dismantling results in a loss to the owner, the person who made the addition shall pay for the loss (1988 Opinion, s. 86).

Under the civil laws of some countries, the finder of unclaimed property may acquire its ownership.[33] Unclaimed property (*bona vacantia*) includes lost things that are recovered, buried or concealed things that are found, and flotsam. Under the GPCL, buried or concealed things that are found and whose owner is unknown, shall go to the State. Lost things that are recovered, flotsam, or stray domestic animals shall be returned to the owner, but any expenses incurred shall be reimbursed by the owner (GPCL, Article 79).

Derivative acquisition of ownership is the acquisition of ownership from an existing owner through a legal event. It includes sale, donation, barter, succession and other means.

Where property is acquired through contract or other lawful means, ownership is transferred at the time the property is delivered, unless the agreement of the parties provides otherwise (GPCL, Article 72, para. 2). If the property has been delivered but the parties agreed to attach a condition to the transfer of the ownership of the property, the ownership of the property is transferred when the attached condition is fulfilled (1988 Opinion, s. 84).

Ownership terminates when:

(a) the ownership is transferred,
(b) the thing is extinguished,
(c) the owner is dead or wound up,
(d) the ownership is renounced, or
(e) the ownership is terminated by the state in accordance with the law (for example, by expropriation).

State Ownership, Collective Ownership and Individual Ownership

The GPCL has separate provisions for state ownership, collective ownership and individual ownership.

The State owns things on behalf of the whole people. The State owns an extremely extensive range of things, some of which may only be owned by the State. For example, only the State is the owner of mineral resources and national defence apparatus, and only the State may operate railways, telecommunications, and radio and television broadcasting. But the State normally does not directly possess, use and manage its property. Usually, the State bestows its property to enterprises and institutions, and the latter has the right to operate the State-owned property.

Collective ownership differs from State ownership in that property under collective ownership is separately owned by individual collective units, while State-owned property is owned by the State as a single entity. Collective units include rural agricultural co-operatives, rural enterprises, retail co-operatives and credit co-operatives, They may own a wide range of things, some of which cannot be owned by natural persons (for example, land, forest, and mountains). But each individual collective unit can only own property according to its nature and scope of business.

Individual ownership has seen dramatic development in the recent years in China, particularly with the emergence of private enterprises. An individual citizen may own his lawful income, house, savings, articles for daily use, cultural objects, books and reference materials, trees, livestock, and means of production which citizens may own within the limits of the law, as well as other lawful property. Individual ownership is protected by the law (GPCL, Article 75).

Co-ownership

Property may be co-owned by two or more persons (GPCL, Article 78, para. 1) Co-ownership is a special form of ownership that involves more than two persons as co-owners. Internally, each owner has certain rights and duties with regard to the property. Externally, the owners are treated as a single subject that owns the property, and they will enter into property transactions with others as one subject.

Co-ownership is divided into co-ownership by shares and joint co-ownership. A co-owner by shares enjoys a portion of the rights and assumes a portion of the duties in accordance with his own share., whereas joint co-owners enjoy rights and assume duties with respect to the whole property (GPCL, Article 78, para. 2) Whether a particular co-ownership is joint co-ownership or co-ownership by shares depends on the relevant provisions of the law and the intent of the parties. In case of a dispute among co-owners as to the nature of their co-ownership, the co-ownership is presumed to be a joint co-ownership (1988 Opinion, s. 88).

Co-ownership by shares typically occurs in partnerships and other co-operative business activities. In exercising their rights over the property, the co-owners should seek consensus, and, failing consensus, they may act according to the intention of those with a majority share. To balance the interests of the majority against those of the minority co-owners, the GPCL provides that each co-owner by shares is entitled to ask that his share of the property be separated or transferred, but if his share is to be sold, the other co-owners have a priority right to purchase his share on equivalent terms (GPCL, Article 79, para. 3).

Joint co-ownership mostly occurs in the domestic context. Co-ownership between spouses and co-ownership among family members is usually joint co-ownership. But partnerships and business ventures may also adopt joint ownership. Each joint co-owner enjoys the same rights and has the same duties towards the property, and the disposal of the property by some co-owners without the consent of the other co-owners is generally deemed void, but the rights and interests of a *bona fide* third party shall be protected. The co-owners who disposed of the property without the consent of the other co-owners shall compensate the other co-owners for any loss sustained (1988 Opinion, s. 89). Upon the termination of a joint co-ownership, the property shall be divided in accordance with the agreement of the co-owners. In absence of such an agreement, the property shall be divided in accordance with the principle of equal division, taking into account such factors as the contribution of the co-owners to the property and the actual needs of each co-owner. The division of property co-owned by spouses shall be governed by the *Marriage Law* (1988 Opinion, s. 90). After division, if a co-owner wishes to sell his shares in the property, other co-owners have priority rights to purchase the property to be sold, if the portion of the property to be sold and the portion of the property obtained by other co-owners belong to one complete unit or are used as a set (1988 Opinion, s. 92).

Usufructuary Rights

Usufructuary rights are the rights to use and benefit from things owned **6.14** by another person. They constitute a limitation on the ownership over the property concerned. As a type of rights *in rem*, they can be claimed against the whole world, including the owner.

Right of State-Owned Enterprises to Operate State Property

The right of State-owned enterprises to operate State property is the right of State-owned enterprises to possess, use, benefit from, and dispose of State-owned property given by the State. The GPCL, Article 82, provides that the right enjoyed by a State-owned enterprise to operate according to law State property given by the State is protected by law.

Under the centrally planned economy, the government, for a long period of time, directly involved itself in the operation of State-owned enterprises and commanded their daily business activities. One of the crucial parts of China's economic reform since the late 1970s has been the separation of State ownership rights and the right to operate State property. When an enterprise is granted the right to operate State property, it may independently conduct business operations which even the State may not interfere with. The nature and scope of such rights are determined by the law (for example, 1988 *State-Owned Industrial Enterprise Law*), and the State exercises regulatory and supervisory authority over the enterprises.

The right to operate State property includes the rights to possess, use, benefit from, and dispose of the State-owned property. It is still short of ownership, as the State reserves according to law the right to benefit from and dispose of the property.

Right to Use

Under the GPCL, the right to use mainly refers to the right to use and benefit from the land and natural resources owned by the State or collective units. State-owned land may be used in accordance with law by State-owned units or collective units. The State protects the rights of such units to use and benefit from the land. The units which use the land are under a duty to manage, protect, and make reasonable use of it (GPCL, Article 80, para. 1). A similar provision applies to State-owned natural resources (GPCL, Article 81, para. 1).

Right of a Contractor to Operate

The right of a contractor to operate is the right under the law or a contract to possess, use, and benefit from property owned by another person. The GPCL provides that the right of a citizen or collective to operate land owned by a collective or the State under contract is protected by law. The rights and duties of both contracting parties are determined by the contract in accordance with the law (GPCL, Article 80, para. 2). A similar provision applies to natural resources owned by the State or a collective (GPCL, Article 81 para. 3). In practice, operation under contract by citizens or collective units have extended also to enterprises owned by the State or collective units. They are not mentioned in the GPCL.

Right of Dien

The right of *dien* is the right of one (the *dien*-holder) to possess, use and benefit from an immovable owned by another (the *dien*-maker) upon the payment of a price. *Dien* is a unique Chinese concept that has

206

existed in China for centuries. It is not mentioned in the GPCL, but is generally recognized in judicial practice.[34] *Dien* is somewhat similar to a pledge of real property in other countries. But, unlike a pledge, which is a security right, *dien* is a usufructuary right, whose creation is not conditional on a principal obligation. *Dien* is usually created under a contract whereby the *dien*-holder pays a price to the owner and takes possession of the immovable. In practice, the amount of the *dien* price is usually fifty to eighty per cent of the sale price of the property. The payment of the price is not a loan for which the right of *dien* provides a security, but a consideration for the right of *dien* itself, *i.e.*, the right to possess, use and benefit from the property within the term of *dien*.

During the term of *dien* (usually 30 years or less), the *dien*-holder may possess, use and benefit from the property and does not have to pay any rent. He may transfer his right of *dien* to another, and has a priority right to purchase the property if the owner intends to sell it. Upon the expiry of the term of *dien*, the *dien*-maker may redeem the property by repaying the original *dien* price to the *dien*-holder. If the *dien*-holder fails to redeem the property, the *dien*-holder may acquire the ownership of the property in the following ways. Firstly, the contract establishing the right of *dien* may provide that the *dien*-holder shall acquire the ownership of the property if the *dien*-maker fails to redeem it upon the expiry of the term. Secondly, where there is no such provision, the *dien*-holder shall acquire the ownership of the property upon the expiry of ten years after the expiration of the term of *dien*. Thirdly, if the contract fails to provide for a term of *dien*, the *dien*-holder shall acquire the ownership of the property upon the expiry of thirty years after the commencement of the right of *dien*.[35]

Right to Exploit Minerals

The right to exploit minerals is the right of citizens and legal persons to exploit or excavate within the limits of law State-owned mineral resources. The GPCL, Article 81, para. 2, provides that State-owned mineral resources may be exploited by State-owned units, collective units and citizens according to law, and lawful exploitation rights are protected by the State. The right to exploit minerals is usually granted to a citizen or legal person through an application procedure. It is primarily governed by the 1986 *Mineral Resources Law*.

Security Rights

Security rights are rights *in rem* created in the property owned by   **6.15**
another in order to secure the performance of an obligation. The property on which the security rights are imposed may be owned by the

obligor or by a third party. Unlike other rights over things which accentuate the rights to possess, use, benefit from and dispose of the property, a security right is auxiliary to the principal obligation and centres on the monetary value of the property rather than its substantive utility. The existence of a security right is dependent on the existence of the principal obligation.

The GPCL contains succinct provisions on pledge and lien in the section on obligations. The 1995 *Security Law* (SL) sets forth elaborate rules on mortgage, pledge, lien, guaranty and earnest money. Guaranty and earnest money are special forms of obligations and will be dealt with later (see para. 6.17).

Mortgage

To secure the performance of an obligation, the obligee (mortgagee) may acquire the right of mortgage in the property which is owned by the obligor or a third party (mortgagor), and the possession of the property is not transferred thereby. The mortgagee has a priority right to obtain compensation from either the value of the property that is converted to money, or the proceeds from the auction or sale of the property (SL, Article 33). The Chinese term for "mortgage" here is *diya*, the same term used in GPCL, Article 89, to denote "pledge". It should be noted that the term *diya* in the GPCL is used in a broad sense that denotes both mortgage and pledge,[36] while the term *diya* used in the *Security Law* is used in a restrictive sense that denotes a security right that does not involve the transfer of the possession of the property concerned.

Another possible source of confusion is that "mortgage" as used in the *Security Law* may apply not only to immovables, but to movables as well. Property that may be subject to mortgage includes, among others, right to use land, houses, machinery, means of transportation, and other property which is owned by the mortgagor or of which the mortgagor has the right to dispose (SL, Article 34).

Mortgage shall be established by a written contract between the mortgagor and the mortgagee (SL, Article 38). The obligation secured by the mortgage shall not exceed the value of the mortgaged property (SL, Article 35). Mortgage over the following property *shall* be registered, and the mortgage contract becomes effective upon registration: right to use land, urban houses and buildings of rural enterprises, forest trees, means of transportation, and equipment or other movables of an enterprise (SL, Article 42). Mortgage over other property *may* be registered and the contract becomes effective when it is signed (SL, Article 43, para. 1). Without registration, a mortgage cannot be invoked against a third party (SL, Article 43, para. 2).

Under the *Security Law*, Article 49, the mortgagor may transfer the mortgaged property that is registered to a third party, only if he notifies the mortgagee and informs the transferee of the existence of the mortgage.[37] The proceeds from the transfer shall be used to repay the secured debt owed to the mortgagee even if it is not yet due, or to be lodged (deposited) with a third party appointed by the mortgagee. If the price of the transfer is obviously lower than the value of the property, the mortgagee may demand the mortgagor to provide additional security.

When the period for the performance of the obligation has expired and the mortgagee has not been paid, he may enter into an agreement with the mortgagor whereby the mortgaged property is converted into money, or the mortgagee is to be paid from the proceeds of the auction or sale of the property. If no agreement can be reached, the mortgagee may bring a lawsuit to the court (SL, Article 53). If the property is subject to more than two mortgage rights, registered mortgage rights have priority over unregistered ones. Among registered mortgage rights, those that are registered earlier have priority over those that are registered later. Among unregistered mortgage rights, the priority goes to those whose mortgage contracts become effective earlier. Mortgagees of the same order of priority shall be paid in the proportion of their rights (SL, Article 54).

Pledge

Pledge includes pledge of movables and pledge of rights. Pledge of movables is to transfer the possession of movables from an obligor or a third party (pledgor) to the obligee (pledgee), using the movables to secure the performance of an obligation. When the obligor fails to perform the obligation, the pledgee has a priority right to obtain compensation from either the value of the property that is converted to money, or the proceeds from the auction or sale of the property (SL, Article 63). Pledge of rights applies to:

(a) bills of exchange, checks, promissory notes, bonds, deposit receipts, warehouse receipts and bills of lading;
(b) shares and stocks;
(c) trademark rights, patent rights and property rights comprised in copyright; and
(d) other rights (SL, Article 75).

A pledgor of rights shall deliver the relevant documents of rights to the pledgee (SL, Article 76). The rules governing pledge of movables also apply to pledge of rights, unless the law provides otherwise (SL, Article 81).

Pledge is established by a written contract, and the contract becomes effective when the pledged property is delivered to the pledgee

(SL, Article 64). The pledgee may receive the fruits of the pledged property, unless the pledge contract provides otherwise (SL, Article 68). He also has the duty to take proper care of the property (SL, Article 69). When the period for the performance of the obligation expires and the obligor has performed the obligation, the pledged property shall be returned to the pledgor; but if by that time the obligee has not been paid, he may enter into an agreement with the pledgor to value the pledged property and credit it against the obligation, or he may auction or sell the property according to law (SL, Article 71).

Lien

Lien is a right of an obligee, who has taken possession of the obligor's movables in accordance with a contract, to retain the possession of the property when the obligor fails to perform a contractual obligation within the agreed time. The lien entitles the obligee to a priority right to obtain compensation from either the value of the property that is converted to money, or the proceeds from the auction or sale of the property (SL, Article 82). The *Security Law*, Article 84, provides that an obligee has the right of lien in regard to storage contracts, transportation contracts and contracts for processing goods. The right of lien may be waived under the contract.

Where the property under lien is divisible, the obligee may only retain part of the property whose value is equivalent to that of the obligation (SL, Article 85). The obligee has the duty to take proper care of the property under lien (SL, Article 86). The contract should provide that after the obligee exercises the right of lien, the obligor shall perform the obligation within no less than two months. Where there is no such provision in the contract, the obligee, after exercising the right of lien, shall set a time limit for at least two months and notify the obligor to perform within the period. If the obligor fails to perform the obligation within the period, the obligee may enter into an agreement with the pledgor to value the property under lien and credit it against the obligation, or he may auction or sell the property according to law (SL, Article 87).

Adjacent Relationships

In exercising their rights to possess, use, benefit from and dispose of property, the owners (or possessors or users) of adjacent immovables often have to afford mutual convenience and accept limitations on their rights. The rights and duties arising from the adjacent relationships are governed by the law or the agreement between the parties. The GPCL lays down the general principle governing adjacent relations. In the case of adjacent immovables, all the parties concerned shall, in the spirit of facilitating production, making life more convenient, harmony and mutual assistance, and fairness and reasonableness, properly conduct adjacent relations such as those with respect to water supply, drainage, passage, ventilation, and lighting. A person who causes an obstruction or damage with respect to his adjacent property shall cease any infringement, eliminate any obstruction, and pay damages (GPCL, Article 83). The specific rules governing adjacent relationships are detailed in 1988 Opinion, ss. 97–103.

Obligations

The law of obligations in a civil law system covers such major areas of **6.16** law as contracts, torts and restitution in a common law jurisdiction. The GPCL sets forth general rules on obligations as part of Chapter 5 on civil rights. These rules are primarily concerned with contractual obligations, while the rules on torts are largely contained in Chapter 6 on civil liability. As the law of contract is dealt with elsewhere in this book, and the rules on torts will be discussed in the next section on civil liability, this section will focus on the general concepts and principles on obligations.

Obligations in General

Concept

An obligation is a relationship of specific rights and duties between specific persons, arising either from terms of a contract or from a provision of law. The essence of an obligation is that the obligee has the right to demand that the obligor performs his duty according to the terms of the contract or the provision of law (GPCL, Article 84).

Obligation is a major kind of civil law relationship. Its subjects are specific parties *of* an obligee (or creditor) who enjoys a right under the obligation and an obligor (or debtor) who bears the duty under the obligation. Parties to a contractual obligation often both enjoy rights and bear duties, and they may be obligor and obligee at the same time. The object of an obligation is prestation, *i.e.*, the act (or forbearance) that the obligee has the right to demand the obligor to perform. The contents of an obligation are the rights and duties arising therefrom. The rights of an obligee are primarily the right to claim prestation and the right to accept prestation. The duty of an obligor is the performance of specific acts (or forbearance) as required by the contract or the law.

Rights arising from an obligation are different from rights over things in several respects. Firstly, rights over things are absolute rights while rights arising from an obligation are relative rights. An absolute right is enjoyed by a specific person against an indeterminate group of persons who have the duty not to interfere with the right. Rights over things may be claimed against the whole world. In contrast, a relative right is enjoyed by a specific person against another specific person and usually cannot be claimed against a third party. Secondly, rights over things are the rights to govern and control things that may be effected without another's acts. Rights arising from an obligation are the rights to claim performance, and can only be effected through the acts of the obligor. Thirdly, rights over things have things as the object, while rights arising from an obligation have acts as the object. Fourthly, the establishment of rights over things is governed by mandatory rules of law, while the rights arising from an obligation, particularly contractual rights, may be established by the free will of the parties.

Sources

Obligations may be created by several legal events. They include contracts, torts, unjust enrichment, management of affairs without mandate and others.

Contracts

A contract is defined as an agreement whereby parties establish, modify, or terminate civil relationships (GPCL, Article 85). The parties to a contract have rights and duties under the contract which form the content of the obligation of contract. Contract is a bilateral civil legal act, and it is the most important source of obligations. The law of obligations in China is primarily law of contracts. An obligation based on contract distinguishes itself from other obligations in that the binding effect of the obligation is derived from an agreement between the parties, and the content of the obligations is largely determined by the will of the parties.

Contract law of China is embodied in the GPCL and numerous laws and regulations on specific types of contracts. In the GPCL, the law of contract is contained in three parts:

(a) the provisions on civil legal acts;
(b) the provisions on obligations; and
(c) the provisions on civil liability.

As contract law is discussed in detail in another chapter of this book, we will only examine the provisions on obligations generally, most of which apply to contracts, except where the special law may provide otherwise.

Torts

A tort is an act of interference with the property or person of another and for which the actor shall bear civil liability. Upon the occurrence of a tortious act, the tortfeasor has the duty to compensate the injured party for his loss, while the injured party has the right to claim such compensation. The obligation of tort stems from a wrongful act that violates the law or public interest. The content of an *obligation* of tort is akin to the *civil liability* for the tort; the duty of the obligor (the tortfeasor) is to pay damages or discharge other forms of civil liability, and the right of the obligee (the injured party) is to claim the performance of the duty. The rights and duties under an obligation of tort are determined by the law, not the intention of the parties.

The provisions on torts in the GPCL are contained in the chapter on civil liability. While the provisions on obligations primarily apply to contracts, certain rules on obligations in general (such as the rules on joint obligations and on transfer of obligations) apply also to torts.

Unjust Enrichment

Unjust enrichment is an event in which one party obtains benefit without contractual or legal basis, resulting in loss to another party. Unfair enrichment gives rise to an obligation whereby the party obtaining the benefit (the obligor) has the duty to return the benefit to the person who suffered the los (the obligee) (GPCL, Article 92).

Unfair enrichment may be caused in various ways:

(a) by the act of the party who suffers loss (for example, the buyer mistakenly paying more than the contract price to the seller);
(b) by the act of the party who obtains benefit (a person using another's property without permission);
(c) by the act of a third party (a carrier delivering the buyer's goods to a wrong person); or
(d) by a natural incident (A's fish entering into B's pond).

Whatever the cause may be, unjust enrichment is obtained without lawful grounds, and the party obtaining the benefit has the duty to return the benefit. The benefit includes the original property plus any fruits. Any other benefit gained through making use of the improper benefit shall be confiscated after a deduction for the value of labour and for management expenses (1988 Opinion, s. 131).

Management of Affairs without Mandate

Management of affairs without mandate (*negotiorum gestio*) refers to one party, without legal or contractual duties, providing care or services to avoid harm to an interest of another party. Management of affairs without mandate gives rise to an obligation whereby the party managing another's affairs (the obligee) has the right to demand that the party who receives the benefit (the obligor) reimburse him for the necessary expenses incurred (GPCL, Article 93).

Management of affairs without mandate is an incidental act (*shishi xingwei* in Chinese), with the actor not intending the legal consequences that result from the act. But the party managing another's affairs shall have the intention to avoid harm to an interest of another party. Management of affairs without mandate is socially desirable and should be rewarded through an obligation based thereon. The obligor shall reimburse the obligee for the necessary expenses incurred which shall include expenses directly resulting from the care or service and actual losses sustained as a result of the care and service (1988 Opinion, s. 132).

Other Events

Apart from the above four major sources, special obligations may arise from certain unilateral acts. For example, an obligation may result from a person's act that causes a contract to be void or voidable, resulting in loss to another,[38] or from an act of necessity (see discussion below).

Types of Obligations

Obligations may be classified in several ways. According to source of obligations, obligations may be divided into contract obligation, tort obligation, obligation of unjust enrichment, obligation of management of affairs without mandate and other obligations.

According to the number of persons that are parties to an obligation, obligations are divided into unitary obligation (both the obligor and the obligee comprise one person) and plural obligations (the obligor and/or the obligee comprise more than one person). Plural obligations may be further divided into obligations by shares and joint obligations.

Obligation by shares has more than one person as obligor (or obligee), each of whom bears the duty (or enjoys the rights) according to his fixed share (GPCL, Article 86). Each obligor has only to perform his part of the duty and may not be required to perform other obligors' duties. Also, each obligee may only enjoy his share of the rights, and may not exercise other obligees' rights. An obligation by share is, in effect, an assemblage of several obligations that arise from the same source over the same, divisible subject matter.

Joint obligation is created by the provisions of law or the agreement of the parties. In a joint obligation, each obligee may demand that the obligor perform the duty; each obligor with a joint duty is obliged to satisfy the entire duty under the obligation; the person who performs the duty has a right to demand that any other joint obligor reimburse him in the amount of the share for which the joint obligor was obligated (GPCL, Article 87). Joint obligation is designed to protect the interests of the obligee who is enabled to claim performance against one of the obligors who is the most capable of performance. The obligation is, in effect, secured by the total property of all the obligors. Joint obligation is created by the provisions of the law[39] or the agreement of the parties.

Performance

It is the obligor's duty to perform an obligation, *i.e.* to effect certain acts (or forbearance) in accordance with the requirements of the obligation. Parties to a contract should perform the contract in strict conformity with the terms of the contract; any deviation constitutes a breach for which the obligor shall bear civil liability. The performance of obligation should follow the principle of good faith.[40] **6.17**

Obligation should normally be performed by the obligor to the obligee. In some situations, a third party may perform the obligation in place of the obligor, or accept performance in place of the obligee. This amounts to a transfer of obligation, and the relevant legal rules are discussed below.

For a contract obligation, the subject matter and the requirements for performance are stipulated in the contract, and the subject matter as delivered, whether goods, services, or money, should meet the requirements set forth in the contract. If the terms of a contract are not clear, and cannot be determined from the content of related provisions of the contract, the rules prescribed in GPCL, Article 88, shall apply:

(a) If the quality requirements are not clear, performance shall be according to the state standard; where there is no State standard, according to the usual standard;
(b) If the time for performance is not clear, an obligor may perform his duty to the obligee at any time, and an obligee may demand the obligor to perform the duty at any time, but in both situations a party shall afford the other party the time necessary to prepare for performance or acceptance thereof;
(c) If the place of performance is not clear, payment of money shall be made at the location of the payee; other obligations shall be performed at the location of the obligor;
(d) If the price provision is not clear, performance shall be according to the State price; if there is no State price, performance shall be made with reference to the market price or the price of similar products or to standard remuneration for similar services.

An obligor's failure to perform the obligation consists in non-performance (including impossibility of performance and repudiation), defective performance and delayed performance, all of which give rise to civil liability, except where the law may provide for justifications.

Security of Performance

Performance of obligation may be secured in several ways. The GPCL, Article 89, sets forth four means of securing performance of an obligation: guaranty, pledge, earnest money and lien. Security of performance of obligations is now governed by the 1995 *Security Law*. Pledge (now divided into mortgage and pledge) and lien are security rights imposed on the property of the obligor or a third party. They are discussed in the section on rights over things above. This section will examine guaranty and earnest money.

Guaranty

Guaranty is an act whereby the guarantor and the obligor agree that the guarantor shall perform the obligation or bear the liability as agreed if the obligor fails to perform the obligation (SL, Article 6). The *Security Law* permits legal persons, other organizations and citizens who are financially able to perform the obligor's obligation to act as a guarantor (SL, Article 7), but prohibits governmental organs, institutions engaging in public interest activities, social organizations, and subsidiary and functionary departments of an enterprise legal person from acting as guarantor (SL, Articles 8–10).

Guaranty, which shall be established through a written contract (SL, Article 13), are divided into two kinds: general guaranty and joint liability guaranty (SL, Article 16). With certain exceptions, a general guarantor has the right to refuse to perform his duty before the dispute over the principal contract has been litigated or arbitrated and the obligee has failed to perform the obligation after enforcement measures are imposed on his property (SL, Article 17). A joint liability guarantor undertakes joint liability with the obligor. If the obligor fails to perform the obligation when the period for such performance under the principal contract has expired, the obligee may demand the joint liability guarantor to perform his duty (SL, Article 18).

During the term of the guaranty, the guaranty shall not be affected if the obligee assigns his rights to another person, unless the contract provides otherwise (SL, Article 22). But the guarantor's written consent is required if the obligee allows the obligor to transfer his duties; the guarantor has no duty in regard to the transferred part of the obligation as to which he gives no consent (SL, Article 23). The guarantor's written consent is also required if the obligor and the obligee agree to vary the principal contract; without the guarantor's consent, he shall bear no duty as a guarantor (SL, Article 24). The guarantor has the right to claim compensation from the obligor after he has performed his duty as a guarantor (SL, Article 31).

Earnest Money

Earnest money is a sum of money that a party agrees to pay to the other in order to secure the performance of the obligation. After the obligee performs the obligation, the earnest money shall be deducted from the price or returned. Where the payer of the earnest money fails to perform the agreed obligation, he shall forfeit his right to reclaim the earnest money. Where the payee of the earnest money fails to perform the agreed obligation, he shall return twice the amount of the earnest money (SL, Article 89).

The earnest money shall be stipulated in a written contract, which should also specify the time limit for the payment of the earnest money (SL, Article 90). The amount of the earnest money is to be agreed upon by the parties, but shall not exceed twenty per cent of the value of the subject matter of the principal contract (SL, Article 91).

Transfer and Termination

Transfer of Obligations

Transfer of an obligation is the change in the subjects of the obligation, **6.18** without affecting the content of the obligation. It includes assignment of rights, delegation of duties and general transfer.

Assignment of Rights

Assignment of rights is the transfer of rights arising from an obligation from the obligee to a third party. Assignment of rights is conditional on the assignability of rights. The parties may agree that certain rights enjoyed by the obligee may not be assigned to a third party. The nature of certain rights as well as the law and public policy may also restrict the assignability of certain rights. For example, rights involving personal trust usually cannot be assigned while rights under a contract requiring governmental approval may not be assigned without governmental approval.

The assignment of rights is usually effected through a contract between the obligee (assignor) and a third party (assignee). The assignment requires the consent of the obligor, and the assignor shall not profit from the assignment (GPCL, Article 91).

Delegation of Duties

Delegation of duties is the transfer of duties arising from an obligation from the obligor to a third party. After the duties are delegated, the third party will perform the duties in place of the obligor. Delegation of duties is subject to the delegability of the duties. The delegation of duties is usually effected through a contract between the obligor and the third party. Since who will be the obligor to performs the obligation has significant impact on the interest of the obligee, the delegation requires the obligee's consent.

If only part of the duty is delegated to a third party, the original obligation is then turned into a plural obligation. The obligor and the third party should agree in their contract whether they will bear liability by shares or joint liability.

General Transfer

General transfer is the transfer of both rights and duties of a party to a third party according to law or the agreement of the parties. One party to a contract may agree with a third party to transfer all his rights and duties under the contract to the third party. General transfer may also occur by operation of law. For example, where an enterprise legal person is divided or merged, all of its rights and duties shall be enjoyed and borne by the legal person or persons resulting from the change (GPCL, Article 44).

Termination of Obligations

Termination of obligation is the extinction of obligation, bringing to an end all the rights and duties thereunder. Termination of an obligation may result in no obligation between the parties, or new obligation between the same parties, or new obligation between a party and a third party or between third parties. The main ways of terminating obligations are as follows:

Performance

Performance by the obligor of all the duties under an obligation terminates the obligation. It is the normal way of concluding an obligation.

Set-Off

Set-off is the discharge of obligations between two parties who are bound to each other by obligations with similar objects and whose performance is all due. Set-off is actually a special form of performance. Where the parties owe to each other obligations that demand similar prestation and that are all due, the obligations may set off against each other. Set-off should not violate the law or the agreement of the parties.

Lodgment

When an obligation is due, but the obligor is unable to perform the obligation because the obligee refuse to accept the performance without proper grounds, or the obligor does not know the whereabouts of the obligee, the obligee may lodge the subject matter with the relevant governmental agency. After the lodgment, the obligor is deemed to have completed the performance, and the obligation between the obligor and the obligee is terminated.

According to the Supreme People's Court opinion, where an obligee rejects without good cause the performance of an obligor and the obligor lodges the subject matter of the performance in the care of an appropriate agency, the obligation shall be deemed performed. Any expenses incurred by the agency in caring for the subject matter should be borne by the obligee. While the subject matter is in the care of the agency, any fruits of the property belong to, and the risk of loss is borne by, the obligee (1988 Opinion, s. 104). The 1995 *Security Law* also provides for lodgment in the case of transfer of mortgaged property (see discussion earlier).

Agreement

The parties may agree to terminate the obligation. The obligee may agree to release the duties under the obligation, or the parties may rescind the contract, or replace it with a new contract. The agreement of the parties shall not violate the law or the public interest.

Merger

Where the obligor and the obligee are merged into one person, the obligations between the two parties are terminated.

Civil Liability

In the civil codes of most other countries, rules on civil liability are **6.19** spread throughout the various sections in the Parts on Rights over Things and Obligations. One of the unique features of the GPCL is that it includes a separate chapter on civil liability where the rules on liability for breach of contract and for torts are comprised. This is to emphasize the important role that the rules on civil liability as a separate body of law play in implementing civil law norms.

General Principles

Concept

Civil liability is the legal consequences brought about by one's breach of civil duties. The GPCL, Article 106, provides that a citizen or legal person who breaches a contract or fails to perform other duties shall bear civil liability; where a citizen or legal person through fault interferes with and causes damage to state or collective property, or to the property or person of another, he shall bear civil liability.

Civil liability differs from civil duties in that a legal duty requires a person to engage in certain activities (acts or forbearance) that are socially desirable, whereas civil liability results from one's breach of legal duties which acts or forbearance are socially blameworthy. Civil liability is based on the existence of civil duties which may arise from the provisions of the law or an agreement between the parties. Civil liability may resemble primary legal duties, in that a person bearing civil liability is also required by the law to act or forbear from acting in a certain way. Especially where, for example, the defendant is ordered by the court to specifically perform the contract, the distinction between the primary duties arising from the contract and the civil liability imposed by the court order is hard to discern, as both require the person to perform the same contract. Thus, civil liability is sometimes deemed as a special form of obligation.[41] But civil liability is in essence a legal compulsion imposed on a person regardless of his will and is backed up by the enforcement power of the State. Failure or refusal to carry out civil liability will usually result in a stiffer penalty against the person than a breach of civil duty.

Civil liability is primarily concerned with property. Failure to perform obligations and invasion of property rights will lead to liability of economic content (payment of damages, specific performance, etc). Infringement of personal rights may also lead to monetary liability. Liability not concerned with property (such as elimination of effects, restoration of reputation and apology) apply to some cases of infringement of personal rights and cases of petty misconduct.

Constitutive Elements

For an act to result in civil liability, the following four elements have to be established.

(1) Damage

The fact that damage has been caused to another person shall be proved for one to bear civil liability. "Damage" is the subversion of normal state of civil law relationships protected by law, resulting in adverse impacts on lawful rights and interests of persons. Damage denotes both tangible loss and intangible invasion. It includes loss of property, which may be actual loss or loss of prospective interest, and injury of person.

(2) Wrongful Act

A lawful act, even if it has caused damage to another, does not result in liability. Wrongful acts are acts that breach legal duties, which include breach of contract and torts. Both breach of contract and torts violate duties sanctioned by law. Civil liability, to a certain extent, penalizes unlawful acts.

The wrongfulness of an act may be exonerated by virtue of certain events that the law deems as justifications of the act. *Force majeure,* self-defence, necessity and the fault of the injured party are justifications that are discussed below.

(3) Causation

To establish civil liability, it must be shown that the damage incurred by one party is caused by the wrongful act of the other party. The causal link between the damage and the act should be ascertained objectively in the intricate matrix of facts, and should not be based on speculations and hypotheses.

In determining causation, it is important to distinguish between cause and condition. A condition makes the occurrence of a certain result possible, but does not play a decisive role in its occurrence. For example, A injures B while riding a bicycle. B goes to a clinic and is given the wrong medication by C. As a result, B dies. Although it is fair to say that, without A's act that injures B, B would not go to the clinic and take the fatal medication, A's act is only a condition and not the direct cause of B's death.

It is also possible that a certain damage may be the result of several causes. In determining civil liability in such a case, it is important to distinguish between major causes and minor causes, and dispense liability accordingly. For example, A creates a mechanical problem in B's car and fails to inform B. B drives the car and injures C. The injury is caused by the acts of both A and B, but A's act is probably the major cause which has a logically more immediate and direct link with the result.

(4) Fault

Fault is a subjective element that must be proved to establish civil liability. Fault refers to the mental state of an actor in regard to his act and its consequences. Fault includes *dolus* (*guyi* in Chinese) and *culpa* (*guoshi* in Chinese). *Dolus*, or wilfulness, is a mental state in which the actor, knowing the consequences of his act, intends or allows them to occur. *Culpa*, or negligence, is the mental state in which the actor fails to foresee the consequences of his act which he should have foreseen, or, having foreseen the consequences of his act, believes they will not occur or will be avoided. Fault represents the social attitude of a person, indicating his indifference or disdain towards the rights and interests of others and the public interest of the society. It is not the injurious consequences of an act, but the fault of the actor, that forms the social blameworthiness of the act, on the basis of which civil liability rests.

The ascertainment of fault in actual cases is not an easy task. Subjectivists focus on whether, as a matter of fact, an actor is able to take the proper care for others, while objectivists focus on whether a reasonable man in like circumstances is able to take the proper care. Chinese scholars mostly favour the combination of the two standards. Fault should be ascertained by considering both the objective circumstances of the act and the subjective mentality of the actor. In particular, account should be taken of the nature of the injurious act, the circumstances in which the act occurs and the personal skills, experience and ability of the actor.

The distinction between *dolus* and *culpa* is not as important in civil law as in criminal law. The law normally does not impose harsher liability for wilful acts than for negligent acts. But a court will probably mete out a higher amount of damages within its discretion against a wilful wrongdoer than a negligent actor. In cases where there are more than two defendants at fault, or where the plaintiff is also at fault, it becomes necessary to weigh the degree of fault of the parties concerned, and the distinction between wilfulness and negligence (and between gross negligence and ordinary negligence) becomes quite pertinent. Also, certain legal rules distinguish between wilful acts and negligent acts, such as, for example, a civil act is void only if it is induced by a wilful misrepresentation (deceit) (see earlier discussions).

Justifications

6.20   Justifications are legal events whose occurrence may exonerate one from civil liability for his injurious acts. The GPCL provides for four types of justifications.

(1) Force Majeure

Force majeure refers to objective situations that are unforeseeable, unavoidable and irresistible (GPCL, Article 153). Where, because of *force majeure*, it is impossible to perform a contract or harm is caused to another, there is no civil liability unless the law provides otherwise (GPCL, Article 107).

Force majeure includes, among others, earthquake, typhoon, flood and war, but it does not include all the unexpected incidents. To invoke the *force majeure* defence, one has to establish that the event cannot be foreseen by the actor and that, under the prevailing social and technical conditions, it can neither be avoided nor overcome. *Force majeure* excuses an actor from the liability for his act, only insofar as the damage is caused by the *force majeure*. If *force majeure* is proven, civil liability will be exempted, unless the law provides otherwise. Unexpected incidents short of *force majeure* usually do not exonerate one from civil liability, although the proof of an unexpected incident may aid the actor in showing that he was without fault.

(2) Fault of the Injured Party

If the injured party and the actor are both at fault in committing a breach of contract or a tortious act, the actor's liability may be exempted or reduced. Although the rule is not expressly prescribed in the GPCL as a general rule, it is accepted by scholars and judicial practice,[42] and is also implied in GPCL, Articles 131, 123 and 127. If the injured party consents to the breach of contract or a tortious act, the breaching party or the tortfeasor is relieved of liability to the extent of the consent. If the damage is caused by an intentional act of the injured party along with an act of the defendant, the causal link between the damage and the defendant's act may well be removed. If the injured party performs a negligent act that contributes to the damage, the defendant's liability may be reduced.

(3) Self-Defence

Self-defence is an exonerating event in tort cases and is governed by GPCL, Article 128. Self-defence is for the protection of lawful rights and interests against ongoing wrongful infringement and should be directed against the party who is committing the wrongful infringement. If self-defence inflicts damage on the party committing the wrongful infringement, the party who performs self-defence has no liability. Self-defence should be limited to what is necessary to stop the infringement; if self-defence exceeds that limit and causes unnecessary damage, the party performing self-defence shall bear appropriate liability. Appropriate liability is not full liability for all the unnecessary damage that has been caused, but should be determined in light of all the relevant circumstances of the case.

(4) Necessity

Necessity (*jinjibixian* in Chinese) is another exonerating event in tort cases, governed by GPCL, Article 129. An act of necessity is for the protection of lawful rights and interests against imminent danger of damage. For example, a driver causes his vehicle to swerve onto the sidewalk to avoid hitting a boy who is crossing the street. A vessel jettisons part of its the cargo during an emergency to avoid the loss of the whole vessel. The person performing such an act should use appropriate means to minimize the damage caused by his act. If his act results in damage to a third party, he shall not bear liability, and the injured party may claim compensation from the person who caused the danger which the act of necessity was intended to avoid. But if the danger resulted from natural causes, the injured party may claim appropriate compensation from the party who benefitted from the act of necessity (1988 Opinion, s. 156). The person performing the act of necessity shall bear appropriate liability to the injured party if he used inappropriate means or his act exceeded the limit of necessity.

Forms of Civil Liability

6.21   The GPCL, Article 134, provides for ten forms of civil liability. They are different types of civil remedy that may be given in various types of civil cases.

(1) Cessation of Infringement

This form of liability applies primarily to tort cases. It serves to prevent further infringement of lawful rights and interests. It only applies to cases where the infringement is continuing. For example, the court may order cessation of infringement to stop emission of toxic wastes or unauthorized production of copyrighted works.

(2) Elimination of Obstruction

This form of liability applies to tort cases where the defendant's act interferes with the plaintiff's normal enjoyment of his property or personal rights. For example, the court may order elimination of obstruction in cases where a construction team blocks the public passageway near the building site, or where the defendant piles things up that obstruct the ventilation or lighting of his neighbour, or where the defendant makes noise or vibration that interferes with the quiet life of others.

(3) Elimination of Danger

This form of liability applies to cases where no actual damage has occurred, but the defendant's act (or forbearance) causes danger to the safety of the person or property of others. For example, the owner of a dangerous house that is about to collapse may be ordered to take steps to eliminate the danger that the house poses to others.

(4) Return of Property

This form of liability serves to protect property rights, and applies typically to cases of unfair enrichment (GPCL, Articles 92 and 61) and to tort cases of conversion (GPCL, Article 117). To claim the return of property, the plaintiff shall have the right to possess the property (such as ownership, the right of *dien* or the right of pledge) and the defendant has no such right. If the defendant is a *bona fide* third party who obtained the property with consideration, his lawful rights and interests should be protected, and the remedy of return of property may not be granted. Return of property may only be ordered if the original property still exists; if the property is already lost, the plaintiff may only claim damages.

(5) Restoration of the Original Condition

This form of liability applies to tort cases where the plaintiff's property is damaged through the defendant's fault. Where the restoration is still practicable and may be performed without substantially decreasing the value and utility of the property, the plaintiff may demand restoration of the original condition.

(6) Repair, Reworking and Replacement

This form of liability applies to breach of contract cases where the goods or service provided by the defendant are defective. If the subject matter, after repair, still fails to conform with the requirements of the contract, the defendant may be ordered to redo the work or replace it.

(7) Payment of Compensation

This remedy is applicable to all kinds of civil cases, including cases where the plaintiff suffers no financial loss. In principle, the defendant should pay full compensation for all of the loss suffered by the plaintiff. But the court often takes into account other relevant circumstances (such as the plaintiff's contributory negligence, the reasonableness of the defendant's act, and the financial conditions of both parties) to mete out a fair and just amount of compensation.

(8) Payment of Liquidated Damages

This remedy applies only to contract cases where the contract or the governing law or regulation provides for the amount of or the method for calculating liquidated damages. It is an essential remedy for most domestic economic contracts.

(9) Elimination of Effects and Restoration of Reputation

This, along with apology, is what is called non-property-related liability. This form of liability applies to tort cases of infringement of personal rights, particularly those where the plaintiff's right to reputation or honour is infringed. For example, a defendant who wrote a defamatory article about the plaintiff may be ordered to give public notice to eliminate the adverse effects on the plaintiff's reputation.

(10) Apology

This form of liability applies to cases of petty misconduct. As a form of legal liability, apology is ordered against the defendant by the court. It may, nevertheless, help preserve the harmonious relations between the parties.

The above forms of civil liability may be used separately or in combination. In addition to these remedies, the court in a civil case may issue admonitions, order repentance, or confiscate property used for illegal activities, or things obtained illegally, and may also impose fines or detention in accordance with law (GPCL, Article 134).

Liability for Breach of Contract

6.22 Detailed discussion on liability for breach of contract may be found elsewhere in this book. Here, we will briefly examine the rules on liability for breach of contract as set forth in the GPCL.

Breach of contract is failure by a party to perform his duties under the contract, or performance by a party not in conformity with the requirements of the contract. It includes non-performance, incomplete performance and delayed performance. The breaching party shall bear civil liability for all instances of breach.

Unlike legal duties involved in tort cases, contractual duties are self-imposed in that they arise from the parties' agreement. But when a valid contract is concluded and becomes effective, the rights and duties under the contract are sanctioned by law, and an act in breach of contract becomes an act violating legal duties. The breaching party is compelled to bear civil liability.

The four elements of civil liability generally apply to breach of contract cases, except for the requirement of fault. Chinese scholars tend to believe that fault is an indispensable element of liability for breach of contract, but that in breach of contract cases, fault is presumed on the part of the breaching party and need not be proved by the non-breaching party.[43] Under the GPCL, a breaching party may escape civil liability only if he proves that his breach was caused by *force majeure* (GPCL, Article 107). If the breach was caused by the governmental organ in charge of the breaching party, the breaching party shall, in accordance with the contract, pay compensation to the other party or take measures to correct the defective performance; the governmental organ shall then be responsible for dealing with the loss that the party sustained as a result (GPCL, Article 116).

If a party breaches the contract, the other party has a right to demand performance, or the taking of measures to correct the defective performance, and has the right to demand compensation for loss (GPCL, Article 111). According to this provision, the court may order specific performance, if the non-breaching party so demands and actual performance is still possible. Specific performance serves to achieve the purposes for which the contract was made and to give full protection to the non-breaching party. It may be ordered even though the breaching party has paid damages. The non-breaching party may also demand the breaching party to take other corrective measures, such as repair, reworking and replacement.

The damages to be paid by a breaching party shall be equal to the loss the other party sustained as a result of the breach. Parties may provide in a contract that when a party breaches the contract, he shall pay to the other party a certain sum of liquidated damages; they may also stipulate in the contact the method for calculation of damages caused by a breach (GPCL, Article 112).

Liquidated damages (*weiyuejin* in Chinese) include agreed liquidated damages that are stipulated in the contract, and statutory liquidated damages that are prescribed in the governing law or regulation for a certain type of contract. They serve the dual purpose of compensating for the loss of the non-breaching party and penalizing the breaching party. Liquidated damages are payable upon breach of contract, even where the non-breaching party has suffered no loss. To a certain extent, liquidated damages secure the actual performance of the contract.

Upon breach of contract, the non-breaching party has a duty of mitigation. If he fails to take prompt measures to prevent an increase in the extent of the loss, the party has no right to demand compensation for the increased loss (GPCL, Article 114).

Liability for Torts .

Concept of Tort

GPCL, Article 106, provides that where a citizen or legal person through fault interferes with and causes damage to state or collective property, or to the property or person of another, he shall bear civil liability (para. 2). Where there is no fault, there shall be civil liability if the law so provides (para. 3). Accordingly, tort may be defined as an act whereby the actor through fault interferes with the property or person of another and for which the actor shall bear civil liability, or an injurious act for which the actor shall bear civil liability according to special provisions of the law.

A tortious act brings about certain legal consequences. The legal consequences are, however, not what the actor intended to have, as the act violates the law and public interest. A tortious act is, therefore, not a civil legal act. A tortious act primarily infringes absolute rights (rights over things and personal rights) of another, although exceptionally interference with another's contractual rights (relative rights) may also give rise to tort liability.

The four constitutive elements of civil liability apply to liability for torts. In a tort case, the plaintiff usually has the burden of proving the damage that he has incurred, the wrongfulness of the defendant's act, the causal link between his damage and the defendant's act, and the fault of the defendant. Tortious acts may be divided into general torts and special torts. Liability for general torts is established upon the proof of the four elements of civil liability. Liability for special torts is governed by special provisions of the law. The four constitutive elements of civil liability do not apply to special torts, nor do the normal rules on burden of proof. The constitutive elements of a special tort as well as the burden of proving them are governed by special provisions of the law. The GPCL provides for seven special torts in Articles 121–127 and 133, that are discussed below.

The GPCL embraces three legal principles for the determination of tort liability, and they apply to different torts. The principle of fault liability is the basic principle that apply to general torts. The principles of presumed fault, liability without fault and equitable liability apply to special torts in accordance with the special provisions of the law.

The Principle of Fault Liability

6.23 The principle of fault liability is set forth in GPCL, Article 106, para. 2 (mentioned above) as the general principle for determining tort liability. This principle postulates that fault is at the heart of a tortious act and it is out of fault, not the injurious consequences of an act, that the social and moral blameworthiness of a tortious act stems. Under this principle, fault is the definitive element of tort liability. The court should examine the fault of both the tortfeasor and the injured party to determine the appropriate liability. Fault may result in civil liability for an actor, even though his act does not directly cause the damage, such as, for example, an actor who through his fault causes another to commit a tortious act may be held liable for the resultant damage (see discussion below on instigation of tort). The fault of the injured party may reduce the liability of the tortfeasor. The burden of proving fault shall be borne by the party who pleads the existence of fault, unless the law provides otherwise.

The basic principle of fault liability applies to general torts. They include the tort of interference with the possession of property (GPCL, Article 117, para. 1), the tort of causing damage to the property of another person (GPCL, Article 117, para. 2), the tort of infringement of intellectual property (GPCL, Article 118), the tort of personal injury (GPCL, Article 119), and the tort of infringement of personal rights to one's name, likeness, reputation or honour (GPCL, Article 120).

In two situations, the application of the principle of fault liability is governed by special rules. Firstly, where two or more persons jointly infringe a right and cause loss to another, they shall bear joint liability (GPCL, Article 130). This is the so-called "joint fault". The provision applies only if the individual faults as well as the actual behaviours of the actors are joined together into a single combined act that causes the damage. If the actors act on their own, and there is no link among their fault, then each actor shall bear his individual liability rather than joint liability for the whole damage. The fault of the actors may be *dolus*, such as the actors wilfully conspire to commit a tortious act; the fault may also be *culpa*, such as, for example, two engineers jointly design a defective machine through negligence. The Supreme People's Court, in its interpretation of the GPCL, refers to a special kind of joint fault. A person who instigates or helps another to commit a tort is a joint tortfeasor and shall bear joint liability (1988 Opinion, s. 148).

Secondly, if an injured party is also at fault with respect to the occurrence of the loss, the civil liability of the tortfeasor may be reduced (GPCL, Article 131). This is the so-called "mixed fault". The provision applies where the injured party failed to take proper care of his own interests, and his fault, along with the tortfeasor's fault, has a causal link with the damage. In certain situations, the fault of the injured party may exempt the tortfeasor's liability (GPCL, Articles 122 and 127).

The Principle of Presumed Fault

The principle of presumed fault is the principle of fault liability in a special form. While it still bases the tortfeasor's liability on his fault, it reverses the burden of proof and holds the defendant liable unless he can prove the plaintiff's damage was not caused through his fault.

The principle of presumed fault applies to situations where the plaintiff is able to show that the damage he suffered was caused by the defendant's acts, but, owning to the special nature of the defendant's act or other circumstances, it is difficult or even impossible for him to prove the fault of the defendant. The principle of presumed fault dispenses with the plaintiff's burden of proving the defendant's fault. The plaintiff has only to prove the other three elements of civil liability, and it is for the defendant to rebut the presumption of fault in order to avoid liability. In many situations, the law will also restrict the means by which the defendant may rebut the presumption of fault; in other words, the law may enumerate grounds on which the defendant may rely to disprove his fault. In other situations (*e.g.*, GPCL, Article 126), the law may impose no restrictions in this respect.

The GPCL, Articles 121–124, 126–127 and 133, provide for the application of presumed fault. The tortious acts governed by those provisions are often regulated by more specific rules of other laws. They are

    (a) tortious acts by a governmental organ or its officers in the course of performing their official duties (Article 121), which are governed by the 1994 *State Compensation Law*;

    (b) tortious acts arising out of defective quality of goods (Article 122), which are governed by the 1993 *Product Quality Law*;

    (c) tortious acts arising out of pollution of the environment (Article 124), which are governed by various laws and regulations on environmental protection, such as the 1989 *Environmental Protection Law*, 1982 *Marine Environment Protection Law* and the 1995 *Air Pollution Prevention and Treatment Law*;

    (d) tortious acts arising out of underground construction and unsafe buildings (Articles 125 and 126);

    (e) tortious acts arising out of attacks by domestic animals (Article 127);

    (f) tortious act by persons of incompetence or limited competence (Article 133).

The Principle of Liability without Fault

6.24 The principle of liability without fault (also known as absolute liability or objective liability) holds an actor liable if his act causes damage to another person, even though the actor has no fault. The principle sets aside the relevance of fault in a tort case and serves not as a social or moral admonition, but a fair allocation of loss. As fault becomes irrelevant, causation becomes the central issue. The defendant may avoid liability if he can refute the causal link between his act and the plaintiff's damage. One way of achieving this is to show that the damage was caused by an intentional act of the injured party.

The principle applies only where the law so provides. The GPCL contains only one provision that prescribes liability without fault. Where engaging in work that poses high hazards to the surroundings, such as work in the upper atmosphere, or work involving high pressure, flammables, explosives, strong poisons, radioactive substances, or high-speed means of transportation, which results in damage to another, there shall be civil liability; if it can be proved that the damage was intentionally caused by the injured party, there is no liability (GPCL, Article 123).

The Principle of Equitable Liability

The principle of equitable liability applies to a tort case where none of the parties was at fault. GPCL, Article 132, provides that where none of the parties is at fault with respect to the occurrence of the loss, civil liability may be apportioned among the parties in accordance with the actual circumstances. The Supreme People's Court further holds that where no party is at fault with respect to the occurrence of the loss, but one party suffered a loss while engaging in activities for the benefit of the other party or of both parties, the party receiving the benefit may be ordered to provide certain monetary compensation (1988 Opinion, s. 157). The principle is also embodied in other provisions of the GPCL and the 1988 judicial interpretation.[44] The principle of equitable liability serves to achieve a fair allocation of loss where no party is at fault, especially where one party benefits from the act that causes damage to the other party. In apportioning the loss between the parties, account is usually taken of the extent of the loss, the extent of the benefit and the financial conditions of both parties.

Notes

[1] The term "obligation" (*zhai* in Chinese) as used in this chapter has the exclusive meaning of a relationship of specific rights and duties between parties, arising either from terms of a contract or from a provision of law, as defined in GPCL, Article 84. The term for constraint or requirement will be "duty" (*yiwu* in Chinese).

[2] *Quanguo Renmin Daibiao Dahui Changwu Weiyuanhui Gongbao* [Gazette of the Standing Committee of the National People's Congress], 1986, p. 208.

[3] The English translation of the GPCL may be found in *Laws of the People's Republic of China (1983–1986)*, pp. 225–249; *Laws and Regulations of the People's Republic of China Governing Foreign-Related Matters (1949–1990)* (China Legal System Publishing House, 1991), Vol. 1, pp. 331–348. This chapter primarily uses the translation by Whitmore Gray and Henry R. Zheng published in the *American Journal of Comparative Law*, Vol. 34, pp. 715–743 (1986).

[4] The English translation of the 1988 Opinion by Whitmore Gray and Henry R. Zheng may be found in *Law and Contemporary Problems*, Vol. 52, no. 2, pp. 59–87 (1989).

[5] The term "civil rights" used throughout this chapter means rights in civil law (*minshi quanli* in Chinese), not constitutional rights and liberties.

[6] See Wang Liming, et al., *Minfa Xinlun* [A New Treatise on Civil Law] (hereinafter, *Xinlun*) (China University on Political Science and Law Press, 1988), Vol. 1, pp. 59–60.

[7] See Tong Rou (ed.), *Zhongguo Minfaxue: Minfa Zongze* [Studies in Chinese Civil Law: General Principles of Civil Law] (hereinafter, *Zongze*) (Chinese People's Public Security University Press, 1990), p. 18; Zheng Li & Wang Zuotang (eds.), *Minfaxue* [The Science of Civil Law] (hereinafter, *Minfaxue*) (Peking University Press, 2nd ed., 1995), p. 21.

[8] See Wang Liming, *Xinlun*, p. 61.

[9] On declaration of death, see GPCL, Articles 23–25.

[10] "Close relatives" refers to spouse, parents, children, brothers and sisters, grandparents and grandchildren (1988 Opinion, s. 12).

[11] "Institutions" refers to non-profit organizations that are created and funded by the government to provide public services to the community. Examples of institutions are public schools, hospitals, public libraries and radio and television stations.

[12] "Social organizations" are associations created by citizens and legal persons that engage in non-profit activities for social, cultural and educational purposes. Social organizations are often funded by the government. Examples of social organizations are trade unions, learned societies, churches and foundations.

[13] See, for example, 1993 *Company Law*, Articles 23 & 78.

[14] Such laws and regulations include, for example, 1982 *Regulation for the Implementation of the Chinese-Foreign Equity Joint Venture Law*, 1988 *Chinese-Foreign Contractual Joint Venture Law*, 1988 *Regulation on Registration of Enterprise Legal Persons*, 1990 *Rules for the Implementation of the Wholly Foreign-Owned Enterprise Law* and 1994 *Regulation on the Registration of Companies*.

[15] There is as yet no regulation on the registration of institutions as legal persons. For social organizations, the 1989 *Regulation on the Registration of Social Organizations* requires social organizations as defined in the Regulation to be registered with the civil affairs departments of the various levels of government upon their establishment.

[16] See, for example, 1993 *Company Law*, Article 11; 1988 *Regulation on Registration of Enterprise Legal Persons*, Article 13.

[17] See Wang Liming, *Xinlun*, pp. 330–333.

[18] An "incident" (*shijian* in Chinese) is an event with civil law consequences that does not directly involve the exercise of human will, such as the elapse of time, the birth or death of a natural person, and the occurrence of a natural disaster.

[19] But expression of intent alone is not a civil legal act. The establishment of a civil legal act may require the expression of intent be accompanied by the delivery of the subject matter, or that the expression of intent be embodied in a special form.

[20] However, civil codes in most countries provide that acts induced by deceit, duress and another's taking advantage of the declarant's distress are only voidable.

[21] The Chinese GPCL does not provide for the legal consequences of incorrect transmission (*unrichtige Übermittlung* in German Civil Code, Article 120). The Supreme People's Court states in the 1988 Opinion that where one's expression of intent is to be communicated by a third party and the third party, due to negligence, miscommunicated or failed to communicate the expression of intent, thereby causing a loss to another person, the declarant ordinarily may be held liable for the loss, unless otherwise provided by law or otherwise agreed by the parties (1988 Opinion, s. 77).

[22] 1993 *Economic Contract Law*, Article 3; 1985 *Foreign Economic Contract Law*, Article 7; 1987 *Technology Contract Law*, Article 9. But the 1993 *Economic Contract Law* permits an economic contract to be in oral form if it is "instantly performed".

[23] See Tong Rou, *Zongze*, p. 240.

[24] See German Civil Code, Article 138(2).

[25] See Tong Rou (ed.), *Zhongguo Minfa* [Chinese Civil Law] (Law Publishing House, 1990), p. 188.

[26] See Tong Rou, *Zongze*, pp. 233–234. Whether a civil legal act may be rescinded if substantial change of circumstances occurs after the act goes into effect is not dealt with in the GPCL. But see 1981 *Economic Contract Law*, Article 27, para. 1, s. 4 (amended in 1993).

[27] See Tong Rou, *Zongze*, pp. 251–252; Tong Rou, *Zhongguo Minfa*, p. 185.

[28] Zheng Li & Wang Zuotang, *Minfaxue*, pp. 134–135. Wang Liming, *Xinlun*, p. 400, suggests that a civil act may be rescinded by the parties if all the parties so agree. Otherwise, the rescission should be decided on by the court or arbitral tribunal.

[29] For example, GPCL, Article 16, para. 3; Article 17, para. 2; 1991 *Civil Procedure Law*, Article 57.

[30] See Tong Rou, *Zongze*, pp. 255–300; Tong Rou, *Zhongguo Minfa*, pp. 211–212; Zheng Li & Wang Zuotang, *Minfaxue*, pp. 152–154.

[31] See 1991 *Civil Procedure Law*, Article 34; GPCL, Articles 144 and 149.

[32] See Qian Mingxing, *Wuquanfa Yuanli* [Principles of Property Law] (Peking University Press, 1994), pp. 393–395; Zheng Li & Wang Zuotang, *Minfaxue*, pp. 259–261.

[33] German Civil Code, Article 984; Japanese Civil Code, Article 240.

[34] See the Opinion of the Supreme People's Court on Certain Questions Concerning the Implementation of Civil Policies and Laws of 30 August 1984, s. 58.

35 *Ibid.* See also the Letter from the Supreme People's Court on Certain Questions over the "Opinion on Certain Questions Concerning the Implementation of Civil Policies and Laws" of 24 February 1985, s. 2.

36 The GPCL does not provide that the possession of property under *diya* is not to be transferred. The Supreme People's Court suggests that the property under *diya* may be possessed by the obligee, or may remain in the possession of its owner (1988 Opinion, s. 114). Therefore, it is obvious that *diya* as used in the GPCL includes both mortgage and pledge.

37 This supersedes the previous rule as stated in the 1988 Opinion, s. 115, which conditions such transfer on the consent of the mortgagee.

38 See Wang Jiafu (ed.), *Zhongguo Minfaxue: Minfa Zhaiquan* [Studies in Chinese Civil Law: Obligations in Civil Law] (hereinafter, *Zhaiquan*) (Law Publishing House, 1991), pp. 37–39.

39 See GPCL, Articles 35, 55, 65, 66, 67, 89 and 130.

40 See Wang Jiafu, *Zhaiquan*, pp. 146–150.

41 *Ibid.*, pp. 226–227.

42 See Wang Liming, *Xinlun*, p. 478; Zheng Li & Wang Zuotang, *Minfaxue*, pp. 643–644; Wang Liming (ed.), *Minfa Qinquan Xingwei Fa* [Civil Law: Law of Torts] (People's University of China Press, 1993), pp. 195–198.

43 See Wang Liming, *Xinlun*, pp. 495–496; Zheng Li & Wang Zuotang, *Minfaxue*, pp. 663–664.

44 GPCL, Article 109, and 1988 Opinion, s. 142, provide that where a person sustains a loss in protecting the property or person of another from damage, the person who receives the benefit may be ordered to give appropriate compensation. Other relevant provisions are concerned with an act of necessity (GPCL, Article 129; 1988 Opinion, s. 156) and liability of persons of incompetence or limited competence (GPCL, Article 133).

CHAPTER 7
CONTRACT LAW

Zhao Yuhong

City University of Hong Kong

Zhao Yuhong, Lecturer in Law, City University of Hong Kong. B.A. in English Language and Literature (Peking University); LL.B (Peking University); Master of Studies in Law (Vermont Law School); Ph.D candidate (City University of Hong Kong).

Introduction

Contracts, known as *qiyue* in ancient China, existed even before the creation of Chinese characters. Written contracts started to appear in the Western *Zhou* dynasty over 2,500 years ago. Barter contracts, sale of goods contracts, loan contracts, employment contracts and even partnership contracts have all been documented.[1] However, modern contract law of the People's Republic of China (PRC) started its life in the early 1950s, and any real and substantial development occurred only after the 1980s. This chapter will present an overall description of the Chinese contract law as it exists today. This first section is a brief introduction of historical development and current situation of the contract law in China. There is then a discussion of the general principles governing contracts in China. The three sections following that each focus on one of the three pieces of contract legislation in China, *i.e.* the *Economic Contract Law* (ECL),[2] the *Foreign Economic Contract Law* (FECL)[3] and the *Technology Contract Law* (TCL),[4] The concluding section points out some problems that exist in the present contract system in China and anticipates the future uniform contract law.

7.01

Historical Development

The PRC contract law is based on an economic system that is developing from pure planned economy to market economy. After the founding of the PRC, the concept of economic contract was introduced to China from the former Soviet Union. It is a product of planned economy and only legal persons or units can become parties to an economic contract prior to the ECL. It is in contrast with civil contract, to which individuals can become parties. Such categorization of contract, which may be abolished by the proposed uniform contract law in the near future, still exists in China today.

The earliest PRC contract law was established by the *Provisional Rules Regarding Contract among Governmental Organizations, State-Owned Enterprises and Collective Units*[5] issued by the Financial and Economic Committee of the then Council for Government Affairs, the predecessor of the State Council, in September 1950. It contained similar basic principles and framework of the current ECL and was intended to facilitate State control over local economic activity. It recognized the role of contract as the basis for economic transaction but subjected it to the approval and supervision of State authorities. The regulation was largely ignored during the late 1950s as the Anti-Rightist Movement substantially downgraded the function of law and the "Great Leap Forward" virtually destroyed the established economic order.

In the early 1960s, as the economic and political situation became gradually stabilized, the National Economic Committee issued the *Interim Regulation on Contract for Ordering Industrial and Mineral Products*[6] on August 30, 1963. To further emphasize the role of contract in the economy and reinforce the mandate of the new rules, the Communist Party Central Committee and the State Council jointly issued their *Notice Regarding Strict Implementation of Basic Construction Procedure and Economic Contracts*[7] on December 10, 1962. The focus of contract regulation in this period was contract enforcement. Economic sanctions were imposed on those who failed to fulfill their contractual obligations. This period did not last long because the ten-year Cultural Revolution starting in 1966 destroyed China's entire legal system, including its contract law.

In short, contract in the 1950s and 1960s was viewed as an administrative and allocative mechanism to control economic exchanges between units and to carry out the State economic plan. The basic purpose of contract was to implement the quotas and allocations of goods and services fixed by the State.

After the economic disasters brought by the Cultural Revolution and as the new market-oriented economic policy began to take shape, the role of contract law was once again emphasized. In 1978 and 1979, various governmental agencies promulgated several interim rules and regulations to fill the legal void in the contract law area. Such development reached its height in 1981 with the promulgation of the ECL, followed by the FECL of 1985 and the TCL of 1987. The ECL was substantially amended in 1993 as China officially announced that a "socialist market economy" is the ultimate goal of the economic reform. The discussion on ECL in this chapter is based on the new 1993 ECL.

Current Situation

The Law of Contracts in China can now be found in five sources: **7.02**

    (a) the *General Principles of Civil Law* (GPCL)[8];

    (b) three individual contract law statutes;

    (c) State administrative regulations over particular types of contracts;

    (d) local regulations and rules; and

    (e) judicial interpretation.

Many provisions of the GPCL are directly related to contracts. Chapter 5 provides for the definition of contract, performance of contract, interpretation of contract, guaranty of contract, and assignment of contract. Chapter 6 prescribes the liabilities for breach of contract. It establishes general principles applicable to both economic contracts (both domestic and foreign) and civil contracts (including technology contracts). Domestic economic contracts are contracts between legal persons,[9] other economic organizations,[10] individual business households[11] and rural leaseholding households.[12] They are entered into for economic purposes and affected by the State economic plan. Foreign economic contracts are those economic contracts where one party is a foreign enterprise or individual. Civil contracts are contracts where one or both parties are individuals. They include consumer contracts, exchange contracts, gift contracts, agency contracts, brokerage contracts and trust contracts. Technology contracts, as a type of civil contract, can be made between legal persons, between citizens, or between a legal person and a citizen. The subject matters of such contract must be related to technology.

    The three contract law statutes, *i.e.* ECL, FECL and TCL, were enacted at different stages of the economic development in China since the 1980s. More detailed discussion of the three statutes is to be found in this chapter.

    Administrative regulations and rules are usually promulgated by the State Council or its subsidiary commissions or ministries under particular statutes. They are more specific and detailed regulations with regard to certain aspects of the law. For example, under the ECL, there are *Regulation on Contracts for the Sale of Industrial and Mineral Products, Regulation on Contracts for the Sale of Agricultural and Related Products, Regulation on Property Insurance Contracts,*

Regulation on Loan Contracts and so on. They are all issued by the State Council. They will be briefly mentioned where necessary in this chapter.

Local regulations and rules are enacted by the provincial or municipal people's congresses or governments to be applied only within their own jurisdiction, for example, *Rules on Foreign Economic Contracts in Shenzhen Special Economic Zone* and *Methods on Management of Economic Contracts in Beijing.* Due to the limited space, this aspect of contract law will not be covered in this chapter.

Judicial interpretation made by the Supreme People's Court in the form of notice or opinion is another very important source of Chinese contract law. In China, the Supreme People's Court is not restricted by the Constitution to adjudicating questions that arise from particular cases or disputes. It has the implied power to issue notices or interpretation with regard to general or specific areas of law when the Court feels that such areas are not clear. Its opinion not only serves as a guideline for lower courts in adjudicating similar cases, but also provides clarification of the law for the legal profession in general. There are four major pieces of judicial interpretation of contract law: *the Supreme People's Court's Opinion on Several Issues Regarding the Implementation of the "Economic Contract Law" (September 17, 1984), the Supreme People's Court's Reply to Several Questions Regarding the Application of "Economic Contract Law" in Adjudicating Economic Contract Disputes (July 21, 1987), the Supreme People's Court's Reply to Several Questions Regarding the Application of "Foreign Economic Contract Law" (October 19, 1987)* and *the Supreme People's Court's Opinion on Several Issues Regarding the Implementation of the "General Principles of Civil Law" (for trial use) (January 26, 1988).* They will be discussed where necessary to clarify certain issues in Chinese contract law.

General Principles of Chinese Contract Law

7.03   A contract is an agreement whereby parties establish, vary or terminate civil relationships (GPCL, Article 85). The general principles refer to the basic tenets applicable to all contracts, regardless of the differences in parties or subject matters of a contract. They are by no means impractical abstractions or generalities, but rather are capable of being applied and cited in analysing and solving real issues of contract law, especially in cases where there are no specific or obvious rules addressing a particular legal issue. Those principles are mostly established by the GPCL, and reiterated in the ECL, FECL and TCL.

Fundamental Principles

Each of the three statutes has its own emphasis with regard to the fundamental principles for forming a contract. The following are generally applicable to all contracts established by the GPCL governing all civil activities.

Equality

GPCL, Article 3 provides that parties have equal status in civil activities. In the context of contract, equality means that parties enter into contract with equal status. Agreement shall be reached after negotiation or consultation carried out on equal basis and no party is allowed to impose its will on the other. The parties are under equal protection of law, which means the same law shall be applied to both parties regardless of their differences.

Voluntariness, Fairness, Exchange of Equivalent Values, Honesty and Good Faith

Civil activities must be carried out in accordance with the principles of voluntariness, fairness, exchange of equivalent values, honesty and good faith (GPCL, Article 4). Voluntariness means a party has independent and free will and shall express his true will in civil activities. A contract therefore must be formed, varied or rescinded by the parties upon agreement based on their true will. A contract formed under fraud or duress is against the principle of voluntariness and therefore shall be void. Fairness is connected to the moral value of a society and the concept of justice. It fills the gap in the law. A contract is voidable in China if it is *obviously unfair* to one party. Exchange of equivalent values means rights and obligations in civil activities shall be correspondent with each other. Except for gift contracts, all contracts need to be supported by consideration. That means a party must give something in exchange for some benefits. The consideration rule is different from the common law rules in that Chinese law has a requirement of equivalent values, even though they may not be of exactly the same value. Common law regards consideration as sufficient if the promisor gets what he has asked for in return for his promise. The court will not inquire into the adequacy of the consideration.[13] The principle of honesty and good faith requires the parties in civil activities to fulfil their obligations honestly and in good faith. They shall not try to evade laws or contracts. According to this principle, a party to a contract should perform his part of the duties under the contract voluntarily.

Breach of contract is viewed as a breach of legal duty and is strongly discouraged by Chinese law.

Compliance with the Laws and Policies of the State

Civil activities shall comply with the law. Where there is no provision of law, activities must be in conformity with state policy (GPCL, Article 6). In addition, civil activities shall defer to social morality. They may not harm public interests of the society, undermine the state economic plan, or disrupt the economic order (GPCL, Article 7).

Formation of Contract

Offer and Acceptance

7.04 Although express provisions on offer and acceptance, fundamental rules in contract law of other legal systems, do not exist in major legislation such as the GPCL, ECL, FECL or TCL, it would be a total misconception to conclude that such rules do not exist in Chinese contract law. The doctrines on offer and acceptance have been extensively discussed by legal scholars in textbooks and treatises, which function as sources of authority for courts and practitioners. Generally speaking, the offer and acceptance rules are similar to their common law counterparts with certain variations.

An offer, also known as proposal to make a contract, is an expression of the intention of one party to enter into a contract based on certain conditions. The person making the offer is known as the offeror, while the person to whom the offer is made is the offeree. To be effective, an offer must contain major terms of the contract and be communicated to the offeree. An offer is different from an invitation to treat, which merely expresses a willingness to enter into a contract and invites the other party to make an offer. Normally, advertisements and catalogues of merchandise are invitations to treat, not offers. An offer may be revoked before it becomes effective, *i.e.* before it is delivered to the offeree. That means if a notice to revoke the offer reaches the offeree before the offer, the offer is effectively revoked, otherwise, the offer becomes effective and is irrevocable by the offeror. An offer is put to an end when the offeree rejects it or makes a counter-offer, when the offeror receives no acceptance within the prescribed or reasonable period of time, when the offeror or the offeree loses his capacity, or when new law makes the offer illegal.

Acceptance is an expression of the intention by the offeree to enter into contract in full conformity with all the terms of the offer. To be effective, an acceptance must be made by the offeree. It must be full

and unconditional acceptance of all the terms of the offer. Any variation will result in a counter-offer, *i.e.* a new offer made to the original
offeror. An acceptance must be made within the time period prescribed
in the offer. Normally, an acceptance becomes effective when it
reaches the offeror, and contract is formed at that time. An acceptance
may be revoked before it becomes effective. The notice to revoke an
acceptance must reach the offeror prior to or at the same time as the
acceptance. The time when acceptance takes effect is different in
common law. *Adams v. Lindsell* established the postal rule which says
that an acceptance by post takes effect as soon as it is posted. It applies
even where the letter of acceptance is delayed in the post, and even
where it is totally lost.[14]

Major Terms

A contract is formed when the two parties reach an agreement upon
the major terms of a contract. Major terms are those necessary terms,
without which the contracts cannot be formed. Generally, they should
include the subject matter of the contract, quality and quantity of the
subject matter, price or remuneration of the contract, time, place and
manner of performance and liabilities for breach of contract. Each of
the three contract statutes provides for a list of major terms for economic contracts, foreign economic contracts and technology contracts,
with certain variations to accommodate the particular features of the
contracts under their regulation.[15]

Formality of Contract

Contracts must be in writing according to Article 7 of FECL and
Article 9 of TCL. However, some domestic economic contracts can be
made orally. According to Article 3 of ECL, a contract can be oral if it
is performed immediately after the conclusion of the contract.

Vitiating Factors

The GPCL provides for the circumstances where a civil act will be
rendered void or voidable and these provisions apply to contracts. Each
of the three contract statutes also specifies vitiating factors that render
a contract void.

    Contracts may be rendered void by incapacity of the parties (GPCL,
Article 58(1) & (2); ECL, Article 7(3)), fraud and duress (GPCL, Article
58(3); ECL, Article 7(2); FECL, Article 10; TCL, Article 21(4)), illegality
or being against public interests of the society, including legal

contracts for illegal purposes (GPCL, Article 58(5) & (7); ECL, Article 7(1) & (4); FECL, Article 9; TCL, Article 21(1)). A contract will also be void if the two parties by malicious conspiracy cause damage to the interests of the State, collectives or third parties (GPCL, Article 58(4)). Economic contracts are void if they are not in compliance with the mandatory economic plan of the state (GPCL, Article 58(6)). According to Article 7(1) of the 1981 ECL, economic contracts are void if they are against the laws or state policies and plans. The term "state policies and plans" is removed in the new 1993 ECL. Now that Article 7(1) reads economic contracts are void if they are against the laws and administrative regulations (of China). The law recognises the severability of contracts. If a contract is partially void, other parts of the contract may still be valid (GPCL, Article 60).

Voidable contract is recognised by GPCL Article 59. A contract is voidable where one party enters into the contract due to *significant misconception* or the contract is *obviously unfair* to one party. In such circumstances, the disadvantaged party has the right to petition the people's court or an arbitral tribunal to vary or rescind the contract.

Where a contract is determined to be void, or where a voidable contract is rescinded, the parties shall return the property acquired under the contract to the injured party. The party at fault is required to compensate the other party for any losses suffered as a result of the contract being void or rescinded. If both parties are at fault, each will be responsible for his share of the liability. Where the two parties enter into contract by malicious conspiracy to harm the interests of the State, the collectives or third parties, the property acquired by the parties shall be returned to the State, the collectives or third parties (GPCL, Article 61).

Performance of Contract

7.05 Chinese law emphasizes full and actual performance of contracts. GPCL Article 88 provides that parties to a contract shall fully perform their duties in accordance with the contract. Only performance that is in full compliance with the terms of a contract is appropriate performance. To ensure full performance of the contract, the GPCL establishes the legal mechanism known as guaranty of contracts which includes the use of a guarantor, pledge, deposit and lien (GPCL, Article 89).

Variation and Rescission of Contracts

Variation of contracts, in a restrictive sense, refers to alteration of the subject matter, its quality or quantity requirements, or other rights and obligations. In a broad sense, variation also includes the change of parties to a contract. However, that is more commonly referred to as assignment of contract in Chinese law. Here in this chapter we adopt the restrictive sense. Rescission of contracts refers to the termination of contract before it is fully performed.

Conditions for Variation or Rescission of Contract

Variation or rescission of contracts is allowed where the parties reach an agreement to amend or terminate a contract for the purpose of achieving better economic efficacy or avoiding unnecessary losses. Such a new agreement must not damage the state interests or public interests of the society. It may also be exercised by one party if he is prevented from performance by *force majeure*, or if the other party fails to perform the contract within the stipulated time set by the contract. Variation or rescission is also allowed where there is a *change of circumstances*, which refers to a situation where the circumstances have changed due to causes unrelated to the parties so that the performance of contract has become *obviously unfair* to one party. This is not mentioned in the ECL, but was clarified as one of the causes to vary or rescind the contract by the Supreme People's Court in its *Minutes of the National Conference on Economic Disputes Adjudication Work* in 1993. It pointed out that if, due to reasons unrelated to the parties, the circumstances for performing the contract have changed fundamentally out of the expectation of the parties so that the performance of the original contract becomes *obviously unfair* to one party, the court may grant variation or rescission of the contract upon the request by either party based on the principle of *change of circumstances*.

Procedures for Variation and Rescission of Contract

Where the parties decide to vary or rescind the contract by agreement, such variation or rescission becomes effective when the new agreement is reached. Such agreement must be in writing (ECL, Article 27; FECL, Article 32).

Where one party decides to rescind the contract due to *force majeure* or because the other party fails to perform the contract in due time, he must notify the other party immediately. Such notification must be in writing (ECL, Article 27; FECL, Article 32). In practice, the party usually explains the reasons for rescinding the contract. He is required to provide a certificate to the other party in case of *force majeure*. Rescission of the contract becomes effective once it is notified to the other party. The effectiveness does not depend on the other party's consent.

Where a contract is varied or rescinded according to the rule of *change of circumstances*, it will not be directly effectuated by either party. The party wishing to vary or rescind the contract must make a petition to the people's court or an arbitral tribunal, who will then affirm the *change of circumstances* and order a variation or rescission of the contract.

Legal Consequences of Variation and Rescission of Contract

The rights and obligations of the parties under the original contract terminate once the contract is varied or rescinded. Article 16 of ECL provides that the party at fault shall compensate the other party for any loss suffered as a result of the variation or rescission of the contract, except where exemption of liability clauses apply. GPCL, Article 115 also provides that variation or rescission of contract does not affect the injured party's right to claim compensation. Variation or rescission of the contract will not affect the terms relating to dispute resolution and accord and satisfaction in the original contract (FECL, Articles 34–36).

Liabilities for Breach of Contract

GPCL Article 106 provides that a citizen or legal person who breaches a contract or fails to perform other obligations must bear civil liability. Where both parties have breached a contract, it is necessary to determine separately the amount of civil liability each should bear (GPCL, Article 113).

Traditionally, Chinese law has shown a strong favour towards specific performance as the primary form of remedy for breach of contract. GPCL Article 111 provides where one party fails to perform his contractual duty, or his performance is not in accordance with the agreed terms, the other party has a right to demand performance, or the taking of measures to correct the defective performance, and has the right to demand compensation for loss. According to GPCL Article 112, the liability for compensation shall be equal to the loss suffered by the other party as a result of the breach. Parties may provide in a contract that when a party breaches the contract he shall pay to the injured party a certain sum of money for the breach (liquidated damages); they may also provide in the contract a method for the calculation of damages. Liquidated damages can be purely compensatory as in FECL and TCL, or both compensatory and punitive as in ECL.

Where a party's failure to perform his contractual duty is caused by its supervisory government organ, GPCL, Article 116 requires the party in breach to pay compensation to the other party or take measures to correct the defective performance in accordance with what is agreed in the contract. The supervisory government organ will then be responsible for dealing with the losses that the breaching party has sustained as a result. This principle was reiterated in the 1981 ECL, Article 33. The provision was deleted in the new 1993 ECL. Where the supervisory government authorities unlawfully interfere with the performance of contract and cause damages to the parties, the injured party may seek remedies according to the *Administrative Procedure Law*.[16] This rule of GPCL, Article 116, however, is still applicable to technology contracts according to TCL, Article 19.

The injured party has a duty to mitigate the loss caused by the breach. GPCL, Article 114 requires the non-breaching party to take prompt measures to prevent an increase in the extent of the loss. If measures are not taken in a timely manner to prevent an increase in the extent of the loss, the injured party does not have the right to demand compensation for the resulting increase in damages.

Liabilities for breach of contract may be exempted by *force majeure*.[17] *Force majeure* generally refers to natural disasters such as earthquake, typhoon, drought, flooding and events such as war or other military actions. It must be unforeseeable, unavoidable and insurmountable by the parties. If one party is hindered by *force majeure* from performing the contract, he must notify the other party immediately and provide a certificate of such event to the other party. The certificate shall be issued by the responsible State agency for the party concerned or by other relevant authorities. It shall certify the occurrence of the *force majeure* and that the non-performance or defective performance is the result of *force majeure*.

Dispute Resolution

Consultation and Mediation

Consultation is the most common method of dispute resolution in China. The procedure is simple, friendly and harmonious compared with other methods. The parties consult with each other directly and on equal status, attempting to reach an agreement as to who bears what amount of liability. Consultation shall be in compliance with the laws and policies of the State and may not be used to injure a third party's interests. **7.06**

Mediation is facilitated by a third party, agreed upon by the parties to a contract, to help them reach a mediation agreement. The agreement must be reached voluntarily and willingly by the parties so that they will implement the agreement voluntarily. In practice, the role of a mediator is usually played by the responsible government agency because it is more familiar with the business operation of the parties than outsiders. Mediation has proved to be an effective method of dispute resolution in China.

Arbitration

To resolve contract disputes by arbitration, there must be mutual agreement by the parties to do so. This is achieved by an arbitration clause in the contract or an arbitration agreement at a later stage when a dispute arises, whereby the parties agree to submit their dispute to an independent arbitral tribunal for resolution. The arbitral award is final and neither party may appeal to the court for further review. Where one party fails to perform his part of the duty according to the arbitral award, the other party may apply to the people's court for enforcement. According to article 217 of the *Civil Procedure Law* (CPL), courts may not allow enforcement of domestic arbitral awards if there are procedural errors in the arbitration proceedings, insufficiency in fact finding or mistakes in application of law. While for arbitral awards involving foreign elements, CPL Article 260 provides that courts may not allow enforcement if there are procedural errors in the arbitration process.

Adjudication

Adjudication of contractual disputes occurs where the parties neither include an arbitration clause in their contract nor reach an arbitration agreement afterwards. The people's courts will not accept cases where an arbitral award has already been made. That is, the parties must choose between arbitration and adjudication. They cannot have both. Nevertheless, if there is a dispute over jurisdiction of an arbitration tribunal and one party brings the case to a court, the court has the power to decide the dispute over the issue of jurisdiction.

Economic Contract Law

7.07   The ECL was first promulgated on December 13, 1981 and became effective on July 1, 1982. It applies to domestic economic contractual relationships. According to Article 56 of the 1981 statute, the State Council has promulgated 13 administrative regulations to supplement the rules established in the ECL. They are *Regulation on Contracts for Construction Project Survey and Design* (May 8, 1983), *Regulation on Contracts for Construction and Installation* (August 8, 1983), *Regula-*

tion on Economic Contract Arbitration (August 22, 1983), *Regulation on Property Insurance Contracts* (September 1, 1983), *Regulation on Contracts for the Sale of Agricultural and Related Products* (January 23, 1984), *Regulation on Contracts for the Sale of Industrial and Mineral Products* (January 23, 1984), *Regulation on Processing Contracts* (November 20, 1984), *Regulation on Loan Contracts* (February 28, 1985), *Implementation Rules on Bailment Contracts* (September 25, 1985), *Implementation Rules on Contracts for Transportation by Highway* (November 8, 1986), *Implementation Rules on Contracts for Transportation by Water* (November 8, 1986), *Implementation Rules on Contracts for Transportation by Rail* (November 8, 1986), and *Implementation Rules on Contracts for Transportation by Air* (November 8, 1986).[18] The ECL was substantially amended on September 2, 1993 by the Third Session of the Standing Committee of the Eighth National People's Congress to accommodate the newly emerging market economy in China.

Application of the ECL

The ECL applies to a contract where both parties are legal persons, other economic organizations, individual business households and rural leaseholding households. The purpose for concluding economic contracts is to clarify each party's rights and obligations so as to realise certain economic goals (ECL, Article 2).

An economic contract is formed in the process of production or exchange of commodity for business purposes or for the purpose of carrying out certain tasks that are assigned by the State. Both parties enter into the contract for certain economic purposes. Thus, the following contracts are excluded from this law: ordinary consumer contracts, where one party intends to obtain goods for personal or family consumption; foreign economic contracts where one party to the contract is a foreign person or entity; technology contracts where the parties are concerned with the development, transfer, consultation or service of technology.

ECL Article 8 contains a list of specific contacts under its governance:

- (a) sale of goods contracts, including contracts for the sale of industrial and mineral products and contracts for the sale of agricultural and related products;
- (b) construction contracts, including survey and design contracts, and construction and installation contracts;
- (c) processing contracts;
- (d) contracts for the transportation of goods;

(e) contracts for the supply and use of electricity;
(f) storage and bailment contracts;
(g) property lease contracts;
(h) loan contracts; and
(i) property insurance contracts.

With limited space, this section will focus on the general principles that apply to all economic contracts.

Formation of Economic Contracts

Basic Principles

7.08 The basic principles for forming an economic contract are: that the parties must comply with the laws and administrative regulations of the State (ECL, Article 4); that the parties must on equal status enter into a contract which is mutually beneficial, and they must reach the agreement through consultation — neither party may impose its own will upon the other party by force and no other unit or individual may interfere with the formation of contracts (ECL, Article 5). Where an economic contract concerns any mandatory plan issued to an enterprise by the State according to needs, it shall be formed between the enterprises concerned according to their rights and obligations prescribed by relevant laws and administrative regulations (ECL, Article 11). This last principle reiterates Article 58(6) of the GPCL, which provides that economic contracts that violate the State's mandatory plans are void.

Major Terms and Formality of Contract

According to the ECL, Article 9, an economic contract is formed when the parties reach an agreement upon the major terms of the contract. Major terms of an economic contract include: subject matter(s) of the contract; quantity and quality; price or remuneration; time, place and manner of performance; liabilities for breach of contract; and other necessary terms required by law or either party to the contract (ECL, Article 12). As for formality, ECL, Article 3 requires all contracts to be in writing except those that are performed immediately after the formation of contract. For example, a transaction whereby the buyer pays the price and in the meantime the seller delivers the goods, may be deemed as an oral contract and is valid under ECL. In practice, there are very few oral economic contracts. A contract is usually in writing if the subject matter involves a large amount of money, even if it can be performed immediately after the formation.

Void Contracts

Vitiating Factors

Incapacity is one vitiating factor. Parties to a contract must have the capacity to enter into contract. Economic contracts are often void because of incapacity in the following circumstances: where legal persons, individual business households or private enterprises enter into contracts before obtaining their business licence pending approval and registration by the administrations for industry and commerce; or where they enter into contracts after their licences are revoked. Where a party enters into a contract that goes beyond its approved scope of business, the part of the contract in excess of its approved scope of business is void.[19] Contracts are also void where the agent of a party goes beyond the authority to make the contract, or where the agent signs the contract in the name of the principal with the agent himself or his other principals (ECL, Article 7(3)).

Illegality is another vitiating factor. According to ECL, Article 7(1), contracts that are against the law or administrative regulations are void. Illegal contracts include both contracts that are against the express provisions of the law and contracts that attempt to evade the regulation of the law. ECL, Article 7(4) adds that economic contracts against State interests or public interests of the society are void.

Contracts formed by fraud or duress are also void (ECL, Article 7(2)). Fraud means one party intentionally provides false information to, or conceals the truth from the other party when entering into a contract. Duress means coercing the other party into making an expression of intention against his true will by causing or threatening to cause damage to the health, property or reputation of the other party, or his family or friends.

Legal Consequences of Void Contracts

The determination of void contracts, *i.e.* the declaration that a contract is void, is made by a people's court or an arbitral tribunal. Void contracts do not have any legal effect from the time of formation. If the determination is made that only part of the contract is void, then the rest of the contract may still be valid (ECL, Article 7).

Article 16 of the ECL provides for the legal consequences of void contracts. They are restitution, compensation, and confiscation. After an economic contract is declared void, a party to the contract shall return the property acquired pursuant to the contract back to the other party. The party at fault shall compensate the other party for any loss suffered as a result of the contract being void. If both parties are at fault, they shall bear the liabilities respectively. As regards contracts that are against State interests or public interests of the society, if both parties have acted wilfully, the property acquired or stipulated to be acquired by the parties shall be confiscated by the State; if only one party has acted wilfully, the wilful party shall return the goods acquired back to the other party, and the property acquired or stipulated to be acquired by the party that has not acted wilfully shall be turned over to the State.

Performance of Economic Contracts

7.09   ECL, Article 6 attempts to ensure full performance of the contracts and discourage any breach. It provides that once an economic contract is formed according to law, it has a legally binding force. The parties must perform the contract fully. Neither party may vary or rescind the contract out of his own will, *i.e.* without the consent of the other party.

Variation and Rescission of Economic Contracts

An economic contract may be varied or rescinded where the two parties have reached an agreement to do so and it will not injure the State interests or public interests of the society, or where full performance of the contract becomes impossible due to *force majeure,* or where the other party does not perform the contract within the stipulated time (ECL, Article 26). The notice or agreement to effectuate the variation or rescission must be in writing (ECL, Article 27).

By Article 30 of ECL, if *force majeure* only partly affects the performance of the contract, the party, after giving the other party notice and certificate of the event, may postpone performance or render partial performance of the contract. It is, in effect, variation of the contract.

Liabilities for Breach of Economic Contracts

Breach of Contract

7.10   Article 29 of the ECL provides that if, due to the fault of one party, an economic contract cannot be performed or cannot be fully performed, the party at fault shall be liable for breach of contract. If both parties are at fault, each party shall be liable for the breach. Therefore, a breach of economic contracts requires two elements: the fault of the party or parties, and the fact that the contract is not performed at all or the performance is defective.

Remedies

The ECL strongly favours specific performance as the primary form of remedy in comparison with monetary damages or other remedies. The parties enter into an economic contract to realize certain economic purposes. Although damages can compensate the loss as far as money can do, it is not a substitute for the economic interests expected by the parties when making the contract. Only continuing and actual performance can let the injured party realize his expected interests under the contract and from a broader perspective, can maintain a healthy economic development.

Specific Performance

Article 31 of the ECL provides that if the injured party requires continuing performance of the contract, the party in breach shall render continuing performance of the contract. The term "continuing performance" has the same meaning as specific performance in common law. In particular, it includes repair, redelivery, repackaging, remake, and exchange for a substitute etc.

Liquidated Damages

The ECL, Article 31 provides that where a party breaches an economic contract, he shall pay liquidated damages to the other party. Liquidated damages are payable to the non-breaching party upon the other party's non-performance or defective performance as a result of his fault. It can be stipulated by law, or agreed upon by the parties. Many regulations on economic contracts stipulate the method for calculating damages in case of breach. For example, *Regulation on Contracts for the Sale of Industrial and Mineral Products*, Article 35(5), Article 36(3) and (4); *Regulation on Contracts for the Sale of Agricultural and Related Products*, Article 18(3) and (5); *Regulation on Loan Contracts*, Articles 15–17. These are known as fixed or mandatory liquidated damages. The parties must follow those rules to calculate their damages. Some regulations give a permissible range, within which the parties may decide the amount of such damages. For example, *Regulation on Contracts for the Sale of Industrial and Mineral Products*, Articles 35(1) and 36(1); *Regulation on Contracts for the Sale of Agricultural and Related Products*, Articles 17(1), (2) and (4) and 18(1) and (2). They are floating liquidated damages. Where the law or regulations do not have specific provisions on the calculation of liquidated damages, or where the regulations on contracts have such provisions but permit the parties to agree otherwise, the parties to an economic contract may agree upon liquidated damages when forming the contract.

Liquidated damages have the double nature of being punitive and compensatory. When the breach causes no actual loss to the non-breaching party, he is still entitled to claim liquidated damages from the breaching party. In this case, liquidated damages are punitive. They act as a penalty to the breaching party. While the breach causes actual loss which is greater than the liquidated damages, it operates as com-pensation to the injured party. Where the loss caused by the breach is smaller than the liquidated damages, it is both punitive and compensatory.

Compensatory Damages

Compensatory damages are payable to the injured party if the contract does not provide for liquidated damages or the economic loss caused by the breach exceeds the amount of liquidated damages. ECL Article 31 provides that an injured party may claim compensatory damages where the actual economic loss exceeds the amount of liquidated damages. It is compensatory by nature. There must be actual economic loss. In case the contract contains a liquidated damages clause, the actual economic loss must be greater than the liquidated damages to entitle the injured party to claim compensatory damages.

Rescission of Contract

Where the other party breaches an economic contract, the injured party has the right by notifying the other party to rescind the contract (ECL, Article 26(1)).

Payment of Damages

Payment of liquidated damages or compensatory damages must be made within ten days after the liability is determined, otherwise the matter shall be treated as an overdue payment (ECL, Article 32). The liability can be determined by court or arbitral tribunal, or through consultation or mediation.

Exemption of Liabilities for Breach of Contract

Liabilities for breach of contracts may be exempted if such breach is the result of *force majeure* (ECL, Article 30). In practice, the extent to which *force majeure* may exempt a party's liability for breach of contract varies. If *force majeure* renders the performance of the con-tract totally impossible, the party is fully exempted from the liability for breaching the contract and may rescind the contract. If *force majeure* only makes a certain part of the performance of the contract impossible, then the party's liability is only partially exempted. If *force majeure* only temporarily prevents the party from performing the contract in due course, then the party's liability for delayed performance is exempted. By Article 30 of ECL, if *force majeure* only partly affects the performance of the contract, the party, after giving the other party notice and certificate of the event, may postpone performance or render partial performance of the contract. This is, in effect, variation of the contract.

Dispute Resolution

Where there is dispute arising from an economic contract, the parties may settle it by consultation or mediation. If they are unwilling or unable to settle the dispute through consultation or mediation, they may resort to arbitration according to the arbitration clause in the contract or an arbitration agreement reached after the dispute arises. If there is neither arbitration clause nor arbitration agreement between the parties, they may bring the case to a people's court for resolution (ECL, Article 42).

The time limit for petitioning for an arbitration of economic contract disputes is two years, and the time starts to run when the party knows, or should know that his rights are infringed. Economic contract disputes are dealt with in the economic chambers of the people's court, the rail transportation courts and maritime courts. Arbitration of economic contract disputes is dealt with in detail in Chapter 11 on "Alternative Dispute Resolution".

Management of Economic Contracts

Management of contracts is a special feature of Chinese contract law. This is one of the areas that strongly demonstrate government intervention in the contract system. Article 44 of the ECL provides that the administration for industry and commerce of the people's government above the county level and other relevant State agencies shall be responsible for the supervision of economic contracts according to laws and regulations. Such supervision is done through certification and notarization, neither of which is mandatory for the parties. Certification is intended to verify the legal capacity of the parties to fulfil their contractual obligations and other related matters. Economic contracts are certified by the administrations for industry and commerce. Notarization is intended to verify the legality and truthfulness of contracts by the state notary bodies.

Foreign Economic Contract Law

7.11 The FECL was promulgated on March 21, 1985 and implemented on July 1 of the same year. In most of the important aspects, the FECL has codified and reaffirmed China's foreign economic practice consistent with international commercial customs. The basic principles of the FECL dealing with formation, performance, liabilities for breach, choice of law, and dispute resolution etc. can all be traced back in some way to the model contracts used or negotiated by the Chinese in international trade transactions in the past.

The FECL is complemented by the following laws and regulations promulgated by the NPC Standing Committee and the State Council: the *Sino-Foreign Equity Joint Venture Law*,[20] the *Sino-Foreign Co-operative Joint Venture Law*,[21] the *Regulation on the Management of Technology Import Contracts*[22] and its implementation rules,[23] and the *Regulation on Chinese-Foreign Co-operative Exploitation of Offshore Petroleum Resources*[24] etc.

Two years after the implementation of the FECL, the Supreme People's Court issued its first formal interpretation of the law on October 19, 1987. The document was entitled *Reply to Certain Questions Concerning the Application of the Foreign Economic Contract Law* (the Reply).[25] It was intended to clarify a number of important issues that have emerged since the FECL was promulgated.

China ratified the 1980 United Nations Convention on Contracts for the International Sales of Goods (CISG) on December 11, 1986, which became effective January 1, 1988.[26] According to the FECL Article 6, where Chinese laws are in conflict with international treaties, to which China is a signatory or a party, the international treaty shall apply, except for provisions on which China has declared reservation. For example, China declared reservation to CISG Article 11 which states that contracts need not be in writing. Therefore, according to FECL, all foreign economic contracts are required to be in writing.

Application of FECL

FECL has covered virtually all foreign commercial activities in China ranging from finance and trade to service and investment. According to Article 2, FECL applies to all economic contracts between Chinese enterprises and foreign business or individuals, except for contracts concerning international transportation. The Reply defines the notion of "economic contracts" by providing a list of such contracts and further explains what constitutes a "foreign" economic contract.

"Economic contracts" include contracts for the sale of goods, equity joint venture contracts, co-operative joint venture contracts, contracts for co-operative exploration and exploitation of natural resources, loan contracts, lease of property contracts, contracts for technology transfer, contracts for supply of whole sets of equipment, processing and labour contracts etc. Contracts for international transport by sea, air, rail or any combination thereof are excluded from FECL (The Reply, s. 1(1)).

"Foreign" economic contracts are contracts between or among enterprises, economic organizations or individuals of Hong Kong, Macau or a foreign country and Chinese enterprises. Where both parties to a foreign economic contract are foreign (or from Hong Kong or Macau) and the contract is either made or performed in China, the FECL should apply (The Reply, s. 1(2)). Taiwan is not mentioned in the Reply. However, according to practice, companies or individuals from Taiwan have been treated as foreign persons. Article 5 of the *Provisions on Encouraging Investment from Taiwan*[27] issued by the State Council provides that Taiwan investors who establish wholly- owned enterprises, equity joint ventures or co-operative joint ventures in mainland China shall be treated as foreign investors and relevant foreign economic laws and regulations shall apply. They are thus entitled to such incentive measures as low-interest loans and tax deduction or exemptions which are available to foreign persons. Article 13 of the recent *Protection of Investment by Taiwanese Compatriots Law*[28] seeks to emphasize such treatment by providing that Taiwanese investment enterprises shall enjoy preferential treatment in accordance with the relevant State Council Regulations for encouraging investment by Taiwanese compatriots.

The FECL does not apply to contracts between Chinese-foreign equity joint ventures, co-operative joint ventures, or wholly foreign-owned enterprises and Chinese enterprises or individuals in China. Since they are entities established in China as Chinese legal persons, the domestic ECL applies in such cases (The Reply, s. 1(3)). The FECL does not expressly provide for a standard to determine the nationality of an enterprise or other economic organizations. According to relevant legislation on foreign investment and foreign enterprise management, nationality of an enterprise is determined by its place of registration.

Formation of Foreign Economic Contracts

Formality of Contract

Foreign economic contracts must be in writing. According to the   **7.12**
FECL, Article 7, a contract is formed when the parties sign a written

agreement. Where an agreement is reached through letters, telegrams or telex, and one party requests a signed confirmation letter, the contract is formed when the confirmation letter is signed. In practice, a fax can also be used to form a written contract. Where, according to the laws or administrative regulations of the PRC, the contract needs to be approved by the state, the contract is formed when such approval is granted. Such contracts include Chinese-foreign equity joint venture contracts, Chinese-foreign co-operative joint venture contracts, technology import contracts, compensation trade contracts, Chinese-foreign co-operative exploration of ocean petroleum contracts etc.

Major Terms

A foreign economic contract shall contain the following terms: name, nationality, principal place of business or domicile of the parties; date and place of contracting; type of contract and type and scope of the subject matter of the contract; technical requirements, quality, standard, specification and quantity of the subject matter; time, place and method of performance; price, currency and method of payment and other related costs; assignability of contracts and conditions of assignment; liabilities for breach of contract; dispute resolution; and languages of the contract and their effects (FECL, Article 12). These terms are crucial for the performance of contract and the determination of breach and remedies.

Void Contracts and Voidable Contracts

The FECL and subsequent judicial interpretation provide for circumstances where a contract is void or voidable.

Void Contracts: Vitiating Factors

Incapacity is one such vitiating factor. The FECL Article 2 provides that foreign economic contracts are made between Chinese enterprises or other economic organizations and foreign enterprises, other economic organizations or individuals. That does not prevent Chinese citizens (individuals) from becoming party to a foreign economic contract if they are granted such capacity with regard to certain types of contracts by law. For example, according to Article 2 of the *Regulations on Administration of Technology Import Contracts*, Chinese citizens can be a party to such contracts.

The Reply lists four situations where contracts are rendered void due to incapacity. It indicates the importance of determining a Chinese entity's status and authority before entering into any kind of contract with it. The four situations are as follows:

(a) where one of the parties does not have the "qualification of a legal subject" at the time of contracting;
(b) where the Chinese party was not granted the "foreign trade authority" by the relevant State organs;
(c) where the Chinese party exceeds its scope of business; and
(d) where the contract is made by a party holding itself out as an agent but who does not have the actual authority to sign on another's behalf. Similarly, a contract is void if it is signed by a party who exceeds the scope of its authority to sign on another's behalf, or whose authority to sign on another's behalf has terminated before it signs the contract (The Reply, ss. 3(1)–(4)).

Illegal contracts and contracts against public interests are also void. FECL, Article 4 provides that the formation of a contract must be in compliance with the laws of China and must not harm the public interests of the society. Contracts against the laws of the PRC or the public interests of the society are void, according to Article 9. Illegal contracts are those which violate the constitution, laws and regulations of China. Contracts that attempt to evade the Chinese laws and regulations are also illegal.

The rule that a contract against public interests of society is void is similar to the doctrine of "public policy" in common law, which enables judges to refuse relief to litigants claiming under contracts which are considered to be injurious to the public good.[29] Under China's socialist legal system, the interpretation of this provision may be different from the common law practice. Contracts that cause harm to the state sovereignty, destruction to China's natural resources, heavy pollution to the environment, injury of people's health and safety, deterioration and corruption of Chinese moral values etc. are all regarded as against public interests. Therefore, contracts for the import of heavy polluting technology or equipments, contracts for the disposal of toxic and hazardous wastes in China, contracts for the import of pornographic publications to China etc. are void according to this doctrine.

The Reply further provides that a contract is void where the parties maliciously conspire to harm the interests of the State, a collective or a third party, and that legal contracts for illegal purposes are also void (The Reply, s. 3(8)).

One point worth noting is that the FECL accords special protection to contracts concerning foreign investment in China or the development of natural resources in co-operation with foreign business. Under Article 40 of the FECL, contracts for Chinese-foreign joint ventures, Chinese-foreign co-operative enterprises or Chinese-foreign co-operation in exploration and development of natural resources, which are performed in the PRC and approved by the State, may continue to be performed according to the contract terms despite new laws that provide otherwise. Such a rule provides a greater degree of certainty to foreign investors who might be concerned that a contract will become void if it is inconsistent with subsequent legislation.

FECL Article 10 provides that contracts made under fraud or duress are void. Section 3(7) of the Reply further explains the principle. Where one party by means of deceit or fraud intentionally makes false representation or conceals the truth from the other party, so as to induce the other party to make a contract on the basis of mistake or misunderstanding; or where one party uses duress or threat of economic loss or other damage to the other party to force the latter to enter into a contract; or where one party takes advantage of the economic distress of another party to enter into a contract based on unfair terms against the will of the other party, such contracts are void.

A contract is also void if, according to PRC laws or administrative rules, it should have been submitted for approval to the Chinese authorities in charge and it did not receive such approval. Further, an approved contract becomes void if significant variations are made, or significant rights and obligations are transferred without obtaining approval from the original approval authorities (The Reply, s. 3(6)).

Voidable Contracts

The FECL does not mention voidable contracts, but the Reply reaffirms the principles established by Article 59 of the GPCL by providing that foreign economic contracts which show *significant misconception* or which are *obviously unfair* to one party are voidable. The disadvantaged party may request the people's court to rescind the contract. Where one party has a misconception with regard to the nature of the contract, the capacity of the other party, the type, quality, specification and quantity of the subject matter of the contract, and method, time and place of performance so that the consequence of his conduct is against his intention and he suffers great loss, the situation is recognised as *significant misconception*. Where one party takes advantage of his position or the lack of experience of the other party to make a contract in which the rights and obligations of the two parties are obviously against the principles of fairness and exchange of equivalent values, it is recognised as being *obviously unfair* to one party. However, according to the *Supreme People's Court's Opinion on Several Issues Regarding the Implementation of the "General Principles of Civil Law (for trial use)"*, the request to rescind the contract must be made within one year after the contract is formed.

Severability of Contract

It is recognized in Chinese law that contracts are severable, *i.e.* where part of the contract is void, other parts may still be valid so long as they are "not affected" by the absence of the voided terms (The Reply, s. 5(1)). This is consistent with Article 30 of FECL, which provides that partial termination of a contract does not affect the rest of the contract when the terms are "mutually independent".

Legal Consequences of Void and Rescinded Contracts

Void contracts and rescinded contracts have no legal effect from the time the contract is made. The rights and obligations of the parties are therefore not protected by law.

Both FECL and the Reply treat the fault causing a contract to be void as a type of breach. Therefore, the party at fault is liable for the losses caused to the innocent party as a result of the contract being void. "Fault" seems to include negligence as well as non-compliance with statutory or administrative rules. Therefore a foreign party may claim damages from a Chinese party where a contract becomes void due to the latter's failure to comply with the PRC approval procedures.

Performance of Foreign Economic Contracts and Suspension of Performance

The FECL Article 16 provides that parties to a contract shall perform 7.13 their parts of the duties under the contract and neither party may unilaterally vary or rescind the contract. However, a party is granted the right to suspend the performance of the contract if he has sufficient evidence that the other party is not able to perform the contract (FECL, Article 17). Such a right is subject to the following limitations: First of all, the party exercising such a right must have sufficient evidence that the other party is not able to perform the contract. Sufficient evidence may be a written notice from the other party that he is not able to perform the contract or is not able to perform the contract according to schedule, or evidence that the other party has lost its ability to perform or has been declared bankrupt, or a certificate showing the other party is not able to perform the contract because of *force majeure*. Secondly, the party exercising such a right must notify the other party of the suspension of performance immediately to avoid or reduce the losses. If the other party, after receiving the notice of suspension of performance, provides adequate guaranty to perform the contract, then the party exercising such a right must continue to perform the contract. Thirdly, a party may exercise such a right only when there is no guaranty terms in the contract or the guaranty is obviously inadequate. If one party provides adequate guaranty when making the contract, the other party does not have the right to suspend the performance.

Assignment, Variation and Discharge of Foreign Economic Contracts

Assignment of Contract

The idea of assignment of contract was introduced by the FECL. Under Article 26, the rights and obligations of a party under a contract may be assigned to a third party, but the assignment must be made with the consent of the other party. According to the FECL Article 27, if a contract is formed with the approval of the State, the approval by the same State authority is required for the assignment of the contract, unless the original contract with state approval has terms to the contrary.

Variation and Rescission of Contract

Contracts may be varied upon agreement by the parties (FECL, Article 28). Rescission of contract is allowed to a party if the other party breaches the contract and the breach has seriously affected the economic interests expected by the non-breaching party when making the contract, or if the other party does not perform the contract within the time limit set by the contract, and fails to perform the contract again within the reasonably extended period (FECL, Article 29(1) and (2)).

   According to the FECL, Article 32, both the agreement for the variation of contract and the notification of rescission are required to be in writing. FECL Article 33 further provides that where the formation of the original contracts requires State approval according to the law or administrative regulations, any substantial variation of such contracts would also require the approval, while rescission notice is only required to be submitted to the approval organ for record. Despite the variation or rescission of a contract, the right of the injured party to claim damages from the other party under the contract is not affected (FECL, Article 34).

Discharge of Contract

Under the FECL, Article 31, contracts may be discharged by performance, by the order of the arbitral tribunals or the courts, or by agreement between the parties. Discharge of contract does not affect a party's right to claim damages from the other party (FECL, Article 34). The contract terms with regard to dispute resolution and accord and satisfaction will not be affected by the discharge of the contract (FECL, Articles 35 and 36).

Liabilities for Breach of Foreign Economic Contracts

The FECL is quite different from the ECL in determining liabilities for breach of contract. For breach, the ECL requires proof of fault before imposing liability on the party in breach (ECL, Article 29). This requirement is absent from the FECL. For remedies, the ECL shows a strong favour for specific performance (ECL, Article 31), which is not expressly provided as a type of remedy and can only be implied as one of those "other reasonable remedies" under the FECL Article 18. As a matter of fact, compensation for losses is the primary form of remedy for breach of foreign economic contracts. **7.14**

Breach of Contract

According to the FECL, Article 18, a breach of contract means one party to a contract does not perform his part of the duties or his performance does not comply with the terms of the contract. The party in breach must provide remedies to the injured party. However, where both parties breach the contract, each of them will be liable (FECL, Article 21).

Liabilities for Breach of Contract

Once the injured party proves breach by the other party and that he suffers economic losses as a result of the breach, he is entitled to remedies.

Compensatory Damages

The FECL, Article 18 provides that an injured party has the right to claim compensatory damages or other reasonable remedies from the party in breach, and if other remedies (as discussed later in this section) are not sufficient to compensate his losses, the injured party may claim damages in addition to those other remedies. But there is a limit to such damages, that is, the amount of the damages shall compensate the injured party's losses, but shall not be more than the amount of losses that the party in breach should have foreseen at the time when the contract is made (FECL, Article 19). The rule of compensation for actual loss and loss of profits and limitations based on foreseeability are consistent with CISG, Articles 74 and 77.

The Reply s. 6(1) further provides that damages for breach of contract include destruction, reduction or loss of property, expenses incurred in reducing or preventing such losses, and interest that could have been earned had the contract been fulfilled. With respect to international sale of goods, the Reply specifies that the interest that could have been earned refers to lost profits, *i.e.* the profits or interests expected from the full performance of the contract by the non-breaching party when he enters into the contract.

Another limitation on the right of the injured party is set by the FECL, Article 22. The non-breaching party has a duty to take proper measures in time to prevent the increase of the loss, *i.e.* to mitigate the loss. If he fails to do so, he has no right to claim compensation for the increased portion of the loss.

Liquidated Damages

Under the FECL Article 20, parties to a contract may stipulate a set amount of money as liquidated damages when forming the contract. When there is a breach of contract, the party in breach will be liable to pay the sum to the non-breaching party. They may also agree upon a method for calculating the damages in the contract. Such liquidated damages are treated as compensation to the injured party for his losses resulting from the breach. Therefore, if the amount of liquidated damages is set too high or too low compared with the actual loss suffered by the non-breaching party, either party may petition the arbitral tribunal or the court to reduce or increase the amount as appropriate. The purely compensatory nature of liquidated damages is further emphasized by the Reply, which defines liquidated damages as a "predetermined amount of compensation" in section 6(2). Because the nature of liquidated damages under FECL is compensatory, a party cannot claim liquidated damages and compensatory damages at the same time, though liquidated damages may be used together with other remedies. In contrast, liquidated damages in domestic economic contracts are both compensatory and punitive by nature. A party may seek and is entitled to claim compensatory damages in addition to liquidated damages if the actual loss exceeds the liquidated damages (ECL, Article 31).

Other Remedies

If one party pays the contract price after the due time set by the contract, the other party has the right to claim interests over the overdue payment. Method for calculation of interest may be stipulated in the contract (FECL, Article 23). Other remedies include suspension of performance (FECL, Article 17) and rescission of contract (FECL, Article 29(1) and (2)). In practice, the injured party may get other reasonable remedies such as a price cut, specific performance, repair, exchange, reprocessing, reconstruction and other remedies.

Exemption from Liabilities

Under the FECL, Article 24, liabilities for breach of contract may be exempted if the breach results from *force majeure*. The parties are allowed to stipulate the scope of *force majeure* in the contract. However, the party whose performance of the contract becomes impossible due to *force majeure* is required, by Article 25 of the FECL, to notify the other party in a timely manner so as to minimize the losses the non-performance may cause to the other party. He must also, within a reasonable time, provide a certificate of *force majeure* issued by the relevant government body to the other party.

Dispute Resolution and Choice of Law

Dispute Resolution

The FECL outlines a basic dispute resolution procedure, including **7.15** consultation, mediation, arbitration and adjudication, with emphasis on consultation and mediation. Consultation and mediation are informal methods for dispute settlement which can be used together with arbitration or adjudication, while the latter two are mutually exclusive of each other.

Article 37 of the FECL allows the parties of a dispute to select an appropriate dispute settlement method. If the parties are unwilling or unable to settle their disputes through consultation or mediation, they may resort to arbitration, which may be conducted within or outside China. In practice, arbitration is favoured to adjudication in international commercial dispute settlement not only because it is less time-consuming (as an arbitral award is final while court decision can be appealed) but also because the arbitrators have more expertise in solving the dispute. One very important reason in favour of arbitration is the ease of recognition and enforcement of foreign arbitral award in countries who are members of the *New York Convention on Recognition and Enforcement of Foreign Arbitral Award*. More discussion on arbitration can be found in Chapter 11 on "Alternative Dispute Resolution".

According to the FECL, Article 38, if there is no arbitration clause in the contract or the parties fail to reach an agreement for arbitration after the dispute arises, they may bring a suit in the People's Court. Although there is no express exclusion of foreign courts as a forum for dispute resolution, this Article clearly gives an advantage to the

Chinese party of a contract who wants to use a Chinese court as the forum. In fact the current practice in China is that many loan agreements between Chinese borrowers and foreign banks cede jurisdiction to courts in New York, Japan and Hong Kong.

Choice of Law

The FECL Article 5 and the GPCL Article 145 provide for the basic principles on choice of law. The Reply illustrates those general rules by more detailed explanations.

Party Autonomy

The FECL adopts a liberal approach to the choice of law in contracts. Parties are allowed to choose the law for the settlement of disputes. However, one exception is that Chinese law shall apply to contracts involving Chinese-foreign equity joint ventures, Chinese-foreign co-operative joint ventures, and the co-operative exploration and development of natural resources in China with foreign business. Where Chinese law fails to have specific provisions, international practice will be followed (FECL, Article 5). However, there is a general qualification for applying foreign laws or international practices in China. They may not be applied if such application will violate the public and social policy of the PRC (GPCL, Article 150; the Reply, s. 2(10)).

The explicit mandate to apply Chinese law for contracts concerning joint ventures and the development of natural resources is intended to protect China's political and economic interests. It should not be a surprise to foreign lawyers for it is consistent with international practice. The law of the host country is usually applied to foreign investment contracts. The contracts that the FECL specifically requires to be governed by Chinese law are those concerning investment in China. They are usually negotiated and performed in China. For contracts involving exploration and development of natural resources, in addition to the fact that the place of contracting and performance is in China, the subject matter of the contract is also in China.

The Reply reaffirms the basic principle of party autonomy established in Article 5 of the FECL, specifying that the parties may choose Chinese law, the law of Hong Kong or Macau, or the law of a foreign country. The parties' choice of law must be made through mutual agreement, and it must be clearly stated in the contract. Where no choice of law is stipulated in a contract, the parties may still agree on their choice of law after a dispute has arisen or after a court has decided to hear the case. But it must be made before the hearing.

The Principle of Closest Relationship

Where the parties fail to choose the law in the contract or the parties cannot agree on the choice of law, the law of the country with the closest and most immediate relationship to the contract shall apply (FECL, Article 5; the Reply, s. 2(6)). The Reply further provides a guideline for courts to determine which law should govern certain types of contracts in the absence of an express choice by the parties. These guidelines are qualified by a provision that where the law of another jurisdiction clearly has a closer relationship to the contract than the law that would be applied according to the guidelines, then the law of such jurisdiction should be applied. The following is a list of the types of contracts and the law usually to be applied:

- (a) Contracts for the international sale of goods: generally the law of the seller's place of business. Exceptionally, the law of the buyer's jurisdiction should be applied if the contract:
  - (i) is negotiated and signed in the buyer's place of business, or
  - (ii) relies principally on terms proposed by the buyer and is executed on the basis of an order by the buyer, or
  - (iii) clearly stipulates that the seller must perform its obligations to tender goods at the buyer's place of business;
- (b) Bank loans or guarantee contracts: the law of the lender's or guarantor's place of business;
- (c) Insurance contracts: the law of insurer's place of business;
- (d) Processing contracts: the law of the processing contractor's place of business;
- (e) Technology transfer contracts: the law of the place of business of the recipient;
- (f) Project tender contracts: the law of the place where the project is located;
- (g) Contracts for scientific and technical consultancy or design contracts: the law of the place of business of the client;
- (h) Labour contracts: the law of the place where the labour is to be performed;
- (i) Contracts for the supply of complete sets of equipment: the law of the place where the equipment is to be operated;
- (j) Agency contracts: the law of the agent's place of business;
- (k) Contracts for the leasing, purchase, sale, or mortgage of real estate: the law of the situs of the real estate;
- (l) Contracts for the leasing of movable property: the law of the place of business of the lessor;
- (m) Storage contracts: the law of the place of business of the bailee.

When an enterprise has more than one place of business, the one with the closest relationship to the contract should be used for determining the "place of business" of the enterprise. Where a party to a contract has no place of business, its domicile or residence of the party should be used (the Reply, s. 2(7)).

International Treaties

The Reply section 2(8) reiterates the principle established in Article 6 of the FECL, that provisions of international treaties to which China has become a party should be applied where those provisions are different from corresponding provisions of PRC law. This rule is subject to the caveat that where China has made a reservation on the treaty provisions, these provisions do not override the relevant Chinese law. China has made such reservations, for example, to the provisions in the CISG governing conflicts of law and the recognition of oral contracts.

Sources of Foreign Laws

The Reply section 2(11) provides the following four sources that a court may consult to determine the content of foreign law:

(a) sources provided by the parties;
(b) sources provided by the Chinese embassy or consulate in the country whose law is to be applied;
(c) sources provided by the embassy or consulate in China of the foreign country whose law is to be applied; and
(d) sources provided by Chinese or foreign legal experts.

The variety of these sources gives Chinese courts much discretion in their determination of foreign law. The Reply provides that if reference to these sources does not provide the court with a clear answer, the case may be adjudicated according to the corresponding Chinese law.

Technology Contract Law

7.16 The TCL was promulgated on June 23, 1987 and implemented on November 1 of the same year. It applies to contractual relationships with regard to domestic technology development, technology transfer, technology consultation and technology service. According to the TCL Article 54, the State Science and Technology Commission promulgated the *Implementation Rules for Technology Contract Law* (TCL Implementation Rules) on March 15, 1989 with the approval of the State Council. This provides much more detailed regulatory mechanisms to supplement the general rules of TCL.

Application of TCL

Article 2 of the TCL provides that the statute applies to contracts between legal persons, between legal person and citizen, and between citizens with regard to technology development, technology transfer, technology consultation and technology services. The subject matter of the contract must be technology products. It does not apply to contracts where one party is a foreign enterprise, other organization or individual. However, the Chinese-foreign equity joint ventures, Chinese-foreign co-operative joint ventures and wholly foreign-owned enterprises established in China according to Chinese law are regarded as Chinese legal persons, and can therefore enter into technology contracts governed by TCL. On the other hand, due to the special status of Hong Kong, Macau and Taiwan, the technology contracts entered into between legal persons or individuals in those regions and a Chinese party are not governed by the TCL, but by the FECL, and the regulations issued under the FECL, primarily the *Administrative Regulation on Technology Import Contracts*, and its Implementation Rules.

The TCL particularly covers the following four types of contract:

(a) technology development contracts;
(b) technology transfer contracts;
(c) technology consultation contracts; and
(d) technology service contracts.

The requirements of the subject matters and rights and obligations of the parties are accordingly different for each type of technology contracts. The following are general rules applicable to all technology contracts.

Formation of Technology Contracts

Formality of Contract

As the subject matter of technology contract has a special complexity which requires accurate, precise and scientific description in the contract, all technology contracts are required to be in writing under the TCL Article 9. Letters, telegrams, telephone records, telex or fax can all be supplementary documents and form part of a valid technology contract, but cannot become substitutes for a written contract. According to TCL the Article 10, a contract is formed once the parties reach an agreement on the major terms of the contract and sign and seal the contract, or, where the contract requires State approval, it is formed when approval is granted. Where a contract requires the guarantee by a third person, the technology contract is formed when the guarantee contract is signed and sealed (TCL, Article 11).

Major Terms of Contract

The law provides that the major terms of a technology contract include: title of the project; content, scope and requirement of the subject matter; plan, progress, duration, place and method of performance; security measures for technology information and materials; bearing of risk; ownership and allocation of technology products; standard and method for inspection and acceptance; price or remuneration and method of payment; method of calculating liquidated damages or compensatory damages; method of dispute resolution; and explanation of technical terms and terminology (TCL, Article 15).

Vitiating Factors

The TCL Article 21 provides that contracts are void if they violate State laws or regulations, or cause damage to State interests or public interests of the society; if the parties illegally monopolize the technology and hinder the technological progress; if they infringe the legal rights and interests of other persons; or if they are formed by fraud or duress. Void contracts have no legal effect from the time of formation.

Performance of Technology Contracts

A technology contract is legally binding once it is formed according to law. Each party to the contract must fully perform his part of the duties under the contract. Neither party may unilaterally vary or rescind the contract (TCL, Article 16).

Variation and Rescission of Technology Contracts

Upon agreement by the parties, a contract may be varied or rescinded. Where the formation of a contract requires State approval, such variation or rescission must also get consent from the approving authority (TCL, Article 23). TCL Article 24 further provides that a party has the right to notify the other party to rescind the contract upon the breach by the other party, the occurrence of *force majeure,* or the disclosure of the subject matter of a technology development contract by a third party. Both the agreement and the notice to vary or rescind the contract shall be in writing (TCL Implementation Rules, Articles 30 and

31). Variation or rescission of the contract does not affect the injured party's right to claim damages (TCL, Article 35).

Liabilities for Breach of Technology Contracts

The TCL Article 17 provides for liabilities for breach of contract. A   **7.17** party is in breach if he does not perform the contract or the performance is not in accordance with the contract. The TCL stresses the remedy of specific performance. If there exists the possibility of continuing performance, the party in breach must render specific performance at the request of the injured party. The non-breaching party also has the right to request other remedial measures and claim damages. The amount of damages shall be equivalent to the losses suffered by the injured party, but shall not exceed the amount the party in breach should have foreseen at the time when the contract was formed. This upper limit based on foreseeability is similar to provisions in the FECL, which are absent in the ECL. The parties may agree upon a fixed amount as liquidated damages, or a method for calculating the damages in the contract. Liquidated damages are compensation for the losses caused by the breach. Unless otherwise provided in a contract, when actual loss exceeds liquidated damages, the court will not consider or try to calculate compensatory damages for the injured party (TCL Implementation Rules, Article 22). The non-breaching party has a duty to mitigate the loss and he has no right to claim damages with regard to the increased loss due to his failure to take proper measures to prevent the increase of loss.

Where one party cannot perform the contract due to reasons attributed to its supervisory governmental organs, it shall compensate the other party's loss or take other remedial measures first, and then request the governmental organs to deal with its losses (TCL, Article 19).

Force majeure may exempt a party's liability for breach of contract (TCL, Article 20). It must be unforeseeable, unavoidable and insurmountable. The parties are allowed to provide for the scope of *force majeure* in their contracts (TCL Implementation Rules, Article 24).

Dispute Resolution

The parties may settle their disputes through consultation or media-   **7.18** tion. Where the parties are unwilling to do so or such measures fail, they may resort to the arbitration according to the arbitration clause in the contract or an arbitration agreement reached after the dispute arises. Where there is neither an arbitration clause nor an arbitration agreement, the parties may bring the case to the people's court (TCL,

Article 51; TCL Implementation Rules, Articles 117, 118 and 120). The time limit for the parties to petition to a court or an arbitral tribunal is one year, starting from the time the party knows or should have known that his legal rights and interests are infringed (TCL, Article 52).

Arbitration is generally favoured due to the highly technical nature of such contracts and thus the requirement for expertise of the adjudicators plus the parties' desire to keep every aspect of the technology undisclosed to the public. To establish a sound and effective arbitration system, the State Science and Technology Commission promulgated the *Arbitration Rules for Technology Contract Arbitral Institutes (for trial use)* in January 1991 with the approval of the State Council. It also established a technology contract arbitration committee to provide supervision over technology contract arbitration nationwide. It promulgated the *Provisional Regulation on the Management of Technology Contract Arbitral Institutes* in January 1991 with the approval of the State Council. According to this regulation, arbitral institutes are established at the municipal, provincial and national levels by the administrative bureaux of science and technology specifically to deal with technology contract disputes.

Adjudication of technology contracts is less favoured than arbitration and one of the reasons is that judges do not have the expertise possessed by arbitrators. There are, however, circumstances where the parties have to bring the case to court to settle their disputes. To cope with the technical nature of technology contracts, the courts in many cities such as Beijing and Shanghai have established a special chamber — intellectual property chamber — to deal with technology contract disputes.

Conclusion — Prospects for the New Uniform Contract Law

7.19 Despite the rapid establishment of a contract system in China in such a short period, there are still many problems with the present contract law system. Firstly, it is still largely influenced by the old planned economy. Its function is to carry out the State plan and that is why individuals are not parties to economic contracts. Secondly, China has been undergoing drastic economic changes since the early 1980s, therefore the contract laws and regulations enacted in the different periods of China's economic reform lack consistency due to the different reform policies at different stages. Thirdly, the overwhelming majority of those laws and regulations were not drafted by the Legislative Affairs Committee of the NPC Standing Committee, but by the subsidiary commissions of the State Council. They tend to take into consideration the interests of their own departments but overlook the whole picture. As a result, inconsistency, redundancy and conflicts can be found in the contract law system. Fourthly, there are still obvious gaps in Chinese contract law due to the immaturity of the current Chinese market. For example, no legislation has mentioned offer and acceptance, which are important to the formation of contract. No legislation has directly dealt with frustration of contracts. Despite the adoption of the *Consumer Protection Law*[30] in 1993, the major contract law statutes do not govern the very common consumer contracts.

Modern market economy requires the modernization of contract law. The idea of creating a uniform contract law emerged at a conference in Beijing in October 1993 while revising the ECL. The Legislative Affairs Committee of the NPC Standing Committee entrusted the actual drafting of the new uniform contract law with the scholars of twelve leading law schools and research institutions. The first draft produced by the twelve institutions was submitted to the Legislative Affairs Committee in November 1994 for further consideration. It is anticipated that the new uniform contract law will come out in 1997 or 1998. Then, most former statutes, regulations, rules, opinions, etc., relating to contract law produced at different stages and by different bodies will be repealed once this code is passed by the NPC. The code contains general doctrines that apply to all types of contracts and specific principles for individual contracts. There will be no more artificial division of contracts into economic contracts or civil contracts. This is a big step forward in the legislative history of Chinese contract law and great expectations have been placed on this uniform contract law to be released in the near future.

Notes

[1] Ye Xiaoxin, ed. *Zhongguo Minfa Shi* 63–73 (Shanghai: Shanghai Renmin Chubanshe, 1993) (*History of Chinese Civil Law* (Shanghai: Shanghai People's Press, 1993)).

[2] *Zhonghua Renmin Gongheguo Jingji Hetongfa* (Economic Contract Law of the People's Republic of China). The original ECL was adopted on December 13, 1981 at the 4th Session of the 5th National People's Congress. An English translation of the statute can be found in 2 *China Law Report* 61 (1982). It was substantially amended on September 2, 1993 in accordance with a decision made at the 3rd Session of the Standing Committee of the 8th National People's Congress. The Chinese text and an English translation of the new ECL can be found in *China Laws for Foreign Business*, paragraph 5-500, at 6,254 (CCH Australia Ltd., 1993 ed.) (hereinafter as *CLFB*).

[3] *Zhonghua Renmin Gongheguo Shewai Jingji Hetongfa* (Foreign Economic Contract Law of the People's Republic of China). It was adopted on March 21, 1985 at the 10th Session of the Standing Committee of the 6th National People's Congress. The Chinese text and an English translation appear in *CLFB*, paragraph 5-550, at 6,442.

[4] *Zhonghua Renmin Gongheguo Jishu Hetongfa* (Technology Contract Law of the People's Republic of China). It was adopted on June 23, 1987 by the 21st Session of the

Standing Committee of the 6th National People's Congress. The Chinese text and an English translation can be found in *CLFB*, paragraph 5-577, at 6,718.

5 *Jiguan, Guoying Qiye, Hezuoshe Qianding Hetong Qiyue Zanxing Banfa* (Provisional Rules Regarding Contract among Governmental Organizations, State-Owned Enterprises and Collective Units). The Chinese text of the regulation can be found in Wang Zhong, Li Quanyi and Zhou Zhiyuan eds. *Jingji Hetongfa Shouce*, 27 (Jilin: Jilin Daxue Chubanshe, 1984). (*Economic Contract Law Handbook* (Jilin: Jilin University Press, 1984)).

6 *Guanyu Gongkuang Chanpin Dinghuo Hetong de Jiben Tiaokuan de Zanxing Guiding* (Interim Regulation on Basic Terms of Contract for Ordering Industrial and Mineral Products). It is replaced by the Regulation on Contracts for the Sale of Industrial and Mineral Products, issued by the State Council in January 1984 according to the 1981 ECL.

7 *Guanyu Yange Zhixing Jiben Jianshe Chengxu, Yange Zhixing Jingji Hetong de Tongzhi* (Notice Regarding Strict Implementation of Basic Construction Procedure and Economic Contracts). The Chinese text of the Notice appears in Wang Zhong, Li Quanyi and Zhou Zhiyuan eds. *Jingji Hetongfa Shouce*, 192 (Jilin: Jilin Daxue Chubanshe, 1984). (*Economic Contract Law Handbook* (Jilin: Jilin University Press, 1984)).

8 *Zhonghua Renmin Gongheguo Minfa Tongze* (General Principles of Civil Law of the People's Republic of China). It was adopted on April 12, 1986 by the 4th Session of the 6th National People's Congress. The Chinese text and an English translation can be found in *CLFB*, paragraph 19-150, at 23,758.

9 According to GPCL Article 37, a legal person must satisfy the following requirement, (a) It is established in accordance with the law; (b) it has necessary property or funding; (c) it has its own name, organization and premises; and (d) it has the ability to independently bear civil liability.

10 Other economic organizations can engage in profit-making activities such as manufacturing, sale, and supply of services, but they cannot bear civil liability independently. They are approved and registered with the administrations for industry and commerce. They are not legal persons according to Chinese law. For more, see Guojia Gongshang Xingzheng Guanli Ju Jingji Hetong Si, *Xin Jingji Hetongfa Jiaocheng*, 21–22 (Beijing: Falu Chubanshe, 1993). (Economic Contract Bureau of the State Administration for Industry and Commerce, ed. *Textbook on the New Economic Contract Law* (Beijing: Publishing House of Law, 1993)).

11 It refers to businesses run by individual citizens who have been lawfully registered and approved to engage in industrial or commercial operation within the sphere permitted by law. GPCL, Article 26.

12 It refers to members of a rural collective economic organization who engage in commodity production under a contract and within the spheres permitted by law. GPCL, Article 27.

13 Robert Upex, *Davies On Contract* (7th ed.), pp. 29–30 (London: Sweet & Maxwell, 1995); J.C. Smith, *The Law of Contract* (2nd ed.), pp. 73–74 (London: Sweet & Maxwell, 1993).

14 Robert Upex, *Davies on Contract* p. 18; J.C. Smith, *The Law of Contract*, p. 32.

15 ECL; Article 9, FECL, Article 12 and TCL Article 15 provide a list of major terms for the three types of contracts.

16 *Zhonghua Renmin Gongheguo Xingzheng Susongfa* (Administrative Procedure Law of the People's Republic of China). It was adopted on April 4, 1989 at the 2nd Session of the 7th National People's Congress. The Chinese text and an English translation can be found in *CLFB*, paragraph 19-558, at 24,536.

17 GPCL, Article 107; ECL, Article 30; FECL, Article 24 and 25; and TCL, Article 20.

18 Guojia Gongshang Xingzheng Guanli Ju Jingji Hetong Si, *Xin Jingji Hetongfa Jiaocheng*, 1 (Beijing: Falu Chubanshe, 1993). (Economic Contract Bureau of the State Administration for Industry and Commerce, ed. *Textbook on the New Economic Contract Law* (Beijing: Publishing House of Law, 1993)).

19 *Zuigao Renmin Fayuan Guanyu zai Shenli Jingji Hetong Jiufen Anjian zhong Juti Shiyong Jingji Hetongfa de Ruogan Wenti de Jieda* (July 21, 1987), s. 4 (Supreme People's Court's Reply to Several Questions Regarding the Application of "Economic Contract Law" in Adjudicating Economic Contract Disputes).

20 *Zhonghua Renmin Gongheguo Zhongwai Hezi Jingying Qiye Fa* (Law of the People's

Republic of China on Sino-Foreign Equity Joint Ventures). It was originally adopted on July 1, 1979 at the 2nd Session of the 5th National People's Congress, and amended on April 4, 1990 at the 3rd Session of the 7th National People's Congress. The Chinese text and an English translation appear in *CLFB*, paragraph 6-500, at 7,638.

[21] *Zhonghua Renmin Gongheguo Zhongwai Hezuo Jingying Qiye Fa* (Law of the People's Republic of China on Sino-Foreign Co- operative Joint Ventures). It was adopted on April 13, 1988 at the 1st Session of the 7th National People's Congress. The Chinese text and an English translation can be found in *CLFB*, paragraph 6-100, at 7,506.

[22] *Zhonghua Renmin Gongheguo Jishu Yinjin Hetong Guanli Tiaoli* (Regulations on Administration of Technology Import Contracts of the People's Republic of China). It was promulgated on May 24, 1985 by the State Council. The Chinese text and and an English translation appear in *CLFB*, paragraph 5-570, at 6,682.

[23] *Zhonghua Renmin Gongheguo Jishu Yinjin Hetong Guanli Tiaoli Shishi Xize* (Implementation Rules for the Regulations on Administration of Technology Import Contracts of the People's Republic of China). It was approved on December 30, 1987 by the State Council and promulgated on January 20, 1988 by the Ministry of Foreign Economic Relations and Trade. The Chinese text and an English translation can be found in *CLFB*, paragraph 5-573, at 6,690.

[24] *Zhonghua Renmin Gongheguo Duiwai Hezuo Kaicai Haiyang Shiyou Ziyuan Tiaoli* (Regulation of the People's Republic of China on the Exploitation of Offshore Petroleum Resources in Cooperation with Foreign Enterprises). It was promulgated by the State Council on January 30, 1982. The Regulation and an English translation can be found in *Zhonghua Renmin Gongheguo Shewai Fagui Huibian 1949–1990 (Vol.1)*, at 220 & 545 (Beijing: Zhongguo Fazhi Chubanshe, 1991). *(Laws and Regulations of the People's Republic of China Governing Foreign-Related Matters)* (hereinafter as *Huibian*).

[25] *Zuigao Renmin Fayuan Guanyu Shiyong "Shewai Jingji Hetongfa" Ruogan Wenti de Jieda* (Supreme People's Court's Reply to Certain Questions Concerning the Application of the "Foreign Economic Contract Law"). It was issued on October 19, 1987. The Chinese text and an English translation can be found in *CLFB*, paragraph 5-555, at 6,638.

[26] See "United Nations Convention on Contracts for the International Sale of Goods", 1 *China Law and Practice*, no. 5, at p. 24 (11 June 1987). The text of CISG as concluded on 11 April 1980 can be found at U.N. Doc. A/Conf. 97/18, reprinted in 19 *International Legal Materials* pp. 668, 677–699 (1980).

[27] *Guowuyuan Guanyu Guli Taiwan Tongpao Touzi de Guiding* (Provisions of the State Council Concerning the Encouragement of Investments by Compatriots from Taiwan). It was promulgated by the State Council on July 3, 1988 and became effective at the date of promulgation. The regulation and an English translation can be found in *Huibian 1949–1990 (Vol. 3)*, 1590 & 1958.

[28] *Zhonghua Renmin Gongheguo Taiwan Tongpao Touzi Baohufa* (Law of the People's Republic of China on the Protection of Investment by Taiwanese Compatriots). It was adopted on March 5, 1994 by the 6th Session of the Standing Committee of the 8th National People's Congress. The Chinese text and an English translation can be found in *CLFB*, paragraph 19-582, at 25,008.

[29] *Pearce and Another v. Brooks* held that the contract for the purpose of prostitution is invalid. Prostitution is not a crime in England but it is morally repugnant. See J.C. Smith, *The Law of Contract* pp. 246–247. For more discussion of the doctrine public policy, see Robert Upex, *Davies on Contract* (7th ed.), pp. 135–144.

[30] *Zhonghua Renmin Gongheguo Xiaofeizhe Quanyi Baohufa* (Law of the People's Republic of China on the Protection of the Rights and Interests of Consumers). It was adopted on October 31, 1993 by the 4th Session of the Standing Committee of the 8th National People's Congress. The Chinese text and an English translation can be found in *CLFB*, paragraph 16-480, at 20,006.

CHAPTER 8

FOREIGN INVESTMENT LAW

John S Mo

City University of Hong Kong

John Shijian Mo, Assistant Professor, Law Department, City University of Hong Kong, LL.B. (Jilin), LL.B. (Monash), LL.M. (Dalhousie), and Ph.D. (Sydney), barrister and solicitor in Australia. Author of *Butterworths Student's Companion: International Commercial Law* (Sydney, Butterworths, 1995) and *International Commercial Law* (Sydney, Butterworths, 1996), and a number of articles in the areas of international trade law, Chinese law and Australian law.

Legal Framework for Foreign Investment

It has been 18 years since China opened its door to the world in 1978. **8.01** As at March 1996, there were more than 250,000 foreign invested enterprises operating in China. China is a land of opportunity. Its potential purchasing power, which is seen not only in the vastness of its domestic markets but also in its US$800 billion foreign currency reserve in 1996, meets the dream of long-term investors.[1] Its naive and somewhat uncoordinated enthusiasm for foreign investment provides a paradise for those adventurous and shrewd investors who are looking to make money quickly. However, China is indeed a land of uncertainty for those investors who do not know much about its culture and law, under which the game of investment has been, and will be played. This chapter provides a concise introduction to the foreign investment law of China.

The legal framework for foreign investment in China consists of laws, regulations, measures and policies of both the national and local governments. The basis of the framework is founded on three laws passed by the Chinese National People's Congress, which are the *Sino-Foreign Joint Equity Ventures Law*, the *Sino-Foreign Joint Co-operative Ventures Law* and the *Solely Foreign-Invested Enterprises Law*. The theoretical basis of the legal framework also extends to Article 18 of the Chinese Constitution, which gives legitimate existence to foreign investment in China's socialist economy. On the basis of the three laws, a great number of national and local regulations, measures and policies have been made. In addition, a number of national laws which have been passed for other purposes are sometimes relevant to foreign investment.

The legal framework for foreign investment consists of the following four groups of laws, regulations and policies:

(a) the national laws on foreign investment, such as the Chinese Constitution (Article 18), the *Sino-Foreign Joint Equity Ventures Law*, the *Sino-Foreign Joint Co-operative Ventures Law*, the *Solely Foreign-Invested Enterprises Law*, *The Company Law*, *Income Tax Law for Foreign-Invested Enterprises and Foreign-Registered Enterprises*, and other laws concerning foreign investment;

(b) the State Council Regulations and departmental rules on foreign investment, such as the Detailed Rules for the Implementation of the Sino-Foreign Joint Equity Ventures Law, the Detailed Rules for the Implementation of the Sino-Foreign Joint Co-operative Ventures Law, the Detailed Rules for the Implementation of the Solely Foreign-Owned Enterprises Law, the Detailed Rules for the Implementation of the Income Tax Law for Foreign-Invested Enterprises and Foreign-Registered Enterprises, the Administrative Rules for Foreign Currency Control, the State Council Measures on Encouragement of Foreign Investment, the State Council Decisions relating to Special Economic Zones (SEZs), Open Coastal Cities and other special economic areas, the State Council Regulations for the Registration of Chinese Legal Persons, and the Implementing Rules for the State Council Regulations for the Registration and Administration of Foreign Representative Office, etc;

(c) the local laws and regulations on foreign investment; and

(d) the foreign investment policies of both national and local governments.

In addition to the above-listed legislation, many other laws, such as the *Arbitration Law*, laws on export and import control, *Labour Law* and laws on environmental control, also affect the operation of foreign investment. This chapter only discusses the laws which are most relevant to foreign investment in China. Tax law, company law, contract law, financial law, civil procedure and environmental law, etc, are examined in the relevant chapters of this book.

The regulations, measures, orders, explanatory notes, policies, issued by the relevant governmental authorities to implement the national law and State Council regulations constitute an important part of the foreign investment law in China. In a sense, besides the judicial interpretation of the law and regulations, the governmental departments also provide their own interpretations to fill in the gaps left by the law and regulations which are only meant to be general and broad principles. The power to make delegated legislation is generally vested in the Executive by the Chinese Constitution, under which the State Council and its departments have made a great deal of delegated legislation. As at March 1996, more than 300 regulations and measures had been issued by various departments of the Chinese central government. The volume of the delegated legislation alone presents a maze to most foreign investors and lawyers who are not so familiar with the operation of Chinese foreign investment law.

Local legislation on foreign investment should not be ignored by foreign investors and lawyers. After 1988, provincial governments have been granted an authority to approve foreign investment projects which do not exceed US$10 million in total value. This authority is theoretically subject to the central government's approval in the following circumstances:

(a) if the project purports to sell within China its products which are subject to import restrictions;
(b) if the project intends to export its products which are subject to export licences or State quotas;
(c) if the project wishes to invest in an area which is restricted by the national law;
(d) if the company is established for the purposes of investment only; and
(e) if the company is set up for providing financial and hire-purchase services.

In order to attract foreign investment, provincial, municipal and regional governments have made various regulations and policies. These regulations and policies must be theoretically consistent with the laws and regulations of the central government. However, they supplement the national laws and regulations in areas where the national laws and regulations are silent, and provide, local incentives to foreign investors. In addition, the local law and regulations may fill the vacuum left temporarily by the national law. The company laws in Shenzhen and Shanghai, which were superseded by the national *Company Law* of 1993, are such examples. Presently, although there is the *Provisional Law on Bankruptcy of State-Owned Enterprises*, the bankruptcy law for foreign invested companies is still locally based and locally initiated in China. Thus, attention must be given to the relevant local law where an investment is to be made. **8.02**

The policy on foreign investment affects the operation of foreign investment. It is an important part of the legal framework for foreign investment in China. Policy is usually not as transparent as the law and regulations. A foreign investor should pay attention to the policy which may affect a particular investment project from time to time.

There used to be considerably different standards for approving Sino-foreign investment and solely foreign-invested enterprises in various areas or projects. This practice has been gradually abandoned. In June 1995, the State Planning Commission, the State Economic and Trade Commission and the Ministry of Foreign Trade and Economic Co-operation (MOFTEC) jointly issued the Provisional Guidelines for Foreign Investment to indicate to potential foreign investors the areas and projects open or closed to them.

The Guidelines divide investment projects into four categories. Foreign investment projects are accordingly encouraged, permitted, restricted and prohibited, as the case may be. The encouraged, restrictive and prohibited areas are specified in the list attached to the Guidelines. The projects falling outside these categories belong to the permitted areas, where foreign investment is allowed without either preferential treatment nor any restriction.

Foreign investment in the following areas or projects is encouraged:

(a) new agricultural technology, comprehensive development of agricultural resources, and development of natural resources, of transportation or of essential raw materials;

(b) new or advanced technology, and technology capable of improving a product, saving energy and raw materials, enhancing productivity or satisfying market needs which cannot be met by domestic industries;

(c) projects capable of meeting the needs of international markets, enhancing competitiveness of a product, developing new markets, and increasing exports;

(d) new technology or equipment for effective use of resources, recycling and environmental protection;

(e) projects developing the resources in the middle and western regions of China in accordance with the law and policy; and

(f) any other projects which may be encouraged by the law and regulations.

The government provides concessions and preferential treatment to foreign investment in the above-mentioned areas and projects. It may also allow long-term and large-size foreign investment in the areas of mining, power industries, infrastructure development and harbour construction. The existence of the encouraged areas and projects suggests that the government has shifted the emphasis of the foreign investment from developing the specially designated zones to the overall development of the national economy.

8.03   The projects and areas where foreign investment is restricted are as follows:

(a) the existing technology which has met the needs of the domestic markets;

(b) the experimental areas or projects which have been designated for attracting foreign investment or the areas where State monopoly applies;

(c) exploration or exploitation of rare and invaluable mining resources;

(d) industries which are subject to State control; and

(e) any other areas restricted by the laws and regulations.

Sino-foreign investment operating in the restrictive areas or carrying out restricted projects must have definite terms of operation. This requirement allows the Chinese government to review the operation of the venture at the end of each term. However, it is unclear why only the joint venture is specified although both the laws on joint ventures and on sole foreign investment require the projects to have a definite term of operation. Projects falling under the restrictive category may be upgraded to the permitted category if exports reach 70 per cent of total products or if State needs to develop the middle and western regions of China are met. The upgrading means the restrictions do not apply even though the project is restricted under the Guidelines. The Guidelines require that the provincial, regional, and municipal governments examine and approve the projects listed in the restrictive category to ensure the enforcement of Guidelines.

The areas and projects where foreign investment is prohibited are as **8.04** follows:

(a) projects which endanger State security and public interest;

(b) projects which cause pollution, destroy the natural environment or endanger public health;

(c) projects which request large tracts of farm land, endanger preservation of soil or the safety and operation of military facilities;

(d) projects based on the unique technology or know-how of China; and

(e) any other areas or projects closed to foreign investment under law and regulations.

The Guidelines have opened those areas which are supposed to be closed to sole foreign investment under the *Solely Foreign-Invested Enterprises Law*. Although inconsistencies arise between the Regulations for the Implementation of Solely Foreign-Invested Enterprises Law and the Guidelines, the prevailing effect of the Guidelines is unmistakable. Sole foreign investment was, and still is under the *Solely Foreign-Invested Enterprises Law*, prohibited in the areas of newspapers, publications, broadcasting, television, postal services, film industry, pure domestic commerce, domestic insurance, and foreign trade. However, foreign investors may carry on restrictive activities in almost all areas except for the areas of building and management of main railways, carriage of goods and passengers by waterways, transport of goods and passengers across borders by road, civil navigation, foreign trade, tourist industries, real estate industries, and service industries, certain car and motorcycle industries, and the manufacturing of certain power generators.

By the same token, a joint Sino-foreign venture can rely on the Guidelines to choose an area of operation, even though the relevant laws may have different requirements. In the restrictive areas, a joint venture is subject to less restrictions than a sole foreign investment. For example, a joint venture can invest in any areas or projects subject to the restrictions, even though in some areas, such as the construction and management of main railways, civil navigation, car-making or motorcycle-making, Chinese control of the invested projects is required.

The relevant governmental departments have recently issued a number of rules and regulations regulating foreign investment in particular industries and sectors of the economy. For example, the State Administration for Industry and Commerce and the MOFTEC formulated in 1995 the Regulations on the Establishment of Sino-Foreign Enterprises in Advertising Industries;[2] the MOFTEC issued a Circular in 1994 on Foreign Investment in BOT Form;[3] it also issued in 1995 the Measures for Examining Foreign Investment in Freight Forwarding Houses,[4] and the Provisional Rules on Foreign Investment in the Investment Companies;[5] the China Civil Navigation Authority issued in 1994 the Explanatory Memorandum on the MOFTEC Policy on Foreign Investment in Civil Navigation;[6] the Ministry for Construction in 1994 issued the Provisional Measures for Construction Contracts Undertaken by Foreign Investment, and the Detailed Rules for the Implementation of the Provisional Measures;[7] and the Ministry for Construction and the MOFTEC published the Rules on Foreign-Invested Construction Companies in 1995.[8] These departmental rules are delegated legislation in China. Inconsistencies are apparent in the laws and regulations on foreign investment. This appears to be inevitable given that every department in the Chinese Government has the general power to formulate delegated legislation. Foreign investors need to check the relevant regulations and rules when investing in a particular project.

Solely Foreign-Invested Enterprises

What is a Solely Foreign-Invested Enterprise?

8.05 Solely foreign-invested enterprises are also known as wholly foreign-owned enterprises. As defined in Article 2 of the *Solely Foreign-Invested Enterprises Law*, a solely foreign-owned enterprise is an enterprise invested wholly by foreign interests. Foreign interests include foreign registered companies controlled by foreigners, and foreign individuals

A solely foreign-invested enterprise can be a Chinese legal person, if the enterprise satisfies the relevant requirements. Article 2(4) of the State Council Administrative Measures for the Registration of Legal Persons provides that a foreign-invested enterprise, whether solely foreign-owned or jointly owned, can be registered as a Chinese legal person. An enterprise applying for registration must satisfy the following requirements:

(a) the applicant should have a business name, administration and a constitution;

(b) the applicant must have a permanent business place and the necessary facilities for carrying on the business concerned;

(c) the applicant should have adequate capital and employees as required by law to carry on the business concerned;

(d) the applicant should be able to take civil liability in its own right; and

(e) the business carried by the applicant must be consistent with the relevant laws, regulations and policies.

A solely foreign-invested enterprise is usually formed as a company with limited liability. Article 19 of the Regulations for Implementation of the Solely Foreign-Invested Enterprises Law provides that a solely foreign-invested enterprise can be established as a company with limited liability. The provision also allows an enterprise to adopt other forms of liability. It is less likely that a foreign investor will establish an unlimited liability company in China. Nor is it reasonable to expect the Chinese government to encourage the establishment of a company whose unlimited liability is borne by someone over whom the government has little control.

A solely foreign-invested enterprise is different from a branch or representative office of a foreign registered company in China. The former is a foreign-owned Chinese legal person; but the latter is a foreign-registered foreign legal person which may or may not be able to operate in China depending on whether it can be registered as a foreign company under *The Company Law*. Presently, a foreign registered company may carry on business in China upon registration and a foreign financial institution may carry on limited operation in China after approval.

A solely foreign-invested company allows a foreign investor to enjoy autonomy in administering the affair of the enterprise. Such autonomy distinguishes a solely foreign-invested enterprise from a Sino-foreign joint venture. A solely foreign-invested enterprise is a convenient vehicle for foreign investors who prefer to operate at their own pace and under their own familiar managerial system.

How to Set Up a Solely Foreign-Invested Enterprise

8.06   A solely foreign-invested enterprise can be established in pursuance of the *Solely Foreign-Invested Enterprises Law* and the relevant regulations made by the MOFTEC. Under the present law, a foreign investor purporting to establish a solely foreign-invested project should take the following steps:

    (a) find an area and project which are suitable for carrying on the intended business;

    (b) submit a proposal and feasibility study to the local authority in charge of foreign investment review;

    (c) the local authority is obliged to inform the applicant of its assessment of the project's feasibility within 30 days after the receipt of the application;

    (d) an intending investor should submit a formal application which includes a number of required documents to the relevant local authority for approval;

    (e) the authority is obliged to make a decision within 90 days after the acceptance of all the required documents; and

    (f) if approved, the investor must register with the local Administration for Industry and Commerce within 30 days after approval.

Since a solely foreign-invested enterprise does not have a Chinese partner, the investor must make an application him/herself to the relevant authority. There are investment agencies in and outside China, which may help those who need assistance. An investor may also authorize a governmental organization, a company or a person in China to make an application on his/her behalf, if the investor appreciates the conditions, nature, implications and risk of the proposed investment project. The investor will have to comply with the relevant standards for land use, environmental protection, work safety and employment contract.

In making a formal application, the following documents must be presented:

    (a) the completed application form (in Chinese only);

    (b) a report of feasibility study;

    (c) the constitution of the company (in Chinese only), indicating its business name, place of business, total assets and registered capital of the company, structure of the company and rules for the administration of the company;

    (d) a list of the board members, and name and nationality of its legal representatives;

    (e) if the investor is a foreign registered company, the certificate of registration;

(f) if the investor is a foreign individual, the personal ID or passport of that person;

(g) proof of the investor's financial standing;

(h) the local government's response to the preliminary inquiry of
the investor;

(i) a list of materials and equipment to be imported for the project;

(j) if more than two investors are involved, the contract to establish the company must be provided; and

(k) any other documents requested by law and regulations.

The above documents can be presented in English and be accompanied
by Chinese translations except where the Chinese version is specified.

A sole foreign investment must also satisfy the relevant quality
standards for the proposed project. There are two alternate tests for
controlling the quality of sole foreign invested projects. The first test is
that the enterprise must adopt advanced technology and equipment
and be capable of developing new products, saving energy resources
and raw materials, improving its products and substituting imported
products. The second test requires the project to export more than 50
per cent of its products and to maintain the balance of its foreign
currency. This means that any sole foreign investment must satisfy at
least one of the two tests to justify its establishment. These tests
suggest that sole foreign investments are allowed to operate in China
only under the conditions that they bring in new technology which is
relatively advanced in China or that they generate sufficient foreign
currency to sustain their operations in China. The standards operate in
conjunction with the Guidelines for investing in the encouraged, permitted, restrictive and prohibited areas or projects.

Operation of a Solely Foreign-Invested Enterprise

This section deals with a number of issues, such as evaluation of   **8.07**
investment, terms of investment, land use, foreign currency control,
import control, domestic sales, taxation and accounting rules, relating
to the operation of a sole foreign investment. The present law on sole
foreign investment does not deal with all issues that are relevant to the
operation of foreign investment. In particular, the administration of a
solely foreign-invested company is largely unregulated and is subject
to the constitution of the enterprise as approved by the relevant authority. Unless a solely foreign-invested enterprise falls under the
scope of *The Company Law*, the managerial matters of the enterprise
are left with the hands of the board.[9]

An investment can be made in the form of cash, technology and
know-how, equipment, and other forms approved by the competent
authority. When investing in cash, a foreign investor can invest in
renminbi generated by any other investment projects in China. When

an industrial or intellectual property is invested, the detailed information on the property must be submitted to the relevant authority for examination and approval. Under the present law, the technology investment cannot exceed 20 per cent of the registered capital of the enterprise concerned. When machines and equipment are invested, they must be evaluated by the authority in charge of the examination of imported and exported goods in pursuance of the rules set out jointly by the State Bureau for the Examination of Imported and Exported Goods and the Ministry of Finance in 1994. A reasonable price of the machinery so invested should be compatible with the prevailing market price of the same or similar product in the world market.

There are time requirements for the making of investment. For example, the *Solely Foreign-Invested Enterprises Law* requires the foreign investor to invest at least 15 per cent of the enterprise's registered capital within 90 days after the issue of its licence and must pay off the total registered capital within three years after the issue of its licence. A failure to comply with these requirements may lead to various penalties, including cancellation of the licence. However, the requirements for making investment have been affected by the Circular of the State Administration for Industry and Commerce and the MOFTEC on the Administration and Registration of Foreign-Invested Enterprises of 1994. The Circular sets out a time framework for substantiating investment according to the value of the registered capital.[10] A foreign investor has to comply with the new requirements even though there are inconsistencies between the laws.

A solely foreign-invested enterprise can obtain the land use right from the relevant local authority. After approval, a certificate of land use right should be issued to the investor. The land use right is not transferable unless written approval has been given by the local authority. When a solely foreign-invested enterprise is transferred to another foreign owner, the land use right is transferred at the same time. The fees for land use right are set out by the State Council. The local governments may vary the charges within the scope allowed by the National Government. A solely foreign-invested enterprise may also contract with the relevant local government to obtain land for development. For example, in 1992, a solely foreign-invested enterprise, based on a consortium of Taiwanese investors, was granted a contract by a local government in Fujian Province to develop a piece of land for shipping, tourist and industrial purposes. The local government reneged on the agreement in 1994 because of a significant increase in the market price for land use. The enterprise took the government to the local court, which found the contract enforceable and ordered specific performance against the local government.[11]

Domestic sales, taxation, accounting, foreign currency balance and labour organizations within solely foreign-invested enterprises are regulated. There is a need to check the relevant law from time to time.

For example, the Ministry of Finance issues regulations and rules for accounting and evaluation of a company's assets, and taxation from time to time; the State Taxation Bureau makes rules and measures for implementing the tax law on foreign-invested enterprises; the State Administration on Foreign Exchange and the People's Bank of China may make detailed rules for foreign exchange control in pursuance of the State Council Measures for Foreign Exchange Control of 1996; and the relevant authorities may issue measures implementing laws and regulations for labour management, quality control, health and safety standards. The *Solely Foreign-Invested Enterprises Law* and its Implementing Regulations provide only general principles in these areas.

Termination of a Solely Foreign-Invested Enterprise

Under the present legal framework for foreign investment, a foreign **8.08** invested enterprise may or may not have a definite term of operation. The proposed term of operation should be approved by the relevant authority on a case by case basis. The approval process enables the Chinese Government to control foreign investment in various sectors of the economy, and to redirect the foreign investment from time to time according to the needs of the economy. It is perhaps deemed to be also necessary in the presently incomplete legal infrastructure, for the government to adjust and to maintain consistency in its foreign investment law and policy without undertaking any indefinite commitment to foreign investments.

The *Solely Foreign-Invested Enterprises Law* and its implementing Regulations sets out general rules for transferring or termination of a sole foreign investment. The rules so set are important in the sense that China has not passed any national bankruptcy law for foreign invested companies. Nor is there a special law governing transactions of assets between foreign investors. *The Company Law* provides only limited guidance to an enterprise which is registered as a Chinese company. In the case where no other law is available, the provisions of the *Solely Foreign-Invested Enterprises Law*, however general and brief they may be, are crucial for determining the interests of the parties concerned.[12] In a liquidation or termination sale, the Chinese company should be given a right of priority to purchase the enterprise's equipment when the terms of purchase are the same between a foreign buyer and a Chinese buyer.

Settlement of Disputes

The *Solely Foreign-Invested Enterprises Law* does not deal with this **8.09** matter at all. Disputes arising from the internal management of the

285

enterprise are governed by the constitution of the enterprise or the law under which the investor (in the case of a corporate investor) obtained its legal status. Under the general principles of conflict of laws a local court does not lose its jurisdiction over a matter merely because it arises from a foreign law. In fact, Article 146 of the Civil Law Principles provides that a Chinese court may apply the law of a place where the tortious act was committed. If a Chinese court can apply a foreign law in a case involving torts, it may also apply a foreign law in a case involving the enforcement of a company's constitution. It can be expected that in the near future any dispute arising from a solely foreign-invested enterprise can be decided by a Chinese court, whether the matter is governed by Chinese law or a foreign law.

Any disputes arising from a solely foreign-invested enterprise can be arbitrated in China. A solely foreign-invested enterprise can submit a dispute to the China International Economic and Trade Arbitration Commission (CIETAC, see Chapter 11 for details). It may also initiate an arbitration proceeding under the *Arbitration Law* (see Chapter 11). In addition, Chinese law generally encourages the parties to a dispute to resolve their differences through negotiation and mediation.

Sino-Foreign Joint Equity Ventures

What is a Joint Equity Venture?

8.10   A joint equity venture (enterprise) is established by Chinese and foreign interests jointly as a Chinese company with limited liability. It is a Chinese legal person and must be registered as such under the Regulations for the Registration of Chinese Legal Persons. Individual Chinese and governmental bodies cannot participate in a joint venture. A solely foreign-invested company established under the Chinese law may be able to participate in a joint venture as a "Chinese company" because neither *The Company Law*, nor the *Sino-Foreign Joint Equity Ventures Law* expressly excludes such possibility.[13] A joint venture so organized may be eligible to wider benefits which are otherwise not available to a solely foreign-invested enterprise.[14] A joint equity venture is established as a limited liability company and is subject to *The Company Law*.

How to Set Up a Sino-Foreign Joint Equity Enterprise

There are two major stages for the establishment of a joint equity venture. The first stage is to submit a proposal and feasibility study.

This can be, and usually is, done by the Chinese partner of the proposed venture. After the proposal has been approved, the parties to the
venture are allowed to negotiate and form an agreement to establish a
joint equity venture and to proceed to the second stage. The *Sino-
Foreign Joint Equity Ventures Law* requires the Chinese party to the
proposed venture to complete the second stage. In doing so, the following documents in Chinese must be presented:

  (a) the completed form of application;
  (b) the report of feasibility study;
  (c) an executed contract for establishing the venture, which must
       clearly define the parties' rights and obligations,[15] and the
       constitution of the venture;
  (d) a list of the chairman and vice chairmen of the board of direc-
       tors, manager, assistant managers and members of the board;
       and
  (e) written approval of the proposal by the relevant authority.

The relevant government authority must make a decision whether to
approve the application with three months after the receipt of the
compliant application. The three months limit may not always be
equal to 90 days depending on the number of days each relevant
calendar month has. The contract and constitution are required to
contain specific types of information. But, there is no guidance as to
how to draft the constitution. The relevant provisions of *The Company Law* may provide some principles for the drafting of a joint
venture's constitution in the future, if the Law is applicable. A joint
venture is required to register with the relevant authority and obtain
the relevant licence for its operation within one month after the
approval. The date on which the business licence is issued is deemed
to be the date on which the joint venture commences its business
operation.

A joint venture must have at least 25 per cent foreign investment.
There is no restriction on the maximum shares held by a foreign
investor. This suggests that maintaining control on the Chinese side is
not a major concern of the *Sino-Foreign Joint Equity Ventures Law*.
Similarly, the amended law provides that the chairman of the board
can be either a Chinese or a foreign national, depending on the agreement of the parties.

An investment can be made in the form of cash, equipment, intellectual or industrial property, land or building. There are specific
standards for the use of equipment, machinery, intellectual or industrial property as investment. The relevant departments, such as the
MOFTEC and the Ministry of Finance have issued a great deal of
explanatory notes or implementing measures setting out rules for the
evaluation of investment in non-cash forms.

There are minimum requirements for the ratios between a venture's registered capital and total investment. The ratios vary according to the value of investment:

(a) if the total value is under US$3 million, the registered capital must be over 70 per cent of the total investment;

(b) if the total value is between US$3 and US$10 million, the registered capital must be over 50 per cent of the total investment;

(c) if the total value is between US$10 and US$30 million, the registered capital can be 40 per cent of the total investment; and

(d) if the total value is over US$30 million, the registered capital can be 33 per cent of the total investment.

Operation of a Joint Equity Venture

8.11   The board of directors exercises the highest power of a joint venture. The law requires a board to have at least three members. The appointment of the board chairman and vice chairmen should be made through consultation between the parties. Generally, the right to make an appointment should be exercised alternately in order to maintain a balance of power between the participating parties. Thus, if the chairman is appointed by one, the vice chairman should be appointed by the other. The term of appointment for each board member is currently four years. The board is required to meet at least once a year to decide the important matters, such as amendments to the constitution of the venture, termination or dissolution of the venture, increase or transfer of the registered capital, and merger. Any amendment to the venture's contract and constitution must be approved by the relevant authority to gain validity. Failure to comply with this requirement makes the amendment so made unenforceable.[16] The other issues of the venture are usually dealt with by the chairman, vice chairmen or managers. Under the present law, a venture is not allowed to reduce its registered capital during the term of operation.

A joint venture can apply to the local government for land use rights. The local government charges a fee for the land use within the scheme set out by the State Council. Local incentives may be given to a joint venture, which is deemed to be beneficial to the local economy. The government undertakes not to adjust the land use fee within the first five years of the operation. The fee scale will be adjusted every three years after the first five years. The land use right is not assignable, but may be transferred with the venture together.

There are restrictions on the domestic sales and purchase by a joint venture. The relevant authorities may from time to time vary the restrictions. The system of control is based on various licences, quotas or permits.

Taxation is subject to the relevant provisions of the *Sino-Foreign Joint Equity Ventures Law* and the *Tax Law for Foreign-Invested Companies and Foreign Companies*. There are incentives for foreign investment made in the specified areas of the economy or in the special economic regions.

There are also restrictions on access to foreign currency. The restrictions are largely seen in the following measures:

(a) a foreign currency account can only be opened in designated banks;

(b) domestic transactions are usually settled in Chinese currency;

(c) the transactions in foreign currency are monitored by the government;

(d) remittance of foreign currency overseas is subject to restrictions; and

(e) access to conversion of foreign currency is subject to restrictions.

Accounting is subject to the relevant provisions of the *Sino-Foreign Joint Equity Ventures Law* and its implementing Regulations. The Ministry of Finance has also issued the Accounting Rules for Foreign-Invested Enterprises. The accounting practice of a joint venture must comply with these laws and regulations.

Workers unions are allowed under the present legal framework for foreign investment. But industrial action in China is rarely seen. A joint venture is required by law to look after the interests of unions and its employees. The labour disputes are subject to the *Labour Law* and relevant regulations.

Termination and Dissolution of a Joint Equity Venture

A joint venture should have a definite term of operation. There is no **8.12** requirement for either minimum or maximum years of operation. The term can be renewed six months before the expiry date. A joint venture may be terminated or dissolved before the end of the expected term. It may also transfer part or all of its interests to another foreign investor.[17] If dissolved, the process of liquidation is governed by the provisions of the Regulations for the Implementation of the Sino-Foreign Joint Equity Ventures Law.

Dispute Resolution

Article 109 of the Regulations for the Implementation of the Sino-Foreign Joint Equity Ventures Law provides that all disputes should be resolved through consultation, mediation, arbitration or litigation. The provision suggests that the government should encourage the use of non-judicial means of dispute settlement, but does not force any settlement outside court.

While there is no rule for consultation and mediation, arbitration is governed by the relevant provisions of the *Sino-Foreign Joint Equity Ventures Law* and its implementing Regulations. *The Arbitration Law* also governs arbitration proceedings involving a joint venture (see Chapter 11). In order to submit a dispute to an arbitral body, the parties must have reached an arbitration agreement in writing. This is expressly stated in Article 110 of the Regulations for the Implementation of the Sino-Foreign Joint Equity Ventures Law, and Article 16 of *The Arbitration Law*. However, Articles 217 and 260 of *The Civil Procedure Law* allow a court to refuse to enforce an arbitral award on the ground, *inter alia*, that no arbitration agreement in writing was reached between the parties concerned. Arbitration is more comfortable than litigation for a joint venture and may indeed produce a more acceptable result for the parties.[18]

Sino-Foreign Joint Co-operative Ventures

What is a Joint Co-operative Venture?

8.13 A joint co-operative venture is based on a contractual arrangement. It can be a loosely connected co-operation between the contracting parties, and may also be an independent Chinese legal person formed on the basis of a contract. A Chinese legal person so established is a limited liability company. If a venture is not a legal person, it cannot carry on business activities in its own name and be responsible for the venture's debt in its own right.[19] Internally, the co-operative parties to a non-legal person venture may be responsible for the venture's debt to the limit of their contributions. This must be noted by foreign investors dealing with a joint co-operative venture. A contract to set up a joint co-operative venture is also subject to the *Foreign Economic Contract Law*. Though the *Sino-Foreign Joint Co-operative Ventures Law* was promulgated in as early as 1988, the Regulations for the Implementation of the Sino-Foreign Joint Co-operative Ventures Law were not formulated by the MOFTEC until 1995. A venture which is not a legal person is subject to Articles 50–54 of the Implementing Regulations, which, however, do not provide sufficient rules to clarify any ambiguity arising from the legal status of such venture.

How to Establish a Joint Co-operative Venture

The Regulations for the Implementation of the Sino- Foreign Joint Co-operative Ventures Law set out the procedure for establishing a joint co-operative venture. Like a joint equity venture, a joint co-operative venture can be approved either by the national government or by local government as the case may be. The general principle is that a joint co-operative venture can be examined by local government, if the sum of the investment is within the maximum sum which can be approved by a local government, if the project does not require funding or assistance in construction or production from the national government, if the exported products of the project are not subject to quota or permit or have been granted a permit, or if the project is allowed under law and regulations. Local approval is supposedly less burdensome than State approval, because of the local government enthusiasm for attracting more foreign investment to the area. A project cannot be approved if it is against Chinese sovereignty, public interest, State security, the relevant law and policy, or causes pollution to the environment.

When making a formal application for the establishment of a joint co-operative venture, the following documents in Chinese are usually required:

(a) an executed contract to establish the venture;[20]
(b) venture's constitution or a similar document;[21]
(c) local government's approval of the proposal and feasibility study to set up the venture;
(d) documents proving the legal status of each party to the venture (in the appropriate language as the case may be);
(e) a list of the board members and of chairman, vice chairmen and managers; and
(f) any other documents required by the government in the circumstances.

The relevant authority is obliged to make a decision as to whether to approve the application within 45 days after the receipt of the application. The venture is obliged to register with the local administration of industry and commerce, which should issue a licence to the venture. But no time requirement has been imposed. The venture commences its operation from the date on which the licence is issued. The Administration for Industry and Commerce can set out deadlines for the parties to fulfil their contractual obligations under the joint venture contract. A failure to comply with the requirement may lead to the withdrawal of the approval and cancellation of the licence.

Parties may invest cash, industrial property rights, know- how, land use rights and other movable or immovable property in the venture. The non-cash form of investment must not be subject to any forms of mortgage or encumbrance. Foreign investment in a venture which is a legal person should normally be more than 25 per cent of the venture's registered capital. The registered capital of a venture refers to the total sum subscribed by the parties as registered with the Administration for Industry and Commerce. The total investment of a venture is the total investment as provided by the contract or constitution of the venture. The proportion of foreign investment in venture which is not a non-legal person is to be set out by the MOFTEC, probably in its administrative directives.

Operation of a Joint Co-operative Venture

8.14 A joint venture can enter legal relationships in its own right, if it is a limited liability company. If a joint venture is not a Chinese legal person, its legal status is unsettled in Chinese jurisprudence. The Chinese law does not expressly state whether or not an unincorporated body which is neither a Chinese legal person nor a natural person can carry on civil activities, even though many organizations which are not Chinese legal persons do exist in China. In theory, an organization which is not a legal person does not have a capacity to enter a legal relationship in its own right and in particular, is not liable in its own name for any debt.[22] In practice, an unincorporated joint co-operative venture has to operate.

Article 50 of the Regulations for the Implementation of the Sino-Foreign Joint Co-operative Law provides that the parties to an unincorporated joint co-operative venture take civil liabilities under the relevant principles of the Chinese law. Article 52 of the Civil Law Principles appears to impose either a joint or individual liability, as the case may be, upon parties to a joint co-operation which has not been set up as a Chinese legal person. This provision seems to suggest that an unincorporated joint co-operative venture may enter commercial transactions in its own right. However, the Civil Law Principles do not recognize the civil ability of an organization which is not a legal person. Thus, the combined effect of Article 50 of the Regulations for the Implementation of the Sino-Foreign Joint Co-operative Ventures Law and Article 52 of the Civil Law Principles is to imply a duty to a party to a commercial transaction with an unincorporated joint co-operative venture to guard against the potential risk in suing the venture which is not capable of being liable for its act in civil law. Therefore, a party dealing with an unincorporated joint co-operative venture must be aware of such risks and should make a contract with one or both parties to the venture, rather than with the venture. Where the venture is not a legal person, at least one of the parties to the venture is normally expected to undertake unlimited liability to the civil activities conducted by the venture. However, if the party is a limited liability company, its unlimited liability to the debt of the venture is limited by its status as a limited liability company in its own right.

A joint co-operative venture which is a legal person is administered   **8.15** by a board of directors, or by a joint administrative committee. The board or committee consists of at least three persons. Its members are appointed by the parties respectively or jointly. The chairman and vice chairman are appointed in pursuance of the venture's constitution under the principle that the chairman and vice chairman must be respectively appointed by the parties. The board or committee must hold general meetings at least once a year and two thirds of the board or committee members must be present for each meeting. The meeting can be called by the chairman or vice chairman, or by one third of the board or committee members. The board or committee is required to notify the members of the meeting at least ten days prior to the scheduled meeting, which can be held also in teleconferencing form. A number of matters, such as the amendment of the constitution, increase or reduction of the registered capital, mortgage of the venture's property, merger or dissolution of the venture, must be resolved by the board or committee. The board or committee also appoint the senior managerial staff and deal with other important administrative matters relating to the venture. If the venture is to be managed by an outsider under a contract, the contract must be approved by all members of the board or committee.

These requirements in practice prevail over the relevant provisions of *The Company Law* in cases of inconsistency. Article 18 of *The Company Law* prevails over the law on foreign investment, and a joint co-operative venture is thus bound by the requirements set out in the Regulations. In addition, the Regulations may prevail because it is assumed that they represent the true position of Chinese law because they were made after the adoption of *The Company Law*.

A venture which is not a legal person is managed by a joint administration. The operation of the joint administration should be subject to any contractual arrangement analogous to the constitution. The joint administration co-ordinates the operation of the venture under the principles set out in the joint venture contract. Though the joint administration is authorized to decide all important matters of the venture under Article 53 of the Implementing Regulations, the administration may not exceed the limits as defined in the contract of co-operation. But, when dealing with outside parties, the administration may act on behalf of the venture. It is the responsibility of the outside parties to appreciate the differences between a legal person and a non legal person.

A joint co-operative venture, whether it is a legal person or not, enjoys limited civil capacity within the scope of the *Sino-Foreign Joint Co-operative Ventures Law*. Under the Law, a joint co-operative venture can make contracts of employment with its employees. It can also open accounts and borrow money from Chinese or foreign financial institutions in its own name. It can be assumed that in these circumstances the court would have to hold the parties to the venture liable whether or not the parties have technically entered the transactions in their own names.

The Implementing Regulations set out a number of rules on the purchase and sale by a joint co-operative venture. There are also rules on profit share and recovery of investment. Due to lack of space, these rules will not be examined in this chapter.

It must be emphasized that the contract is the foundation of a joint co-operative venture. Parties' contributions to the venture are determined by the contract. So are their liabilities and their entitlement to share profits. The parties can agree upon the form of the respective contributions and their values in the contract. In short, everything can be settled in the contract as long as the parties so agree. This is one of the advantages that the joint co-operative venture has over the joint equity venture.

Termination of a Joint Co-operative Venture

8.16 A joint co-operative venture can be terminated according to the terms of the contract. It may also be terminated according to the general principles of contract law. Thus, under Article 48 of the Regulations for the Implementation of Sino-Foreign Joint Co-operative Ventures Law a joint co-operative venture can be terminated if a party's breach has made the continuation of the venture impossible, if co-operation cannot continue because of frustration,[23] if a subsequent condition to the joint venture contract has arisen, or if the venture has been ordered to close down by the government or court. The contracting parties may also terminate a joint venture contract by agreement.[24] By the same token, a contract may be found invalid if it does not reflect the true intentions of the party or has failed to comply with the statutory requirements for its validity.[25]

The Regulations for the Implementation of the Sino-Foreign Joint Co-operative Ventures Law sets out a number of rules for the termination or dissolution of a joint venture. For example, a venture can renew the permit for its operation 180 days prior to the scheduled termination date. However, the Regulations do not allow a venture to continue beyond its term if the foreign investor has recovered his or her investment unless that investor is to make a new investment in the venture.

Dispute Resolution

8.17 Disputes in a joint venture can be settled by negotiation, mediation, arbitration and litigation. Negotiation and conciliation can be carried out in any manner that both parties agree to (see Chapter 11). Article 26 of the *Sino-Foreign Joint Co-operative Ventures Law* stipulates that if the parties have agreed to arbitrate the dispute in writing, the dispute should be submitted to a Chinese or foreign arbitral body as agreed. If there is no any agreement in writing, a party can take the matter to the court. This provision implies that the existence of an arbitration agreement in writing presents a bar for the parties to submit a dispute to the court. This proposition is supported by Article 5 of *The Arbitration Law*. Similarly, the parties are effectively barred from litigating on the same matter unless the arbitration agreement or the arbitral award can be challenged on one of the grounds set out by law.

Operation of Foreign Companies and Foreign Representative Offices

What is a Foreign Company or a Foreign Representative Office?

Article 199 of *The Company Law* defines a foreign company as a company established under a foreign law. This provision allows a foreign company to carry on business in China after registration. Article 203 of *The Company Law* provides that a foreign company is not a Chinese legal person, but the company is liable for its commercial activities in China. These provisions make the Chinese law compatible with the company laws of most countries. **8.18**

A foreign representative office is a local establishment of a foreign registered company. It is not meant to carry on business in China, but serves as a liaison office. It was the only legal way in which a foreign registered company could establish its presence in China until 1993 when *The Company Law* was passed. A foreign representative office is presently subject to the State Council Provisional Regulations for the Administration of Foreign Representative Offices and implementing rules promulgated by different ministries, including MOFTEC.

Registration of Foreign Companies and Foreign Representative Offices

The registration of foreign companies should be regulated by the State Council regulations to implement *The Company Law*, which are yet to be formulated. The registration is currently done under internal policies and other relevant regulations.

Under the Provisional Regulations, a foreign company may set up a representative office in China. But the office is not allowed to carry on business, except for the activities involving liaison functions, exhibition, market research and exchange of information. The Provisional Regulations allow a foreign representative office to have access to basic facilities and privileges, such as right of residence, banking services and the right to import means of transport, which are essential for its daily operation. The Implementing Rules issued by MOFTEC explain the procedure and requirements for the registration of foreign representatives in the areas of trade, manufacturing, freight forwarding, contractors, consultation, advertising, investment and leasing. They set out detailed prerequisites for the establishment, renewal, change and termination of a representative office in China.

The registration of certain foreign companies and foreign representative offices may also be regulated by the State Council Regulations for the Registration and the Administration of Legal Persons and Enterprises and the Detailed Rules for Implementing the Regulations for the Registration and the Administration of Legal Persons and Enterprises issued by the State Administration of Industry and Commerce in 1988. Article 2 of the State Council Regulations requires the registration of "any other enterprises whose registration is required by law". Article 2 of the Detailed Rules extends the registration requirements to "other enterprises". The expression "other enterprises" may include certain foreign companies and foreign representative offices, although neither the State Council Regulations nor the Detailed Rules use the words "foreign companies" and "foreign representative offices". This proposition is supported by a 1988 State Administration for Industry and Commerce document entitled "A Circular Dealing with the Numbering of 'PRC Legal Person's Business Certificate', of 'PRC Business Certificate' and of 'Registration Certificate for Foreign Representative Office'". This Circular provides that a local branch of a foreign bank, which is certainly not a Chinese legal person, can receive a PRC Business Certificate and a foreign representative office may obtain a Registration Certificate for Foreign Representative Office. These inconsistencies need to be clarified by law.

Operation of Foreign Registered Financial Institutions

8.19 Certain financial services, such as the banking services in foreign currency and insurance services, are the only areas where a foreign financial institution may carry on a limited business in its own right. If a foreign bank sets up a banking operation in China under the laws governing foreign invested enterprises, the company so established is a Chinese company and a Chinese legal person. But the Chinese law presently allows a foreign financial institution to be engaged in specified operations in China as a foreign company. A foreign bank was allowed to operate in Shenzhen in 1982. Many more banks were allowed in a number of special economic zones and coastal open cities. At the end of 1994, 109 foreign banks, five foreign financial institutions and four foreign insurance companies had been approved to operate in China.[26] In 1996, there are 36 foreign insurance companies operating in China. These foreign financial institutions are exclusively engaged in foreign currency related services. Their customers are largely foreign invested companies, foreign nationals and foreign registered companies in China. Presently, a foreign financial institution cannot apply for a banking licence unless it has been in China for more than two to three years, depending on the requirements of the relevant local law.

Foreign Invested Enterprises and Chinese Company Law

The Company Law is discussed in more detail in Chapter 10. This **8.20** section will briefly examine the major issues arising from the co-existence of *The Company Law* and the laws on foreign-invested enterprises.

A foreign investor appears to have an option to set up a limited liability company under either *The Company Law* or the laws on foreign-invested enterprises. One of the obvious reasons affecting his or her decision is that a company established under the *Law on Foreign-Invested Enterprises* will receive benefits and privileges which are theoretically unavailable to a company established under *The Company Law*. However, *The Company Law* does not expressly prohibit treating a foreign-invested company established under *The Company Law* as a foreign-invested company. In fact, Article 18 of *The Company Law* states that when a foreign-invested company is set up under the Law, the company is subject to the provisions of the relevant law on foreign investment if there is any inconsistency between *The Company Law* and the relevant law. Thus, a foreign-invested company established under *The Company Law* should be eligible to the benefits and privileges available to it as if it had been formed under the relevant law on foreign investment.

The Company Law and the laws on foreign-invested enterprises have different requirements for registered capital. Under Article 23 of *The Company Law*, the registered capital of a limited liability company is the paid-up capital. But, Article 21 of the Regulations for the Implementation of the Sino-Foreign Joint Equity Ventures Law and of the Regulations for the Implementation of the Solely Foreign-Invested

Enterprises Law, and Article 16 of the Regulations for the Implementation of the Sino-Foreign Joint Co-operative Ventures Law provide
that the registered capital of a foreign-invested enterprise is the capital
subscribed by the foreign investor(s). The implication is that under the
laws on foreign-invested enterprises, a foreign investor has more time
to pay the registered capital. This may be one of the considerations for
a foreign investor to decide on which law to resort to. Article 18 of *The
Company Law*, which gives prevalence to the laws on foreign investment, may not be able to reconcile the differences because such prevalence would undermine a number of basic principles, *e.g.* calculation of
the registered capital, of *The Company Law*.

Article 18 of *The Company Law* may resolve a number of other
inconsistencies between *The Company Law* and laws on foreign investment. For example, the laws on foreign investment impose restrictions on the transfer of interests from a participating party to third
party, but *The Company Law* allows such a transfer if the board of the
company so desires. In such cases, the relevant provisions of the laws
on foreign investment prevail. Similarly, the board of a foreign invested enterprise does not have to follow strict rules of operational
procedure, but the board of a limited liability company under *The
Company Law* must adopt the procedural rules set out in the Law.
In such cases, a foreign-invested company should be able to rely on
the less formal requirements under the relevant law. As a general
rule, Article 18 of *The Company Law* provides guidance for most
inconsistencies.

Local Laws on Foreign Investment

8.21 Local laws on foreign investment form a significant part of the legal
framework for foreign investment in China. Local governments have
considerable authority in approving foreign investment proposals and
extensive powers in making local laws, regulations and policies on
foreign investment. The constitutional principle is that a local government can make laws, regulations and policies in the area of foreign
investment as long as the laws, regulations and policies so made do not
conflict with the laws, regulations and policies of a higher government.
In the areas where the laws, regulations and policies of the national
government are scarce or silent, local regulations and policies can fill
the vacuum legitimately. This constitutional principle explains why
many local laws, regulations and policies on foreign investment
co-exist with the laws, regulations and policies of the national
government.

Generally speaking, foreign investments in a number of Special
Economic Zones, Open Coastal Cities, Special Development Areas and

similar areas enjoy lower tax rates and lower import duties. Depending on the nature of the investment, a foreign invested company may also be given better access to funding and markets, or benefits, privileges and concessions relating to the use of land, facilities and infrastructure. A local government may also reduce or exempt a foreign-invested company from local tax or various local levies. There is a need for a foreign investor to investigate the availability of local concessions and to negotiate the best deal in the circumstances given. In addition, it is also possible that a deal can be made locally even though the national law appears to be disapprove of such a deal.

Administration of Foreign Investment

This section deals briefly with the administrative structure for foreign investment. The administration of foreign investment in China is based on a two-tier structure, namely the national government and local governments. The national government formulates guidelines for foreign investments. The local governments implement the guidelines. Local governments' power to examine and approve foreign investments is granted by the State Council in pursuance of the national law. The local governments are thus bound by the State Council's regulations and policies on foreign investment.   **8.22**

The State Council is the highest authority in approving and supervising foreign investment. In 1994, the Co-ordination Committee for Foreign Investment was set up under the State Council. The Committee is responsible for studying, co-ordinating and guiding foreign investment policies throughout the country. It does not have formal decision-making power, but, its proposals, decisions and opinions can always be implemented through the State Council's executive power and delegated legislative power.

The State Council departments administer foreign investment in the relevant sectors of the economy. The major departments are the MOFTEC, the Ministry of Finance, the State Administration of Industry and Commerce, and the People's Bank of China. These departments formulate detailed rules to implement and interpret foreign investment laws and regulations. The MOFTEC has the authority to approve important foreign investment applications which do not fall under local authority. The Ministry of Finance implements and interprets tax laws and regulations. The State Administration of Industry and Commerce is in charge of the registration of foreign invested companies. The People's Bank shares responsibility for making foreign exchange policies. Other governmental departments, such as civil navigation, textile industry, light industry, electronic industry, oil and petroleum, have the power to formulate foreign investment policies within their own departments in pursuance of the national laws and regulations. There is a need to examine the relevant regulations and policies of each department in most circumstances.

A local government administers foreign investments through its special agency or body. Such an agency or body can be a commission, a committee or a departmental office. A local governmental department may also be directly responsible for examining and approving foreign investment proposals in the area administered by it. There is a need to ascertain the administrative authority for approving foreign investment within each local government. In addition, a foreign investment proposal also needs the approval from a number of governmental authorities in charge of relevant areas, such as labour relations, environmental protection, land management, or product standards. Often after a proposal has been approved by the responsible commission or committee, the proposed enterprise has to satisfy the specific requirements of each responsible authority before it can be issued a licence to commence operation.

After commencement, a foreign-invested enterprise is subject to the administration and supervision of the relevant governmental authorities. Various certificates and permits may be required to enable the enterprise to carry on its business operations. This is the same as any business operating in industrial countries, where a company has to comply with the relevant governmental regulations and policies from time to time.

Chinese Foreign Investment Law and the Agreement on TRIMS

8.23 "The Agreement on TRIMs" refers to the Agreement on Trade-Related Investment Measures, which is an inherent part of the Agreement on the World Trade Organization (WTO Agreement). The agreement was made in the 1993 Uruguay Round of GATT negotiations and came into existence with the WTO Agreement in January 1995. The purpose of this agreement is to prohibit the WTO members from using the trade-related measures to restrict and control foreign investment. This is the first time in the GATT history that foreign investment was regulated by its members.[27]

The Agreement on TRIMs contains a list of measures which are regarded as prohibitive. The agreement aims at restricting, reducing and eliminating the use of such measures. The major measures prohibited in the agreement are as follows:

(a) a trade-related measure which is a prerequisite for a foreign investor to obtain an advantage or benefit;

(b) a measure which requires a foreign investor to purchase or use domestic products or products of domestic origin in specified volume, value or proportion;

(c) a measure which sets out limits or ratio on a foreign investor's importing capacity according to the volume or value of his or her exporting capacity;

(d) a measure which sets out limits on a foreign investor's access to foreign exchange according to his or her foreign currency earning capacity; and

(e) a measure which sets out limits on a foreign investor's exporting capacity by reference to volume, value or proportion of his or her local production.

The above categories of TRIMs illustrate what are prohibited under the Agreement on TRIMs. Many provisions of the present Chinese investment law and policy fall under the above categories. An obvious example is the approval of solely foreign-invested enterprises, where a sole investor must either provide advanced technology or export 50 per cent of the enterprise's products. Similarly, the Chinese requirement that a foreign invested company should balance its own foreign currency account is also prohibited under the Agreement on TRIMs.

The Agreement on TRIMs allows a phase-out period for WTO members to comply with. China's entry into the WTO is only a matter of time. After it becomes a WTO member, it will have to implement the Agreement on TRIMs. Although the agreement does give a developing country like China some extra time for compliance, China will have to face the issue sooner or later. It can be expected that China will streamline its foreign investment laws and regulations at a reasonable speed. The length of a reasonable time for compliance is yet to be negotiated or considered by the other WTO members and the Committee on Agreement on TRIMs. It is yet to be seen how fast China can comply with the Agreement on TRIMs and how such compliance will affect the legal framework for foreign investment in China.

Notes

[1] Examples of successful foreign invested enterprises can be seen in Pengqin Li and Others eds, *An Introduction to China's Import of Foreign Investment* (Beijing, China Foreign Trade Press, 1995, in Chinese, *Zhong Guo Li Yong Wai Zi Ji Ben Zhi Shi*), pp. 181–187.

[2] Foreign investment can be made in the form of a joint equity venture or in the form of a joint co-operative venture.

[3] BOT stands for "Build, Operate and Transfer", which is similar to a turn-key type of investment. It is a vehicle for attracting foreign investment in the construction of

roads, railways, power stations and industrial waste processing factories, or similar projects which require a considerably large investment.
4 Only Sino-foreign joint ventures are allowed to act as freight forwarders in China. There are different requirements for the minimum registered capital of the forwarders engaged in road carriage, air carriage and sea carriage. Such requirements do not appear to be reasonable because a forwarder often has to engage in a multi-mode of carriage to complete a contract. It can be expected that any requirements inconsistent with commercial practices will soon be modified.
5 The rules regulate investment houses or the trust established for the purpose of investment.
6 The Memorandum explains the requirements for the ratio between Sino and foreign investment in a project and the areas open to Sino-foreign joint ventures.
7 Joint ventures and sole foreign investment are allowed to undertake construction contracts.
8 Sole foreign investment is not allowed to be set up as a construction company for the time being, even though the Provisional Measures for Construction Contracts Undertaken by Foreign Investment allow a sole foreign investment to undertake a major construction contract in China.
9 For some cases and comments, see Thomas G Guo and Others eds, *A Concise Analysis of the Recent Foreign Economic Cases of China* (Beijing, Chinese University of Political Science and Law Press, 1994, in Chinese *Dang Dai Zhong Guo She Wei Jing Ji Jiu Feng An Jing Xi*), pp. 393–398.
10 The time requirements are as follows:

    (a) if the registered capital is less than US$0.5 million, the full sum must be invested within one year from the date the licence is issued;
    (b) if the registered capital is between US$0.5 and 1 million, the full sum must be paid within one and half years from the date the licence is issued;
    (c) if the registered capital is between US$1 and 3 million, the full sum must be paid within two years from the date the licence is issued;
    (d) if the registered capital is between US$3 and 10 million, the full sum must be paid within three years from the date the licence is issued; and
    (e) if the registered capital is above US$10 million, the time of payment is to be negotiated.

11 Thomas G Guo and Others eds, see above note 9, pp. 521–527.
12 Article 10 of the *Solely Foreign-Invested Enterprises Law* states that dissolution, merger or any important changes in the structure of a solely foreign-invested enterprise must be approved by and registered with the relevant authority. A sole Taiwanese investor of a cloth manufacturing factory in Shenzhen transferred all his interests in the factory to another Taiwanese investor. The transaction was not approved by any governmental authority. The seller later refused to deliver the factory to the buyer, who sued the seller at court. The court held, *inter alia*, that the agreement to transfer the factory was invalid because the transaction was not approved and thus ordered the seller to return the purchase money to the buyer. This decision was affirmed by the appellate court. Ruifu Liu and Others eds, *A Complete Collection of Annotated Cases of PRC* (Beijing, International Culture Press, 1995, in Chinese, *Zhong Hua Ren Min Gong He Guo Xian Xing Fa Lu Pan Li Fen Xi Qian Shu*), pp. 1695–1698.
13 In 1992, a limited liability company solely owned by a Taiwanese investor entered into a contract to establish a joint venture with another Taiwanese investor to set up a textile operation. The contract was never approved and the "venture" was not formally registered. The latter alleged that the former had breached the contract. While the case was pending decision at a Chinese court, the commentators were of an opinion that the contract was invalid for a non-compliance with the registration requirements. Nor was the venture deemed to be legal for the same reason. See Thomas G Guo and Others eds, see above, pp. 409–412.
14 For example, a joint venture can invest in certain restrictive areas or projects, but a sole foreign investment cannot.
15 In 1986, a joint venture to develop solar energy was established between a Chinese company and a Hong Kong company in Jiang Su Province. The contract stated that the Hong Kong company would invest US$80,000 and be responsible for introducing new

equipment to be used by the venture. The contract stipulated the price of the equipment. The Hong Kong company made a considerable gain by purchasing the new equipment from a Canadian company at a lower price and selling it to the venture at the agreed price. The parties later could not reach agreement on a number of matters which were not dealt with in the contract. The Chinese company alleged that the Hong Kong company had breached the contract and made a huge profit in reselling the equipment to the venture. CIETAC found that the contract stipulated the price of the equipment and there was no basis for alleging the illegality of the Hong Kong company's act. The venture was dissolved because the parties could not reach any solution to their difference. See Thomas G Guo and Others eds, see above 9, pp. 403–408.

[16] Article 17 of the Regulations for Implementing the Sino-Foreign Joint Equity Ventures Law provides that any amendment to the venture's constitution and contract to set up the venture must be approved by the relevant authority. In 1986, a Chinese company and a Hong Kong company set up a joint venture to build a hotel. In the first board meeting of the venture, the board added new terms to the original contract. The amendment was not reported to and approved by the relevant authority. The Chinese company later alleged that the Hong Kong company breached the terms of the joint venture contract. The Hong Kong company argued that the Chinese company failed to comply with the new terms added to the contract. CIETAC decided, *inter alia*, that the amendment to the venture's contract was invalid because of non-compliance with the statutory requirement. See Thomas G Guo and Others eds, *Ibid.*, pp. 398–402.

[17] For example, in 1984 three Chinese companies and one Hong Kong company (A) set up a joint venture in Xiamen city. In 1987, the Hong Kong company (A) withdrew from the venture, whilst another Hong Kong company (B) stepped in to succeed A as a participating party. Company A sued the venture for unpaid interest on the money invested. The court mediated the dispute and decided that the agreement to replace A with B was enforceable and the venture was obliged to pay interest to A. See Thomas G Guo and Others eds, *Ibid.*, pp. 417–419.

[18] For example, there was a joint venture which could not continue to operate because the board members could not work together. The dispute was submitted to an arbitral body, which made an award on the basis of an agreement reached by the parties in the process of mediation. The award terminated the joint venture contract and ordered the parties to share the venture's debts and costs of arbitration on an equal basis. See Thomas G Guo and Others eds, see above, pp. 413–416.

[19] Article 54 of the Civil Law Principles provides that only a natural or legal person can enjoy civil rights and take civil liabilities.

[20] A contract must contain necessary information, *e.g.* parties' names, business addresses, place of registration, nationalities (if applicable), venture's name, business address, scope of business operation, registered capital, total investment, contributions of the parties, transfer of property between the parties, share of profit and costs, matters relating to the board of directors, details on equipment, technology to be used and marketing, foreign exchange balance, accounting matters, procedure for amending the contract, duties for breach of the contract, the term of operation and dispute resolution.

[21] The constitution must provide basic information on the venture, *e.g.* name, address, scope of operation, legal representatives of the parties, names and business of the parties, conditions and forms of the parties' contributions, share of profit and costs, the operation and constitution of the board of the directors, managerial rules, accounting arrangement, amendment procedure, and principles for dissolution and liquidation.

[22] Besides Article 54, Articles 106–110 of the Civil Law Principles appear to suggest that only natural persons and legal persons are liable for their contractual or other civil activities.

[23] For example, in 1990 a Chinese fishing company and a Hong Kong company concluded a contract to establish a joint co-operative venture. According to the contract, the Chinese party provided office space and labour, and the Hong Kong company provided two fishing vessels. In 1992 during the first fishing trip of the venture, the two fishing vessels were withdrawn by their owners because the Hong Kong company failed to pay the charter charges to the owners. The Chinese party had to fly its crew members from Singapore back to China, and claimed damages against the Hong Kong

company for an alleged breach of contract. CIETAC could not determine whether the Hong Kong company had breached the contract because that decision depended on the nature of the dispute between the Hong Kong company and the ship owners. It ordered the contract to be terminated and the Hong Kong party to pay the costs arising from the accident in 1992 to the Chinese Party. Ruifu Liu and Others eds, see above note 12, pp. 1684–1689. Depending on further information, this case may be, arguably perhaps, an instance of frustration (suppose the Hong Kong party did not breach the terms of the charter party).

24 For example, a joint co-operative venture had four parties: three Chinese companies and one Hong Kong company. The venture went into *de facto* dissolution because of a lack of co-operation among the parties. The parties agreed to dissolve the venture, but disagreed on the share of losses. One of the Chinese parties applied for a court order to distribute the losses. The trial court refused the application on the grounds that the identity of the defendants were unascertained. The appellate court ordered a retrial on the ground that there was a serious issue of law to be tried and the parties involved were ascertained. Ruifu Liu and Others eds, see above note 12, pp. 1689–1892.

25 For example, the parties to a joint co-operative venture made a supplementary agreement in 1985 to amend the 1982 agreement. The agreement was not approved by the relevant authority. The communications between the parties after the making of the supplementary agreement showed some disagreement on the terms of the supplementary agreement. When the matter went to CIETAC's Shenzhen branch, the Commission found the supplementary agreement was unenforceable because it did not represent the true intention of the parties and it failed to comply with the requirement for approval. Thomas G Guo and Others eds, see above note 9, pp. 420–423.

26 Pengqin Li and Others eds, see above note 1, p. 91.

27 In order to avoid confusion, it is necessary to point out that the GATT was succeeded by the WTO in 1995. The history of GATT is now regarded as part of the history of the WTO.

CHAPTER 9
FAMILY LAW

Zhang Xianchu

City University of Hong Kong

Zhang Xianchu, University Lecturer, Faculty of Law, City University of Hong Kong; LL.B. (China University of Political Science and Law, Beijing PRC); MCL (Indiana University School of Law, Bloomington); JD (Indiana University School of Law, Bloomington).

The major areas covered by family laws in China are marriage and divorce, adoption, and succession as well as special protection for women and children. From a practical perspective, family laws are the most extensively applied group of laws in China. According to the Annual Working Reports of the Supreme Court, the number of marriage/divorce cases tried in 1995 by the people's courts of all levels reached 1,313,910 from 610,893 in 1987. Family relation cases alone represent approximately 48 per cent of total civil cases with an average yearly increase of 8.75 per cent since 1987. It was reported following the latest plenary Session of the Standing Committee of the National People's Congress at the end of October 1996 that a revision of the current *Marriage Law* is on the agenda of the Committee.

Marriage Law

The marriage system in China is based on the constitutional principles **9.01**
of the freedom of marriage, of monogamy, and of equal rights for each gender. These principles are further articulated by *The Marriage Law* of 1980.

Substantive Conditions

Necessary Conditions

(a) Under Articles 3 and 4 of the Law, a marriage must be based upon the complete willingness of both the man and woman. Neither party shall use compulsion on the other, and no third party is allowed to interfere.[1] Any marriage contracted through arrangement, coercion, money dealing or fraud shall be void.

(b) Article 5 of the Law provides that no marriage shall be contracted before the man has reached 22 years of age and the woman 20 years of age. Late marriage and late childbirth should be encouraged. The Law raises the lawful marriage age from 20 for a man and 18 for a woman with the aim of further enforcing the family planning policy and slowing down the increase in population. As such, the lawful marriage age is different from the age where citizens can obtain their full civil capacity under the General Principles of Civil Law (This is 18 years of age).[2] Article 36, however, allows autonomous regions to formulate their own adaptation or supplementary provisions in the light of the specific conditions of local nationalities with regard to marriage and family. As a result, the lawful marriage age has been lowered to 20 for men and 18 for women in most autonomous regions.

(c) Monogamy is strictly enforced and any marriage violating this rule shall be void. Any married person who, with spouse alive, either marries a third person or lives with a third person to constitute a *de facto* marriage shall be subjected to a criminal penalty against bigamy.

Prohibitive Conditions

(a) To prevent both birth defects and incest, marriage is not permitted under Article 6(1) where the man and woman are lineal relatives by blood, or collateral relatives by blood up to the third degree of kinship. In practice, the main focus is on marriage between first cousins, a custom which has lasted for centuries in China on the basis of patriarchal clan system.

(b) By Article 6 (2), no marriage shall be contracted if the man or woman is suffering from leprosy, a cure not having been effected, or from any other diseases which are regarded by medical science as capable of rendering a person unfit for marriage. Under the *Law Concerning the Protection of Maternal and Infant Health* of 1994, both marrying parties shall present pre-marriage medical examination certificates issued by certified medical institutions. The items under examination include serious genetic diseases, listed infectious diseases and certain mental diseases. In such cases, doctors shall advise on the postpanement of marriage during the contagious period for infectious diseases, and the effecting period for mental diseases.

Sexuality is not mentioned in the current Law. However, the fact that the Law deletes the factor from the law of 1950 suggests that it is not generally prohibited for a person without sexual ability to get married as long as the marriage is based on the parties' informed decision.

Procedural Conditions

Article 7 of *The Marriage Law* stipulates that both parties should   9.02
register in person with the marriage registration office. The husband-
wife relationship shall be established upon the acquisition of the
marriage certificates issued after the proposed marriage is found to
conform with the Law. In order to implement this provision, the
Ministry of Civil Administration has promulgated three regulations on
marriage registration applicable to all domestic marriage registrations
since 1980 with the latest one becoming effective on January 12, 1994.

   (a) According to the latest Regulation, the office responsible for
       marriage registration is the people's government of the town-
       ship, villages in the countryside or in small cities; or the local
       civil administration office in a large city. The regional jurisdic-
       tion of a marriage registration office is based on the parties'
       household registers. If the parties' household registers are es-
       tablished in different places, either office is empowered to
       review the applications and issue the marriage certificates.
   (b) To safeguard freedom of marriage and facilitate examination,
       applications must be made by the parties in person and any
       delegation is disallowed. The application shall also be filed
       together with the necessary documents, including personal
       identity document, certificate of marital status, and pre-
       marriage health examination certificate. If one party desires to
       marry after divorce, he or she must produce the necessary
       documents, such as the divorce registration certificate or court
       divorce judgement to prove that the divorce has become effec-
       tive. It should be noted, however, that all the documents shall
       only be used as references and the final decision on the validity
       of the proposed marriage will be made by the marriage registra-
       tion office on the basis of examination of the overall substan-
       tive conditions rather than completeness of documentation.

Thus, a valid registration may be granted even if the parties may not be able to submit all the documents required.

The marriage registration office shall examine the application of the parties to determine whether all substantive conditions provided by the Law are met. If necessary, the office may make further inquiries, conduct investigations, or direct the party towards certain medical appraisal. Under Article 12 of the Regulation, any proposed marriage shall not be registered where either or both parties fail to satisfy with any legal conditions. The registration office shall inform the parties of reasons for denial in writing.

Where after divorce, both parties desire to resume their husband-wife relationship, they shall apply in person for registration of remarriage with the marriage registration office. By the same procedure as marriage registration, the certificate shall be issued for the resumption of the relationship and the divorce certificate shall be recalled at the same time. For remarriage registration, a medical examination may not be required.

The registration office shall declare a marriage void by cancelling the marriage registration with a fine of up to 200 renminbi after cheating or fraud is discovered. The office is also under the duty to report any bigamous case to the people's procuratorate if the spouse of the offender fails to do so. On the other hand, the marrying parties may challenge the decision made by the registration office of refusal of their marriage application by requesting a reconsideration or even filing an administrative lawsuit against the office in accordance with the *Law of Administrative Litigation Procedures*.

Special Regulations Relating to Marriages between Overseas Chinese or Chinese from Hong Kong or Macau and Citizens of Mainland China

9.03 The legal authority on this matter is the Provisions Concerning Registration Procedure for Marriages between Overseas Chinese or Chinese from Hong Kong or Macau and Citizens of Mainland China promulgated by the Ministry of Civil Administration on March 10, 1983.

According to the Provisions, both parties of a proposed marriage, if they choose to register their marriage in mainland China, shall apply together in person for the marriage certificate with the marriage registration office at or above county level, where the household register of the domestic citizen is established.

For overseas Chinese to file the marriage application, the documents demanded by the Provisions include the passport of the party issued by the Chinese diplomatic mission in the country and proof of unmarried status issued by a local notary public office and attested by

the Chinese diplomatic mission, or directly issued by the mission in
the country. A Chinese resident from Hong Kong or Macau is required
to present

   (a) his or her personal identity document;
   (b) the marital status certificate issued by the Registrar of Mar-
      riage of Hong Kong and attested by a local lawyer authorized by
      the Ministry of Justice of China together with the statements
      made by the applicant and certified by a local lawyer to declare
      that the applicant is single; or a marital status certificate is-
      sued by the Macau Administrative Bureau or Police Bureau.

In addition, overseas Chinese and Chinese residents from Hong
Kong and Macau also need to produce evidence of their occupation and
reliable economic income as well as a medical examination report
from a hospital in China at or above county level designated by the
marriage registration office. Those who have been married before the
application, have to submit the proof of valid divorce or death of
spouse.

An overseas Chinese or Chinese resident from Hong Kong or Macau
may resume his or her marriage with a domestic citizen after divorce
by applying together in person with their proof of unmarried status for
remarriage with the marriage registration office.

Registration Procedures for Intermarriages Between Chinese and Foreigners

The detailed procedures are stipulated in the Regulations Concerning   **9.04**
Registration Procedures for Intermarriages between Chinese and Foreigners by the Ministry of Civil Administration on August 26, 1983.

A Chinese national and a foreigner who desire to marry in China
shall apply in person with the marriage registration office designated
by the people's government of the province, autonomous region or
municipality directly under the central government where the Chinese
partner has his or her permanent domicile.

To apply for marriage registration, the foreigner must present

   (a) passport or other identity certificate;
   (b) resident card issued by the Chinese Public Security Bureau, or
      identity certificate issued by the Ministry of Foreign Affairs, or
      entry or residence certificate;
   (c) marital status certificate issued by the foreign ministry of his
      or her country, or issued by the notary public office of the
      country which has been verified by the Chinese embassy or
      consulate in the country, or directly issued by the Chinese
      diplomatic mission.

For foreign nationals residing in China, a marital status certificate may be issued by the people's government of the county level or above, or by his or her working unit with personal and marital information and the name of the person he or she wishes to marry. Both parties shall also submit health certificates issued by the hospital designated by the marriage registration office.

Under the Regulations, certain Chinese are not allowed to marry those foreigners who are servicemen, diplomatic personnel, public security officers, persons engaged in confidential or any important work prescribed by the State authority, and those being reformed through labour or serving prison terms.

Engagement, Wedding and *De Facto* Marriage

9.05 Engagement was a necessary procedure for a valid marriage in ancient China. The practice, however, is no longer recognized by the Law so as to safeguard the freedom of marriage and to prevent arranged marriages and other problems arising from difficulties that may occur after engagement. A wedding is not a necessary formality for a valid marriage any more either. On the contrary, government propaganda has been used extensively to promote thrift in managing a household.

De facto marriage in China is defined as the man and woman living together publicly as husband-and-wife without marriage registration but being nevertheless acknowledged as a married couple by the local community. It has been one of the most serious and complicated problems in family law for a long time in China and has obliged the Supreme Court to issue several instructions, in order to give lower courts the judicial guidance needed to remedy the silence of the law in this area.

Most *de facto* marriages are contracted by unmarried couples with the purpose of establishing a husband and wife relationship. The only defect is that the parties fail to carry out the marriage registration. A large number of *de facto* marriages are the result of non awareness of the law and strong resistance of certain traditional and local marriage customs. Some de facto marriages are the result of improper or incorrect application of the law and policy by some offices and units, such as refusing to issue certain certificates as a means to enforce a local late marriage policy even though the marrying parties have reached the lawful age for marriage.

By taking into account of the complex reality of *de facto* marriage and the policy to protect lawful rights and interests of women and children and to stabilize family relationships, the Supreme Court opinion of December 13, 1989 allows recognition of a marriage relationship created by *de facto* marriage under some conditions during a certain period. The time line dates from March 15, 1986 when the Regulations of Marriage Registration of 1986 became effective. On one hand, a *de facto* marriage taking place before this date shall be recognized if both parties meet all the substantive conditions for a valid marriage. *De facto* marriages after this date, on the other hand, shall be treated as unlawful cohabitation. Certain principles applicable to divorce and succession to determine property division, child custody and debt sharing are, however, virtually employed to handle the issues in termination of *de facto* relationships.

De facto marriage may subject a party to criminal liability against bigamy. In 1994 the Supreme Court reconfirmed its holding that criminal penalties against bigamy shall still be imposed where a married person unlawfully cohabits with an unmarried person or with another married person with the knowledge of the marriage in the name of husband and wife after the Marriage Registration Regulation of 1994 became effective.[3] Recently a Hong Kong businessman was sentenced for one year's imprisonment for bigamy. He continued to live with his divorced second wife even though the first marriage was still valid.[4] In this circumstance, regardless of the imposition of the criminal liability, the second relationship must be renounced.

Family Relationship

Husband-wife Relationship

Under Article 9 of *The Marriage Law*, both husband and wife shall   **9.06** have equal status in the family. Both husband and wife have the freedom to engage in work, study and to participate in social activities. Neither party may restrict or interfere with the other. Both have the right to use their own surname and given name. Children may adopt either their father's or mother's surname.

The property acquired by the husband and wife during the marriage period shall be under their joint ownership, unless they have agreed otherwise. By agreement, the husband and wife may provide instructions on how to divide the property acquired by them either before, during, or after the period of their marriage so long as the agreement reflects the true intention of the parties free from any fraud, duress or coercion without violation of the law or lawful interests of a third party. Such an agreement shall be made in writing, or verbally in the presence of at least two witnesses.

Article 14 of the Law provides that both husband and wife have a duty to maintain each other. If one party fails to perform this duty, the other party in need shall have the right to demand maintenance payments. By consideration of the income gap between most husbands and wives, the people's courts have taken the view that even the agreement made by the husband and wife on their property shall not exempt a party's duty to maintain the other. Under Article 18, both husband and wife have the right to inherit each other's property.

Parent-child Relationship

Article 15 provides that parents have a duty to bring up and educate their children. If parents fail to perform their duties, children who are minors or are not capable of living on their own shall have the right to demand the costs of upbringing from their parents. Criminal liability may even be imposed on parents who refuse to perform their duties in this respect, which constitutes abandonment. Moreover, to combat gender discrimination against females the Law prohibits infanticide by drowning or any other acts causing serious harm to infants. Article 32 of the *Law Concerning Protection of Maternal and Infant Health* of 1994 further prohibits technical tests to determine the gender of the foetus unless medically necessary.

Article 17 allows parents the right to subject their children to discipline and to protect them. Thus, the parents shall be held liable for compensation for any damages caused by their children. In 1991, the *Law Concerning Protection for People under Age* was adopted to give special legal protection to minors under the age of 18. The duties of parents under *The Marriage Law* are further articulated in Chapter 2 of the *Minor Protection Law* which include the duty to guard and financially support, not to abuse and abandon; not to discriminate against female and disabled children; to respect a child's right to education; to guide children with a healthy ideology; to prevent children from, and stop them smoking, drinking, gambling, drug abuse, and prostitution; and not to allow or coerce children under age to marry or arrange marriages for them. Parents or other guardians may be subjected to legal liability or be deprived of their guardianship if they fail to carry out their duties under the Law.

According to Article 19 of *The Marriage Law*, children born out of wedlock shall enjoy the same rights as ones born in wedlock. No one may harm or discriminate against them. By taking into account the difference of income earning ability between males and females in China, the Law further explicitly requires the father of a child born out of wedlock to bear part or all of the child's living and educational expenses until the child is able to support itself.

Article 15 also imposes a duty on children to support and assist their parents. If children fail to perform their duties, parents who are unable to work or have difficulty in providing for themselves shall have the right to demand support payments from their children. Parents and children have the right to inherit each other's property. The relevant provisions of the laws governing the relationship between parents and children are also applicable to the relationship between step-parents and their step-children who receive care and education from them.

Relationships Between Other Family Members

Article 22 of the Law provides that grandparents who can afford it shall have the duty to bring up those grandchildren who are minors and whose parents are dead. Grandchildren, who can afford it, shall also have the duty to support their grandparents whose children are dead. The Supreme Court expands this provision on grandparent's duty of bringing up their grandchildren to circumstances under which one parent is dead and the other is not able to perform parental duty, or both parents are no longer able to perform their duties to their children. The grandchildren's duty to support their grandparents is also extended to cover those situations where the children of the grandparents have no means to support and assist them.[5] Elder brothers or sisters who can afford it, shall have the duty to bring up their younger brothers or sisters who are minors, if their parents are dead or if they have no means to bring them up.

Divorce

A dual track system of divorce exists in China, under which divorce   **9.07** may be effected either through the agreement of both parties or through legal proceedings.

Divorce through Agreement of the Parties

Article 24 of *The Marriage Law* allows divorce by agreement by both husband and wife. The effectiveness of such divorce, however, depends on three conditions:

(a) divorce is the true desire of both parties;
(b) appropriate arrangements have been made for child care and disposition of property; and
(c) both parties apply to the marriage registration office for divorce registration with their identity certificate, divorce agreement and marriage certificate as well as a reference letter issued by their place of work or the neighbour committee. After these conditions are met, a divorce certificate shall be issued within a month.

Divorce by agreement, however, does not apply to the following situations:

(a) just one party desires to divorce;
(b) both parties desire divorce, but can not reach an agreement on other matters;
(c) one or both parties have only incomplete or no civil competence; or
(d) the marriage has never been registered.

The rules discussed above will also be applicable to divorce by agreement between a domestic citizen and overseas Chinese or Chinese from Hong Kong and Macau. This procedure, however, is not available for divorce between a Chinese citizen and a foreigner, for which divorce proceedings with the court must be pursued.

Divorce through Legal Proceedings

Divorce Proceedings

Under Article 25, the organization concerned, such as the working units of the parties or the neighbour committee, may carry out mediation first where one party alone desires to divorce. The party may, nevertheless, file directly to a people's court to start divorce proceedings.

It should be noted that there are two special provisions regarding divorce proceedings in the Law. Article 26 affords special protection for a marriage where a service person in action is a party, by providing that the start of a divorce proceeding shall be conditioned by the consent of the service person. The rule, however, does not apply to a marriage between two service persons. Under Article 27, in order to protect the lawful rights and interests of women and children, a husband is not allowed to apply for divorce within a year after his wife has given birth or at the time his wife is pregnant. This restriction shall not apply to a case where the wife applies for divorce, or the people's court considers it necessary to accept the divorce application made by the husband.

Divorce through Mediation

In dealing with a divorce case, the people's court is required by law to carry out mediation as a necessary procedure in all stages of divorce proceedings with the purpose to restore relations between the parties. If the efforts fail, the court may then mediate the disputes between the parties over child custody, property division or other matters. Upon agreement on all matters being reached under the direction of the court a certificate of divorce through mediation shall be issued by the court with the same legal authority as a judgment.

Divorce by Judgment

Under Article 25, divorce shall be granted if mediation fails because mutual affection between husband and wife has broken down. The legal test seems an indication that the traditional divorce permissible on a fault basis has made way for the new concept of freedom of divorce.

In practice, however, the legal test was considered very difficult to apply because of the ambiguity of the wording and the virtually unrestricted discretion left to the court until the Supreme Court issued the long awaited circular entitled Certain Opinions on How to Determine Breaking Down of Mutual Affection between Husband and Wife in Divorce Proceedings on December 13, 1989.

According to the Circular, whether mutual affection has broken down should be examined from the following four aspects:

(a) the basis of the marriage: consideration should be given as to whether the marriage was contracted recklessly or by arrangement of a third party, or by deceit or fraud;

(b) the condition of mutual affection after the marriage: what may be taken into account includes the duration of living together and separation, or the failure to establish mutual affection between the parties under an arranged marriage despite living together for years;

(c) the reasons for the divorce: the listed conducts that may justify a divorce include adultery; illicit cohabitation; polygamy; habitual gambling; refusal to work, to carry out family duties or to improve unacceptable behaviour despite repeated admonition; committing a crime; abuse; abandonment; or disappearance for a term of two years;

(d) the possibility of restoration of mutual affection: this will depend on whether the party at fault decides to change their behaviour, whether the parties accept the court's mediation, or whether relations between the parties have improved after the court's first denial of their petition for divorce.

These four aspects provide a legal test with an objective basis and to some extent, revert to the traditional legal standards for divorce based on fault. For instance, even if a divorce is granted on the grounds of the breaking down of mutual affection, the court is required to tell who the party at fault is in its decision.[6] Thus, the no fault divorce legislation must be applied together with the Supreme Court Circular aimed at stabilizing family and social relationships and protecting the innocent party.

Child Custody and Property Division

Child Custody and Support

9.08   Article 29 provides that the relationship between parents and children shall not come to an end with the divorce of the parents. After divorce, regardless of who is granted the right of custody, they shall remain the parents of the children and shall still have the rights and duties to bring up and educate their children.

In principle, the mother shall have the custody of an infant after divorce. Over disputes on the custody of older children, the people's court shall make a decision based on the rights and interests of the child and the actual condition of the parents. The detailed guidelines are provided in the circular issued by the Supreme Court on November 3, 1993.[7] Generally a child under the age of two shall be under the custody of the mother unless the father and mother agree otherwise and the healthy growth of the child will not be negatively affected under such an agreement, or the mother is the party at fault in failing to perform her duty to the child, or she has healthy or financial difficulties. Both parents are entitled to the custody of a child above the age of two. The priority, however, will be given to the party who can no longer have any children; who lives with the child longer than the other party and where a clearly negative impact would be experienced by the child as the result of the change of living environment; who does not have any children while the other party has either from previous marriage or adoption; and who has advantageous conditions for the healthy growth of the child. If the conditions of the two parties are equal, the relations between the child and his or her paternal and maternal grandparents as well as their ability to look after the child may even be taken into account to decide the preference. The opinion of a minor above the age of 10 should be considered in deciding custody. Alternating custody may be granted if the parents so agree.

After divorce, the non-custodian parent shall still bear part or all of the child's living and educational expenses. According to the Circular, the payment for child support in principle is capped at twenty to thirty per cent of the party's fixed monthly income in the case of a single child, and fifty per cent in case of two or more children involved. This support shall be given until the child reaches the age of eighteen unless the child is able to live on his or her own earnings which must correspond to the average local living standard after the child reaches the age of sixteen. The support duty of the parents may continue if the child has not lived on his or her own and is still studying, or is unable to make a living due to either total or partial loss of his or her capacity to work, or is unable to live independently. Any agreement or court judgment on the payment of child support shall not prevent the child from making a reasonable request, when necessary, to either parent for an amount exceeding what was agreed to in the agreement or judgment.

Property Division

Under Article 31 of the Law, at the time of divorce, the husband and wife shall seek agreement on the disposition of their jointly owned property. Article 31 and the Supreme Court Circular stipulate that in court proceedings as a general principle, the property shall be divided equally between the husband and wife. The principle, however, is subject to many detailed qualifications based on special consideration of the actual conditions of the property, for the special protection of the rights and interests of the wife and the child, for the actual needs of living and production, and for the favourable treatment of the innocent party.

For example, the means of production shall be awarded to the party competent to operate and manage them while the other party may be compensated with money equal to half the amount of its value. The accommodation shall be given to the party who is bringing up the child and favourable treatment will be awarded to the innocent party. A wife shall be treated favourably on the grounds that in most families, husbands usually are better positioned to earn more income. In certain circumstances, one party shall be entitled to appropriate treatment in division of jointly owned property for the yet to be received economic interests from an intellectual property right that is created during the marriage by the other party. Recently the Supreme Court issued another Circular to give judicial guidance on assigning contract rights concerning public housing in divorce proceedings.[8]

The debts incurred jointly by the husband and wife during the marriage shall be paid out of their jointly owned property. They shall not include, however, the debts that under the agreement by the husband and wife shall be borne by one party and that are incurred by one party without the consent of the other for supporting relatives or friends to whom the party does not own any legal duties, or for the purpose of business, of which no income has been used in the marriage. The debts that are not classified as joint debts shall be paid by the party who incurred them with his or her own personal property.

The party who illegally conceals, transfers, damages, or refuses to hand out the jointly owned property shall be penalized during the legal proceedings by less awards or even deprivation of his or her property rights. Under Article 33 if, at the time of divorce, one party has difficulty in supporting himself or herself, the other shall be under a legal duty to render appropriate financial assistance.

Sanctions

9.09 Article 34 provides that persons who violate the Law shall be subject to administrative, or legal sanctions. Administrative sanctions shall apply to minor violations which yet constitute any crimes including warning or dismissal from work. In addition, the public security office may also impose sanctions against those who cause social disorder in the way of marriage law violation. For example, warnings, fines or detention may be imposed as penalties against the abuse of a family member.[9]

Legal sanctions include impositions of civil liabilities and criminal penalties. The former will be carried out mainly by economic means, such as the return of property in arranged marriages, and enforcement of financial support on family members. Methods of restoration of lawful relations are also widely employed, such as restoration of reputation, extension of apology and signing a statement of repentance. The latter can be used against crimes of interfering with the freedom of marriage by force, bigamy, serious abuse, abandonment and the infringement of marriages of service persons.

Law Concerning Divorce Involving A Foreign Party

9.10 Under *The Law of Civil Procedure*, the people's court shall have jurisdiction over any divorce action to which a Chinese citizen is a party to if he or she desires that the hearing be conducted in China even after the action is denied by a foreign court on the grounds of nationality or marriage being established under the Chinese law. The Chinese law shall be applied to proceedings conducted in China.

A divorce judgment rendered by a foreign court shall not have any legal effect until it is recognized by a people's court through the application of the party concerned. However, according to the Provisions on Procedure for Recognition of Foreign Divorce Judgment Applied by Chinese Citizens issued by the Supreme Court on August 13, 1992, once a people's court has registered a divorce action for hearing, any application for recognition of a foreign divorce judgement shall be denied. Moreover, the foreign judgement may not prevent a party from filing a new divorce action in a people's court if the application for the recognition has yet been filed. The people's court may not accept a divorce action involving a foreign party only if the application for the recognition is filed before the initiation of the domestic action.

To apply for recognition of a divorce judgment rendered in a foreign country, the Chinese party has to file a written application with the foreign judgment and the attested Chinese translation, to the intermediate people's court in the place of the applicant's domicile. Where the applicant has moved abroad, the jurisdiction shall be exercised by the court in the place of original domicile of the applicant.

The court, after receiving the application, may further require the applicant to produce proof of the foreign judgment having become effective and proof of the defendant having been served and subpoenaed in accordance with the law by the foreign court, if the applicant is the plaintiff in the foreign action. The foreign judgment, nevertheless, may be presumed valid and effective upon the presence of copies of the proceeding notice and subpoena to appear before the court if the applicant, as a Chinese citizen and defendant in the foreign action, has difficulties to produce the aforementioned notarized and verified documents. Application for recognition of a foreign judgment may be conducted through attorneys.

The application shall be denied in any of the following findings:

(a) the foreign judgment has not become effective yet;
(b) the foreign court does not have jurisdiction over the case;
(c) the foreign judgment is entered by default in violation of the defendant's right to due process;
(d) a people's court is hearing or has heard the divorce case between the two parties, or the foreign judgment rendered by a court of a third country has been recognized by a people's court; and
(e) the foreign judgment either violates the basic principles of the Chinese law or harms the sovereignty, security or public interests of China.[10]

Although the application procedure is stipulated for Chinese citizens and there is no time limit on the application, the Supreme Court holds that the marriage registration office shall not register a proposed marriage involving a foreign party who has divorced a Chinese spouse in foreign proceedings until the foreign judgment has been recognized by the people's court. It has further ruled that a marriage registration must be revoked on the grounds of violation of the Chinese law where the Chinese spouse objects to the foreign divorce judgment which is not recognized by the people's court while the foreign party has registered a new marriage with another Chinese citizen.[11]

Some different rules and policies, applicable to divorce and related issues involving parties from Taiwan are adopted on the basis of recognition of the historical separation and the reality. According to the Supreme Court, all divorce judgments rendered by people's courts are valid regardless of the presence of the parties involved and the service procedure. A couple may not be allowed to resume their marriage relationship unless both of them have remained single. The people's court will treat the later marriages contracted by the parties without termination of the previous marriage relationship as valid ones. It shall exercise its jurisdiction over any action brought by a party from

Taiwan to divorce his or her spouse in Taiwan where the plaintiff has settled in mainland China.[12]

As far as property, alimony or child support is concerned, the Supreme Court takes the position that it will not entertain any action by a party from Taiwan on property left to the spouse on the mainland before 1949 unless such property still exists and is worth an anount more than warranting a leftover after satisfying the living of the spouse and child, if any on the mainland.[13]

Family Planning

9.11 China is adhering firmly to its birth control policy. Article 25 of the Constitution calls on the State to promote family planning in order to stabilize population growth in accordance with economic and social development. Article 12 of *The Marriage Law* further provides that both the husband and wife shall have a duty to practice family planning. The specific implementation of these laws, however, depends on local legislation which varies significantly.

Improvement of birth quality is another important aspect of family planning in China. In addition to the requirement for medical examination prior to a marriage, Article 15 of *The Law Concerning Protection of Maternal and Infant Health* of 1994 further provides that the husband and wife shall take necessary measures if medically advised to avoid a birth after either or both parties are found to have a serious hereditary disease. Article 18 authorizes the doctor to advise the would be parents on terminating the pregnancy if the antenatal diagnosis determines that the foetus has a serious hereditary disease or physical defect or that the life or health of the mother may be in danger. Article 20 requires that both the husband and wife take a medical examination in a designated medical institution if the wife has a history of defective birth.

Adoption Law

9.12 *The Adoption Law* was promulgated by the Standing Committee of the National People's Congress in 1991. Since then several supplementary procedure rules for both domestic and foreign adoptions have been adopted by the Ministry of Civil Administration, the organ responsible for adoption registration under the Law. The Supreme Court has also interpreted the Law through its Circular or replies to lower court requests on certain issues.

The General Principles

To protect the lawful adoptive relationship and to safeguard the rights and interests of parties involved, some important principles are established by *The Adoption Law*: (a) Adoption shall be practised for the interests of upbringing and growth of adopted minors. (b) Adoption shall be in conformity with the principle of equality and voluntariness. (c) Adoption shall not violate social morality. Article 19, for instance, provides that buying or selling a child or doing so under the guise of adoption is strictly forbidden. Article 9 requires an age difference of over 40 years for a male without spouse to adopt a female child in order to prevent any moral or ethical violation. Adoption of a grandchild by grandparents is disallowed by the Supreme Court.[14] The judicial practice also rejects adoption by a cohabiting couple on the grounds of a lack of legitimate and stable family basis. (d) Adoption shall not contravene laws and regulations on family planning. Generally a person who already has child shall not be allowed to adopt another child. To stop the practice of placing female children up for adoption in order to continue to became pregnant again in the hope of having a male child, Article 18 explicitly provides that persons having placed a child for adoption may not bear any more children in violation of the regulations on family planning.

Establishment of an Adoptive Relationship

Parties to an Adoptive Relationship

Adoptee

According to Article 4, the adoptee must be a minor under the age of 14 who is an orphan, abandoned infant, child whose parents cannot be found, or child whose parents are unable to rear him or her due to unusual difficulties including death, injury, disability, sickness, financial difficulties, or divorce.   **9.13**

Adopter

Where a person with spouse intends to adopt a child, the decision shall be made on the basis of joint consent by the couple. Under Article 6, an adopter must meet three requirements simultaneously:

(a) Childlessness. This requirement applies to both single and married people who have neither any adopted child nor step-child. In the case of second marriage, adoption on childless grounds will not be allowed as long as one party has a child. A

person may be eligible to be an adopter if the spouse has passed
away and no step-relationship exists between the person and
the child of the deceased;

(b) Capable of rearing and educating the adoptee. This is measured
by the adopter's financial conditions, civil competence, morality and other elements that ensure the adoptee is supplied with
a good education and growth environment;

(c) Having reached the age of 35. The age requirement is applied to
both husband and wife in case of adoption by the couple.
Moreover, as a result of Article 9 which provides for an age
difference of over 40 years between a male adopter without
spouse and female adoptee, the minimum age of such an
adopter shall be at least 40.

There are some exceptions. Under Article 7, any childless citizen
who has reached the age of 35 may adopt a child of a blood relative of
the same generation and up to a third degree of kinship, irrespective
of the conditions of unusual difficulties for placing out for adoption, of
age difference of 40 years between the male adopter and the female
adoptee and of the requirement of the age of 14 for the adoptee. This
exception shows the legislative special consideration to the custom of
adoption between relatives in China. Also according to Article 8(2),
orphans or disabled children may be adopted irrespective of the restrictions that the adopter must be childless, have reached the age of 35 and
may adopt one child only. Moreover, Article 14 allows a step-parent,
with the consent of the biological parents to adopt the step-child
regardless of the requirements for an adopter and restriction on the age
of the adoptee as well as the unusual conditions for the placing family.

The Parties Who Place out Children for Adoption

Based on Article 5, citizens or institutions that may place out children
for adoption include guardians of an orphan, social welfare institutions
and parents unable to rear their children due to unusual difficulties.

Article 10 provides that the parents must act on the basis of joint
consent if they intend to place out their child for adoption. The Supreme Court by its Circular of August 30, 1984 further held that either
parent will have veto power on the proposed adoption. However, no
objection to the knowledge of the placing out will be deemed as
consent. This rule is also applicable to divorced parents as well as
parents of a child born out of wedlock. An adoption based on the
placing out by one parent shall be void unless one parent cannot be
ascertained or found.

A guardian may not place a minor out for adoption, if both parents
of the minor do not have complete civil capacity, unless they may
cause serious harm to the minor. Where a guardian intends to place out
an orphaned minor for adoption, he must obtain the consent of the

person who has the obligation to support the orphan. Article 21 stipulates that the wish of the adopter and the person placing out the adoptee to keep the adoption secret shall be respected.

Domestic Adoptive Procedure

Procedure for Adoption of an Abandoned Child or Orphan

Article 15 of the Law provides that whoever adopts an abandoned **9.14** infant or a child whose parents cannot be found or an orphan in the care of a social welfare institution shall register the adoption with an office of the Ministry of Civil Administration. Accordingly, the Ministry has issued Certain Regulations on Adoption Registration by Chinese Citizens of April 1, 1992, which are applicable to all such adoptions in mainland China by Chinese citizens as well as overseas Chinese and Chinese from Hong Kong, Macau and Taiwan.

Article 5 of the Regulations requires the adopter to go in person to register the adoption. In case of adoption by the husband and wife, a signed and notarized power of attorney for the adoption must be presented where one party cannot be in the registration office in person. The adoptee is also required to be present if he or she has reached the age of 10.

Under Article 7 of the Regulations, the adopter shall file an application to state the purpose of the adoption and promise not to abuse, abandon and to ensure the healthy development of the adoptee. In addition, the adopter is required to present

(a) his or her identity document;

(b) the sealed certificate issued by the working unit or local government office showing the age, marital status, family members and capability to rear and educate the adoptee; and

(c) the certificate of consent issued by the social welfare institution in case of the adoption of an orphan; or the certificate issued by the institution concerned as the evidence that the parents cannot be found in case of adoption of an abandoned infant or child. If the adoptee is disabled at the time of adoption, an additional certificate concerning the condition of his or her disablement issued by a medical institution at county level or the welfare institution, of which the adoptee has been in care, will be needed.

According to Article 8 of the Regulations an adoption certificate will be issued by the registration office if its review finds that all required documents have been presented and all legal conditions are met. The adoptive relationship is established at the date when the application for registration is approved.

Procedure for Adoption of a Minor Who is Not an Abandoned Child or Orphan

Under Article 15 of the Law, a written agreement on adoption shall be concluded by the adopter, and the parents or other person placing out the child for adoption in accordance with the law. Although notarization is treated as an optional procedure under the Law, in practice, however, it is still an advisable procedure to prove the validity of, and prevent any dispute arising from, the adoption. Under the Joint Notice on Transfer of Household Register and Staple Food Supply of Adoptees issued by the Ministry of Commerce and the Ministry of Public Security on May 16, 1992, for instance, notarization for the adoption is required as a necessary document where the household register and staple food supply of the adoptee needs to be transferred to the place of the adopter as the result of the adoption.

Procedure of Adoption Involving Overseas Chinese or Chinese from Hong Kong, Macau or Taiwan

9.15   In addition to the conditions above, an adoption must meet substantive legal requirements of both mainland China and the home country or place of the adoptee, so that the adoption will be valid on both sides. Moreover, a person may not be allowed to adopt a child in China if he or she does not have the right of permanent residence in the country or area where he or she is residing.[15]

According to Article 7 of the Regulations, overseas Chinese are required to produce an identity document; notarized certificate showing age, marital status, family members, occupation, financial and health conditions, issued within six months and attested by both the department of foreign affairs of his or her residing country and the Chinese diplomatic agency there; and proof that the intended adoption shall not violate the law of his or her living country. For Chinese from Hong Kong or Macau, an identity card and a notarized certificate with the same content as described above issued within six months by an attorney entrusted by the Ministry of Justice in Hong Kong or Macau is reqiured for such a registration. In addition to the identity card and notarized certificate, an effective travel document issued by the State authority needs to be presented by those Chinese from Taiwan.

Procedure for Adoption by a Foreign Party

9.16   Under Article 20 of the Law, a foreigner may adopt a child in China through mandatory registration and notarization procedures. The detailed authority for carrying out this requirement is the Operational

Procedure for Adoption by Foreigners in China of November 10, 1993 jointly issued by the Ministry of Justice and the Ministry of Civil Administration.

According to Articles 2 and 3, the Procedure will govern adoption of Chinese adoptee(s) by foreign adopter(s) within China, even if only one party of the adopting couple is a foreigner. The adoption shall violate neither the *Adoption Law of China*, nor the law of foreign country.

The foreign adopter must file the application, together with the required documents and proof to the Chinese institution responsible for adoption authorized by the Chinese government through either the foreign government or the institution authorized by it. The required documents, which must be notarized and attested by both the foreign affairs department of the foreign country or its designated institution and the Chinese diplomatic mission there, include

(a) adoption application;
(b) birth certificate;
(c) marital status certificate;
(d) proof of occupation, income and financial condition;
(e) health certificate;
(f) a clean criminal record;
(g) proof that the country where the adopter resides in allows the intended adoption;
(h) family references including proof of suitability of the adopter, family conditions and health records, reasons for the adoption as well as proof of good character in caring for children.

Upon receiving the application with all required documents, the Chinese office responsible for adoption shall assist the adopter to look for an adoptee if its review finds all the legal requirements are met.

Under Article 6 of the Procedure, the parents, guardian or the welfare institutions who place children up for adoption by foreign adopters shall also produce their own and the adoptee's identity documents as well as the written consent for the placing. The guardian's consent shall be presented with his or her guardianship certificate. For a placing out by a welfare institution, certificate of the adoptee as an abandoned infant or child or orphan as well as the proof of the death of, or failure to find, the adoptee's parents shall be needed. In case of a disabled child being placed out for adoption, a certificate concerning the physical condition of the child issued by a medical institution above county level shall be required.

The Chinese adoption agency will then provide the intended adoptor with the information of the proposed adoptee and his or her family through the foreign government or the authorized institution and notify the adopter to come to China to complete further procedures.

Article 8 of the Procedure provides that the foreign adopter should make a written agreement with the party who places the child out for adoption after the adopter decides to adopt the child. Then all the parties involved in the adoption should go to the branch office of the Ministry of Civil Administration above county level where the household of the adoptee is registered to register the adoption.

For adoption registration, the foreign adopter shall submit

(a) the notification issued by the Chinese adoption organ to the foreign adopter requesting him or her to come to China to complete the adoption procedures;
(b) identity document and pictures of the adopter; and
(c) the adoption agreement reached between the adopter and the party who places the child out for adoption.

All the parties to the adoption are required by Articles 11 and 12 of the Procedure to go in person to have the adoption notarized after registration. The foreign adopter also needs to go through exit formalities for the adoptee with the adoption certificate and the notarization paper at the public security office where the household of the adoptee is registered. In addition to a fee to be paid to the Chinese adoption organ for its services, the foreign adopter may confer with the party who places the child out for adoption on the terms of reasonable compensation.

Effects of Adoption

9.17 Article 22 of the Law provides that as of the date of establishment of the adoptive relationship, the laws governing the relationship between parents and children shall apply to the adopter and adoptee and the relationship between the adoptee and his or her biological parents shall terminate at the same time. The same principle is applicable to the relationship between adoptees and their close adopting and biological relatives. With regard to the name of the adoptee, however, Article 23 provides that the adoptee may adopt the surname of the adopter, or may retain his or her original surname if so agreed through consultation between the parties involved.

Termination of Adoptive Relationship

Conditions for Termination of Adoptive Relationship

Article 25 of the Law provides that an adopter may not terminate the adoptive relationship before the adoptee comes of age, unless the adopter and the party who places the child out for the adoption agree on such termination. If the adoptee involved has reached the age of 10 at the time, his or her consent for the termination shall be obtained.

Where an adopter fails to raise the adoptee adequately or commits maltreatment, abandonment or other acts of encroachment upon the lawful rights of the minor adoptee, the party who places the child out for adoption shall have the right to demand termination of the adoptive relationship. The adoptive relationship may also be terminated by an agreement between the adopter and the adult adoptee if the relationship between them deteriorates to such a degree that their living together in a same household becomes impossible.

Procedure for Termination of Adoptive Relationship

Under Article 27, to terminate an adoptive relationship, the parties concerned shall conclude a written agreement. Where the adoptive relationship is established through registration, the parties shall complete the termination by registering it with a branch office of the Ministry of Civil Administration. If the adoptive relationship is notarized, the parties shall have the termination notarized also. Where the parties fail to reach an agreement on the termination, a lawsuit may be brought to the people's court.

Effects of Termination of Adoptive Relationship

Article 28 of the Law provides that upon termination of an adoption, the relationship between the child and his or her biological parents and close relatives shall be restored automatically. However, whether the relationship will be restored between an adult adoptee and his or her biological parents and close relatives may depend on the consultation of the parties concerned.

Regardless of the termination, an adult adoptee who has been raised by the adoptive parents shall provide them with financial support if they have lost the ability to work and are short of income. If the adoptive relationship is terminated on the grounds of maltreatment or desertion of the adoptive parents by the adult adoptee, the parents are entitled to compensation from the adoptee for the living and educational expenses incurred during the period of adoption. If the termination is requested by the biological parents of the adoptee, the adoptive parents may demand reasonable compensation unless the adoptive relationship is terminated on the grounds of maltreatment or desertion of the adoptee by the adoptive parents.

Legal Liabilities

Article 30 of the Law imposes criminal and administrative liabilities on offenders against the Law. Whoever abducts and traffics in children under the cloak of adoption shall be subject to criminal penalties ranging from a five year prison term to the death penalty depending on the severity of the particular offence. For those who abandon an infant or sell their own child, a fine of a maximum amount of 1,000 reminbi shall be imposed by the public security organ; if the circumstances are so flagrant as to constitute a crime, the offender shall be subject to criminal liability of abandonment, which may lead to a maximum term of five years imprisonment.

Succession Law

9.18 Succession, defined as a system under which the personal property lawfully belonging to the deceased passes to the successors in accordance with the law, has a long history in China. The current laws governing succession include *The Law of Succession* of 1985 and certain Circular of the Supreme Court, such as Opinions on Implementing Law of Succession of 1985 ("OILS") and Opinions on Implementation of the General Principles of Civil Law of 1988.

General Provisions

The legislative purpose is to protect the rights of citizens to inherit private property under the basic principles of equal entitlement; of promotion of mutual help and support among family members and relatives; and of mutual rights and duties.

Opening of Succession

Article 2 of the Law provides that succession begins on the death of a citizen. This provision is further interpreted by the OILS to include natural death and declaration of death. Where more than one family member dies in the same accident, among whom inheritable relationships exist and the exact time point of the death of each person cannot be ascertained, the person without any successor shall be assumed to have died first. If each of the deceased has his or her successors, then the eldest person shall be assumed to have died first. Where all deceased are in the same generation, death at the same time shall be assumed to the effect that there will be no succession between them, and the personal property of each of the deceased will be inherited by his or her own successors respectively.

The Scope of Estate

Article 3 of the Law, together with the provisions of the General Principles of Civil Law, the OILS and some State regulations define an estate for succession as the lawful property owned by the deceased personally at the time of his or her death composed of the following:

(a) personal income;
(b) houses, personal savings and daily used articles;
(c) forest, trees, livestock and poultry;
(d) artistic objects, books and reference materials;
(e) means of production lawfully owned;
(f) property rights pertaining to intellectual property; and
(g) other lawful property rights such as rights of land use granted to the deceased, or rights on securities and other creditor's rights.

The estate, however, shall not include the property of others. Article 26, for example, provides that in partition of the jointly owned property acquired by the deceased and his or her spouse during their matrimonial life, half of such property shall be first allotted as the personal property of the surviving spouse unless otherwise agreed upon by the parties. Also if the estate is a component part of a common property entitled to the deceased and other family members, the portion of such property belonging to the other members of the family shall be first separated at the time of the partitioning of the decedent's estate.

In addition, under the current policy articulated in various official documents and the opinions of the Supreme Court, the rights enjoyed by the decedent under the contracts to conduct agricultural production on a certain piece of land, to operate a business or to rent a home from the working unit of the decedent are generally are not heritable.

Disinheritance

Under Article 7, a successor shall be the disinherited by judgment of the people's court based upon his or her commission of any of the following cases:

(a) murder of the decedent;
(b) murder of any other successors with the purpose of acquiring the estate;

(c) abandoning or seriously maltreating the decedent; and

(d) serious acts of forging, tampering with or destroying the will. In practice, a will may be held wholly or partially void if the successor who committed the murder is one of the receivers of the estate under the will. The seriousness of other acts shall be judged by the particular circumstances and will not be conditioned by the imposition of criminal liability. A successor, nevertheless, may not be disinherited for abandoning or seriously maltreating the decedent if the successor shows real signs of repentance and was forgiven by the decedent before his or her death.

Statute of Limitation

Article 8 of the Law provides that the time limit of instituting of legal proceedings pertaining to disputes over the right to inheritance is two years, counting from the date on which the successor knows, or should have become aware of, the violation of his or her right to inheritance. No legal proceedings, however, will be instituted after the expiry of a period of 20 years from the date on which the succession begins in any event.

Types of Succession

Three major types of succession are provided by the Law: statutory succession, testament succession, and succession under the agreement for legacy in return for support. In addition, the legacy and the estate without successor or legatee are also treated by the Law as supplementory ways of disposition of the estate.

Concerning the legal effect of different types of succession, Article 5 recognizes the priority of an agreement for legacy in return for support over the others, followed by testamentory and statutory succession. In cases of conflict, the prior type shall prevail.

The Agreement for Legacy in Return for Support

9.19   Article 31 of the Law provides that a citizen may enter into a legacy-support agreement with a party, who under the agreement assumes the duty to support the former for his lifetime and to bury him after his death and shall inherit the estate of the decedent. The agreement for legacy in return for support, as the prior way of succession, is promoted in China because of its reflection of both China's social policy and beliefs based on mutual assistance and benefit.

According to the Supreme Court and the Ministry of Justice, the supporting party can be either organizations or citizens who are not successors under the Law and are capable of supplying support. Where no such agreement is reached between the decedent and the organization, it shall still be entitled to paid expenses from the estate incurred while supporting the decedent.[16] The judicial practice, however, does not recognize the legal effect of an agreement made between the decedent and his children on the grounds that they bear the legal duty to support their parents in the first place and, therefore, they are not eligible for the compensation.

The agreement, once reached, may be modified or even terminated based on mutual consent. The Supreme Court held in Article 56 of the OILS that where the agreement is terminated as the result of breach by the supporter without proper reasons, neither entitlement to any legacy nor to any refund for his expenses incurred for the support shall be allowed. In case of breach by the legator, he shall compensate the person or the organization for all supporting expenses incurred.

To promote the legacy-support agreement the Ministry of Justice issued the Detailed Provisions on Notarization of Agreement of Legacy in Return for Support on April 3, 1991 to specify the required terms. Under the Provisions, notarization of the agreement shall have the legal effect to the extent that without the consent of the supporter, the legator shall not dispose of his property covered by the agreement.

Testamentary Succession and Legacy

Article 16 of the Law allows a citizen to dispose of his property by means of a will in accordance with the Law and to appoint a testamentory executor. A citizen may, by making a will, designate one or more of the statutory successors to inherit his personal property; or donate his personal property to the State, or a collective; or bequeath it to persons other than the statutory successors by way of legacy. Despite the legislative silence, the judicial practice has seen joint wills made by husbands and wives. **9.20**

Under the provisions of the Law and the opinion of the Supreme Court, to be a valid will, the testament must meet four conditions:

(a) The testator must have attained full age with complete civil competence, otherwise the will shall be void. In determining civil competence, the focus should be based on the time of the will. Thus, a testament made by patient with intermittent insanity or a person without civil competence may still be valid as long as it can be proved that at the time of willing he is sane or he has not lost his full competence. Moreover, the

will shall be the manifestation of the genuine intention of the
testator free from duress or fraud.

(b) By a will, the testator can only dispose of his own lawful
property. Any part of such testament that infringes the lawful
property rights of his or her spouse, or other parties shall be
void.

(c) The testament must meet the condition of legal formalities.
Article 17(5) of the Law provides that a nuncupative form will
may only be used in emergency situations, in which the testator is dying or facing imminent danger. To guarantee accuracy
and prevent fraud, the Law requires the testament to be witnessed by at least two witnesses and the testament to be
replaced by a will in other forms when the emergency situation
is over, otherwise the nuncupative form will shall become void.

Article 18 articulates the persons who shall not act as a witness of
a will: persons with either no or limited civil competence; successors
and legatees; or persons whose interests are related to the successors
and legatees.

Articles 17(3) and (4) respectively provide that a testament hand-
recorded by a third person on behalf of the testator or sound recorded
shall be witnessed by at least two witnesses including the recorder.
The Supreme Court holds that the content concerning disposition
of the personal property of the decedent in a posthumous paper signed
by him with the specific date may be treated as a will if his true
intention can be ascertained and no contradictory evidence is
presented.[17]

A will may also be made by the testator through a notary agency.
Under the Law, a notarial will must be made by the testator in person
and a notarial will certificate bearing the signature of the testator and
the date of the will shall be issued by the agency. A notary public,
nevertheless, cannot handle such matters for himself, his spouse, his
close relatives or any person with whom he has interests with.

Under Articles 19 and 28, reservation of a necessary portion of an
estate shall be made in a will for an unborn successor and a successor
who neither is able to work nor has any source of income. According
to the Supreme Court, the time point for determination of the reservation for such a successor should be the time when the will becomes
effective. If the will fails to make the required reservation for such
successors, the people's court shall take the necessary portion from the
estate first at the time of partitioning of the estate and then divide the
rest according to the principle established by the will.[18] In addition to
the reservation, under the general legal principle the will shall not
violate or be intended to evade other laws.

Article 20 provides that a testator may revoke or alter a will previously made, explicitly or tacitly. As far as explicit revocation and

alternation are concerned, the testator may do so by making either a statement or a new will. In practice, where the testator has made several wills in different forms that are in conflict with each other in content, the latest notarial one shall prevail; if there is no notarial will, the last one shall prevail.

With regard to tacit revocation and alternation, the Supreme Court takes the position that the testament shall be deemed to be wholly or partially revoked if before the opening of the succession the property disposed by the testament has been wholly or partially extinguished, or the ownership of such property has been wholly or partially transferred due to the conduct of the testator which negates the previous testament.

At the opening of a testamentary succession, an executor must be ascertained. If the testator fails to appoint an executor or the appointed executor refuses appointment, or for natural reasons is not able to carry out his duty, one or more executors may be selected by the successors and legatees from either among themselves or others. The duty of a testamentary executor may also be performed by the working unit or organization that the decedent belonged to before his death, by a public notary agent, or a lawyer on the basis of the agreement by all parties concerned. Where a dispute over the appointment of an executor is brought to a people's court, it may either appoint one or more executors for the succession or supervise the partition of the estate by itself in accordance with the will.

A testamentory executor has the power and duty to carry out the contents of the will in accordance with the law and stop any interference or infringements. The successors or legatees have the right to dismiss an executor and recover the damages if the executor violates the will, due procedure or other legal provisions.

Article 21 of the Law allows a testator to attach obligations to testamentary succession or legacy, which the successors or legatees shall have a duty to perform. Failure to do so without due cause may, upon request by a relevant organization or individuals such as beneficiaries or executors, lead to nullification of the right of the successors or legatees to inheritance by the people's court.

Statutory Succession

Generally, statutory succession, as the type of succession most used in China today, shall be employed when neither any agreement for legacy in return for support, nor any will exists. In some circumstances, however, the existence of a will may not exclude application of statutory succession. Under Article 27, the part of the estate in the following circumstances shall be dealt with in accordance with statutory succession where: **9.21**

> (a) a successor or a legatee disclaims his portion under the will or the legacy;
> (b) a testamentory successor is disinherited;
> (c) a testamentory successor or legatee predeceases the testator;
> (d) an invalidated portion of the will involves part of the estate; or
> (e) no disposition is made under the will for the part of the estate.

The range of successors in statutory succession are provided in Articles 10, 11 and 12 of the Law to include spouse, children, parents, brothers and sisters, grandparents, and the direct lineal descendants of the predeceased child in subrogation of succession for the decedent, as well as a widowed child-in-law under certain circumstances.

As far as the spouse in statutory succession is concerned, the valid marriage relationship is the basis of determining entitlement although the judicial practice may also admit concubines contracted before 1949 and spouses in certain *de facto* marriages as successors. A divorced spouse and relationships based on unlawful cohabitation, however, are not recognized by the Law.

The term of children in the Law includes legitimate children, illegitimate children and adopted children as well as step-children who either supported, or were supported by, the decedent. Principally, the adopted children may no longer have the right to inherit the estate of their biological parents once the adoptive relationship is established. But if such a relationship no longer exists, the right of the children to inheritance may be restored if they have renewed their relationship with their biological parents. With regard to step-children, their rights to inheritance shall depend on whether a relationship of mutual support exists between the deceased step-parents and the step-children. Moreover, according to the Supreme Court, the fact that a step-child has inherited the estate of his step-parent shall not affect his status as a successor to the estate of his biological parents. The dual succession rule for step-children is justified on the grounds that they may have to carry out double duties to support both their step-parents and biological parents. Furthermore, under *The Adoption Law*, the step-parent and child relationship may be turned into an adoptive parent-child relationship if the step-parent adopts the child. Consequently, the adoption rules rather than the step-parent and child rule shall be applied to those issues concerning inheritance rights.

The term parents in the Law includes biological parents and adoptive parents as well as step-parents who supported or were supported by the decedent. By the same token as described above, the inheritance by step-parents of the estate of their step-children shall not affect their status as successors to the estate of their biological children.

9.22   The terms of brothers and sisters in the Law cover blood brothers and sisters, brothers and sisters of half blood, adopted brothers and sisters as well as step-brothers and step-sisters who supported or were supported by the decedent. The Supreme Court by its opinion excludes the right to inheritance between an adoptee and his blood brothers and sisters on the grounds that their relationship based on the ties of blood is extinct once the adoptive relationship is established. Also the rights to inheritance among step-brothers and sisters shall rely on the existence of the relationship of mutual support between them and the succession from step-brothers or step-sisters shall not affect the right of the successor to inheritance to the estate of his blood brothers or sisters.

Grandparents under the Law includes both paternal and maternal grandparents. In judicial practice, adoptive grandparents may also be taken into consideration.

Widowed children-in-law under the Law may have the right to inherit the estate of their parents-in-law only if they have made predominant contributions in maintaining the parents-in-law and the right to inheritance shall not be affected by remarriage at a later date. The predominant contribution in maintenance, according to the Supreme Court, means the supply of the main source of income or labour assistance to the decedent during his lifetime.[19]

Article 10 provides two orders for inheritance based on the intimacy with the decedent. The successors first in order include spouse, children and parents as well as widowed children-in-law who made the predominant contributions in maintaining the parents-in-law while brothers and sisters and grandparents are placed second in the list of the successors. When succession opens, the successors first in order shall inherit to the exclusion of the successors second in order. The successors second in order shall inherit in default of any succession first in order. In another words, the successors second in order may be allowed to inherit the estate only if none of the successors first in order will, or are able to, inherit.

Where a decedent survives his child, the direct lineal descendants of the predeceased child inherit in subrogation. Descendants who inherit in subrogation generally shall take only the share of the estate their parent is entitled to. As a result, the descendants cannot inherit in subrogation if their parent as the successor has been disinherited. They may, however, be granted an appropriate amount of the estate if they have carried out major duties to support the decedent or they are not able to work and have no source of income.[20]

In practice, inheritance in subrogation by the descendants of the predeceased successor is often confused with inheritance by passing on. The latter is defined as the right to inheritance being passed on to the descendants of the successor where the successor dies without manifestation of giving up after the succession is open, but before the estate is distributed.[21] The two are different in that inheritance in subrogation is preconditioned by the survival of the decedent of the successor while inheritance by passing on requires the survival of the successor of the decedent; that the descendants in inheritance in subrogation are limited to the direct lineal descendants of the predeceased successor whereas in inheritance by passing on, the persons entitled to the right to inheritance, in addition to the children of the successor, also include all other lawful successors recognized by the Law; and that inheritance in subrogation can only be applied to the successor first in order in statutory succession, while inheritance by passing on may be used in all the ways of succession.

In addition, under Article 14 an appropriate share of the estate may be given to a person who depends on the support of the decendent and who is unable to work or has no source of income, or to a person who was largely responsible for supporting the decedent during his lifetime although he is not a successor in all the types of succession. Moreover, according to the Supreme Court, the amount given to such a person may be either more or less than what the statutory successors may inherit depending on the extent and degree of the dependence by, or support given from, the person as compared with other successors.[22]

Article 13 provides that the successors shall, in general, inherit in equal shares. Due consideration, however, shall be given to successors who are unable to work and have special financial difficulties. The successors who have made the predominant contributions in maintaining the decedent or have lived with the decedent may also have a larger share. For those who were in the position to and were able to maintain the decedent but failed to fulfil their duties, none or a smaller share of the estate shall be given. The successors may take unequal shares if an agreement to that effect is reached among them.

Disposition of the Estate

9.23   Article 23 provides that after the opening of succession, a successor who has knowledge of the death of the decedent should promptly notify the other successors and the testamentory executor. If no one among the successors knows of the death or the successors are not able to make such notification, the organization to which the decedent belonged to before his death or the neighbour committee at his place of residence shall make the notification. Article 24 further stipulates that anyone who has in his possession the property of the decedent, shall take due care of such property and no one will be allowed to misappropriate it or contend for it. For those who are found guilty of such wrong doing, a deduction of shares may be imposed by the peoples' court.

A successor is entitled to his shares only after he accepts the inheritance. The acceptance can be either made explicitly through a statement or a legal proceeding to claim his rights; or presumed tacitly by the absence of any disclamation. Article 25 imposes a duty for a successor or legatee who disclaims inheritance to make known his decision either by a written or oral statement before the disposition of the estate. In practice, revocation of such a disclamation with good reason before the disposition of the estate may be admitted by the court. No revocation, however, shall be allowed after the disposition.

To prevent people from purposefully avoiding duties under the law to support family members or duties to pay back personal debts, the Supreme Court is of the opinion that any disclamation will be void should such an act cause the successor to be unable to carry out his legal duties.

Together with the ascertainment of the successors, the type in which the estate shall be disposed of must be determined before the distribution. For instance, the disposition of the entire estate by the agreement for legacy in return for support, may end any further enquiry whereas the partial disposition by such an agreement may bring procedures for testamentory succession and legacy as well as statutory succession into play. Thus, the complexity of a succession case largely depends on the extent and type of disposition of the estate by the deceased before his death.

The Law establishes some principles in estate distribution that are applicable to every type of succession. Article 28, for example, provides that at the time of the partitioning of the estate, a reserved share shall be made for an unborn child. The share reserved shall, if the baby is stillborn, be dealt with in accordance with statutory succession. Article 29 provides that the partitioning of the estate shall be conducted in a way beneficial to the needs of production and livelihood; it shall not diminish the usefulness of the estate. If the estate is unsuitable for partitioning, it may be disposed of by such means as price evaluation, appropriate compensation or co-ownership. Also according to the Supreme Court, a smaller portion of the estate shall be partitioned by the people's court on those who have abused the deceased, forged or destoryed the will, misappropriated or contended the estate, if the degree of such acts are not serious enough to justify disinheritance.

Under the legal principle of mutuality of rights and obligations, Article 33 provides that the successors to the estate shall pay all taxes and debts owed by the decedent in accordance with the law, up to the actual value of such estate. The successor who disclaims inheritance assumes no responsibility for such payments. This rule, however, is qualified by the holding of the Supreme Court that the successors should be responsible for the debts incurred by the decedent due to the failure of the successors to perform their legal duties to support him even if the estate proves insufficient to cover such debts. It further held that the appropriate portion reserved from the estate for a successor who is neither able to work nor has any source of income for his livelihood shall be taken out first before the aforementioned rule is applied even if the amount of the estate is not enough for the payment of taxes and debts owed by the decedent at the opening of the succession.[23]

The statutory successors shall bear the duty to pay back the taxes and debts owed by the decedent with the estate inherited first where both statutory and testamentory or legacy succession procedures are used in a single case of succession. The testamentory successor or legatees may have the duty to make the payment for the decedent proportional to the amount of the estate they inherited, only if the amount paid by the statutory successors falls short. The duty shall be on testamentory successors or legatees in a pure testamentory succession or legacy proportional to their inherited estate.

Article 32 stipulates that an estate which is left with neither a successor nor a legatee shall belong to the State or, where the decedent was a member of an organization under collective ownership before his death, to such an organization. This provision, nevertheless, is interpreted by the Supreme Court in Article 43 of the Opinion Concerning Certain Issues of Implemention of Civil Policies and Law of August 30, 1984 to be applied to the effect that where the estate shall belong to the State or an organization under collective ownership, the people's court may, however, allow an appropriate amount to a person who depended on the support of the decedent and is unable to work or has no source of income, or who was largely responsible for supporting the decedent before his death upon the requst of such a person.

To combat the corrupt custom in China that the estate left by a male decedent shall still belong to his clan and should not be taken away by his surviving wife by way of remarriage after her inheritance, Article 30 explicitly provides that a surviving spouse who remarries is entitled to dispose of the property he or she has inherited free from interference of any other party.

Succession of Estate Outside China

9.24   Both Article 76 of Succession Law and Article 149 of the General Principles of Civil Law provide that the law of domicile of the decedent shall apply to inheritance of movable property while the law of the place where the property is located shall govern in case of inheritance of immovable property. However, this principle is applicable only to testamentory succession. As a result, the legal status of domestic citizens who otherwise may have the right to inheritance under Chinese law may depend on the legal provisions of the particular country or place concerned or on the scope of successors in the case of statutory succession with an estate outside China.

With regard to the validity of a testament made outside China, in the absence of any special legislation, the judicial practice has held that such a will shall be valid as long as it is made in accordance with the local rules and its content does not violate the principles of the law and the public interests of China.[24]

Notes

[1] Also see Article 49 of the Constitution and Article 103 of the General Principles of Civil Law.

[2] Under Article 21 of the General Principles of Civil Law, a citizen shall be deemed to have full civil capacity when he reaches the age of 18.

[3] The Reply of the Supreme Court to the High Court of Sichuan on the issue of imposition of criminal penalties against bigamy after the enactment of the Marriage Registration Regulation of December 14, 1994.

[4] Ming Bao, 20 April 1996, at A2.

[5] Part 3 of the Certain Opinions Concerning Implementation of the Civil Policies and Law by the Supreme Court of August 30, 1984.

[6] *Idid*. Part 1, (3).

[7] Certain Opinions Concerning Child Custody in Divorce Proceedings by the Supreme Court on November 3, 1993.

[8] The Explanation Concerning Issues of Using and Renting Public Housing in Divorce Trials issued by the Supreme Court on February 5, 1996.

[9] See Article 22 of the Revised Regulations on Public Security and Administrative Penalties of May 12, 1994.

[10] Article 12 of the Provisions. The same provision can also be found in the bilateral judicial assistance agreements signed between China and more than twenty foreign countries.

[11] The Supreme Court Reply to the Marriage Administration Division Concerning the Marriage Registration between Cao, Baoxin and Wang, Xuli of January 22, 1993.

[12] Section I of the statement made by Mr. Ma, Yuan, the Vice President of the Supreme Court on the news conference held on September 9, 1988.

[13] *Idid*. Section II.

[14] The Supreme Court Reply to the High Court of Henan Concerning the Intended Adoptive Relation between Mao, Yutang as the grandparent and Mao, Xinguo as the grandson of January 30, 1993.

[15] The Statement made by the Marriage Division of the Ministry of Civil Administration on the conditions and registration procedure of adoptions by overseas Chinese or Chinese from Hong Kong, Macau and Taiwan. See The Trial Division of Civil Cases of the Supreme Court: Selected Laws and Regulations on Marriage and Adoption, the People's Court Press, 1994, p. 140.

[16] Article 55 of the OILS.

[17] Article 40 of the OILS.

[18] Article 37 of the OILS.

[19] Article 30 of the OILS.

[20] Article 28 of the OILS.

[21] Article 52 of the OILS.

[22] Article 31 of the OILS.

[23] Article 61 of the OILS.

[24] Chen, Guoying: Legal Issues on Succession Cases Involving Foreign Countries, 5 Legal Studies 117, 1992.

CHAPTER 10

LAW OF BUSINESS ORGANIZATIONS

Yu Guang Hua
and revised by
Zhang Xianchu

University of Hong Kong
and
City University of Hong Kong
(*respectively*)

Yu Guanghua, Lecturer of Law, Department of Law, University of Hong Kong;
BA (Shangha Maritime Institute); LL.M. (Osgoode, York); LL.B. (Toronto); SJD
(Toronto).

Zhang, Xianchu, University Lecturer, Faculty of Law, City University of Hong
Kong; LL.B. (China University of Political Science and Law, Beijing PRC); MCL
(Indiana University School of Law, Bloomington); JD (Indiana University
School of Law, Bloomington).

Introduction

The development of laws on business organizations in China is closely **10.01**
related with the continuing economic reform. From 1949 to 1978, the
Chinese economic system was based on a planned model. Within
such an economy, the means of production was owned mostly by the
State, leaving a minor portion in the hands of enterprises under so-
called collective ownership. Virtually all decision-making powers for
macroeconomic activities and for the daily operation of enterprises
was concentrated in the hands of the State. While the market still
existed in name, since currency-commodity relations remained, the
basic means by which the various targets were realized were mandatory plans drawn up by the State hierarchy. The enterprises immediately responsible for production had to follow State orders in all their
activities, including finance, management, marketing, employment,
wage policy and expansion with hardly any independence. As the
economic benefits of enterprises were not linked with their perform-

341

ance, enterprises with significant profits had no right to dispose of their profits while enterprises operating with heavy losses were subsidized by the State. Economic information was transmitted vertically between the higher and lower levels in the administrative system in the form of instructions and reports. Within this system, the role of law on business organizations was extremely limited.

China's economic reform began in rural areas where the contractual responsibility system was adopted. That system increased the role of market as more agricultural products were circulated on the market. From 1978, urban enterprises were given more autonomy in managing their own affairs. They were allowed to retain part of their profits. In 1984, the Central Committee of the Communist Party adopted the Decisions on Reforming the Economic System. These Decisions initiated the reform of enterprises in urban areas. The concept of separation between ownership and management was recognized. The General Principles of the Civil Law (the Civil Law) provided the basic framework of business operation by facilitating the establishment of various forms of organizations such as individual business, leaseholding farm households,[1] individual partnerships,[2] legal persons (for detailed treatment, see Chapter 6),[3] and other economic associations.[4]

The transition from a planned economy to a market economy has significantly increased the role of law. Considering the increasing need of laws and regulations, the State Council adopted the Provisional Regulations on Administration of the Individual Industrial and Commercial Households in Urban and Rural Areas (the AIICH) in 1987. While the AIICH only permits the individual owner to hire not more than seven people, the Provisional Regulations on Private Enterprises (the Private Enterprise Regulations) promulgated by the State Council a year later allows individual investors and owners to employ more than eight people. Thus, an artificial distinction, based on the number of employees, has been created by these different regulations for sole proprietorships.

On April 13, 1988, the Seventh National People's Congress adopted the *Law on Industrial Enterprises Owned by the Whole People* (the IEOWP). This Law specifies the nature, rights and duties of State-owned enterprises. According to this Law, an industrial enterprise owned by the whole people (State-owned enterprise) shall be a unit of socialist commodity production. While the property of the enterprise shall be owned by the whole people, they enjoy the rights to possess, utilize and dispose of the property which the State has authorized them to operate and manage. Consequently, the enterprise bears civil liability with the property conferred upon by the State. Quickly following this Law, the State Council promulgated the Regulations on Rural Collectively-owned Enterprises in 1990 and the Regulations on Urban Collectively-owned Enterprises in 1991.

In the 1990s, a consensus has been reached among economics and legal scholars as well as some governmental officials that reform of the enterprise system must move towards a market oriented economy. In early 1992, Deng Xiao Ping visited Southern China to further fromote economic reform and to advocate the establishment of a market economy in China. The Regulations for Converting the Status of the Enterprises Owned by the Whole People adopted by the State Council in 1992 were intended to push State-owned enterprises onto the market.

Meanwhile, some State-owned enterprises started to adopt the form of companies. That practice was based on two documents entitled the Opinion on the Standardization of Limited Liability Companies and the Opinions on the Standardization of Joint Stock Companies respectively issued by the State Economic Structure Reform Commission of the State Council. It has then been generally recognized that companies are an essential part of a modern enterprise system. Thus, *The Company Law* was soon enacted at the end of 1993. It has to be pointed out that it is relatively easier to promulgate some laws and regulations than to make these laws operate in reality. Whereas various private companies have been established in accordance with *The Company Law*, State-owned enterprises still have difficulties in applying this Law.

Another feature in the development of China's business organization law is the change of emphasis. In the past, the laws and regulations on business organizations were organized in accordance with the nature of ownership. The laws on State-owned enterprises, collectively-owned enterprises, and foreign investment enterprises, to name only a few, followed this line. It is expected that future development of the laws in this area will be organized along the lines of the nature of organization. It may be foreseen that a sole proprietorship law and a partnership law will be enacted by the National People's Congress soon. This chapter briefly discusses the laws and regulations on sole proprietorships, partnerships, and companies. Considering that State-owned enterprises and collectively-owned enterprises still play significant roles in the economy, the laws and regulations on State-owned enterprises and collectively-owned enterprises are briefly examined.

Sole Proprietorships

Sole proprietorship is generally defined as a form of business in which **10.02**
one person owns all the assets of the business in contrast to a partnership or a corporation. The sole proprietor is solely liable for all the debts of the business. Currently, a sole proprietorship in China may take the name of individual industrial and commercial households (*Geti gongshang hu*) or of private enterprises (*Si ying qiye*) where the

sole proprietor employs more than eight employees[5], or of individual business.

The Constitution of China provides the legal basis for people to establish and operate the business by adopting the form of sole proprietorships. The State permits the existence and development of private and individual economy as a complement to the public social-ist economy within the limits prescribed by law. The State protects the lawful rights and interests of the private and individual economy and at the same time, guides and supervises it.

Currently, three major pieces of legislation are applicable to sole proprietorships. The Civil Law provides some general provisions. Sec-ondly, the AIICH regulates sole proprietorships which employ one or two helpers and/or three to five apprentices. Pursuant to the AIICH, the maximum number of staff the investor may have is seven. Thirdly, the Private Enterprise Regulations apply to those with more than eight employees. The distinction of assigning different names to the seem-ingly same type of business organizations is undoubtedly unsound. It has been criticized with the hope that these regulations will soon be replaced by a sole-proprietorship law.[6]

These regulations indicate that sole proprietorship does not have separate legal entity. Article 26 of the *Civil Law* stipulates that indi-vidual business refers to business run by individual citizens who have been approved to engage in industrial or commercial operation within the sphere permitted by law and have lawfully registered their busi-ness. Under Article 29, the debts of an individual business shall be secured with the individual's property if the business is operated by an individual and with the family's property if the business is operated by the family. The AIICH has the same provisions for individual indus-trial and commercial household business run by an individual or by his or her family. Similarly, Article 8 of the Private Enterprise Regulations states that the investor of the sole proprietorship has unlimited liabil-ity for the debts of the business. Pursuant to these regulations, the assets of the other non-investing spouse may be implicated if the business is run by the family. This point seems to be based on equita-ble ground that if the spouse receives benefits by participating in the business, he or she shall also be held to share the burden. An alterna-tive interpretation is that the business is a quasi-partnership.

The AIICH only lists three categories of people who may apply to engage in individual industrial and commercial household business. They include unemployed in urban areas, farmers in the rural areas, and others permitted by the policy of the State.[7] The last category seems to be quite vague. The Implementation Measures of the Private Enterprise Regulation, however, provide explanation of some very similar categories contained in the Private Enterprise Regulations. According to these Measures, persons permitted by laws, regulations and policies mainly include:

    (a) retired scientific and technical persons;[8]
    (b) scientific and technical persons who are currently employed but without receiving remuneration from their institutions;
    (c) retired persons from enterprises and institutions; and
    (d) specified retired people from the Communist party and governmental bodies.

The AIICH provides a non-exhaustive list of sectors or trades where business is permitted. They include industry, handicrafts, construction, transportation, commerce, food and beverages, services, repair, and other trades.[9] Detailed explanations of these sectors or trades are given by the Implementation Rules of the AIICH.[10] The Private Enterprise Regulations add a category of consultancy.[11] The Implementation Measures of the Private Enterprise Regulations further expand the scope to trades or services related to culture, arts, travel, sports, food production, medicine and medical services, fishing and other trades. While the AIICH does not specify any prohibited area of business, the Private Enterprise Regulations state that private enterprises are prohibited from engaging in business in the military or financial industry or from producing prohibited products.[12]

Whether to engage in business as a private enterprise or as an individual industrial and commercial household, a business licence must be obtained from the local State Administration of Industry and Commerce (SAIC). To operate an individual business, the applicant has to submit the formal household registration. Sometimes, documents approved by competent authorities have to be submitted. For instance, consent from the public security bureau is required for a hotel operation or printing business.[13] For food and beverage business, a certificate from a health and sanitary supervisory body is needed.[14]

Individual industrial and commercial household business shall be carried out at places where the sole proprietor has household registration. If that person wants to do business elsewhere, the original approval SAIC has to be notified. Further, a temporary business licence has to be obtained from the SAIC located at the intended place.[15] For private enterprises, the applicant needs to submit his identification card.[16] Although the individual identification card is still linked to the household registration system, it is nevertheless an area where economic mobility has been enhanced. The Implementation Measures of the Private Enterprise Regulations further provide that private enterprises may set up branch factories and stores. The investor may also establish enterprises elsewhere although business licences from the SAICs of the intended places are required.[17] Obviously, the Private Enterprise Regulations are a major step forward in facilitating economic mobility.

The applicant for individual business has to provide the local SAIC with the following items: name of the applicant, name of the business,

number of persons of the household business including the sole proprietor, family members, helpers and apprentices, registered capital,
scope of business, and premises of the business.[18] If some of these items
are changed during the course of business, modification of the former
registration is required. If the business ceases, the relevant SAIC has
to be informed and the business licence returned.[19] Similarly, if any
division, merger, transfer of business, or relocation of a private enterprise is carried out, modification of the original registration or re-
registration is required.[20]

Once a business licence is received, the applicant of the sole proprietorship has to go through tax registration with the local tax authorities. For private enterprises, the amount of the fund for expansion of
the business, investment in other enterprises, repayment of loans and
offsetting any losses of the enterprises should not be less than 50
percent of after-tax profit. For any other uses, approval from the tax
authorities is required.[21]

One significant difference between the individual industrial and
commercial household business and private enterprises is that the
latter is able to set up equity or contractual joint ventures with foreign
investors. Further, private enterprises are permitted to engage in compensation trade, processing, assembling, and manufacturing activities
for foreign business entities.[22]

The SAICs at various levels are the major supervisory bodies of
these individual business and private enterprises. Basically, these
bodies are responsible for registration, modification of registration, re-
registration and cancellation of registration. They have the power to
check that those individual business and private enterprises do not
exceed the scope of their business as registered. In addition, tax authorities, price control authorities and labour authorities are empowered to supervise these business enterprises in their respective
areas.

Partnerships

10.03 As mentioned, a partnership law is currently on the agenda of the
Standing Committee of the National People's Congress. Before this
law is finally enacted, the relevant laws governing partnerships are
sketchy. *The Civil Law* has several provisions applicable to partnerships. As this law only provides some basic principles with insufficient
details, the Judicial Committee of the Supreme People's Court promulgated on January 26, 1988 Certain Opinions on the Implementation of
The Civil Law.

The Civil Law divides partnerships into two categories, individual
partnerships and enterprise partnerships. Individual partnerships refer

to two or more natural persons associated in a business and working together, with each providing funds, materials, skills, intangible properties according to a partnership agreement.[23] Rights and duties between partners, methods of profit distribution, conditions of joining and withdrawal from a partnership, liabilities for debts of the partnership shall be spelled out in the partnership agreement. The operational activities of an individual partnership shall be decided jointly by the partners, each of whom shall have the right to carry out these activities. Partners may delegate their powers to a responsible person or other persons. If that is the case, all partners shall bear civil liability derived from the operational activities of the responsible person or other persons.[24] With respect to the debts of the partnership, each partner is jointly liable towards creditors. However, internally after satisfying the claims of the creditors, a particular partner may seek indemnity from other partners for the amount exceeding his or her proportion as specified in the partnership agreement.

Under *The Civil Law*, enterprise joint operation is specified in Article 52. Basically, if enterprises conduct joint operation but do not have a legal person status, each party to the association shall, in proportion to its respective contribution of investment or according to the agreement made, bear civil liability with the property each party owns or manages. If the law or their agreement so provides, the parties shall assume joint liability.

According to the Supreme Court's opinion, partners may specify ways of withdrawal from a partnership. It may be still permissable even if there are no provisions in the partnership agreement on the issue of withdrawal. Where losses are caused to other partners by such a withdrawal, damages may be awarded, taking into account the reasons of withdrawal and the liability of both parties. As for the debts of the partnership, the withdrawing party is liable if he has not paid his portion as agreed. But even though the withdrawing partner has paid his agreed share, he may still be liable for the debts of the partnership so long as the partnership does not have sufficient assets to satisfy all the creditors at the time of withdrawal. With respect to distribution of assets of a partnership when the partnership ceases its business, the partnership agreement shall be respected. In a case where there is no ex ante or ex post agreement on that issue, the majority's view shall prevail.

Partnerships are widely used in China. Currently, a great number of law firms and accounting firms adopt this business form. In addition, a large number of small business prefer the structure as the partnership agreement and relevant laws provide them with the necessary degree of control over their business. Furthermore, hundreds of thousands of enterprises have voluntarily chosen to set up joint operations by utilizing the form of partnerships. Since 1980, horizontal economic integration has been encouraged by the government. In 1980, the State

Council issued the Provisional Measures on the Encouragement of Economic Integration. Pursuant to these Measures, economic integration shall not be affected by industries, locations, ownership, relevant authorities of the respective enterprises. In March 1986, these Measures were replaced by another State Council document entitled Provisions on Certain Issues Concerning Further Promotion of Horizontal Economic Integrations. The Provisions aim at reduction of the impact of regionalism and helping good enterprises voluntarily acquire some declining or insolvent enterprises. As a result of the enactment, economic integration is very popular in the 1990s.

Companies

10.04 Limited liability companies and joint stock companies are separate legal entities in the sense that shareholders are distinct from their companies. The liability of both types of companies is limited, which means each shareholder in such a company assumes liability toward the company to the extent of the amount of shares held by him, but the company shall be liable for its debts to the extent of all its assets.[25]

Formation of Companies

The number of shareholders in a limited liability company shall be between two and fifty. There are, however, at least two exceptions. First, an institution or a department authorized by the State may establish a wholly State-owned limited liability company.[26] Second, a foreign individual or company may set up a wholly-owned foreign invested limited liability company pursuant to the *Law on Foreign-Capital Enterprises*. Foreign-invested companies are subject to the Company Law. Where the laws on foreign invested enterprises, however, provide otherwise, these latter laws shall prevail.[27] In contrast to a limited liability company, there are no restrictions on the number of shareholders in a joint stock company. *The Company Law* only mentions that there must be more than five promoters in a joint stock company.[28]

Unlike some common law jurisdictions, Article 23 stipulates that a company shall have a minimum capital. The minimum registered capital of a limited liability company varies in accordance with the nature of particular business. *The Company Law* specifically provides that the minimum registered capital of a limited company shall be:

(a) RMB500,000 for a company whose main business is related to production;

(b) RMB500,000 for a company whose main business is wholesale;
(c) RMB300,000 for a company whose main business is retail;
(d) RMB100,000 for a company whose main business is the development of science and technology, consultancy or the provision of services.

For banking and insurance companies, the minimum registered capital is much higher than specified in these relevant laws. Naturally, higher minimum registered capital for joint stock companies is imposed. Thus, the minimum amount of the registered capital of a joint stock company shall be RMB10 million.[29] The total amount of a listed company's registered capital must amount to at least RMB50 million.[30] The law not only imposes a minimum capital requirement but also requires that the registered capital shall be the amount of capital actually paid in at the time of registration.[31] Given the irregular financial and economic activities in China, it is extremely difficult to catch those who do not have the necessary amount of capital but bribe officials to obtain a business licence, or those who borrow money to incorporate companies and quickly withdraw their capital. To deter this, China has provided heavy administrative penalties and criminal sanctions. For instance, where a company makes a false declaration on the registered capital, it shall be subject to a fine of not less than RMB10,000 and not more than RMB100,000.[32] The individual applicant or a responsible person of a company may be sentenced for a term of less than three years for falsifying the registered capital, or of five years for falsifying the registered capital and withdrawing capital after incorporation.[33]

A company shall have a fixed site and the necessary conditions for production and operation. Further, it shall have the articles of association of the company. There are two kinds of provisions in the articles. *The Company Law* mandates certain provisions relating to the name and domicile of the company, the name of the shareholders or promoters, the rights and obligations of the shareholders, the governance of the company, the conditions for transferring the shares of the shareholders, the legal representative of the company, the conditions for dissolution of the company and liquidation procedures, the scope of business of the company, etc. The shareholders may adopt other provisions suitable to their respective cases.

The Company Law does not specify the liability of a company towards third parties when the directors or officers act beyond the scope of business of the company. It merely states that a company's business activities shall be limited to its registered scope of business. Change of the registered scope of business is possible so long as the relevant legal procedures are followed and registration of such amendments with the SAIC is completed.[34] Furthermore, the Regulations for the Administration of Company Registration issued by the State

Council in 1994 provide administrative penalties against activities going beyond the registered scope of business. It is relatively clear, however, that the *ultra vires* doctrine is not recognized in the eyes of the law. Article 49 of *The Civil Law* provides that an enterprise as a legal person shall bear liability for the directors' or managers' decisions which result in activities going beyond the registered scope of business of the company.

It is much easier to establish a limited liability company than a joint stock company. Except for engaging in trades such as the production of food and drugs where approval from relevant authorities is required, registration for a limited liability company will be obtained if the specified conditions in *The Company Law* are satisfied. The establishment of a joint stock company requires the prior approval of the departments authorized by the State Council or by the relevant provincial People's Government.[35] The rationale for such approval is micro-control of the capital flow in China and protection of the public.

The establishment of a joint stock company may be through the method of promotion or public issue. Promotion means that all the shares to be issued by the proposed company are purchased by the promoters themselves whereas public issue refers to the method where promoters purchase only a portion of no less than 35 per cent of the total shares to be issued by the proposed company with the remaining shares being offered to the general public for subscription.[36]

Governance Structure

10.05 The shareholders' meeting is the organ of authority of a company and shall exercise its powers in accordance with *The Company Law* and its articles.[37] *The Company Law* mandates that the following functions and powers shall be exercised by the shareholders' meeting: to determine the business policies and investment plans of the company; to elect and remove directors and to determine compensation for directors; to appoint and dismiss supervisors of the supervisory board; and to fix compensation for supervisors; to review and approve reports of the board of directors and of the supervisory board or the supervisors; to review and approve the annual financial budget and final accounts of the company; to review and approve plans for the distribution of profits of the company and for the recovery of losses; to decide upon the increase or reduction of the registered capital of the company; to decide upon the issue of debentures by the company; to approve the transfer of capital from a shareholder to a non-shareholder; to adopt resolutions on any merger, division, termination and liquidation of the company; and to amend the articles of association of the company.[38]

Pursuant to *The Company Law*, certain matters must receive two thirds of the votes from shareholders. Resolutions on the merger, division, dissolution, amendment of articles of association, increase or reduction of registered capital of a limited liability company shall be adopted by an affirmative vote of the shareholders representing two thirds of all the voting rights of a limited liability company or two thirds of the casted voting rights of a joint stock company.[39]

Shareholders' meetings are divided into regular meetings and interim meetings. Regular shareholders' meetings shall be convened as stipulated by the articles of association. Provisions on shareholders' procedural rights of demanding interim meetings differ between limited liability companies and joint stock companies. For limited liability companies, interim shareholders' meetings may be convened upon request by the shareholders representing one-fourth of the voting rights, or by one-third of the board of directors, or supervisors.[40] As for joint stock companies, an interim shareholders' meeting shall be convened within two months if a request is made by shareholders holding more than ten per cent of the shares, or by the board of directors or by the supervisory board.[41] Like many other countries, a shareholder's right to vote at the shareholders' meeting shall be in proportion to the capital he has contributed or the shares he holds. Each share entitles the shareholder one vote.[42] Similarly, shareholders in joint stock companies may appoint an agent to attend the shareholders' meetings.[43]

Differences concerning notice of shareholders' meetings of limited liability companies and joint stock companies are obvious. Shareholders in limited liability companies shall be notified of a shareholders' meeting at least fifteen days prior to the scheduled date of the meeting.[44] In contrast, shareholders in joint stock companies shall be notified of the matters to be considered at a shareholders' meeting at least thirty days before such a meeting is held. *The Company Law* further provides that no resolutions may be adopted in respect of matters not included in the notice at interim shareholders' meetings. In case of invalid notice, the shareholders concerned shall be entitled to apply for an injunction in the People's Court to terminate the violation or infringement.[45]

A limited liability company shall have a board of directors, the number of which shall comprise between three and thirteen.[46] Given the large size, a joint stock company shall have a board of directors comprising between five and nineteen.[47] The board of directors of a limited liability company established by State-owned enterprises or State invested entities shall have employee representatives elected by the employees of the company.[48]

The board of directors shall be responsible to the shareholders' meeting. It shall exercise the following functions and powers: to convene shareholders' meetings and to report its work to the shareholders' meeting; to implement the resolutions of the shareholders' meeting; to decide the business plans and investment plans of the company; to formulate the annual financial budget and final accounts of the company; to formulate plans for the distribution of profits and the recovery of losses of the company; to formulate plans for the increase or reduction of the registered capital; to propose plans for any merger, division, dissolution and liquidation of the company; to decide upon the establishment of the management organs of the company; to appoint and dismiss the general manager; and upon recommendation of the manager, to appoint and dismiss the deputy manager(s) and persons in charge of the financial affairs of the company and to determine their remuneration; and to determine the basic management system of the company.[49]

While the rules of procedure may be specified in the articles by the shareholders of limited liability companies, *The Company Law* stipulates clearly that a board meeting of a joint stock company shall only be convened if more than half of all the directors are present.[50] Any resolution requires the affirmative vote of more than half of all the directors in a joint stock company.[51] Unlike the laws in other countries where directors may be removed at any time without cause provided compensation is paid, Articles 47 and 115 state that a director may not be removed from his office without cause prior to the expiration of his term.

10.06   Either a limited liability company or a joint stock company may have one general manager. Such a manager shall be responsible to the board of directors and shall exercise the following functions and powers:

(a) to be responsible for the production, operation and management of the company and for organizing the implementation of the resolutions of the board of directors;

(b) to organize the implementation of the annual production, operation, and investment plans of the company;

(c) to draft plans for the establishment of the internal management organs of the company;

(d) to propose plans for the basic management system of the company;

(e) to formulate detailed rules and regulations of the company;

(f) to recommend the appointment and dismissal of the deputy manager(s) and of persons in charge of the financial affairs of the company;

(g) to appoint and dismiss managerial personnel except those to be appointed and dismissed by the board of directors;

(h) and to exercise other powers specified in the articles of association of the company or conferred upon by the board of directors.[52]

Unlike company laws on the governance structure in the common law jurisdictions, *The Company Law* follows the German law in that it requires a supervisory board be set up. Large-sized limited liability companies and joint stock companies shall have a supervisory board with more than three members. Where a limited liability company has a small number of shareholders and is small in size, it may have one or two supervisors in lieu of a supervisory board. In order to perform the monitoring tasks meaningfully, *The Company Law* provides that directors, managers and responsible persons in charge of the financial affairs of the company may not serve concurrently as supervisors.[53]

The supervisory board shall be comprised of both shareholder and employee representatives. A reasonable proportion of employee representatives shall be provided for by the articles of association of the company and shall be elected by the employees.[54] Generally, the supervisory board or the supervisors shall exercise the following functions and powers:

(a) to examine the financial affairs of the company;

(b) to supervise the work of the directors and the general manager and to ascertain if any violation of the law, administrative regulations or the articles of association of the company has occurred during the performance of their duties;

(c) to demand that the directors and the managers rectify any wrong doing which has adversely affected the interests of the company;

(d) to propose the holding of interim shareholders' meetings;

(e) and to exercise other functions and powers provided for in the articles of association of the company.[55]

Consistent with past practice, the functions of trade unions are recognized in *The Company Law*. A company's employees may, in accordance with the law, organize a trade union to carry out activities and protect the lawful rights and interests of the employees. Further, a company shall provide the trade union with facilities necessary for the trade union to carry out its activities.[56] It should be mentioned that traditionally the trade unions did not have the right to demand wage increases as these matters were dealt with through managerial plans. Their roles were limited to handling other welfare benefits of the employees and recreational activities.

The Company Law requires the management to consult with the trade union prior to making decisions on certain matters involving the interests of its employees such as their salaries, welfare, production safety, labour protection, labour insurance, etc. On these matters, representatives of the trade union shall be invited to attend meetings although these representatives shall not have the right to vote.[57] Furthermore, a company shall take into account the opinions and suggestions of the trade union and the employees of the company when deciding important matters of production and operation, and when formulating major rules and regulations.[58]

Management Liability

10.07 Directors, supervisors and managers have considerable powers in managing the affairs of a company. As they do not receive the full benefits of their major decisions, they are likely to engage in some activities to maximize their self-interest. Such activities may harm the company or the shareholders whose interest is aligned with that of the company. To curtail these activities, *The Company Law* imposes strict legal duties and sanctions on these players for breach of their duties. Furthermore, remedies are provided for in *The Company Law*.

Directors, supervisors and managers of a company shall comply with the articles of association of the company, perform their duties faithfully and uphold the interests of the company and shall not use their position in the company to seek any personal gain. They shall not, by using their position in the company, take bribes, accept other unlawful income or misappropriate the property of the company.[59] Directors and managers shall not misappropriate or lend company funds to a third party. Nor shall they deposit any company funds in their personal accounts or the accounts of other persons. Furthermore, they shall not use the property of the company as collateral for the personal debts of the shareholders or for the debts of other persons.[60]

Self-dealings and competition with the company are strictly prohibited under *The Company Law*. Generally speaking, directors and managers shall not engage personally in, or assist others in the business operation of a company which carries out the same business as the company in which he is serving a term or, activities which may adversely affect the interests of the company in which he is serving. They must account to the company for the benefits derived from the aforesaid business operation or activities. In addition, directors and managers shall not enter into any contract or conduct any transaction with the company unless the articles of association provide otherwise or unless the consent from shareholders on a meeting is obtained.[61] However, the law is not clear on whether the director or the manager, who is also a shareholder, may vote.

Article 63 provides that directors, supervisors and managers shall be personally liable for the damages caused to the company by their violation of laws and administrative regulations as well as the articles of association while performing their duties. Article 118 further stipulates that in a joint stock company, directors shall be held responsible for the resolutions adopted by the board of directors. Each director shall be personally liable for the damages to the company caused by any board's resolution that violates laws, regulations or articles of association unless it can be proved by the minutes of the board meeting that he casts a dissenting vote in the proceedings.

Mergers and Divisions

Any merger or division of a limited liability company shall be decided   **10.08**
by shareholders' meetings.[62] For a joint stock company, decisions of
any merger and division shall be approved by the authorized departments of the State Council or by the relevant provincial People's
Government.[63]

There are basically two methods of carrying out a merger plan.
Thus, a merger may take the form of merger by absorption or by new
establishment. The former means that one company takes over another and the party that is taken over dissolves. The latter refers to
where two or more companies merge together to establish a new
company and the parties to the merger dissolve.[64]

In case of a merger or division, creditors are entitled to require the
company to satisfy their debts or to provide a guarantee for their debts
within a certain period. No merger or division shall be allowed to
proceed if the company fails to satisfy its debts or to provide the
guarantee. The claims and debts of the creditors of these companies to
a merger shall be succeeded by the acquiring company or the newly
established company as a result of the merger. As for a division of a
company, the debts of any original company shall be assumed by the
companies that have resulted from the division in accordance with the
division agreement.[65] When mergers or divisions are implemented,
registration or amendment of the original registration is required. If a
company is dissolved, it shall apply for cancellation of its registration
in accordance with the law.[66]

Insolvency, Dissolution and Liquidation

According to Article 190, a company may be dissolved if certain events   **10.09**
specified by law or the articles of association of the company occur.
Specifically, a company may be dissolved if the term of business
operation contained in the articles of association of the company
expires or an event stipulated in the articles of association takes place.
In addition, dissolution may also be demanded by shareholders at a
shareholders' meeting. Furthermore, a merger or division may also lead
to the dissolution of a company.

Dissolution resulting from the operation of law occurs if a company
violates the law or administrative regulations.[67] In addition, insolvency
of a company will cause the dissolution of a company by the operation
of the law.[68] Currently, The *Law on Enterprise Bankruptcy* of 1986
(*The Bankruptcy Law*) applies only to State-owned enterprises. It is
expected that a bankruptcy law applicable to all types of enterprises
will be enacted soon. Before that, however, enterprises other than

State-owned ones are subject to the relevant provisions in *The Company Law* and *The Civil Law* on a national level. Generally speaking, legal provisions in these laws are very brief and vague.

Where a company is dissolved in accordance with the provisions in the articles of association, a liquidation committee shall be established within fifteen days thereafter.[69] A liquidation committee of a limited liability company shall be composed of the shareholders. Membership of a liquidation committee of a joint stock company shall be decided upon by the shareholders' meeting. If a company is dissolved as a result of violating laws and administrative regulations, the department in charge shall organize the shareholders, other relevant departments and relevant professionals to form a liquidation committee.[70] The application of the above provisions may cause some problems. For State-owned enterprises, it is relatively easy to identify the department in charge. However, it may be difficult to find out which department is in charge of a non State-owned enterprise in some cases.

Where a company is lawfully declared insolvent for having been unable to satisfy its debts, the people's court concerned shall, in compliance with relevant laws, organize the shareholders, persons from the relevant departments and relevant professionals to form a liquidation committee for the liquidation of the assets of the company.[71] It is difficult to understand why the creditors are not included. In cases of insolvency, it is the creditors who risk their loans or credits as the shareholders' equity capital has virtually been wiped out.

In the liquidation process, the liquidation committee of a particular company shall exercise the following functions and powers:[72]

    (a) to ascertain the assets of the company by preparing a balance sheet and a detailed inventory of assets;

    (b) to serve notice upon the creditors or make a public announcement;

    (c) to complete the company's unfinished business in relation to the liquidation;

    (d) to prepare a list of the claims and debts of the company;

    (e) to pay taxes owned by the company;

    (f) to dispose, after repayment of the debts of the company, the remaining assets;

    (g) and to take actions or defend in civil proceedings on behalf of the company.

Once a liquidation committee is set up, the committee shall inform the creditors of the company of its establishment within ten days following the date of its establishment, and make a public announcement in a newspaper at least three times within sixty days following the aforesaid date. The creditors shall submit their claims to the committee within thirty days after the date on which they received notice or, where notice has not received, within ninety days after the date of the first public announcement. A creditor shall specify the relevant items of the claims and produce documentary evidence in support of the claims for the claim registration with the liquidation committee.[73]

When liquidation proceedings are concluded, the liquidation committee shall prepare a liquidation report and submit the same to the shareholders' meeting or to the department in charge for endorsement. The company shall also request the Company Registration Authority to cancel the registration of the company and make a public announcement of the termination of the company.[74] It has to be pointed out that the provision does not require the committee to report to the creditors.

Foreign Investment Company

Company Law legislation creates a new vehicle for direct foreign investment. However, the Law does not map out the way for foreign companies' investment operations in China except for a few provisions on branches of foreign companies. In order to fill the gap, the Ministry of Foreign Trade and Economic Cooperation (MOFTEC), the State organ in administration of foreign investment, issued two regulations in 1995. The first one is entitled Provisional Regulations on Certain Issues Concerning Establishment of Foreign Investment Company Limited by Shares (the "Regulations"). The second is Provisional Provisions Concerning Establishment of Investment-type Company by Foreign Business Investment (the "Provisions"). **10.10**

According to Article 2 of the Regulations, a foreign investment company limited by shares is a company whose shares are jointly held by Sino-foreign shareholders with the foreign shareholding being more than 25 per cent of the registered capital. It may be established by promotion or public issue when the following conditions are met:

(a) at least one of the promoters must be a foreigner; in addition, in the case of establishment by public issue, at least one of the promoters must have a profit record for a successive length of three years prior to the public offering;

(b) the minimum registered capital shall be RMB30 million; and

(c) the application for the establishment has been approved by the relevant State authority.

A foreign investment company limited by shares may be set up through new establishment; conversion of existing equity or contractual joint ventures or wholly owned foreign enterprises that are not in the form of a joint stock company; or acquisition of existing State-owned enterprises or collective enterprises. Provisions on the details of application for establishment and public issue, contents of the promoting contract and other issues are also stipulated in the Regulations.

A foreign investment-type company is, by its nature, a holding company with limited liability for the purpose of either sole or joint investment in China. The requirements for the establishment of such a holding company are provided in Article 2 of the Provisions:

(a) Foreign investors must have a good credit standing and sufficient economic resources. Such conditions can be met by the proof of the foreign investors' total assets of no less than US$400 million in the year immediately proceeding the application, existence of their investment enterprises in China with paid-in registered capital of more than US$10 million, and obtainment of government approval of more than three investment projects proposed by them. Alternatively, the requirement can be satisfied by showing that more than ten investment enterprises on production or infrastructure sector in China have been established by them with a paid-in registered capital of more than US$30 million.

(b) In case of joint investment, the Chinese investors are also required to have total assets of no less than RMB100 million in order to prove their creditworthiness and financial capability.

(c) The minimum registered capital of such a holding company must not be less than US$30 million.

In addition, an application to establish a foreign investment holding company must be submitted to MOFTEC for final examination and approval after the local government's review and approval are obtained.

The business areas that a foreign investment holding company may engage in include direct investment in the permitted sectors of industry, agriculture, infrastructure and energy and supply of services to its invested enterprises, such as the procurement of equipment and materials, after-sales service, assistance for foreign exchange balance, recruitment, market development and consultation. The investment activities of a holding company are not restricted to the place of registration of the company. Moreover, its invested enterprises may enjoy the preferential treatment available to other foreign investment enterprises if the foreign investment in the invested enterprises is made up of 25 per cent of the registered capital.

The Provisions also allow foreign investors to establish a holding company by their wholly-owned subsidiaries. However, some concerns have been expressed about Article 12, which requires the foreign parent company to guarantee not only the capital contribution of their subsidiary to the holding company, but also the registered capital and technology transfer contracted by the holding company in its investment projects. Such a requirement may not be reasonable because it may create an excessive burden and liability on foreign investors if a holding company is jointly owned by both Chinese and foreign investors.[75]

Other Forms of Business Organizations

In addition to sole proprietorships, partnerships and companies, there are still some other special business organizations. Equity and contractual joint ventures discussed elsewhere in this book are two obvious examples. This section, however, is not intended to examine these organizations. Instead, it will focus on two particular forms of business organizations. They are the State-owned enterprises and the collectively-owned enterprises. These forms of business organizations used to dominate the Chinese economy and still play significant roles. At present, there exist several pieces of legislation governing each category. The relevant laws and regulations will be briefly examined.   **10.11**

State-owned Enterprises

The laws relating to State-owned enterprises were enacted relatively recently and were intended to enhance the efficiency of these enterprises. Under the planning model, State-owned enterprises were instrumental in carrying out the State's economic plan. They did not have any independent legal status nor any autonomy. The evolution of the laws on State-owned enterprises can only be understood by China's continuing economic reform policies discussed in the introduction. The policy goal is to change the rigid planned economy to a market economy with some minor governmental intervention. While this macro-economic reform is intended to solve the information and coordination problem of the planning system, the micro-economic reform is to solve the structural problems of the State-owned enterprises.

The government wants to make it clear that the State will not bear unlimited liability for the debts of these enterprises. In these State-owned enterprises there shall exist complete separation between ownership and management. Thus, *The Civil Law* provides that State-owned enterprises may obtain the status of legal persons when they have sufficient funds as stipulated by the State, have articles of association, organizations and premises, have the ability to independently bear civil liability; and have been approved and registered by the competent authority.[76] Like other legal persons such as companies, a State-owned enterprise shall bear civil liability with the property that the state authorizes it to manage.[77] This legal issue became clearer when China adopted *The Bankruptcy Law*, which only applies to

State-owned enterprises. While this law has been in existence for many years, it is not always strictly enforced. This fact indicates the difficulty of reforming State-owned enterprises. A transition from a planned economy to a market economy requires not only a few laws but also comprehensive adjustment policies and a wide range of social welfare programmes.

The IEOWP mandates that an enterprise owned by the whole of the people shall obtain the status of a legal person. A State-owned enterprise shall be a socialist commodity production and operation unit which shall, in accordance with law, make its own managerial decisions, take full responsibility for its profits and losses and practise independent accounting. While the property of the enterprise is owned by the whole people, the enterprise shall enjoy the rights to possess, utilize and dispose of, according to law, the property which the State has authorized it to operate and manage.[78] A fundamental defect clearly exists in the complete separation between ownership and management. As symbolic shareholders, the people simply will not be interested in monitoring the activities of the management of these State-owned enterprises as the costs will alway exceeds the benefits to any particular shareholder. These collective action problems and free rider problems considerably undermine the internal monitoring mechanism.

In order to ensure that State-owned enterprises have the autonomy of managing their business, the IEOWP spells out some important rights of these enterprises. Specifically, a State-owned enterprise shall have the right to arrange its own production needed for society or the provision of services for society;[79] to choose the suppliers for itself and purchase from them materials needed for production;[80] to negotiate and sign contracts with foreign parties; to budget and use its retained funds subject to state regulations;[81] to determine such forms of wages and methods of bonus distribution as appropriate to its specific conditions;[82] to employ or dismiss its staff members and workers subject to labour regulations;[83] to engage in joint operations with other enterprises or institutions or to invest or hold shares in other enterprises; and to issue bonds subject to the approval of the State authority.[84]

Moreover, State-owned enterprises shall have the right to reject the exaction of its manpower, materials and financial resources in the form of apportionment by any State organ or unit. Exaction by apportionment is defined as any demand on the enterprise by any State organ or unit in any form for the provision of manpower, materials and financial resources except as otherwise stipulated by the laws and regulations.[85]

10.12 It has to be pointed out that there are still many constraints on these State-owned enterprises. For instance, the enterprise must fulfil any mandatory plans.[86] As the State may change the prices of certain products or raw materials, the enterprise is provided a limited right of requesting for an adjustment of these mandatory plans. It is, however, relatively clear that the enterprise has the right to reject production assignments given by any State department or unit outside the mandatory plans.[87] Furthermore, such an enterprise undertaking production according to a mandatory plan shall have the right to market for its own products manufactured in excess of the planned quota.[88]

The above provisions breed a market distortion in that the price of products or resources allocated through the mandatory plan is different from that of those allocated by the market force. Generally speaking, the prices of materials allocated within the mandatory plan are lower than those on the open market. This artificial restriction or distortion may result in rent seeking activities as more enterprises desire to obtain more resources within the planning system while selling more products on the open market. Fortunately, economic reform has significantly reduced the portion of products allocated through mandatory plan.

The Regulations for Converting the Status of the Enterprises Owned by the Whole People promulgated by the State Council in 1992 (CSER) represented the new efforts to push State-owned enterprises onto the market. The CSER makes the rights contained in the IEOWP more specific and concrete. For instance, a State-owned enterprise must implement and improve a director responsibility system with the director being the legal representative of the enterprise. The enterprise is responsible for the business conduct of the legal representative and other persons on behalf of the enterprise. Liability is limited to the assets managed by the enterprise in accordance with the authorization of the State.[89]

The factory director shall be appointed by the competent department of the government or elected by the staff and workers' congress of the enterprise.[90] The factory director shall exercise leadership relating to production, operation and management of the enterprise. Specifically, the factory director shall exercise the powers and functions to decide on the various plans of the enterprise or report them for examination and approval in accordance with law and the provisions of the State Council; decide on the administrative setup of the enterprise; to propose to the competent department of the government the appointment or removal, employment or dismissal of leading administrative cadres at the level of a vice-director of the factory; appoint or remove, employ or dismiss the intermediate-level leading administrative cadres of the enterprise; propose plans for wage adjustment and bonus distribution; design important rules and regulations, and refer them to the staff and workers' congress for examination and approval; propose programmes for the use of welfare funds and make suggestions regarding such other matters as are important for the well-being and benefits of the staff and refer them to the staff and workers congress according to law; and submit to the competent department of the government proposals for rewarding or punishing leading administrative cadres at the level of a vice-director of the factory.[91]

As the factory director and other officials of the company are agents of the enterprise, monitoring the activities of these agents is essential to make sure that they are working for the best interests of the enterprise and not just for themselves. The relevant governmental agencies have the power to check the indicators of maintaining or increasing the assets and profits or losses of the enterprise through auditing work,[92] to determine the ratios, methods or quotas of profit distribution between the State and the enterprise in accordance with the regulations of the State Council, to decide and approve productive construction projects, to decide or approve the methods of management and establishment, division, merger (excluding takeovers), termination, auction, takeovers and bankruptcy, to decide or approve the appointment, removal, and rewards and punishment of the factory director, to provide regulations concerning asset management and monitoring, to approve the reporting of bad debts, offset and management of vital assets of the enterprise.

A State-owned enterprise may be terminated for reason of violation of laws and regulations, being dissolved by decision of the competent department of the government made in accordance with the provisions of the laws and regulations, being declared bankrupt in accordance with law, or other matters.[93]

Collectively-owned Enterprises

10.13   Collectively-owned enterprises in rural areas and in towns and cities are respectively governed by the Regulations on Rural Collectively-owned Enterprises of 1990 (the Rural Enterprise Regulations) and the Regulations on Urban Collectively-owned Enterprises of 1991 (the Urban Enterprise Regulations). Both urban collectively-owned enterprises and rural collectively-owned enterprises are deemed as the part of the State economy.

The Rural Enterprise Regulations do not define the term "rural collectively-owned enterprise". It specifically mentions, however, that the Regulations do not apply to agricultural producers' cooperatives, agricultural supply and marketing cooperatives and agricultural credit cooperatives.[94] In contrast, the Urban Enterprise Regulations provide a definition and some criteria. An urban collectively-owned enterprise is collectively-owned by the people of the enterprise where they make joint contributions and the remuneration is mainly based on the contribution of labour of each individual person.[95] Such an enterprise may be a single entity or combined by several entities. Both urban and rural collectively-owned enterprises may obtain the status of legal persons as specified in the Civil Law.[96]

Establishment, Change of Registered Matters and Termination

An enterprise shall have a name, proper organization and articles of association, have business premises and facilities which shall comply with sanitary and safety conditions, have the necessary funds and staff corresponding to the scale of business operation or services, have clearly specified business scope, etc.[97]

If the conditions of the establishment are met, the enterprise shall obtain the approval from the competent authority in charge of either rural or urban collectively-owned enterprises. Furthermore, the enterprise has to be registered with the local SAIC and receive a business licence or an enterprise legal person business licence depending on whether the enterprise is a legal person. If the enterprise is not a legal person, the owner may be personally liable for the debts of the enterprise.

In case of any merger, division, cessation of business, relocation, name change, or change of other registered items, the enterprise has to obtain approval form the original competent authorities and to vary the original registration.[98] The enterprise may be terminated for being unable to continue its business, violation of laws and regulations, becoming insolvent, or being merged or divided, etc.[99]

Governance Structure

The governance structure of collectively-owned enterprises is quite different from that of State-owned enterprises. Peasants' meetings or peasant representative meetings exercise the ownership right.[100] The nature of business, methods of operation, appointment and methods of selection of factory directors or managers shall be determined by the owners or their representatives on these meetings. In addition, distribution of after-tax profits, matters concerning mergers, divisions, relocation, petition of bankruptcy, termination of business of the enterprise shall be resolved at the peasants' meetings or peasant representatives meetings. The power of running the day to day business is delegated to the factory director or manager.[101] Similarly, urban collectively-owned enterprises shall establish the system of staff meetings if the number of staff of the enterprise is below one hundred or staff representative meetings if the number of staff exceeds three hundred.[102] At these meetings, the staff or representatives of the staff can exercise the powers to propose or amend the articles of association, to elect, remove, appoint or dismiss the factory director or manager or deputy factory director or deputy manager, to review various proposals submitted by the factory director or manager and to resolve significant matters of staff remuneration, wage adjustment policies, distribution of bonus and dividends, matters of staff welfare, to decide upon the methods of punishment or rewards of staff and other regulations, etc.[103] Other daily business matters are also assigned to the factory director or manager.[104]

Conclusions

10.14 This chapter has examined the laws on business organizations in China. It should be mentioned that the laws of business organizations in China are historically arranged in accordance with ownership of the means of production. As discussed in the introduction, State-owned enterprises and collectively-owned enterprises used to dominate the economy. Economic reforms from 1978 have greatly changed the nature of the economy. The allocation of resources through economic planing has been replaced by the allocation of resources through voluntary contractual means by various market participants. Change or amendment of laws needs to be understood from its evolution in response to the economic reforms in China. As the laws in this area are still in a state of flux, readers are expected to frequently check new laws and regulations and their amendments to ensure the accuracy of the legal position on a particular issue of business organization.

Notes

[*] This chapter was written by Dr Yu Guang Hua, who provided the initial draft, and Zhang Xianchu, who made some revisions and additions.
[1] Articles 26 and 27 of *The Civil Law*.
[2] *Ibid.* Articles 30 to 35.
[3] *Ibid.* Articles 36 to 50.
[4] *Ibid.* Articles 51 to 53.
[5] Article 2 of the Private Enterprise Regulations.
[6] Zhao Xu-dong, "A Study of Sole Proprietorship Legislation" (1995) 1 Forum of Law and Politics 65.
[7] Article 2 of the AIICH.
[8] There are two categories of people included under retired persons. One category (*li xiu ren yuan*) refers to those who have achieved certain levels or satisfied certain criteria and are entitled to better retirement benefits. The other category (*tui xiu ren yuan*) include those who have reached their normal retirement age and are entitled to normal retirement benefits.
[9] Article 3 of the AIICH.
[10] These rules were promulgated by the State Administration of Industry and Commence on September 5, 1987; Article 5.
[11] Article 12.
[12] *Ibid.*

[13] *Ibid.*
[14] Article 3 of the Implementation Rules of the AIICH.
[15] Article 9 of the AIICH.
[16] Article 9 of the Private Enterprise Regulations.
[17] Articles 6 and 10.
[18] Article 8 of the AIICH.
[19] *Ibid.* Article 11.
[20] Article 16 of the Private Enterprise Regulations.
[21] *Ibid.* Article 38.
[22] *Ibid.* Article 22.
[23] Article 30 of *The Civil Law.*
[24] *Ibid.* Article 34.
[25] Article 3 of *The Company Law.*
[26] *Ibid.* Article 20.
[27] *Ibid.* Article 18.
[28] *Ibid.* Article 75.
[29] *Ibid.* Article 78.
[30] *Ibid.* Article 152.
[31] *Ibid.* Articles 23 and 78.
[32] *Ibid.* Article 206.
[33] Articles 1 and 2 of the Decisions of the Standing Committee of the National People's Congress on Sanctions of Criminal Conduct in Contravention of the Company Law of February 28, 1995.
[34] Article 11 of *The Company Law.*
[35] *Ibid.* Article 77.
[36] *Ibid.* Articles 74 and 83.
[37] *Ibid.* Articles 38 and 102.
[38] *Ibid.* Articles 38 and 103.
[39] *Ibid.* Articles 39, 40, 106 and 107.
[40] *Ibid.* Article 43.
[41] *Ibid.* Article 104.
[42] *Ibid.* Articles 41 and 106.
[43] *Ibid.* Article 108.
[44] *Ibid.* Article 44.
[45] *Ibid.* Article 11.
[46] *Ibid.* Article 45.
[47] *Ibid.* Article 112.
[48] *Ibid.* Article 45.
[49] *Ibid.* Articles 46 and 112.
[50] *Ibid.* Articles 49 and 117.
[51] *Ibid.* Article 117.
[52] *Ibid.* Articles 50 and 119.
[53] *Ibid.* Articles 52 and 124.
[54] *Ibid.*
[55] *Ibid.* Articles 54 and 126.
[56] *Ibid.* Article 16.
[57] *Ibid.* Article 55.
[58] *Ibid.* Article 56.
[59] *Ibid.* Article 59.
[60] *Ibid.* Article 60.
[61] *Ibid.* Article 61.
[62] *Ibid.* Article 182.
[63] *Ibid.* Article 183.
[64] *Ibid.* Article 184.
[65] *Ibid.* Article 185.
[66] *Ibid.* Article 188.
[67] *Ibid.* Article 192.
[68] *Ibid.* Article 189.
[69] *Ibid.* Article 191.
[70] *Ibid.* Article 192.
[71] *Ibid.* Article 189.
[72] *Ibid.* Article 193.
[73] *Ibid.* Article 194.
[74] *Ibid.* Article 197.
[75] Kaiguan Tao and Yapu Zhang: The Law Related to Foreign Investment Companies in China, Vol, 5 No. 1 *Asia Pacific Law Review*, Summer 1996, at 99.
[76] Article 41 of *The Civil Law.*
[77] *Ibid.* Article 48.
[78] Article 2 of the IEOWP.
[79] *Ibid.* Article 23.
[80] *Ibid.* Article 25.
[81] *Ibid.* Article 28.
[82] *Ibid.* Article 30.
[83] *Ibid.* Article 32.
[84] *Ibid.* Article 34.
[85] *Ibid.* Article 33.
[86] *Ibid.* Article 35.
[87] *Ibid.* Article 23.
[88] *Ibid.* Article 24.
[89] Article 23 of the CSER.
[90] *Ibid.* Article 44.
[91] *Ibid.* Article 45.
[92] *Ibid.* Article 42.
[93] Article 19 of the IEOWP.
[94] Article 2 of the Rural Enterprise Regulations.
[95] Article 4 of the Urban Enterprise Regulations.
[96] Article 41 of *The Civil Law.*
[97] Article 12 of the Urban Enterprise Regulations and Article 13 of the Rural Enterprise Regulations.

[98] Article 15 of the Rural Enterprise Regulations and Article 15 of the Urban Enterprise Regulations.
[99] Articles 15 and 17 of the Urban Enterprise Regulations and Article 15 of the Rural Enterprise Regulations.
[100] Article 18 of the Rural Enterprise Regulations.
[101] Article 19 of the Rural Enterprise Regulation and Article 22 of the Urban Enterprise Regulation.
[102] Article 27 of the Urban Enterprise Regulations.
[103] *Ibid.* Article 28.
[104] *Ibid.* Article 34.

CHAPTER 11
ALTERNATIVE DISPUTE RESOLUTION

John S Mo

City University of Hong Kong

John Shijian Mo, Assistant Professor, Law Department, City University of Hong Kong, LL.B. (Jilin), LL.B. (Monash), LL.M. (Dalhousie), and Ph.D. (Sydney), barrister and solicitor in Australia. Author of *Butterworths Student's Companion: International Commercial Law* (Sydney, Butterworths, 1995) and *International Commercial Law* (Sydney, Butterworths, 1996), and a number of articles in the areas of international trade law, Chinese law and Australian Law.

Introduction

Alternative dispute resolution (ADR) is an expression from the United States. It embraces a number of methods or means of dispute resolution which are regarded as alternatives to litigation, a traditional means of settling a dispute. ADR has no fixed content. By definition, any method of, or approach to, dispute resolution which provides an alternative to litigation can be regarded as an ADR method. **11.01**

ADR in this chapter refers to any method of dispute resolution available in China, which provides an alternative to litigation at a Chinese court under formal judicial proceedings. The Chinese are well-known for their preference of non-judicial means of dispute resolution to court proceedings. This attitude has its historical and cultural bases. Traditionally, the Chinese did not have much interest in seeking a court victory if the costs and complications were too great or the enforcement was too difficult.

In this chapter, ADR includes negotiation (consultation), mediation (conciliation) and arbitration. Mediation includes the process of court-conducted mediation which is different from formal judicial proceedings and is not bound by the procedural law. As we will see later, it is sometimes an inherent part of a court proceeding, though it is not compulsory. It should be regarded as a method of ADR because it provides an alternative to formal judicial proceedings. The court is required to mediate disputes in most cases. It is also required to obtain

367

consent of the parties before commencing a process of mediation. However, the court has a discretion in determining whether a proposal to mediate should be made to the parties.

There is no any uniform legal framework for ADR in China. Presently, arbitration is regulated by law. Negotiation is not, nor should it be. Mediation is partly regulated, in particular in mediation by the People's Mediation Committee (PMC),[1] court-conducted mediation and labour mediation. It is not necessary to have a uniform legal framework to institutionalize ADR, nor is it possible.

Negotiation or Consultation

11.02 There is no law to regulate the process of negotiation or consultation. This is because the method of negotiation is meant to be a free, voluntary and direct discussion between the disputing parties. However, a great number of Chinese laws and regulations, such as Article 51 of the *Civil Procedure Law*, the *Sino-Foreign Joint Equity Ventures Law*, the *Sino-Foreign Joint Co-operative Ventures Law*, the *Foreign Economic Contract Law*, the *Economic Contract Law* and its implementing rules (19 subordinate regulations were made to implement the *Economic Contract Law*) and the State Council Measures for Resolving Labour Disputes in Enterprises, provide negotiation as a preliminary method for settling a dispute by mediation, arbitration or litigation.

Negotiation or consultation is the most direct and primitive means of dispute resolution. Humans are born with an ability to compromise and a capacity for resolving conflicts by negotiation. Offer, counter-offer, bargaining and compromise are the tactics employed to negotiate. Justice and fairness are what the negotiators are capable of perceiving to be, or willing to accept as, just and fair. Unequal bargaining powers may not always lead to disharmony when counterbalanced by the fully informed consent of the parties. Any agreement reached on the basis of voluntary concessions, whether or not it squarely matches the solution which can be offered by a court of law, can indeed resolve a dispute and is as effective as, if not more than, a judicial decision. This is why negotiation or consultation is the most commonly used means of dispute resolution.

There is no any meaningful distinction between "negotiation" and "consultation". In fact, the Chinese word *xieshang* can be translated as either "negotiation" or "consultation". Both words refer to a direct, unfettered and voluntary discussion between the parties concerned. The law does not tell the parties how to negotiate. Balanced fairness or justice and fully-informed voluntariness are always implied in a process of negotiation. A party can take advantage of the other. A party may also make concessions which would appear to be unfair to an outsider. But, both parties must be happy and willing to be bound by the agreement reached in a process of negotiation. A dissatisfied party may renege on the agreement and resort to other means of settlement, such as arbitration or litigation. Thus, a process of negotiation must be conducted in a manner which appears to be fair, appropriate, acceptable and controlled in the eyes of the parties concerned.

As stated, the Chinese are well-known for their preference for negotiation and their patience for negotiating a bargain. Chinese value time differently from most of their Western counterparts. While negotiation has assisted parties to resolve many differences and maintain amicable business relationships, it is also capable of being used as a tactic to prolong the process of dispute resolution. This may be a negative factor that has discouraged westerners from negotiating with the Chinese. In addition, a party may sometimes employ the tactic of sending a negotiator with limited authority as a means to gain an advantage. As a result, a party may discover that the other negotiator cannot honour his or her words after an agreement has been reached. These possibilities offset the advantages of negotiation being a direct, voluntary and efficient means of dispute resolution.

The Chinese law specifies negotiation or consultation as the initial step in resolving most commercial, civil, industrial, family, or neighbourhood disputes. A great number of Chinese laws and regulations adopt the order of negotiation, mediation, arbitration and litigation.[2] The order does not have any legal effect unless the relevant law so specifies.[3] The specification of such an order suggests that the Chinese government encourages the use of negotiation or consultation as a preliminary step for dispute resolution. A strict interpretation of the law may lead to the conclusion that the disputing parties have a legal duty to negotiate if the law provides negotiation as the first option for dispute resolution. Such a legal obligation, if it does exist, is easy to comply with because any gesture of discussion, or any communication for resolving the dispute, could be arguably regarded as evidence of attempted negotiation. No one would breach this obligation as long as he or she has attempted to draw the attention of the other party to his or her views of the dispute concerned. When, however, reading the provision in context, negotiation in Chinese law is not a legal obligation. There has been no court case illustrating the "obligation" to negotiate in Chinese law.

Negotiation and consultation, though capable of being abused, should be encouraged in resolving commercial disputes, in particular, the disputes involving foreign parties. If rationale prevails and a dispute is resolved by way of negotiation, the parties can certainly save time, money and their business relationship. It indeed deserves to be the first option, as promoted by Chinese law. In addition, Article 51 of the *Civil Procedure Law* allows the parties to resolve the dispute by negotiation at any stage of court proceedings. The parties may attempt to negotiate a solution at any time during a trial before the court delivers a judgement. Similarly, parties to an arbitration proceeding conducted by the CIETAC or CMAC, or under the *Arbitration Law*, are also allowed to negotiate a settlement at any time prior to the making of an arbitral award.

Chinese lawyers play an important role in negotiating a settlement on behalf of their clients. In most economic and family cases, lawyers often communicate with each other on behalf of their clients and discuss disagreements on facts and law. Many disputes arise from parties' lack of appropriate understanding of the relevant law or facts. Sometimes, only one party is legally represented. The involvement of the lawyer may help the parties to narrow down the issues in disagreement and facilitate the process of negotiation. However, there is no guarantee that negotiation carried out by the lawyer on behalf of the clients is necessarily more effective than negotiation conducted by the parties themselves. The availability of a lawyer provides at least one more option for the parties to attempt a settlement by negotiation.

Mediation or Conciliation

What is Mediation or Conciliation under Chinese Law?

11.03 The expressions "mediation" and "conciliation" are not clearly defined in Chinese law. Either of them can be regarded as an adequate translation of the Chinese word *tiaojie*. The expressions are not legally distinguishable, and are interchangeable in this chapter.

Mediation refers to a process of dispute resolution in which a third party acts as a mediator either to assist the parties to reach a solution, or to persuade the parties to accept a solution. The fundamental difference between mediation in common law countries and in China is that a mediator may insist on the parties accepting a solution and that the parties may eventually give in to the persuasion.[4] This strong persuasion is often seen in the process of mediating a domestic or neighbour dispute, but is less popular in commercial dispute resolution.

Mediation in China can be divided into six broad categories: those conducted by the PMC (people's mediation), those conducted by someone with certain official capacity (administrative mediation), those conducted by friends or community leaders (voluntary or private mediation), those conducted by the court of law (court-conducted mediation), labour dispute mediation and Beijing Mediation Centre for international commercial disputes. People's mediation is regulated by the State Council Organizational Rules for People's Mediation Committees. The Rules set out principles for the appointment of mediators and conduct of mediation sessions. Local government officials, officers of a government authority, village committees, resident committees and responsible officers of State owned enterprises may also carry out mediation wherever necessary. Mediation is only one of the roles these officials and committees are expected to perform. In addition, mediation is often carried out from time to time, by friends, neighbours or community leaders in a very informal manner. This type of mediation is not regulated and is taken for granted by both the voluntary mediators and disputants. Labour disputes in enterprises are mediated by the mediation committee set up in pursuance of the *Labour Law* and the relevant regulations. The Beijing Mediation Centre is set up under the China Chamber of Commerce (the China Council for the Promotion of International Trade).

The China International Economic and Trade Arbitration Commission (CIETAC) and the China Maritime Arbitration Commission (CMAC) also provide services of mediation or conciliation during the processes of arbitration conducted by them. This type of mediation is an inherent part of their arbitral proceedings. The disputants have an option to ask the commissions to mediate, rather than arbitrate, a dispute. This type of mediation is examined under the arbitral proceedings conducted by the CIETAC and CMAC.

Court-conducted mediation is largely based on the *Civil Procedure Law*, which authorises a court of law in Articles 9 and 85 to 91 to resolve a dispute by mediation if the disputing parties so agree. In addition, Article 25 of the *Marriage Law* makes the process of mediation compulsory when a court adjudicates an application for divorce. The court of law may attempt to mediate all disputes of a civil and commercial nature, except for those cases involving a judicial review of administrative decisions,[5] or the commission of economic offences punishable by fine or imprisonment.[6]

Mediation by the People's Mediation Committee

The People's Mediation Committee is defined by Article 2 of the State   **11.04**
Council Organizational Rules for the People's Mediation Committees
as an organization of the people set up within each village committee
or urban resident committee. The same definition is provided in Article 16 of the *Civil Procedure Law*. There are four different views on the
status of the PMC.[7] The first view regards the PMC as a mediation
organization of the masses.[8] The second view treats the PMC as an
autonomic organization of the masses. The difference between an
organization and an autonomic organization is in the suggestion that
an autonomic organization implicitly has more administrative power
than an organization because the former exercises an autonomy on
behalf of the masses concerned. The third view argues that the PMC is
an inherent part of the people's judicial system of China. The fourth

view insists that the PMC is an auxiliary system of the people's judicial system. The difference between the third and fourth view is that the third one regards the PMC as part of the judicial system, but the fourth view considers the PMC as supplementary to the formal judicial system. Some of the debate on the nature of the PMC does not have much practical implication at all.

The PMC is a means of social control. This can be seen in the appointment of the mediators. For example, Article 3 of the Organizational Rules of the People's Mediation Committees provides that a "unit" can re-appoint a mediator to replace the one who is not suitable for the position. "Unit" suggests that the committee is a fabric of the organized Chinese society. The same provision also allows a "unit" to recall a mediator on the ground of misconduct. In addition, Article 5 of the Organizational Rules requires the mediator to advocate the law, regulations, and governmental policies and to educate the citizens to obey the law and to respect social morals. These provisions indicate that the PMC is part of the State machine, although the committee is elected, and financed by a local community (unit).

A PMC should have three to nine mediators appointed from two sources. A member of a village or urban resident committee can be *ex officio* of the local PMC, if he wishes to be involved. The rest are elected by the local community. If the local community consists of several units, *e.g.*, an urban resident committee of 700 households may be subdivided into the units of street or road,[9] each subdivision can elect a mediator. The elected members serve a three-year term and can be re-elected. The mediator is required to have good character and high moral standards. He or she must be able to communicate with the local community and be enthusiastic. Adequate knowledge of law and policy is also essential for a mediator. A mediator can be replaced in situations of incapacity or misconduct.

Article 6 of the Organizational Rules sets out the following principles for conducting a session of mediation:

(a) the session of mediation should be conducted in pursuance of law, regulations and relevant policies;
(b) in the absence of the law, regulations and policies, mediation can be conducted according to the prevailing moral standards;
(c) voluntariness is the basis of mediation;
(d) equality between the parties is essential;
(e) the mediator has no power to impose mediation as a precondition for litigation; and
(f) the mediator has no power to prohibit the parties from resorting to litigation when he or she has failed to mediate the dispute.

The mediator's role in a session of mediation is threefold. First, he or she is an investigator who must find out the facts of the dispute.

Secondly, he or she is an educator, who must tell the parties what is right and what is wrong according to the law, policy and moral standards. Thirdly, he or she must be a persuader, who will patiently and persistently convince the parties that a compromise is the best option for the interests of themselves and the public. The mediator of the PMC plays a much more active role than any mediator in common law countries.

The mediator is subject to a number of disciplinary measures in the Organizational Rules. The following rules govern the conduct of the mediator in mediation or in carrying out activities relevant to mediation:

(a) the mediator must not abuse power and manipulate the process of mediation for his or her own purpose;
(b) the mediator must not suppress or take revenge upon the disputant(s) when conducting mediation;
(c) the mediator must not insult or punish the disputant(s) when conducting mediation;
(d) the mediator must not disclose the privacy of the disputant(s); and
(e) the mediator must not take bribes.

These rules imply that the PMC exercises certain State power when mediating a dispute. A mediator whose authority solely derives from the parties' voluntary consent has no power to suppress or take revenge upon anyone. Nor can he or she abuse the power to the extent that the parties are unable to control the conduct of mediator. The fact that the law clearly imposes disciplinary measures upon the mediator suggests that the mediator has some official power or status which must be fettered and controlled to ensure the integrity of the governmental administration.

Depending on the severity of any breach of disciplinary measures by a mediator, different consequences will follow. If the breach is not serious, the relevant village or urban resident committee, or the relevant local government can reprimand the mediator. The local government has the power to set aside or change any mediation settlement made by the mediator's wrongful interpretation of the law and policy, or procured by his or her misconduct. If a breach is severe, the mediator can be replaced.

The agreement reached by the parties to resolve the dispute can be either in oral or written form. The Organizational Rules require the mediator to keep written records of the mediation process and result. The written agreement is not required in a simple dispute, unless the parties so request. A written agreement should be signed by the disputants and the mediator, and also bear the seal of the relevant PMC.

The agreement reached by the parties is not enforceable in law. Article 9 of the Organizational Rules imposes a moral obligation upon the parties to comply with the agreement. A party dissatisfied with the mediation result is entitled to request the matter to be further dealt with by the local government, or be heard by the local court. The local government can affirm, change or set the agreement aside, but has no power to deprive the disputing parties of their right to litigate the matter.

Administrative Mediation

11.05 Mediation is a method used to resolve social conflicts. It is used in China by local government, the governmental authority, the village committee, the urban resident committee and the mediation committee of a State-owned enterprise which is still an essential part of the Chinese economy. Mediation by these organizations refers to a process of dispute resolution in which an officer or a person (or persons) is authorized by law to mediate a dispute on behalf of the organization concerned. Unlike mediation by the PMC, administrative mediation is largely unregulated. The organizations have a general power and obligation to resolve small disputes falling within their jurisdiction in order to strengthen social stability. Mediation is an effective means of serving this purpose.

Most local governments, particularly in rural areas, have a judicial assistant, who co-ordinates legal education and provides the necessary assistance to the courts. The judicial assistant has the power to supervise the work of the PMC and to examine the mediation settlement brokered by the PMC, the village committee or the urban resident committee. He or she may also mediate a dispute as he or she thinks fit. It can be presumed that the judicial assistant is subject to the same conduct rules applicable to local government officers. At the end of mediation, the parties may reach a written agreement, which will be signed by the parties and the mediator, and stamped by the local government. If the parties cannot reach any agreement, the judicial assistant may make an award on behalf of the local government to resolve the dispute. It appears therefore, that the real function of the judicial assistant is to resolve the dispute, rather than mediate the dispute. Neither the agreement sealed by the local government, nor the award given by the judicial assistant on behalf of the local government is enforceable in law.

Mediation can be also carried out by a governmental authority, which could be invited as mediator because of its jurisdiction over the matter or the parties in dispute. *The Economic Contract Law* used to have a provision stating that the governmental authority in charge of the relevant contract can mediate the dispute. The provision was repealed in 1993. Presently, Article 42 of *The Economic Contract Law* encourages the parties to mediate their dispute, but does not specify the governmental authority as the mediator. However, this provision does not prohibit a governmental authority being chosen as a mediator either. If the disputing parties are controlled by the same governmental department, the department may be invited as a mediator to facilitate a solution. This process of mediation is not regulated and the administrative pressure or persuasion is expected. The possibility of administrative pressure was probably the reason for the amendment to *The Economic Contract Law* in 1993. Under the present law, the parties are not obliged to accept the results of mediation, even the department may have some administrative influence over the settlement. An unwilling party may proceed to arbitration (if an agreement has been reached) or resort to a court of law, even if the process of mediation has begun. A settlement of mediation is not enforceable in law, but may be complied with voluntarily because of the parties' participation.

China passed *The Organizational Law of the Village Committees* (Tentative) in 1987. The purpose of this legislation is to establish the village committee in rural areas as the basic unit of social control. The local government is the lowest level of government administration. The village committees can be set up under a local government to assist its work. *The Organizational Law* defines in Article 2 the village committee as the autonomous organization of the masses for the purposes of self-management, self-education and self-service. One of its functions is to mediate local disputes. A PMC is usually established under each village committee. In the areas where the local population is too small to justify the establishment of the PMC, a member of the village committee will be in charge of mediation. The conduct of the committee member in mediation is subject to the Organizational Rules of the People's Mediation Committees by analogy. The agreement mediated by the village committee member has the same effect as an agreement mediated by the PMC.

In 1989 China passed *The Organizational Law for the Urban Resident Committees*. The committee so established is an autonomous organization of the urban residents for the purposes of self-management, self-education and self-service. It is a means of social control since the committee is expected to provide assistance to local government and the local police station. The urban resident committee succeeds the urban resident committee set up in 1954 under the Organizational Rules of the Urban Resident Committee. The urban resident committee has a duty to mediate disputes between local residents. A committee with a sufficient population may have the PMC within its structure. If the population is small, one of the members of the urban resident committee should be responsible for mediation. *The Organization Law* does not set out rules for mediation conducted by the committee member. It can be assumed, however, that the Organizational Rules for People's Mediation Committees may provide guidance to the committee member mediating a dispute. Thus, the process of mediation, conduct of the mediator and effect of the mediation agreement can be dealt with by analogy to the relevant rules of the PMC.

Mediation of Labour Disputes

11.06 Most labour disputes in Chinese enterprises (companies) are mediated by the mediation committee of each enterprise set up under the State Council Measures for Resolving Labour Disputes in Enterprises.[10] The Measures require an enterprise to adopt a dispute resolution system based on negotiation, mediation and arbitration to resolve internal labour disputes. According to the Measures, a dispute can be either mediated or arbitrated within the system. Arbitration of labour disputes will be discussed in more detail later. The labour dispute system in China is based on Articles 77 to 84 of *The Labour Law*, which provide the legal basis for the State Council Measures.

The disputes arising from employment contracts, dismissal of em ployees, salary disputes, work compensation, worker's welfare, and workplace safety, etc., are to be negotiated, mediated or arbitrated within the enterprise. A dispute arising from an enterprise should be mediated by its mediation committee. If the process of mediation fails, the party may take the matter to the relevant arbitration commission. Article 6 of the Measures recommends negotiation as the first step in resolving a labour dispute, which is followed by mediation, and arbitration. But, a party is allowed to go to the arbitration commission directly, and to proceed to a court of law late if necessary. Therefore, negotiation and mediation are not compulsory for resolving labour disputes.

The mediation committee consists of representatives of the employees, the management and the union. The size of each committee is to be negotiated between the employees (or their delegates) and the management. The management's representatives should not exceed one third of the total members of the committee. The employees' representatives are elected by the employees directly or by their delegates. The representatives of the management and union are appointed by the management and union respectively. The chair of the committee must be taken by the union representative. If there is no union in an enterprise, the constitution of the committee is to be negotiated by the employees and the management.

Although the mediation committee is set up under the law, it has no compulsory power to impose a settlement of mediation upon the parties. Voluntariness of the parties is protected in the sense that the parties can decide whether to proceed with the process of mediation and whether to reach a settlement. Thus, the mediation committee can commence a process of mediation if requested by one party, but cannot proceed with the process if refused by the other party.

A speedy settlement is intended by the Measures. Article 10 of the Measures provides that if the parties cannot reach a settlement within 30 days from the date an application for mediation is filed, the process of mediation is deemed to have failed. This requirement is necessary for resolving labour disputes which are often concerned with the daily life of the employee and the normal operation of an enterprise.

The Measures do not deal with the effect of a settlement of mediation. It can be assumed that a settlement mediated by the mediation committee in pursuance of the Measures does not have any binding effect. The party cannot ask the court to enforce it. Nor can a party prevent the other party from submitting the same matter to arbitration. The parties to a labour dispute arising from an enterprise do not have direct access to the court of law until the matter has been arbitrated by the arbitration commission. Thus, a party dissatisfied with a process of mediation or the settlement of mediation has to try arbitration before he or she can resort to judicial proceedings. The procedure must be complied with, because Article 111(3) of *The Civil Procedure Law* states that the court will direct a plaintiff to submit the dispute to a competent authority which has jurisdiction over the dispute under law.

Court-Conducted Mediation

The Chinese courts can initiate a session of mediation in most civil cases, except for cases involving judicial review of administrative decisions,[11] or economic cases involving criminal sanctions against one or both parties.[12] This power of mediation derives from *The Civil Procedure Law*. Articles 9 and 85 of the Law provide that the court may mediate a dispute if such mediation can be voluntarily accepted by the parties. The process of mediation can be initiated at any stage of litigation. A court may attempt to mediate a dispute at the beginning of a trial, in particular, in family disputes. It may also mediate a dispute after the hearing of substantial issues. In fact, the court often switches to the mode of mediation after it has investigated the major facts and has examined and explained to the parties their legal positions in a trial, or even before it delivers a judgment at the end of the trial.[13]

A session of mediation can be conducted by either a single judge or a court of three. Article 86 of *The Civil Procedure Law* does not prejudice one form against another. The only requirement is that the process of mediation shall be conducted in the place where the proceeding is. The court intending to commence a session of mediation is required to notify the parties in an informal manner which is

11.07

convenient to both parties and sufficient for the purpose of mediation. The court may also call for support from the relevant individuals or the parties' employers, such as witnesses (when necessary) or a conciliator, when conducting mediation. The relevant individuals or companies are obliged to co-operate with the court under Article 87 of *The Civil Procedure Law*.

The court mediating a dispute cannot force the parties to reach a settlement. Nor can it make an award of mediation. The parties have the right to terminate the session of the mediation at any stage of the mediation. A party is entitled to refuse to reach a settlement at the end of mediation. If a settlement is reached, the court will normally issue an order, which contains the cause of litigation, the agreed facts and the agreement of settlement. In special circumstances, for example, when a divorcing couple have been reconciled, when parties to a maintenance dispute have reached a settlement, when a settlement can be implemented immediately or when the dispute is too trivial to require a settlement document, the court does not have to make an order. In such cases, the court is required to record only the detail of the dispute and the settlement.

The court order has the force of law upon the signature of the parties and certification of the court and can be enforced under Articles 207 to 215 of *The Civil Procedure Law*.[14] A party to an effective order of mediation may apply to the court for its enforcement under Article 216 of *The Civil Procedure Law* if the other party refuses to comply with it. The party is expected to sign the order when it is delivered to him or her. The order is deemed ineffective until the recipient accepts it, even though it has been certified by the court. A party is entitled to renege on any agreement which has not been signed by him or her. If so, the party is allowed to litigate the same matter at the court, which is obliged to adjudicate the matter as soon as possible. Where there is no court order, the settlement becomes effective when the parties and the court have signed the court record. This means that the parties to a settlement which is not evidenced by a court order are not allowed to renege on the settlement once the record containing the settlement has been signed by them.

The order of mediation can be reviewed, or the matter mediated may be re-heard by the court under Articles 177 and 188 of *The Civil Procedure Law*. These provisions deal with the procedure for trial supervision, a procedure allowing a decision or judgment of the court which has become enforceable, to be reviewed by a competent court. Article 180 of *The Civil Procedure Law* states that a party to an effective order of mediation are entitled to apply for a re-trial if the evidence shows that the process of mediation was conducted in contrary to his or her free will or that the order of mediation is inconsistent with the law. In addition, the National High Court Directive number

174 of 1992, directs a lower court on its own initiative to review a defective order of mediation under the procedure for trial supervision, even though the parties to mediation have not applied for a review. However, Article 111(7) of *The Civil Procedure Law* disallows the plaintiff to re-litigate certain matters concerning divorce or adoption if the matter has been mediated within the previous six months.

The method of mediation may also be used by an appellate court. Article 155 of *The Civil Procedure Law* provides that the appellate court may mediate an appeal case. If the parties agree to a settlement, the court will issue an order of mediation. The order must be signed by the judges and the court clerk recording the proceedings. It must also be sealed by the court. There is no requirement for the disputing parties to sign the order, which is regarded as effective when delivered to the parties concerned. The order of mediation issued by an appellate court supersedes any judgement or order made by the lower court. It appears that mediation can be regarded as an inherent part of the judicial means of dispute resolution in China.

Court-conducted mediation is an alternative way for a court to settle a dispute. The process of mediation is less formal than the court proceedings. The court is not bound by any evidential rules, although it must be impartial and fair to both parties. It may interpret the relevant law and regulations to the parties as a mediator, thus persuading the parties to compromise voluntarily on the basis of the court's construction of the facts and law. Such compromise could be better received by the parties concerned, because it is still largely a decision of their own. This is perhaps the major rationale for allowing mediation of a dispute during the trial.

Voluntary Mediation

Mediation has its cultural basis in Chinese society. Many domestic, **11.08** family or neighbourhood disputes have been mediated in various ways by third parties who are known to the disputing parties. This type of mediation is entirely voluntary. The parties are not under legal or administrative pressure to attempt mediation, although they may be pressed to mediate by their friends and family. Such pressure, if exercised, is beyond the regulatory regime of the government. The parties have a choice of either going along with mediation, or resorting to other means, such as litigation. The existence of such mediation is based purely on the belief that friends should help each other to reach an amicable solution in order to maintain harmony within the local community. Based on the same principle, parties to any commercial disputes, including foreign investment disputes, may appoint a mediator of their choice, who may facilitate a mutual acceptable and beneficial agreement by applying any means which are both practical and effective. There is nothing wrong with this type of mediation just because it is voluntary. Nor is there any unfairness, because either party is entitled to resort to legal proceedings before, during or after the process of mediation.

The Beijing Mediation Centre for International Commercial Disputes

11.09 The Beijing Mediation Centre was set up in 1987 under the China Chamber of Commerce (China Council for the Promotion of International Trade). It deals with international commercial mediation and maritime mediation. The centre's headquarters are situated in Beijing. It presently has about 25 local branches throughout the country and about 250 listed mediators. The centre was set up in response to demands for international commercial mediation and maritime mediation from the China Chamber of Commerce.

The centre's mediation rules were made by the China Chamber of Commerce. Unlike the arbitration rules of CIETAC and CMAC, there is no doubt that the centre's mediation rules are private in nature. They are binding upon the parties by agreement only. The rules reflect the voluntary characteristics of mediation.

The centre's power to mediate a dispute is based on the parties' voluntary submission. The agreement to mediate can be made either orally or in writing, or either prior to, or after, the occurrence of a dispute. The centre may also commence a process of mediation at the request of one party and proceed with the process with the consent of the other. A considerable flexibility is seen in these arrangements.

The centre's rules are generally flexible, but incomplete in some respects. For example, the centre will certainly mediate a dispute submitted to it jointly by the parties, however the rules do not deal with this situation. This omission appears to be a defect in the rules, and gives rise to an incorrect presumption that the centre does not accept joint submission, and can lead to uncertainty when there is a joint submission. The omission is probably due to a misbelief that the centre is a Chinese "authority" which has the power to mediate international commercial disputes and maritime disputes, rather than an institution providing assistance in mediation. The same misbelief can be seen in the CIETAC Arbitration Rules and the CMAC Arbitration Rules, which only serve to make the committees look like exclusive international arbitral "authorities" in China, rather than institutions providing arbitration services.

The usual procedure for commencing a process of mediation starts from an applicant submitting an application for mediation to the centre. The centre will inform the respondent of the process and obtain his or her consent. The process of mediation can be conducted by two mediators appointed respectively by the parties from the centre's panel, or by a single mediator jointly appointed by the parties. The centre may also appoint a mediator or mediators on behalf of the parties if they so wish. The centre also has the power to appoint a single mediator if the parties wishing to be mediated by a single mediator cannot reach an agreement on the appointment. This power impinges upon the voluntary principle of mediation, and is practically inoperative because any party may terminate the process of mediation if he or she does not like the mediator chosen by the centre. Therefore, the centre should only appoint a mediator if the parties have given informed consent.

A mediator can conduct the process of mediation as he or she thinks fit. He or she can interview each parties separately or jointly, and conduct necessary meetings, etc. The conduct of mediator is subject to the centre's Rules of Conduct for the Mediator. The parties do not have to proceed with the process if they do not like the way the mediator acts. Article 15(3) of the centre's rules implies that any party may terminate a process of mediation by giving written notice to the mediator. The mediator's discretion to choose proceedings is counterbalanced by the parties' right to terminate the process. Thus, the process of mediation conducted by the centre is largely controlled by the parties themselves even though a number of the centre's authorities appear to be inconsistent with the autonomy of the parties in mediation.

The process of mediation is subject to the principle of confidentiality. A mediator may disclose information to each party as he or she considers necessary. But, he or she cannot reveal a party's confidential information to the other party. A party must specifically inform the mediator of the confidential nature of the information to override the mediator's discretion in disclosing necessary information. The confidentiality extends to the evidence and information provided, or admissions made, by the parties in the process of mediation. The evidence, information and admissions cannot be used by any party in subsequent proceedings of arbitration or litigation.

The settlement should be signed by the parties and the mediator. However this settlement does not appear to have any legally binding force at all. The rules do not prohibit the parties from submitting the mediated matter to an arbitral body or the court of law. Nor is there any law prohibiting the parties to a settlement of mediation from litigating on the same matter. This feature of the mediation settlement is consistent with the international practices. The centre's fee for mediation is based on a progressive fee schedule. Depending on the sum in dispute, the centre charges a percentage of the sum, ranging from 0.5 per cent to 6 per cent.

Arbitration

Legal Framework of Arbitration

11.10 The legal framework for arbitration in China is based on *The Arbitration Law*, which is supported by a number of laws, regulations and rules whose existence is authorized by *The Arbitration Law*. The legal framework consists of the following major legislation and rules:

(a) *The Arbitration Law*;
(b) *The Civil Procedure Law*;
(c) The Arbitration Rules of the China International Economic and Trade Arbitration Commission (CIETAC);[15]
(d) The Arbitration Rules of the China Maritime Arbitration Commission (CMAC);[16]
(e) *Foreign Economic Contract Law*;
(f) Relevant provisions of the laws on foreign-invested enterprises;
(g) Relevant provisions of *The Labour Law*;
(h) State Council Measures for Resolving Labour Disputes in Enterprises; and
(i) Relevant provisions of the laws on contractual management of farming land.

Types of Arbitration in China

11.11 Arbitration is an important part of dispute resolution in China. It is commonly used in dealing with economic or commercial disputes. According to the arbitral bodies involved, arbitration can be divided into five categories: international commercial arbitration by CIETAC, maritime arbitration by CMAC, arbitration of labour disputes by the labour arbitration commission, arbitration of contractual disputes involving farming of collective land and arbitration of all disputes by the arbitration commission set up under *The Arbitration Law*.

These categories reflect the present state of arbitration in China. The precise relationships between the arbitration commission set up under *The Arbitration Law* and other specialized arbitration commissions are yet to be clarified. *The Arbitration Law* establishes the arbitration commissions in all medium-sized cities. It does not specifically deal with the co-existence between the arbitration commission and the specialised arbitration commissions. It can be assumed that the continuous existence of the above-mentioned four types of arbitration is warranted under *The Arbitration Law*, because none of them appears to be significantly inconsistent with *The Arbitration Law*, though necessary changes must be effected to ensure the consistence between them. These categories of arbitration will be examined in turn.

International Commercial Arbitration by CIETAC

What Is International Commercial Arbitration?

In China, international commercial arbitration refers to arbitration of   **11.12** commercial disputes arising from the legal relationships between a Chinese legal or natural person and a foreign legal or natural person, or between two foreign legal or natural persons. Arbitration of a commercial dispute between two Chinese legal or natural persons also falls within the definition if the dispute involves international commercial or economic relationships, such as foreign economic contracts or overseas property. Thus, a commercial dispute can be international by virtue of the parties involved or by reason of the subject-matter concerned. Arbitration of such a dispute is regarded as international commercial arbitration.

What is CIETAC?

CIETAC stands for the China International Economic and Trade Arbitration Commission, which is attached to the China Council for the Promotion of International Trade. The China Council for the Promotion of International Trade is said to be an unofficial organization. It presently performs also the functions of the China Chamber of Commerce. Thus, CIETAC is said to be an unofficial arbitral institution. But it is difficult to treat the China Council for the Promotion of International Trade and CIETAC as unofficial organizations in the same way as private arbitration institutions in Western countries, because of the administrative and financial connections between these organizations and the Chinese government. Given the historical environment from which CIETAC was created, it can be regarded as a semi-private and semi-official institution, which is currently being transformed into a fully private status, like the International Chamber of Commerce, American Arbitration Association, the Netherlands Arbitration Institute, and the Arbitration Institute of the Stockholm Chamber of Commerce, etc. However, the fact that CIETAC was substantially government funded does not affect its status as an independent and impartial arbitrator in resolving international commercial disputes.

CIETAC was initially established in 1956 as the Foreign Trade Arbitration Commission under the 1954 Decision of the Executive Council of the Central Government to Set Up the Foreign Trade

Arbitration Commission within the China Council for the Promotion of International Trade. The Foreign Trade Arbitration Commission was renamed in 1980 as the Foreign Economic and Trade Arbitration Commission, which in 1988 became CIETAC. Presently, CIETAC remains a body established within the China Council for the Promotion of International Trade, which, however, also became the China Chamber of Commerce after China joined the International Chamber of Commerce. *The Arbitration Law* requires an international arbitration institution to be part of the China Chamber of Commerce. Therefore, CIETAC is regarded as part of the China Chamber of Commerce, even though no structural change has been made to effect this transformation.

The first arbitration rules of CIETAC were formed in 1956. They were replaced by the Arbitration Rules of CIETAC in 1988. The 1988 rules were amended in 1994, and again in 1995 to incorporate the requirements of *The Arbitration Law*. The arbitration proceedings of CIETAC are exclusively governed by the Arbitration Rules, which were formulated by the China Chamber of Commerce in September 1995.

CIETAC has grown significantly since its inauguration in 1956. In 1956 there were 21 listed arbitrators of Chinese nationality. Between 1959 and 1965, the Commission received only 27 cases.[17] Between 1967 and 1979, the Commission arbitrated 11 cases and mediated 60, and also provided advisory opinions to several hundred cases.[18] The number of arbitrators increased to 65 in 1980, and 71 in 1983.[19] The Commission's caseloads grew rapidly in the 1980s. For example, the Commission accepted 37 cases in 1985, 75 in 1986, 129 in 1987, 162 in 1988, 310 in 1988,[20] and 182 in 1989.[21] The growth continued in the 1990s. CIETAC received 238 cases in 1990,[22] 274 in 1991 (205 resolved), 267 in 1992 (236 resolved), 504 in 1993 (486 resolved), 829 in 1994 (574 resolved) and 902 in 1995 (867 resolved).[23] CIETAC presently has about 291 listed arbitrators, of whom 203 are Chinese and 88 are foreign nationals.[24] CIETAC's headquarters are currently situated in Beijing. It has branches in Shanghai and Shenzhen.

Status of the CIETAC's Arbitration Rules

11.13   The CIETAC's Arbitration Rules were made by the China Chamber of Commerce. The status of the Rules may be arguable in theory. If the Council is an official body, it would be able to exercise its delegated legislative power under the Chinese Constitution and the relevant regulations of the State Council. If it is an unofficial organization, it cannot in theory exercise delegated legislative power. Nor should an unofficial body make any regulations or rules which have the force of law. Article 1 of the CIETAC Arbitration Rules is rather confusing. It provides that the rules are made in pursuance of *The Arbitration Law* and other relevant laws, the 1954 Decision of the former Executive Council of the Central Government to set up CIETAC and the State Council's notice and approval. This provision suggests that the China Chamber of Commerce has been authorized to make the rules. Such authority is unnecessary for an unofficial body to make its private rules, although the rules so made must be consistent with law.

The CIETAC Arbitration Rules are largely inflexible. Presently, the parties cannot by agreement modify the arbitration proceedings conducted by CIETAC. Nor are they allowed to adopt another set of procedural rules while submitting the dispute to CIETAC. Although the same practice has been adopted by arbitral institutions in a number of countries, *e.g.*, the American Arbitration Association, the rigidity in insisting on the use of the CIETAC Arbitration Rules could rather be discouraging to parties who are more comfortable with flexible arbitration practices. The CIETAC Arbitration Rules must be accepted in entirety. Once a dispute has been submitted to CIETAC for arbitration, the CIETAC's Arbitration Rules are deemed to have been accepted by the parties by virtue of Article 7 of the CIETAC Arbitration Rules.

No matter whether or not the CIETAC Arbitration Rules have the status of law, the application of the rules is subject to the limited supervision of the court. Article 260(1) of *The Civil Procedure Law* allows the court to refuse to enforce an arbitral award of any Chinese international arbitration authority, such as CIETAC and CMAC, on the grounds that there was no arbitration agreement to submit the dispute to the authority. Article 260(2) authorizes the court to set aside an arbitral award on the grounds that the applicant did not receive the notice of arbitration, or on the grounds that the applicant was denied natural justice. Article 260(3) empowers the court to set aside an arbitral award, if the constitution of the arbitral tribunal or the procedure of the tribunal has contravened the relevant law. Article 260(4) makes an award unenforceable if the arbitrator did not have authority to arbitrate the matter concerned or if the enforcement contravenes the public interest. These provisions cover most of the CIETAC Rules, although the interpretation of the rules is an issue yet to be judicially considered in China.[25] It must also be pointed out that Article 260 may not apply to a party which is deemed to have waived the right to challenge procedural irregularities by acquiescence under Article 45 of the CIETAC Arbitration Rules.

Arbitration Agreement and CIETAC Arbitration

Arbitration agreement is the basis of the CIETAC authority to arbi- **11.14** trate a dispute. As set out in Articles 3 to 6 of the Arbitration Rules, an agreement must be in writing. It can be made as either part of a contract or an independent document, and formed either prior to, or after, the occurrence of the dispute. It can be evidenced by any written forms, such as letters, telegrams, faxes, or other documentation, but whether the written form extends to electronic messages is not yet established. An agreement to arbitrate may also be inferred from the communications between the parties, because CIETAC has the power to rule on the existence and validity of an arbitration agreement, as well as the appropriateness of its own jurisdiction. The CIETAC's power to rule on its own authority to hear a dispute is a wide and arbitral power and should be subject to the court's supervision. This is why in 1995, Article 4 of the Arbitration Rules was amended to incorporate the statement that if one party requests CIETAC to rule on the existence of an agreement or the appropriateness of its jurisdiction but the other party submits the matter to a court, the matter shall be determined by the court. It must be pointed out, however, once CIETAC has ruled on the said matters, the ruling may not be challenged under Article 260 of *The Civil Procedure Law* for the generality of Article 260. Depending on the judicial interpretation of Article 260, the CIETAC's ruling on the appropriateness of its jurisdiction may not fall under the provision at all.

The CIETAC Arbitration Rules do not require the parties to specify the matter to be arbitrated. Sometimes, the parties may only wish an arbitral body to determine a point of law which will provide a basis for their future negotiation. If so, it is the responsibility of the parties to ensure that the scope of arbitration has been clearly defined in the arbitration agreement. If not, there may be a risk that CIETAC may arbitrate the whole dispute for the parties. The Rules only require the existence of a written agreement as the basis of CIETAC's authority to arbitrate, but does not define the meaning of "dispute". Moreover, if CIETAC has power to determine its own jurisdiction, there is always a risk that it may, by mistake perhaps, give itself more authority than has been mutually agreed. Thus, it is always a good practice to clearly define the "dispute" which is to be submitted for arbitration. If CIETAC exceeds the authority actually agreed by the parties, the party can only ask the court to deny the enforcement of the award under Article 260 of *The Civil Procedure Law*. Given the ambiguity of the relevant laws, it may not be easy to say the tribunal did not have authority to hear a matter after the CIETAC had ruled that it had an appropriate jurisdiction over the matter.

Commencement of Arbitration Proceedings

11.15 An arbitration proceeding is initiated by an applicant submitting a dispute in pursuance of an arbitration agreement to CIETAC. The proceeding commences from the date when CIETAC issues a notice of arbitration. Both parties should choose an arbitrator from the panel of CIETAC within 20 days from the date of receiving the notice of arbitration, or authorize the chairman of CIETAC to appoint arbitrators on their behalf. If a party fails to do so, the chairman of CIETAC will appoint an arbitrator on behalf of him or her. The respondent should submit a statement of defence within 45 days from the date of receiving the notice of arbitration. His or her failure to comply with this requirement does not prevent the tribunal from hearing the case according to the schedule. If the respondent wishes to file a counter-claim, he or she must do so within 60 days from the date of receiving the notice of arbitration. A respondent who fails to comply with the requirement will presumably lose his or her right to make a counter-claim. The tribunal's discretionary power to allow the applicant to amend the statement of claim and to allow the respondent to amend the counter-claim does not appear to extend to the filing of a counter-claim after the expiry of the 60 day limitation period. The time requirements must be complied with by the parties as the CIETAC's authority to hear the dispute cannot be seriously challenged late, because CIETAC has power under Article 42 of the Rules to make a default award. The CIETAC Rules require the applicant to deposit a sum of arbitration fees with it according to the schedule of fees. The parties' request to preserve each other's property as security is to be heard by the competent court in the place where the property is located. If a party requests CIETAC to preserve the evidence obtained in the proceedings, the request should be ruled by the Intermediate Court of the place where the evidence is collected.

Constitution of an Arbitral Tribunal Under the CIETAC's Rules

The tribunal consists of either three arbitrators or a single arbitrator. For a three member tribunal, two arbitrators should be appointed by the parties one for each side and a third, who is the president of the tribunal, is either appointed jointly by the parties or chosen by the chairman of CIETAC if the parties so wish. The chairman has the power to appoint all three arbitrators if the parties so authorized, or if the parties failed to comply with the procedure. It appears that once CIETAC's machine has been activated, the parties only have a limited autonomy to choose arbitrators, because the combined effect of Articles 16, 24 and 26 is that all three arbitrators would be appointed by the chairman if the parties failed to appoint anyone within the time specified. If the tribunal consist of a single arbitrator, he or she can be jointly appointed by the parties or by the chairman in pursuance of the rules. A request to withdraw an arbitrator from the proceedings can be made 15 days prior to the first hearing, but may also be made in special circumstances anytime before the tribunal delivers its award.

Hearing by CIETAC

A tribunal may arbitrate a dispute by way of hearing, or by written submissions only if the parties so wish. The tribunal is obliged to notify the parties of the time of the first hearing at least 30 days prior to the date of hearing. Any request to postpone the first hearing must be made at least 12 days prior to the scheduled date and is subject to the discretion of the tribunal. The 30 day notice rule applies to the first hearing only. If a party wishes to challenge an arbitral award on the grounds that no sufficient notice was given prior to the subsequent hearings, he or she must prove why the notice was insufficient in the circumstances concerned.

The hearing is normally conducted in private. If both parties wish to have a public hearing, the tribunal will determine whether a public hearing is suitable. The tribunal cannot allow a public hearing if only one of the parties so wishes. The confidentiality of the hearing prohibits unauthorized disclosure of the confidential information by the persons attending the hearing, eg., the parties, their legal representatives, experts, witnesses and tribunal staff.

The parties are entitled to have legal representation. They can provide evidence, experts and witnesses to support their cases. The tribunal may also call its own evidence, experts and witnesses when making an investigation. No rule of evidence is set out in the CIETAC Arbitration Rules. The tribunal makes the final decision as to the admissibility or reliability of any evidence or expert's opinion. The tribunal's award cannot be challenged for non-compliance of any evidential rules or of even any acceptable practice, unless any provision of the Arbitration Rules has not been complied with by the tribunal.

Mediation During the Arbitration Proceedings

11.16 The CIETAC Arbitration Rules allow a tribunal to mediate a dispute during the proceedings. The power to mediate is based on the voluntary consent of the parties, which can be obtained by the tribunal at the request of one of the parties. The tribunal does not have to follow the procedure of the Arbitration Rules when conducting mediation. Nor can it force the parties to reach a settlement when mediating. If the parties can reach a settlement, they should sign a written agreement of mediation. They are entitled to decide the legal effect of the settlement so reached. If they do not reach an agreement on the effect of the mediation agreement, the tribunal has the power to grant an arbitral award on the basis of the agreement. The difference between the two results is that the award so made will be enforceable unless it can be challenged under law. The Arbitration Rules do not provide an express answer to the situation where the parties to a mediation agreement made in a non-award form, want to arbitrate the same matter. According to Article 44 of the CIETAC Arbitration Rules which gives the chairman of CIETAC discretion in determining whether to accept a dispute that has been settled by private mediation outside CIETAC during a previous proceeding, the said situation may also be subject to the discretionary power of the chairman. The parties to a non-award form of mediation agreement appear to have the right to litigate the same matter, because *The Civil Procedure Law* does not expressly deprive them of the right.

The CIETAC Arbitration Rules also allow the parties to reconcile their differences outside CIETAC whilst a CIETAC proceeding is going on. If a settlement has been reached by the parties in negotiation, the tribunal will allow the parties to withdraw from the proceedings if they so wish. If the parties reconciled their differences after the tribunal has commenced a process of mediation, the private settlement is regarded as the result of mediation, rather than negotiation. This means that the tribunal will make an award in pursuance of the terms of the settlement, if the parties do not object to the making of this award.

The process of mediation conducted by a tribunal is subject to the principle of confidentiality and the principle of "without prejudice". If an attempt to mediation fails, the parties are not allowed to use the information or evidence obtained in the process of mediation to challenge the other party's position, or to strengthen his or her own position, in the resumed arbitration proceedings. Nor can the tribunal make an assessment on the basis of the information disclosed in the process of mediation.

The Making of an Arbitral Award

The tribunal is required to make an award on the basis of relevant **11.17** facts, law, contractual terms, commercial customs and usage. It must also act impartially and independently, and apply equitable principles and the notion of fairness if necessary. The exercise of the above-power is not subject to judicial supervision, because the tribunal is a private body whose authority to arbitrate is based on the parties' consent. Nor is the making of an arbitral award subject to any administrative review for the same reason. The relevant Chinese laws either disallow an appeal from an arbitral award or provide no access to the review of an arbitral award made by CIETAC.[26]

The tribunal is required to deliver an award within nine months after its constitution. It is required to provide reasons for its decision. The majority's view is regarded as the tribunal's decision. In the case of a hung-decision, the president's view prevails. The minority arbitrator is entitled to reserve his or her dissenting opinion in the tribunal's record, and does not have to sign the award if he or she so wishes. An arbitrator is expected to consult CIETAC about the formality of an award before delivering his or her decision, although CIETAC cannot influence the independence of the arbitrator in making the award. The award becomes effective from the date when it is signed and sealed by CIETAC. The tribunal has the power to determine the fee payable and to order costs against a party.

The tribunal can, at the request of a party, make an interim award or partial award. The effect of such an award is not clear. It should be enforceable in law. But whether or not the non-compliance of a party with such an award can affect his or her position in the final award is unclear. Article 57 of the Arbitration Rules says that a refusal by a party to perform an interim or partial order neither affects the continuation of the proceeding, nor the making of the final award. If a party is allowed to ignore an interim or partial award against him or her, the authority of the law will be undermined. Article 57 may suggest that the proceeding of arbitration continues whether or not an interim or partial award has been complied. However, if the party against him or her the award has been made, refused to comply with it, the loss flowing from the refusal should be taken into account in the making of the final award.

After the making of an award, the parties may request the tribunal in writing to correct any mistakes in the award within 30 days from the time he or she receives the award. The tribunal has the power to rectify any errors in the award within 30 days from the time it delivers the award to the parties. If the parties request the tribunal to make a supplementary award on any matter which should have been dealt with in the award, the request must be made in writing within 30 days after the receipt of the award. Similarly, the tribunal may also make a supplementary award at its own initiative within 30 days from the delivery of the award.

The Effect of an Arbitral Award

11.18 Article 60 of the CIETAC Arbitration Rules provides that the arbitral award of CIETAC is final. A party is not allowed to appeal to the court of law for a review of the award. Nor can he or she apply for a review of the award to any other authorities, such as the government or an administrative review authority. This provision effectively deprives the parties of the right of appeal against a CIETAC award unless a ground of appeal has been specifically provided for by a particular law. This is consistent with international practice.

The CIETAC's arbitral award can be enforced either by the parties voluntarily or by a court order. But, the court may refuse to enforce an arbitral award in certain circumstances. As we have seen, an award made by CIETAC can be set aside by a court of law under Article 260 of *The Civil Procedure Law*. This provision provides the following grounds on which a CIETAC's arbitral award may be regarded as unenforceable:

- (a) there is no agreement of arbitration;
- (b) the applicant did not receive the notice of arbitration;
- (c) the applicant was not given an opportunity to state his or her case;[27]
- (d) the constitution of the arbitral tribunal contravened the CIETAC Arbitration Rules;
- (e) the proceedings contravened the CIETAC Arbitration Rules;
- (f) the tribunal exceeded the authority given by the arbitration agreement;
- (g) the tribunal did not have authority to arbitrate the matter concerned; or
- (h) the enforcement of the award contravenes the public interest or public policy.

The above grounds suggest that an award cannot be challenged on the grounds of error of law, or misinterpretation of a custom or usage. In other words, the reasoning process of an award is generally not challengeable. If a tribunal has grossly abused or misused its power, the award may be challenged on the public policy or public interest grounds. However, any technical error or insignificant misinterpretation of law does not render a CIETAC award reviewable by a court of law in China. This practice is consistent with the New York Convention on the Enforcement of Foreign Arbitral Awards.

The right to challenge the enforcement of an award may be lost by acquiescence. Article 45 of the Arbitration Rules states that if a party knew or ought to have known the non-compliance of any provision of the Rules, but still proceeded with the proceedings and failed to raise his or her objection in writing, he or she is deemed to have waived the right to object to the irregularities. Can this provision prevail over Article 260 of *The Civil Procedure Law*? Article 260 does not expressly impose estoppel against the applicant. Nor does it appear to be legalistic to deprive a person of his or her right of judicial review under *The Civil Procedure Law* by a waiver provision of a document which probably does not have the force of law. The interpretation of Article 45 is yet to be seen.

Enforcement of the CIETAC's Award Overseas

11.19 China ratified the New York Convention in 1986. It made two reservations when giving effect to the Convention. The first reservation is that China only enforces the Convention on the basis of mutual recognition, thus refusing to enforce an award made in a country which does not enforce the awards made in China. The second reservation is that in China the Convention only applies to the disputes arising from the contractual or non-contractual relationships which are recognized in Chinese law, thus making certain arbitral awards concerning arguable commercial relationships, such as some State-engaged commercial activities, unenforceable in China.

A number of CIETAC arbitral awards have been enforced in foreign courts of law, such as the United States, Canada, France, Germany, New Zealand, Japan and Hong Kong.[28] For example, a contractual dispute arose in 1988 from a contract for the sale of paper pulp by a New Zealand company to a Chinese buyer. The Chinese party submitted the dispute to CIETAC pursuant to the arbitration clause of the contract. The New Zealand company refused to appear before the tribunal, which made an award in default against the New Zealand company. The award was recognized by the New Zealand court, which made an order in default against the New Zealand company to enforce the award. The New Zealand company was eventually closed because of its inability to repay its debts.[29]

Most overseas enforcement of CIETAC awards take place in Hong Kong, because of the extensive commercial contacts between China and Hong Kong. A foreign applicant may seek enforcement of a CIETAC award in Hong Kong against a Chinese party. He or she may also wish to enforce an award against another foreign party, because there are so many foreign establishments in Hong Kong. However, most cases of enforcement arise between Chinese applicants and Hong Kong companies. For example, a Chinese applicant from Shenzhen sought to enforce a CIETAC award against a Hong Kong company in 1991. The respondent relied on the English version of the contract which chose Hong Kong as the forum of arbitration and also argued that the CIETAC Arbitration Rules of 1988 were not applicable because the 1956 Rules were chosen. The Hong Kong court found that the English version relied upon by the respondent had been replaced by a Chinese-English version which specified Beijing as the forum of arbitration, and that the 1988 Rules are similar to the 1956 Rules and are more favourable to the respondent. Accordingly, the court enforced the award against the Hong Kong company.[30]

Simplified Proceedings of CIETAC

A tribunal may adopt a simplified proceeding on its own initiative to arbitrate a dispute involving less than Renminbi 500,000 yen. It may also apply a simplified proceeding with the parties' consent, even though the value of the dispute exceeds 500,000 yen. A simplified proceeding is simpler in all aspects than a formal proceeding. Only one arbitrator is needed to constitute a tribunal. The parties must file a statement of defence and a counter-claim, if any, within 30 days from the time of receiving the notice of arbitration. If a hearing is required, the tribunal is required to give a notice of the hearing ten days prior to the scheduled date of hearing. There is only one hearing for the proceeding. The tribunal can make an award in default. In a trial by way of hearing, the tribunal is required to deliver its award within 30 days from the date of the hearing. If it is a trial by submissions only, the tribunal is required to deliver an award within 90 days after the constitution of the tribunal. An award made in a simplified proceeding has the same effect as one made in a formal proceeding, and is subject to the same procedure of court supervision.

Arbitration of Disputes Involving Bond Dealers and Stock Markets

In 1994 the State Council Securities Commission authorized CIETAC **11.20**
as the sole arbitral authority to arbitrate disputes arising between bond dealers or securities houses, or between the dealers and the management of stock markets. These disputes are not necessarily international, but need to be arbitrated by an institution which has adequate resources and expertise. In the absence of an adequate domestic commercial arbitral institution, the State Council Securities Commission has chosen CIETAC to perform the task.

CIETAC will form special arbitration rules for arbitrating disputes arising between the bond dealers, securities houses, or between the dealers and the management of stock markets. It has formed a special panel for arbitrating these disputes. The panel currently consists of 62 arbitrators. An arbitrator can be listed on both the panel for international commercial arbitration and the panel for securities-related disputes. Presently, only CIETAC's headquarters in Beijing can hear these disputes. But, there is no reason why the branches in Shanghai and Shenzhen cannot hear them once the relevant rules have been finalized. CIETAC's role in arbitrating these disputes is yet to be developed.

Maritime Arbitration

What Is CMAC?

11.21 CMAC stands for China Maritime Arbitration Commission. It was initially established in 1959 as the Maritime Arbitration Commission as a subsidiary to the China Council for the Promotion of International Trade by the order of the State Council. In 1988, the State Council renamed it the China Maritime Arbitration Commission, which remains within the China Council for the Promotion of International Trade. *The Arbitration Law* requires international arbitration institutions of China to be managed by the China Chamber of Commerce. Maritime arbitration is subject to this requirement by virtue of Article 65 of *The Arbitration Law*. Thus, CMAC is presently a subsidiary to the China Chamber of Commerce, whose functions are performed by the China Council for the Promotion of International Trade.

CMAC has the same status as CIETAC. It is said to be an unofficial arbitral institution, but is different from any private arbitral institutions in western countries. Given that the China Council for the Promotion of International Trade (China Chamber of Commerce) is in the process of being transformed into a private organization, CMAC may be "privatized" if the transformation of the China Council for the Promotion of International Trade is successful. However, the ambiguous status of CMAC as an unofficial arbitral institution does not affect its ability to act as an independent and impartial arbitrator in maritime cases. CMAC is situated in Beijing and has about 66 arbitrators.[31] Its caseload is much smaller than that of CIETAC. For example, CMAC received 10 cases in 1990, 8 in 1991 and 14 in 1992.[32] The present CMAC Arbitration Rules were made by the China Chamber of Commerce in 1995. They are identical in most aspects to the CIETAC Arbitration Rules.

Jurisdiction of CMAC

CMAC deals with all maritime cases, whether domestic or international. The written arbitration agreement, which can be either part of a contract or an independent document, forms the basis of CMAC's jurisdiction over the matter in dispute. The commission has the power to determine the validity of an agreement or the appropriateness of its jurisdiction if necessary. But, if a party submits the validity of the agreement or the appropriateness of the CMAC's jurisdiction to a court of law, the issue should be adjudicated by the court. Under Article 2 of the CMAC Arbitration Rules, the following categories of cases can be submitted to CMAC:

(a) disputes arising from salvage and general average;

(b) disputes arising from collision between vessels, or from damage caused by a vessel to the structure and installation on the sea, waterways connected with sea, in the harbour as well as the submarine or underwater installation;

(c) disputes arising from management, operation, chartering, mortgage, agency, towage, raising, sale, repair, building, demolition, of seagoing/river vessels, as well as carriage by sea by virtue of contracts of affreightment, bill of lading or other documents, and marine insurance;

(d) disputes regarding the utilisation of the marine resources and pollution damages to the marine environment;

(e) dispute arising from contract of freight forwarding, supply of ship's stores, employment of seaman aboard a foreign vessel, fishery production and fishing; and

(f) other maritime disputes submitted for arbitration by agreement between the parties.

The above grounds effectively embrace all marine-related disputes that could been submitted to CMAC voluntarily by the parties.

Commencement of CMAC Proceedings

Like the CIETAC proceeding, the CMAC proceeding commences **11.22** when the applicant files the complaint documents with the commission. The respondent should appoint an arbitrator within 20 days after receipt of the notice of arbitration. If he or she fails to do so, the chairman of CMAC will appoint an arbitrator on his or her behalf. The respondent should file a statement of defence, or a counter-claim if any, within 45 days after the receipt of the notice of arbitration. Failure to comply with the requirement by the respondent may not affect the progress of the proceedings because the tribunal may deliver an award in default.

Constitution of the Tribunal

The tribunal consists of either three arbitrators or a single arbitrator. If three arbitrators are required, each party should appoint an arbitrator of his or her choice and jointly appoint the third presiding arbitrator. The parties may also authorize the chairman of the commission to appoint all arbitrators. The single arbitrator can be appointed jointly by the parties, or by the chairman of the commission in pursuance of the Rules. The party can, when necessary and reasonable, request an arbitrator to withdraw from the proceedings any time before the closing of the last proceeding. The request is subject to the discretion of the chairman of the commission.

Proceedings of the Tribunal

The tribunal can have a private hearing, or deal with the case by way of submissions. If a hearing is to be held, CMAC must notify the parties of the time and venue at least 30 days prior to the first hearing. Public hearings are held only at the request of the parties. Legal representations are allowed. Evidence, experts and witnesses may be called for by the parties. The tribunal has the power to carry out its own investigation and call necessary evidence, experts and witnesses. The tribunal has the power to mediate a dispute provided that it has obtained the parties' consent. If the parties reach a settlement outside the proceedings, they can withdraw the case from the tribunal. If the parties wish to re-submit a case which has been settled by the parties themselves, the chairman has the discretion in determining whether to accept the case.

Most of the CMAC cases involve bills of lading and charter parties. The salvage cases usually go to the maritime court of China by the parties' optior. The disputes heard by CMAC have arisen from damage to goods, short delivery, damage to vessels, calculation of laytime, withdrawal of vessels, loss arising from the detention of vessel, loss arising from incorrect orders, cargo inspection charges, demurrage, seaworthiness of the vessel, loss arising from the late return of vessels, negligence of tallymen and stevedores, the agency, master's right to choose the correct route and payment of radio charges etc.[33] CMAC's practice is consistent with international standards. The cases are dealt with on the basis of the bills of lading, charter parties, customs, usage, and common international practices.

Arbitral Awards of the Tribunal

The tribunal is obliged to give an award within nine months after the constitution of the tribunal. The majority's view is deemed to be the decision of the tribunal. If necessary, the tribunal can make an interim or partial award, whose effect has not been clearly stated in the Rules. The tribunal may also make an award on the basis of the agreement of mediation. The parties are not able to stop the tribunal from turning the agreement of mediation into an arbitral award. The award of the tribunal is final. A party cannot submit the same dispute to a court of law if dissatisfied with the award. Nor can he or she ask any other authorities to review the award. But, the enforcement of the award is subject to Article 260 of *The Civil Procedure Law*.

Arbitration of Labour Disputes

The Legal Framework for Arbitrating Labour Disputes

Labour disputes are subject to *The Labour Law* and State Council   **11.23**
Measures for Resolving Labour Disputes in Enterprises. The Regulations on Labour Management in Sino-Foreign Joint Equity Ventures
although they have not been repealed, may not have any practical
implication at all because a joint equity venture is a Chinese legal
person and thus an "enterprise" with the meaning of *The Labour Law*
and State Council Measures. Any enterprise, whether it is a Chinese
legal person or not, is governed by *The Labour Law* and the State
Council Measures as long as it is an enterprise. The labour disputes
arising from a governmental organization or an unincorporated body
are subject to the same law.

The State Council Measures for Resolving Labour Disputes in Enterprises regulate labour dispute system. Under the Measures, a labour
mediation committee is set up within each enterprise and the labour
arbitration commission is established at the local government in each
county, municipality or district within a municipality. The system of
labour dispute arbitration has been retained under *The Arbitration
Law*, which purports to streamline the national system of arbitration.
One of the essential characteristics of labour arbitration is that the
process of arbitration is compulsory before the parties can resort to a
court of law.[34]

Mechanism of Arbitration

The labour arbitration commission is a governmental authority set up
within a certain level of local government. It is usually established at
the level of a county government, a municipal government when the
municipality does not have districts under its jurisdiction or a district
government when the municipality has districts under it. Each commission is responsible for arbitrating labour disputes within its jurisdiction. There is no appellate arbitration mechanism at a higher level of
government to supervise the lower government. Article 17 of the
Measures appears to suggest that in a municipality with districts the
arbitration commission can be set up within both the municipal government and the district government. Even so, the wording of this
provision implies that the commissions at the two levels of government
have different responsibilities which are not of a supervisory nature.

The arbitration commission consists of representatives of the labour
department, the unions, and the relevant governmental departments as
nominated by local government. The representative of the labour department acts as the chairman of the commission. The commission

can nominate full-time or part-time arbitrators from the governmental departments, unions, experts and legal professionals to constitute a panel of arbitrators.

Labour arbitration is compulsory. The arbitration commission has the power to appoint arbitrator(s) for the parties, when the dispute is submitted to the commission. The commission can appoint either three arbitrators or a single arbitrator (in a simple dispute) to constitute a tribunal. The parties do not appear to have any right to choose their own arbitrators, even though the autonomy to choose arbitrators is one of the basic rights of the parties in most proceedings for commercial arbitration.

Proceedings of Labour Arbitration

11.24   An applicant must commence an arbitration proceeding in writing within six months from the time he or she knew or ought to have known of the violation of his or her rights. The tribunal is obliged under Article 23 of the Measures to hear the dispute if the elapse of the limitation period was not caused by the applicant's fault. This provision is potentially litigious for two reasons. First, the commission has an obligation to hear a dispute, rather than a discretion in determining whether to hear it, once the applicant has proved that the delay had been caused by an event beyond his or her control, or that the delay had been reasonable in the circumstances concerned. However, whether or not the applicant has proved the delay was not caused by his or her fault is subject to the discretion of the tribunal. If the tribunal is not satisfied with the evidence that the delay was not due to the applicant's fault, its obligation to hear the dispute does not arise. The applicant may wish to challenge the decision of the tribunal when an action has been denied, even though there is a lack of clear guidance in law to warrant such a challenge.

Secondly, the applicant whose action at the tribunal is time barred may also be arguably denied access to the court. The present system of labour dispute resolution makes arbitration a prerequisite for litigation. *The Civil Procedure Law* has no provision to deal with the situation. If *The Civil Procedure Law* is construed as allowing the applicant to have the last recourse at the court of law, the construction may encourage the applicant to a labour dispute to circumvent the compulsory arbitration by an inactivity within the limitation period. If *The Civil Procedure Law* is interpreted as denying access to a court of law after the expiry of the limitation period, the combined effect of the Measures for Resolving Labour Disputes and *The Civil Procedure Law* is that the applicant's right to legal protection will be deprived of by an executive authority exercising limited judicial power, which, however, is not subject to any judicial supervision.

The arbitration commission must reply to the applicant within seven days after receiving the application whether to hear the dispute. If accepted, the commission must inform the respondent of the proceedings and appoint a tribunal within seven days from the date of acceptance. The respondent must submit a statement of defence within 15 days from the time when the notice of arbitration is received. The tribunal must notify the parties of the date of hearing at least four days prior to the scheduled hearing. If the respondent fails to make submission or to appear at the hearing, then the tribunal can make an award in default. If the applicant fails to attend the hearing, the tribunal may regard the application as having being withdrawn.

The tribunal encourages the parties to reconcile their differences or to mediate their dispute during the arbitration proceedings. The parties are allowed to negotiate a settlement after the commencement of the proceedings. The tribunal will also initiate a mediation process if it thinks there is any possibility of a voluntary settlement. It will make an agreement of mediation if the dispute has been settled. The agreement so made has legal effect under Article 28 of the Measures and is enforceable in the same way as an arbitral award according to Article 31 of the Measures.

The tribunal should deliver its award within 60 days from the date of its constitution. The commission may allow a 30 day extension when necessary. The majority's decision forms the tribunal's award. The tribunal is expected to consult the arbitration commission and follow its decision in important and difficult cases. This suggests that the tribunal is not an independent body. In fact, the Measures do not provide an independent status to the arbitration commission at all. It can be argued that the award of the commission is not different from an administrative decision, although the award is enforceable in law. The party intending to appeal against an award must do so within 15 days from the date of receiving the award. After an award becomes effective, the party intending to challenge it can only rely on Articles 177 to 185 of *The Civil Procedure Law* to ask a court to review the award.

Arbitration of Contractual Disputes involving Farming of Collective Land

Article 77 of *The Arbitration Law* states that labour disputes and **11.25** internal disputes arising from contractual management of collective-owned farming land are subject to special law. This provides the basis for the existence of an independent arbitration system for resolving disputes arising from contractual management of farming land within a collective. The system is meant to resolve farming contract disputes arising between collective members. However, there is presently no national law regulating the arbitration system and the matter is entirely subject to various types of local legislation, made by local authorities ranging from a provincial government to a county government.

According to the local governments' practices, the arbitration commission is usually set up at the level of county or township as part of the local government. The commission is an administrative authority with a governmental official as the chairman. Some local governments require an arbitration agreement to commence the arbitration proceedings, the rest allow the proceeding to be commenced by a party's unilateral submission. The administrative discretion is inevitably exercised when the commission assumes the power to arbitrate on the basis of one party's submission. Mediation is also emphasized in the proceedings conducted by the arbitration commission. Because of the nature of farming land disputes, the arbitration commission has often ordered or allowed one party to proceed with the contract after the party has provided adequate undertaking to the commission.

The award of the commission is enforceable in law. Because of the lack of national law in this field, the enforceability of the award is subject to the discretion of the local court. Some local governments allow a dissatisfied party to appeal against the arbitral award at the court of law. Some permit the dissatisfied party to appeal only to an appellate arbitral commission which is a higher government authority. Whether or not these local laws can effectively deprive parties of their access to the court of law is an unsettled question. *The Civil Procedure Law* does not provide an answer to the question. The system needs urgent streamlining by the national government if it is to continue as part of the arbitration mechanism in China.

Arbitration under *The Arbitration Law*

Chinese Arbitration System and The Arbitration Law

11.26 *The Arbitration Law* is the most important legislation in the Chinese arbitration system. It covers all types of arbitration except for those whose independent status is conferred by *The Arbitration Law*. In other words, *The Arbitration Law* governs arbitration of all disputes except for those discussed in the previous subsections. We discuss this Law at the end of this section for two reasons: first, the Law was promulgated in 1994 and came into effect on the September 1, 1995, and thus its implications to the present arbitration system are yet to be fully appreciated; secondly, in the absence of detailed information on the implementation of this new law, it appears rational to discuss this law at the end of this section on arbitration to emphasize that this law covers all other types of disputes which have not been dealt with in previous discussions.

The Arbitration Law applies to all commercial or property disputes involving citizens, legal persons and other organizations, except for the disputes arising from marriage, adoption, custody, maintenance and inheritance. The Chinese word *gongmin* means citizens. But, the word, whether or not it has been correctly used, actually means "individuals". This proposition is supported by Articles 65 to 73 of *The Arbitration Law*, which makes the Law applicable to international arbitration in China. International arbitration as conducted by CIETAC applies to disputes arising between Chinese citizens/companies and foreign citizens/companies, or between foreign individuals/companies and foreign individuals/companies. Therefore, *The Arbitration Law* applies to the disputes involving foreign citizens.

The Status of the Arbitration Commission

The Arbitration Law streamlines the arbitration system in China. In **11.27** particular, it purports to replace various arbitration authorities established under various contract regulations or legislation on patent, intellectual property or other matters. *The Arbitration Law* establishes the arbitration commission at the level of provincial government, the municipalities which are under direct control of the national government, (*i.e.* Beijing, Tianjin and Shanghai) or certain large-sized or medium-sized municipalities which are divided into districts. The commission, which is meant to be an authority independent from the administration, or any individuals or organizations, is not set up according to the hierarchy of the government administration. The administrative level at which the commission is established indicates the scope of the commission's jurisdiction. There is no administrative connection between an arbitration commission at the provincial level and the one set up in a municipality under the provincial government. *The Arbitration Law* does not allow a party to appeal against any arbitral award to another arbitral body or the court unless the award can be set aside by the court under Articles 217 and 260 of *The Civil Procedure Law*.

The Arbitration Law requires the Chinese Arbitration Council (or Association) to be established as the national umbrella body of arbitration. The arbitration commission in each province or municipality is the member of the Council, which is established as an incorporated association exercising self-regulation. The constitution of the Council is formed by the general meeting of its members. The Council enforces the constitution and disciplinary measures within the association. This supervisory and disciplinary power of the Council also applies to the arbitrators and individual members of each arbitration commission. The Council is authorized by *The Arbitration Law* to formulate arbitration rules in pursuance of *The Arbitration Law* and *The Civil Procedure Law*. The arbitration rules so made should not have the force of law because the China Arbitration Council is unquestionably not a law-making authority.

The legal status of the arbitration commission is not clearly stated in *The Arbitration Law*. The draft of *The Arbitration Law* described the arbitration commission as a non-profit organization which is a Chinese legal person. This description was considered to be misleading and was thus omitted. Article 10 of *The Arbitration Law* simply says that the arbitration commission must have its name, address, constitution, necessary property, members and arbitrators. This provision does not deal with the status of the commission. One of the crucial issues arising from the ambiguity of the commission's status is whether the commission members or the commission itself are liable in a civil action to a party who has suffered losses because of their acts. This uncertainty probably requires the arbitration commission to insert a clause of waiver when obtaining parties' consent to arbitration.

The arbitration commission is to be created jointly by the relevant local government and the local chamber of commerce. Each commission should have a chairman, two to four vice chairmen and seven to eleven commission members. They are appointed from people with practical experiences. But, at least two thirds of the commission members should have a legal, economic or trade background. The commission should appoint persons of high moral standard to be arbitrators. They must also meet the requirements of practical experience or qualifications, *e.g.* eight years experience in arbitration, legal practice, adjudicating, or being a law professor, or a person with high qualifications and adequate legal knowledge of economic and trade related works. These requirements suggest a legal professional-based team of arbitrators. Is this new arbitration system an informal justice system based on voluntary consent of the parties? Is the purpose of this system to create a semi-judicial mechanism outside the formal court system? These questions can only be adequately addressed in the forthcoming years. Each commission is supposed to list the arbitrators according to their specialities.

Arbitration Agreement

11.28 Arbitration agreement forms the basis of arbitration. The commission has no power to hear a dispute if only one party wishes to submit the dispute to the commission. Article 16 of *The Arbitration Law* requires the parties to make a written agreement to submit the dispute to arbitration. The written agreement can be made any time prior to the submission of the dispute. It can also be part of a contract or an independent agreement. But, it must clearly express the parties' intention to submit the dispute to a particular arbitration commission and define the matter(s) to be arbitrated. Failure to reach an agreement on the matter to be arbitrated or on the commission to hear the dispute in the arbitration agreement makes the agreement ineffective. An effective arbitration clause contained in a contract continues to operate under Article 19 of *The Arbitration Law* even if the contract has been modified, terminated or avoided. This provision ensures certainty in arbitration and the arbitration commission has the power to decide the validity of a contract.[35] The arbitration commission also has the power to determine the validity of an arbitration agreement. This power cannot be exercised if a party has asked the court to determine the validity of the agreement. The court is obliged under Article 26 of *The Arbitration Law* to enforce a valid arbitration agreement, which, however, can be invalidated by both parties participating voluntarily in a court proceeding.

Commencement of Arbitration Proceedings

The proceedings commence when an applicant submits the arbitration agreement and application for arbitration to the commission chosen in the agreement. The commission decides whether to hear the dispute within five days after receipt of the application. When accepting the case, the commission must notify the respondent of the proceedings within the time limit to be specified in the arbitration rules of the relevant commission. The respondent must file a statement of defence or a counter-claim, if applicable, within the required time. The request to take the other party's property as security must be determined by the local court.

Constitution of the Arbitration Tribunal

A tribunal consists of either three arbitrators or a single arbitrator. If three arbitrators are required, two arbitrators are chosen by the parties respectively and the third (president) by them jointly. The parties may authorize the chairman of the commission to appoint any or all of the arbitrators. The chairman also has the power to appoint an arbitrator if any party fails to exercise the right to choose an arbitrator within the specified time. The arbitrator is required to withdraw from the case if he or she has a conflict of interests. A request to withdraw an arbitrator can be made at any time, when necessary, prior to the end of the last hearing and must be accompanied by valid reasons. The chairman or the commission has the power, as the case may be, to determine whether the withdrawal is necessary in a particular case.

Proceedings of the Tribunal

The tribunal usually carries out proceedings by way of hearing. If both parties wish, the tribunal may also hear the case by submission only. The session is private unless both parties request to be public. However, if a State secret is involved, the proceedings must be confidential. The commission is required to notify the parties of the time of hearing according to the arbitration rules. If the applicant fails to attend the hearing or withdraws from the proceedings without permission, he or she is regarded as having withdrawn from the proceedings. If the respondent fails to appear in the proceedings, the tribunal has the power to deliver an award in default.

The parties can have legal representation and use evidence, experts or witnesses to further their cases. The tribunal may investigate any issues of its concern and for this purpose, call its own evidence, experts and witnesses. Both parties should be given an equal opportunity to argue their cases and to answer the other's case. If a party requests to preserve evidence which needs to be preserved, the tribunal is obliged to pass it to the local court for preservation provided that the necessity has been proved. Potential disputes may arise from this power because the tribunal has to be satisfied of the necessity to preserve the evidence before the obligation to preserve it arises.

The tribunal allows the parties to negotiate a settlement. It may either make an award pursuant to the settlement or allow the parties to withdraw the case if they so wish. *The Arbitration Law* allows a party to renege on a negotiated settlement or on an agreement to withdraw the arbitration application. In such situations, the matter may be re-arbitrated by the commission. The tribunal is obliged to mediate the dispute before making an award. If mediation succeeds, the tribunal will make an award according to the agreement of mediation. The award becomes effective when received by the parties and has the same effect as any other awards made by the tribunal. If a party reneges on the agreement of mediation before the award is made, the tribunal is obliged to arbitrate the dispute as soon as possible.

The award must be signed by the arbitrator and sealed by the commission. It becomes effective when signed and sealed. The award represents the view of the majority arbitrator. In the absence of any majority, the president's opinion prevails. The tribunal has the power to make a partial award. This partial award is enforceable on its own. In other words, the tribunal has the power to make separate awards if the circumstances so demand. Any technical errors or omission of important matters in the award must be rectified within 30 days from the time the award becomes effective. These issues may not be relied upon by an applicant as the grounds for setting aside the award after the elapse of time.

Enforcement of the Award

An award can be enforced by a court of law. But, the court cannot **11.29**
enforce an award if the other party has commenced or is to commence
a proceeding to set aside the award. The party has the right to apply to
a court under Articles 217 or 260 of the *Civil Procedure Law* for setting
aside an award in the following circumstances:

(a) when there is no arbitration agreement;
(b) the tribunal has no authority to decide the matter concerned;
(c) the constitution of the tribunal contravened the arbitration
rules;
(d) the proceedings of the tribunal are inconsistent with the arbitration rules;
(e) the award was made on false evidence;
(f) a party has hidden significant evidence from the tribunal;
(g) the arbitrator took bribery or abused his or her power as an
arbitrator; and
(h) the award contravenes the public interest.

The application for setting aside an award must be made within six
months from the time the applicant receives the award. A court must
decide on the application within two months after receiving it. It may
ask, but does not have the power to direct, the tribunal to re-arbitrate
a dispute. If the tribunal refuses to do so, the court has to determine the
matter in question.

Notes

1 The committee mainly deals with "neighbourhood disputes", which refers to any
family and civil disputes arising between parties resident in adjacent areas.
2 For example, *The Sino-Foreign Joint Equity Ventures Law, The Sino-Foreign Joint Co-
operative Ventures Law, The Foreign Economic Contract Law, The Economic Contract Law*, and the rules for implementing *The Economic Contract Law* (19 separate
pieces of legislation). In addition, a number of laws, such as *The Inheritance Law, The
Prairie Law, The Fishery Law*, and *The Mineral Resources Law*, etc, specify negotiation as the first option of dispute resolution, although they have not listed all of the
other three options.
3 For example, Article 6 of the State Council Measures for Resolving Labour Disputes
in Enterprises implies that the parties must submit the dispute to the relevant
arbitration commission before resorting to the court proceedings.
4 For example, in many reported cases of mediation by village or resident committees,
the mediators resolved the conflicts by persistently educating or talking to the parties
or by pointing out what was right and what was wrong to the parties, or urging the
parties to reach a comprise. Chunxiang Li and Other eds, *Handbook for People's
Mediation* (Beijing, Beijing Press, 1989, in Chinese *Ren Min Tiao Jie Shou Ce*), pp.
267–381.

⁵ Article 50 of the *Administrative Review (Judicial Decisions) Law*. The National High Court of China decided in the Gazette No 4 of 1985 that disputes involving judicial reviews of administrative decisions cannot be mediated by a court because the court is expected to make a decision as to whether the executive power in question has been correctly exercised.

⁶ The National High Court stated in the Gazette No 128 of 1985 that the court should not mediate a dispute arising from an economic contract if the conduct of a contracting party has attracted fine or criminal penalties.

⁷ Chunshuang Li and Xiaming Puan, "Our Views of the Debate on People's Mediation" [1990] *Zheng Fa Lun Tan* (in Chinese), Vol. 2, pp. 16–20.

⁸ The word "masses" in China has the same meaning as "people", but is less formal and official than "people".

⁹ Article 6 of the Organizational Rules for the Urban Resident Committees provides that an urban resident committee can cover the population of 100 to 700 households.

¹⁰ The word "enterprises" normally refers to company-like organizations, as opposed to what is known as unincorporated bodies in common law. But, presently, many Chinese enterprises are not incorporated companies, although they may be transformed into companies at some stage of the reform. "Enterprises" thus refers to both companies and State-owned enterprises.

¹¹ Article 50 of the *Administrative Review (Judicial Decisions) Law*.

¹² The High Court' Opinions on a Number of Issues Arising from the Enforcement of the Economic Contract Law, see *Gazette of the National High Court of the People's Republic of China* No 3 of 1985.

¹³ Article 128 of *The Civil Procedure Law* allows a court to mediate a dispute before delivering a judgment. The court exercised this power in a case involving a copyright dispute. See Guiguo Wang *Business Law of China* (Hong Kong, Butterworths, 1993), pp. 526–527.

¹⁴ It was reported that in 1989 the Intermediate People's Court in Huanshi City of Hubei Province mediated a dispute between a factory and a bank. The order of mediation stated that the factory would repay the outstanding debt to the bank in several instalments within the next three years. The factory failed to implement the order according to the time schedule. The bank sought court enforcement in 1990. When the factory failed to comply with the court order to perform, the court froze the factory's assets and imposed criminal sanctions upon several managers of the factory who hindered the enforcement of the court. *Re Detention of Yuechao QI, Maoqing YU and Kezhi CHEN for Their Hinderance of Court Enforcement*, in *Chinese Legal Data Base*, Law Department, City University of Hong Kong. The case is also collected in Guiguo Wang, *ibid.*, pp. 528–529. See also Guiguo Wang, p. 529 for a similar case.

¹⁵ CIETAC Arbitration Rules form part of the legal framework even though they are only private rules. For a detailed discussion on CIETAC see paras 11.12–11.20.

¹⁶ CMAC Arbitration Rules which are of a private nature are part of the legal framework too. For details of CMAC, see paras 11.21–11.22.

¹⁷ Chunming Tao and Shenchang Wang, *Procedural Theories and Practices of China's International Economic and Trade Arbitration* (Beijing, People's China Press, 1992, in Chinese, *Zhong Guo Guo Ji Jing Ji Mao Yi Zhong Cai - Chen Xu Li Lun Yu Shi Wu*), p. 3.

¹⁸ *Ibid.*, p. 5.

¹⁹ *Ibid.*, p. 7.

²⁰ *Ibid.*

²¹ *Ibid.*, p. 10.

²² Information provided by Prof Houzhi Tang, Vice Chairman of CIETAC

²³ Information provided by Prof Zhiming Xiao, Chairman of the CIETAC Shenzhen Committee.

²⁴ Arbitration Research Institute of the China Chamber of Commerce *Collected Documents of Foreign Economic Arbitration* (Beijing, ARI of China Chamber of Commerce, 1995, in Chinese, *She Wai Jin Mao Zhong Cai Wen Jian Hui Bian*), pp. 28–39.

²⁵ It was reported that a dispute arose between the partners to a joint equity venture in Henan Province. It was alleged that two of the three partners refused to perform the contract on the grounds of the State's export quota control. The other partner submitted the dispute to CIETAC, which decided in 1992 that the other two partners were not justified in relying on the export quota to breach the contract. In May 1993, the

successful party to the arbitral award applied to the Intermediate People's Court of Zhengzhou Municipality for the enforcement of the award. The court refused to enforce the award on the grounds of public policy consideration, which is set out in Article 260(4) of *The Civil Procedure Law*. In November 1992, the Provincial High Court changed this decision through its internal directive to the Intermediate Court on the grounds that there was no public policy against the enforcement of the arbitral award. See Dejun Chen and Others, *International Usage and Practice of Foreign Arbitration* (Beijing, Chinese Youth Press, 1993, in Chinese, *Guo Ji Guan Li He She Wai Zhong Cai Shi Wu*), pp. 258–260. Because of the scarcity of officially reported cases on the enforcement of arbitral awards, the meaning of Article 260 of *The Civil Procedure Law* is yet to be judicially clarified.

[26] Article 10 of *The Administrative Review (Administrative Decisions) Law* does not allow an applicant to apply for an administrative review of an arbitral award, or a mediation agreement. Article 11 of *The Administrative Review (Judicial Decisions) Law* does not specify the abuse of power or misapplication of law by an arbitrator as grounds of judicial review. Article 12 of *The Administrative Review (Judicial Decisions) Law* states that the court cannot review an arbitral award of an administrative body whose award is regarded as final in law.

[27] It must be pointed out this ground of refusal was relied upon by the Hong Kong court in *Paklito Investment Ltd v Klochner East Asia Ltd* to refuse the recognition of an award made by CIETAC in Hong Kong. See Dejun Chen, Michael Moser and Shengchang Wang, *International Arbitration in the People's Republic of China* (Hong Kong, Butterworths, 1995), p. 85.

[28] *Ibid.,* p. 85.

[29] *Ibid.,* pp. 260–261.

[30] *Ibid.,* pp. 262–263.

[31] *Ibid.,* pp. 473–475.

[32] Shan He and Shui Xiao, *Outline of Arbitration Law* (Beijing, China Law Press 1995, in Chinese, *Zhong Cai Fa Gai Yao*), p. 119.

[33] A number of case summaries are collected in Dejun Cheng, Michael Moser and Shengchang Wang, see above, pp. 125–145.

[34] See Article 79 of *The Labour Law* and Article 6 of the State Council Measures for Resolving Labour Disputes in Enterprises.

[35] This is another potentially litigious power, and is vulnerable to abuse by a commission wishing to have the authority to arbitrate the matter in dispute.

CHAPTER 12

LAW OF CIVIL PROCEDURE

Zhang, Xianchu

City University of Hong Kong

Zhang, Xianchu, University Lecturer, Faculty of Law, City University of Hong Kong; LL.B. (China Unviersity of Political Science and Law, Beijing PRC); MCL (Indiana University School of Law, Bloomington); JD (Indiana University School of Law, Bloomington).

Introduction

The current *Law of Civil Procedure* was adopted in 1991 to replace *The Law of Civil Procedure* (on trial) of 1982. The revision and supplementation were demanded by judicial practice for a long time to deal with many new issues in trials, to promote judicial efficiency under the pressure from the sharp increased number of cases tried under *The Law of Civil Procedure* from 1,072,600 in 1985 to more than 4 million in 1995; and to facilitate dispute resolution with foreign parties.   **12.01**

As compared with the structure of the five parts and 205 articles of the 1982 Law, the new Law is arranged into four parts, 29 chapters and 270 articles, which demonstrate the development and sophistication of the judicial practice in this area in China today. As a result, many new procedural issues are dealt with in the Law for the first time, such as property preservation, time limitation of trial instances, imposition of burden of proof on the parties to the actions, procedure for hastening debt recovery, procedure for public notice for assertion of claims, bankruptcy repayment procedure for legal persons, execution procedure including search and compulsory measures, and jurisdiction over cases involving foreign parties.

Despite being better armed, however, the Law is still facing various other challenges. Unfair and biased judgments, for instance, have been entered under the local government's influence in favour of local interest, or with the same reason some courts have refused to carry out effective judgments made by other jurisdiction. Certain incidents of abuse of judicial powers have also caught national attention.

General Provisions

12.02   The general provisions are provided in the first part of the Law which contains 11 chapters and 107 articles and are applicable to all stages of civil proceedings.

Scope of Application

Under Article 3, the Law shall apply to civil actions resulting from disputes over property rights and personal relationships among or between citizens, legal persons and other organizations. According to the current division of the adjudication powers and two Provisions of the Supreme Court concerning trial procedures of economic cases,[1] the Law shall be applied to cases handled by civil, economic, intellectual property divisions of a people's court as well as maritime courts. The Law shall govern all these actions conducted within the territory of China. A foreign national or enterprise or organization shall have the same litigation rights and duties as a Chinese party does in legal proceedings in China. However, this rule shall be applied under the reciprocity principle.

Mediation

Mediation has been a notable feature of Chinese civil procedure. According to the Law, mediation may be conducted at any stage of the proceedings from pre-trial meeting to execution of judgment. However, Article 9 alters the emphasis on mediation as a mandatory procedure under the old law to a voluntary one by providing that mediation shall only be carried out on the bases of both parties' consent, their willingness to participate, verification of facts and determination of faults and responsibilities in order to promote judicial efficiency and to prevent mediation from being used as a strategy to force a party to accept an unfair deal. The Law further stipulates that a judgment should be rendered promptly if mediation fails.

Mediation may be conducted by either a single judge or the collegiate bench on the spot as far as possible. In addition to the parties and witnesses, relevant units, such as the parties' company or plant, or individuals such as the parties' close relatives or friends may be invited by the court to take part in facilitating the mediate. A mediation certificate should be made with the details of the claims, facts and settlement upon the agreement being reached by the parties. It shall become legally effective when signed and accepted by the parties. The parties, however, are allowed to change their minds before the mediation certificate is delivered, which shall lead the court to enter its judgment without delay.

Mediation certificates may not be needed for agreements reached by parties that do not require any further court execution. For example, where the parties are reconciled through mediation in divorce proceedings, or an adoptive relationship is maintained through mediation, the agreement recorded in the court file becomes legally effective when the parties, the judges and the court clerk sign or seal it.

In addition to court mediation proceedings, Article 16 authorizes the people's conciliation committee as a private organization, to mediate civil disputes under the guidance of local government and the basic people's court although the procedure and the agreement reached will not prevent a party from filing a lawsuit at the court.

Jurisdiction

Jurisdiction refers to the issue of which court should have the proper **12.03** authority to adjudicate the case of the first instance. The matter is classified into jurisdiction on the basis of ranks of courts and jurisdiction on the basis of locations of courts. The former deals with jurisdiction of different levels of the people's courts whereas the latter defines jurisdiction of courts of a same level but in different places. The provisions of the Law are further detailed by various circulars issued by the Supreme Court.

Jurisdiction of Courts at Different Levels

A basic people's court at the county level shall have jurisdiction for first instance over most civil actions. According to the Law, a basic people's court is competent to handle civil cases involving foreign parties provided they are not classified as major cases on the basis of the amount of money or property involved, complexity, and number of the participants in the cases.[2]

Article 19 provides that an intermediate people's court at the prefectural level shall exercise jurisdiction for first instance over major cases involving foreign interest and cases of major importance within its jurisdiction. In addition, the Supreme People's Court may authorize intermediate courts jurisdiction over cases that represent new challenges to the judicial system. Since the adoption of the Law, the Supreme Court has, by virtue of the provision to grant intermediate courts jurisdiction over some patent and maritime cases.

A high court at the provincial level, as the top level of local courts, shall have jurisdiction for first instance over civil cases of major importance within its jurisdiction. The Supreme Court is competent for first instance of civil cases that either have great significance to the nation as a whole, or are considered as necessary ones to be tried by itself. All courts above intermediate level are competent for second instance of civil cases appealed from the lower courts.

Territorial Jurisdiction

Once the rank of courts with proper jurisdiction has been determined, the following issue is which local court should have the jurisdiction over the case considered. Under Article 22, as a general principle of regional jurisdiction, a civil action shall be filed at the people's court in the place of the defendant's domicile, or main business or management office. Where the defendant's domicile is different from his residence, the action comes under the jurisdiction of the court at the place of his usual residence. The exercise of jurisdiction by the court that has already recorded the case shall not be affected by the change of domicile or residence of the defendant to the action. If several defendants with household registers or residences in different places are involved in an action, all the courts concerned have the jurisdiction over the case.

Article 23 provides certain exceptions to the general principle. As a result, the jurisdiction over a civil action shall be exercised by the people's court in the place of the plaintiff's domicile or usual residence where the action is brought against defendants who do not reside within the territory of China; who are under rehabilitation through labour or in prison; whose whereabouts are unknown; or who have been declared missing.

Moreover, Articles 23 through 31 stipulate, in addition to the general principle, the methods of determining territorial jurisdiction in certain types of cases. For example, the parties to a contract may select a court by a written agreement to hear a potential dispute from various choices provided by the law including the place of implementation, the place of signing, the place of the plaintiff's domicile, or the location of the contracted object. Even if the parties fail to make such selection in their contract, Article 24 allows the plaintiff to choose between the place of the defendant domicile and the place of implementation to file his lawsuit.

Other types of civil actions that may come under the jurisdiction of two or more people's courts under the Law include disputes arising from insurance contracts, transportation contracts, negotiable instruments, tortious acts, compensation as the result of transportation accidents, or collision of ships. It should be noted that the general rules in determining the jurisdiction are further supplemented by the Supreme Court's interpretation and instruction. For instance, Article 29 of the Law stipulates that a tort action can be either filed in the place where the tortious act is committed or the place of the defendant's domicile. The possible jurisdiction, nevertheless, may further be exercised by the court of the place where the damages or injuries as the result of the tortious act occur. In a product liability case, the jurisdiction may even be extended to the place in which the products are manufactured or sold.[3]

Jurisdiction over the claims for compensation for salvage services shall belong to the people's court in the place of the salvage or the place of the first arrival of the salvage vessel. With regard to an action claiming general average, the case shall be heard by the court in the place where the vessel first docked after the general average, the place where the general average adjustment is conducted, or the place where the voyage ended.

Article 34 provides exclusive jurisdiction for three types of civil **12.04** actions under which neither courts that are not authorized by the Law shall exercise their jurisdiction over the actions, nor the parties may choose or change jurisdiction by their agreement: actions concerning immovable property shall be heard by the court in the place of the property; jurisdiction over actions concerning harbour operations shall be exercised by the court in the place of the harbour; actions for inheriting property shall come under the jurisdiction of the court in the place of the domicile of the deceased before his death or the place of the principal estate.

According to Article 35 where two or more courts may have jurisdiction over an action as provided by the Law, the plaintiff may elect to file the lawsuit in any one of the courts. The court that first registers the case for hearing shall have the jurisdiction if the plaintiff institutes his action in two or more competent courts. The growing concern with local protectionism in judicial practice in recent years has made the Supreme Court issue a Circular on December 22, 1994 entitled Some Provisions on Strict Implementation of Civil Procedure Law of China in Trials of Economic Cases. The Provisions stipulate that in the case of two or more courts being competent, other courts shall transfer all the files to the court that first registered the case within seven days upon being informed of the first registration regardless of their own registrations. The same principle also applies to more than two lawsuits filed by the plaintiff based on same legal relationship or same legal facts to different courts.

Transferred and Designated Jurisdiction

Articles 36 through 39 together with the Circular of the Supreme Court provide ways to solve jurisdiction conflicts. When a people's court finds out that a case having been registered for hearing is not within its jurisdiction, it shall transfer the case to the competent court.

The competent court must accept the case since the transfer may only be made once. If a court discovers that the case that it accepts through transfer does not come under its jurisdiction, it shall report the matter to the court at the higher level for its final decision and may not transfer the case to any other court itself.

Where the competent court is unable to perform the duty to exercise its jurisdiction due to special reasons, the court at the higher level shall designate jurisdiction. According to Article 37, when the matter of jurisdiction is disputed between courts, they should resolve the dispute through consultation. Their common superior court may also designate jurisdiction upon the request of the lower courts if the consultation fails.

Moreover, the Supreme Court has ruled in the Circular that in jurisdiction disputes the court involved must stay any proceedings of disposing substantive matters and cannot render any judgment. Their common superior court shall designate jurisdiction within 30 days upon receiving the lower court report on the matter. It should revoke any judgment forestalled by the lower courts before the resolution of the jurisdiction dispute on the grounds of violation of due procedure and shall transfer or designate the case to a competent court, or hear the case itself.[4]

The Supreme Court further points out that a court may not claim its jurisdiction over an action by taking pre-trial preservation of the property that is not a principal part in a domestic economic dispute. It rules that all local provisions on the regional jurisdiction are null and void and regulations on allocation of jurisdiction within a province, autonomous region, or municipality directly under the central government adopted by the high court concerned shall not become effective until approved by the Supreme Court.[5]

The parties to a civil action may challenge the court's jurisdiction and may appeal the matter to the court at the next higher level if its first petition is denied. Article 39, as a switching device, provides that a higher court is empowered to conduct as first instance, a trial of a case which is under the jurisdiction of a court at a lower level. It may also assign a case under its jurisdiction of first instance to a court at a lower level. Conversely, a court at a lower level may request a higher court to hear a case as first instance on the grounds of necessity although the case comes under the lower court's original jurisdiction. In practice, this article is invoked in situations of novel or complicated cases, or lack of experience by the lower court.

Trial Organization

12.05 Two types of trial organizations are provided in Articles 40 through 43: collegial panel and single judge bench. The former is used in most of trials with an odd number of members. In first instance, a collegial panel may be composed of either judges and assessors, or judges alone while an entire judge bench is required for second instance. A single judge bench shall be employed to hear cases under special procedures.

A presiding judge shall be designated by the president of the court or the head of the division of the Court for the collegial panel. If the president or the head participates in the trial, he himself shall serve as the presiding judge. A collegiate shall decide a case by a majority vote.

To combat abuse of judicial power and corruption, for the first time the Law explicitly provides that judicial personnel shall not accept any gifts from the parties or their attorneys. For those involved in corruption, accepting bribes, or bending the law for personal gain, the legal liability up to imposition of criminal penalties shall be pursued.

Moreover, Article 45 lists three situations in which a member of the judicial personnel must withdraw from the hearing either by their own initiation or upon request of the parties to the action:

(a) he is a party to the case or close relative of a party or an attorney to the case;
(b) he has personal interests in the case; or
(c) he has some other relations with a party to the case which may prevent him from handling the case impartially.

This provision shall also be applicable to clerks, interpreters, experts, witnesses and inspectors. A request for withdrawal shall be made before the start of the hearing. If the facts concerning the withdrawal are not known until after the trial has begun, the request may be made any time before the conclusion of the court debate. Upon the request the person against whom the withdrawal is filed shall temporarily suspend his participation in the proceedings before the court makes any decision, except for any emergent measures that need to be taken. The court shall decide within three days of the request on the matter and the requesting party may apply once more to the court for reconsideration if he disagrees with the decision. The second decision to be issued within three days shall be the final one.

Participants in Proceedings

Under Article 49, parties to a civil action may include citizens, legal persons, and other organizations. Legal persons and organizations shall be represented by their legal representatives, principals in charge or other authorized persons in an action.

Parties to an action shall have the right to appoint their attorneys, to request withdrawal, to collect and produce evidence, to participate debate, to request mediation, to lodge an appeal and apply for execution of a judgment. They may also decide to settle the dispute, or waive or modify their claims. However, parties shall exercise their litigant rights in accordance with the Law, observe the order of proceedings and carry out their obligations under legally effective judgments, rulings and mediation agreements.

Article 53 provides that several actions may be heard combinatively through a joint action upon the approval of the court and the consent of the parties if one or both parties include two or more in number with common objectives of litigation, or objectives of the same type. Where litigants on one side to a joint action have common rights and obligations regarding the litigant objective, they shall not be bound by any litigant act taken by one of them unless the act is ratified by the rest of them.

In a case with ten or more persons, two to five representatives may be selected and their acts in litigation shall be binding on all other members except for certain significant decisions, such as replacing representatives, waiving claims or negotiating settlements must be approved by all the members of the party.

Where some members of a party in a joint action are not yet ascertained because of sheer numbers, the people's court may, by public notice with the case particulars and claims, notify potential claimants to register their claims with the court within a period of no less than 30 days. The judgment and rulings of the case shall be binding not only on the registered claimants but those who do not register their claims but nevertheless bring separate actions on the same grounds within the statute of limitation.

A third party may participate in the proceedings by claiming his own rights. Article 56 classifies such parties into two categories: a third party with independent rights to the objective disputed by the plaintiff and the defendant may participate in the action by filing his own lawsuit against other parties; a third party without independent rights to the disputed objective may join the proceedings by applying to the court, or by being notified by the court if his participation is indispensable to the outcome of the action.

Any individual without civil capacity to engage in litigation shall be represented by his guardian as his legal representative. In cases of evading responsibility between two or more legal representatives, the people's court shall appoint one such person for participation in the action. Each party or its legal representative may entrust one or two attorneys to represent him in the action, who may include lawyers, close relatives of the party, individuals recommended by a social organization, a working unit of the party or other citizens approved by the court.

A power of attorney with specified items entrusted by the party shall be submitted to the court. However, under Article 59, special powers from the party are required for an attorney to admit, waive or modify claims, settle the dispute, file a counterclaim or an appeal. A power of attorney executed by overseas Chinese shall be attested by the Chinese diplomatic mission in the foreign country. The party has the duty to inform the court of any change or termination of the attorney's power. In certain cases, such as divorce proceedings, the appointment of attorneys shall not exempt the parties from appearing before the court, even if they are unable to express their will, unless some other special reasons make them incapable of doing so.

Evidence

Article 63 lists seven types of evidence which may be used in civil **12.06** actions after being verified (as same as the provision in *The Criminal Procedure Law*): documentary evidence, material evidence, video-audio material, testimonies of witnesses, statement of parties concerned, conclusion of expected corroboration, and records of inspection.

The significant change regarding the burden of proof under the new Law is that the main portion of the burden has been shifted from the court to litigating parties. Article 64 stipulates that whoever claims shall be liable for producing the relevant supporting evidence. However, the court's duty is not totally exempted. When the parties or their attorneys are not able to collect evidence by themselves for reasons beyond their reach or control, or the court believes that certain evidence is necessary, it should examine and collect it.

In order to be used as a valid basis for the court's decision, evidence must be collected legitimately. The Supreme Court ruled in 1995 that an audio record taken without the consent of the party could not be used as evidence in a trial because this conduct is illegal.[6] The court should examine and verify all evidence comprehensively and objectively in accordance with the legal procedures.

All evidence shall be presented in the courtroom and cross-examined by the parties concerned except those involving State secrets, trade secrets and personal privacy which shall not be displayed on an open trial. Originals shall be presented as documentary and material evidence as far as possible. Copies are not allowed unless there are genuine difficulties in presenting the originals. Notarized documents shall be *prima facie* evidence for ascertaining the relevant facts subject to rebuttal by sufficient contradictory evidence. Any documentary evidence in a foreign language must be presented with a Chinese translation.

Article 70 provides that any unit or individual who has knowledge of the case shall have an obligation to testify before the court. A written testimony may be submitted to the court if a witness has difficulties appearing at the trial. Persons who are unable to express themselves accurately are not qualified to offer any testimony.

The parties to an action may apply to the court for preservation of evidence where the evidence will possibly be lost or destroyed or is difficult to obtain at a later date. If the circumstance so requires, the court may also take security measures to preserve the evidence on its own initiative.

Property Preservation and Execution Prior to Judgment

12.07   The people's court may, upon the application of the party concerned or on its own initiative, take measures to preserve the property of the other party by ruling where the other party's conduct or other existing reasons may cause execution of the judgment to be rendered at a later time difficult or impossible. Provision of security may be a condition for the court to adopt these measures when the preservation is requested by one party to the action.

Under Article 92 the court is bound to make its decision within 48 hours in cases of emergency with the measures becoming effective immediately. In certain urgent circumstances, the preservation measures may even be taken before initiating the lawsuit under the conditions of the provision of security by the applicant. Such measures, however, shall be cancelled if the applicant fails to institute any legal proceedings within 15 days of implementing the measures.

The methods for such preservation may include sealing up, confiscation, freezing of assets or others prescribed by law. The property subject to preservation shall be limited to the extent of the claims relevant to the action. The party whose assets are frozen by the court ruling shall be notified immediately and may apply to the court for cancellation of the preservation by providing security. The party is entitled to damages to his property caused by any wrongful preservation against him.

Execution prior to judgment refers to a temporary measure by which the people's court may, upon the plaintiff's request, order the defendant to carry out his obligation by making certain payment to the plaintiff before the judgment is rendered. This measure, according to Article 97, may be invoked in claims for alimony, payment of maintenance, payment of child support, medical expenses, claims for labour compensation, or other urgent situations.

The purpose of this measure is to provide the plaintiff with urgently needed relief and to avoid a social tragedy caused by the delayed delivery of justice. Therefore, this measure will not be applied unless the following conditions are met:

   (a) there are clear rights and relationship of a obligation between the parties;
   (b) the claims must be for certain payment;

418

(c) any delay of the payment would seriously affect the plaintiff's living or business operation;

(d) the defendant is capable of carrying out the obligation.

If possible, the court may order the applicant to execute the measures prior to judgment to provide security. He shall compensate the defendant for any losses caused by the execution of the measure if he loses the action. The parties subject to the measure of property preservation or execution of the measures prior to judgment may apply the court for reconsideration one more time but the execution of the measures shall not be suspended by such an application.

Coercive Measures Against Hinderance to Civil Actions

The people's court may coercively summon the defendant who is required to appear before the court and refuses to do so without due cause after a summons has been served to him twice. Fines, detention or even criminal penalties may be imposed against violation of the rules of the court, contempt of court and assaulting judicial personnel. Article 102 explicitly lists six types of activities that may subject both the directly responsible person and the person in charge of the unit concerned to legal liability. The Law also imposes duties on all units involved to assist the court in investigating the case and to execute the judgment. Otherwise they shall face legal liability as well as administrative discipline. **12.08**

Under Article 104 the fine shall be limited to RMB1,000 to individuals and RMB30,000 to a unit and detention shall be no longer than 15 days. Procedurally, imposition of coercive summons, fines and detention must be approved by the president of the court. The party subject to coercive measures may apply to the court once more for reconsideration, which will not cause suspension of the execution of the measures.

Court Costs

Court costs are provided by the Law with the purpose to lessen the State financial burden, to prevent the abuse of rights to legal proceedings, to deter civil violation, and to enable the judicial branch to improve its adjudicating work. The current measures governing the payment of court costs was formulated by the Supreme Court on July 12, 1989 in its Measures of Charge of Court Costs. In 1990, the Supreme Court adopted the Measures of Charge on Distraint of Vessels. **12.09**

Under Article 107, court costs are divided into two categories: case acceptance fees and other court costs. The parties of non-property cases are required to pay only an acceptance fee based on the nature of their cases. The acceptance fee for a divorce action, for example, ranges from RMB10 to 50 according to the complexity of the case and the living standards of the particular area; lawsuits against violation of right to name, portrait, reputation and honour are charged from RMB50 to 100. The amount of the acceptance fee for cases of property dispute is calculated on the basis of the disputed amount on a progressive rate as the following list shows:

Disputed amount (RMB)		Acceptance fee
less than 1,000		RMB50
part of	1,000–50,000	4%
part of	50,000–100,000	3%
part of	100,000–200,000	2%
part of	200,000–500,000	1.5%
part of	500,000–1,000,000	1%
above	1,000,000	0.5%

In addition, the parties of property cases may have to pay other court costs including the court's expenses of service, inspection, corroboration, public notice and translation, if needed; expenses incurred by witnesses, experts, translators for their transportation and accommodation to participate in the trial and the subsidies for the delay of their work; expenses for preservation of property prior to judgement; the execution costs; and other necessary costs.

The court costs shall be paid in advance by the plaintiff within seven days of the court notice before the trial. In a joint action, the parties shall pay their court costs in proportion with their respective claims. In cases of counterclaim, the defendant is also required to pay. Failure to make such a payment on time by a competent party shall be treated as withdrawal of the case. The court, however, may permit deduction and delay or even exemption of payment of court costs if the party has financial difficulties. Certain cases do not require payment before the trial. The payment of the costs in bankruptcy repayment proceedings, for instance, may not be made until conclusion of the proceedings from the bankrupt property.

At the end of litigation, the parties' responsibility for sharing the court costs shall be determined by the guidelines provided by the Supreme Court: whoever lost the case should bear the burden of the payment; parties' responsibility should be proportionate to their rights and duties decided in the trial if each party is entitled to part of his claims; parties' payment should be determined through consultation in case of successful mediation of the parties' dispute; the plaintiff should pay if he withdraws the case; the parties' portion to the costs in a divorce action shall be decided by the court according to the parties' responsibility in the merit of the case; and the party subject to execution shall bear the burden of the cost for his failure to carry out his legal obligation in time. The aforementioned principles are also applied to appeals.

According to the Supreme Court, two kinds of cases are not subject to the requirement of court costs. All the cases heard in accordance with the special procedures are exempted on the ground that they are not of true litigation. The cases tried under the trial supervisory procedures are not subject to any payment simply because the litigant parties should not pay for any mistakes made by the court.

Trial Procedures

In China, a case shall conclude with two instances of trials except for **12.10** the Supreme Court who takes the case for the first instance. Although the general principles, such as jurisdiction, mediation and withdrawal are embodied in both stages, different procedures may be used in each instance. In addition, some special procedures may also be used in practice.

Ordinary Procedures of First Instance

A litigation starts by the plaintiff's pleading with a written, or verbal if **12.11** he is unable to write, statement of complaint to the people's court. In order to be valid, four conditions must be met: the plaintiff has direct interest in the case in question; the defendant is specified; there are specific claims with supporting facts and reasons; and the court has jurisdiction over the case.

Upon receiving the indictment, the people's court shall conduct an examination and decide within seven days whether the pleading should be accepted or rejected on the grounds of lack of necessary conditions. In the latter situation, the court shall advise the party of the grounds of rejection and the alternatives available to him. The rejection is interlocutarily appealable to the court at the next higher level.

The court shall serve the defendant with the copy of the indictment within five days after the case is recorded for a hearing. The defendant is required to respond by filing his reply within 15 days after receiving the copy. The reply shall be served to the plaintiff within 15 days of receipt by the court. However, the proceedings will not be affected by the defendant's failure to reply.

A collegial panel shall be formed for the hearing and the parties shall be notified within three days of its formation. It must carefully examine the file, investigate the facts, collect evidence and notify other indispensable parties. If necessary, the court may entrust a court of another area with specific requests and items to conduct an investigation. Without due cause, the entrusted court shall complete the investigation within 30 days from being commissioned.

All civil actions shall be heard by open sessions except those involving State secrets, personal privacy or other situations provided by the Law. Proceedings of divorce and cases involving business secrets may not necessarily warrant close trials unless the parties to the action so request. Depending on the circumstances, a trial may be conducted either in the courtroom or on a particular site, such as a party's workplace or place of residence, in order to promote awareness of Law.

Under Article 122, the court shall notify the parties and other participants to the action three days before the trial. In cases of open session, the parties' names, the subject matter of the case, and the time and venue of the hearing shall also be announced publicly. Although in practice, such short notice has long been criticized for the hardship imposed against the parties and their attorneys in order to get ready for the trial, the recent slight amendment to *The Law of Criminal Procedures* on this issue indicates that the old ways are still adhered to.[7]

According to Articles 123 through 134, a trial shall be proceeded in four stages.

Session Opening

The court clerk shall ascertain the presence of the parties and other participants to the action and announce the rules of the court. Then the presiding judge shall check the identity of the parties and the scope of authorization to the parties' attorneys; announce the subject matter of the hearing and the composition of the bench including the court clerk; inform the parties of their rights and duties concerning the litigation; and inquire whether the parties wish to request any member at the bench to be withdrawn.

Court Investigation

The investigation shall be conducted in the order provided by Article 124 as

    (a) the parties' presentation of their cases to the court by their statements;
    (b) testimony of the witnesses;
    (c) display of documentary, material, audio or video evidence;

(d) reading out of the conclusion of expert corroboration;

(e) reading out of the record of the site inspection.

The parties may, subject to the court's permission, introduce new evidence, cross-examine the witnesses, experts or inspectors and request re-investigation, re-corroboration or reinspection. During the court investigation, additional claims requested by the plaintiff, counter claims raised by the defendant and the other litigant request filed by a third party may be combined for the hearing.

The significant change in the procedure as well as the court's function in a civil action under the Law is that by deleting the provision on the court's inquiry of the parties and witnesses in the old procedure on the trial basis, the adversary system in fact has been introduced in the civil procedures.

Court Debate

The debate shall be started with the opening statement of the plaintiff or his trial attorney and followed by the defendant's; and the third party's, if any. Then the parties may debate with each other without the restriction of the first round order. At the end of the debate, the presiding judge shall ask the parties to state their final opinions by following the first round order.

After the court debate, new efforts to mediate the dispute between the parties may be made by the court based on the merits revealed by the court investigation and debate. However, the judgment shall be entered without delay should the effects fail.

The written court record shall be either read out to the parties and other trial participants or read by themselves in the courtroom immediately after conclusion of the trial or read within five days of the trial. The parties or the participants have the right to correct any errors and make up any omissions. They shall also sign or affix their seals to the record. Any refusal to do so shall be recorded on the file.

Pronouncement of Judgment

All judgments shall be publicly pronounced by the court regardless of the trials being publicly or closely conducted. A pronouncement may be made either immediately after the conclusion of the trial in the courtroom with the written judgment to be delivered within 10 days; or on a fixed date with the written judgment to be issued immediately after the pronouncement. At the same time the parties shall also be informed of their rights to appeal, of the time limitation to appeal and the competent court to hear the appeal.

12.12

A judgment by default may be entered by the court if the parties refuse to appear before the court without proper cause after being subpoenaed, or leave the trial without the court's permission. A plaintiff may not be allowed to withdraw the case after the conclusion of the trial and before the pronouncement of the judgment unless the court so permits.

Under Article 132, a hearing may be postponed in the following situations where an indispensable party or other litigant participants fail to appear before the court with due course; a party requests for the withdrawal of the member of the bench at the opening of the trial; a new witness needs to be summoned, new evidence needs to be collected; or new corroboration, inspection or further investigation needs to be conducted; or other justifiable circumstances entail a postponement.

According to Article 136, a trial should be suspended where

(a) one party dies, entailing a stay for his successor to decide whether to take part in the case;

(b) a legal representative needs to be appointed after a party has lost his capacity to conduct litigation;

(c) the new party has not been ascertained after a legal person or organization as a party to the action was terminated;

(d) one party is prevented from participating in the trial because of *force majeure*;

(e) the decision of the case in question must be dependent on the outcome of another case whose hearing has not yet concluded; and

(f) other situations justify the suspension. The trial shall resume once the above causes are removed.

Article 137 provides that a trial should be terminated if

(a) the plaintiff dies without any successor, or the successor has denounced his litigant right;

(b) the defendant dies without any estate or any person to undertake his obligation;

(c) one of the parties dies in divorce proceedings or an action to claim alimony, maintenance payment, payment of child support or to terminate an adoptive relation.

Judgments and rulings are the forms of court documents for adjudicating different substantive and procedural issues. Rulings should be used by the court to decide issues concerning rejection of a pleading, objection to the jurisdiction of the court, dismissal of a complaint, application for security preservation and payment prior to judgement, application for withdrawal of a case, suspension or termination of the trial, correction of errors in a judgment, suspension or termination of execution, application for enforcing an arbitral award or notarized obligation document, or other necessary matters. Among them, only the rulings over acceptance or denial of a suit and jurisdiction matter may be interlocutorily appealable.

Generally, a judgment is the judicial decision made by the court to the merit of a lawsuit. It shall specify the subject matter of the case, claims, facts and reasons disputed by the parties, the facts and reasons determined by the court, the grounds for application of the relevant laws, the result of the trial and the parties' responsibility for the litigant costs, the time limitation for appeal and the competent appellate court. A judgment, however, may be used to dispose part of a suit if the facts concerned are already evident and certain circumstances may prevent the whole case from being concluded without delay.

All judgments and rulings rendered by the Supreme Court and the judgments and rulings that either are unappealable or are not appealed within the time limitation shall be legally effective.

In addition to judgment and rulings, the people's courts are also allowed by the Law to use decisions as a method to safeguard the smooth progress of the proceedings. The issues to be determined by decisions include permission of a party's request for withdrawal, extension of certain time limitation; deduction, delay or exemption of payment of the court costs; adoption of compulsory measures; and a new trial after a mistake is found in a legally effective judgment or ruling. Such decisions may be made in writing, or verbally but are recorded later into the written file. Under the Law, decisions are unappealable. The party, however, may request the deciding court to reconsider the decision one more time.

A civil case tried under the ordinary procedures of first instance shall be completed within six months of the date of recording the case for hearing. The president of the court has the authority to approve an extension for another six months in extra-ordinary situations. Any further extension must be approved by the people's court at a higher level.

For a trial of first instance, summary procedures may be applied to simple cases defined by Article 142 as those where the facts are evident, the relation of rights and obligations between the parties is definite and the dispute is minor. The features of the summary procedures include that the plaintiff may start a lawsuit by a verbal indictment, or both parties may go together to the court for instant adjudication; the hearing should be conducted by a single judge; the judge may not be bound to follow the normal provisions for summoning parties or witnesses, for public announcement of the trial venue and time, for the order of the trial procedures; and the trial should be finished within three months of the date of recording the case. Summary procedures may be transformed into ordinary proceedings if during the trial the court finds that the case is a major and complicated one.[8]

Procedures of Second Instance

12.13   An appeal against a judgment of first instance shall be filed to the
people's court at the next highest level within 15 days of the date of
delivery of the judgement. In case of appeal against a ruling, the time
limitation is 10 days.

An appeal may be filed either through the court of first instance,
which will submit the petition to the appellate court with the respondent's response as well as the complete file and evidence, or directly to
the appellate court. In the latter case, the appellate court shall transmit
the appeal petition within five days to the court of first instance,
through which the copies of the petition shall be served to the other
party with a period of 15 days to respond.

Article 151 has modified the provision of the old procedures that the
appellate court should conduct an overall review of the trial of first
instance by requiring it to review only the part of the facts and application of law appealed by the parties. As a result, more duties are
imposed on the parties to exercise their litigation rights. In practice,
the appellate court may inform the parties to add more items of appeal
if a mistake is found outside the scope of the appeal and is not realized
by the parties because of insufficient legal knowledge.

The procedures of first instance may be applicable to second instance except provided otherwise by the Law. The court of second
instance shall form a collegial panel to review the file, conduct its own
investigation, and question the parties in order to verify the facts. The
way of trial, however, is at the court's discretion. It may hold an open
hearing, or may enter its decision without a hearing at all, if it is
deemed unnecessary. A hearing, if needed, may be held in its courtroom, in the place where the dispute arose, or in the location of the
court of first instance in order to facilitate the parties' participation.

After a hearing, an appellate court shall dispose of the appeal according to Article 153: the appeal shall be dismissed and the judgment of
first instance shall be affirmed where the facts are verified clearly and
the law is applied correctly; the original judgment should be amended
if the law is incorrectly applied in the first instance; where it is found
that the original judgment incorrectly or unclearly verified the facts
with insufficient evidence, the appellate court may quash it and remand the court of first instance to conduct a new trial, or alternatively
enter a new judgment itself after clarification of the facts. In case of
legal procedure violation in first instance which may have prejudiced
the correctness of the judgment, the case should be remanded to the
original court for a new trial with the original judgment being quashed.

All judgments and rulings of second instance are final. Thus, the
differences between a new trial remanded to the court of first instance
and a judgment entered directly by the appellate court is that in the
former, the judgment of the new trial is still appealable whereas in the

latter, the judgment is not. Rulings shall be used by the court of second instance to dispose all appeals against rulings of first instance.

During a hearing by the court of second instance, it may also try to mediate the dispute between the parties. Once an agreement is reached, a mediation certificate shall be made and served to the effect that the original judgment has been quashed.

Disposition of an appeal against a judgment shall be concluded within three months of the date of the appeal being recorded for second instance. The president of the court may approve an extension of the time limitation in extraordinary situations. In cases of appeal against a ruling, the disposition shall be finished within 30 days without any extension.

Special Procedures

Chapter 15 of the Law provides some special procedures for the people's court to hear certain legal requests that differ from ordinary civil actions. For instance, actions for declaration of a person as missing or dead, for determination of a person as lacking complete civil capacity, and for judgment ascertaining property as ownerless are not litigated by the parties, but only requested by the interested party of one side. As a result, these special procedures are independent from ordinary procedures and shall be applied first to the listed actions. **12.14**

A single judge bench shall be responsible to hear the cases under the special procedures except those that are important or complicated or involve voter eligibility. However, regardless of the forms of the trial organization, all the judgments entered by the bench shall be final. A special procedure shall be terminated and a litigant proceeding should be started by the party filing a separate indictment where the procedures find that a genuine dispute concerning the parties' civil rights and interests exist.

The special procedures shall be concluded within 30 days of the case being recorded or of the expiry of public notice. This time limit may be extended with the approval of the president of court except in voters' eligibility cases.

A citizen may institute a lawsuit in the basic people's court at the place of the electoral district five days before election day if he contests the decision of the election committee on his appeal for voting eligibility. The hearing must bring all the parties concerned including the complainant, the representative of the election committee and other interested parties before the court and must be concluded before election day with the notification to all the parties involved.

An interested party (a wife, for example) may apply for declaration of a person (e.g. husband) as missing or dead to the basic people's court of the place of the missing person's domicile. The written application shall specify the facts and time of the disappearance, with a certificate issued by the public security or other relevant office to confirm it. The court, upon receiving the application, shall make a public notice to look for the missing person.

A person may be declared missing by a judgment if his whereabouts have not been known for two years and the court's public notice expires after three months. A judgment declaring death may be made by the court against the missing person where he has been missing for four years, or has disappeared after an accident for two years, or has been verified by the relevant state authority unlikely to survive after an accident and the public notice has expired after one year for disappearance and three months for missing after an accident since the date of issuance. Such a judgment shall be revoked upon the application of the interested party if the person re-appears after a declaration for missing or death is made.

Close relatives or interested parties may apply for determination of a person as being incapable or with limited capacity for civil conduct to the basic people's court of the place of the person's domicile. The court shall enter its judgment based on its review of the supporting facts and grounds submitted by the parties and expert corroboration, if necessary. The person shall be represented by his close relatives. A new judgment should be made based on the application of the person himself or his guardian to revoke the previous one if the causes of the person's incapacity or limited capacity have been removed.

Any individual, legal person or other organization may apply to ascertain certain property as ownerless to the basic court of the place where the property is located. The property shall be declared to be ownerless if the court's public notice expires after one year since its issuance without anyone claiming it. Such a judgment will result in the property being reverted to the State or the relevant collective. The court shall enter a new judgment to restore the ownership if the original owner or his successor appears and claims the property within the statute of limitation.

Procedure for hastening debt recovery: a creditor may petition the competent people's court for an order of payment to recover pecuniary debt or commercial instruments against a debtor. The court shall notify the petitioner of its acceptance of the case within five days of the filing if the parties are not involved in any other claim dispute and the order of payment can be served on the debtor. Where the court's examination finds that the request is well supported by the facts and law, the order of payment shall be issued within 15 days of the date of registration of the case. The creditor may request the court to execute the order if the debtor neither settles the debt, nor lodges his written dissent to the court within 15 days after receipt of the order. The procedure shall be terminated upon the court's receipt of the written dissent from the debtor, which will render the order invalid and will lead to an action if the creditor wants to enforce his rights.

Procedure for public notice for assertion of claims: any holder of an endorsable bill of exchange may apply for public notice for assertion of claims to the people's court of the place where the bill is to be paid if it is stolen, lost or destroyed. The court, if it accepts the application, shall notify the payer to suspend payment and issue a public notice within three days to request interested parties to assert their claims with a duration of not less than 60 days. During the period, any transfer of the rights on the instrument shall be void.

Upon receiving the claims from the interested parties, the court shall terminate the procedure by issuing a ruling and notifying the applicant and the payer. Where conflicts of claims exist, either the applicant or the claimant may file a lawsuit with the court. A judgment to invalidate the instrument may be rendered if no one asserts a claim. The applicant may demand the payment from the payer after the judgment is publicly announced. If any due reasons prevent an interested party from asserting his claim before the announcement of the judgment, he may institute a lawsuit at the court within one year of the date of his actual or constructive knowledge of the judgment.

Bankruptcy repayment procedure for enterprises with legal person status: since *The Enterprise Bankruptcy Law* of China (on trial) has been adopted to govern bankruptcy proceedings of state owned enterprises, the procedure in *The Law of Civil Procedure* is designed to deal with bankruptcy of other business organizations, mainly collective, private and foreign investment enterprises. The procedure, however, does not apply to enterprises without legal person status, such as individual business households or individual partnership.

According to Article 199, either the creditor or the debtor may **12.15** petition the court in the place of the enterprise location for the start of the procedure where severe losses make the enterprise unable to settle a debt when it is due. The court shall notify the ascertained creditors and the debtor within 10 days of the court's ruling to commence the procedure and make a public announcement accordingly.

Personally notified creditors shall file their claims to the court within 30 days of the receipt of the notice from the court and unnotified creditors shall petition within three months of the public announcement, otherwise their rights are considered as abandoned. The creditors may organize a creditors' meeting to discuss the plan of disposition and distribution as well as a settlement agreement. The court, on the other hand, shall set up a liquidation group to be composed of the responsible State authority at an upper level, other relevant State departments, such as taxation, planning, finance, labour and busines administration, and professionals. Being responsible to the court, the liquidation group is empowered to custody, sort out, appraise, dispose and distribute the property of the debtor. The court may approve the settlement reached by the creditors' meeting and the liquidation group, with a public announcement to suspend the procedure.

The secured creditors under Article 203 shall have priority in distribution of the debtor's property. However, unlike most of the bankruptcy laws of other countries, the secured part of the property is not deemed as bankruptcy repayment property. According to Article 204, after secured creditors have taken their parts, the bankruptcy repayment property shall be distributed in the following order: bankruptcy expenses; wages and labour insurance premiums; unpaid tax; unsecured creditors. Where the bankruptcy repayment property proves insufficient to satisfy the claims of the same order, proportional distribution shall be made.

The procedure, together with other bankruptcy legislation, has been criticized for its ambiguity, inoperability, unfair treatment to secured creditors over tax and wage liability, and destruction of the unified legal system of bankruptcy.[9] Currently, the revision of the existing bankruptcy laws are underway and some significant changes can be expected in the near future.

Trial Supervisory Procedure

12.16 Trial supervisory procedure is special in China in that it will only be applied to a situation where a mistake is found in a legally effective judgment or ruling. Thus, it is independent from normal trial procedures with the sole purpose of providing the wronged party with a procedural remedy.

According to Articles 177 through 188, trial supervisory procedure may be initiated by any one of the four ways:

(a) the president of the court submits the case to the trial committee to decide whether a new trial is necessary after a mistake is discovered;

(b) the people's court at a higher level, after finding a mistake in the lower court's decision, may either conduct a hearing itself or remand the lower court to retry the case;

(c) a party to the action may petition the original trial court or the court at a higher level to retry the case. A new trial should be conducted if the party proves that new evidence exists conclusive enough to reverse the original decision; the key evidence to support the original decision is not sufficient; the law was wrongly applied; the legal procedure in the original trial was violated so seriously that the correctness of the decision would be prejudiced; or corruption was committed by the trial person-

nel during the trial. The execution of the original court's decision however, shall not be suspended until the new trial is
ordered.

(d) a people's procuratorate, as a State institution responsible for
trial supervision, may protest against a court decision on the
ground of procedural or substantive violation which may also
lead to a new trial.

A mediation certificate may also be subject to the trial supervisory
procedure if the party produces evidence showing the mediation proceedings violated the principle of voluntariness or the content of the
settlement violated the law. The procedure, however is not available to
the parties to divorce proceedings after the judgment has become
effective. The statute of limitation for applying for a new trial is two
years from the date on which the original court's decision becomes
effective.

The new trial to be conducted by the court shall follow its original
trial instance. For example, if the mistake found in the appellant
court's decision warrants a new hearing, it should be retried as second
instance. The trial conducted by a higher court shall always be of
second instance. For a new trial, a new collegiate bench must be set up.
The personnel from the people's procuratorate shall be present where
the new trial results from its protest against the original decision.

Procedure of Execution

All civil judgements or rulings that have become effective shall be **12.17**
executed by the people's court of the first instance. Other legal documents subject to execution, such as arbitral awards and notarized
obligation deeds, shall be enforced by the court of the domicile of the
party subject to execution or the place of the property.

The methods a people's court may use for execution include freezing and transferring bank deposits; withholding income; and confiscat-
ing, freezing, auctioning or foreclosing property. The application of
these methods, however, shall be limited within the scope of the
obligation for which the party subject to execution is liable and subject
to the condition that essential living expenses of the party and his
family dependents have been preserved.

A people's court may issue a search warrant if the party subject to
execution is suspected of concealing the property. In addition, interest
at double the highest bank loan interest rate at the time shall be
charged against the party for his failure to carry out his obligation
under the judgment, court rulings or other legal documents. The legal
obligation of the party subject to execution shall continue if he is

unable to pay off his debts even after the aforementioned enforcement methods have been used. The creditor may petition the people's court for continuation to execute the judgment anytime when more property of the party subject to execution is found.

A people's court, by executing a judgement or other legal document, may also enforce the party to perform some specific acts. It may, for example, summon both parties involved before it to effect the delivery of certain property or commercial paper with compulsory measures to be taken if necessary. It may enforce eviction from a building or from land and transfer of the title of property. In the course of execution, all relevant units must follow the court's order and provide their assistance. All the expenses incurred by the court and other units for the execution shall be borne by the party subject to execution.

Under Article 212, the execution may be suspended if the party subject to execution provides security for his debt and the provision is consented to by the execution applicant. The estate of the party subject to execution shall be used to satisfy the judgment if the party dies before or during the execution. In case of termination of a legal person or organization as the party subject to execution, the entity that inherits its rights and obligations shall assume the duty to fulfil the obligation under the judgment.

Article 234 provides that execution may be stayed when the applicant agrees the extension of the period for the other party to perform its duty; a successor is needed after a party dies or closes business; a third party raises a well grounded objection to the object of the execution; and other necessary situations warrant a stay. The execution shall be resumed upon removal of these situations.

According to Article 235, execution shall be terminated if the applicant withdraws his application for execution; the legal document for execution is repealed; the party subject to execution dies without any estate to satisfy, or any successor to assume the legal obligation; he has difficulties in living without any source of income, any collateral to take a loan or any ability to work; the party who is entitled to the payment of alimony, payment of maintenance or child support dies; or other necessary situations call for termination.

A party may apply to a competent people's court to enforce an arbitral award or notarized obligation deed if the other refuses to carry out its legal obligations. It should be noted here that unlike enforcement of an international artitral award, the people's court may review the substance of the award in domestic proceedings, in addition to procedural matters. Article 217 authorizes the court to reject an application for execution of arbitral awards if the other party can prove that there is insufficient evidence to support the finding and the law is incorrectly applied. The refusal to execute an award may give the parties a choice to either agree on new arbitration proceedings or start a lawsuit at a court.

The statute of limitation for execution is one year if one of the parties is a natural citizen; six months if both parties are legal persons or other organizations. The people's court may entrust the execution to another if the property is located in another area.

Execution of a civil judgment has been a serious social and judicial concern in China for a long time. Unavailability of certain judicial doctrines such as lifting the corporate veil, local protectionism and insufficient judicial resources for enforcement have rended many judgments as nothing more than mere scrap paper.

Special Procedures Applicable to Civil Cases Involving Foreign Interests

The Law has a special part with six chapters to deal with procedures for civil actions involving foreign interests, which are defined by the Supreme Court to include cases with one or both parties being foreign nationals, enterprises or organizations, with facts concerning establishment, alteration or termination of civil legal relations between the parties taking place in a foreign country, or with the object of the litigation being located in a foreign country.[10]   **12.18**

Under Articles 238 and 239, the provisions of an international treaty acceded to by China shall prevail if they differ from or conflict with the provisions of the Law except those on which China has declared its reservation. Any civil actions against a foreign national, organization or international organization enjoying diplomatic privileges and immunities shall be handled with the relevant domestic laws and international treaties entered into by China.

Articles 243 through 246 stipulate that a people's court may exercise its jurisdiction over a dispute involving a foreign party by virtue of

(a) close nexus of contractual relations to China;
(b) the parties' choice;
(c) the foreign party subjecting itself to the court's jurisdiction by defending itself without challenging the court's competence over the case; or
(d) the provisions of the law for exclusive jurisdiction of a Chinese court, such as disputes arising from joint venture operations and co-operative exploitation of natural resources in China.[11]

According to the Supreme Court, where both Chinese and foreign courts have jurisdiction over a dispute and each party files a lawsuit to the courts in different countries respectively, the people's court may accept the case and enter its judgment accordingly, which will preclude the other party from applying for recognition of the foreign judgment in China unless an international treaty, of which both China and the foreign country are the member states, provides otherwise.

Under Article 241, a foreign party must appoint a lawyer from China as its trial attorney if so needed. According to the Supreme Court, however, the provision shall not prevent the foreign party from entrusting a lawyer or another national of his own country to be his litigation representative without a lawyer's capacity in China.[12] Chinese shall be used in hearings involving foreign parties and translation may be provided at the foreigner's own expense.

Under Article 247, legal process of civil action may be served on a foreign party without domicile within China by the following methods:

(a) any method provided by an international treaty acceded to by both China and the foreign country;[13]

(b) through diplomatic channels;

(c) through a Chinese diplomatic mission if the party to be served is a Chinese national;

(d) through an attorney authorized by the recipient;

(e) through the representative or branch office or a business agent stationed in China of the party to be served;

(f) through mail service if the law of the country of the recipient so permits and the circumstance warrants constructive receipt such as no-return of the mail service within six months;

(g) Where the service can not be made by the methods mentioned above, service by public notice for 6 months will be used.

By taking the foreign elements into consideration, the law extends the period to respond indictment and appeal petition and the period to file appeal from 15 days for domestic proceedings to 30 days from the date of receipt of the copy of the indictment, appeal petition, or the judgment of first instance if the foreign party does not have a domicile in China. The party may even request further extension of the period, subject to the court's discretion.

12.19   By the same token the usual period for completion of first and second instance within six and three months as provided for domestic proceedings shall not apply to civil proceedings involving foreign interests. The period in which an applicant shall start a lawsuit after the court grants property preservation on his request is also stretched to 30 days.

A valid arbitration agreement entered into by the parties either in their contract or after the dispute arises shall prevent the parties from instituting a lawsuit in a people's court. The validity of an arbitration clause may not be affected by the discharge or termination of the contract.

A party may apply to the intermediate court where the other party's domicile or the property is located to execute an arbitral award made by a Chinese arbitration tribunal if the other party fails to perform the obligation under it. The court, however, may disallowed the application if the evidence proves that

(a) there is no valid arbitration agreement between the parties;
(b) the party's right to due process is violated;
(c) the composition of the arbitration tribunal or the proceedings violates the relevant arbitration rules;
(d) the items decided by the award are not within the scope of the jurisdiction of the arbitration provided by the agreement; and
(e) the award violates social and public interests in China.

A Chinese arbitration tribunal may submit an application for property preservation to the people's court upon the request of a party to arbitration proceedings involving a foreign party and the court may grant its approval under the condition that security is provided by the requesting party.

A people's court and a foreign court may request each other's assistance in delivery of legal documents, investigation, collection of evidence and other judicial acts related to civil litigations in accordance with an international treaty acceded to by both countries, or under the principle of reciprocity.[14] As a matter of fact, in 1995 alone, 562 assignments of such judicial assistance were completed. According to the Supreme Court, such judicial assistance may extend to foreign courts without any relations with China under international treaties or the reciprocity principle as long as the request is made through diplomatic channels.[15] The people's court, however, will refuse to provide any assistance if the requested item by a foreign court is deemed harmful to the sovereignty, safety and social and public interest of China. A translation text in Chinese or other languages provided by the international treaty shall be attached to the request from a foreign court when submitted to a people's court.

Any judicial assistance provided by a people's court shall be conducted by following the procedures stipulated by the laws of China. The court may carry out the assistance by using a special method requested by the foreign court so long as the method does not contravene any laws of China.

No foreign organ or individual may conduct any judicial activities concerning service, investigation, and evidence collection in China unless permitted by the State authority. The exception is that without taking any compulsory measures, a foreign diplomat in China may conduct the aforementioned activities to its nationals within the scope of the laws of China.

A judgment rendered by a people's court may be executed by either a party's application to, or the people's court request under an international treaty or principle of reciprocity for, a competent foreign court for recognition and enforcement of the judgment if the party subject to execution or its property is not within China. An arbitral award entered by a Chinese tribunal, however, may only be enforced through the party's application.

A party or a foreign court may apply to the competent people's court to recognize and enforce a judgment rendered by the foreign court if there is obligation based on an international treaty or relation under the reciprocity principle. In 1994 an application for enforcing a judgment rendered by a Japanese court against a debtor's property in China was denied on the grounds that there existed neither any obligation based on an international treaty nor relationship under the reciprocity principle.[16] A foreign arbitral award may also be recognized and enforced by an intermediate court at the domicile of the party subject to execution or the place of the property through the party's application.[17]

The people's court may not entertain an application for enforcement of a foreign judgment if its review finds the judgment violates the basic legal principles, national sovereignty and safety, social and public interest.

Notes

[1] Certain Provisions Concerning Application of Ordinary Procedure To Economic Cases of the Supreme Court on November 16, 1993 with the issuing number (1993) 34 and Certain Provisions Concerning Application of Summary Procedure to Economic Cases of the Supreme Court on November 16, 1993 with the issuing number (1993) 35.
[2] Point 1 of the Certain Opinions Concerning Application of Law of Civil Procedures of the Supreme Court of July 14, 1992.
[3] Ibid. Points 28 and 29.
[4] Points 1 through 4 of the Certain Provisions for Strict Implementation of the Law of Civil Procedure on Economic Trials by the Supreme Court of 1994 with the issue number 29.
[5] Ibid. Points 6 through 8.
[6] The Supreme Court Reply to High Court of Hebei on March 6, 1995 with the Reply No. 2.
[7] Notice given three days prior to the trial is still provided in most situations in The Law of Criminal Procedures as amended on March 17, 1996. See Article 151.
[8] See above note 1, point 3 of the Provisions Concerning Summary procedure with the issuing number (1993) 35.
[9] See Tang, Wei Jian: The Legal system of Survival of the fittest — Principles of Bankruptcy, Edited by Jiang Ping, Chapter 15 (pp. 229–253), Gui Zhou People's Press, 1995.
[10] See above note 2, point 304.
[11] See Article 5 of the Law on Economic Contract Involving Foreign Interest 1985.
[12] See above note 2, point 308.
[13] China has joined the Convention On The Service Abroad Of Judicial And Extrajudicial Documents In Civil Or Commercial Matters (Hague) of November 16, 1965 in 1991. Accordingly, the Joint Notice On The Procedure Of Implementation of the Convention was issued by the Supreme Court, Ministry of Foreign affairs, and Ministry of Justice on March 4, 1992.

[14] So far China has signed agreements on judicial assistance with 25 countries.
[15] See above note 2, point 319.
[16] The details of the case were reported at the Bulletin of the Supreme Court, Issue 1 of 1996 (March 20 1996), at 29.
[17] The UN Convention On The Recognition And Enforcement Of Foreign Arbitration Awards (New York) of 1958 has been acceded to by China in 1986.

CHAPTER 13

INTELLECTUAL PROPERTY LAW

Bryan Bachner

City University of Hong Kong

Bryan Bachner is a graduate of Tufts University and the Washington College of Law at the American University. He is an Associate Professor of Law at the City University of Hong Kong. He is Managing Editor of the *Asia Pacific Law Review*. He is chair of the Hong Kong Environmental Law Association. His research interests include environmental law and law concerning intellectual property.

Introduction

Intellectual property law covers a broad area of laws designed to regu-   **13.01** late the ownership and use of intellectual property. Intellectual property may be divided up into three general categories: copyright, patents and trademarks. Generally speaking, the purpose of copyright is to protect the use of an expression of ideas, such as books or software programmes. Patent law is intended to regulate the use of inventions and trademark law is meant to regulate the use of commercial marks representative of companies.

Due to the vast increase in cultural and commercial activities relating to intellectual property in China arising out of the implementation of the Open Door Policy[1] as well as the international pressure brought to bear on China,[2] the importance of a stronger and more effective intellectual property law has become readily apparent.[3] Indeed since 1978, the Chinese government has been involved in a comprehensive reform of the copyright, patent and trademark laws[4]. Comments from the *White Paper on Intellectual Property* issued on June 16, 1994 underline China's commitment to improving the enforcement of intellectual property rights[5] and bear repeating:

> China cannot remain satisfied with the achievements it has already made. China is a developing country and still has much work toward optimizing its intellectual property system.... China is confident that the implementation of all the important

measures contained in the [laws] will mark a great new step forward in the nation's efforts to ensure the protection of intellectual property rights.[6]

The purpose of this chapter is to introduce the regulatory framework that enshrines these intellectual property rights within the People's Republic of China.

Copyright Protection

Historical Background

13.02 The first copyright law for China in the twentieth century was entitled the *Law of Author's Right of the Great Qing* promulgated in 1910. This law basically allowed copyright protection in a work of the author for the lifetime of the author plus 30 years and imposed a scale of fines for unauthorized use of an author's work if the use was not within the fair dealing exception as stipulated. Although the language of the statute is clear, no evidence could be found to affirm whether or not the law was implemented with any effect.[7]

The Qing Imperial Court had signed a treaty with the United States in 1903 extending mutual agreements concerning copyright protection.[8] Under the agreements protection was extended to foreign works, but limited to books, maps, prints or engravings, that were intended for special use by the Chinese people. Basically the objective of the agreement was to assure that English versions of these works were not reproduced. Translations were not necessarily protected by the treaty. Although there is mention in Articles 9 and 10 about the protection of trademarks and patents, the extent of that protection could not be substantiated.

Following the fall of the Qing Dynasty, the Nationalist Government under Sun Yat-sen and the Northern Warlord Government had promulgated specific statutes concerning copyright in 1906, 1914, 1928, 1930, 1937 and 1943.[9] The Northern Warlord Government, under a separate jurisdiction, enacted the *Law of Author's Right,* a copyright law which interestingly included specific limitations on the freedom of speech and press.

The Nationalist Government adopted a largely "Europeanized" version of copyright. The first author's rights law, signed into law on May 14, 1928, provided the author with exclusive reproduction rights over books, musical compositions, photographs and works of sculpture and other works concerning letters, sciences and the arts. Registration was a prerequisite to protection. The duration of protection usually extended to the life of the author plus 30 years. If authorship included a group of people, the duration would extend from the death of the last living person plus 30 years. Generally foreigners were extended national treatment in China.[10]

In 1946 the Nationalist Government signed a new treaty with the United States, entitled "The Treaty of Friendship, Commerce and Navigation".[11] This treaty provided some copyright protection to American authors against illegitimate reproduction and sale of U.S. works in China.

The establishment of the People's Republic of China in 1949, however, marked a dramatic change in the nation's approach to copyright. The objective of copyright rules during the early part of Communist rule is probably best captured by a statement by Mao Tse-tung where he explains how the creation of cultural expression must serve the overall social interest. He wrote

> [our purpose is] to ensure that literature and art fit well into the whole revolutionary machine as a component part, that they operate as a powerful weapon for uniting and educating the people and for attacking and destroying the enemy, and that they help the people fight the enemy with one heart and one mind.[12]

In 1949 the Communist government repudiated the existent domestic copyright law and all copyright agreements which had been signed between the Nationalist Government and other foreign countries.[13] Prior to conquering the mainland, the Communist party, while living in the areas of liberation, had not enacted any legislative directives to protect the rights of authors or create copyrights.[14]

One year after the Communist Party had established control over the mainland, the Central Committee declared an intent to create a viable copyright system.[15] That year the Government Administrative Council of the Central People's Government issued a *Decision on Awards for Inventions, Technical Improvements and Rationalization Proposals Relating to Production* (Decision).[16] The rule was meant to reassure authors that copyright was on the legislative agenda and promote the establishment of an author's rights regime to protect against the reproduction of works without consent.

Also in 1950 the *Resolution on the Improvement and Development of Publishing Work* (Resolution) was adopted. It set out more clearly how publishers and authors should determine the royalty payment for a publication. Article 12 of the Resolution stipulated that a royalty ought initially account for three factors: the reader's interest, the author's interest and the publisher's interest. The final calculation should also consider the nature and quality of the work, the number of Chinese characters and the number of copies printed.

Despite the comprehensive consideration of the value of a work stated in the Resolution, the mid-1950's marked a period of time when author's rights were substantially marginalized. In 1957 the policy with regard to royalty payments changed dramatically and the value of the author's contribution to the work was drastically reduced. The Central Committee confined the determination of royalties to consideration of the number of characters in a text and the number of copies of the text distributed. In 1961 the Central Committee further limited the author's payment to a per character basis. Furthermore a contract form commonly used in those days entitled *Contract for Publication of Works by the People's Press* (Publication Contract)[17] provided that the publisher gained the exclusive right to publish a contracted work throughout China. The contracting author agreed not to allow any publication of the work by any other publisher and the author assumed liability for any breach. The contract form also stipulated the publisher's right to compel the author to make appropriate revisions.

13.03   While it may be fair to say that rules concerning copyright were being formalized, the infringement of an author's or publisher's copyright in a work remained common. For example, in the early 1950's World Knowledge Press in Beijing had published an account of the Korean War.[18] A short time after the original publication, the Dalian Bookstore, a branch of the New China Bookstore, had reproduced 5,000 copies of the work and re-entitled it *The International Situation After the Korean War* with the inscription "First Edition Dalian", "All Rights Reserved" and "No Reproduction Allowed" on the book's copyright page. World Knowledge Press sought damages from this blatant copying; the General Publishing Office was assigned to adjudicate the dispute. They found that Dalian had never obtained permission to use the original book, found them guilty of violating World Knowledge Press's rights and implicitly acknowledged the need for a better system of copyright. The final report stated

> We believe that the action of the Dalian Bookstore in reproducing another publication just after the adoption of Resolutions at the Publishing Conference is extremely improper; even if readers urgently need this material, the Bookstore should first have consulted the publisher and asked for its agreement. Before obtaining that agreement the Bookstore should not have reproduced (the book) of its own accord.

In response to the weaknesses in the copyright system highlighted in the Dalian case, the Government Administration Council promulgated in 1952 the *Provisional Regulations on Management of Book and Periodical Publishing, Printing and Distribution* (Provisional Regulations).[19] For the first time in the new People's Republic copyright, although not specifically defined, was, in some sense, protected. The regulations stipulated that publishers must not infringe the author's copyright and that the author of a particular work had a right to its copyright. An infringement could result in penalties ranging from a warning from the General Office to a revocation of a publisher's licence to publish books.

The promulgation of *Regulations on the Editorial Structure and the Work System of State-Run Publishing Houses* soon after the enactment of the provisional regulations highlighted the government's early reluctance to protect the author's right in a work; through these regulations the government sought to encourage the protection of copyright through the use of comprehensive contracts. It has been argued that as a result of the increasing use of contracts to govern copyright, disputes between publishers and authors over copyright were reduced and those disputes that did arise were usually settled through consultation or mediation.[20]

The gradual development of copyright law through contractual negotiations and regulatory mechanisms was suspended, however, as a result of the implementation of repressive cultural policies during the Cultural Revolution. One Chinese publishing official commented that

> The publishing work of our country since the liberation has made rapid progress. From 1949 to 1978, 302,000 new titles have been published in a total of 50,309,000 copies. After 1966, due to interference and sabotage by the Gang of Four, the publication of books suffered unprecedented atrophy. Many publications were forbidden. The titles were so depleted that most bookstores had no books to sell and most readers had no books to read. This extremely abnormal phenomenon ended with the downfall of the Gang of Four.[21]

Fundamentally, during the Cultural Revolution, the State took away any moral rights the author may have had in a work; in other words the integrity of the work could no longer be protected or claimed by the individual author: at creation, the work became State property and the work itself was subsumed by the interests of State.[22] The author lost basic publication rights, the right to protect the character of the work and the right to have the author's name mentioned as the creator of the work.[23] A maxim popularized during the Cultural Revolution illustrated this point:

> Is it necessary for a steel worker to put his name on a steel ingot which he produces in the course of his duty? If not, why should a member of the intelligentsia enjoy the privilege of giving his name on his intellectual product?

During the Cultural Revolution, the Central Committee eliminated the administrative agencies responsible for publishing.[24] Piracy of works proliferated due to a Government policy to reclaim as State property all previously copyrighted works. The Central Committee also abolished contracts between author and publisher and eradicated all payment beyond the base salary, thereby excluding the previously allowed per word royalty.

Following the demise of the Gang of Four and the discontinuation of the policies of the Cultural Revolution, the development of the author's right to protect his or her work noticeably improved. In 1978 the Central Committee issued the *Directive on Trial Methods for News and Publishing Royalties*. This directive regranted to authors, rights to receive a minimal remuneration for publication of works. The directive stipulated a royalty based on a per-character standard, the quality of the mechanical writing and the type of material published. Similar to the 1961 directive, the publisher would not be allowed to substantiate the royalty fee on the basis of the number of copies produced or the quality of the work itself.[25] The promulgation of the 1980 *Provisional Regulation on Book Royalties* reiterated the dismantling of the policies of the Cultural Revolution by allowing a dual system of per-word and per-copy royalties.[26] Another major piece of legislation with regards to author's rights was the 1983 *Notice of the State Council Approving the Circulation of the Interim Measures on the Management of Audio-Visual Manufacturers*.

By 1985 the State Council had established the National Copyright Administration and a year later, the National People's Congress had passed the *General Principles of Civil Law*.[27] Articles 94 and 118 respectively included reference to the regulation of copyright in China. Article 94 stipulated that citizens should enjoy the right of authorship and that in accordance with the law, such authors should have the right to sign works, to publish their works and to receive payment for their works. Article 118 asserts that where plagiarism, distortion or passing off arises, the injured party has the right to demand that the infringement cease, its effects be eliminated and damages paid. By 1990, the People's Republic of China had reversed the policies of the Cultural Revolution and had enacted its first copyright legislation.

Modern Copyright Law

13.04   Copyright law in the People's Republic of China is a difficult area to survey. The problematic nature of the law may best be illustrated by the fact that the drafters had difficulty in deciding whether or not to define the law in terms of copyright or author's rights.[28] In a compromise between the two positions, the title of the fundamental legislation translates into "author's rights" while Article 52 of the legislation states that author's rights and copyright are to mean the same thing. In light of this complexity the aim of this section is only to describe the regulatory framework concerning copyright in the PRC.[29] This section will basically discuss three laws: *The Copyright Law of the Peoples' Republic of China* (and its implementing regulations); *Regulations for the Implementation of International Copyright Treaties*; and *Regulations for the Protection of Computer Software*.

The Copyright Law of the People's Republic of China

Due largely to international obligations[30] and the necessity of clarifying issues of copyright liability,[31] the People's Republic of China, since 1980, had committed itself to establishing a comprehensive copyright legal system. On September 7, 1990, the People's Republic of China adopted *The Copyright Law of the People's Republic of China* (Copyright Law) at the 15th meeting of the Standing Committee of the 7th National People's Congress. The law went into effect on June 1, 1991.[32]

According to Article 8, the National Copyright Administration (NCA) governs the enforcement of copyright law in China. In particular, the NCA must investigate important infringement cases, regulate the administration of foreign based copyright issues, establish administrative agencies and arbitration agencies on copyright disputes, look after State owned copyrights and monitor enforcement activities of local copyright authorities[33]. While the NCA is responsible for national issues, the local copyright administration have been established to administer local issues.

The Copyright Law governs Chinese citizens, legal persons as well as units that do not have the status of legal persons in China.[34] Foreigners also gain protection under the law where the law is extended to them through relevant international treaties.[35] The following subjects are entitled to protection under the copyright law: musical, dramatic and choreographic works; literary works; oral works; works of fine art; photographic works; television and video works; maps and schematic drawings; and computer programmes amongst others.[36] Other works protected under the law include: adaptations, translations, annotations and collations of work that have already been copyrighted.[37] Items such as laws, regulations, administrative or judicial documents, and their official translations as well as news on current affairs and calendars among other things are excluded from copyright protection. The law also stipulates that a copyright may not be implemented where a violation of the Constitution will result or the public interest will be harmed.[38]

The author of a work is normally considered to be the copyright holder in China. The copyright holder has the authority to determine whether or not a particular subject matter is published, to demand attribution from users, to amend his subject matter and to prohibit others from misrepresenting or distorting the subject matter.[39] According to the reasonable use exception, however, there are certain times when the author of a work may not restrict the use of his or her work.[40] These exceptions include: the use of a published work for academic study or research; translation of a small amount of a published work for use in a classroom; use by a State organization for the performance of official responsibilities; reproduction of a work by a library or museum for the sake of preservation; and non commercial performances of a published work. Generally speaking copyrights subsist for the life of the author plus 50 years except for copyrights in cinematographic, television and photographic works as well as video and sound recordings where protection lasts for 50 years from the work's first publication[41].

Infringement of the copyright law gives rise to a series of civil and criminal penalties.[42] Infringements include: plagiarising; wrongful attribution of authorship for fine art; unauthorized reproduction and distribution of that work for profit; publication of a book where someone else has the exclusive right of publication; unauthorized production and distribution of a sound or video recording of a live performance; and unauthorized reproduction and distribution of a radio or television programme. Some criminal sanctions for copyright infringement exist.[43]

Regulations for Implementation of International Copyright Treaties

13.05   In order to assure that China properly enforces international obligations with regard to copyright, the State Council enacted on September 25, 1992 the *Regulations for the Implementation of International Copyright Treaties.*[44] They went into force on 30 September 1992. The international agreements which are referred to in the Regulations include: the Berne Convention for the Protection of Literary and Artistic Works (15 October 1992); the Universal Copyright Convention (30 October 1992); and the Convention for the Protection of Producers of Phonograms Against Unauthorized Duplication of their Phonograms (30 April 1993) and other relevant multinational and bilateral agreements. According to the regulations when an international treaty comes into force, foreign works entitled to copyright protection will be given protection in accordance with Chinese copyright law. Where Chinese citizens or legal entities have use or possession of a foreign work prior to the accession of the international treaty, the user may continue to use the work without being held liable as long as the user does not unreasonably prejudice the original copyrighted work.[45]

Protection of Computer Software

According to Article 53 of the Copyright Law, independent regulations were to be promulgated in order to govern copyright protection of computer software.[46] On June 4, 1991, the State Council approved the *Regulations for the Protection of Computer Software* (Regulations). They came into effect on October 1, 1991. In addition to the software Regulations, the Ministry of Machine-Building and Electronics Industry (MMBEI) approved the *Measures for the Registration of Copyright in Computer Software* on April 6, 1992.[47]

According to the Regulations a computer programme is defined as a coded sequence of instructions which are performed by a computer in order to achieve a particular consequence or a symbolic instruction sequence that can be converted into code. The source and object codes included in the programmes are dealt with as if they were the same.[48] The documentation of the programme may include amongst other things the user's manual, flowcharts, content, functional specifications and developmental situations.[49] Copyrightable software must be original and fixed in a tangible medium.[50]

PRC citizens, legal persons and foreigners who first publish their software in China will be able to enjoy the rights protected by the Regulations.[51] Foreigners who first publish their software programmes elsewhere but wish to enjoy copyright protection in China will be subject to bilateral or multilateral international copyright agreements entered into by China. The authority responsible for administering the registration of the software programmes is the Ministry of Electronics Industry (The MMBEI has, since the original approval of the registration measures, split up into two ministries). The China Software and Assessment and Registration Centre is responsible for examining and deciding whether to approve applications for registration.

There are five fundamental rights for the copyright owner of a software programme protected by the Regulations.[52] They are: the right to publish; the right of developership; the right of exploitation (*i.e.* copying, exhibiting, distributing, amending, translating, annotating so long as the use does not conflict with social norms); the right to licence and receive compensation for use of the programme by others; the right to transfer the right of usage and licensing to other interested parties. Normally the software programme is entitled to protection for the first 25 years after publication. Extensions may be applied for prior to the expiration of the first 25 years.

The Regulations also specify certain reasonable uses by legitimate holders of software programmes in which these holders need not seek the consent of the copyright owner[53]. The holders may install the software in a computer in accordance with the relevant use of the programme. The holder may make back-up copies, but these back-up copies may not be given to others for use. Once the holder loses his legitimate claim to use of the software programme, the back-up copies must be totally destroyed. The holder may make necessary changes to the nature of the software programme in order to make the software compatible with his or her computer, however, at no time may a third party take possession of this revised programme without consent of the original copyright owner. If the software is being used for a non-commercial purpose such as classroom teaching, scientific research or official business by State organizations, a small number of copies of the programme may be made without getting the consent of the copyright owner. When used the software must be properly attributed to the software developer and no other rights of the copyright owner should be infringed.[54]

Legal liability for infringement[55] will arise where a software programme is published without the consent of the owner; publishing a piece of software developed by others; publishing a piece of software without the consent of the cooperative developers; a software programme is changed without the consent of the copyright owner; a software programme is copied without the consent of the copyright owner; a software programme is publicly distributed without the consent of the copyright owner; or a licence for use of a software programme is given without the consent of the copyright owner.[56] Remedies for infringement include orders to cease the infringement, eliminate the effects of the infringement, make a public apology or compensate for losses suffered. The National Software Administration has the authority to demand confiscation of illegally obtained income, payment of fines and other administrative punishments deemed suitable.

Patent Law

13.06   Patent laws have existed in the People's Republic of China since the earlier part of the founding of modern China, (e.g. *Provisional Regulations on the Protection of Invention Rights and Patent Rights* (August 11, 1950)); however, few patents were ever received under the early regime.[57] New rules concerning invention were enacted in 1963, namely *Regulations to Encourage Inventions* and *Regulations to Encourage Improvement in Technology*. They served to extend considerable control over a patent to the State while providing only some honourary or financial awards to the inventors.[58] During the Cultural Revolution the enforcement of patent law was further neglected. It was not until the end of the Cultural Revolution and the death of Mao Zedong that the reform of patent law received serious consideration from the Government.

The controversy surrounding the reform of patent law is illustrative of the more general difficulties with the implementation of the law reform arising during the late 1970's and early 1980's.[59] There were a number of arguments in favour of patent law reform. First, patent law reform was necessary in order to eliminate the "iron rice bowl" system which, it was argued, rewarded technological mediocrity and ordinariness, and to replace it with an incentive-based system where inventors would be adequately rewarded and protected for creating useful inventions.[60] Advocates also appreciated that multinational corporations were reluctant to invest and apply their technology in a country without sufficient intellectual property protection and argued that stronger patent laws were necessary if China wished to attract more foreign investment and import more technology from abroad.[61] Conversely it was stated that if China did not enact an adequate patent law, China could not belong to any international patent agreements and therefore China's own inventors would not be able to obtain reciprocal protection of their Chinese-made inventions in foreign jurisdictions.[62]

While arguments supporting the passage of a patent law seemed strong, contentions against the patent law were no less effective. One school of thought argued on pure ideological grounds that a patent law was contrary to the socialist principles upon which the political system underlying the People's Republic of China was based and that the granting of patents would allow a few elite to control and, thereby, misallocate the use of technology that was necessary for the benefit of the masses.[63] Others criticized the implementation of a patent law by claiming that it promoted a western system of technological innovation that was inherently prejudicial to the development of an indigenous science; moreover, it was suggested that the liberal nature of the patent system would allow foreign enterprises to control and dominate Chinese technology.[64]

The sharp division of opinions resulted in the government's failure to reach any consensus on the issue of patents and required the intervention of Deng Xiaoping who decided that China needed to reform its patent law in order to effectively implement the Open Door Policy. In April 1985 China finally enacted *The Patent Law of the People's Republic of China* and the supplementary implementing regulations. Additional examples of regulatory protection for patents include the promulgation of the *Decision of the Standing Committee of the National People's Congress Concerning the Amendment of the Patent Law of the People's Republic of China* following an agreement with the United States in early January of 1992; *Regulations on the Administrative Protection of Pharmaceutical Products* and the *Regulations for the Administrative Protection of Agricultural Chemical Products*. In 1993, the Patent Office of the PRC revised its "Examination Guidelines" and, for the first time, made them publicly available.[65]

The Patent Law governs inventions, utility models, designs[66] and pharmaceutical items produced by chemical processes. Animal and plant varieties as well as scientific discoveries may not be patented.[67] Inventions are protected for 20 years while utility models and designs are protected for ten years[68]. Like trademarks, the patent law abides by the "first to file" rule; so the first inventor to file application for patent has the right to the award for that particular invention. Applications for patents may be sought through the Patent Agent in Beijing, China Patent Agent (Hong Kong) Ltd or the NTD Patent and Trademark Agency Ltd in Hong Kong. In addition, China has acceded to several important international patent treaties, including the Paris Convention for the Protection of Industrial Property and the Patent Cooperation Treaty.

An invention or utility model will receive a patent if it is characterized by novelty, inventiveness and usefulness.[69] The concept of novelty refers to a condition whereby prior to filing, no identical invention or utility model has been publicly disclosed nor has a patent application been made for the same invention or utility model. The concept of inventiveness refers to the notion that an invention or utility model must be distinguishable in a substantive manner from other similar products and must in some way be better than the other similar products. The concept of usefulness refers to the notion that an invention or utility model must have the capacity to produce positive results.

If a patent holder's right is infringed, the patent holder may bring a claim to the administrative authority or go directly to the People's Court.[70] The patent holder is limited to bring his or her suit within two years of the discovery of the infringement. If the patent holder has sought administrative relief but is not satisfied with the decision, he may bring an action to the People's Court within three months of knowing the administrative decision. Administrative remedies include ordering the cessation of the infringement or compensation for the damages caused.[71]

Trademark Law

13.07   During the early years of the People's Republic of China, the enforcement of trademark rights was extremely problematic. It has been recorded that unauthorized use of trademarks was extensive in the 1950's.[72] Part of the trademark protection problem originated in the ideological contradiction of a socialist government trying to enforce a proprietary trademark law. The law of trademark was originally intended to establish private proprietary rights in a commercial mark in order to protect the commercial interests of a manufacturer and the consumer interests of citizens. According to Alford, by the late 1950's, most capitalist businesses in China had been converted to socialist enterprises and the administration of trademark was seen merely as a means to assure the quality of a product while the issue concerning exclusive rights of use and ownership of a trademark disappeared.[73]

After the Cultural Revolution China tried to return to its prior trademark position. The State General Administration for Industry and Commerce and the China Council for the Promotion of International Trade were made responsible for re-implementing trademark regulation, bringing some order back to the domestic trademark system and attempting to re-establish China's position in the international trademark legal framework.[74] By the early 1980's, due to the economic growth and increase in the use of intellectual property precipitated by the implementaiton of the Open Door Policy, China was prepared for and required the implementation of a new trademark system.

The Trademark Law of the People's Republic of China (Trademark Law) was established on March 1, 1983 and was supplemented by the *Detailed Implementing Regulations of the Trademark Law* in January of 1988. China approved the *Supplementary Provisions for the Punishment of Crimes of Passing Off Registered Trademarks* in 1993. The purpose of these regulations is to set out the administration, registration and protection of trademarks in the People's Republic of China.[75] *The Trademark Law* was amended in 1993; the implementing regulations were amended in 1988, 1993 and 1995. *The Criminal Law* was also revised in 1993 to cover the counterfeiting of registered trademarks.[76] The mainland employs the international classification of trademarks as stipulated in the *International Classification of Goods and Services*. As of 1989 China became a member of the *Madrid Agreement for the International Registration of Marks*, an agreement which facilitates reciprocal protection amongst member countries.

The objective of *The Trademark Law* is to protect the exclusive right of a trademark owner or user to employ a trademark, while protecting the consumer's interest and encouraging the development of the socialist market economy.[77] The law covers both service marks and commodity trademarks. A trademark is identified as a word or, design or their combination that has distinctive characteristics so as to facilitate identification.[78] The law adopts a "first to file" approach; in other words, the first to file a unique trademark will have the right to protection. Trademark protection lasts for ten years and each renewal may extend the legal protection for another ten years.[79] There are a variety of administrative offices established to allow for registration and enforcement of *The Trademark Law* at national and local levels. The primary offices include: The State Administration of Industry and Commerce, the Trademark Office, the Trademark Review and Adjudication Board, China Trademark Service and China Trademark Agency.

In order to register a trademark, an applicant must first report the class of goods and the designation of goods for which the trademark is intended to be used.[80] When a proper application has been made, the Trademark Office will perform a preliminary examination of the trademark and publicly announce its decision.[81] Opposition to the approval of trademark by third parties is allowed.[82] Appeals to rejections of a trademark application must be filed with the Trademark Review and Adjudication Board within 15 days of receiving notification of the rejection.[83] Furthermore, a registered trademark will be revoked where it is found that a word or design has been altered without authorization, the registrant's name or address is changed without appropriate notification, the registered trademark is assigned without authorization or the registered trademark has not been used for three years.[84]

Where a trademark is infringed the injured party has two possibilities to redress the problem.[85] First he may inform the responsible administrative authority, the Trademark Review and Adjudication Board and ask it to pursue the case. Second, the injured party may make a claim directly to the People's Court. Challenges of an administrative decision may be either appealed to the next highest administrative authority, or be brought before the People's Court. Remedies include the prohibition of all sales of the trademarked products, the destruction of all of the infringing product, fining the offender, as well as ordering the payment of compensation to the injured party.[86] Criminal sanctions also provide for the option of imprisonment of the offenders.[87]

Notes

I would like to thank Professor Zhang Yurui of the Law Institute of the China Academy of Social Sciences for his help in identifying relevant source materials and Kong Chi Keung for his research assistance.

[1] "White Paper Hails Property Protections", *China Daily* June 17, 1994, p. 4. See generally, Joshua Floum, "Counterfeiting in the People's Republic of China: Perspective of the Foreign Intellectual Property Holder", *Journal of World Trade*, Volume 28, Number 5, October 1994 35–59.

[2] See, *e.g.* Helene Cooper and Marcus Brauchli, "US Threatens Sanctions Against China in Reprise of Last Year's Copyright Fight", *The Wall Street Journal*, January 23, 1996, p. 2. See also David Silverstein, "The US-China Trade Dispute over Intellectual Property Protection: Timely Resolution or Time Bomb", *North Atlantic Regional Business Law Review*, Spring 1995, 105–118. But see Chen Yanni, "IPR Gets Full Legal Backing", *China Daily*, June 6, 1996, p. 1 (arguing that regardless of the outcome of forthcoming talks with the United States, China will give full protection to intellectual property rights).

[3] The best analysis of the law concerning intellectual property in the People's Republic of China that I have read is William Alford, *To Steal a Book is an Elegant Offence: Intellectual Property Law in Chinese Civilization* (Stanford: Stanford University Press, 1995).

[4] See Derek Dessler, "China's Intellectual Property Protection: Prospects for Achieving International Standards", *Fordham International Law Journal*, Volume 19, October 1995 181–246. See further Michael Schlesinger, "A Sleeping Giant Awakens: the Development of Intellectual Property Law in China", *Journal of Chinese Law* Volume 9, Spring 1995, 93–140. See also Jianyang Yu, "Protection of Intellectual Property in the PRC: Progress, Problems and Proposals", *UCLA Pacific Basin Law Journal* Volume 13, Fall 1994, 140–162.

[5] China's commitment to the protection of intellectual property rights is further illustrated by China's ratification of the Agreement on Trade-Related Aspects of Intellectual Property Rights, Including Trade in Counterfeit Goods. See Information Office of the State Council, "White Paper on Intellectual Property Protection in China", June 1994, p. 21.

⁶ See above note 5.
⁷ Owen, "Copyright in China", Vol. 1, No. 3 *Rights, Copyright and Related Rights in the Service of Creativity* (Autumn, 1987).
⁸ Pub. L. 93-618, 88 Stat. 1978, 19 U.S.C. 2101 *et seq.*
⁹ Shen and Yu, *Banauanfa Qiantan* (1982) 100; Shen, "Banquan yu Banquan Baohu", 8 *Baike Zhishi* (1980) 192; Zhang, "Xinwen Yeyao Lifa", 18 *Baike Zhishi* (1981) 976 as cited in Authors in China.
¹⁰ Lavagna, "Le Droit d'Auteur en Chine" 1 *Il Diritto Di Autore* (1937).
¹¹ 1946 Treaty of Friendship, Commerce and Navigation, *Copyright Law and Treaties of the World* (19).
¹² *Quotations for Chairman Mao Tse-Tong* (1967) 173.
¹³ Baumgarten, "Copyright Relations Between the United States and the People's Republic of China — the Seventeenth Annual Jean Geiringer Memorial Lecture", 23 *Bulletin of the Copyright Society of the USA* 421.
¹⁴ Sidel, "The Legal Protection of Copyright and the Rights of Authors in the People's Republic of China, 1949–1984: Prelude to the Chinese Copyright Law", 9 *Columbia Journal of Art and Law* 479.
¹⁵ For a discussion of the historical context of the early copyright law in the People's Republic of China, see Zhang Chengsi, "The Future Chinese Copyright System and Its Context", Vol. 15, No. 2 *International Review of Industrial Property and Copyright Law* 144.
¹⁶ 1 *Zhongyang Renmin Zhengfu Faling Huibian* (Laws and Decrees of the Central People's Government) (1950) 460.
¹⁷ 3 *Chung Hua Jen Min Kung Ho Kou Min Fa Ts an K'ao Tzu Liao* (Reference Materials on *The Civil Law* of the People's Republic of China) published by the Chinese People's University as cited in Goldstein, "Copyright Relations Between the United States and the People's Republic of China: An Interim Report", 2 *Brooklyn Journal of International Law* 403, 414.
¹⁸ Shen and Yu, *Banquanfa Quiantan* at 106.
¹⁹ *Ibid.* at 482.
²⁰ *Ibid.* at 485.
²¹ Carnese, "China Diary — U.S. Publishers In Historic Visit Discuss Copyright and Other Book Related Matters", *Publisher's Weekly*, June 4,1979 at 27.
²² See generally, Zhang Chengsi, "The Future of Chinese Copyright System and Its Context".
²³ Some have argued that this failure to respect the author's contribution to the work was a result of the government's intention to censor thought and to undermine intellectuals as a political force. One Chinese writer noted:

> The absence of a comprehensive statute for copyright protection supports the theory that the Chinese since 1949 have become increasingly wary of according extraordinary rights to creative individuals by law for fear of contributing to the establishment of an elite group . . . In the field of literary and artistic achievement, there has been no comparable countervailing motive powerful enough to overcome the regime's distaste for legislating extensive rights for an elite group. Especially since the Cultural Revolution, that distaste has expanded to include almost all types of what the Westerner would consider creative literature. The Belles-Lettres are at a nadir in the People's Republic of China.Hsia & Haun, "Law of the People's Republic of China on Industrial and Intellectual Property", 38 *Law and Contemporary Problems* 290 (1983).

²⁴ *Authors in China* at 486.
²⁵ *Authors in China* at 488.
²⁶ The liberalization of copyright policy in the People's Republic of China was further highlighted by the emergence of an internationalization of copyright concerns. In 1980 the PRC deposited an instrument of accession with the World Intellectual Property Organization (WIPO) to join the Paris Convention and the Berne Convention.
²⁷ Joseph Simone, "Copyright in the People's Republic of China: A Foreignor's Guide", (1988) *Cardoza Arts and Entertainment Law Journal* Volume 7, Number 1, p. 4.
²⁸ Zheng Chengsi, "The First Copyright Law of the PRC", [1990] *European Intellectual Property Review* volume 10, p. 376.
²⁹ For a more comprehensive analysis of Chinese copyright law, see above note 26.

30 Zheng Chengsi, "The First Copyright Law of the PRC" at 376.
31 See Zheng Chengsi with Michael Pendleton, "China's First Court Decision on Copyright: Jiang v Qiao and the Film 'Hospital Ward No. 16'", [1990]*European Intellectual Property Review*, Volume 6, p. 217.
32 Joseph Simone, "Copyright Law Finally Enacted", 22 November 1990, *IP Asia*, p. 21.
33 Article 7 of Regulations for the Implementation of Copyright Law of the PRC (1991).
34 Article 2, *Copyright Law of the People's Republic of China.*
35 *Ibid.*
36 Article 3, *Copyright Law of the People's Republic of China.*
37 Article 12, *Copyright Law of the People's Republic of China.*
38 Article 4, *Copyright Law of the People's Republic of China.*
39 *Intellectual Property Guide — People's Republic of China* at p. 13.
40 Article 22, *Copyright Law of the People's Republic of China.*
41 Joseph Simone, "Copyright Law Finally Enacted", *IP Asia* 22 November 1996, p. 21.
42 Joseph Simone, "Copyright Law Enters Into Effect", *IP Asia* 4 July 1991, p. 21.
43 See the Decision of the Standing Committee of the NPC on Cracking Down Crimes of Infringement of Copyrights of July 5, 1994.
44 *Intellectual Property Guide — People's Republic of China* at p. 16.
45 Article 17 of the Regulations.
46 See generally KH Pun, "A Critique of Copyright Protection for Computer Software in the People's Republic of Chian", *European Intellectual Property Review*, Volume 16, June 1994 and Zheng Chengsi, "The Protection of Computer Programs Under the Chinese Copyright Law", *European Intellectual Property Review*, Volume 7, July 1995.
47 For a review of some problems related to the drafting of the registration measures, see Joseph Simone, "Copyright: Software Registration", *IP Asia* November 28, 1991, p. 24.
48 Article 3 of the Regulations. See also Lu Song, "Computer Software Protection — New Development in the People's Republic of China" *Software Protection* Volume X, Number 1 (June 1991), p. 1.
49 Article 3, *Regulation on the Protection of Computer Software.*
50 Article 5, *Regulation on the Protection of Computer Software.*
51 Jia Zhao, "Computer Software Protection: New Regulations Go Into Effect", *East Asian Executive Reports*, October 1991, p. 9.
52 Article 9 of the Regulations.
53 Article 21 of the Regulation.
54 Article 22 of the Regulations.
55 Chapter 4 (Articles 30–37) of the Regulations.
56 Article 30 of the Regulations.
57 *Intellectual Property Guide — People's Republic of China* at 18.
58 *Ibid.*
59 William Alford, *To Steal a Book is an Elegant Offence: Intellectual Property Law in Chinese Civilization* (Stanford: Stanford University Press, 1995) at 67.
60 *Ibid.* at 67.
61 *Ibid.*
62 *Ibid.* at 68.
63 *Ibid.*
64 *Ibid.* at 69.
65 KH Pun, "Patentability of Computer Software in China", *European Intellectual Property Review*, Volume 8, August 1995.
66 Article 2, *Patent Law of the People's Republic of China.*
67 Article 25, *Patent Law of the People's Republic of China.*
68 Article 45, *Patent Law of the People's Republic of China.*
69 Article 22, *Patent Law of the People's Republic of China.*
70 Article 60, *Patent Law of the People's Republicof China.*
71 Article 60, *Patent Law of the People's Republic of China.*
72 *To Steal a Book is an Elegant Offence: Intellectual Property Law in Chinese Civilization* at 61.
73 *Ibid.*
74 *Ibid.* at 65–66.
75 *Intellectual Property Guide — People's Republic of China* at p. 3.

76 Jianyang Yu, "Protection of Intellectual Property in the PRC: Progress, Problems & Proposals", Volume 13, [1994] *UCLA Pacific Basin Law Journal* , 140, 141.
77 M Schlesinger, "A Sleeping Giant Awakens: the Development of Intellectual Property Law in China", Volume 9 [1995] *Journal of Chinese Law* 93, 101.
78 Article 7, *Trademark Law of the People's Republic of China.*
79 Article 24, *Trademark Law of the People's Republic of China.*
80 Article 11, *Trademark Law of the People's Republic of China.*
81 Article 16, *Trademark Law of the People's Republic of China.*
82 Article 19, *Trademark Law of the People's Republic of China.*
83 Article 21, *Trademark Law of the People's Republic of China.*
84 Article 30, *Trademark Law of the People's Republic of China.*
85 Derek Dessler, "China's Intellectual Property Protection: Prospects for Achieving International Standards", Volume 19 [1995], *Fordham International Law Journal* 181, 193.
86 Article 43, *Trademark Law of the People's Republic of China.*
87 Article 40, *Trademark Law of the People's Republic of China.*

CHAPTER 14
LABOUR LAW

Lin Feng

City University of Hong Kong

Lin Feng, Assistant Professor of Law, Faculty of Law, City University of Hong Kong; formerly Assistant Professor of Law, Faculty of Law, Fudan University, Shanghai, China; LL.M., Victoria University of Wellington, New Zealand, 1992; LL.B., Fudan University, 1987; B.Sc. in Physics (equivalent), Fudan University, 1985.

Introduction

China's labour legislation has undergone rapid changes since the adoption of *The Labour Law* of the People's Republic of China (hereinafter as Labour Law) in July 1994. The enactment of the Labour Law is very essential to the development of labour legislation in China in the sense that it has set up the structure of labour legislation and put an end to the situation under which there was no comprehensive national Labour Law. The promulgation of the Labour Law has also made it possible to streamline the existing labour legislation both at national and local levels. At national level, the Ministry of Labour issued seventeen regulations shortly after the adoption of the Labour Law.[1] Many local governments have amended or are amending their local regulations on labour management and are in the process of implementing national labour legislation. A detailed and comprehensive analysis of labour legislation in China well deserves a book and is beyond the scope of this chapter. What this chapter intends to do is to outline the structure and the main contents of Chinese labour legislation.

After the introduction, part two will briefly describe the historical development of labour legislation in China. It will reveal that China's labour legislation is mainly a product of its economic reform in the last decade and half. Part three will examine and analyse the main contents of labour legislation, including the guiding principles, the scope of

14.01

application, labour contract system, working hours, wages, protection of female and juvenile workers, social insurance and welfare, trade union and labour dispute resolutions, and labour supervision and inspection. A quite comprehensive system of labour legislation has already been established though it still lacks sufficient detailed provisions in certain aspects such as social insurance. The next major task for China is to implement these legislations as vigorously as possible.

The Historical Development of Labour Legislation in China

14.02 The Communist Party of China (CPC) came into power in 1949. But labour legislation had begun well before 1949, and had served as the basis for the PRC labour legislation. The development of China's labour legislation went through a rough journey over the next 45 years, which can be divided into three periods.

The period from 1949 to 1956 was described as the establishment and formation period of Chinese labour legislation. The basic structure of labour legislation was formed by the end of that period. But the majority of the legislation was focused on State-owned and collectively owned enterprises because one of the main objectives during that period was the transformation of private ownership of productive means into State or collective ownership.

The second period was from 1956 to 1976, during which the entire legislative progress in China, including the drafting of Labour Law, was interrupted and almost halted by several political movements, "the Struggle against the Rightists", the "Great Leap-forward", and the "Cultural Revolution". During that period, few regulations were promulgated. Some enacted labour legislation was described as restraints imposed by revisionists upon workers, and was therefore not implemented in practice.

The third period is from 1976 onwards. China entered into a new period of development after the Cultural Revolution ended officially in 1976. The third session of the 11th Plenum of the CPC was held in 1978, which was regarded as a turning-point in China's modern development. It was announced at that session that China would start economic reforms. Legislation was put at the top of the agenda of the NPC and its Standing Committee. This period has been claimed as the recovery and development period of China's labour legislation. Having realized the importance of law, the State Government has enacted many labour legislation, including laws and regulations on labour system, wages, labour protection, social insurance, vocational training

of workers, democratic management of enterprise workers, labour discipline, labour dispute resolution and so on. As private ownership of
businesses was not permitted from the late 1950s, it was, therefore,
logical that most labour legislation in this period was applicable only
to State-owned or collectively owned enterprises.

From 1979, China started to introduce foreign investment to assist
the development of its economy. With the progress of economic reform
and opening-up of China to foreign investors, various kinds of enterprises with different combinations of ownership have co-existed.
Labour systems and relationships have become diversified and
complicated. Even with State-owned or collectively owned enterprises,
a contract employment system has been introduced to many of them
since 1983. The mobility of employees has increased. Enterprises also
enjoy autonomy to a certain extent in choosing their employees. After
taking into account international customs, the need to provide preferential treatment to foreign investors, China's practical experience,
and the need to facilitate external economic and technological communication and cooperation, different sets of legislation have
been promulgated to govern enterprises with different ownership, *i.e.*
State-owned and collectively owned, privately owned, and foreign
investment enterprises.

With regard to the enactment of the Labour Law, the Ministry of
Labour resumed its drafting work and submitted a draft in 1983 to the
Legislative Affairs Commission (LAC), which is the institution in
charge of the revision of draft laws before they are submitted to the
NPC or its Standing Committee. However, the State Government,
including the Ministry of Labour, had not made up its mind about the
labour policy, *i.e.* how China's economic system, including the labour
system, should be reformed. It was held that the time had not come yet
for the enactment of the Labour Law. That uncertainty eventually led
to the withdrawal of the draft by the Ministry of Labour from the LAC.

The 14th Plenary of the Communist Party of China made it clear
that China would develop a socialist market economy and its labour
system should be reformed accordingly. The Decision adopted at the
Plenary regarded a healthy labour market as an integral part of a
socialist market economy and the development of such a market as
one of priority in cultivating a market economy. The Decision also
stated that the establishment and improvement of a socialist market
economy required the regulation and guarantee of a comprehensive
labour system. Having had a clear understanding of the objectives of
the reform to labour system, the Legislative Affairs Bureau of the State
Council, together with the Ministry of Labour and All-China Federation of Trade Unions, thoroughly studied, elaborated and revised the
draft Labour Law and then submitted it for discussion to the 14th
standing meeting of the State Council on January 7, 1994. The State
Council approved the draft in principle. It was then submitted to the

sixth session of the eigth Standing Committee of the NPC for its examination on February 18, 1994. It was from then that the LAC was formally involved and started its research on the draft Labour Law and collection of opinions in order to submit the draft to the next NPC Standing Committee meeting for its examination and scrutiny. At the sixth session, consensus was reached on the necessity of the enactment of the Labour Law. Four months later, the Labour Law was adopted at the eighth session on July 5, 1994.

In the process of drafting the Labour Law, the Ministry of Labour was also preparing a series of labour regulations. This is because the Labour Law, as a national legislation, only lays down the framework and main principles. Its implementation relies on more detailed subsidiary legislation. The Ministry of Labour promulgated seventeen new labour regulations shortly after the enactment of the Labour Law, which was further followed by 100 opinions on the implementation of the Labour Law.

The Main Contents of Labour Legislation

14.03   The concept of labour legislation is a broad concept in Chinese law, including not only legislation relating to employment issues, but also legislation on social welfare. For example, chapter nine of the Labour Law is on social insurance and welfare. In this chapter we will examine the main contents of China's labour legislation as covered by the Labour Law. In order to better understand the Labour Law, its application and possible implication against the PRC's background of continental legal tradition, it is necessary to look first at its objectives and the guiding principles.

The Guiding Principles of the Labour Law

Protection of Workers' Rights and Interests

According to China's Constitution, the working class is the leading class in the society. Workers are the masters of the State and enjoy very high political status in society. However, it has never been made clear how that important political and legal status is guaranteed in practice, especially in employment relationships. For example, what are the exact identities of the workers in an employment relationship: masters or servants? How are the interests of the workers protected by law? Under the previous system of planned economy, enterprises were owned by the State and jobs were all allocated by the State Government. The workers were regarded as masters of the enterprise where they were working. Enterprises did not have the autonomy to dismiss any workers. With the change from a planned to a market economy and the increase of market competition, workers' rights to employment will no longer be as secured as they were. The Labour Law has put the protection of lawful rights of workers as the guiding principle. Though this is also provided in China's Constitution, constitutional rights cannot be directly enforced, they have to be incorporated into some specific legislation in order to be enforced in practice. Workers' rights have been guaranteed under the Constitution. The Labour Law has made the protection of the lawful interests of workers an important principle. Section 1 states clearly that the protection of the legitimate rights and interests of labourers is one of the objectives of the Labour Law. In order to achieve this objective, other chapters of the Labour Law have detailed provisions on the lawful rights of the workers and the duties and obligations of employing units. For example, the discretion of workers to conclude long-term service contracts if they have worked for their employers for more than 10 years. This provision aims at the prevention of exploitation by employers. An examination of the chapter on legal liability under the Labour Law will also reveal clearly the intention of the Legislature to protect the lawful rights of workers. There are altogether twelve sections on the liabilities of the parties to labour relationship if either party fails to fulfil its legal obligations. Among them, eleven are to prescribe the liabilities of the employing units, only one is about the liability of the workers for violation of the Labour Law. Restriction of overtime work is another example. Overtime should normally not exceed one hour per day. If there are special reasons, then working hours may be further extended, but to no more than three hours per day. Remuneration for overtime should be higher than the workers' usual wage. All these provisions aim to discourage overtime in order to protect the health of workers. There are many other provisions aimed at the protection of workers' rights, such as those on termination of a labour contract by 30 days prior notice, minimum wages, special protection for women and inexpenenced workers and so on.

Guarantee of the Autonomy of Enterprises

A market economy is still a relatively new concept to China and the Chinese people because a planned economy has been in place ever since the CPC took power in 1949. Under a planned economy, the supply and demand relationship of the labour force was mainly regulated by the administration. However, under a market economy, the allocation of the labour force shall be determined by the demand of the market. In order to facilitate the development of a socialist market economy, especially a healthy labour market, the Labour Law has laid down an objective to "establish and safeguard a labour system that suits the socialist market economy and promotes economic development and social progress". One prerequisite for a labour market is the employment autonomy of employers. The Labour Law has granted autonomy to the employers in conclusion of employment contracts, determination of wages, conditions for the dissolution of employment contracts.

Balance of the Two Principles

It seems that a balance needs to be struck between the protection of workers' rights and the guarantee of the autonomy of employing units when they are in conflict with each other. However, the Labour Law does not provide any guidance as to how to strike this balance. Sometimes it is unavoidable that one has to be given preference over the other. Given that much emphasis has been put on the protection of workers' rights, it may well be the case, at least thoeratically, that the legitimate rights and interests of workers shall prevail.

Scope of Application

14.04 The scope of application of the Labour Law has been a controversial issue from the start of the drafting to the promulgation of the Labour Law. The original draft submitted by the State Council to the NPC Standing Committee provides that:

> This law is applicable to the enterprises, institutions, state bodies, social organizations and individual economic organizations, as well as to the workers who have formed a labour relationship with them.
>
> Where laws and regulations contain special provisions for the labour relationship between state bodies, institutions, social organizations and their workers, such provisions shall be complied with.

Under a planned economy, jobs were allocated by the State Government. All employees, either in State organizations, institutions or different kinds of enterprises, were socialist workers. Their wages, social welfare, retirement benefits etc. were all provided for by the State Government. Labour relationships were therefore between workers and the State. However, the execution of economic reform and open-door policy has brought much change to labour relationships in China. Contractual employment relationships have been adopted in many enterprises since 1983.

The draft intended to make the Labour Law applicable to all employees regardless of their employers. Some legislators argued that the scope of application was too wide under the draft. They held that State organizations and institutions were different in nature from enterprises. Thus certain provisions that applied in enterprises might not be applicable to State bodies or institutions.

Different views were expressed as to whether or not the Labour Law should be applied to the employment relationship between institutions, social organizations and their employees. Institutions are diversified. Some like universities and research institutes are funded by the State government, where labour contracts are usually not signed between the institutions and their employees. Instead, letters of appointment are issued to some employees. But whether or not letters of appointment can be treated as labour contracts is not clear because there are no clear legal provisions and policy guidelines available at the moment. The officials from the LAC prefer to treat letters of appointment as labour contracts. Some other institutions are established to absorb surplus employees from relevant State organizations which are under quota restriction. They still perform certain administrative functions. There are also institutions which are self-financed and managed as enterprises. The diversity of institutions makes it unrealistic for the adoption of a uniform system among them.

Employment relationships in social organizations have also been controversial. Social organizations were traditionally part of the administration. As such, their management has always been conducted according to the State personnel system and many of their employees are governmental cadres. The employees' relationship with the organizations is not based on a labour contract. Instead, they are delegated their jobs by the government. The 14th CPC Congress made it clear that the Regulation on Civil Servants is applicable to the Party's organs and other 18 social communities, including the All-China Federation of Trade Unions, the League of Communist Youth and the Federation of Women.

At the end, the necessity to protect by law the letigimate rights and interests of all employees, whether they are workers, peasants, intellectuals or civil servants, was agreed upon. This is provided in China's Constitution. However, due to the different nature of employment relationships, the interests of different kinds of employees should be protected through different laws and regulations respectively. The Labour Law, under the demand of a socialist market economy, should mainly regulate the labour relationships established through labour contracts between employing units and workers. Peasants and civil servants should not be included.

Based on this consensus, the scope of application has finally been **14.05** provided as follows:

> This law is applicable to the enterprises and individual economic organizations (hereinafter referred to as employing units) within the territory of the People's Republic of China, as well as to the workers who have formed a labour relationship with them.
>
> The establishment of a labour contract relationship between workers and State bodies, institutions and social organizations shall be conducted in accordance with this law.

Enterprises here include State-owned, collectively-owned, privately owned, and foreign investment enterprises. Individual economic organizations are interpreted under the opinions issued by the Ministry of Labour on the Implementation of the Labour Law to be a private employer with no more than seven employees. Two different criteria are adopted to determine the applicability of the Labour Law. For enterprises and individual economic organizations, the criterion is the existence of a "labour relationship", which means the workers have become members thereof and provide work for remuneration. For State organs, institutional organizations and societies, the criterion is the existence of a "labour contract relationship". The opinions issued by the Ministry of Labour state that the Labour Law will be applied to service staff who have concluded or should have concluded employment contracts with State organs, institutions and social communities; employees of institutions adopting enterprise management; and other workers concluding labour relationships through labour contracts with State organs, institutions and social communities. But the terms of labour relationships and labour contract relationships are not defined in the Labour Law. One official from the Ministry of Labour is of the opinion that a labour contract is just one means to establish a labour relationship. It means a labour relationship can be established without concluding any employment contracts. One semi-academic interpretation refers to a labour relationship as that formulated in the working process between workers and their employing units. Whether or not all the provisions in the Labour Law shall be applicable to interim workers remains unclear, and needs further interpretation from either the Standing Committee of the NPC or the Supreme People's Court. The Opinions expressly exclude civil servants, those employees with institutions and social communities who are treated in a similar way to civil servants, peasants, soldiers in service and domestic maids.

This does not mean that none of the provisions in the Labour Law shall be applicable to civil servants or those working in certain institutions and social communities. This is because the Labour Law is quite broad covering both employment issues and social insurance and welfare. Those provisions on labour protection, working hours, rest and

holidays, social insurance, welfare, together with the general principles of the Labour Law, should be equally applicable to all workers,
including civil servants and staff employed by State bodies, institutions and social organizations. It is unrealistic for the relevant legislation on civil service to provide for a completely separate system or to
repeat the same system. This view can be seen to be supported by the
comments made by one official from the Ministry of Labour. But the
interpretation seems to be contradictory to the literal interpretation of
Section 2 of the Labour Law and the interpretation given by officials
from the LAC. Potential danger exists with regard to the scope of
application due to different understandings. Any disputes arising
later should be referred to the Standing Committee of the NPC for
interpretation.

On the one hand, the provision on the scope of the Labour Law has
shown the advantage of flexibility. With the deepening of economic
reform and the adoption of a market economy, it is likely that
more and more institutions will establish labour relationships with
their employees by concluding labour contracts. They shall then fall
within the jurisdiction of the Labour Law. On the other hand, such a
provision reflects clearly the characteristics of a labour system in
transition. It does not seem logical that institutions should be subject
to different treatment. Neither is it reasonable that these provisions
will be applicable immediately after an institution adopts a labour
contract system but not before. Furthermore, it is the general practice
that many institutions only adopt a labour contract system with new
employees, not with those already employed. This means different
rules apply to different employees. However, there do not seem to be
any satisfactory solutions available. Only after the transition is
completed can these issues be properly addressed and finally resolved
by the unification of the two criteria into one, *i.e.* the adoption of a
labour contract.

The Labour Contract System and Its Implementation

The labour contract system is a relatively new employment system **14.06**
implemented by the Communist Government in China. However,
chapter three of the Labour Law, labour contract and collective contract, is the longest chapter and is claimed to be the core of the Labour
Law. It covers the formation, validity, vitiating factors, discharge of
employment contracts and collective contracts. In order to better understand the labour contract system and its implementation, an overview of the development of China's employment system since 1949 is
justified.

The Development of China's Employment System

When the Communist Party took over power, it transplanted into China the employment system of the former Soviet Union. There used to be three kinds of workers in China, permanent workers (iron rice bowl), contractual workers and interim workers, of which the majority were permanent workers. They maintained long-term (or permanent) labour relationships with their employing units. Their recruitment, allocation and arrangements were under the control of labour and personnel departments at various levels. After the introduction of economic reforms in 1979, the State Government realized that the system of permanent workers was too rigid as workers could not be dismissed once recruited, and the government was responsible for too much. In order to strengthen labour discipline, to motivate workers, to increase productivity and enhance vitality of enterprises, the State Council introduced a labour contract system on a trial basis in 1983. After three years of practice, it formally decided to reform the existing labour system in 1986 and promulgated four important interim regulations to facilitate this reform.[2] The objective is to gradually move toward a labour contract system with the coexistence of a variety of employment means. As a first step of the transitional measures, the Regulations on Recruitment focused on the implementation of a labour contract system for newly recruited workers from 1986. During this period, contractual workers' system and permanent workers' system coexisted and both kinds of workers enjoyed equal rights in enterprises.

The second step is to reform the law with regard to existing permanent workers, which is a more sensitive issue. It was not until 1992 that universal contract employment was encouraged nationwide. Certain local governments, such as Shanghai, have decided their own measures as to how a universal contractual employment system can be implemented. Shortly afterwards, the Ministry of Labour issued a notice to standardize the handling of some issues arising from the implementation of a universal contractual employment system. It is State policy that enterprises run their business autonomously. The State will only be in charge of macrocontrol and business will be able to compete fairly under market principles. A universal contractual employment system is a means to change State employment to enterprise employment, administrative management to contractual management. The pace in adopting a uniform contract employment system varies from place to place.

The third step is to abolish the permanent employment system and to adopt a contractual employment system in all kinds of enterprises irrespective of their ownership. However, it seems that China is still at the second stage. It may take many years for it to complete the transition. However in Shanghai, which is leading the country in reforming its labour systems, it is planned to implement a contractual employment system by the end of 1996.

The Implementation of a Contractual Employment System and the Labour Law

The main controversy during the deliberation of the Labour Law draft was how to incorporate a labour contract (contractual employment) system. One opinion was that once the labour contract system was incorporated into the Labour Law it should be implemented nationwide. However, most legislators do not believe that China is ready to implement a universal contractual employment system. This is because the implementation of a labour contract system requires as a prerequisite, a comprehensive social insurance system, including unemployment insurance, retirement insurance, medical insurance and so on, which are not yet fully established in China. Though a labour contract system has been promoted since 1986, many enterprises have not yet implemented it. For example, only four out of more than 50 enterprises under the Beijing Construction Material Group Corporation had implemented the system in 1993. It is in practice very difficult either to retain technical personnel or to dismiss redundant staff through labour contracts. The suggestion is that the Labour Law should make it clear that the labour contract system will be implemented gradually. The final adopted version on the issue of labour contracts is:

> A labour contract is an agreement between a worker and an employing unit establishing their labour relationship and specifying the two parties' rights and obligations.
> A labour contract should be concluded to establish labour relations.

This provision has confirmed the conclusion of a labour contract as a means to establish a labour relationship. The literal interpretation of the second paragraph suggests that the conclusion of the labour contract is the compulsory means for the establishment of a labour relationship. But Section 160 of the Labour Law puts a proviso to the implementation of this provision by authorizing the people's governments at the provincial level to determine the pace of implementation of the labour contract system.

As to exactly how the labour contract system should be implemented, the opinion of an LAC official is that all enterprises must conclude labour contracts because the Labour Law aims at a universal system in which all workers shall participate. However, exceptions are allowed for State-owned enterprises. The pace for the adoption of a universal labour contract system varies from one locality to another. **14.07**

The Shanghai Municipal Government has determined to lead the country in this aspect with the objective to implement a labour contract system in all State-owned enterprises by the end of 1996.

The Opinions issued by the Ministry of Labour further explain with whom an employing unit should conclude labour contracts. Labour contracts should also be concluded between employing units with their surplus employees who have not been assigned any work to do, employees on long leave, employees lent to other employing units, employees pursuing further study on paid leave. The terms of labour contracts with those employees may be varied through the consultation of the two parties. Labour contracts should also be concluded with employees on long sick leave, employees who choose to keep their posts without payment and are now willing to come back. The party secretary and chairman of the trade union should also conclude their labour contracts with the employing units unless otherwise provided for by legislation. Managers and managerial personnel in any companies should conclude labour contracts with the board of directors according to *The Company Law*. Those who are sent by their original employing units to work in foreign investment enterprises should conclude labour contracts with their original employing units, which will conclude labour service contracts with foreign investment enterprises, specifying relevant benefits such as wages, insurance welfare, leave and so on.

If the employing units do not conclude labour contracts with their employees intentionally, but a *de facto* labour relationship exists between the two, then the labour administrative organ should intervene requesting the employing units to rectify the matter. The employing units should pay the employees compensation for any damages caused to them.

The Forms, Contents and Types of Labour Contract

The Labour Law provides that "a labour contract should be in written form". The purpose is that the supervision of labour contracts will be easier if the rights and obligations of the parties to labour contracts are in written form. Moreover, the settlement of potential disputes between the parties will also be easier. However, oral labour contracts have not been excluded by the Labour Law. But there are no provisions in the Labour Law nor in the General Principles of Civil Law on the conditions under which oral contracts can be concluded.

Section 19 of the Labour Law provides that a labour contract should contain certain clauses such as the term of the labour contract, job description, labour protection and conditions, remuneration, labour discipline, conditions for terminating the labour contract, and liability for breach of the labour contract. The exact contents of the provisions shall be left for the parties to decide, which should be done on the basis of equality, voluntariness and consensus. It also says that the clauses mentioned above are compulsory, which in turn proves the interpretation that "should" actually means "must". Failure to include any of the provisions in Section 19 will make the labour contract partially invalid. The remaining portion of the contract shall not be affected and still remain valid. However, it is not clear what can and should be done if any disputes arise with regard to an area which is not covered by the labour contract. In addition to the required items, the parties may also agree on any other contents through consultation.

A probation period should be specified in the term on the duration of the labour contract which should not exceed six months. It can be included in labour contracts concluded with new employees or reemployed staff. For those permanent employees transferring to a contractual employment system, a probation period may not be necessary.

Section 20 of the Labour Law lays down three kinds of labour contracts: fixed term, flexible term and commissioned for specific work. For those employees who have worked in one employing unit continuously for ten years, labour contracts with flexible terms should be concluded upon the request of the employees. For those transferring from permanent employment to a contractual employment system, contracts with flexible terms may be signed. The main purpose is to protect older employees in State-owned enterprises and employees in foreign investment enterprises.

Dissolution of a Labour Contract

The general principle is that the dissolution of a labour contract should **14.08** be based on the mutual agreement of the parties. The parties can either specify the conditions of termination of their labour contract or reach a separate termination agreement later. The Labour Law also provides three areas under which the employing unit can unilaterally dissolve a labour contract.

The first category is based on the fault of workers, and includes three clauses:

(a) the failure to satisfy recruitment conditions during the probation period,
(b) serious violation of labour discipline or the employing unit's rules and regulations,
(c) guilty of serious dereliction of duty or graft resulting in major damage to the employing unit, prosecuted according to law.

The employing unit can immediately dissolve the labour contract if any of the above mentioned grounds exist. It should be noted that these

are the only three grounds under which termination is allowed without prior notice.

The second category is based on incapability of the workers, and
includes three grounds:

   (a) failure to engage in original or any other assigned work due to
       illness or non-industrial injury,
   (b) incompetence even after training or for a new job,
   (c) major change of circumstances.

The only limitation imposed upon an employing unit here is that a
written notice should be given 30 days in advance. Whether or not 30
days prior notice is sufficient to protect the interests of the employees
remains arguable because employing units may have been given too
much discretion. The real issue here is how the balance should be
struck between the protection of the employees' interests on the one
side and the autonomy of the employing units on the other. This issue
becomes more serious and can lead to much more discussion when
dismissal for economic reasons is raised.

Dismissal for economic reasons mainly occurs when major difficulties arise in the production or operation of an enterprise. It becomes
essential for the enterprise to reduce workers in order to improve its
business management so as to increase its economic efficiency. This is
within the autonomy of the enterprise under a market economy. However, different opinions have been expressed with regard to whether
dismissal for economic reasons, especially by State-owned enterprises,
should be allowed.

No dispute exists on

   (a) the necessity to grant autonomy to employing units in employ-
       ment under a socialist market economy;
   (b) that autonomy should be equal between State-owned and non-
       State-owned enterprises,
   (c) that dismissal for economic reasons has proved to be possible
       after trial implementation in some localities.

Meanwhile it was also realized that workers' legitimate interests
should also be protected, which is beneficial to social stability.

The Labour Law provides that reduction of workers is allowed for an
enterprise

   (a) during the period of statutory readjustment,
   (b) on the verge of bankruptcy, or facing major difficulties in
       production or operation.

But a strict statutory procedure has been laid down in the Regulations
on the Dismissal of Employees For Economic Difficulties, which needs
to be followed by the employing units. The employing unit has to

explain to the trade union or all the workers 30 days in advance and provide information on the condition of production and operation; it should then submit a proposal for the reduction of workers, the time and method for its implementation, and economic compensation for the workers as required under relevant legislation and collective contract; the proposal should be submitted to the trade union or all the workers to seek their opinion and may be amended and improved; the employing unit should submit a report to the relevant labour administrative department and seek their opinion; finally the employing unit will announce the proposal and go through the formalities for the dissolution of labour contracts, pay economic compensation, and issue a certificate of reduction. However, these are merely procedural requirements upon employing units because the explanation and report requirements do not mean that the employing unit actually needs the consent and approval from the entire employees, the trade union, or the labour administrative organ. It is, therefore, very doubtful how effective they are in preventing the employing unit from employing new staff after letting the old staff go.

One effective measure seems to be section 27 which requires the employing unit to give priority to hiring the staff it previously laid off if it wants to hire workers within six months of reducing workers for economic reasons. This compulsory requirement will make the employing unit think twice when laying off workers because its business could be affected for up to six months. Otherwise, it has to bear legal responsibilities under section 98, *i.e.* to be ordered by the labour administrative department to make corrections and to pay compensation if damages have been caused to workers.

The trade union in the enterprise concerned also has a role to play **14.09** under section 30. Firstly, the trade union can raise an objection if it considers the termination of the labour contract inappropriate. Secondly, the trade union can request the matter to be dealt with anew if an employing unit violates laws, regulations or the labour contract. However, it is not clear what would happen if the objection and the request of the trade union were ignored by the employing unit. It does not seem that the trade union can, under the Labour Law, initiate any further action. The other effective step could be for the worker to lodge an application of arbitration or litigation to which the trade union can render its assistance.

For unilateral dismissal on any grounds, the employing unit has to pay economic compensation to the dismissed workers. Compensation should be paid according to the Economic Compensation Methods for Violation and Dissolution of Labour Contract issued by the Ministry of Labour in December 1994. The employing unit should pay the reduced worker one month wages for each year of service. If the employing unit fails to do so, a penalty of 50 per cent of the amount payable will be imposed.

There also exist circumstances under which the employing unit cannot dissolve the labour contract for any reasons. They include

- (a) when a worker is afflicted with an occupational disease or is injured in work and has been affirmed as having lost or partially lost the ability to work;
- (b) when a worker is still under medical treatment for illness or injuries;
- (c) when a female worker is pregnant or nursing a child;
- (d) other circumstances provided for by laws and administrative regulations.

These provisions aim to protect certain disadvantaged persons. However, prohibition of dismissal for employees who have only partially lost the ability to work may be too harsh to the employing unit and is also likely to restrict the mobility of workers. Such a provision is the result of a clear legislative intention to protect disabled workers and the difficulty in ascertaining the degree of partial disability. The suggestion is that this will put some pressure upon employing units to improve their production safety measures in order to reduce their possible financial burden. Section 29 is open-ended and gives the Legislature and also the Administration, especially the Ministry of Labour, certain leeway provided that other circumstances arise in the future to justify the restrictions upon the employing unit to dismiss workers.

On the other hand, if the workers want to terminate contracts, they can do so at any time provided that written notice is given 30 days in advance. The workers may terminate contracts immediately during the probation period, or under coercion of violence, threat or illegal limitation of personal freedom, or failure to pay remuneration by the employing units and so on.

The above discussion reveals clearly that provisions on the termination of labour contracts is biased towards the interests of workers. That is to a certain extent understandable as they enjoy, compared to their employers, weaker bargaining power.

Collective Contracts

14.10 Collective contracts are another important measure to protect workers' rights, which have a much longer history in China. The Labour Law provides that collective contracts can be concluded between workers and employing units on such matters as labour remuneration, working hours, rest, holidays, labour safety and hygiene, insurance, welfare and so on. The Ministry of Labour issued a Regulation on Collective Labour Contracts in December 1994. It provides for the conclusion, scrutiny, and handling of disputes of collective contracts.

Under the Labour Law and the Regulation on Collective Labour Contracts, workers in an employing unit may be represented by their trade union or their selected representatives, if no trade union is organized, with the support of more than half of the workers. It is questionable whether a trade union can truly represent the entire workforce. It is justifiable if all workers are union members. However, the question will arise if some workers, who are not members of the trade union, object to the collective contract. This issue is further complicated by the provision that a collective contract, once concluded, is binding on the enterprise and all the workers. It does not make sense that those workers who are not union members and object to the collective contract should be bound by it. Though the Labour Law provides that collective contract should be submitted for discussion and approval to the workers' representative assembly or all the workers, it does not require unanimous assent. The issue therefore, still remains unsolved.

The labour administrative department plays an important role in the conclusion of collective contracts. Any collective contracts should, according to the Regulation on Collective Contracts, be submitted to the relevant labour administrative department for scrutiny within seven days of its conclusion. The labour administrative department will follow a statutory procedure to examine certain contents such as the qualification of the two parties, the compliance with legal requirements for the conclusion of the collective contract, and the specific labour standards in the collective contract. A collective contract shall take effect if the labour administrative department raises no objection within 15 days after receiving the text of the document. In other words, the approval of the relevant labour administrative department is required.

Any disputes concerning the conclusion of collective contracts shall be handled by the relevant labour administrative department as provided under the Regulation on Collective Contracts. The Regulation on Collective Contracts does not provide whether or not the decision from the relevant labour administrative department shall be final, what other remedial methods are available to the aggrieved party. Disputes concerning the implementation of collective contracts shall be handled according to the 1993 Regulation of the PRC on the Handling of Labour Disputes within Enterprises.

Wages

The right to receive payment is the most fundamental right that a **14.11** worker is entitled to. In order to deal with non-payment of wages, the Labour Law has one chapter with specific provisions on various aspects of the payment of wages.

Equal Pay for Equal Work

The principle of equal pay for equal work for men and women alike is set in the International Labour Organization (ILO) Convention No. 100. It has in fact been well recognized and implemented by the Communist Government for quite a long time and has been incorporated into China's Constitution. Therefore, its incorporation by section 46 of the Labour Law is not only to fulfil the international obligation undertaken by China under the ILO Convention No. 100 but also to implement its constitutional principle.

Payment of Wages

Under the Labour Law, the general principle for the distribution of wages is that wages shall be distributed according to work undertaken. The Central Government shall exercise macroscopic adjustment over the total amount of wages at a national level and wages shall be gradually raised along with the level of economic development. But the actual distribution methods and wage levels are within the autonomy of individual employing units and are mainly determined by their economic efficiency. However, they are required to pay wages to the workers monthly in the form of currency and payment may not be delayed without any proper justification. This provision is due to the need to balance various kinds of interests. On one hand, the workers' entitlement to wages is acknowledged and should be protected. On the other, the actual situation is that some State-owned enterprises are often in serious financial difficulty and close to bankruptcy. But the State Government cannot declare them bankrupt for the sake of social stability even though they cannot pay their wages on time. There also exist other situations such as production low seasons and natural disasters, which may cause the delay in the payment of wages. All these situations may be classified as proper reasons which are justifiable under the Labour Law.

Apart from the provisions in the Labour Law, the Ministry of Labour issued an Interim Regulation on the Payment of Wages in December 1994. According to the Interim Regulation, wages should be paid to workers according to the stipulation of labour contracts while they are on annual leave, marriage leave, and any other statutory leave. Workers should also be paid wages if the production or operation of the enterprises is interrupted due to any reasons other than the fault of the workers within one wages payment period (usually one month). If production is interrupted for more than one wages payment period, workers should be paid no less than minimum wages if they have provided labour during that period. Otherwise the problem should be dealt with according to relevant State provisions.

The Labour Law provides that wages should not be deducted without proper reason. This provision on deduction of wages is different from that under the draft law, *i.e.* wages should not be deducted unlawfully. The scope covered under the final version is wider than that under the draft. Not only unlawful but also other kinds of improper deduction are prohibited by the Labour Law. However, deduction is not completely prohibited. Deduction with due reason, such as according to the provisions under labour contracts or the rules of the enterprises, are permitted so long as the latter are not contradictory to the Labour Law. The Interim Regulation provides that if the workers caused economic losses to the employing units, the latter can request the workers, as agreed under labour contract, to compensate, which can be deducted from the wages of the workers. But monthly deduction cannot exceed 20 per cent of the workers' monthly wages. If the remainder after deduction is lower than local minimum wages, then minimum wages should be paid to the workers. The employing units may also deduct personal income tax, various social insurance expenses, and other costs as permitted by legislation.

Minimum Wage

The requirement of minimum wage is set down in the ILO Convention No. 26, entitled the Adoption of the Mechanism for Determining Minimum Wages. Convention No. 26 requires each member state undertake its obligation to adopt or maintain a mechanism for determining minimum wages so as to protect workers employed in certain sectors of industry. In determining the minimum wages, relevant employers and employees should be consulted and their views be taken into account. However, member states have been given the discretion under section 3(1) of Convention No. 26 to make the decision on the nature, form and implementation of their own mechanisms.

Section 48 of the Labour Law requires the implementation of a guaranteed minimum wage system. The actual standards of minimum wages will be determined by the People's Government at provincial levels. The Labour Law is consistent with the ILO Convention No. 26. Moreover, the mechanism under China's Labour Law seems more comprehensive than that under the ILO Convention. This is because the Labour Law sets up a national mechanism whereas the ILO only intends to protect certain sectors of industry.

The Ministry of Labour issued a notice in October 1994 to amend the 1993 Regulation on Minimum Wages in Enterprises issued by itself. The notice requires each province, autonomous region and municipality directly under the Central Government to set or adjust its minimum wage standard and report to the Ministry of Labour. The standards can then be submitted to the local people's government for approval and promulgation if the Ministry of Labour does not suggest any changes within 25 days of submission.

An employing unit is required to pay minimum wages. The Labour Law provides that wages paid by employing units shall not be lower than minimum wage standards in their localities. Different views were expressed as to who should be granted the authority to make provisions on minimum wages: the State Council, or provincial people's government or provincial people's congress. It has finally been determined that "actual standards of minimum wages shall be formulated and submitted to the State Council for the record by the people's governments of the provinces, autonomous regions and municipalities directly under the central government". It is a balance between central supervision and decentralization of powers and efficiency. This does not mean that there should only be a uniform minimum wage legislation in the province. Instead, there may be different minimum wage standards for different cities in the same provinces. But they all need to be promulgated by the Provincial People's Government.

As to the determination of the exact minimum wage, five factors should be taken into account. They are the average minimum living expenses of workers and their dependents, the average wage level of labour productivity, the employment situation, and differences in economic development levels between regions. In Shenzhen, for example, a formula has been created for the calculation of minimum wages.

The Opinions issued by the Ministry of Labour state that the precondition for the payment of minimum wages is that workers have fulfilled their employment duties within working hours. Even if the workers do not complete the work as required under labour contracts, they should still be paid minimum wages. But those workers who are not currently at their posts will only be paid living subsidies which can be lower than the minimum wage. Exceptions are provided for female workers during maternity, or breast-feeding. They will be entitled to original wages. For workers who are under medication due to illness or non-work-related injury, their payment or subsidy can be lower than the minimum wage but should not be lower than 80 per cent of the minimum wage.

Working Hours

14.12 In order to set appropriate provisions on working hours, reference has not only been made to the ILO Conventions ratified by China but also to other Conventions which China has not ratified yet. Among the ILO Conventions on working and resting hours, China has only acceded to Convention No. 14, which requires that workers be given a minimum of 24 hours of continuous rest every seven days. Nevertheless attention has also been paid by legislators to the ILO Convention No. 47

concerning a working week of 40 hours, as well as some other Conventions.

The provision on working hours under the Labour Law is eight hours per day or 44 hours a week on average. It has been acknowledged that this is a transitional measure and will eventually converge with the international standard, *i.e.* 40 hours per week. Shortly after the enactment of the Labour Law, the State Council made a decision in March 1995 to amend the Regulation on Working Hours issued by itself in February 1994. The decision adopts an eight hours per day and 40 hours per week working system, which came into force on May 1, 1995. For institutions which have difficulty in implementing the new working hours, they may delay its implementation. The phrase "on average" is added to give flexibility to some special business such as navigation, fishery and so on, which normally require flexible working hours and adopt different leave systems. It could mean that in one week a worker may work more than 44 hours while working less than 44 hours in another week, so long as the average working hours per week are no more than 44 hours. Even though flexibility is allowed, one day off per week should normally be guaranteed by employing units. Again the above requirements are not without exception. If an enterprise is unable to meet these requirements due to special production characteristics, they may implement other work and rest systems after obtaining approval from the relevant labour administrative department.

In order to regulate exceptional cases, the Ministry of Labour issued the Examination and Approval Method on the Adoption of Flexible and Accumulated Working Hours Systems in December 1994. Flexible and accumulated working hours systems are two different systems. The Method allows a flexible working hours system to be applied to certain employees such as managerial personnel, employees on duty trips, salespersons, drivers on long distance transportation, taxi drivers, service staff at railways, ports, warehouses or other employees whose work cannot be arranged according to standard working hours.

An accumulated working hours system is allowed for some other employees whose nature of work requires such a system. For example, transportation, railway, post, aviation, fishery which have special characteristics that require employees to work continuously. Geographical work, natural resource exploration, construction, tourism are restricted by seasons and natural conditions and some of these employees have to work very hard during high seasons. The period for accumulation can be a week, month, season or year.

The most controversial issue is the extension of working hours. The **14.13** international standard under the ILO Convention for overtime work is one hour per day. But overtime work in non-State-owned enterprises in China is very common, varying from three to seven hours. An investigation into foreign investment enterprises in Guangdong and Fujian

Provinces shows that the working hours in most enterprises are 11 hours per day. Some are even as long as 17 hours and without a day off per week. The maximum overtime work per month can reach 200 hours in certain enterprises. Moreover, there are other practical problems in China. Sometimes, overtime work is agreed by both parties to the contract. For some export-oriented enterprises, their work depends largely on the orders and the deadlines set down by clients. Overtime work also exists in some State-owned enterperises due to the imbalance of production tasks or the influence of seasonal demands on their products. After balancing the needs to meet international standards and China's domestic practical conditions, taking into account the objective to protect the health of workers, the final provision in the Labour Law is one hour per day, or three hours per day under special circumstances and no more than 36 hours per month.

Extra payment should be made for overtime work. For work during extended working hours, remuneration of no less than 150 per cent of the workers' wage shall be disbursed. For overtime work during the workers' leave days when compensation time cannot be arranged, remuneration of no less than 200 per cent of the workers' wage shall be disbursed. For overtime work during statutory holidays, remuneration of no less than 300 per cent of the workers' wages shall be disbursed. There are two considerations that require employers to pay higher wages for workers during their days off or vacation. One is that workers are entitled to compensation by working during their time off or vacation periods. The second purpose is to discourage or indirectly restrict overtime work since it is not good for the health of the workers.

Protection of Female and Juvenile Workers

14.14 As female and juvenile workers are more vulnerable than other employees, special statutory protection has been provided under labour legislation. For juvenile workers, the minimum age requirement is laid down in the ILO Convention No. 59, on the Minimum Age for the Permission of Children to Work in Industry. Industry is defined and distinguished from commercial business and agriculture in the Convention. The Convention has special provisions for China, *i.e.* the minimum ages are 15 and 12 respectively, depending on the actual types of work involved in the industry. Apart from the Labour Law, the Ministry of Labour issued the Regulation on Special Protection of Juvenile Workers in December 1994. The protection for juveniles under the Labour Law and that Regulation is better than that under the ILO Convention No. 59. Minimum age is higher under the Labour Law as employing units cannot employ those under 16 years of age. Exceptions are only allowed for specific activities, such as artistic, athletic and special handicraft units. Even for them, special examination and approval procedures provided by State regulations must be followed and the juveniles' rights to education must be guaranteed. Juvenile workers may not be assigned to work in mines and pits, work involving danger of harm or poisoning or heavy labour work and so on. In order to ensure their healthy growth, their employing units are required to conduct regular physical examinations for them.

Special protection is also available to female workers. Apart from the Labour Law, the Ministry has also issued Measures on Labour Protection of Female Workers. Female workers cannot be required to work in mines, or work with Grade IV physical labour intensity or any other heavy manual work. During menstruation, pregnancy, and breast-feeding periods, they shall not be required to engage in Grade III physical labour tasks. During menstruation, they cannot be required to work high above the ground, under low temperatures, or in cold water. Female workers pregnant for seven months or longer, or while breast-feeding cannot be required to extend their working hours or work night shifts. In addition, women are entitled to 90 days of maternity leave with pay.

Social Insurance and Welfare

In order to provide enterprises with real autonomy in employment and **14.15** to implement a contractual employment system, the setting-up of a social insurance scheme and its satisfactory operation is an indispensable condition. The Labour Law provides that the State promotes social insurance services, sets up a social insurance system and establishes a social insurance in order to provide assistance and compensation for workers in the event of old age, sickness, on-the-job injuries, unemployment and childbirth. At present, insurance for workers in State-owned enterprises are undertaken almost completely by the State Government. Foreign investment enterprises have a legal obligation to pay insurance premiums for their workers. As for privately owned enterprises, most of them do not provide any insurance for their workers.

From January 1, 1995 when the Labour Law came into force, all employing units and workers must join social insurance and pay social insurance premiums in accordance with the law. Under the Labour Law, social insurance covers retirement, sickness, injury, disablement from an injury on the job or occupational disease, unemployment, childbirth and dependent pensions for surviving dependents of the deceased. Before the promulgation of the Social Insurance Law, which is under draft, the payment of social insurance premiums will be made according to relevant regulations governing State-owned enterprises. The main legislation in this aspect is the Labour Insurance Regulation of the People's Republic of China issued by the State Council in 1951 and the Amended Detailed Rules for Its Implementation issued by the Ministry of Labour in 1953. The Regulation covers work-related injury and disability, illness, non-work-related injury and disability, old age benefits and maternity benefits. Employees who are not trade union members are only entitled to half of certain kinds of benefits such as wages and subsidies during periods of illness and recovering periods of non-work-related injuries, retirement subsidies and so on. Since then the Ministry of Labour has issued several notices on the payment and management of pension funds. Labour administrative departments in various regions have issued their own rules respectively. Employees will contribute no more than three per cent of their wages to the fund. The percentage to be paid by employers shall be determined by local governments. For foreign investment enterprises, the contribution to be paid by the enterprises shall be determined by local government. In the case of Shanghai, for example, the percentage is 30 per cent of the total wages paid to employees.

Unemployment insurance is governed by the 1986 Interim Rules on Unemployment Insurance of Workers in State-owned Enterprises issued by the State Council. The employers shall contribute one per cent of the total wages of all employees to the fund which will be subsidised by local finance. Foreign investment enterprises will make the same contribution to the fund, *i.e.* one per cent of total wages of Chinese employees.

The Ministry of Labour issued the Trial Measures for Child-birth Insurance for Workers in Enterprises in December 1994. The amount of payment to be paid by the enterprises shall be determined by local governments, but it should be no more than one per cent of the total wages of the employees. Employees are not required to pay any contribution.

Trade Unions

The Legal Status of the Trade Union

14.16 The 1992 *Trade Union Law* (hereinafter as TUL) states that trade unions are the mass organizations of the voluntary unity of the working class. Their status seems higher than an ordinary social organization because the working class is still called the leading class in China.

The legal status of the trade unions have been reflected through their aims and objectives. Section 5 of the TUL requires the unions to educate workers to exercise their democratic rights according to the stipulations of the Constitution and laws, to give play to their roles as the masters of the State, to participate in the management of national affairs through various means and forms, to administer the economic, cultural and social affairs, to assist the people's governments in carrying out their work, to protect the socialist regime which is under the people's democratic dictatorship. Trade unions should also educate workers to apply a good attitude towards their work, to take good care of State properties and enterprises, to comply with labour disciplines and so on. It seems that the trade unions are actively involved in the administrative activities of the State and act in the interests of the State.

On the other hand, the trade unions are also required to protect the legitimate interests of the workers. According to the TUL, they must liaise with workers, listen and reflect their opinions and demands, look after their lives, and help them to solve difficulties. Thus, they play a double role. With regard to the advantages and disadvantages of this relationship, one commentator has remarked that[3]

> Its close relationship with the government in a sense provides the union with improved access with which to influence government and enterprise policies that may affect the interests of the workers. But such a system also makes it difficult for the union to maintain its distinctive identity. In cases of conflict between the interests of employees and the interests of the State, union leaders may find it difficult to vigorously defend the interests of the union members. The recent trend, however, is to further emphasize the independence of the union. As the economic reforms enhance the autonomy of State-owned enterprises and the authority of enterprise managers, the union will likely enjoy more independence from the government.

Though the comment was made before the 1992 TUL was promulgated, it still seems valid nowadays as the aims and objectives of *The Trade Union Law* was not changed when the 1950 TUL was amended in 1990.

The Functions and Powers of the Trade Unions

The functions and powers of the trade unions in the PRC have been **14.17** mentioned in various laws, regulations and documents. The TUL provides that the general trade unions at or above county level may provide legal consultation services to the unions under them and staff members and employees. Trade unions may also act as advisers to the people's government. The latter will consult and solicit the views of trade unions concerning the interests of staff members and employees, or when they formulate national economic and social development plans, draft bills, regulations and decrees, or when the government departments at or above the county level formulate their main policies and measures on wages, production safety, labour protection and labour insurance.

On the other hand, grassroots organizations especially have an obligation to protect the legitimate interests of the employees. The trade unions have the power to submit opinions on the protection of the exercise of the democratic management authority of staff members and employees in accordance with Chinese laws and regulations if any State-owned or collectively owned enterprises have violated the rights of the assembly of employee representatives and other democratic management systems. The trade unions may appoint representatives to make investigations concerning breaches of the legitimate interests of employees in the enterprises where the unions are located. The concerned entity should provide the appropriate assistance.

When enterprises and institutions violate labour laws and regulations, or infringe the legitimate rights of the staff members and employees, *e.g.* lengthy overtime work, violation of special interests of female employees, then the trade unions can request them or the relevant authority to deal with the issues seriously. The trade unions may help and provide guidance to the staff members and employees on the conclusion of labour contracts with enterprises, institutions and administrative agencies. They may also represent staff members and employees and sign collective contracts with the latter. If this is the case, the draft of the contract must be submitted to the congress or the assembly of employee representatives for discussion and approval.

The trade unions should be informed of the reasons for dismissal of or disciplinary actions against any employees. If they deem the decisions inappropriate, they can submit their opinions and request reconsideration of those decisions. When the legitimate interests of employees are infringed upon, the trade unions may offer their opinions for conciliation and provide support to the employees if they bring legal action to the people's court.

The trade unions have the authority to submit their opinions on labour conditions, safety, hygiene, potential danger and occupational detriment within the existing enterprises or those under construction or expansion. They will participate in the handling of accidents and the like, the investigation of other serious problems that may endanger the health of employees. They can also request immediate resolutions.

The trade unions will carry out their tasks concerning the collective welfare of the employees, functions regarding wages, labour protection and labour insurance. The trade unions may, together with the administration, organize after-hours cultural, technological study and vocational training to enhance cultural and professional quality. They should also organize artistic and sports activities outside working hours. The trade unions will also be involved in the mediation of labour disputes.

14.18   Within State-owned enterprises, the participation of trade union

representatives in a management committee is required. Their participation is also required for meetings held within enterprises on wages,
welfare, safe production, labour protection, labour insurance, and other
matters relating to the fundamental interests of the staff members and
employees. For collectively owned enterprises, the requirements are
not as strict. But trade union committees within enterprises are required to support and organize staff members and employees to participate in democratic administration and supervision, and to protect their
rights to elect, recall managerial staff, as well as to make decisions on
important business and management issues.

Some of the trade unions' rights and obligations mentioned above
are exclusive to State-owned and collectively owned enterprises. According to the Explanation Report delivered to the NPC on the draft
TUL by Wang Hanbing, the deputy chairman of the NPC and the
director of the LAC, the basic principles of the TUL are also applicable
to foreign investment enterprises. The term "enterprises" in the TUL
consists of State-owned, collectively owned, foreign investment, and
private enterprises. Foreign investment enterprises are different from
State-owned and collectively owned ones. That is why it is specifically
stated in the TUL that some provisions are only applicable to State-
owned or collectively owned enterprises. Two articles in the TUL are
exclusive to foreign investment enterprises. The specific powers and
obligations of trade unions in foreign investment enterprises are stipulated in the laws on foreign investment.

Within foreign investment enterprises, the employees shall have the
right to set up grassroots trade union organizations and to carry out
trade union activities in accordance with the provisions of the TUL.
The trade unions represent the interests of the employees, have the
right to conclude collective labour contracts with enterprises on their
behalf, and to supervise the execution of labour contracts. When an
enterprise holds discussions on problems concerning the commenda-
tion and punishment of workers and staff members, the wage system,
welfare benefits, labour protection and labour insurance, development
plans, production and operational activities, representatives of the
trade union shall have the right to attend the discussions as non-voting
attendants. The enterprise should listen to their opinions and aim to
gain their cooperation. An enterprise shall give active support to the
work of the trade union of the enterprise, and in accordance with
the provisions of the TUL, provide the trade union organization with
the necessary offices and equipment for handling its work, holding
meetings, and conducting such collective undertakings as welfare benefits, and sports activities for the staff members and employees. Every
month, the enterprise shall appropriate a sum equal to two per cent of
the actual total amount of wages and salaries of Chinese employees for
the administration of trade union outlay, as formulated by the All-
China Federation of Trade Unions.

Comparing the provisions in laws on foreign investment enterprises with the TUL, the functions of the trade unions in foreign investment enterprises are much more limited in management than the unions in State-owned or collectively owned enterprises. The focus is rather on the protection of employees' material interests. Nevertheless, the unions also play a supervisory role in making sure the implementation by foreign investment enterprises of various laws, and has a limited advisory role on matters affecting the interests of employees.

Trade unions have not yet been established in most township and some foreign investment enterprises. Questions have arisen in some of those enterprises where the legitimate interests of the employees have not been properly protected due to the lack of trade union organizations. Therefore, it has been urged by the All-China Federation of Trade Unions that trade unions should be organized as soon as possible in those enterprises "where the conditions are already ripe for the establishment of the labour unions".

Labour Dispute Resolution

14.19   China's preference for non-adversarial methods to resolve disputes has a long tradition and has actually been incorporated into various types of legislation. The same attitude has also been adopted for the resolution of labour disputes. The Regulation on the Dispute Resolution in the Enterprises in the People's Republic of China was promulgated in 1993. The Labour Law has incorporated the general structure laid down in the Regulation.

There are four mechanisms available for labour dispute resolution, *i.e.* consultation, mediation, arbitration and litigation. Mediation is conducted by the employing unit's labour dispute mediation committee which consists of representatives of workers, the employing unit and the trade union. Mediation can also be conducted in the process of arbitration and litigation by arbitrators and judges respectively. While mediation has its own advantage, it is vulnerable to the criticism that it may be biased given the fact that the trade union is not an independent organization of workers and may lean to the employer's side if the enterprise is a State-owned one. The labour dispute arbitration committee may be even more vulnerable to similar criticism since it is composed of representatives of the labour administrative department, a trade union at the corresponding level and the employing unit. If the dispute happens in a joint venture between a foreign partner and a Chinese State-owned enterprise, the foreign investor or foreign employee involved has every reason to think in this way.

However, the mechanisms designed under the Labour Law seem to be good enough to dispel these misgivings. Under ordinary civil cases, the parties can choose either arbitration or litigation. Normally only one mechanism is available and the ruling is binding. In labour cases, however, either party, who disagrees with the arbitration ruling, may file a suit at the people's court within 15 days after being notified of the ruling. The resort to the people's court is always available if the parties doubt the fairness of the other mechanisms for labour dispute resolution.

Labour Safety

Before the promulgation of the Labour Law, safety legislation was not applicable to foreign investment enterprises due to China's tradition to legislate according to ownership. However, many accidents happened in those enterprises. It has therefore been decided that, from now on, distinction will not be made between enterprises of different kinds of ownership. Under the Labour Law, all employing units must set up and complete a labour safety and sanitation system, strictly implement State rules and standards for labour safety and sanitation, conduct education in labour safety and sanitation for workers, prevent accidents at work, and minimize occupational hazards. A distinction is made between old enterprises and newly built, modified and expanded projects. For old ones, their equipment must meet relevant standards or requirements. For new ones, labour safety and sanitation facilities shall be designed, constructed and put into production and be used in principal projects. This is the first stage of safety requirement, *i.e.* the installation of safety equipment. **14.20**

For safety in the course of work, rules for safety operations must be strictly complied with. In practice, some privately owned enterprises and foreign investment enterprises use out-dated equipment and do not pay much attention to labour safety issues. Even worse, some enterprises force their workers to work in violation of the safety rules. Section 56 of the Labour Law provides that workers have the right to refuse to work at risk and can sue the management for actions that endanger the safety of their lives and health.

Another issue closely related to labour safety is vocational training. This is now provided for under the Labour Law, and vocational training systems should be established in employing units. Those workers who do technical work must undertake training before taking up their posts.

Supervision and Inspection

The main task of supervision and inspection is undertaken by labour administrative departments within county and high-level people's governments. Their authority includes the supervision and inspection of **14.21** the ways in which an employing unit abides by labour legislation and regulations, to stop any act that violates labour legislation and regulations and to order the unit to make corrections. There is a possibility that the authority may be abused if no restriction is imposed upon the authority. In response, two restrictions are imposed under section 86. Firstly, the scope of investigation is restricted to the method of carrying out labour legislation and regulations, the examination of the necessary records and the inspection of the working area. Secondly, the personnel who conduct supervision and inspection must be appropriately qualified. While carrying out their duties, they should comply with relevant regulations. The existing regulations on labour supervision was issued by the Ministry of Labour in August 1993.

Apart from the official supervision provided by the labour administrative department, trade unions, social or business organizations and individuals all have a role to play in labour supervision. They can either report to the labour administrative department or initiate a charge against the employing unit. Should the supervision be in advance or afterwards? It seems that it could be both ways. From the viewpoint of effectiveness of supervision, supervision in advance should be encouraged. However, China's practice and the frequent occurrence of industrial accidents prove that advanced supervision is far from enough. At present, at county level, there exist labour supervision brigades within labour administrative departments. However, human resources are extremely limited, which makes it impossible for them to undertake advanced supervision for every enterprise.

However, the importance of labour supervision and inspection has been realized by both central and local governments. In order to strengthen labour supervision, some local governments such as Guangdong Prorince have issued or are drafting their own detailed regulations on labour supervision.

Conclusion

14.22 The above discussion reveals that labour legislation is biased towards the protection of workers' rights, which is consistent with the objectives and guiding principles of the Labour Law, *i.e.* the protection of the legitimate rights and interests of the workers.

The Labour Law bears clear marks of a system which is still in a transitional period from a planned economy to a market economy. For example, the impossibility of implementing a comprehensive labour contract system and incomplete compliance with international labour standards with regard to working hours. There are plenty of other examples to be found. This is understandable given that China has just started the development of its market economy.

Many undefined words and phrases have been used in the Labour Law, which may lead to uncertainty in interpretation. This may then further lead to the sacrifice of enterprises' autonomy or to the detriment of the workers' lawful interests. Fortunately, the Ministry of Labour has already taken some remedial measures by issuing 17 more regulations and 100 opinions on the implementation of the Labour Law.

After the enactment of so much legislation, the next task for China is to enforce the legislation effectively as up to now the enforceability of labour legislation has not been satisfactory. This remains a daunting task for Chinese government.

Nevertheless, the Labour Law signifies great progress and will contribute to the protection of lawful interests of workers. It has provided for the first time, important laws regulating labour relations in China and laid down the framework for future labour legislation. It has put an end to former practices in labour legislation, *i.e.* legislation according to the ownership of enterprises, and made it possible to establish a unified labour law system in China.

Notes

[1] The seventeen regulations are:

> Notice from the Ministry of Labour on the Implementation of the Minimum Wage Guarantee System (October 8, 1994);
> Measures on Occupational Guideline (October 27, 1994);
> Management Measures on Labour Inspectors (November 14, 1994);
> Regulations on the Dismissal of Staff by Enterprises for Economic Reasons (November 14, 1994);
> Interim Provisions on Inter-provincial Employment Management of Workers from Countryside (November 17, 1994);
> Provisions on Medical Period for Sick or Non-work-related Injury (December 1, 1994);
> Measures on Economic compensation for Breach or Dissolution of Labour Contract (December 3, 1994);
> Provisions on Collective Contract (December 5, 1994);
> Interim Provisions on the Payment of Wages (December 6, 1994);
> Provisions on Occupational Training (December 9, 1994);
> Provisions on Special Protection of Juvenile Workers (December 9, 1994);
> Approval Measures for Enterprises to Implement Flexible and Combined-calculated Working Hours (December 14, 1994);
> Provisions on the Management of Occupational Training Entities (December 14, 1994);
> Implementation Measures on the Safety Supervision of Mines' Constitution Projects (December 14, 1994);
> Measures on the Management of Mines' Safety Inspectors (December 14, 1994);
> Provisions on Occupational Training (December 9, 1994).

[2] The four regulations were promulgated on July 12, 1986. They include: Interim Regulation on the Implementation of Labour Contract System in State-owned Enterprises;

Interim Regulations on the Recruitment of Workers by State-owned Enterprises; Interim Regulations on Dismissal of Workers Breaching Disciplines by State-owned Enterprises; Interim Regulations on Unemployment Insurance for Workers in State-owned Enterprises.

[3] Henry R. Zheng, "An Introduction to the Labour Law of the PRC"; in R.H. Folsom & J.H. Minan *Law in the People's in Republic of China — Commentary, Readings & Materials*, Martinus Nijhoff Publishers, 1989, (pp. 515–543), at p. 523.

CHAPTER 15

LAWS ON THE FINANCIAL SYSTEM

Stephen Foo

City University of Hong Kong

Stephen Foo, LL.B., PCLL, M.A. (City University of Hong Kong); ACIArb; Lecturer, Faculty of Law, City University of Hong Kong; Barrister-at-law, Supreme Court of Hong Kong.

Introduction

As early as the late 1970's when China first adopted an open-door   **15.01**
policy, the Chinese government started its reforms of the financial
system. Prior to the reforms, the Chinese economy was extremely
centralized, with everything under the tight control of the State. There
was little room for the development of a market financial system
because of the limited commercial activities. Ironically, there was an
institution called a "bank" at that time in China, but by no means did
it operate as a bank in western terms. Virtually, the only established
bank in China was the People's Bank of China (the "PBOC") which
operated as the cashier of the government. The PBOC, the central bank
of China, was charged with implementing policy as decided by the
State Council, such as extending credit and granting subsidies to State-
owned enterprises. The PBOC's monopoly was broken when a couple
of State-owned banks were subsequently set up or restored in the
1970's and 1980's as the result of decentralization.[1]

The State Council's Decision to Reform the Financial Sector in 1993

The economic reforms in China over the past 15 years have served to   **15.02**
make China more closely connected with the world economy. The
sharp increase in international trade and foreign investment in China

has resulted in China's realization that the existing financial system can no longer adapt to the conditions of the new economic environment. According to the decision of the Third Plenary Session of the 14th Congress of the Chinese Communist Party, China is committed to transforming its traditional planned economy into a socialist market economy. Agricultural and industrial reforms cannot stand by themselves without a compatible financial system. To implement the policy of building up a market economy and to strengthen the macro-economic control by the PBOC, the State Council promulgated the Decision to Reform the Financial Sector (the "State Council Decision") on December 15, 1993.[2] The principal objectives of the Decision are:

> (a) to establish a macro-control system by the central bank, *i.e.* the PBOC, under the leadership of the State Council, for the purpose of implementing monetary policies independently;
>
> (b) to establish a financial entity system under which "policy" finance and commercial finance are separated and under which the State-owned commercial banks play a dominant role, with the co-existence of multifold financial entities; and
>
> (c) to establish a market financial system with a unified open market, orderly competition and close supervision.

To achieve the goals of the Decision requires, *inter alia*, the adoption of relevant legislation. Four major laws were accordingly adopted in 1995, including *The Law on the People's Bank of China* (the "*People's Bank Law*"),[3] *The Law on Commercial Banks* (the "*Commercial Bank Law*"),[4] *The Law on Negotiable Instruments* (the "*Negotiable Instrument Law*")[5] and *The Law on Insurance* (the "*Insurance Law*").[6] These laws, in addition to various rules and regulations which have already been in force, constitute the milestone for the legal framework for the new Chinese financial system. This chapter attempts to discuss the reforms on the banking sector and negotiable instruments.

Banking Reforms

15.03   Since its establishment in 1948, the PBOC has been acting as the nascent central bank of China though without a legislative mandate. For many years, the PBOC assisted in managing the allocation of public funds, operating as the cashier for the Chinese Government. Meanwhile, it also exercised lending powers as a "bank" until 1978 when such lending functions were transferred to the four State-owned specialized banks pursuant to the decision of the Third Plenum in 1978.

Its role as the central bank of China was further crystallized in 1983 when the State Council adopted the Decision to Require the PBOC to Function as a Central Bank. Three years later, the Provisional Regulations on the Administration of Banks were promulgated.[7] The Provisional Regulations outlined the contemporary banking system in the 1980's and provided a solid ground for the recent round of reforms. To a certain extent, *The People's Bank Law* and *The Commercial Bank Law* are based on the Provisional Regulations and other related administrative regulations. Under that system, the PBOC was the central bank of China, in charge of the overall operation of the system; the State-owned commercial banks played the dominant role whilst credit co-operatives, other banks and foreign financial institutions acted as supplementary institutions.

This system did not work satisfactorily in the early 1990's. Banking operation has been subject to strong administrative interference. This regulatory regime, framed by scattered regulations in the absence of a national law, brought disorder to the Chinese financial system in the early 1990's which has been described in the following words:

> "[F]or many years, the People's Bank of China's regulation of the money supply and supervision of financial institutions was subject to political interference and required the use of cumbersome credit allocations. Banks themselves operated under severe pressure to make or roll over loans to politically favoured customers on preferential terms. Commercial transactions were conducted in an uncertain legal context that imposed few penalties on defaulting borrowers . . ."[8]

As demonstrated in the State Council Decision, the Chinese Government believes a strong central bank which is capable of carrying out macro-economic control efficiently and effectively to be the solution to the problem. To give the PBOC more ammunition to resume orderly operation to the Chinese financial system, Vice Premier Zhu Rongji personally took the office of the President of the PBOC in 1993. He immediately called for a 16-point programme to stop the malpractice and disorder of the financial system. Since then, the PBOC has been able to exercise its statutory functions properly. The position is further codified with the adoption of *The People's Bank Law*.

The Figure 15.1 summarizes the structure of the current banking system.

Powers of the Central Bank

Article 4 of *The People's Bank Law* prescribes the functions and powers of the PBOC as follows:

(a) to formulate and implement monetary policies;
(b) to issue *Renminbi* and control its circulation;

Figure 15.1: China's Banking System

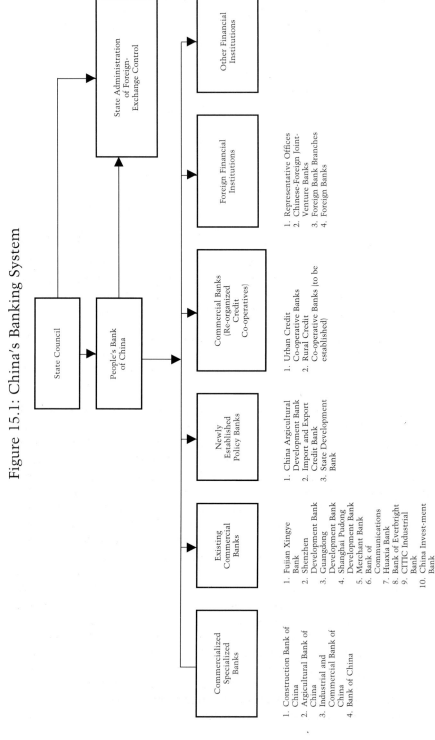

(c) to approve, supervise and administer financial institutions;

(d) to supervise and control the financial market;

(e) to promulgate rules and regulations on the supervision and administration of the financial sector;

(f) to hold, administer and manage the country's foreign exchange reserves and bullion reserve;

(g) to manage the State treasury;

(h) to maintain the normal operation of the payment, clearing and settlement system;

(i) to be responsible for preparing statistics, investigations, analysis and forecasting for the financial industry;

(j) to engage in relevant international activities as the central bank of China; and

(k) to carry out other activities as assigned by the State Council.

To fully understand the central bank's role, Article 4 should be read in conjunction with the rest of the Law. On the one hand, Articles 3 and 4 empower the PBOC "to formulate and implement monetary policies" with the view "to stimulate economic growth by maintaining the stability of the currency value"; on the other hand, Article 5 places limitations on the exercise of such powers. Article 5 states:

> "Decisions of the PBOC in respect of the annual money supply, interest rate, exchange rate and other matters specified by the State Council shall, prior to their implementation, be approved by the State Council..."

Despite this provision, the residual power in policy making exercised by the PBOC is very broad. Decisions in respect of matters other than those stipulated may, however, be implemented by the PBOC upon adoption and submission to the State Council for the record. So long as the objectives under Article 2 require, the PBOC may adopt the necessary measures as it deems fit.

In the past, the PBOC often came under pressure to tailor its credit and supervisory policies for various favoured interests.[9] This is largely due to its status as a branch of the government and its internal structure that was set up according to the administrative structure of the government.[10] Its regional offices were jointly supervised by the head office and local governments. Therefore, local governments were given ample opportunities to exert considerable interference, for example, by influencing matters like personnel appointment and appraisal. This has been considered a major source of administrative interference.[11] In this regard Article 7 of *The People's Bank Law* provides the PBOC with the weapons to resist such local interferences. It states that the Bank will independently perform its functions as well as duties and should be free from interference from local governments, departments at various levels, social entities and individuals. Article 12 further provides that the PBOC adopts a centralized and unified management system towards its local branches to minimize local government intervention.[12] Under Article 36, the Bank must also establish and refine its internal audit and inspection system, and strengthen its internal management.

The PBOC is led by a president with the assistance of several vice-presidents. According to Article 9 of *The People's Bank Law*, the appointment of the president is nominated by the State Council and approved by the National People's Congress. In this regard, the *People's Bank Law* attempts to strike a balance between the administration and the legislature. Having the power to appoint the president, the National People's Congress may exercise certain influence on the policy-making of the PBOC. Under Article 6, the PBOC is required to submit working reports to the Standing Committee of the National People's Congress on matters concerning the monetary policy and the supervision and management of the financial sector.

Pursuant to Article 10, the PBOC adopts the "presidential responsibility system"[13] under which the president is responsible for the entire operation of the Bank. Nevertheless, a number of provisions in *The People's Bank Law* give the State Council ample opportunities to exercise direct or indirect influence on the PBOC. Articles 2 and 7 expressly subordinate the PBOC to the leadership of the State Council. Article 5 requires major monetary decisions to be approved by the State Council, which also controls the appointment of vice-presidents. In short, the PBOC operates as a functional ministry of the State Council.

The People's Bank Law in effect overturns the suggestion by some Chinese banking experts that the PBOC be made a statutory body, accountable only to the NPC. Since 1983, discussions have focused on whether China should model its regulatory regime on the US's Federal Reserve System. As a matter of fact, it was one of the major issues heatedly debated in the National People's Congress when the *People's Bank Law Draft* was being considered. After all, Articles 2 and 7 of the Law demonstrate that the power to formulate monetary policy and to regulate the financial system is too important for the central government to relinquish at this stage.[14]

Formulation of Monetary Policies

15.04   As far as the formulation of monetary policies is concerned, a designated policy committee shall be set up within the PBOC pursuant to Article 11 of *The People's Bank Law*. In fact, there has been considerable debate on the question of whether this committee should be under the State Council, the National People's Congress or the PBOC. The current provision represents a compromise among various authorities. While the committee is set up within the Bank, its functions, constitution and procedures are to be decided by the State Council, and the National People's Congress will be kept informed of the decisions.

It appears that the establishment of the Monetary Policy Committee is only on a pilot basis. Whether it is a policy-making body or merely an advisory body was not decided in the Law. The prospect of the committee will certainly depend upon how it works in the coming years.

In carrying out the monetary policies, the PBOC is empowered to adopt the following measures:[15]

(a) to require financial institutions to place a deposit reserve fund at a required ratio;

(b) to determine the base interest rate of the central bank;

(c) to provide re-discount business for the financial institutes which have accounts with the PBOC;

(d) to provide loans for commercial banks;

(e) to trade treasury bonds, other government bonds and foreign exchange in the open market; and

(f) to adopt other monetary tools as stipulated by the State Council.

This provision signifies a gradual departure from traditional practice. Direct credit control and mandatory loans are no longer the sole or prime monetary tools. Instead, some tools widely adopted by western countries such as determination of the prime interest rate are introduced.

Commercial Banking Operation

China's commercial banks, in the true sense, came into being only **15.05** after 1986. At present, there are 14 commercial banks, of which four are national commercial banks: Bank of Communications, CITIC Industrial Bank, China Everbright Bank, Hua Xia Bank; five are regional share holding banks: Merchants Bank, Guangdong Development Bank, Shenzhen Development Bank, Fujian Industrial Bank and Shanghai Pudong Development Bank; another is the China Investment Bank which is wholly owned by the Construction Bank of China; and four urban co-operative commercial banks.

The adoption of *The Commercial Bank Law* is another major step taken by the Chinese government in formulating the new banking system to suit the needs of a socialist market economy. The objectives are to "protect the lawful rights and interests of commercial banks, depositors and other customers; standardize the acts of commercial banks; raise the quality of credit and assets; strengthen supervision and administration; and safeguard the sound operation of commercial bank and maintain financial order".[16]

Article 2 of *The Commercial Bank Law* defines commercial banks as body corporates established in accordance with *The Commercial Bank Law* and *The Company Law* which may take money deposits from the public, extend loans, provide settlement services and conduct other related businesses. There is an explicit provision in *The Commercial Bank Law* that any establishment, form and structure of organization, merger and division are also governed by *The Company Law*.[17] Under Article 4, commercial banks enjoy autonomy in operation and they must be responsible for their profits and losses. Article 4 also directs them to conduct their business on a commercial basis in accordance with the principles of "profitability, safety and liquidity."

Chapter Two of the Law governs the establishment of commercial banks. All applications should be examined and approved by the PBOC.[18] Without the approval, no other entity or individual may take part in banking business or use the title "Bank". Article 13 sets out the minimum registered capital requirement: Rmb 1 billion for each commercial bank; Rmb 100 million for an urban credit co-operative bank; and Rmb 50 million for a rural credit co-operative bank.[19] Such requirement aims at ensuring the adequacy of capital of commercial banks. An applicant must also:[20]

(a) have qualified managerial personnel, such as directors, a general manager and other senior personnel, who possess relevant professional expertise and experience;
(b) have a sound organization and management structure; and
(c) have a suitable business site, safety measures and other facilitates.

Obviously, some existing banks have not met the above requirements. Article 17 resolves the problem by providing that such banks are temporarily exempted from the above requirements in the transitional period and that the date by which they have to strictly comply with the requirements will be specified by the PBOC later.

Under *The Commercial Bank Law*, a commercial bank may engage in the following activities:[21]

(a) taking deposits from the public;
(b) extending short, medium and long-term loans;[22]
(c) providing domestic and international settlement services;
(d) discounting bills;
(e) issuing financial bonds;
(f) acting as an agent of issuing, cashing and underwriting government bonds;
(g) dealing in government bonds;
(h) carrying out inter-bank loan business;

(i) dealing or acting as an agent in foreign exchange transactions;

(j) providing letters of credit services and guarantees;

(k) acting as an agent in collection and payment and insurance businesses;

(l) providing safe deposit box services; and

(m) doing other businesses approved by the PBOC.

In general, commercial banks are authorized to carry out activities which are normally conducted by the banks in other developed countries. They are required to abide by "the principles of equalities, voluntariness, fairness, honesty and good faith" in their business operation[23] and to protect their customers' lawful rights and interests from encroachment by any organization or individual.

Although Article 3(7) allows a commercial bank to engage in trading in government securities market and conduct certain activities in the financial bonds market, Article 43 prohibits them from engaging in investment in domestic real estate except for their own use, and in non-banking financial institutions. They are prohibited from engaging in such activities directly or through their subsidiaries indirectly. Article 43 resembles the US *Glass-Steagall Act* which created barriers between the banking and securities industries in order to ensure the stability of the banking industry during depressions.[24]

Control on Lending

Chapter Four of *The Commercial Bank Law*, supplemented with the **15.06** *Lending Provisions* which contain thorough guidelines on lending, provides the framework for the lending business of commercial banks. Commercial banks must take into consideration the need for the development of the national economy and social progress and follow the guidance of the State industrial policy.[25] In conducting loan business, a commercial bank must examine the capability and form of repayment by the borrower,[26] and in general require security collateral.[27] To promote safe and sound banking practice and to control the overheated economy, commercial banks should examine the credit worthiness of both the borrowers and their guarantors, and the value and liquidity of the security collateral.[28] Only in cases where the borrower has high credit rating and is able to show that he virtually has the ability to repay the loans may a guarantor not be required.

To ensure autonomy in the lending business, Article 41 of *The Commercial Bank Law* stipulates that no organization or individual may compel a commercial bank to extend loans or provide guarantees.[29] Commercial banks may refuse any application for loans or guarantee. Failure to comply with this provision may cause criminal liability under Article 85 if the circumstances of the case are serious.

However, *The Commercial Bank Law* does not free the four State-owned specialized banks entirely as Article 41 provides that State-owned commercial banks have to grant loans for specific projects approved by the State Council. To eliminate the adverse impacts of this provision, the State Council will take appropriate remedial measures for any losses sustained by the commercial banks as a result of granting such loans.

Article 18 of the *Commercial Bank Law* is another potential source of interference from the PBOC and other government departments. It provides that each State-owned bank should set up a supervisory board consisting of representatives of the PBOC, government departments and financial experts. The board is responsible for supervising the quality of credit and assets, asset-liability ratio, maintenance of the value and appreciation of State-owned assets, and acts of senior management personnel.

Meanwhile, commercial banks may not grant unsecured loans, or loans with preferential terms to related persons under Article 40.[30] "Related persons" include:

(a) members of the Board of Directors or the Board of Supervisors, managerial personnel, and the staff of the credit business department of commercial banks and their close relatives; and

(b) the company, enterprise or other economic entity wherein the aforesaid persons have made investment or assumed senior managerial positions.

Article 25 of the *Lending Provisions* places further restrictions on banks in conducting lending business. In particular, no loans may be granted for financing:

(a) interest payment;
(b) projects expressly prohibited by the State;
(c) projects not falling into any approved investment plan; and
(d) projects in violation of environmental protection regulations.

Besides, no bank may grant loans to a person who has seriously violated foreign exchange regulations or committed major offences.

When conducting their businesses, commercial banks are required to follow the principle of fair competition.[31] To be specific, commercial banks may not raise or lower interest rates or use other unjustifiable means in violation of the relevant provisions in order to attract deposits or grant loans. For example, commercial banks must follow the guiding circulating capital loans rates prescribed by the PBOC; their interest rates are allowed to fluctuate within the permissible range, *i.e.* 20 per cent up or 10 per cent down.[32] Before the adoption of *The Commercial Bank Law*, it was reported that a number of banking officials involved in unfair competition were sacked or subject to administrative penalties in early 1995. Now, similar cases will be dealt with pursuant to Article 83 which imposes both civil and criminal liabilities for non-compliance with these provisions.

Surveillance and Supervision

With regard to administration and supervision of financial institutions, Chapter Five of *The People's Bank Law* entrusts such duties to the PBOC with all necessary powers.[33] For example, Article 31 confirms the PBOC's authority in approving establishment, alteration, termination of financial institutions and their scope of business. Article 32 confers the PBOC the authority to carry out its supervision over various matters, such as deposits, loans, settlement, bad debts, etc. Article 33 empowers the PBOC to demand reports from financial institutions on their financial conditions and operation. To facilitate effective supervision and administration, the PBOC established two internal organs in 1994, namely, the "Administrative Judicial Review Committee" and the "Legal Advisory Office". These two organs were established on the one hand to promote the Judicial Review Committee of the local branches of the PBOC at provincial or municipal levels and address applications for judicial review; on the other hand, to carry out advisory services on financial legislation to the PBOC.[34]

15.07

The Commercial Bank Law also contains specific requirements on the conduct of bank staff and provides legal liabilities for failure to carry out their duties. Article 52 stipulates that staff of commercial banks must abide by the law, administrative regulations and other rules. It further prohibits them from:

(a) taking advantage of their positions to demand or accept bribes, or accept commissions or service fees under any pretext;
(b) taking advantage of their positions to commit graft, misappropriation or unlawful possession of the funds of any bank;
(c) providing loans or guarantee to relatives or friends in violation of regulations;
(d) holding positions concurrently in other economic institutions; and
(e) committing other acts in violation of the law, administrative regulations and rules in business management.

Article 60 requires commercial banks to set up and improve their internal systems for examining and inspecting deposits, loans, settlement and doubtful accounts. Before the promulgation of *The Commercial Bank Law*, these matters were prescribed by the Interim Provisions on Auditing and Supervision by the PBOC issued by the PBOC on July 5, 1985, Provisions on the Penalties for Financial Auditing and Examination issued by the PBOC on May 5, 1989, etc. In 1994, for instance, regular examination on over 1,000 financial institutions were conducted. In addition, the PBOC carried out special examinations on the implementation of macro-economic-regulations policies and measures by 279 financial institutions, on fixed asset loans of 1,200 financial institutions, on call money market activities of 127 financial institutions and credit disbursement for agricultural product procurement at local branches of the Agricultural Bank of China. To strengthen off-site supervision and administration, the PBOC promulgated the Interim Provisions on Off-site Auditing and Supervision on April 5, last year. According to a study by the PBOC, by the end of 1994, all banks in China had employed internal auditing staff of 30,000![35]

Banks in violation of these provisions are subject to a fine, or in serious cases, suspension of business. Individuals in violation may be even subject to criminal liability. Like *The Company Law*, *The Commercial Bank Law* does not contain specific provision for imprisonment. On June 30, 1995, the Standing Committee of the NPC adopted the Decision Concerning Punishment on Crimes for Disturbing Financial Orders which provides specific punishment on serious criminal offences. It serves to supplement *The Commercial Bank Law*. Upon its adoption, it was reported that a banker in Guangdong was sentenced to death for embezzlement.[36]

Administration of Foreign Financial Institutions

15.08   Foreign banks, Chinese-foreign joint venture banks, branches of foreign banks and other financial companies with foreign interests are collectively referred to as foreign financial institutions according to Article 2 of the Regulations on the Administration of Foreign Financial Institutions (the "FFI Regulations").[37] Although the FFI Regulations were promulgated before *The Commercial Bank Law*, Article 88 of *The Commercial Bank Law* expressly provides that banks with foreign interests are also governed by other laws and administrative regulations as prescribed by the government, and that in case of conflict such laws and regulations shall prevail. Therefore, banks with foreign interests are subject to a more stringent regulatory framework, they must comply with the provisions of both *The Commercial Bank Law* and the FFI Regulations.

In the past, there was very little room for foreign financial institutions in the Chinese financial system.[38] Since China adopted an open-door policy in the late 1970s, which resulted in a rapid inflow of foreign capital, many foreign financial institutions have been exploring the possibility of setting up representative offices,[39] branches or even Chinese-foreign joint venture banks in China.[40] At present, there are 519 representative offices of overseas financial institutions and 137 foreign financial businesses in China, including 117 foreign bank branches, five Chinese-foreign joint venture banks, five wholly foreign-owned banks, five foreign-owned financial companies, four insurance companies and one Chinese-foreign joint venture investment bank.[41] According to Mr Yin Jieyan, vice-president of the PBOC, the total assets of foreign financial institutions in China had reached US$ 20 billion by the end of 1995, 40.7 per cent more than that of the previous year.[42] These foreign financial institutions have supplied US$ 12 billion in loans and attracted US$ 3 billion in deposits.[43] Their businesses focus on the following areas:[44]

    (a) syndicated loans for big infrastructure and industrial projects;
    (b) State-owned companies securities' listing and related matters;
    (c) foreign exchange transactions; and
    (d) foreign exchange business for Chinese-foreign joint venture companies.

Establishment of a foreign financial institution in China, like setting up a commercial bank, requires approval from the PBOC.[45] However, the FFI Regulations provide relatively more stern requirements for foreign bankers:[46]

    (a) the applicant institution must possess assets of not less than US$ 10 billion;[47]
    (b) the applicant institution must have had a representative office in China for at least two years; and
    (c) the home country of the applicant institution has a sound supervisory and administrative framework for the financial system.

The FFI Regulations allow the paid-up capital of foreign financial insitutitons to be different from their registered capital.[48] Foreign financial institutions are required to maintain their paid-up capital to the level of not less than 50 per cent of their registered capital. This provision represents a sharp departure from China's practice of *The Company Law* under which all companies and banks must have their registered capital fully paid before commencing their businesses. It appears that the FFI Regulations prevail in this regard by virtue of Article 88 of *The Commercial Bank Law*. It must also be noticed that Article 32 of the FFI Regulations mandates those foreign financial institutions whose paid-up capital is less than its registered capital to withdraw 25 per cent of its after-tax profits to make up the deficiency until the sum of its paid-up capital and reserves equals to its registered capital.

    The minimum amount of the registered capital of a foreign bank or a Chinese-foreign joint venture bank is Rmb 300 million, whilst the minimum registered capital of a financial company with foreign interest is Rmb 200 million. A foreign bank branch, although not having a separate legal personality, is required to be allocated Rmb 100 million as working capital by its head office. All paid-up or working capital must be in the form of freely convertible currency.

With regard to supervision and administration of foreign financial institutions, the PBOC has gradually introduced two major methods of on-site and off-site examinations which have been applied to domestic financial institutions. The PBOC head office is in charge of the overall supervision and administration[49] whilst the day-to-day supervision and administration are delegated to the branches of the PBOC in the localities. Although foreign financial institutions are entitled to autonomy of their business management, certain matters such as deposit and loan interest rates and rates of service charge for handling other transactions must comply with the stipulations of the PBOC.[50]

A foreign financial institution taking deposits must place an interest free deposit reserve in the local branch of the PBOC.[51] The ratio of the deposit reserves is determined and may be adjusted by the PBOC according to the circumstances. The FFI Regulations limit the total assets of a foreign financial institution to 20 times of the sum of the paid-up capital and the reserves[52] and the fixed assets to 40 per cent of the sum of its paid-up capital and reserves. Besides, the total amount of deposits taken up by a foreign financial institution may not exceed 40 per cent of its total assets. Save with the approval of the PBOC, loans to a single borrower, including its associates, are limited to 30 per cent of the paid-up capital and reserves of the foreign financial institution concerned.[53] All these provisions help to ensure the liquidity of foreign financial institutions.

Meanwhile, the FFI Regulations contain specific provisions concerning interests taken by foreign financial institutions. Unless approved by the PBOC, the total investment made by a foreign financial institution may not exceed 30 per cent of the sum of its paid-up capital and reserves.[54] This Article represents relaxation of Article 43 of *The Commercial Bank Law*, which prohibits commercial banks from engaging in high-risk investments such as investments in the stock market or real estate business. By virtue of Article 88 of *The Commercial Bank Law*, this Article will prevail and foreign financial institutions may engage in all sorts of investments provided that they do not exceed the 30 per cent limit. To achieve equal treatment among domestic and foreign financial institutions, amendment to the FFI Regulations in this regard is expected.

Despite the aforesaid provisions, international financial crises such as the Barings incident provide the necessity of the PBOC to strengthen co-operation with the supervision authorities of other countries. In line with the principle of the Basel Committee on Banking Supervision, the PBOC has strengthened the exchange of information and co-operation with foreign supervisory authorities in the process of examination of foreign financial institutions.[55] That is the reason why the PBOC has to ensure the home country of a foreign financial institution has a sound supervisory and administrative framework before approving its application under Article 6 of the FFI Regulations.

Articles 17 to 21 set out the scope of permissible business of foreign financial institutions subject to the approval of the PBOC:

(a) foreign exchange deposits;
(b) foreign exchange lending;
(c) foreign exchange note discount;
(d) approved foreign exchange investment;
(e) foreign exchange remittances;
(f) foreign exchange guarantees;
(g) import and export clearing;
(h) foreign exchange transactions for its own account and for clients;
(i) agency services for the exchange of foreign currencies and foreign exchange note;
(j) agency services for foreign currency credit card payment;
(k) custody and safe deposit box services;
(l) credit investment and advice; and
(m) approved domestic currency business and other foreign currency business.

One notable breakthrough in the FFI Regulations is that a foreign financial institution may engage in *Renminbi* business with the approval of the PBOC. Although such approval has yet been given, Article 17 paves the way for the opening of *Renminbi* business in the future. Currently, the business of foreign financial institutions is still confined to foreign currency transactions. Over the last few years, China has been under tremendous pressure to open its domestic currency market to foreign financial institutions. Due to the infancy and the backwardness of the financial system, China is reluctant to allow foreign financial institutions to enter into the market at this moment so that Chinese domestic banks will not have to face the probable intense competition from foreign banks.[56]

Although foreign financial institutions do not have current access to the *Renminbi* market, these financial institutions still play an indispensable role in the Chinese financial system. China's officials have repeatedly assured that efforts would be made to create conditions for foreign banks to deal with *Renminbi*, along with the promise to apply national treatment to foreign financial institutions in the future in a "planned and step-by-step" manner. It is believed that these restrictions will be removed as soon as the *Renminbi* becomes freely convertible in international markets.

Establishment of Policy Banks and Commercialization of Specialized Banks

15.09   To separate "policy" finance from commercial finance, three policy banks were established pursuant to the State Council Decision to spur the commercialization of the four State-owned specialized banks. This is a very difficult task resulting from the insolvency and triangle debts among State-owned enterprises. Until and unless the specialized banks are liberalized from such burdens, the objectives of *The Commercial Bank Law* cannot be achieved.[57] For example, the State-owned specialized banks will not be able to compete with other commercial banks without government protection if they are not commercialized. They will only be on equal footing if policy finance is entirely taken over by the newly established policy banks. A report released by a research centre of the State Council indicates that three out of four specialized banks suffered hefty losses in the first six months of 1995; for example, the Industrial and Commercial Bank of China made a loss of more than Rmb 6 billion![58]

The four State-owned specialized banks used to carry out policy finance, *i.e.* to extend loans to enterprise in accordance with the State policy. Loans were usually given without conducting any feasibility studies and checks on the credit-worthiness of debtor enterprises. Bad or doubtful debts have accumulated to an alarming level which hinder the development of the Chinese economy.[59] To rectify this situation and to avoid abuse, three policy banks, namely the State Development Bank, the China Agricultural Development Bank and the Import and Export Credit Bank were established.[60] These policy banks will refrain from engaging in competition with other commercial institutions and operations will be on a "break-even" basis.

Pursuant to Article 36 of *The People's Bank Law*, the PBOC is responsible for guiding and supervising policy banks. With regard to the progress of the commercialization of specialized banks, the PBOC made the following evaluation in 1995:[61]

> "Significant progress has been made by State specialized banks in the transition to State commercial banks. All specialized banks have separated policy credit and commercial credit in their operations and accounts, and have gradually transferred the responsibility of policy lending to policy banks. On the basis of separating policy banking and commercial banking, the specialized banks have launched comprehensive asset-liability ratio management set by the PBOC. Through conducting and improving internal audit, constraint mechanism and loan responsibility system, specialized banks are gradually forming risk prevention and self regulating mechanism."

504

Since its founding in 1994, the State Development Bank has opened four subsidiaries and three representative offices throughout China. Pursuant to the State Council Decision, the Bank serves as both the administrative body of the Construction Bank of China and the State investment institutions. It is responsible for extending policy loans to and providing discounting services for key State construction projects in the form of stocks, with funds allocated by the State. For example, the Three-gorges Dam Project in Wuhan and the Qinshan Nuclear Power Plant are financed by the State Development Bank. Statistics show that a total of Rmb 170 billion has been extended in policy loans which were used to finance more than 400 projects.[62] The capital of the State Development Bank comes from three sources:

(a) funds allocated by the Ministry of Finance as capital and key construction project funds;
(b) funds raised through issuing or guaranteeing commercial bonds; and
(c) deposits taken by the Construction Bank of China.

The China Agricultural Development Bank is responsible for making policy loans to boost the development of agriculture, allocating and supervising the use of the State funds in the agricultural sector on behalf of the State. Acting in concert with the Agricultural Bank of China and rural credit co-operatives, the China Agricultural Development Bank is designated to help agricultural development in China. Unlike the State Development Bank, the China Agricultural Development Bank is a legal person with its capital contributed by the Agricultural Bank of China. The Bank takes over the policy loans to agricultural sector by the Agricultural Bank of China and the Industrial and Commercial Bank of China.

In addition to the contribution from the Agricultural Bank of China, the capital of the Bank also comes from the issuing of financial bonds, funds allocated by the State, overseas-raised funds and deposits by enterprises using agricultural policy loans. However, before March 1996 when the PBOC's approval for issuing bonds had not been secured, the interbank loans from the PBOC constituted the primary source of capital of the China Agricultural Development Bank.[63]

The Import and Export Credit Bank of China was set up in April 1994 with the task to provide medium and long-term policy loans to China's exporters of large-scale mechanical and electrical products. Its capital was mainly from the State, approved by the Ministry of Finance.

Since its operation in July 1994, the Bank has already granted loans of Rmb 7 billion[64] and successfully built up business relations with more than two hundred major banks across the world and set up correspondent relations with 71 banks.[65] With regard to credit lines, the Import and Export Credit Bank is also bound by the credit ceiling set by the PBOC aimed at curbing the high inflation rate which has been the prime job of the Chinese government over the past few years. According to Tong Zhiguang, chairman of the board of directors, the Bank will carefully examine each company before approving the loan applications to improve the quality of credits. A debtor company must have a sound record of business performance and management; its products must be highly competitive in the international market and the company must have great potential for further growth.[66]

Apart from extending policy loans, the Import and Export Credit Bank also handles the bills discounting and credit guarantees for the export of mechanical and electrical products. Export credit guarantees in China are currently conducted exclusively by the Import and Export Credit Bank and the People's Insurance Company of China. In 1995, the Bank extended Rmb 213 million in export credit insurance and guarantees.[67] These services are crucial to the development of China's foreign trade.

According to the State Council Decision, each policy bank should have a supervisory board which is composed of representatives from the Ministry of Finance, the PBOC and other relevant government departments. The supervisory board supervises the operation of the policy banks on behalf of the State. The board is also responsible for assessing the performance of the bank's president and proposing their appointment and removal.

Establishment of Co-operative Banks

15.10 Re-organization of credit co-operatives in urban and rural areas is also an important task of the recent banking reform under which credit co-operatives are all crystallized into sophisticated urban and rural credit co-operative banks. Prior to the reform, there were more than 5,000 urban credit co-operatives in China, providing financial services to local medium and small enterprises, private firms and urban residents. Rural credit co-operatives handle mainly loans and deposits in rural areas and are administered by the Agricultural Bank of China.[68] Nevertheless, the limited financial resources of a single individual co-operative can no longer meet the demands of the growing economy. It was also reported that some credit co-operatives were poorly managed and that some had ceased to be financial institutions and converted to be complexion.[69]

The recent case *Jinwei Urban Credit Co-operative* vividly illustrates the poor administration of credit co-operatives. The suit was filed by the Shenzhen Jinwei Urban Credit Co-operative ("Jinwei") against the Shenzhen Branch of PBOC (the "Shenzhen Branch") for infringing its rights. An on-site investigation of Jinwei conducted by the Shenzhen Branch in February 1994 revealed that Jinwei violated a number of provisions, namely, failing to pay up the company capital, granting loans to related enterprise and other credit co-operatives, operating beyond its approved scope of business, allowing unauthorized loans to senior officers, adjusting lending interest rates without approval, etc. By the end of 1995, outstanding loans accounted for Rmb 61.9 million, 87 per cent of the total loan balance; and Rmb 5.96 million in interest was also defaulted by borrowers.

The Shenzhen Branch decided to reconstruct Jinwei, but Jinwei rejected and applied to the People's Court to review the Shenzhen Branch's decision on the basis that the latter had infringed its autonomy. Pending the decision of the People's Court, the Shenzhen Branch set up a working group to take over the management of Jinwei.

On May 30, 1995, the Shenzhen Branch issued a notice stating that prior to the granting of its industrial and business licence, Jinwei had already been carrying out financial business contrary to the law. The unlawful lending and borrowing of loans involved up to Rmb 20 million. In order to restore financial order and protect the interest of public depositors, the Shenzhen Branch revoked the Jinwei's licence.

To address the issue of the Shenzhen Branch's authority over the credit co-operative which was raised in the trial, a document entitled *Financial Institution Inspection System* was issued by the PBOC on September 26, 1995, under which a local branch of PBOC is empowered to inspect and supervise financial institutions annually.

Before the re-organization, services provided by credit co-operatives were confined to deposit, loan and settlement transactions. When they are transformed into commercial banks, the scope of business is broadened. Nevertheless, their focus on circulation of capital for local economic development means that they will only develop as regional banks in the near future.[70]

At present, there are four urban credit co-operative banks in China. All were established in late 1995 or early 1996, located in Beijing, Shanghai, Shenzhen and Nanjing. It is reported that 35 cities across the country are planning to establish the same this year.[71] With the success of the four re-organized urban credit co-operative banks, the reform will be extended to the rest of China.

The inter-region clearance among the four co-operative banks, which is estimated to reach Rmb 100 billion in 1996, is currently conducted by the Shanghai Urban Credit Co-operative Bank. Some banking officials suggested that a nationwide clearing centre be set up in Shanghai with the expansion of credit co-operative banks.

Meanwhile, the re-organization of rural credit co-operatives has yet to commence. According to Dai Xianglong, the President of the PBOC, the Bank will speed up the reform of the rural credit co-operatives this year. Relevant provisions are expected to be issued by the PBOC later this year.[72]

Law on Negotiable Instruments

General Provisions

15.11 Although negotiable instruments play an important role in the operation of a market economy, there was no national law governing them until 1995. Prior to 1995, activities involving negotiable instruments — bills of exchange, promissory notes and cheques — were governed by numerous local regulations and administrative regulations issued by the PBOC, for example, the Procedures for Bank Settlements, issued by the PBOC on December 19, 1988. An example of the important local regulations is the Interim Provisions on Negotiable Instruments of the Shanghai Municipality, initially adopted in June 1986 and amended on July 24, 1989. Increase in economic activities[73] called for the enactment of the first national *Negotiable Instrument Law* which was one of the proposed principal legislation in the State Council Decision. In fact, prior to the issue of the State Council Decision, a law-drafting working group under the PBOC was established in 1990 and the first draft of the *Law* was prepared in November 1990 accordingly.

The Negotiable Instrument Law was finally promulgated on May 10, 1995 and became effective on January 1, 1996.[74] It consists of seven chapters and 111 articles, providing detailed provisions for activities involving bills of exchange, promissory notes and cheques. The *Law* is a consolidation of the established principles concerning negotiable instruments in various rules and regulations as well as the international conventions.

The purpose of the *Law* is to facilitate the commercial transactions and to protect the legal rights and interests of the parties in activities involving negotiable instruments (Article 1). By providing a proper framework, the *Law* promotes the use and circulation of negotiable instruments. The Detailed Implementing Regulations are expected to be issued soon by the PBOC.[75]

Under Article 2, "negotiable instruments" include bills of exchange, promissory notes and cheques. The definitions of them are similar to those commonly adopted by developed countries. Article 19 defines a bill of exchange as "an instrument, signed and issued by the drawer, authorizing to pay unconditionally a sum certain in money to the payee or to holder at sight or at a specified time". Under Article 73, a "promissory note" refers to a banker's note, which is "an instrument signed and issued by the drawer promising to pay unconditionally the payee or the holder a sum certain in money at sight". Article 82 states that a cheque means "an instrument signed and issued by the drawer, authorizing the bank or other financial institution which conducts current account business to pay unconditionally a certain sum in money to the payee or to the holder at sight".

Issue of a negotiable instrument requires the drawer to sign the instrument and bear the liabilities thereon (Article 4). Other debtors who sign the instrument must also bear the liability according to the stipulations therein. When exercising the rights on a negotiable instrument, that is, the rights to demand payment and to recourse, the holder must sign and present the instrument in accordance with the relevant procedure.[76]

Under Article 5 of *The Negotiable Instrument Law*, an agent may sign a negotiable instrument on behalf of its principal provided that the agency relationship is expressly stated in the instrument. An agent acting in excess of its scope of authority is liable therefor. Thus a legal person may issue negotiable instruments through its representative. Article 7 specifies that "the signature of a legal person or other institution on an instrument shall be the official seal of the legal person or the institution, accompanied by the signature of its legal representative or authorized agent".

Where a party with no capacity or limited capacity for civil conducts signs a negotiable instrument, the signature is invalid but it does not affect the validity of other signatures (Article 6). The signature of an incapable endorser, therefore, does not invalidate a negotiable instrument but the signature of an incapable drawer does because the instrument is void *ad initio*. The General Principles of Civil Law also contain similar provisions.[77]

Any discrepancy in the amount expressed in Chinese character and that in numeric figures invalidates an instrument (Article 8). Article 9 requires that a negotiable instrument must comply with the provision of the *Law* with regard to the necessary stipulations.[78] Any alteration of those stipulations also renders an instrument invalid unless such alteration is made and endorsed by the drawer.

Activities involving a negotiable instrument must be conducted in good faith and reflect the genuine transaction and a creditor-debtor relationship between the parties as well (Article 10). Any person who acquires a negotiable instrument by fraud, theft, duress, or obtains the instrument *mala fides* with knowledge of any of the above circumstances, cannot enjoy the rights on the instrument (Article 12). To ensure the high degree of negotiability, Article 13 provides that a debtor of a negotiable instrument[79] may raise no defence against the holder founded on his relation with the drawer or any prior holder, subject to an exception when a holder had prior knowledge of the existence of such defence. Thus, the rights of a holder in due course remain unaffected regardless of any prior claims between the parties. Under Article 13, however, a debtor may raise a defence against the holder if there is privity of contract between them and the holder has failed to carry out its underlying contractual obligation.

The following case exemplifies the operation of Article 13 and how   **15.12** a holder of negotiable instrument is protected. In 1994, a company (the drawer) issued a bill of exchange in favour of a Mr Wu (the payee). The underlying contract concerned a sale of steel where the company was the buyer and Mr Wu was the seller. When the bill was mature, the Industrial and Commercial Bank of China (the drawee bank), upon receiving a request from the drawer company, refused to pay on the grounds of non-delivery of steel by the seller. The case was determined by the Intermediate People's Court which held that any dispute be-tween the parties regarding the underlying contract should be dealt with by the parties concerned either through litigation or by media-tion. It had nothing to do with the bill. The drawee bank should disregard any dispute of the underlying contract and assume its liabili-ties on the instrument and it was for the buyer to recover his loss from the seller. On the basis on this finding, the parties were able to resolve matters by way of a settlement agreement.[80]

Consideration for acquiring a negotiable instrument must be mutu-ally agreed between the parties and given unless it falls within the situations set out in Article 11, namely, through taxation, inheritance or gift.

A holder may exercise his rights on the instrument within the prescribed times set out in Article 17 of *The Negotiable Instrument Law*, otherwise the rights on the instrument are extinguished. An aggrieved holder may recover his losses from the drawer or the acceptor concerned in the People's Court. The prescribed times are as follows:

(a) for bills of exchange or promissory notes payable at sight, the instrument is valid for two years from the date of maturity as against the drawer or the acceptor;

(b) for cheques, the instrument is valid for six months from the date of issue as against the drawer of the cheque;

(c) for a holder's rights of recourse against the prior parties, the instrument is valid for six months from the date of non-acceptance or non-payment; and

(d) for a holder's rights of re-recourse against the prior parties, the instrument is valid for three months from the date of settle-ment or commencement of action.

Where an instrument is lost, the holder should notify the drawee to suspend payment within reasonable time. Upon receiving such notice, the drawee has the obligation to refuse payment. The holder may, within three days of giving the notice of suspension of payment, or after the loss of the instrument, apply to the People's Court for publi-cation of notice for assertion of claims or initiate legal proceedings in the People's Court in accordance with Article 15 of *The Negotiable Instrument Law*.

Bills of Exchange

Chapter Two of *The Negotiable Instrument Law* specifically deals **15.13** with bills of exchange, including such matters as the issue, endorsement, acceptance, guarantee and payment, and rights of recourse.

On issue of a bill of exchange, the drawer undertakes that the bill will be accepted and paid. In the event of non-acceptance or non-payment, the drawer must assume the liability to pay the sum and the expenses incurred (Article 26). Under Article 20, the issue of a bill means the act of signing, issuing and delivering the bill to the payee. In addition to the requirements under Article 10, Article 21 stipulates that a drawer should authorize the drawee to make payment and should have sufficient financial means to settle the sum specified in the bill of exchange.

Article 22 provides that absence of any of the following items renders a bill null and void:

(a) the term "bill of exchange";
(b) an order to pay unconditionally;
(c) a sum certain in money;
(d) the name of the drawee;
(e) the name of the payee;
(f) the date of issue; and
(g) the signature of the drawer.

The date of payment, place of payment and place of issue may be stipulated in a bill by the drawer. If nothing is specified, the presumptions under Article 23 will apply in that: the bill is payable at sight; the place of payment is the business premises, domicile or habitual evidence of the drawee; and the place of issue is the business premises, domicile or habitual residence of the drawer. The drawer may also specify the date of payment in one of the following ways as provided in Article 25:

(a) payable at sight;
(b) payable on a fixed date;
(c) payable on a determinable date after issue; or
(d) payable on a determinable date after presentation.

A holder of a bill of exchange payable on a fixed date or on a determinable date after the date of issue should present the bill to the drawee before the date of maturity for acceptance (Article 39). A bill of exchange payable on a determinable date after sight should be presented to the drawee within one month of the date of issue for acceptance; otherwise the holder loses his right of recourse against his prior parties by virtue of Article 40. "Presentation for acceptance" and "acceptance" bear the same meaning as that of international practice. When a bill is presented for acceptance, the holder is demanding a promise to pay the sum certain on the date of maturity from the drawee. Where such promise is given, the bill is "accepted" by the drawee (Article 38). The drawee must pay the bill on the date of maturity if it has been accepted (Article 44). All bills of exchange, except those which are payable at sight, require presentation and acceptance before payment is made (Article 40). If the bill is payable at sight, no acceptance will be required.

Article 41 requires the drawee, within three days upon presentation, to decide whether to accept the bill or not. To be valid, an acceptance must be unconditional, otherwise it will be deemed a dishonour, *i.e.* non acceptance by the drawee, under Article 43. If the drawee decides to accept a bill, he should sign it and state his acceptance as well as the date thereof on it (Article 42). Where it is a bill payable on a determinable date, the date of payment should also be specified.

Under Article 53, the holder of a bill of exchange must present it to the drawee for payment within the following prescribed times:

(a) for a bill payable at sight, within one month after the date of issue; or

(b) for a bill payable on a fixed day, on a determinable date after issue or after sight, within ten days after the day of maturity of the bill.

Presentation for payment may be handled by a collecting bank or financial institution which is duly authorized by the holder. For the purpose of Article 53, such presentation is deemed to be made by the holder in person. Failure to present a bill for payment within the above prescribed times requires the holder or its authorized agent to account for the reason. However, Article 53 provides that the drawee remains liable for the payment. Under Article 43, the drawee must pay the bill in full on the day upon presentation for payment by the holder in accordance with the preceding paragraph.

Upon payment of the bill, the drawee must ensure that:

(a) the holder has signed the receipt acknowledging payment (Article 55);

(b) the chain of endorsements of the bill is unbroken (Article 57); and

(c) the legal identity and validity of the identification certification of the person presenting the bill has been examined (Article 57).

The drawee or his agent will be responsible for his own liability if payment is made out of malice or with gross negligence. Accordingly, the drawee is at his own risk if he decides to pay the bill before the date of maturity.

A bill of exchange may specify payment to be made in a foreign currency; however, under Article 59, the payment will be made, subject to any agreement to the contrary, in *Renminbi* according to the prevailing market exchange rate on the date of payment.

The rights on a bill of exchange may be transferred by endorsement and delivery unless the term "non-negotiable" is expressly specified in the bill (Article 27). Article 29 defines "endorsement" as the act of recording the relevant details and signing on the back of the bill or on an "allonge". An "allonge" is usually used and attached to a bill of exchange if there is insufficient space on the bill for recording items.

In the event of an endorsement, both the endorsee and endorser should sign the bill. In exercising his rights on the bill, a holder is required to prove the uninterrupted chain of endorsement. Where the bill is obtained through other lawful means, evidence of such acquisition is required (Article 31). Under Article 33, endorsement must be unconditional. Any conditions attached thereto, including those which purport to transfer part of the sum or to transfer the bill to two or more endorsees severally, are ineffective.

In line with the established principles on endorsement, by endorsing a bill, an endorser undertakes that the bill will be accepted and paid, and that if the bill is dishonoured, the endorser will bear the liability (Article 37). An endorser may restrict his liabilities by stipulating that the bill is "non-negotiable", and in that case, his liabilities will be absolved by virtue of Article 34 if his subsequent party re-endorses the bill to further parties. No endorsement is valid if the bill has been refused for acceptance or payment, or the time of payment has lapsed (Article 36).

The Negotiable Instrument Law recognizes the practice of guarantee in bills of exchange. Under Article 45, a bill may be guaranteed by a person other than the debtor of the bill. A guarantor undertakes the rights and obligations on the bill except for one which is invalidated because of non-compliance of Article 46 (Article 49). Article 46 requires the guarantee to be in writing on the bill or on the allonge and contain the following mandatory particulars:

(a) the word "guaranteed";
(b) the name and domicile of the guarantor;
(c) the name of the guarantee;
(d) the period of the guarantee; and
(e) the signature of the guarantor.

Article 48 provides that a guarantee must be unconditional and any condition imposed will have no effect upon the liability of the guarantor. The guarantor and the guarantee, *i.e.* the principal debtor, are jointly and severally liable for their debts. Where there is non-payment, the holder of the bill is entitled to demand payment from the guarantor (Article 50). The guarantor must pay in full accordingly but Article 52 provides him a right of recourse against the guarantee and his prior parties after payment of the principal debt.

Promissory Notes

15.14 As mentioned in the above, only promissory notes issued by a bank are recognized in *The Negotiable Instrument Law*. Under Article 74, the drawer must have sufficient financial means to pay the amount specified in the note and undertake its payment. Article 75 further provides that only those banks which meet the qualification requirements prescribed by the PBOC may issue promissory notes.

A promissory note must contain the following items which are set out in Article 76 and absence of any of them will render the note null and void:

    (a) the term "promissory note";
    (b) the promise to pay unconditionally;
    (c) the sum certain;
    (d) the name of the payee;
    (e) the date of issue; and
    (f) the signature of the drawer.

The drawer is the ultimate party to pay the promissory note according to its stipulations (Article 78) when it is presented for payment within the period prescribed in Article 79, which is two months from the date of issue. Pursuant to Article 80, if the holder fails to present the note for payment within the prescribed time, he will lose his right of recourse against his prior parties, but the drawer will remain liable.

Article 81 stipulates that the provisions with regard to endorsement, guarantee and payment of promissory notes are the same as those applicable to bills of exchange as discussed earlier.

Cheques

15.15 Chapter IV of *The Negotiable Instrument Law* deals with cheques. Not every account holder in China is entitled to open a current account. An applicant for a current account must be financially creditworthy and he is required to deposit at the bank a sum which is fixed by the bank concerned according to Article 83 of the *Law*. Of course, the applicant must register with his true name and submit the relevant identification certification.

Under Article 84, both cash cheque and crossed cheque may be drawn. A crossed cheque which is used for settlement on account should expressly state so on its face. Article 85 requires that every cheque, regardless of whether it is a cash or crossed cheque, must contain the following items:

    (a) the word "cheque";
    (b) the instruction to pay unconditionally;

    (c) the sum certain;
    (d) the name of the drawee;
    (e) the date of issue; and
    (f) the signature of the drawer.

Omission of any of the above renders a cheque null and void. It should be noted that the amount of the sum certain or the name of the payee, or both, may be subsequently filled in by a person other than the drawee with his authorization (Articles 86–87).

Under Article 88, a drawer should not draw a cheque for an amount exceeding the balance of his deposit with the paying bank at the time of the payment. Besides, no drawer should issue a cheque of which the signature or the seal does not comply with the specimen previously submitted to the bank for record pursuant to Article 89. Violation of Articles 88 and 89 will render the application of Article 103 which imposes criminal penalties on the offenders. These provisions are considered to have vital importance, especially as the banking system in China is still in its early stages. The *Law*, however, does not address the consequences of an overdraft on current accounts and the issues are expected to be dealt with in the forthcoming Implementing Regulations promulgated by the PBOC.

All cheques are payable on sight. If the balance of the drawer's account is sufficient to pay, the drawee bank must pay the cheque in accordance with the relevant procedure pursuant to Article 90. No post-dating shall be accepted under *The Negotiable Instrument Law.* The holder of a cheque should present the cheque for payment within ten days of the date of issue; otherwise the drawee is discharged from its obligation to pay the cheque (Article 92).

This ten-day period seems to be rather short, but in light of the conditions of the Chinese economy, such restrictions may help to avoid abuse and fraud.[81] It should be noted that the ten-day limit is only applicable to cheques where the drawer and bearer are from the same place. Where the place of issue and place of presentation are different, the period for presentation for payment will be prescribed by the PBOC, according to Article 92.

Right of Recourse

Under *The Negotiable Instrument Law*, a holder in due course of a **15.16** negotiable instrument has the right of recourse against his prior parties, including the drawer, endorser and other debtors of the instrument, on certain occasions.[82] Article 61 provides that such rights may be exercised when the instrument has become mature, or upon occurrence of the following events prior to its date of maturity:

    (a) the instrument is refused for acceptance;

(b) the drawee or acceptor has died or absconded; or

(c) the drawee or acceptor has been declared bankrupt pursuant to law or has been ordered to cease its business on the ground of violation of the law.

According to Article 68, the drawer, endorser, acceptor and guarantor of a negotiable instrument are jointly and severally liable to the holder, who may exercise his right, without prejudice to the priority of their liability, against any of them as he thinks fit.

Where the payment or acceptance of an instrument is refused, the acceptor or the drawee is obliged to provide a certificate of refusal or a "dishonour memorandum" with the grounds therefor (Article 62). The certificate or memorandum is essential for the exercise of the right of recourse. Article 65 stipulates that by failing to provide such a document, a holder loses his right of recourse although the acceptor and the drawee remain liable for the instrument. The People's Court or the administrative authorities may issue the relevant certificate for the purpose of exercising the right of recourse resulting from situations other than non-acceptance.

To exercise the right of recourse, the holder should give notice within three days of the receipt of the relevant certificate to his immediate prior party in writing (Article 66). Other debtors of the instrument may also be notified. Where there is more than one endorser, each should promptly inform his prior party. Anyone who fails to give notice within the prescribed period will be liable for any loss sustained by the delay.

Article 70 provides that the holder, in exercising the right of recourse, is entitled to claim:

(a) the outstanding amount of the instrument;

(b) the interest on the unpaid amount, at the rate prescribed by the PBOC, from the date of maturity to the date of payment; and

(c) the expenses incurred in issuing relevant certificate and notice.

Any endorser, guarantor or acceptor who has made the payment upon the exercise of the right of recourse by a holder is entitled to the same rights as the holder, and may exercise the right of re-recourse against other debtors to recover any sum paid, and interest and expenses incurred (Article 71).

Foreign-related Instruments

15.17 Foreign-related instruments are governed by Chapter Five of *The Negotiable Instrument Law*. Under Article 95, "foreign-related instruments" refer to those of which the acts of issue, endorsement, acceptance, guarantee or payment take place both inside and outside the territory of China. Presumably, this provision also applies to cases where part of the transaction is done in Hong Kong, Macau and Taiwan whilst the rest is completed in China.

It should be stressed that Article 95 deals with specific acts related to negotiable instruments. The nationality of the party conducting the act is immaterial. This approach is different from the provisions of most Chinese laws which contain a definition of "foreign elements".

With regard to the capacity for civil conduct of a debtor of an instrument, the law of the debtor's jurisdiction applies. In cases where a debtor is regarded as a person with no capacity, or limited capacity for civil conduct under the law of his own country, the principle *lex loci actus* applies in that if he is competent under the law of the place of his conduct, such law will apply (Article 97). This provision gives the maximum protection to the holder's rights on a negotiable instrument.

The principle of *lex loci actus* is also applicable to the issue, acceptance, payment and guarantee as well as the determination of the limitation period for the exercise of the rights on instruments (Articles 98–100). In other words, they are governed by the law of the place where the act in question took place. Likewise, matters relating to the presentation of instrument are governed by the law of the place of payment (Article 101). The only exception lies in the case of cheques where the parties to a cheque may choose to apply the law of the place of payment rather than the law of the place of issue (Article 98).

In line with Article 142 of the General Principles of Civil Law, Article 96 provides that international treaties to which China is a signatory prevail over the provisions of *The Negotiable Instrument Law* in case of any conflict save those provisions where China has made reservations. When no provision can be found in either *The Negotiable Instrument Law* or international treaties, Article 96 further provides that international practice will apply.[83]

Conclusion

In addition to the legislation discussed above, several other laws were adopted in 1995, namely *The Law on Insurance* and *The Law on Security*.[84] These enactments form the milestone of the new financial system for the market economy in China. Nevertheless, implementing regulations of these laws have yet to be issued. Seeing that enforcement is a current problem in China, it may be too early to give a fair evaluation on the impacts of the reforms. Besides, much depends on the State-sector reforms. However, these laws do set the legal framework and produce the requisite foundations for strengthening the reforms laid down in the State Council Decision.

Meanwhile, the on-going negotiations for the WTO entry will definitely speed up the reforms of the financial sector in China. To gain
entry to the WTO, China has to make some concessions and open the
domestic market to foreigners. According to an official of the PBOC,
Renminbi will soon be internationally convertible, and foreign
financial institutions may be allowed to deal with *Renminbi* business
on a pilot basis. The introduction of foreign competition will certainly
help the re-construction of the financial system for a market economy.

Notes

[1] The four major State-owned banks are the Industrial and Commercial Bank of China,
the Agricultural Bank of China, the People's Construction Bank of China and the
Bank of China, each specializing in different fields. The People's Construction Bank of
China (recently renamed as the Construction Bank of China) and the Agricultural
Bank of China were first established in 1954 and 1955 respectively but they ceased
their operation in the 1960's and 1970's. These two banks, together with the Bank of
China, were re-established in 1979. The Industrial and Commercial Bank of China
was established in 1984.

[2] *guo fa* [1993], No. 91.

[3] Adopted at the 3rd Session of the Standing Committee of the 8th NPC and promulgated on March 18, 1995, effective as of the date of promulgation.

[4] Adopted at the 13th Session of the Standing Committee of the 8th NPC and promulgated on May 10, 1995, effective as of July 1, 1995.

[5] Adopted at the 13th Session of the Standing Committee of the 8th NPC and promulgated on May 10, 1995, effective as of January 1, 1996.

[6] Adopted at the 13th Session of the Standing Committee of the 8th NPC and promulgated on May 10, 1995, effective as of October 1, 1995.

[7] Promulgated by the State Council on January 7, 1986.

[8] Lester Ross & Mitchell Silk, "Reforms aim to put the financial sector on more solid
ground", *China Business Review*, November 1, 1995.
        The problem is also revealed in the lowering of the credit-rating of the four
specialized banks for long term debt from A3 to Baa1 by Moody's Investors Services in
April 1995. It was believed that Moody's decision was out of a fear for the Chinese
government's withdrawal of support for the four banks.

[9] *Ibid.*

[10] The PBOC has four tiers of offices: the head office, and offices at provincial, municipal
and city levels.

[11] Yuan Mu, "Actively and Steadily Establishing the Commercial Banks", the *People's
Daily*, February 16, 1994.

[12] Pursuant to Article 12, the PBOC plans to replace its 30 provincial branches with 10
regional branches, whose jurisdiction will no longer correspond to provincial boundaries so that administrative interferences from local governments is discouraged. *See*
Joan Zheng, "Battling China's Inflation", *Far Eastern Economic Review*, March 30,
1995, at p. 34.

[13] This system has been adopted in many State-owned enterprises for years and is subject
to criticisms because of limited checks and balances on the president. *See* Guiguo
Wang & Stephen Foo, "The Banking Law Reforms in China — Difficulties and
Prospects", *World Competition*, (1995) Vol. 18 No. 4, at p. 36.

[14] *See* Joan Zheng, above note 12, at p. 34.

[15] *The People's Bank Law*, Article 22.

[16] *The Commercial Bank Law*, Article 1.

[17] *Ibid.*, Articles 17 & 25.

¹⁸ *Ibid.*, Article 11.
¹⁹ Article 13 sets out the minimum requirements only. In approving commercial bank applications, the PBOC usually requires more than the prescribed capital in order to ensure a sound and safe operation basis. Besides, the PBOC may adjust the prescribed amounts in accordance to the circumstances; for example, the Bank may take into consideration factors like inflation.

Similar requirements can commonly be found in other jurisdictions. For example, the minimum registered capital of a bank in Germany is *DM* 6 million; *SFr* 2 million in Switzerland; and 1 billion *yen* in Japan.
²⁰ *The Commercial Bank Law*, Article 12.
²¹ *Ibid.*, Article 3.
²² The duration of these loans are prescribed in Article 10 of the General Provisions on Lending (For Trial Implementation) (the "Lending Provisions"): Short-term loans refer to loans with a term of less than one year; medium loans, from one year to five years; and long-term loans, five years or more. In general, no loans may exceed 10 years, otherwise they have to be reported to the PBOC for the record pursuant to Article 14. The Lending Provisions were promulgated by the PBOC on July 27, 1995.
²³ *The Commercial Bank Law*, Article 5.
²⁴ Mitchell Silk & Lester Ross, "The Powers and the Supervision of Commercial Banks in the PRC", *China Law & Practice*, February 1996, Vol. 10 No. 1, at pp. 44–48. Please note that such barriers have been slowly lowered by regulatory action but generally remain in place.
²⁵ *The Commercial Bank Law*, Article 34.
²⁶ *Ibid.*, Article 35.
²⁷ *Ibid.*, Article 36.
²⁸ According to Article 11(2) of the Lending Provisions, secured loans may take the form of "guaranteed loan", "mortgage loan" or "pledge loan". A "guaranteed loan" means a loan granted on the precondition that a third party undertakes to guarantee the liability. A "mortgage loan" refers to a loan granted against the property of the borrower or another as mortgaged property. A "pledge loan" is a loan granted against a personal property or a right of the borrower or another.
²⁹ *cf* the Lending Provisions, Article 59.
³⁰ *cf* the Lending Provisions, Article 60.
³¹ For example, Article 47 of *The Commercial Bank Law* provides that commercial banks may not improperly raise or lower interest rates, or adopt other improper means too attract deposits or loans.
³² Some banks, like the Agricultural Bank of China, are experimenting with asset-liability ratio management, which allows them to lend based on a ratio of their assets to liabilities, rather than on a fixed quota set by the PBOC. The Guidelines of the PBOC on the Administration of Assets and Liabilities Ratio of Commercial Banks are issued by the PBOC on February 15, 1994.
³³ *The People's Bank Law*, Articles 30–35.
³⁴ *China Financial Outlook 1995*, the People's Bank of China, China Financial Publishing House, p. 49. Review of the administrative acts of the PBOC can be sought pursuant to the Measures on Administrative Review, issued by the PBOC on 1 March 1992 pursuant to *The Law on Administrative Litigations*. The Administrative Judicial Review Committee was established in accordance with Article 15 of the Measures.
³⁵ *Ibid.*, p. 60.
³⁶ See "Death sentence for corrupt banker", *South China Morning Post*, October 31, 1995, at p. 11.
³⁷ Adopted at the 14th Session of the State Council on January 7, 1994, promulgated on February 25, 1994 and effective as of April 1, 1994.
³⁸ Prior to 1985 when the PBOC first issued licences to foreign financial institutions, foreign financial institutions had been paralysed by the restrictions of business imposed by the Chinese government in that they were only given limited business opportunities in China. For many years, they were merely allowed to set up representative offices. However, a representative office generated no revenue but could offer supporting services like liaison and conducting research for its head office only. Conduct of representative offices is now governed by the Administrative Measures on the Establishment of Resident Representative Offices by Foreign Financial Institutions in China, issued by the PBOC in 1991.

519

[39] Establishment of a representative office is essential for developing banking business in China because it is one of the criteria for the PBOC in determining an application to set up a foreign financial institution in China under Article 6(2) of the FFI Regulations.

[40] *See* Michael Ipson, "How foreign banks can enter the China market", *China Banking & Finance*, September 5, 1994, at pp. 1–3.

[41] "Foreign Banks to enter China Step by Step", *Xinhua English Newswire*, April 27, 1996.

[42] Information was disclosed at the 16th Annual Session of the Asia-Pacific Bankers' Club held in Beijing in April 1996.

[43] Ren Kan, "Curbing Inflation No. 1 Aim", *China Daily*, January 15, 1996, at p. 1.

[44] Brett Cole, "Foreign bank branches set to expand their services in China", *China Banking & Finance*, April 8, 1993, at pp. 1–2.

[45] The FFI Regulations, Articles 9–12.

[46] *Ibid.*, Article 6.

[47] Note that the total assets of not less than US$ 20 billion are required for establishing a foreign bank branch in China. *See* the FFI Regulations, Article 7(2).

[48] The FFI Regulations, Article 5.

[49] *Ibid.*, Article 4. *Cf* Article 4(3) of *The People's Bank Law.*

[50] *Ibid.*, Article 22.

[51] *Ibid.*, Article 23.

[52] *Ibid.*, Article 25.

[53] *Ibid.*, Article 26.

[54] *Ibid.*, Article 27.

[55] *China Financial Outlook 1995*, see above note 34, p. 59. To do this, the PBOC usually contacts the supervisory authority of the parent country in advance, and then solicits from the latter a specific appraisal of the applicant bank's overall financial situation and its management level.

[56] The banking sector is not fully prepared for the opening of the market because the on-going transformation of specialized banks into commercially viable operations has been blocked by the slow pace of reform of the State-owned enterprises. Under such massive debts, the State-owned banks will not be able to act in a real business way. *See* Zheng Jie & Chen Qide, "Foreign banking on more access to market", *China Daily*, October 31, 1995, at p. 5.

[57] *The Commercial Bank Law*, Article 1. In addition, Article 4 of *The Commercial Bank Law* assures that commercial banks enjoy autonomy in their operation. Thus the possibility of administrative interference is reduced and fair competition among commercial banks is encouraged.

[58] *See* "Climate Improves For Foreign Banks", *China & North Asia*, (1995) Vol. 2 No. 9, at p. 7. The only specialized bank run with profits is the Bank of China which serves as China's principal foreign exchange bank. Profit of the Bank of China mainly comes from its foreign exchange operation.

It is worthnoting that Chinese banks seldom make public their profit and loss matters. They usually publish the figures of their deposits and lendings only. The release of such information indicates significant headway in the Chinese banking system which is becaming more visible.

[59] According to a recent study by the World Bank, China currently has 104,000 State-owned enterprises but most of them are running at loss. Some Chinese bankers estimate that bad debts of banks have reached at least Rmb 1 trillion (20 per cent of their loan portfolio to State-owned enterprises). The insolvency of State-owned enterprises are crippling efforts to commercialize the banking system. To prevent it from worsening, the PBOC introduced a licence system in April 1996, under which no enterprise may obtain loans from banks or other financial institutions unless the enterprise can produce a licence issued by the PBOC recording the enterprise's financial and credit standing. *See* Foo Choy Peng, "Controls put on enterprise loans", *South China Morning Post*, April 1, 1996, at p. 1.

[60] For a discussion of the establishment of policy banks, see also "Policy banks — China's new experiment in banking reform", prepared by the Hong Kong & Shanghai Banking Corporation, *China Banking & Finance* January 27, 1995, pp. 7–9.

[61] *China Financial Outlook 1995*, see above note 34, p. 51.

[62] "China's Policy Bank Branches Out", *Xinhua News Agency — CEIS*, May 7, 1996.

[63] Ding Xuemei, "Policy Bank Steps Up Farm Loans", *Business Weekly*, July 24, 1995, at p. 3.

[64] Zheng Jie, "Export Bank to Set Up Loans", *China Daily*, January 12, 1996, at p. 5.

[65] Liu Weiling, "Policy Bank's Deal To Help Export", *China Daily*, May 16, 1995, at p. 5.

[66] Zheng Jie, "Export Bank to Set Up Loans", see above note 64.

[67] Tong Ting, "Export Credit Scheme to Widen", *China Daily*, May 6, 1996, at p. 5.

[68] Pursuant to Article 6 of the Interim Provisions on the Administration of Rural Credit Co-operatives, the PBOC delegates its authority to the Agricultural Bank of China to carry out the supervision. The Interim Provisions were issued by the PBOC on October 12, 1990.

[69] Ding Xuemei, "Reforms Target Urban Co-operative Lenders", *Business Weekly*, February 27, 1995, at p. 1.

[70] Laurence Brahm & Stephen Lu, "Opening a bank in China under the new *Commercial Banking Law*", *China Law & Practice*, March 1996 Vol. 10 No. 2, at p. 30.

[71] "China to Establish Nationwide Urban Co-operative Bank Network", *Xinhua English Newswire*, May 16, 1996.

[72] Ren Kan, "Curbing Inflation No. 1 Aim", *China Daily*, January 15, 1996, at p. 1.

[73] Figures concerning the use of negotiable instruments in the business sector submitted to the Standing Committee of the NPC indicate that there have been 54 million bills of exchange, 58.6 millions promissory notes and 1 billion cheques escalating in China's economy every year. Ma Chenguang, "Draft on Negotiable Instrument Discussed", *China Daily*, February 24, 1995, at p. 2.

[74] Adopted at the 13th meeting of the Standing Committee of the 8th NPC on May 10, 1995, promulgated by the President of the Country on the same day by Order No. 49.

[75] *Ibid.*, Article 110. On December 7, 1995, the PBOC issued the Circular on Questions Concerning the Implementation of Negotiable Instrument Law. The Circular provides general clarifications on various matters which are unclear under *The Negotiable Instrument Law*.

[76] *Ibid.* For example, Article 16 requires the holder to carry out matters regarding exercise or preservation of his rights on the instrument in the business premises of the debtor during office hours, or in their domiciles if there are no business premises.

[77] *See*, the General Principles of Civil Law, Articles 11–13.

[78] See also Articles 22, 76 and 86 which provide the mandatory details to be specified in a bill of exchange, promissory note and cheque.

[79] The *Law* does not define the term "debtors of a negotiable instrument". Presumably the term "debtors" includes those who have the obligations to pay under the instrument, *i.e.* the drawer, drawee (payer) and the endorser.

[80] Decision of the People's Court: Cases and Commentaries (*Renminfayan Anlixuan*), Vol. 13 No. 3 of 1995, at pp. 136–138. Although the case was decided prior to the promulgation of *The Negotiable Instrument Law*, the principle on negotiability of an instrument remains unchanged.

[81] Xiangmin Xu & Robert Caldwell, "An analytical perspective on China's *Negotiable Instrument Law*", *China Banking & Finance*, Dec 95/Jan 96, No. 10, at p. 4.

[82] *The Negotiable Instrument Law*, Section 6 of Chapter II. Section 6 also applies to promissory notes and cheques pursuant to Articles 81 and 94.

[83] Note that the major international conventions regarding negotiable instruments include the *Geneva Conventions* and the *UNCITRAL Conventions on International Bills of Exchange and Promissory Notes* and *on International Cheques*. China is not a signatory of any of them. However, in many respects, *The Negotiable Instrument Law* follows the international practice. *See* Xiangmin Xu & Robert Caldwell, "Analytical Perspective on China's *Negotiable Instrument Law*", note 4 at p. 5.

[84] Adopted by the 14th Session of the Standing Committee of the 8th NPC on June 30, 1995 and came into affect on October 1, in the same year.

CHAPTER 16

ENVIRONMENTAL LAW

Bryan Bachner

City University of Hong Kong

Wang Xi

Wuhan University

Bryan Bachner is a graduate of Tufts University and the Washington College of Law at the American University. He is an Associate Professor of Law at the City University of Hong Kong. He is Managing Editor of the *Asia Pacific Law Review*. He is chair of the Hong Kong Environmental Law Association. He research interests include environmental law and law concerning intellectual property.

Wang Xi is a Professor of Law at the Research Institute of Environmental Law, Wuhan University. He is also a member of the Commission on Environmental Law of the IUCN — The World Conservation Union and Director of the Comparative Environmental Law Programme at the Research Institute of Environmental Law. His research interests include international and comparative environmental law.

Introduction

Environmental law includes a broad range of legal measures designed   **16.01**
to regulate activities by individuals and organizations which effect the
natural environment. The topic of environmental law is traditionally
divided into two sections: pollution control and conservation. The law
concerning pollution control largely governs industries that discharge
pollution into the land, water or air. Conservation law is more concerned with preserving the natural habitat, (*i.e.* forests or wetlands) and
protecting it against any ecological damage caused by man.

   In light of the volatile economic development inaugurated by
the implementation of the Open Door Policy in 1978, the need for
environmental protection in the People's Republic of China (PRC) is

considerable. While care and concern about the protection of natural resources of China can be traced back many centuries, the commitment to the protection of the environment, illustrated by the present government's extensive utilization of financial and human resources, has likely never been greater. The aim of this chapter is to introduce the institutional and regulatory framework that makes up the environmental legal system of the People's Republic of China.[1]

Institutional Structure

16.02   The establishment and enforcement of environmental policy and law largely fall under the domain of three centralized organs.[2] The Environment and Resources Committee (ERC) of the National People's Congress (NPC), the Environmental Protection Commission of the State Council (EPCSC) and the National Environmental Protection Agency (NEPA). They are responsible for setting forth standards and regulations for national, provincial and local enforcement. Further analysis of the governmental relationship amongst national, provincial and local enforcement agencies is essential to understand the efficacy of environmental law, but that study goes beyond the scope of this chapter. For now the role of the principal national environmental institutions will be examined.

The ERC was established on March 29, 1993 at the 7th Plenary Meeting of the 1st Session of the 8th NPC. It is noteworthy that the ERC, led by former NEPA head, Qu Geping, was the only new special committee set up by the 8th NPC. The role of the Committee is to draft natural resource and environmental legislation and policy, evaluate natural resource and environmental proposals and assist the Standing Committee of the NPC in its role of supervising environmental law enforcement.

The EPCSC has been in existence since 1984 and as a result its responsibilities have been further developed than the ERC. The Office of the EPCSC was originally a part of the Ministry of Urban and Rural Construction and Environmental Protection (MURCEP). When the NEPA was separated from MURCEP in 1988, it took the function of running the Office of EPSCS from the MURCEP. Since then, the NEPA has been working as the Secretariat for the EPCSC. Originally the EPCSC consisted of 27 member organizations including the State Council, the General Logistics Department of the Chinese People's Liberation Army, the State Economic Commission, the Ministry of Forestry and the Ministry of Metallurgical Industry. The purpose of the EPCSC is to study and examine China's major principles, policies and measures for protecting the environment and coordinating economic development as well as to propose and evaluate relevant technological and economic policies on environmental protection for consideration by the State Council.

During its first four years the EPCSC enacted the Provisions on the Technical Policies for Preventing and Controlling Pollution by Coal Smoke as well as established policies on strengthening environmental management structures, and integrated approaches to urban environmental management. In 1988, the EPCSC increased its numbers to 44, appointed Song Jian, a State Councillor, as its chairman and invited Qu Geping, then the Administrator of NEPA, as a vice chairman. From 1988 to 1993, it took a variety of decisions on industrial policy concerning the environment, the control of acid rain, the disposal of radioactive waste as well as Beijing's environmental policy vis a vis the bid for the 2000 Olympic Games. Its members and advisors took a proactive role in inspecting and monitoring the environmental work of provinces, autonomous regions and municipalities under central government control.

In 1993, the EPCSC took a number of important decisions on national and international environmental law. It approved the Draft Resolution on Further Strengthening the Check on the Enforcement of Environmental Protection Laws and Severely Cracking Down on Unlawful Activities, the Main Points for the Plan for the Work of the EPCSC, and the Proposal that Beijing, Tianjin and Shanghai should use high quality coal. The EPCSC has created a leading group with the responsibility to check on the enforcement of environmental law. The group is composed of NEPA, the Ministry of Public Security, the Ministry of Justice, the Ministry of Supervision, the Ministry of Construction, the Ministry of Foreign Economic Relations and Trade, the Ministry of Radio, Film and Television, the Ministry of Water Resources, the Ministry of Agriculture, the Ministry of Forestry, the Ministry of Commerce, the State Administration for Industry and Commerce, the General Administration of Customs, the Bureau of Legislative Affairs of the State Council, the Xinhua News Agency as well as the People's Daily. On the international front, the EPCSC read and agreed to China's Agenda 21, The Framework Convention on Climate Change, the Convention on Biodiversity and Proposals for the Principled Statement on the Forest Issue.

The National Environmental Protection Agency was officially started in 1988 following the dismantling of the MURCEP; NEPA today answers directly to the State Council. It must carry out the specific work set out by the EPCSC. Environmental protection first became institutionalized in May 1974 with the establishment of the Environmental Protection Leading Group of the State Council located originally within the State Planning Commission and then the State Construction Commission before being integrated into MURCEP. The main purpose of NEPA is to unify the establishment and management of national environmental law, prevent and control pollution and other public hazards, protect and improve the living and ecological environment and to encourage sustainable economic and social development.

Among other things NEPA formulates the principles, policies, laws and statutes of the State for environmental protection. It is responsible for assisting subordinate departments establish administrative regulations and supervising their implementation of the law. NEPA sets the State's environmental plan and has a significant role in advising the State in the establishment of the national economic and social development plan. NEPA issues the national standards for environmental quality, discharge of pollutants, and environmental methods. It also must supervise and manage environmental concerns such as atmospheric protection, water pollution, solid wastes, soil conservation and marine protection. NEPA administers problems dealing with trans-provincial pollution and international pollution control. Finally NEPA coordinates national responses to international environmental legal issues (*i.e.* United Nations Environment Programme, United Nations Conference on Environment and Development and a number of other international environmental conventions.

Environmental Law and Policy

16.03   The national law and policy which these institutions have had a hand in establishing and enforcing are embodied in China's Agenda 21 and the variety of laws and regulations that relate to environmental protection. Among them, China's Agenda 21 is a key document because it sets out the policy framework that will guide the implementation of pollution control and conservation regulatory measures.

China's Agenda 21

China's Agenda 21[3] is the national response to the 1992 United Nations Conference on the Environment and Development (Rio Conference) held in Brazil. The Rio Conference set out a plan to achieve global sustainable development. This plan was manifested in five internationally approved agreements: Rio Declaration, Agenda 21, the Non-Legally Binding Authoritative Statement of Principles for a Global Consensus on the Management, Conservation and Sustainable Development of all Types of Forests, and the Convention on Biological Diversity and Convention on Climate Change. The concept of sustainable development, however, predates the Rio Conference.

The World Commission on Environment and Development, otherwise known as the Brundtland Report, had drafted a definition of sustainable development in 1987 that has been recognized as the international standard. It states that

> Sustainable development is development which meets the needs of the present without compromising the ability of future generations to meet their own needs.[4]

The concept of sustainable development deals with three main principles: the principle of intergenerational equity, social justice and transfrontier responsibility.[5] The principle of intergenerational equity refers to the need of present consumers to consider the effect their economic decisions will have on future generations. The principle of social justice highlights the notions that poverty is the main source of environmental and human degradation and that the elimination of poverty is a prerequisite for eliminating environmental deterioration. Finally the principle of transfrontier responsibility suggests the importance of national actors thinking in international terms; in particular, because pollution does not recognize boundaries State governments must take responsibility for controlling transfrontier pollution.

Leading international legal scholars recognize that economic and social development must be defined in terms of sustainability and that the role of law in achieving sustainable development, whilst underevaluated, is essential.[6] In 1972 at the first United Nations Conference on the Environment entitled the United Nations Conference on Human Environment (the Stockholm Conference), the Secretary General of the Conference, Maurice Strong declared that it was necessary to draft and enact rights and obligations of citizens and states to protect the human environment.[7] Twenty years later, at the Rio Conference the identification of environmental rights and obligations were expanded to consider not only the ecological but also the developmental needs of the community.[8]

China's voice in the debate concerning the establishment of the concept of sustainable development has been considerable and sheds light on how to understand the enforcement of present and future environmental laws in China. Since the Stockholm Conference, China has advocated the need to recognize that a balanced and healthy ecosystem cannot be achieved if economic development is curtailed. The commitment by the State to economic development and environmental protection must be balanced. Economic development on the one hand addresses the problems of poverty and other social ills that lead to environmental deterioration but on the other hand, economic development, if left unfettered, may also lead to more severe environmental deterioration. As a developing country China understandably resisted the demands of developed countries to impose excessive environmental standards that while controlling pollution also stifle economic development. As one Chinese delegate at the Stockholm Conference stated "We must not give up eating for fear of choking, nor refrain from building our own industry for fear of pollution and damage to the environment".[9]

It would be unfair, however, to characterize the Chinese position as callous toward environmental protection. Chinese society has historically shown respect for the environment[10] and their position in Stockholm was no exception. The Chinese could not support the universalist argument for stricter national environmental standards because that position would lead to developing countries subsidizing the clean up of and prevention of pollution that they were not originally culpable of generating. It is only within the last 20 years that the majority of developing countries such as China have industrialized their economies and begun to contribute proportional shares of pollution. The point by China was, and continues to be, that the developed countries had initiated the environmental crisis which existed and therefore should pay for its clean up.

The Chinese delegation's arguments at the Stockholm Conference bears repeating. They claimed that China ought to receive special treatment with regard to international demands for environmental protection in order:

> to develop their national economy, build a modern industry and modern agriculture and achieve complete economic independence so as to safeguard and consolidate their national independence, in contrast to other developed countries who must bear some responsibility for the destruction of the environment of other countries and the impairment of the environment in the world.[11]

It is important to note that the Chinese position, as early as 1972, was not only concerned with issues of economic fairness but was imbued with the importance of protecting and defending the sovereign right to decide its own environmental policy in the face of (rightful or wrongful) international criticism.

During the Rio Conference two decades later similar themes were revisited and amplified. Li Peng, the Premier of the PRC, stated that:

> economic development should go hand in hand with environmental protection; that environmental protection is the common responsibility of all mankind but the developed countries should assume a bigger share of the responsibility; that strengthening international cooperation should be founded on respect for national sovereign rights.[12]

Qu Geping, the head of China's delegation to the Rio Conference specifically called for developed countries to provide China with financial and technological resources to support its efforts to protect the environment.[13]

Today all three of China's leading environmental officials, Song Jian,[14] Qu Geping[15] and Xie Zhenhua[16] appreciate the difficulty associated with the integration of economic development and environmental protection goals, but, nevertheless remain optimistic. According to them, China is on the correct path toward environmental and economic integration. The primary reason for their sense of optimism rests on the State Council's decision to adopt China's Agenda 21. The document basically describes China's blueprint for sustainability.

The impact of China's Agenda 21 on the enactment and enforcement of environmental law will be considerable. According to Song Jian, there are five basic elements to China's sustainable development policy.

(a) sustainable development must maintain the level of economic growth achieved since the implementation of the Open Door Policy;

(b) the creation and application of all relevant laws should be improved;

(c) the discharge of pollution resulting from economic growth ought be strictly controlled; likewise biodiversity conservation should be promoted;

(d) foreign investment into environmental protection technology ought be encouraged in order to free up domestic funds for other important investments;

(e) scientific research in the fields of population control, environmental protection and biodiversity protection need be enhanced.

China's Agenda 21 stipulates that the policy of sustainable develop- **16.04** ment will be implemented through legal measures.[17] According to China's Agenda 21 the foundation for sustainable development has already been established in the form of a series of economic laws and regulations, science and technology laws, environmental and natural resource laws and significant welfare legislation. China admits to a number of shortcomings including the need to improve coordination between economic development and environmental protection, drafting and enforcement of legislation and reconciliation with appropriate international standards. Amongst the specific legislative modifications planned are: improved population control measures; sustainable development impact assessments for social policies, economic plans and planning approvals; review of national and local legislation to assure compliance with international environmental standards; better public consultation; and comprehensive development of research and education in the field of sustainable development. The government is committed to ensuring that administrative and judicial processes incorporate legal mechanisms to allow the relevant authority to consider issues of sustainable development. Finally the supervisory role of the National People's Congress and the Chinese People's Political

Consultative Conference must be enhanced to insure that the policy of sustainable development is being applied.

Recently China's Agenda 21 has been reconfirmed by and integrated into China's Ninth Five Year Plan of National Economic and Social Development and the Outline of Long-Term Targets for the Year of 2010.[18] The Five Year Plan and Long-Term Targets calls for two important economic readjustments. The first is to transform the highly centralized economic system into a socialist market economic system. The second is to transform the mode of economic growth from one based on "extensive resource consumption" to one based on "intensive resource utilization". The achievement of sustainable development in China is dependent upon the effective implementation of these two economic reform policies. Chapter 9 of the Economic Plan sets out China's goals of protecting natural resources, maintaining a reasonable level of environmental quality and establishing specific environmental legal measures to help acheive these goals.

Environmental Law

16.05 Whilst the sustainable development policy may illustrate the theory underlying the future trends in the application of environmental law, it is to the law itself we should turn now in order to examine the regulatory framework of the present legal system. In this section we will explain two basic parts of environmental law in the People's Republic of China: first, the sources of the environmental law will be discussed and second, the official principles guiding the implementation of the law itself will be examined.[19]

Primary Sources of Environmental Law

There are five primary sources of environmental law in the PRC:

(a) the Constitution;
(b) the basic laws;
(c) international environmental treaties and agreements that have been ratified by the NPC;
(d) Regulations promulgated by the State Council and its subordinate institutions; and
(e) laws established by the provinces, autonomous regions and municipalities.

Constitutional, Criminal and Civil Laws ₁

The 1982 Constitution sets out the basic framework upon which all environmental and natural resource law in China is based. According to Article 26, "the State protects and improves the living environment and the ecological environment, prevents and controls pollution and other public hazards." Article 9 stipulates that "mineral resources, waters, forests, mountains, grassland, unreclaimed land, beaches and other natural resources are owned by the State, that is, by all the people, with the exception of forests, mountains, grassland, unreclaimed land and beaches that are owned by the collectives in accordance with law." The State is responsible for assuring the rational use of these natural resources and for protecting the same resources against exploitation.

Additionally the General Principles of Civil Law (GPCL)(1986) and *The Criminal Law* of the PRC (CL) (1979) provide specific mention of environmental liabilities. Articles 80 and 81 of the GPCL specify that the economic or administrative units that use natural resources are responsible for the reasonable use of it. Article 83 points out that no person may harm a neighbour as a result of economic activities. All persons must be guided by the principles of facilitating production, making life more convenient, living in harmony, mutual assistance, fairness and reasonableness, correctly conducting neighbourhood relations especially with regard to water supply, drainage, passage, air and light.[20] Article 98 stipulates that all persons have the right to life and health. Article 123 specifies that where high risk activities cause harm to others, civil liability will arise. Article 124 states that where a polluting activity has been deemed a violation of the state environmental law, and that pollution causes harm, civil liability will arise against the polluter.

The CL creates criminal liability for certain environmental offences. According to Article 114 criminal liability arises for workers or management where their wrongdoing has led to an industrial accident where injury, death or other environmental harm has been caused. Article 115 stipulates that any misuse of explosive, combustible, radioactive or poisonous product which causes a major accident will give rise to criminal liability. Wrongful use of forests,[21] aquatic resources[22] or wildlife[23] may also lead to criminal punishment.

Environmental Protection Laws

The Environmental Protection Law of China (EPL) was enacted in 1989. This basic law serves as the charter or blueprint for national and local enforcement measures. The EPL replaced the environmental protection law for trial implementation of 1979. The EPL is currently under review for purposes of revision.

The prime objectives of the EPL are to provide a framework to protect and improve the ecological environment, to prevent and control pollution, to protect health and to promote the socialist modernization of the PRC. The "environment", according Article 2, includes air, oceans, land, mineral resources, forests, pastures, wildlife, historical sites, nature reserves, tourist areas, urban and rural areas. The EPL sets out the rights and duties of the variety of State and economic enterprises that concern environmental protection.

According to Article 7, the EPCSC and NEPA have the role of national coordinator with regard to environmental protection.[24] The provincial, autonomous and municipal governments mostly have the responsibility of assuring that their local jurisdictions meet appropriate environmental quality standards. Article 24 states that economic enterprises are obliged to incorporate environmental protection strategies into their business plan; establish environmental management systems; effectively control and prevent pollution. Article 27 requires the polluter to apply for and register its discharge of pollution. According to Article 6, all individuals and units have the duty to protect the environment or to sue polluters for environmental transgressions.

There are three forms of liability that arise from environmental wrongdoing: administrative, civil or criminal punishments. The administrative remedies include fines, the temporary prohibition of the operation of the infringing economic enterprise or the permanent shutting down of the infringing enterprise. The civil remedies include the compulsory elimination of the pollution or the payment of damages to the injured party. Criminal liability is stipulated in the CL.[25]

The Standing Committee of the NPC have also enacted a number of specific laws that relate to controlling pollution or conserving natural resources. They include: *The Forestry Law of the PRC* (1979); *The Water Pollution Prevention and Control Law* (1984); *The Air Pollution Prevention and Control Law* (1987 and as amended 1995); *The Law of the PRC on Preventing and Controlling Environmental Pollution Caused by Solid Waste* (1996); *The Law of the PRC on Land Management* (1988); *The Mineral Resources Law of the PRC* (1986); and *The Urban Planning Law of the PRC* (1989).

Finally it should be pointed out that the EPL and *The Law of the PRC on the Prevention and Control of Water Pollution* are currently under consideration for amendment. One major revision being studied for both pieces of legislation involves the inclusion of a section which stipulates that the following principles must be taken into account when applying the laws: sustainable development; prevention and precaution; effective protection of the environment; polluter-pays principle; economic and resource efficiency; integrated pollution prevention and control; effective control of transboundary pollution; public information and participation; integration of environmental protection with other state policies and decisions based on available scientific data.

International Environmental Law

China has actively participated in the development of the extensive   **16.06**
international environmental regulatory framework.[26] International
environmental treaties ratified by the government are superior in status to domestic legislation. Esamples of international environmental
agreements entered into by China include: Convention on Wetlands
of International Importance, Especially as Waterfowl Habitat (1971);
Convention on International Trade in Endangered Species of Wild
Fauna and Flora (CITES, 1973); Vienna Convention for the Protection
of the Ozone Layer (1985); Basel Convention on the Control of Transboundary Movements of Hazardous Wastes and Their Disposal (1989),
UN Convention on Biological Diversity (1992); UN Framework Convention on Climate Change (1992); UN Convention to Combat
Desertification in Those Countries Experiencing Serious Drought and/
or Desertification, Particularly in Africa (1994).

State Council Regulations

The State Council is another source of environmental law that must be
understood. The State Council may directly issue administrative regulations concerning environmental law. These administrative regulations, while subordinate to the laws promulgated by the NPC, must be
followed by the pertinent enterprises. Additionally, ministries under
the State Council, such as NEPA, may issue administrative rules,
which are subordinate in status to administrative regulations.

Some examples of administrative regulations include: Regulations
of the PRC on Nature Reserves (1994); Regulations of the PRC for the
Implementation of the Law on Prevention and Control of Water Pollution (1989); Regulations on Emergency Management of Nuclear Accidents in Nuclear Power Plants (1993); Administrative Regulations of
the PRC on Prevention and Control of Pollution and Damages Caused
by Coastal Construction Projects to the Marine Environment (1990);
the Decision on Further Strengthening Environmental Protection
Work (1990); Regulations on Environmental Management in Special
Economic Areas Open to the World (1986); Provisions on Strengthening Environmental Management of Rural, Township and Neighbourhood Enterprises (1984); Regulations on Ocean Dumping (1985).

Examples of administrative rules include: Administrative Penalty
Measures for Environmental Protection (1992); Administrative Measures for Marks of Environmental Supervision and Management and
Law Enforcement (1992); Administrative Measures for Supervising
Pollution by Automobile Exhaust Gas (1990); Provisions on Environmental Protection Management in Capital Construction Projects
(1986); Implementing Provisions of Air Pollution Prevention and Control Law (1991).

Environmental quality standards also fall within the category of administrative rules. At the end of 1995, NEPA had established 325 environmental standards. Examples of the standards include the Standard for Atmospheric Environmental Quality; Maximum Allowable Concentration for Atmospheric Pollutants for Protection of Farm Crops; Standard for Surface Water Environmental Quality; Integrated Standard for the Discharge of Sewage; and the Urban Regional Environmental Noise Standard.

Local Laws

16.07   The local People's Congresses for provinces, autonomous regions and municipalities directly under the authority of the central government have the discretion to promulgate their own environmental protection laws. Such laws will normally take the form of a regulation, decision or order. The national laws are supreme and any local law which is in conflict with a national law will be deemed unconstitutional. Local governments also have discretion to set their own environmental quality standards. The level of the local standards, however, must not be lower than the national standards.

Judicial Process, Administration and Environmental Law

Conflicts between environmental laws (*i.e.* conflict between the national administrative regulations and rules, or an administrative conflict between the application of a national and local standard) may be referred to the judiciary. The judiciary has the jurisdiction to settle cases where a concrete problem arises. A "concrete" case is a case where an individual or unit asserts that the individual or unit has been wronged or has been injured as a result of the misapplication of the administrative law. In such cases, the court may order a remedy for that particular "concrete" dispute. However, the court's decision will not necessarily be binding upon other cases because in the Chinese constitutional system, the courts do not have the authority to create law or to determine which of a variety of interpretations or applications of the law is correct. The court may not entertain an action against the administrative authority to challenge its administrative decision if such a decision does not create a concrete case. Alternatively, where a court believes that a decision is unclear as to the application of the law, the court is obliged to refer the case to the Supreme People's Court. The Supreme People's Court will then have the discretion to decide the correct interpretation of the abstract law or to refer it to the State Council for their advice and decision.

Environmental Legal Principles

It is important to understand the official principles which underlie the environmental law because these principles provide a guiding reference for the officials responsible for the application of the law. There are four basic principles that ought to be understood:

(a) the coordination of economic development and environmental protection;
(b) prevention and control strategies;
(c) polluter's environmental responsibilities; and
(d) public participation.

Economic Development and Environmental Protection

The fundamental guiding principle for environmental protection in China is that all urban and rural construction should be planned, conducted and developed so as to achieve economic, social and environmental benefits simultaneously. "Simultaneous" is the key word in the principle's construction and seems to refer to the goal that a rational use of natural resources needs to be proven at every stage of the planning process for an economic project to gain State approval. In other words, it is insufficient for the State to approve a project simply on the basis of its potential economic benefits to the community if it is shown that the project construction will lead to the discharge of serious pollution. Likewise once a project is approved, developers must not ignore safe environmental standards even if the developer believes that the inclusion of these standards does not contribute to the project's value. It has been emphasized that such simultaneous planning must apply to industrial development, urban development, rural development, agricultural development.

The "three simultaneity" system as incorporated in the EPL perhaps provides the best illustration of how the government expects to coordinate economic development and environmental protection. Article 26 of the EPL states that the pollution prevention and control facilities in any construction project should be designed, built and put into operation at the same time as the project itself. This basically provides a rough application process for an environmental impact assessment report. The reason for the three simultaneity system is to prevent the abuse of a development approval procedure. For example a planning process which might allow environmental requirements to be considered after construction had already started, would only marginalize the efficacy of any environmental protection requirements. According to the "three simultaneity" system, developers would be required to incorporate environmental standards into the blueprint, construction and operational phases of the project.

Prevention and Control Principles

16.08 The principles of prevention and control are straightforward. The State is committed to controlling the discharge of present pollution and preventing the harmful generation of future pollution. For instance, China's land use policy identifies particular environmentally sensitive areas and prohibits the construction of facilities likely to create pollution.[27] Additionally the EPL specifies that NEPA is responsible for setting environmental quality standards and objectives and for implementing such standards through licensing strategies or other legal measures.

Polluter's Environmental Responsibilities

The Polluter's Environmental Responsibility principle bears a striking resemblance to the Polluter-Pays Principle. According to this principle the polluter is obliged to control or suspend the discharge of pollution. Also the polluter must pay for the clean-up costs associated with eliminating the waste. The government has instituted an assortment of environmental charges and fees to induce compliance with State standards and to reimburse the State for the costs of cleaning up excessive pollution.

The theory justifying this principle is that if a polluter is responsible for paying the costs of cleaning up pollution, the polluter will have a financial incentive to pollute less. This theory, however, may be difficult to apply in China. There are a variety of reasons for this but due to the limited nature of this paper, we will only briefly survey the problem. On the one hand, the poor economic conditions of many economic enterprises prevent local authorities from strictly enforcing environmental measures such as charges or fees; on the other hand, the level of charges and fees has been traditionally insufficient to deter polluters to pollute. The result is a very uneven application of environmental law and ineffective results.

The solution to this problem may lie in further economic reform and marketization of the highly centralized economy. For example, the implementation of economic reform should lead to the decentralization of State owned enterprises. As a result of the decentralization the survival of economic enterprises will depend upon their own independent ability to make profits; enterprsies will not be able to rely on state subsidies to stay in business. This phenomena should have a drastic effect on the effectiveness of the implementation of environmental law. Because enterprises will have to pay for charges or fines out of their own budgets, they will have an incentive to avoid transgressions and will be more likely to comply with environmental standards.

Public Participation

The Chinese government is committed to improving the transparency of the environmental legal process by involving greater public participation. There are a variety of legal means through which citizens may participate in the law making and enforcement process in the People's Republic of China.

First the people's congresses afford the possibility of public participation. It has been claimed that national legislators take into consideration the views of the public, interested ministries and departments during the process of legislation.[28] Additionally a variety of constitutional supervisory activities exist to hold the legislator accountable. These activities include: the submission of environmental reports by environmental protection commissions; the submission of proposals to the National People's Congress; the submission of inquiries directly to the relevant environmental protection department; the enactment of resolutions by local people's congresses; the inspection of environmental problems organized by local people's congresses; and the delivery of critical speeches during a people's congress.

The Chinese People's Political Consultative Conference (CPPCC) also plays an important role in the development of a transparent environmental law making process.[29] The CPPCC, under the political leadership of the Communist Party, provides the leading forum for inter party debate in China. Members of the CPPCC, including all lawful parties, grass roots and professional organizations, have been known to express their views publicly on State policies that raise serious environmental concerns. For example their criticism of the Three Gorges Project provoked the government to undertake further feasibility studies and environmental impact assessments in order to assure the project's environmental efficacy.

Citizens may also take their environmental concerns to any of the eight lawful political parties who have the lawful right to investigate and report on the matter.[30] Moreover, according to Article 6 of the EPL, citizens have the right to submit complaints to relevant environmental protection departments and these departments are obliged to respond to the complaints in a reasonable period of time. The law additionally allows citizens to bring actions against environmental transgressions. Resident's and villager's committees as well as worker and staff representative conferences also provide a forum for citizens to air environmental complaints. Finally newspapers, radio and television have also proven to be an effective means to address environmental problems.

Having said this, however, public participation in environmental affairs has not yet reached a satisfactory level. A number of problems exist which prevent effective public participation. For example,

constitutional supervision on the performance of the executive governmental departments needs to be improved through new legislation.
The supervisory role of the CPPCC and the democratic parties also
needs to be specified through legislation. It is also important that the
efficiency of executive officer's responses to public enquiries and criticisms be enhanced. Parties concerned with the environment currently
have no clear role in assuring that laws are applied fairly; these parties'
rights ought be protected by detailed procedural legislation and administrative rules. Finally only when the public is adequately informed
about environmental problems will they be able to participate in the
environmental decision making and enforcement process. The government should devote greater resources to assure that the public receives
proper environmental education. It goes without saying that the improvement of public participation in environmental protection depends upon further progress in the nation's economic and political
reform.

Notes

[1] For the definitive work on this subject to date, see Lester Ross & Mitchell Silk,
Environmental Law and Policy in the People's Republic of China (Indiana: Indiana
University Press, 1987).

[2] *China Environment Yearbook 1994* (Beijing: China Environment Yearbook, Inc. 1994)
pp. 199–221 [hereinafter "Yearbook"].

[3] *China's Agenda 21: White Paper on China' Population, Environment, and Development in the 21st Century*, adopted at the 16th Executive Meeting of the State Council
on March 25, 1994 (Beijing: China Environmental Science Press, 1994) [hereinafter
"China's Agenda 21"].

[4] World Commission on Environment and Development (1987) *Our Common Future*
(Oxford: Oxford University Press, 1987), p. 43.

[5] Graham Haughton & Colin Hunter, *Sustainable Cities* (London: Regional Studies
Association, 1994), p. 16.

[6] Patricia Birnie & Alan Boyle, *International Law and the Environment* (Oxford:
Clarendon Press, 1992), p. 7.

[7] *Greening International Law* (London: Earthscan, 1993), p. 2.

[8] See above note 5.

[9] Kraus, *Economic Development and Social Change in the People's Republic of China*
(1982), p. 224.

[10] Wang Xi & Robert Blomquist, "The Developing Environmental Law and Policy of the
People's Republic of China: An Introduction and Appraisal", 5(1) *Georgetown International Environmental Law Review* (1992), 37–40. See also *Lao-Tse* (604BC-531 BC)
who wrote "Men depend on the land; the land depends on the heavens; the heavens
depend on the law of nature; the law of nature depends on the thing itself".

[11] *Report of the UN Conference on the Human Environment*, Stockholm, June, 5–16
1972, at 5, UN Doc A/Conf.48/14/Rev.1 (1972).

[12] *Editorial Views Outcome of Earth Summit*, Foreign Broadcast Information Service,
July 9, 1992 at 17.

[13] *Daily Reports on Qu Geping Speech at Rio Summit,* Foreign Broadcast Information
Service, June 10, 1992, at 1.

[14] Chairman, EPCSC, "China: A Land of Hope" in the *Yearbook* at pp. 128–137.

[15] Chairman, ERC of the National People's Congress,"The Situation in China's Environment and Resources and the Measures for Their Protection" in the *Yearbook* at pp. 137–149.

[16] Administrator, NEPA, "Environmental Problems and Policies in China" in the *Yearbook* at pp. 149–161.

[17] China's Agenda 21at 14–21.

[18] *People's Daily* (Overseas Edition), March 30, 1996, p. 4.

[19] Adopted from Wang Xi, *Chinese Environmental Law in Action* (Wuhan: Research Institute of Environmental Law, 1992). For a further analysis of the enforcement of environmental law in China, see Bryan Bachner, "Regulating Pollution in the People's Republic of China: An Analysis of the Enforcement of Environmental Law", 7(2) Colorado Journal of International Environmental Law and Policy (Summer 1996) 373–408. See also Bryan Bachner, "Coming Home to Roost: Pollution. Law and Economics in the People's Republic of China", 5(3) Georgetown International Environmental Law Review (Summer 1993) 635–650.

[20] Compare with the common law of nuisance. See Bryan Bachner, *Hong Kong Tort Law* (Hong Kong: Longman, 1996), pp. 80–96.

[21] *The Criminal Law of the PRC*, Article 128.

[22] *The Criminal Law of the PRC*, Article 129.

[23] *The Criminal Law of the PRC*, Article 130.

[24] See above footnote 1 and accompanying text.

[25] See above notes 19, 20 & 21 and accompanying text.

[26] See above notes 5–10 and accompanying text.

[27] See *The Law of the PRC on Land Management* and *the Law on Urban Planning*.

[28] *Chinese Environmental Law in Action* at pp. 37–38.

[29] *Ibid.* at pp. 42–44.

[30] *Ibid.* at pp. 44–46.

CHAPTER 17

LAND LAW

Priscilla M F Leung

City University of Hong Kong

Priscilla M F Leung is Associate Professor of Law, City University of Hong Kong, lecturing on the Chinese legal system, the Hong Kong SAR Basic Law and Commercial Law of PRC. She has been an adjunct Associate Professor of the People's University of China since 1991.

Evolution of Land Prescriptions in China

Land is one of the most valuable natural resources on earth. In Chinese history, distribution of land has always been a critical issue for the success of its rulers as it affects the well being of every citizen. According to Chinese lore, "Clothing, food, housing and transportation" are the four essential needs of every human being. Lack of one of the above may make a society very unstable. Among these four needs, housing is mostly related to land. Some societies regard land as a commodity rather than a public good which has led to the enormous growth in land prices.   **17.01**

In early Chinese history, the rulers of different dynasties adopted different land policies to meet the needs of society. In the Qin Dynasty and the dynasties prior to the Qin, land was wholly owned by the emperors. In B.C. 216, Grand Emperor Qin ordered all people to report to the government on how much land they owned. This order subtly implied that the government had recognized the possession of land by the common people. It was regarded as the first sign of the privatization of land in feudal China.[1]

Following the Qin Dynasty, the government of West Jin Dynasty attempted to implement the system that "land would be wholly owned by the people who cultivated it" and "transactions of this privately-owned land were allowed".[2] In the same period, the system of "Lawned Sale" was introduced, which differed from the ordinary sale of land in that after the lawned sale, the vendor still owned the land for a certain period of time and during that period, the vendor could foreclose the sale whereas in an ordinary sale, once the land was sold, the ownership would be transferred.[3] It had, therefore, some similarity to the modern concepts of a "mortgage".

In the Han Dynasty, most of the land was owned by the government, and was strictly forbidden to be transferred. Those who breached this regulation would be sentenced to death. For private land, transactions were allowed, but if the tenants were found to be infringing on the rights of ownership of the feudal lords, they would be subject to very heavy penalties.[4] The feudal lords, therefore, forced the peasants to rent their land for a lifetime by means of contract and the peasants had, for their whole life, to work for the feudal lords because of this land contract.

In the Tang Dynasty, the laws stipulated that every farmer was entitled to a piece of land. The land, however, was wholly owned by the State. Transactions were strictly forbidden. Moreover, the laws also stated that no government official was allowed to own more than certain Chinese acres ("*mu*")[5] of land. It seemed that the Tang Dynasty attempted to narrow the gap between the peasants and landlords and attempted to provide a fairer system to the people. From the records of the Chinese history, the rulers of the Tang Dynasty were the most popular.

The Tai Ping Dynasty, a very shortlived dynasty, also attempted to establish an ideal system by practising ownership of land by the people. Yet, the system was not in place for very long before the dynasty was overthrown.[6] When it came to the Kuomintang period, the classical system of private ownership of land was widely practised. In the 1930's, the Kuomintang government promulgated *The Land Law* which differentiated public land from private land. Only public land was publicly owned by the State while private land could be privately owned. This classification of land ownership is still practised in Taiwan today.[7]

China is a rural country where farmers account for about 80 to 90 per cent of the population. Under these circumstance, in the Chinese history, the uneven distribution of land and the high rents were the main causes for uprisings to overthrow the government.

Being fully aware of this situation, after the emancipation of China in 1949, the Communist government made land reform its first task. Article 3 of the Common Program of 1949 laid out the steps of transforming the "feudalist land ownership system" to the system of "land wholly-owned by the peasants" as the first task, which was actually one of the promises made by the Communist Party to the peasants before they came into power. Article 27 of the Common Program stipulated the necessity of land reform for industrialization. In the 1950's, the first piece of land law was promulgated in China, which abolished the "feudalist land ownership system" and realized the system of "land wholly-owned by the peasants".[8]

In the 1950's, because of political movements such as the "One Hundred Flowers Campaign" and the Great Leap Forward, chaos over ownership of land occurred especially in the people's communes in the rural areas. To deal with the situation, the Chinese Central Government promulgated the Amendment Draft of the Working Regulations for the People's Communes in the Villages which stipulated clearly that land within the communes including farm plots of cropland and hilly land allotted for private use were wholly owned by the commune. Nobody was allowed to rent or sell the land owned by the commune or to possess the land without the approval of the people's commune.[9]

Not until the above policies were carried out was the system of "Collective Land Ownership" really consolidated. This system was the basic model for land ownership in the PRC until economic reforms were introduced in 1979.

Following the economic reforms starting from the late 1970's, the legal construction for the establishment of a new land system began a golden period. The State Council passed the Trial Regulations of the Sino-foreign Joint Ventures for Construction Land and the Regulations for State Acquisition of Construction Land in 1980 and 1982 respectively, to clarify the government policies on land use. In 1986, the Standing Committee of The National People's Congress promulgated *The Land Administration Law of the People's Republic of China* to clearly define the legal relationship of the ownership, possession, use, management and exploitation of land. The legal relationship concerning land was once again consolidated by the General Principles of Civil Law promulgated in 1986, which stipulate that land and its derived legal rights shall be considered as a kind of capital or a commodity which may be transferred.[10]

The year of 1987 was a "bottleneck" of land reform in China. The classical interpretations of Marxist thoughts on the value of land were challenged. New Marxist thoughts reconstrued the concept of land values, *i.e.* "land itself does not have any value; only the labour upon the land had economic value".[11] It was advocated that land together with the rights embedded with the land, such as the rights of ownership, possession, use, profit, and management have economic values. These views eventually led to a series of legislation in respect of the above land-related rights. Regional legislation came much quicker especially in southern China and in coastal cities like Shanghai, both of which have been influenced by Hong Kong and other market economies.

As discussed earlier, according to some dogmatic interpretation of Marxist thoughts, land does not have any independent value; it is only the real estate property above the land which has value. Thus, land has value only when labour has been put into it.[12] Nonetheless, some scholars believe that land itself, as well as the rights derived from land, has independent market value. The value of real estate property should

17.02

be distinguished from the value of land. In other words, even though no labour might have been put into it, land itself and the rights derived from land should have their own economic values. Based on this view, there are four kinds of rights derived from the right of ownership, namely the right of possession, the right of use, the right of profit and the right of management.[13]

Based on the above arguments, recent legislation and policies stipulate the separation of land and real estate property upon the land when calculating the economic values of both. The assessment of the value of land is actually based on the value of the land-use rights. According to Chinese law, only the land-use rights may be transferred in the market while the right of land ownership by the State is an innate and inseparable right which may not be transferred.

Land-use Rights under Chinese Law

Types of Land in China

State-Owned Land

17.03 According to Article 9 of the Constitution, "all mineral resources, waters, forests, mountains, grasslands, unreclaimed land, beaches and other natural resources are owned by the State and by the whole people with the exception of the forests, mountains, grasslands, unreclaimed land and beaches that are owned by collectives in accordance with the law." Article 10 of the Constitution stipulates that, "land in the cities is owned by the State." In the same Article, it further stipulates that "the State may, in the public interest, requisition land for its use in accordance with the law." Under Chinese law, State-owned land includes:

a) land in the cities;

b) part of the rural land and suburban areas, which was allocated to the State at the discretion of the people's governments at city level or above;[14]

c) land lawfully requisitioned by the State from the enterprises, government units, schools or communes;

d) land lawfully nationalized or forfeited by the State in accordance with the law;[15]

e) State owned land lawfully allocated to the units owned by the whole people, or owned by the collectives or owned by the rural collective economic organizations or allocated to be used by individuals; and

f) unreclaimed land, beaches, grasslands, forests, mountains, waters and other unused land owned by the State in accordance with the law.[16]

State-owned land may be allocated to the units owned by the whole people or by the collectives or even to individuals who contract to operate the land.[17] Contractors of State-owned land may use the land, but they are also obliged to administer, protect and make reasonable use of the same.[18]

Collective-Owned Land

As stipulated by the Chinese Constitution and *The Land Administration Law of People's Republic of China* ("Land Administration Law"),[19] "Land in the rural and suburban areas is owned by collectives except for those portions which belong to the State in accordance with the law; house sites and privately farmed plots of cropland and hilly land are also owned by collectives." Among these types of land, the land use rights of house sites may be inherited.

Under Chinese law,[20] where a town or township or village enterprise needs land for construction, for public works or public welfare construction, or a non-agricultural household needs land to build residences, it must first obtain the approval of the people's governments at the county level. The standard of the construction, the size of the land and the project plan must be in accordance with the stipulations of the relevant approval authorities.[21] Compensation and resettlement subsidies must be paid to the collective concerned for the requisition of the land according to the compensation scale provided for by the State.[22] When the State requisitions land from the collectives, it must also compensate or provide them for resettlement subsidies before allocating or granting the land to any unit.[23]

Ownership of Land and Land Use Rights

In China, all land belongs to either the State or collectives and no land ownership can be transferred. The real estate property above the land or land use rights may be transferred without affecting the land ownership.[24] Under Chinese law, ownership of land by the State is a permanent exclusive right. **17.04**

As discussed earlier, there are four basic rights derived from the right of ownership, among these four rights, the land owner may grant, allocate or transfer the land use right to a party it deems fit. The land use right holder then by law enjoys the rights embedded with the land use right which includes the right to possess, the right to use and the right to profit; however, the land use right holder does not have the final power to manage the land. Land must be used as stipulated in the land-grant contract; and only for the purposes so stipulated may the land use right holder use the land. For example, if a piece of land is decided upon for the construction of educational institutions according to government planning, the land use right holder may not use it for building a factory. The land use right holder may only use, make a profit from, as well as possess the land in the way stipulated in the land grant or the allocation certificate. The land use right holder, however, does enjoy a limited scope of power to manage the land in the actual operation according to the construction plan. In fact, even the land owner is not allowed to determine the nature and use of land arbitrarily. The land owner must determine the nature of land in accordance with the law.

Acquisition of Land Use Right

17.05   There are two kinds of land in the PRC: compensatory land and non-compensatory land. Compensatory land is allowed to be freely transferred in the market whereas "non-compensatory" land is not allowed to be freely transferred unless a certain sum of money is paid to the government for changing the nature of the land. Usually it is paid in terms of a "land compensation fee". Failure to pay this fee may cause problems to the status of land and to the whole project in question.

Land use rights may be acquired by granting or allocation. Granting of land-use rights refers to the State granting land users the right to use the State-owned land for a certain number of years. The users must pay the State a fee for the land-use right as agreed upon in the granting contract.[25] A certificate of land use right will be issued thereafter.

Granting of land use rights must conform to the overall planning for land utilization, urban planning and the annual plan for land to be used for construction based on the quota set by the people's governments at or above the provincial level.[26] Collectively owned land which is located in urban planned areas may be granted for compensation only after it has been properly converted into State-owned land. The "land grant" right, as the ultimate management right, lies upon the State, which is not enjoyed by the land-use right holder. The land use right may be granted in the mode of auction, bidding or agreement between the two parties. [27]

The allocation of land refers to the acts that the people's governments at or above the county level approve in accordance with the law to allocate the land to a land user after the latter has paid compensation and expenses for resettlement, etc, for the allocated land; or gratuitously allocate the land use right to the land user.[28] Such land may be allocated without a definite term.

The land use right may also be allocated upon approval by the people's government at or above the county level in accordance with the law as follows:

    a) land used for State organs or military purposes;

    b) land used for urban infrastructure or public facilities;

    c) land used for projects of energy, communications or water conservancy, etc. which are selectively supported by the State;

    d) land used for other purposes as provided by the laws, administrative rules and regulations.[29]

Acquisition of land use rights does not mean that the right may not be interrupted. When any of the following circumstances occur, the land use rights concerned may be terminated:

    a) The unit using the land has been closed down or has moved;

    b) Land requisitioned for state construction has not been used continuously for two years;[30]

    c) The nature of the land has been changed because of a change of land planning scheme;

    d) The land has been used in an unapproved way and the land owner resumes the land use right;

    e) House sites contributed by the commune members who have moved and/or demolished the houses upon the land are rearranged by the rural economic associations;

    f) The period for the land use right has terminated according to the contract;

    g) The land use right holder gives up the land use right.

Transfer of Land Use Right and Real Estate

There are two kinds (classes) of transfer of land-use right: the transfer of land use right from the State to private party is a Class I transfer which is called an assignment (*chu-rang*) through which the government stipulates the nature of the intended use of the land such as industrial or commercial land, whereas the transfer of the land use right from one private party to another is a Class II transfer called *zhuan-rang*, which is basically a transfer based on the market value.[31] It is a re-assignment of a private party to another private party. Yet, no party in a Class II transfer may change the nature of the land.

    Transfer of real estate is an act that an obligee of real estate transfers his real estate right to another person through sale, donation or other legal means.[32] It is, however, worthwhile to note that under certain circumstance,[33] transfer of land-use rights is forbidden:

    (a) Where the land use right is obtained by the mode of granting, but no land grant fee has been paid off yet or a land use certificate is not obtained;

17.06

(b) Where the rights of the real estate are sealed up by order of the court or administrative authority;

(c) Where the land use right is revoked in accordance with the law;

(d) For jointly owned real estate, where the written consent of other co-owners has not been obtained;

(e) Where the ownership is under dispute;

(f) Where the real estate is not registered in accordance with the law and the certificate of ownership is not obtained; and

(g) Other circumstances under which transfer is prohibited by the provisions of law, administrative rules and regulations.

By law, the terms of land use rights differ according to the utilization of land.[34] The maximum term with respect to the assigned right to the use of land shall be determined respectively in the light of the purposes as follows:

a) 70 years for residential purposes;

b) 50 years for industrial purposes;

c) 50 years for the purposes of education, science, culture, public health and physical education;

d) 40 years for commercial, tourist and recreational purposes; and

e) 50 years for comprehensive utilization or other purposes.

The above provision is also reflected in the local regulations. The regulations adopted by the Dongguan County of Guangdong Province and Shanghai governments, for example, have similar stipulations in this regard.[35]

Legal Grounds for Transfer of Land Use Right

The Legal Framework

17.07 Since 1978, a lot of land development projects have been carried out especially in southern China and in the coastal cities.[36] The fast development land forced local governments to formulate rules regulating land development activities. In 1986, the Shanghai Municipal Government for instance advocated the policy for developing the real estate property as a commodity in the market. In the same year, the Shanghai Municipal Government promulgated the Trial Implementation of the Supervision of the Qualification of the Real Estate Property Development Enterprises and the Trial Implementation on the Price Management of the Commercial Houses [Commodity Real Estate Property]. In November 1987, Shanghai Municipal Government also promulgated the Methods for Assignment of Land Use Right with Compensation. To meet the overwhelming demand of the society, the Constitution of the PRC was amended in 1988 to resolve the issue of transferability of land-use rights. Article 2 of the Constitution after the 1988 Amendment states: "the right to the use of land may be transferred according to law." It was first time since 1949 that the PRC had allowed the transferability of land use rights. The effect of the Constitutional Amendment is to ensure that land-use rights may be traded as a commodity in the market. The Constitutional Amendment also led to the formation and momentum of the real estate market.[37]

The third effect of the Constitutional Amendment was the intensification of competition among local governments. All local governments were keen to improve their locality as soon as possible. The methods they adopted included loosening the measures and policies on land development; for the first time land development was considered an easy money making business. With the development of this situation, the Central Government soon began controlling land development in the south. At the same time, purchasers, developers and overseas investors were urging for better legal protection as more and more purchasers complained about existing projects or about the abrupt change in policy by the local authorities.

Though many land developers might prefer less government control in the local markets, many investors prefer certain guarantees from the Central Government to secure their investments. Moreover, criticisms about the overheated market and queries over the constitutionality of local legislation have been aired, which have forced the Central Government to take action in the coastal cities and in Guangdong Province to slow this unhealthy development.

Subsequent to the Constitutional Amendment, several pieces of national legislation[38] and administrative regulation[39] on land transactions have been promulgated. They are:

(a) *The Real Estate Administration Law;*
(b) *The Trial Implementation of Land Added Value Tax of the People's Republic of China;*[40]
(c) *The Land Assignment Regulation;*[41]
(d) *Interim Measures for the Administration of the Foreign-Invested Development and Management of Tracts of Land;*[42] and
(e) *The Land Administration Law of the People's Republic of China.*[43]

Real Estate Developer

The Real Estate Administration Law stipulates that in order to carry   **17.08**
out real estate business in China, a real estate development enterprise
must be established which shall meet the following requirements:[44]

a) to have a name and institutional structure of its own;
b) to have fixed premises for business operation;
c) to have registered assets conforming to the provisions of the State Council;
d) to have sufficient professional and technical personnel;
e) conditions required by other laws and regulations.[45]

Under Chinese law, a real estate development enterprise must have a business licence issued by the State Administration of Industry and Commerce or the local administrative department for industry and commerce according to the size and scale of the project.[46] In order to establish such a real estate development enterprise, the form of wholly foreign owned enterprises, equity joint ventures, contractual joint ventures, limited liability companies or joint stock companies may be adopted.

The Land Management Regulation stipulates that foreign investors who intend to invest for tract development may invest in the form of equity joint ventures, contractual joint ventures and wholly foreign owned enterprises, which are generally referred to as "development enterprises"[47] in the Land Management Regulation and are subject to the respective governance of *The Law of the People's Republic of China on Chinese-Foreign Equity Joint Ventures, The Law of the People's Republic of China on Chinese-Foreign Contractual Joint Ventures and The Law of the People's Republic of China on Foreign Capital Enterprises.*

It should be noted that there are two types of land development projects: land development projects (成片土地開發) and individual land development projects (個別項目土地開發). The definition of "tract development" under the Land Management Regulation usually refers to large scale land development, such as the Yangpu Industrial Zone in Hainan Island, the Shekou Industrial Zone in Shenzhen as well as other economic development zones of which the development plans are set by the relevant provincial government. And, according to Article 2 of the Land Management Regulation, the same term means that after obtaining the right to the use of State-owned land, the investors shall carry out, as planned, comprehensive development and construction on the land, including leveling the ground and constructing such public works as water supply and drainage systems, power and heat supply systems, roads and communications networks, and communications facilities, so that conditions shall be created for the land to be used for industrial or other construction purposes. The investor shall then transfer the right to the use of the land for operating public utilities, or proceed to construct such above-ground buildings as industrial houses and the supporting facilities for production and everyday life services and engage in the business activities of transferring or leasing these above-ground buildings. Definite development targets shall be specified for tract development and there shall be definite construction projects that are intended to make use of the developed land.

Moreover, under the Land Management Regulation, a tract development project of 2,000 *mu* or less and whose amount of investment falls within the limits of the approval authorities of the people's government of the provinces, autonomous regions or municipalities directly under the Central Government,[48] approval may be granted by the relevant local authorities. A "tract development" project which is to take up more than 2000 *mu* of land and whose amount of investment for comprehensive development exceeds the limits of approval ceilings of the local authorities must be approved by the Central Government.[49] This is adhered to by the local regulations. For example, according to the Shanghai Municipal Implementation Rules of the Land Administration Law of the People's Republic of China promulgated by the Standing Committee of the Shanghai Municipal People's Congress on HFebruary 4, 1994 (Hereinafter referred to as the Shanghai Implementation Rules), a land development project which is to make use of agricultural land of more than 1,000 *mu* and other land 2,000 *mu* or "an individual construction project"[50] which uses agricultural land of less than 1,000 *mu* but with a total use of land of more than 2,000 *mu*, the approval of the State Council is required.[51]

Development projects below the above scale may be classified as "individual development" projects which may be subject to the approval of the municipal government as stipulated by law. If the scale is relatively small, it may be approved by the county or district government. For example, according to the *Shanghai Implementing Rules*, if the use of agricultural land or requisitioned land is less than 50 *mu*, or the State-owned land allocated is less than 50 *mu* or the land requisitioned or other land is less than 100 *mu*, then the project may be subject to the approval of the county people's government; if the land requisitioned or the agricultural land is less than 30 *mu*, or the State-owned land is allocated or other land in total is less than 60 *mu*, the project may be approved by the district people's government.[52]

Real estate development enterprises in the form of limited liability companies or joint stock companies are governed by *The Company Law of the PRC*.[53] In practice, real estate development projects involving foreign investment usually adopt the form of wholly foreign-owned enterprises, equity or contractual joint ventures. In some areas, however, the real estate development enterprises have adopted other forms. Shanghai is a case in point.

In Shanghai, there are different types of real estate development companies including state-owned enterprises, corporations, wholly foreign owned enterprises, joint ventures as well as joint stock and limited liability companies. Among these real estate development companies, two kinds are worth mentioning. They are the real estate

17.09

comprehensive companies and the real estate project companies. Real estate comprehensive companies are authorized to develop land, to run the business of real estate property or to do fund raising for the real estate development business and have the status of an enterprise legal person. The real estate project development companies are companies established purely for the construction of a particular project. They also have the status of a legal person. In this regard, Shanghai has developed a very sophisticated system. The Shanghai Government has also developed different classes of real estate development companies. See Appendix I.

Because of the nature of land development and the fact that foreign investment has been concentrated in the south and coastal cities, regional legislation in relation to land development has developed much faster than the national laws. For instance, the Guangdong Provincial Government and the Shenzhen Special Economic Zones adopted their own regulations well ahead of the Central Government. Shanghai came a bit later in adopting the rules relating to land development. Nevertheless, its rules are quite comprehensive and exemplify the emphasis and concerns of local governments.

According to the Trial Rules on the Utilization of the Development and Domestic Sales of Commercial Houses approved by the Shanghai Municipal People's Government on December 28, 1993 (Hereinafter referred to as the Shanghai Domestic Sales Rules), foreign investment on the development and domestic sales of commercial houses may use the mode of equity joint ventures, contractual joint ventures and wholly foreign owned enterprises. This is consistent with the provisions of the Land Management Regulation regarding development enterprises. Yet, the Shanghai Domestic Sales Rules require, furthermore, that the developers have to establish a comprehensive real estate property company or a specialized company for different development projects. It is also required that the Chinese party of a joint ventures, either equity or contractual, shall not use land use rights as conditions for co-operation.[54] This provision seems to be inconsistent with the national legislation on equity joint ventures and *The Real Estate Administration Law*. Some Chinese scholars argue that "the land use right" stipulated in this provision should be "the land use right of government allocated land", which has to be changed to compensatory land before it can be used as a condition of cooperation.[55]

Approval Authorities Procedure

17.10 Obtaining approval for land development projects is an important procedure for overseas investors. According to the relevant provisions, approval for land development may be granted at various levels of the administration depending on the size of the projects concerned. The essential approvals for land development projects include:[56]

a) Licence for land-use rights from the State Land Bureau or its branches;
b) Licence for the transfer of land-use rights;
c) Licence for land-development rights;
d) Licence of commencing to construct from the local branches of the Ministry of Construction;
e) Approval from the Public Security Bureau;
f) Approval from the Environmental Bureau or its local branches;
g) Approval from the State Planning Commission or its local branches;
h) Approval from the Ministry of Construction or its local branches;
i) Licence for domestic sales.

Some local regulations such as those of Dongguan and Shenzhen, require contracts relating to land and real estate property to be notarized, otherwise, the document is not considered as legally valid. This requirement, however, seems not to be in compliance with China's contract law and contract practice, where notarization of contract is only voluntary. This local provision shows that local governments do not favour pre-selling more than once after the contract has been notarized. Investors however prefer not to notarize the contract. As a result, they always defer the notarization process until the very last purchaser who intends to use the real estate property for residential purposes.

The requirement of notarization varies from city to city and from province to province. For example, in Panyu of Guangdong Province, the local regulation does not require contracts for real estate transaction to be notarized. Purchasers, in order to save the notarization fees, prefer not to notarize such contracts.

Taxation

There are many miscellaneous taxes and fees concerning land transactions, which vary from region to region and from province to province. The basic taxes are summarized as follows: **17.11**

Income Tax

Prior to 1991, the income tax laws governing enterprises with foreign investment were *The Income Tax Law on Sino-Foreign Joint Ventures* and *The Income Tax Law of Wholly Foreign-owned Enterprises*. On

April 9, 1991, *The Income Tax Law of the People's Republic of China for Enterprises with Foreign Investment and Foreign Enterprises* was adopted at the 4th Session of the Seventh National People's Congress (the "EFI and FE Income Tax Law") which became effective as of July 1, 1991, replacing *The Income Tax Law on Sino-Foreign Joint Ventures* and *The Income Tax Law of Wholly Foreign-owned Enterprises*.

The taxpayers defined in Article 2 of the EFI and FE *Income Tax Law* include sino-foreign joint ventures, sino-foreign co-operative joint ventures ("CJV") and wholly foreign-owned enterprises established in China ("EFIs"), which are applicable to the land development projects. According to these tax laws, foreign enterprises and economic organizations which have establishments or sites in China and engage in production or business operations and which, though without any establishment or site in China, have income sources within China ("FEs") must also pay income taxes. This applies to real estate development enterprises as well.

In addition, governments at provincial and city levels may grant further tax reductions and exemptions to foreign investors in accordance with the circumstances of their respective districts.

Real Estate Tax

City Maintenance and Construction Tax

The tax rate is determined in accordance with the location where the taxpayer is residing. Taxpayers in urban areas are subject to a tax of seven per cent, whilst taxpayers in the towns and the country level cities are subject to five per cent tax. Other taxpayers are subject to a one per cent rate. The tax base is the aggregate amount of the products tax, value-added tax and business tax.

The taxpayers for property tax are the owners of properties. The tax base can either be the original value of the property or the rental income. The tax rate for the taxable amount calculated on the value of the property is 1.2 per cent. The rate for rental income is 12 per cent. When calculating the value of the property, the taxpayer is allowed to deduct 10 per cent to 30 per cent from the original value of the property.

Cultivated Land Use Tax

The lowest rate of tax is RMB 1–5 per square metre, whilst the highest being RMB 2–10 per square metre. No more than 50 per cent increase in tax may be applied to land use in the Special Economic Zones, Economic and Technology Development Zones and the areas where the economy is advanced or the per capita cultivated land is small.

While paying tax, the taxpayer must produce the land use certificate issued by the government at county level and above.

City and Town Land Use Tax

The taxpayers under the city and town land use tax are entities and individuals entitled to use land in the cities, county level cities, towns, and industrial and mining areas. The tax payable is determined by the

TABLE 17.1
General Stipulations for Tax on Land Transactions in the   17.12
Pearl River Delta Area[57]

Fees/tax	Estimated percentage
Rent from the government *i.e.* initial land transaction from the government to the land users.	Varies in accordance with the market and the site. The State Land Bureau of the relevant province should be in charge of collecting rent, approving rental reduction or exemption subject to an exceptional application. When implementing the granting of a leasehold under consideration, the land price collection should be the sum of the annual rent during the period of use.
Fees for assignment of leasehold *i.e.* transaction from the first hand user to the second hand user of the land, who rents the land from the government.	The fees for the assignment of leasehold are essentially the return to the government of increases in land value. $$V = SP - (C + P + T)$$ where V = Increase in land value SP = Selling price C = Costs P = Planned profit T = Business tax cost includes project expense (land price), administrative expenses (3% of project expense) interest on loans: business tax calculated by the tax department.
Transfer fee from non-commercial land to commercial land-use purposes *i.e.* paid to the government.	Varies according to the valuation of the relevant authorities.

Note   This fee is important. Failure to pay this fee may cause problems for future projects.

TABLE 17.2
Tax on Property Transactions in the Pearl River Delta Area[58]

Fees/tax	Estimated percentage
Deed tax includes: • sales and purchase tax • Dian[#] tax • Bestowed tax • Service charge	6% of purchase price 3% of *Dian* 6% of present value 0.7% of deed tax Overall tax rates for sales of purchase tax or bestowal tax = 6.42%
[#] *Dian* is defined as a transaction whereby a person transfers personal property, land or a building to another person in exchange for a fee and after a fixed time limit, the property, land or building is returned to the owner, who pays the fees. **Note** In Shenzhen Special Economic Zones, Hong Kong and Taiwan, foreign nationals shall be exempted from deed tax.	
Lease administration fees (for buildings owned by farmers, residents or collectives)	5% of total revenue from rent; Shenzhen has the rate set at 5%
Property tax	Varies according to provinces (e.g. 18% of the revenue from rent on buildings leased out by building administration departments in Shenzhen SEZ;
Notarization fee	0.9%

TABLE 17.3
Progressive Tax Rate of Land Added Value (Land Appreciation Tax)[59] (General tax applied nationwide)

Land value-added tax	Progressive tax rate
1. Amount of the added value-project cost =/< 50%	30%
2. 50% =/< Amount of the added value-project cost =/< 100%	40%
3. 100% =/ < Amount of the added value-project cost =/< 200%	50%
4. 200% =/< Amount of the added value-project cost	60%

For Shanghai and Xi'an, please see table 4 and table 5.

TABLE 17.4
Progressive Tax Rate of Land Added Value of Xi'an

Land value-added	Progressive tax rate
20% =/< Amount of land added value =/< 100%	20% of land added value
101% =/< Amount of land added value =/< 200%	40% of land added value
201% =/< Amount of land added value =/< 300%	60% of land added value
300% =/< Amount of land added value	70% to 90%

Note The progressive tax rate will be deducted by 5% of each assignment.

The above taxes will be paid accordingly where appropriate.

TABLE 17.5
Main Components of Property-related Fees/Tax
on Property Transactions in Shanghai (translated by
Priscilla M F Leung)

Fees/Tax	Estimated Percentage
Deed tax includes: • sales and purchase tax* • *Dian* tax • Bestowed tax • Registration fee • Service Charge	6% of purchase price 3% of *Dian* 6% of present value 5 RMB 1% of purchase price of the real estate property from both parties;
	1% from successor of estates or receipient of gifts;
	20% from private seller to enterprises if the purchase price is over 200% of the estimated market price of the Municipal Real Estate Administration Bureau;
	5% from private seller to private purchaser if the purchase price is over 200% of the estimated market price of the Municipal Real Estate Administration Bureau.

* If the price of exchange of the property are the same, tax is exempted.

(Source: *Shanghai Real Estate Property Investment Practice*, p. 70)
(Translated by Priscilla M F Leung)

land used by the taxpayer. The annual tax per square metre is as follows:

1. large cities: Rmb 0.50 to Rmb 10;
2. medium size cities: Rmb 0.40 to Rmb 8;
3. small cities: Rmb 0.30 to Rmb 6; and
4. county level cities, towns, and industrial and mining areas: Rmb 0.20 to Rmb 4.

Governments at provincial level may determine the applicable tax in accordance with the infrastructure and economic development of the city in question. The city and town land use tax may be reduced by not more than 70 per cent by the government at provincial level. Such tax reductions should only be made for economically less developed areas.

But sometimes, *The Land Value Added Tax* in the region will vary slightly from the national legislation. For example, the local regulation on land value added tax in Xi'an and Shanghai may both vary from province to province. Please refer to Tables 17.1 to 17.5 for the differences in taxation of selected provinces and cities in our study.

Presale of Commercial Houses

Legal Conditions and Procedure

17.13 According to *The Real Estate Administration Law*,[60] for the presale of commercial houses, the following conditions shall be met:

a) to have paid all the fees for the granting of the land-use right and obtained the certificate of the land-use right;
b) to have a permit for construction project planning;
c) to have invested the funds into the development construction of more than 25 per cent of the total investment for the project and to have ascertained the completion date of the project;
d) to have registered the presale with the administrative department above county level in charge of housing property;
e) to have obtained the certificate of permission for the presale of commercial houses; and
f) to use the proceeds obtained from the presale of commercial houses for the relevant construction project.

Condition (f) refers to the chaotic situation especially in the southern China and Shanghai where foreign investors often use the presale proceeds of commercial houses for other purposes without completing the construction projects, resulting in large losses for customers.

Local governments have also adopted provisions on the presale of commercial houses. According to the rules of Shanghai, any presale of the assignment of compensatory land-use right and transfer of real estate property must meet the following conditions:

a) have an approved construction design;
b) have a construction licence;
c) have completed the leveleing works on the land and the basic construction work; and
d) have confirmation on the progress of the construction work and the payment schedule.[61]

Before any presale, a real estate developer must apply for approval of the presale. For this purpose, the following documents have to be submitted:[62]

a) Agreements with construction subcontractors;
b) Certificate of qualified basic construction works from local government concerned;
c) Deed of Mutual Covenants[63] for the use, management and renovation of the real estate property;
d) Proposal of supervisory body or management body; and
e) Any other documents required by law.

Apart from applying for presale approval from the local authority, a presale contract must also be signed, which should include the particulars of the parties, the location of the property, the price of the property and a clause for the binding force of the deed of mutual covenant on the use, management and renovation of the real estate property and liability for breach of contract, etc. After the presale contract is signed, the contract should be registered with the local Real Estate Registrar. Different regions have different policies to regulate the presale activities. For example, in Shanghai, once the presale contract is registered, the property may not be presold to another party.[64] Whereas in Shenzhen, there is no such restriction for presale activities once 25 per cent of the purchase price has been paid.

For sales involving a foreign party, *some local provisions* require a new contract to be signed.[65] The new contract has to be approved by the relevant authorities according to the scale of the investment and the size of the project. In order to get the approval of the new contract, a lump sum must be paid to the government, which is the difference of the original land grant fee for domestic sales and that for foreign sales.[66]

Mortgage of Real Estate

According to *The Real Estate Administration Law*, mortgage of real **17.14** estate is considered as a kind of transaction of real estate. Mortgage refers to the acts that a mortgagor[67] provides the mortgagee[68] security [usually the real estate property][69] for the payment of a debt with his legal real estate in the manner that the possession of his real estate [the mortgagor's][70] is not transferred [to the mortgagee],[71] but the mortgagee has the right of priority to get compensation from the proceeds obtained from auction[72] of the mortgaged real estate after the amount of land grant fees has been paid in accordance with law.[73] For the mortgage of real estate, the mortgagor and the mortgagee must enter into a written mortgage contract.[74]

It should be noted that *The Real Estate Administration Law* does not provide detailed regulations on mortgage activities, for land transactions are often subject to local legislation. For example, the rules of Shanghai[75] stipulate that certain real estate property cannot be mortgaged according to law. They include those real estate properties which are built on land allocated by the government for a particular purpose such as for memorial purposes or for public housing purposes; and those properties that by law cannot be mortgaged to a third party.[76] Only the real estate property of which the land use right is legally granted or the right to obtain the real estate property on completion being protected by the contract or within the period stipulated for the completion of construction can be mortgaged.[77] The Shanghai Real Estate Mortgage Rules also stipulate that any additional real estate property built after a mortgage is granted may not be classified as mortgaged property.[78]

As *The Real Estate Administration Law* requires all mortgage contract to be in writing, the Shanghai Real Estate Mortgage Rules further stipulate the mandatory provisions of a standard mortgage contract.[79] With regard to notarization and registration, the Shanghai Real Estate Rules provide that all mortgage contracts signed between citizens, or between a citizen and a legal person in China must be notarized. If the mortgage contract is signed between a domestic legal person and a foreign legal person, the mortgage contract has to be notarized. If the mortgage contract is signed between two legal persons inside China, the parties concerned may decide if they would like the mortgage contract to be notarized.[80]

Whilst the mortgage contract is signed inside China, the place of notarization can either be the place of signing the contract or the place where the property is located. If the mortgage contract is signed in Hong Kong, Macau and Taiwan, the contract should be notarized in one of the recognized notary offices; if the mortgage contract is signed overseas, the contract should then be notarized by the notary public in that country with the recognizance of the embassy of the People's Republic of China or her business representative.[81]

Conclusion

Trends and Prospects

Since 1994, the real estate property market has come to a standstill. It   **17.15**
is predicted that the market will revive again in the next few years, but
subject to at least one prior condition, namely how the local governments handle all the problems that have arisen from existing projects.
It is clear that western investors are still very interested in the Chinese
market. Investors are willing to invest in projects with a guarantee
from established enterprises in China. Yet even the established enterprises in China have become more prudent in allowing their names to
be associated with real estate property projects or guaranteeing these
projects. In recent practice, the foreign party of a joint venture will
raise funds in the overseas stock market and then the money will be
pooled into the joint venture through the foreign party. Successful
cases have occurred in Australia with investments mainly coming
from the Singaporean or Malaysian Chinese.

Despite the continued interest in China, investors are more cautious and are keen to protect their own interests. At the same time
China is considering entering into a memorandum of understanding
with those countries that have been ranked the highest in the list of
China investment which include Australia and Japan. This memorandum mainly concerns the requirement of mutual notification if a
Chinese project is to be listed in the securities market overseas. This
requirement has both pros and cons. On one hand, it is good to ensure
that projects are listed abroad after they have been properly approved in
terms of procedure as well as policy in China; however, on the other
hand, there is the fear that the Central Government is becoming too
involved.[82]

Apart from the changing policies, overseas investors feel vulnerable towards the real estate market in China for the following
reasons:

(a) They are unfamiliar with the rights available *e.g.* the difference
    in the term "land use right" instead of "leasehold";[83]
(b) The ownership of land still rests with the State, not the indi-
    vidual; there is always the potential risk that the State can
    requisition the land on the grounds of public interest;
(c) The laws on land value added tax are chaotic and relatively
    high, thus, discouraging overseas investors to invest in the
    market;
(d) The basic conditions for land development such as water, elec-
    tricity, gas, sewage, etc are still underdeveloped in many areas
    of China;
(e) Local market cannot digest the inflation rate and rapid increase

of land prices; rent becomes unaffordable for ordinary citizens, who, demand control of rents and land prices;

(f) A well developed mortgage system is still lacking. Chinese banks[84] do not have enough cash to be the mortgagee while the overseas banks[85] are only willing to grant a mortgage at a maximum of 50 per cent. This relatively low mortgage percentage discourages purchasers from purchasing real estate property in China. The relatively slow sales rate also leads to a relatively slow market in real estate; together with the newly arising problems of incompleted projects. It is believed that middle sized overseas investors are becoming even more sceptical. These investors usually do not have the capital to survive a cooling period, which may last several years. Any disputes with the government or with the purchasers may lead to construction being stopped, and, may even lead to the closure of the developer or the bankruptcy of individual investors. However, these disputes over relatively small size land development projects may not affect those international corporations with long term plans.

It is predicted that laws relating to the real estate market will develop in parallel with the development of other laws in China. The national laws in relation to the real estate market must develop hand in hand with other laws such as laws on securities, banking, mortgaging and taxation. Although China promulgated *The Real Estate Administration Law* in 1994, it has proved insufficient to effectively regulate the real estate market. Apart from passing more legislation, the Chinese Government should also secure the confidence of overseas investors by keeping its laws and policies stable. Moreover, a more open and fairer system is essential for the establishment of a real estate market.

Notes

[1] Zhang Jinfan (ed)., *The Chinese Legal History*, the Mass Publisher, 1983, p. 42.
[2] *Ibid.*, p. 537.
[3] Nan Luming and Xiao Zhiyue, *The Legal System of Land in the People's Republic of China*, Publishing House of Law, Nov, 1992, p. 2.
[4] Zhang Jinfan (ed), *The Chinese Legal History*, the Mass Publisher, 1983, p. 42.
[5] Chinese *mu* is a measurement in China. One *mu* is equivalent to 666.66 square metres.
[6] See Zhang Jinfan (ed), p. 216.
[7] Lin Jidong (ed), *The Collection of the Six Laws*, Taiwan, 1986, p. 183.
[8] Department Head of the State Land Bureau for Law and Policies (ed), *The Collections*

of the Policies and Laws on Land Management, Vol. 3, the Agricultural Publisher, 1988, p. 7.

[9] *Ibid.*, p. 127.

[10] See Nan Luming, p. 11.

[11] Unpublished articles on land policies in China in June 1993.

[12] Unpublished article on land policy in China in June 1989.

[13] Tong Rou, *The Ownership of The State*, The Publishing House of Law, 1988, p. 35.

[14] Article 15, *Land Reform Law*, 1950.

[15] For example, if a piece of land does not have an ownership record or the owner is dead or is permanently missing for more than 4 years (Article 23 of the General Principles of Civil Law) and there is no successor, the land can be nationalized by the State lawfully.

[16] Article 11 of *Land Administration Law* and Article 80 of the General Principles of Civil Law adopted on 12 April 1986 by the fourth Session of the Sixth National People's Congress.

[17] Article 12 of *Land Administration Law* and Article 80 of the General Principles of Civil Law.

[18] See Article 81 of the General Principles of Civil Law.

[19] Article 10 of the Constitution 1982 and Article 6 of *The Land Administration Law*, promulgated by the Sixteenth Meeting of the Sixth Session of the National People's Congress Standing Committee on June 25, 1986 and amended on December 29, 1988.

[20] Article 39 of *The Land Administration Law*.

[21] Article 40 and Article 41 of *The Land Administration Law*.

[22] *Ibid.*

[23] Lin Zengjie, Shen Shaoyu (ed), *Legal Studies of Land*, People's University Press, 1989, pp. 179–181.

[24] It is still arguable whether land ownership is transferred under requisition. One view holds that "requisitioning of land" does not pass the ownership of land from the collective to the State, but only passes the land use right. The other view is that after land requisition with proper compensation or resettlement subsidies, the land ownership should be considered as having been transferred from the collective to the State as only after a proper transfer of ownership may the State have the right to determine the use of land by way of grant or allocation. This debate stopped at the passing of *The Land Administration Law* and *The Real Estate Administration Law*, both of which make it clear that the ownership of the land requisitioned from the collective belongs to the State.

[25] Article 38 of *The Law of People's Republic of China on Administration of Urban Estate* adopted at the Eighth Meeting of the Standing Committee of the Eighth National People's Congress of China on July 5, 1994 (*"Real Estate Administration Law"*).

[26] *Ibid.*, Article 9 and Article 10.

[27] *Ibid.*, Article 12.

[28] *Ibid.*, Article 22.

[29] *Ibid.*, Article 23.

[30] *Ibid.*, Article 25. It should be noted that several pieces of legislation on land stipulate that if construction is not commenced within two years from the date of commencement of the land-use right, the competent authorities may revoke the land use right without compensation, except where delays are unavoidable or are the fault of the government authorities in question. For example, under Article 20 of the Shanghai Implementation Rules, where real estate development companies plan to develop real estate by stages, investment amounts must be deposited in phases as stipulated in the land grant contract and as appropriate for the scale of the project but not to delay the commencement of the construction works for more than 2 years.

[31] See Nan Luming, pp. 134–135.

[32] Article 36 of *Real Estate Administration Law*.

[33] See Article 38 of *The Real Estate Administration Law*.

[34] Article 12 of the Interim Regulations of the People's Republic of China Concerning the Assignment and Transfer of the Right to the Use of the State-owned Land in the Urban Areas, promulgated by Decree No. 55 of the State Council of the People's

Republic of China on 19 May 1990 and effective as of the date of Promulgation ("Land Assignment Regulations").

[35] See the Shanghai Municipal Rules for Implementation of *The Land Administration Law of the PRC*, promulgated by the Tenth Session of Shanghai Municipal People's Congress Standing Committee on February 4, 1994.

[36] The 14 coastal cities are Shanghai, Tianjin, Datong, Qinghuangdao, Qingdao, Yantai, Lianyungang, Nantong, Ningbo, Wenzhou, Fuzhou, Guangzhou, Zhangjiang and Beihai.

[37] After this Amendment, the development of the real estate market in the coastal cities and the Pearl River Delta region jumped tremendously. For example, in Shanghai in 1990, the volume of the sales of the commercial houses reached 1.036 billion RMB and 8,626,000 USD for domestic sales and sales involving foreign interests respectively. According to official statistics, the transactions on real estate property from 1986–1990 amounted to 129,200,000 RMB. Though the development of the real estate market in Shanghai was disturbed by the 1989 student movement, it was revived by the southern visit of Deng Xiao Ping in 1992. Since then, the property market in Shanghai has mourished. From January to May 1992, an unofficial record indicated that Pudong by itself had attracted foreign investment of 5,193,500 USD from Taiwan, Thailand, Singapore and other places. In 1992, foreign investment amounted to 2 billion USD in Pudong. This boom lasted until late 1993 when the Central Government started to take measures to control the chaotic situation in land allocation by the local governments to foreign investors.

The same happened in Pearl River Delta Region. Shortly after Deng's visit, the transactions of the rights to use land, approvals on the development projects from the local authorities, as well as all kinds of joint ventures on the newly developed land were mourishing especially in southern China, where a lot of investment came from Hong Kong.

[38] It should be noted that according to Chinese legal hierarchy, there are, strictly speaking, four levels of laws. They are the Constitution, the national law, the administrative regulations and the local or provincial legislation. The legal authority of these four levels of laws descends according to their order of hierarchy. Thus, when local legislation is inconsistent with national legislation, national legislation prevails. It is also argued by many Chinese scholars that there should be a fifth level of law, namely, the administrative rules some times in the form of departmental orders and circulars. The administrative rules are promulgated by government departments. As the courts are not bound by the administrative rules, some scholars also argue that they should not be classified as one level of law.

[39] It should be noted that national legislation promulgated by the National People's Congress or its Standing Committee and the administrative regulations promulgated by the State Council are two levels of laws in Chinese legal hierarchy. They are applicable nationwide, but when a national legislation and an administrative regulation contravene each other, the national legislation shall prevail.

[40] Promulgated by the State Council, in December 1993 effective from January 1, 1994 (hereinafter referred to as the Land Added Value Regulation).

[41] Promulgated by Decree No.55 of the State Council of the People's Republic of China on May 19, 1990 and effective as of the date of Promulgation (hereinafter referred to as the Land Assignment Regulation).

[42] Promulgated by Decree No. 56 of the State Council of the People's Republic of China on May 19, 1990 and effective as of the date of Promulgation (hereinafter referred to as the Land Management Regulation).

[43] Promulgated by the Sixteenth Meeting of the Sixth Session of the National People's Congress Standing Committee on June 25, 1986 and amended according to the 1988 Constitutional Amendment in the Fifth Meeting of the Seventh Session of the National People's Congress Standing Committee on December 29, 1988 (hereinafter referred to as *The Land Administration Law*).

[44] *The Real Estate Administration Law*, Article 29.

[45] Such laws should include for instance those governing joint ventures, limited liability companies, etc.

[46] *The Real Estate Administration Law*, paragraph 3, Article 29.

[47] Article 4, Land Management Regulation.

[48] Land Management Regulation, Article 3.

⁴⁹ *Ibid.*, Article 3.
⁵⁰ "Individual construction project" differs from "tract development project" mainly on the scale of the project. The plan for an independent construction project is usually initiated by private developers while tract development projects are within a city planning and usually involve the use of land around 2000 *mu.*
⁵¹ The Shanghai Implementation Rules, Article 42.
⁵² *Ibid.*, Article 45.
⁵³ Promulgated by the National People's Congress Standing Committee in December 1993 and effective on July 1, 1994.
⁵⁴ Shanghai Domestic Sales Rules, 1993, Article 8. Under Chinese law, if the local provisions are inconsistent with national legislations, the latter should prevail.
⁵⁵ This argument was made by Professor Long Yi Fei of the People's University of China in his seminars in the City University of Hong Kong in 1995.
⁵⁶ Priscilla M F Leung, "The Real Estate Market" in Joseph Cheng and Stewart Macpherson (eds) *The Pearl River Delta Development in Southern China- A Report on the Pearl River Delta Region including the Special Economic Zones*, Longman, 1995, p. 275.
⁵⁷ *Ibid.*, p. 272.
⁵⁸ *Ibid.*, p. 273.
⁵⁹ Article 7, Trial Regulation of Land Added Value of the People's Republic of China, promulgated by the State Council, December 1993, effective from January 1, 1994.
⁶⁰ *Real Estate Administration Law*, Article 44.
⁶¹ Shanghai Real Estate Property Investment Practice, p. 123.
⁶² The following list is cited from *Shanghai Real Estate Property Investment Practice*, p. 123.
⁶³ The terminology of "Deed of Mutual Covenants" appears to have been copied from the common law terminology.
⁶⁴ *The Shanghai Real Estate Property Investment Practice*, p. 124.
⁶⁵ Article 12, *Real Estate Administration Law*.
⁶⁶ *Ibid.*
⁶⁷ It is usually the owner of the real estate property.
⁶⁸ It is usually a bank.
⁶⁹ It is usually the real estate property.
⁷⁰ It is usually the mortgagor's real estate.
⁷¹ It is usually to the mortgagee.
⁷² Auction is a means to sell the security if the mortgagor fails to pay. The proceeds of the security is for paying debt. The mortgagee usually ranks the top priority of setting back the debt. In the auction, the mortgagee has to take reasonable care for the sales.
⁷³ *The Real Estate Administration Law*, Article 50.
⁷⁴ *Ibid.*, Article 49.
⁷⁵ They are the Shanghai Temporary Provisions on Renminbi Mortgage Loan Administration (1990), the Shanghai Temporary Provisions on Foreign Exchange Mortgage Loan Administration and the Shanghai Municipal Real Estate Property Mortgage Rules, promulgated by the Shanghai Municipal People's Government No. 74 on 22 August, 1994, effective on January 1, 1995 (hereinafter referred to as the Shanghai Real Estate Mortgage Rules).
⁷⁶ The Shanghai Real Estate Mortgage Rules, Article 7.
⁷⁷ *Ibid.*, Article 6.
⁷⁸ *Ibid.*, Article 16.
⁷⁹ *Ibid.*, Article 19.
⁸⁰ *Ibid.*, Article 21.
⁸¹ *Ibid.*, Article 22.
⁸² As previously discussed, projects under the investment size of USD 30 million require local approval in many provinces and local approval is sufficient for projects under 10 million USD unless the projects involve the interest of military, defence or other State interests. Thus, the memorandum will lead to the fear that the Central Government will interfere even more than before.
⁸³ "Leasehold" is a term used by the common law system to describe the right the leaseholder has: *e.g.* exclusive possession for a period of time. "Land use right" in Chinese law terms also enhances the land use right holder to the right of exclusive

possession, etc. But "leasehold" is used in reference to freehold and land-use right is used in reference to land ownership.

[84] In China, the Bank of Agriculture and the Bank of Construction are the most active banks for mortgaging activities over land projects. Usually, they are willing to give 50 per cent of mortgage to the purchasers.

[85] In Hong Kong, the most active bank is the Bank of East Asia, which is willing to give a mortgage of up to 50 to 60 per cent to developers on land development projects.

APPENDIX I

There are three types of real estate development companies in Shanghai.

The conditions for Class I company are:

   i) having a capital of more than 30,000,000 RMB;
   ii) having more than 40 management personnel with more than 20 personnel at middle management level or above;
   iii) having both senior engineers and senior accountants;
   iv) having completed projects of a residential area over 100,000 square metres or above; and 100% of all completed projects have passed the required standard and 20% of the completed projects have reached "credit" or above, and the total amount of investment has reached 0.1 billion RMB or above.[1]

Class II company:

   i) having a capital of more than 15,000,000 RMB;
   ii) having more than 15 management personnel with at least 10 personnel at middle management levle or above;
   iii) having both senior engineers and senior accountants;
   iv) having completed projects of a residential area of more than 50,000 square metres or above with 100% of completed projects having passed the required standard and 20% having reached "credit" level, and the total amount of investment having reached 50,000,000 RMB.[2]

Class III company:

   i) having a capital of more than 5,000,000 RMB;
   ii) having more than 10 management personnel with at least five personnel at middle management level or above;
   iii) having senior engineers and senior accountants;
   iv) having independently completed projects of residential areas of over 30,000 square metres or above and 100% of the completed projects having passed the required standard and 20% having reached the "credit" level, and the total amount of investment having reached 30,000,000 RMB.[3]

For Class I and Class II companies, conditions (i) (ii) (iii) are compulsory; if condition (iv) cannot be met, the company will be downgraded one level; for Class III companies having the conditions (i) (ii) (iii) but not getting condition (iv), they will be *temporarily* classified as Class III.[4]

Companies not reaching 20% of "credit" level in their completed projects in the year will receive a warning from the local authority; if the company does not improve in the coming year to reach a 20% of "credit" level, the company will be downgraded or may even have its business licence forfeited.[5]

Companies not belonging to either one of the three classes but approved to enter into real estate business will have to have the required capital to develop and complete the existing construction projects; after such construction projects are completed, the company has to be dissolved.[6]

It should be noted that a Class I company is allowed to develop projects of a construction areas of residential zones up to 200,000 square metres and can invest in residential, industrial and commercial areas of all levels of technology to be used without limitation; A Class II company is allowed to develop projects of a construction area of residential zones up to 200,000 square metres and can invest in residential, industrial and commercial projects with levels of technology not involving complicated specialized technology; A Class III company is allowed to develop projects up to 120,000 square metres and can invest in residential, industrial and commercial areas up to a maximum level of 12 storeys and a width not wider than 24 metres.[7]

Notes

[1] *The Shanghai Real Estate Property Investment Practice. Ibid.*, p. 2.
[2] *Ibid.*, p. 3.
[3] *Ibid.*, p. 3.
[4] *Ibid.*, p. 3.
[5] *Ibid.*, p. 11.
[6] *Ibid.*, p. 5.
[7] *Ibid.*, p. 10.

INDEX

569

Market economy, 2.09, 7.19, 10.01
  beginnings, 1.11, 3.07, 7.01, 14.02
  constitutional principle, 2.03
  legislation concerning the, 1.02, 7.07,
    10.11, 15.02
  plans, 16.04
Marriage
  application, 9.02, 9.03, 9.04, 9.10
  bigamy, 4.11, 9.05
  conditions, 9.01
  diplomatic personnel, of, 9.04
  engagement before marriage, 9.05
  freedom of, 2.19, 9.02, 9.05
  husband-wife relationship, 9.05, 9.06
  intermarriage
    Chinese and foreigners, 9.04
    with overseas Chinese, 9.03
  joint ownership in, 9.06
  monogamy principle, 9.01
  not allowed, 9.01, 9.04, 9.05, 9.06
  offenses of disrupting the family as
    crimes, 4.11
  regional jurisdiction in, 9.02
  registration, 6.11
  sanctions for violation of marriage law,
    9.09
  under fraud or duress, 9.01, 9.06, 9.07
  wedding procedures, 9.05
Martial law, 2.12, 2.13
Marxism, 2.04, 17.02
Marxism-Leninism, 2.02
Medals and titles of honour, 2.09, 2.12
Mediation (*tiaojie*), 7.06, 7.10, 11.03,
    11.05, 14.19
  and arbitration proceedings, 11.16
  by the People's Mediation Committee,
    11.04
  certificate, 12.02, 12.13, 12.16
  Court-conducted, 11.07
  divorce through, 9.07
  mediators, 11.04, 11.05, 11.09
  People's Mediation Committee, 11.04,
    11.5
  third parties role in, 7.06
  voluntary, 11.08
  see also Arbitration, Conciliation,
    Negociation
Medical and health services, 2.19
Medical expenses claims, 12.07
Meijer, M.J., 4.11
Mentally ill persons, 6.04, 6.05
Merchants Bank, 15.05
Mergers and divisions, 6.12, 10.08, 10.12
  laws, 15.05
Military
  compensation, 3.11
  court, 2.16
  jurisdiction, 5.02
  law, future, 3.11
  personnel, crimes by, 4.11, 5.02
  Procuratorate, 2.09

Protection Department, 5.02
  service, 2.20
Militia, 2.15, 2.20
Mineral resources
  exploitation of, 6.14, 8.02, 8.03
  ownership of, 6.13
  right to use, 3.05
Ministry of
  Agriculture, 16.02
  Civil Administration, 9.02, 9.14, 9.16,
    9.17
  Commerce, 9.14, 16.02
  Construction, 8.04, 16.02
  Electronics Industry, 13.05
  Finance, 8.07, 8.10, 8.22, 15.09
  Foreign Economic Relations and Trade,
    16.02
  Foreign Trade and Economic Co-
    operation, 8.07, 8.22, 10.10
  Forestry, 16.02
  Justice, 9.03, 9.16, 16.02
  Labour, 14.02
  Machine-Building and Electronics
    Industries, 13.05
  Metallurgical Industry, 16.02
  Public Security, 5.01, 5.06, 9.14, 16.02
  Radio, Film and Television, 16.02
  State Security, 5.02
  Supervision, 3.13, 16.02
  Urban and Rural Construction and
    Environmental Protection, 16.02
  Water Resources, 16.02
Minorities, 2.08, 2.13, 2.18
Minors, 6.04, 6.05, 9.12, 9.14
  see also Adoption, Children
Missing persons, 12.14
Mitigation, 4.08
Mobilisation orders, 2.12
Monetary policies, 15.02, 15.04
Monetary Policy Committee, 15.04
Monetary tools, 15.04
Moral values, traditional, 1.05
Mortgages, 6.15, 6.17, 17.01
  contracts, 6.15
  in Hong Kong, Macau, Taiwan, 17.14
  property, transfer of mortgage, 6.15
Movements, political
  Against Five Evils, 1.09
  Against the Three Evils, 1.09
  Anti-rightist, 1.10, 7.01
  of Agricultural Cooperation, 1.09
  of Judicial Reform, 1.09
  of Rectification, 1.10
Municipalities, 2.04, 2.05, 8.02, 16.05,
    17.08
Mutiny, 5.02
**Mutuality of rights and obligations
    principle**, 9.23

Nanjing, 15.10
Narcotics *see* **Drugs**

579